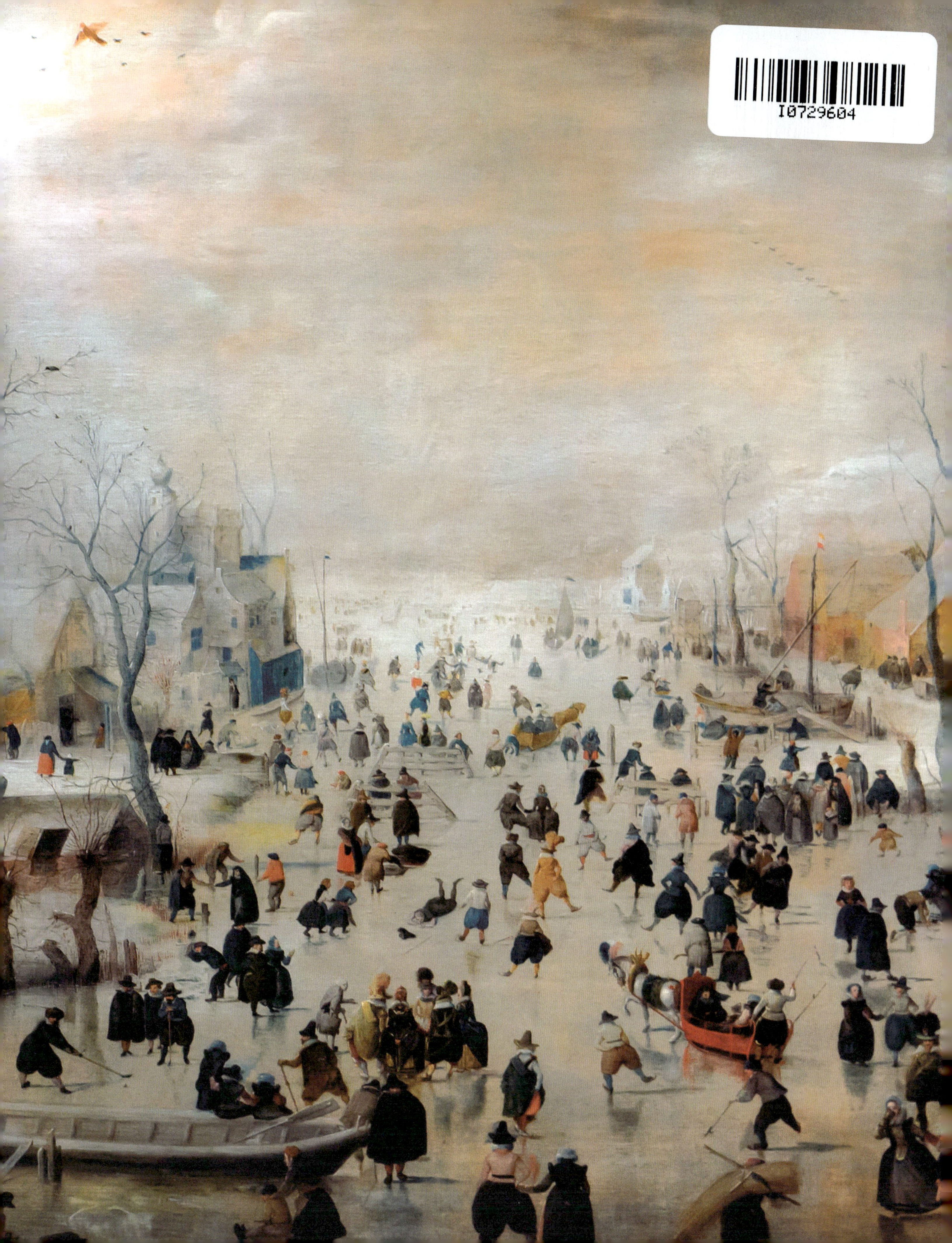
I0729604

THE MASTER PAINTERS OF THE
DUTCH GOLDEN AGE

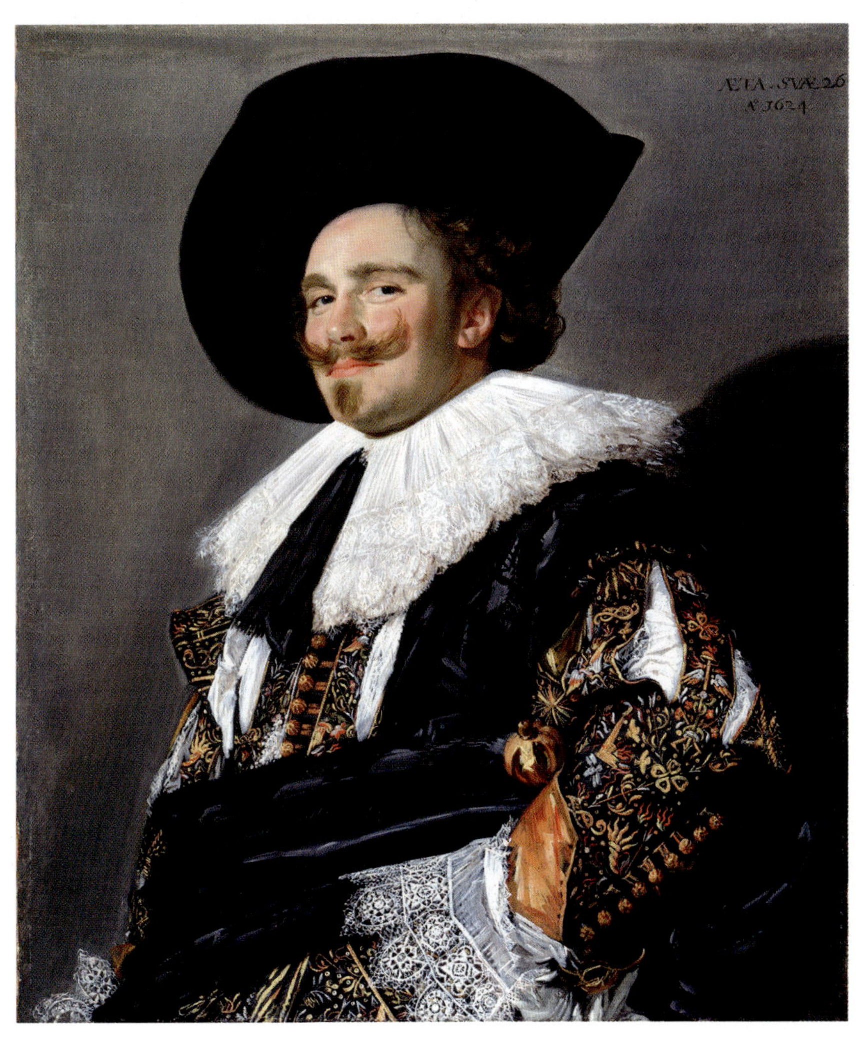

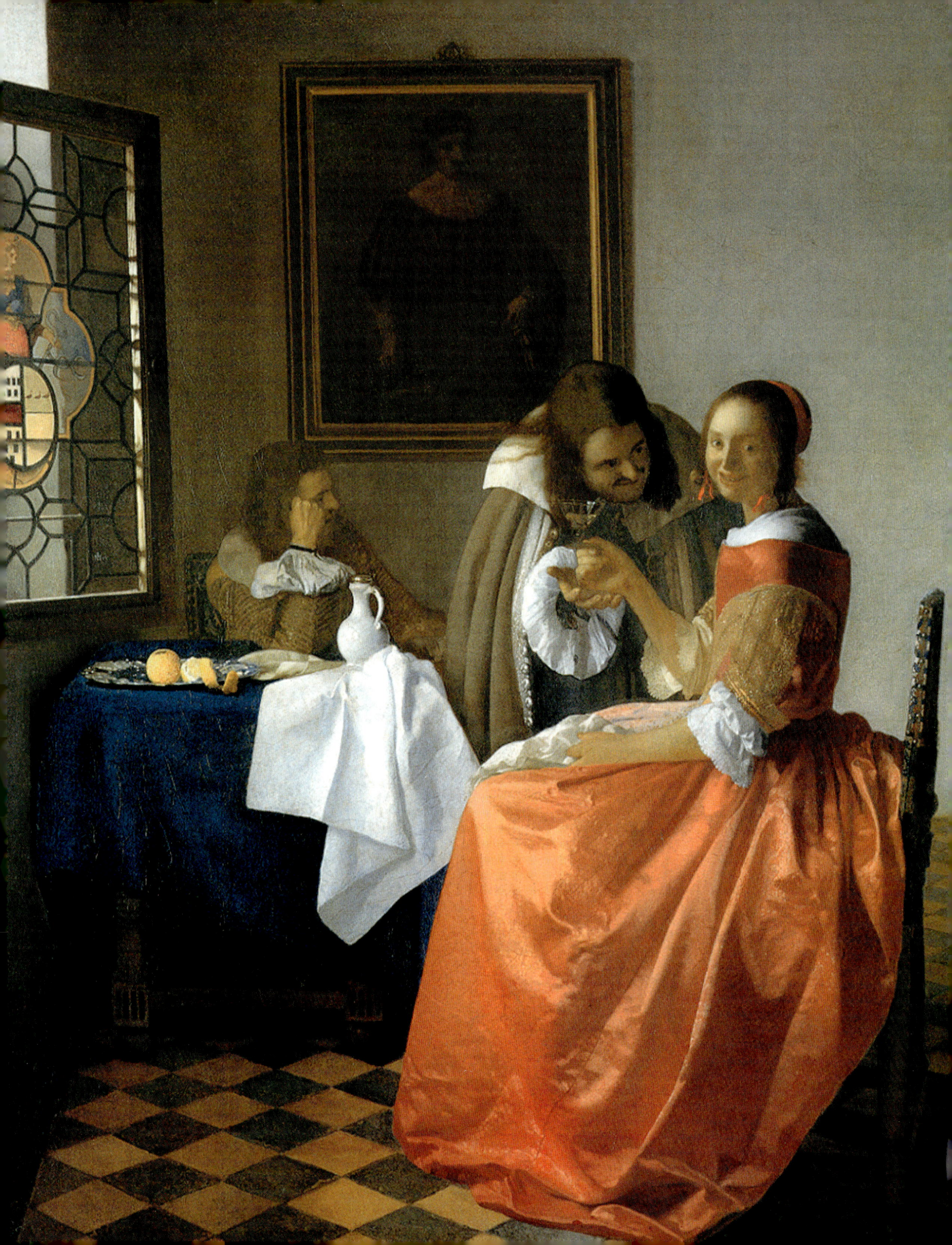

THE MASTER PAINTERS OF THE
DUTCH GOLDEN AGE

THEIR LIVES AND WORKS IN 500 IMAGES

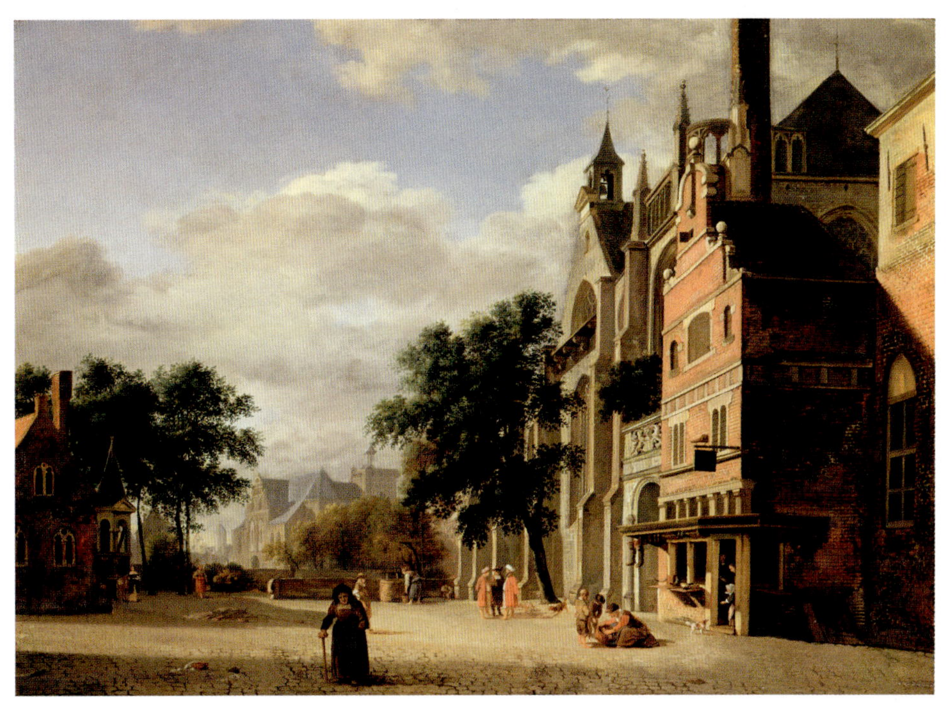

SUSIE HODGE

LORENZ BOOKS

CAPTIONS TO PRELIMS

Front endpaper: see page 161; 1: *The Laughing Cavalier*, Frans Hals, 1624, Wallace Collection, London, UK; 2: *Girl with a Wine Glass,* Vermeer, 1659–6, Herzog Anton Ulrich Museum, Braunschweig, Germany; 3: *A Capriccio of a Town Square*, Jan van der Heyden; 4: *Man and Woman with Two Dogs or 'Teasing the Pet'*, Frans van Mieris the Elder, 1660, Mauritshuis, The Hague, Netherlands; 5 left: *The Guitar Player,* Vermeer, c.1672, Kenwood House, London, UK; 5 centre: *Flowers in a Glass Vase,* Dirck de Bray, Los Angeles Museum of Art, California, USA; 5 right: *A Mother Delousing her Child's Hair, or A Mother's Duty*, Pieter de Hooch, c.1660-61, Rijksmuseum, Amsterdam, Netherlands; back endpaper: see page 79.

Published by Lorenz Books
an imprint of Anness Publishing Ltd
www.lorenzbooks.com; info@anness.com
© Anness Publishing Ltd 2022

Publisher: Joanna Lorenz
Design: Nigel Partridge
Index: Marie Lorimer
Production: Ben Worley

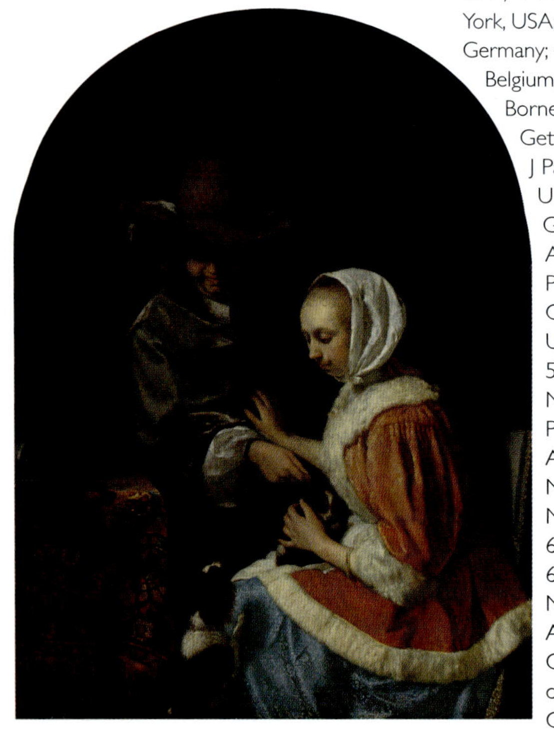

ADDITIONAL PICTURE NOTES

6bl Metropolitan Museum of Art, New York, USA; 6t World History Archive; 7l Musée des Beaux-Arts, Lille, France; 6r Prado, Madrid, Spain; 8 Mauritshuis, The Hague, Netherlands; 10t Rijksmuseum, Amsterdam, Netherlands; 10b Gemäldegalerie Alte Meister, Kassel, Germany; 11t National Gallery, London, UK; 11b Rijksmuseum, Amsterdam, Netherlands; 12 Private Collection; 13tl Ashmolean Museum, Oxford, UK; 13tr Gemäldegalerie, Berlin, Germany; 13b Museum of Dordrecht, Netherlands; 14t Private Collection; 14b Royal Collection, London, UK; 15t Palazzo Comunale, Prato, Italy; 15b National Gallery, London, UK; 16 Private Collection; 17tr Frans Hals Museum, Haarlem, Netherlands; 17bl Musée de Louvre, Paris, France; 17br Staatliches Kunstsammlungen, Dresden, Germany; 18t Private Collection; 18b Musée de Louvre, Paris, France; 19t Alte Pinakotheck, Munich, Germany; 20b Centraal Museum, Utrecht, Netherlands; 22 National Gallery of Art, Washington DC, USA; Rijksmuseum, Amsterdam, Netherlands; 25b National Museum of Women in the Arts, Washington DC, USA; 26 The Wallace Collection, London, UK; 35b Rijksmuseum, Amsterdam, Netherlands; 36t Metropolitan Museum of Art, New York, USA; 37t Museum de Lakenhal, Leiden, Netherlands;; 37b Honolulu Academy of Arts, Hawaii, USA; 38t 39b Museum of Fine Arts, Houston, USA; 40t Rijksmuseum, Amsterdam, Netherlands; 41t Mauritshuis, The Hague, Netherlands; 44b National Gallery of Art, Washington DC, USA; 45t Metropolitan Museum of Art, New York, USA; 45b Metropolitan Museum of Art, New York, USA; 46t Staatliches Museum, Schwerin, Germany; 46b Museum of Fine Arts, Antwerp, Belgium; 48l Museo Nacional Thyssen-Bornemisza, Madrid, Spain; 48r J Paul Getty Museum, Los Angeles, USA; 50b J Paul Getty Museum, Los Angeles, USA; 51b Alte Pinakotheck, Munich, Germany; 52l Kremer Collection, Amsterdam, Netherlands; 53tl Private Collection; 53tr National Gallery of Art, Washington DC, USA; Musée de Louvre, Paris, France; 55b Rijksmuseum, Amsterdam, Netherlands; 56 Musée de Louvre, Paris, France; 57tl 59bl Rijksmuseum, Amsterdam, Netherlands; 60b National Gallery, London, UK; 62bl Musée de Louvre, Paris, France; 63tr Musée de Louvre, Paris, France; 65tl Rijksmuseum, Amsterdam, Netherlands; 65br Rijksmuseum, Amsterdam, Netherlands; 67b Private Collection; 68l Metropolitan Museum of Art, New York, USA; 69r Royal Collection, London, UK; 76t Private Collection; 76b State Hermitage Museum, Saint Petersburg, Russia; 77tl Rijksmuseum, Amsterdam, Netherlands; 77tr State Hermitage Museum, Saint Petersburg, Russia; 80l Musée des Beaux-Arts, Lille, France; 80r Apsley House, London, UK; 81t Museum of Fine Arts, Houston, USA; 81bl National Gallery, London, UK; 81br Rijksmuseum, Amsterdam, Netherlands; 84t Musée de Louvre, Paris, France; 84bl Mauritshuis, The Hague, Netherlands; 85t Los Angeles Museum of Art, California, USA; 89l National Gallery of Ireland, Dublin, Ireland; 89r National Gallery of Ireland, Dublin, Ireland; 91t Rijksmuseum, Amsterdam, Netherlands; 93b National Gallery of Art, Washington DC, USA; 98bl Mauritshuis, The Hague, Netherlands; 101t National Gallery of Art, Washington DC, USA; 101b Rijksmuseum, Amsterdam, Netherlands; 105l Galleria degli Uffizi, Florence, Italy.

PICTURE AGENCY CREDITS

AKG: 13b, 17tr, 17bl, 17br, 18t, 18b, 19t, 21b, 28b, 29r, 31tl, 31tr, 31br, 32tr, 33b, 48l, 52l, 53tr, 61l, 62bl, 63tr, 65tr, 68r, 74l, 75r, 76b, 80r, 82r, 91b, 95tl, 104br, 104l, 104tr, 105r, 122t, 130c, 143t, 154t, 168t, 174b, 179t, 192b, 210t, 211t, 213b, 218t, 220b, 222b, 223b, 233t, 236b, 242b, 242c, 249b, 249t, 250t

ALAMY: 6t, 15b, 19b, 21c, 25t, 28t, 32bl, 34t, 36b, 38b, 39t, 40t, 40bl, 40br, 41b, 44b, 62tr, 66l, 67b, 67t, 69l, 72t, 79t, 83b, 84br, 90r, 93b, 95br, 103b, 109t, 117b, 118b, 119t, 127t, 128t, 129b, 131, 132t, 140b, 145, 153c, 170b, 170t, 177t, 178t, 180b, 181t, 190b, 196c, 200t, 204b, 205t, 207t, 209t, 212b, 215t, 224b, 225t, 226b, 226t, 227b, 230b, 235t, 239b, 246b, 247b, 248b, 248c

BRIDGEMAN: 3, 7l, 7r, 10b, 11t, 12, 13tl, 13tr, 14t, 14b, 15t, 20t, 21t, 22, 24t, 25b, 27tl, 27tr, 29l, 30, 33t, 34b, 35t, 37c, 38t, 43tl, 43tr, 44t, 47t, 47b, 49t, 50t, 51t, 51b, 51r, 54, 55tl, 55tr, 56, 57tl, 57b, 57tr, 58t, 58b, 59t, 59br, 61r, 64, 66r, 70t, 70b, 71t, 71b, 72b, 73t, 73b, 74r, 75l, 77b, 77tr, 78l, 78r, 79b, 82l, 83t, 85b, 86, 87t, 87bl, 87br, 88l, 88r, 90l, 92l, 92r, 93t, 94l, 94r, 96l, 96r, 97t, 97b, 98tr, 99tr, 99bl, 100t, 100b, 101t, 102tl, 102br, 103t, 105l, 106t, 106b, 107t, 107b, 108l, 108r, 109b, 110tr, 110bl, 111t, 111b, 112, 114, 115, 116b, 117t, 118t, 119b, 120t, 121b, 123t, 123b, 125b, 126b, 128b, 130t, 130b, 132b, 134t, 134b, 135b, 137b, 138b, 139t, 139b, 140t, 141, 142t, 143b, 144t, 146t, 146b, 147b, 147t, 148t, 148b, 149t, 149b, 150t, 151b, 151t, 152, 153t, 153b, 154b, 155t, 155b, 156t, 156b, 157b, 159t, 159b, 160, 163t, 163b, 164t, 165t, 165b, 166b, 167t, 167b, 168b, 169t, 169b, 171t, 171b, 172t, 172b, 175t, 176b, 178b, 179b, 180t, 181b, 182t, 183t, 183b, 184t, 184b, 185b, 186t, 186b, 187t, 187b, 188, 189, 191t, 191b, 193t, 194t, 194c, 194b, 195, 196b, 197t, 198t, 198c, 199t, 199b, 203t, 203b, 206t, 208, 209b, 210b, 213t, 214t, 215b, 216, 217, 231t, 231b, 233b, 234b, 235c, 239t, 242t, 244t, 250b, 251t, 252t, 252b

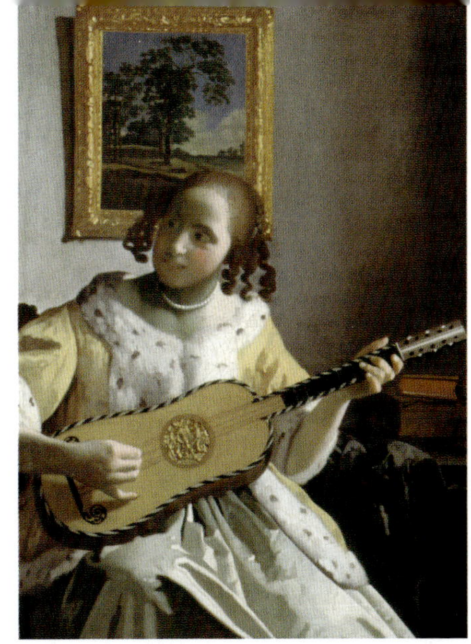 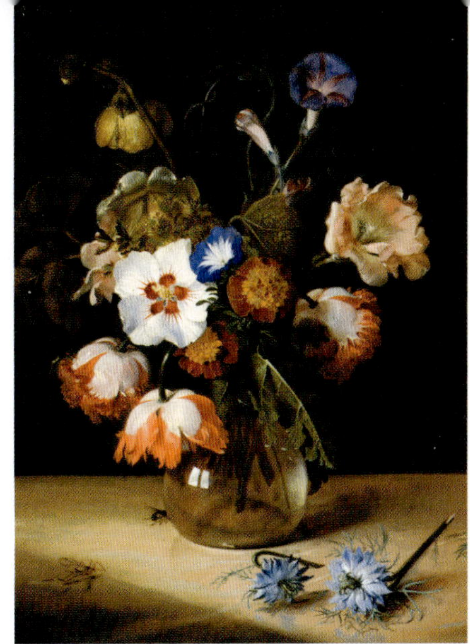 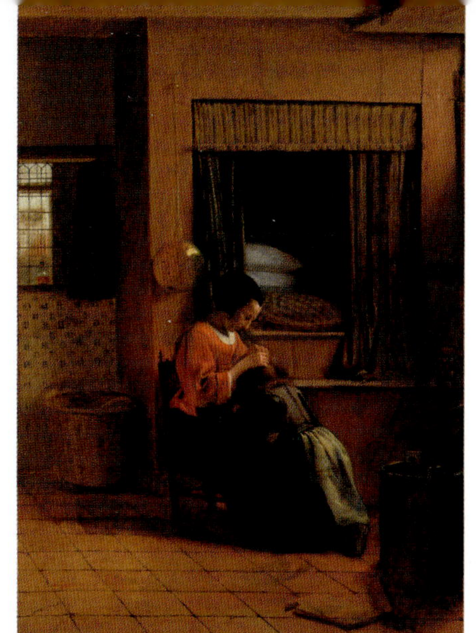

CONTENTS

Introduction — 6

A NEW ERA — **8**

THE PAINTERS — **22**

THE GALLERY — **112**

GENRE — 114

LANDSCAPES — 160

PORTRAITS — 188

HISTORY AND RELIGION — 216

STILL LIFE — 240

Index — 254

INTRODUCTION

The Golden Age was a period when the Dutch Republic was the most prosperous nation in Europe, leading in trade, science and art. Named retrospectively, the Golden Age is generally considered to have started in the later part of the Eighty Years' War (1568–1648) and continued until the end of the century.

The period from the middle to the end of the 17th century became known as the Dutch Golden Age. Trade flourished and cities thrived, and this new wealth created confidence, which in turn led to wonderful achievements, especially in the arts and sciences.

Independence made the Dutch Golden Age possible. From 1384, the Seventeen Provinces of the Netherlands – which were also known as the Low Countries – were ruled by the House of Valois-Burgundy and from 1482 by the House of Habsburg. During that time, the Low Countries were also known as the Spanish Netherlands or the Habsburg Netherlands.

The people of the Netherlands eventually rebelled against Habsburg rule, which evolved into a protracted

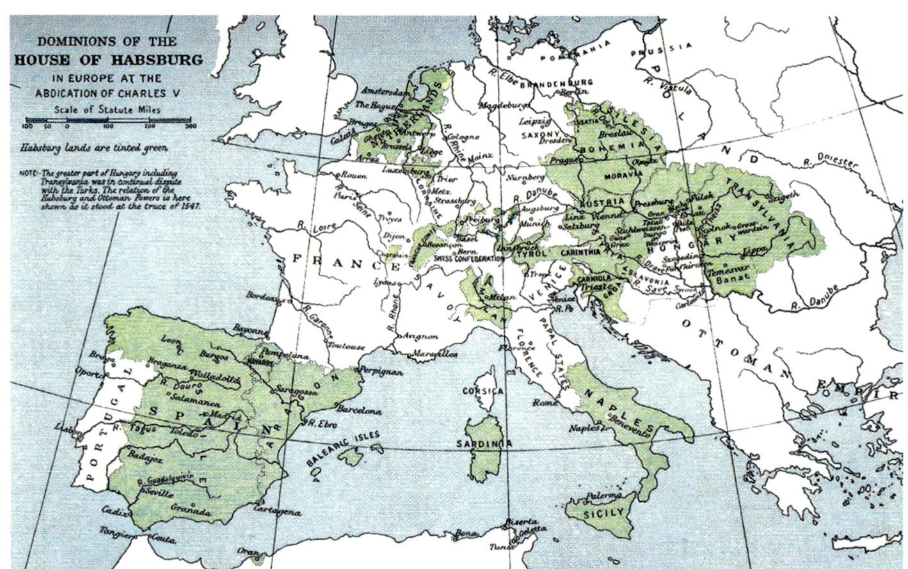

Above: This map shows – in green – the vast areas of Europe ruled by the House of Habsburg in the 16th century.

eighty-year war, ending in 1648 with Dutch autonomy and a new balance of power in Europe. The new Dutch Republic grew to become rich, influential and as we shall see, one of the most creative nations in Europe.

THE HOUSE OF HABSBURG

From the late 15th century, the House of Habsburg controlled vast areas of Europe. Heir of three of Europe's most powerful dynasties, Charles V of Spain (1500–58) ruled over the Netherlands, the Spanish Empire and the Holy Roman Empire. This inspired both jealousy and fear, and Charles's reign became dominated by war, which he funded by imposing heavy taxation on his subjects. Charles was in fact fairly liberal-minded, and having been born in Ghent in Belgium, he retained an affinity for the Low Countries. However, his son and successor, Philip II (1527–98), had a narrower outlook. He had been born in the Spanish capital of Valladolid and he appointed a Governor-General as Regent to take charge of the Low Countries, while he turned his attention to the Italian and Ottoman Wars. A zealous Catholic, he proclaimed himself

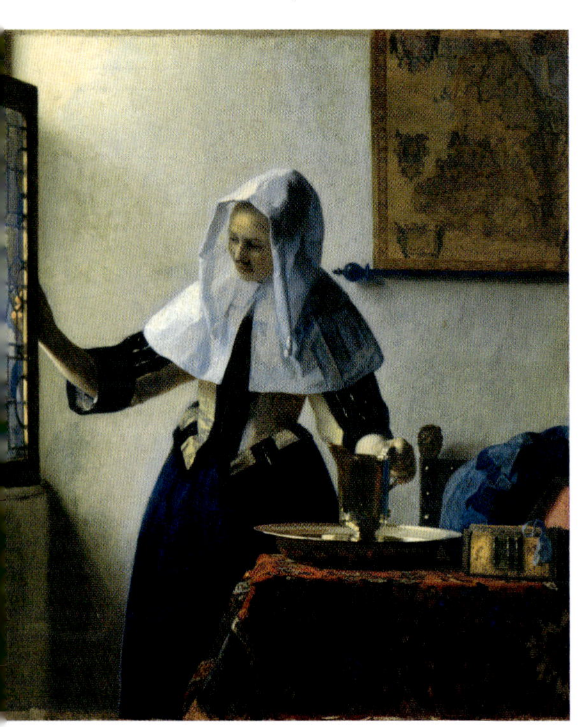

Below: One of the most famous artists of the Dutch Golden Age, Johannes Vermeer is known for his light-filled interiors, such as this work: Young Woman with a Water Pitcher, c.1662.

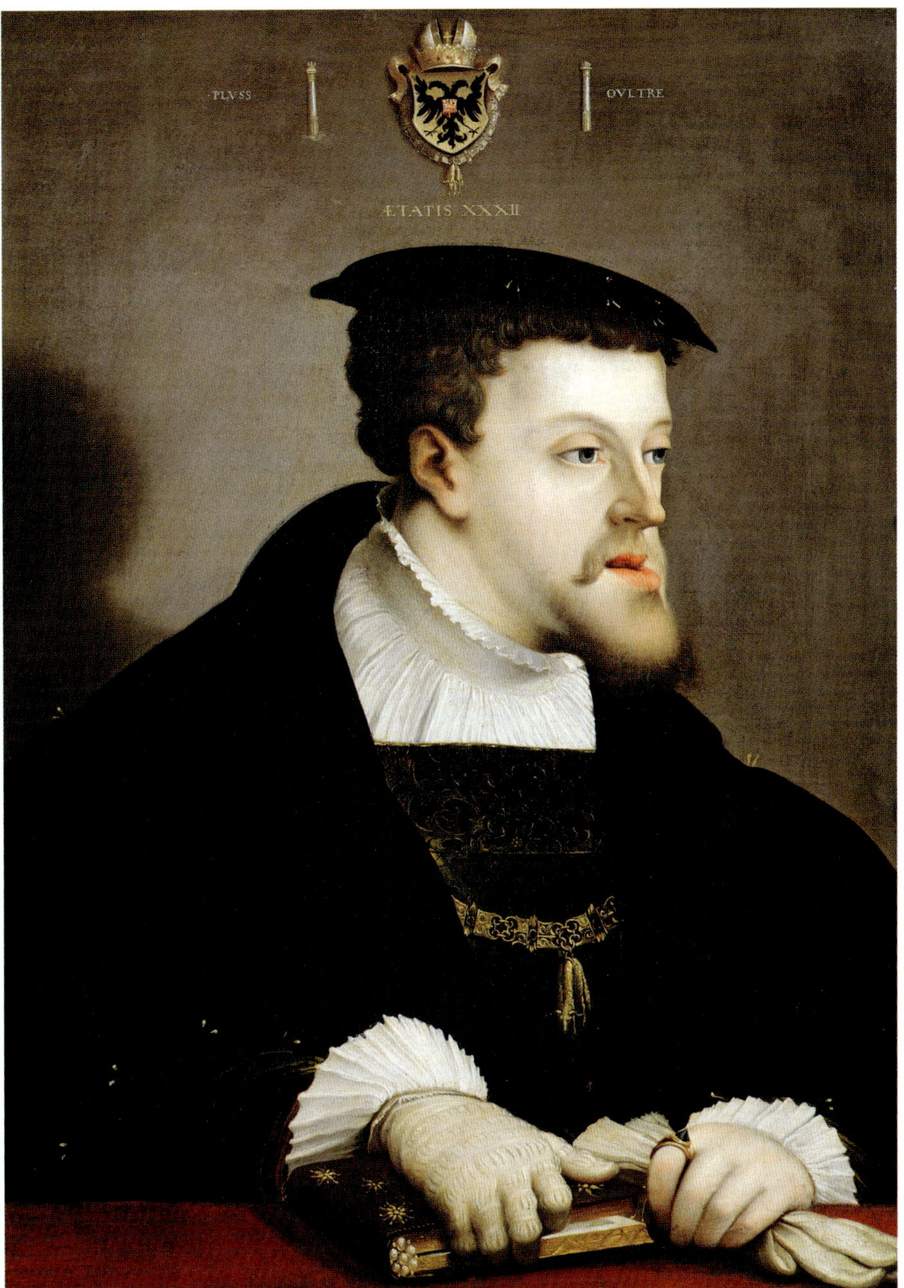

Above: Painted by Christoph Amberger (c.1505–c.1562), a portrait of Charles V, ruler of the Holy Roman Empire, the Spanish Empire and the lands of the former Duchy of Burgundy.

protector of the Counter-Reformation, aiming to eradicate Protestantism.

REBELLION AND WAR

Charles V outlawed any form of heresy, of which Protestantism was one, but he did not enforce it. Philip II, however, ordered the oppression of all Protestants in his lands. Along with heavy taxation, art in Protestant churches and other religious institutions was prohibited. This persecution ultimately exploded in rebellion, and soon after, in an all-out war. After eighty years of fighting, the largely Protestant northern Netherlands was finally recognized by Spain as independent, while the southern Netherlands, or Flanders (roughly modern-day Belgium), remained under the control of Spain and the Catholic Church.

THE ARTISTIC LEGACY

The newly independent Dutch Republic unleashed a creative storm. From 1600 to 1680, it is estimated that more than

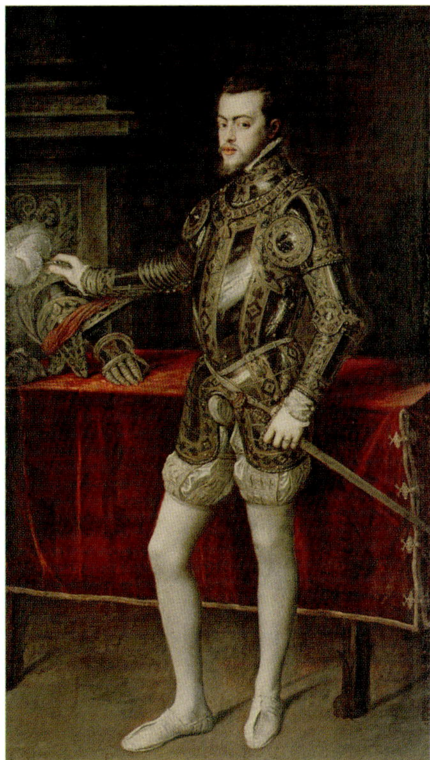

Above: Painted by Titian (c.1488–1576) in 1550, this is Philip II of Spain, whose empire included territories on every continent then known to Europeans, including the Philippines.

four million paintings were produced, and the accomplishments in realism and naturalism, by a large number of Dutch artists, were unprecedented.

After sharing their heritage for so long, there remained many similarities between Dutch and Flemish painting, but also distinctions. Similarities included technical accuracy and detailed realism; differences included an avoidance by Dutch artists of idealised subjects and the portrayals of splendour that were so prominent in Baroque art. On the whole, Dutch artists were also less interested in artistic theory than their counterparts in Flanders and other parts of Europe, and while in Catholic countries, including Flanders, the Church was the main commissioner of art, in the Dutch Republic, nearly all commissions and sales were private.

This book explores the paintings and profiles of the most influential individual artists, and the genres and themes in which they worked, in the period of the Dutch Golden Age.

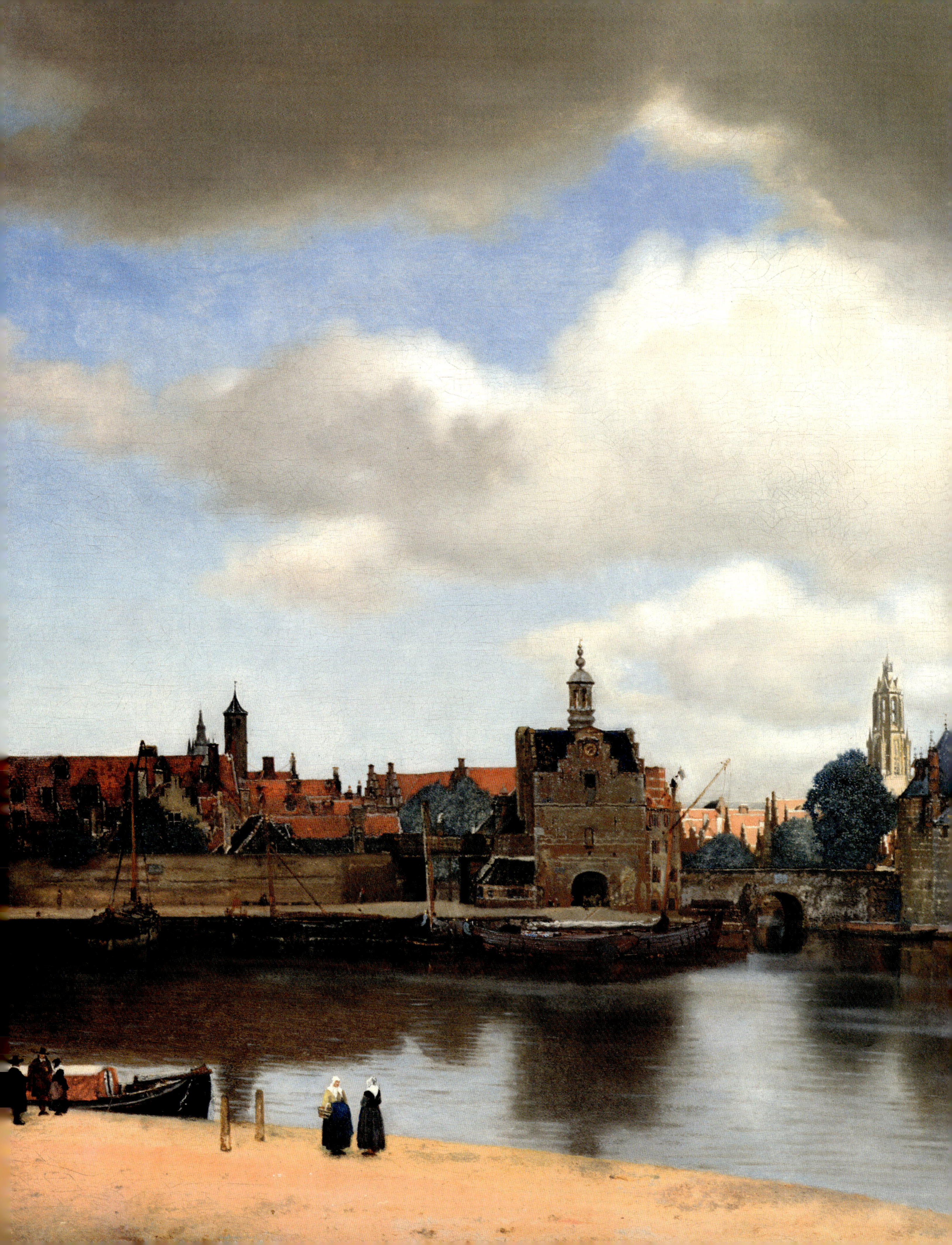

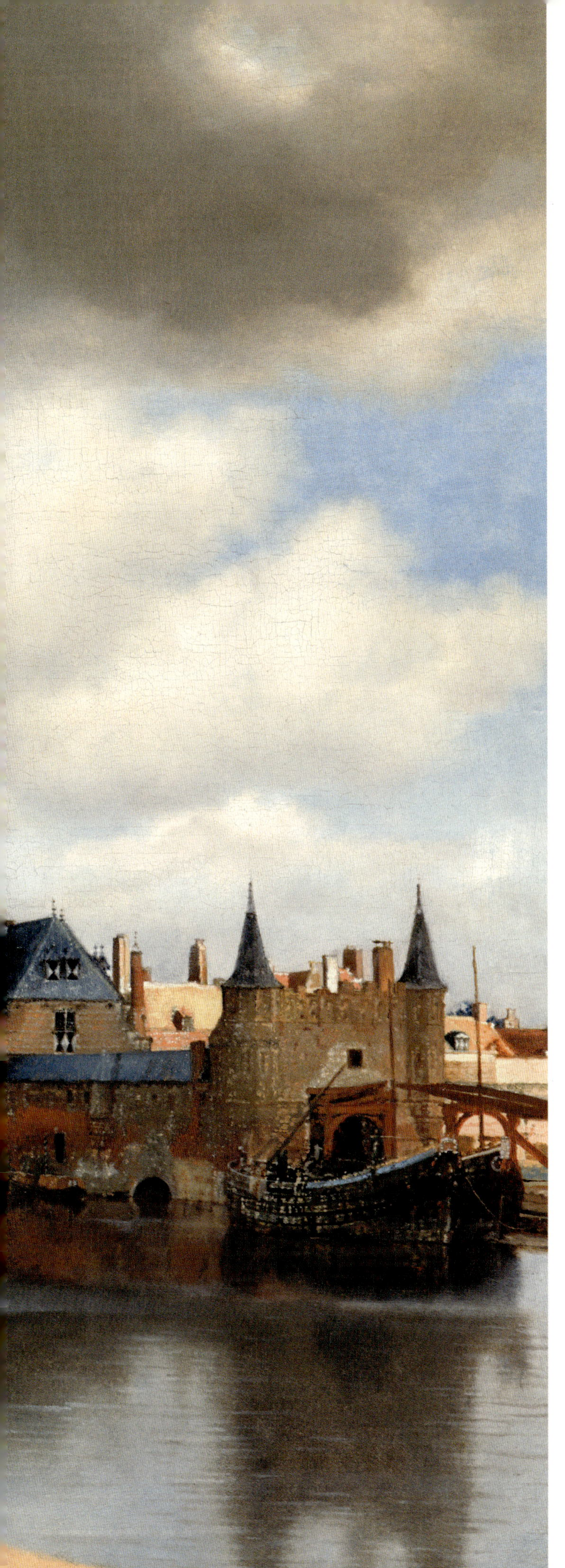

A NEW ERA

After years of domination by a foreign power and then the decades of war, the people of the Dutch Republic were freed. Wealth increased, and religious and intellectual tolerance made the new Republic a sanctuary for other European immigrants and refugees. The population surged, adding to its strength and power. The era began with a destruction of art that became known as Beeldenstorm, or The Iconoclastic Fury. Determining to rid his territories of Protestants, Philip II sent out his formidable Inquisition. In retaliation, in 1566, mobs of Protestants across the Low Countries attacked the art in Catholic churches. The Governor-General of the Netherlands, Philip's half-sister the more tolerant Margaret of Parma (1522–86), granted freedom of religion in exchange for an end to the violence. Yet the unrest continued, and Philip replaced Margaret with Fernando Alvarez de Toledo, the 3rd Duke of Alba (1507–82), whose heavy-handed repression escalated the conflict into war. After the granting of independence, the new art could flourish. Secular subjects were painted with naturalistic colours and tones, and technical skill was admired, and as prosperity increased, the market for paintings grew.

Left: View of Delft, *Johannes Vermeer, c.1660–61. Independence created the Dutch Golden Age, and the great wealth the Republic achieved resulted in mansions, canals, churches, city walls and harbours being built., and which were celebrated in many paintings.*

THE WAR OF INDEPENDENCE

Although Charles V was generally tolerated in the Netherlands, he caused great resentment once he raised taxes to defend his vast domains. Not only were the taxes begrudged, but his wars were considered detrimental as they were directed against many important trading partners of the Netherlandish people.

In 1560, the population of the Netherlands was almost three million. It was the largest urban presence in Europe, and Spain intended to retain control of it. In the fourteen northern provinces, Dutch dialects were spoken, while Walloon was the language of the three southern provinces. Yet despite this diversity, there was strong national unity and patriotism across them all.

Protestantism spread across the Dutch provinces and, perceived as heresy by the Catholic Church and a threat to the stability of the Habsburg political system, Philip sought to suppress the new faith, which made him an enemy of the Netherlandish people. He was also cold and arrogant

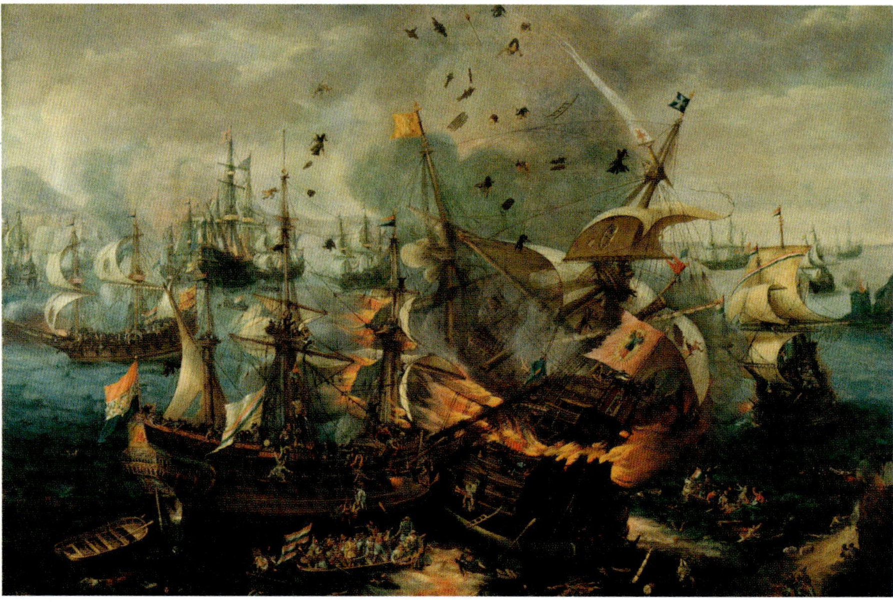

Above: Battle of Gibraltar in 1607, *by Cornelis Claesz van Wieringen, c.1621, depicting a Spanish flagship being hit by a smaller Dutch warship and exploding in the Bay of Gibraltar.*

THE THIRTY YEARS' WAR

Within the eighty-year war between Spain and the Netherlands, there were connected conflicts involving several other European nations. What became known as the Thirty Years' War took place from 1618 to 1648. It began when the future Holy Roman Emperor Ferdinand II (1578–1637), king of Bohemia at the time, attempted to impose Roman Catholic absolutism on all his territories. As in the Netherlands, many newly Protestant nobles of both Bohemia and Austria rose up in rebellion, initiating a chain of events that involved most of the great European powers. As it continued, the war became less about religion and more about the balance of power, and with eight million casualties, it was one of the longest and most destructive conflicts in European history. When the Peace Treaty was signed in 1648, the religious and political map of Europe had irrevocably changed.

towards them, and they became increasingly discontented with Habsburg rule. Philip and his ministers were also angered when actions were taken in the Netherlands without his permission, but as requests sent to Spain took at least four weeks to be answered, it was often impractical to wait. Finally, when the Duke of Alba brought in Spanish troops to suppress the Iconoclastic Fury – the destruction of art in Catholic churches by Protestent protestors – and he ordered the execution of about 3,000 rebels, it greatly intensified the unrest.

WILLIAM OF ORANGE

The Eighty Years' War began with the Battle of Heiligerlee in the province of Groningen in 1568. Although it was a success for the Dutch, Philip II soon regained control, however the war continued as those in the northern Netherlands refused to give up. In 1581, they established the Republic of the Seven United Netherlands, or the Dutch Republic. The leader of the Dutch Republic was William I, Prince of Orange (1533–84), also known as William the Silent. William was a

Below: William I The Silent *by Anthonis van Dashorst Mor, c.1552. William I was the leader of the Dutch revolt against the Spanish.*

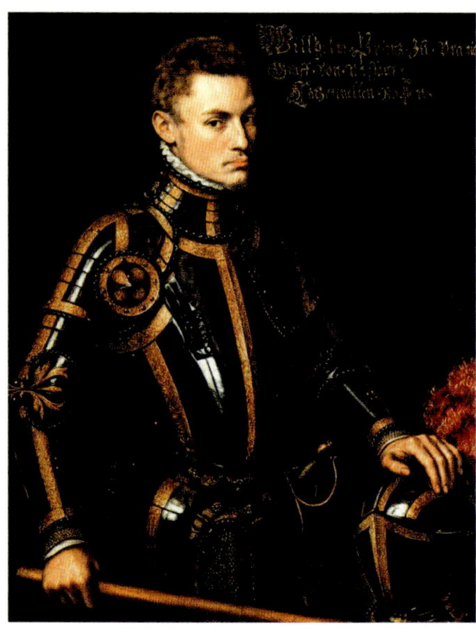

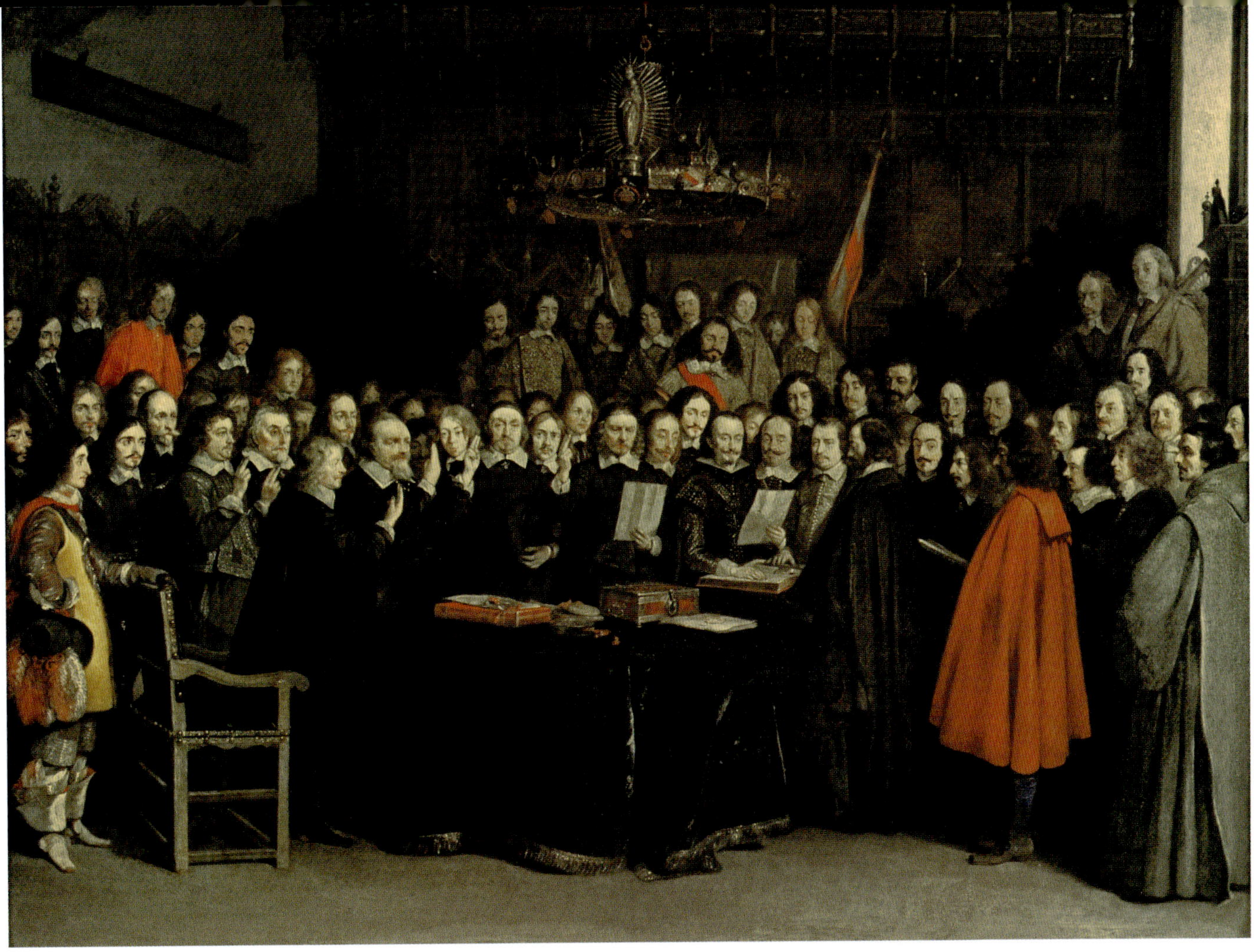

Above: The Swearing of the Oath of Ratification of the Treaty of Münster, *Gerard ter Borch, 1648 – painted in oil on copper, this records the Peace of Westphalia that ended the Dutch 80-year struggle with Spain.*

wealthy nobleman and member of the Habsburg court of Margaret of Parma, but he became horrified at the tyranny of Spanish rule and eventually turned against the Habsburgs to lead the Dutch uprising, intensifying the rebellion into an extensive war. Under his direction, the army won several territories, but he was assassinated in Delft in 1584. His son Prince Maurits of Orange (1567–1625) took control and after Maurits died, his half-brother Prince Frederik Hendrik (1584–1647) assumed power.

THE END OF THE WARS

During the Anglo-Spanish War of 1585–1604, the Dutch had some help from Britain, which angered Philip so much that he focused his resources on the ill-fated Spanish Armada's invasion of England, which resulted in his

bankruptcy. In October 1648, the Peace of Westphalia was signed that ended the Eighty Years' War between the Netherlands and Spain, and the Thirty Years' War between other European sovereignties. This peace treaty resulted in the formal recognition of the Dutch Republic as an empire, completely

independent from the Spanish crown. In addition, large areas of the southern Netherlands became part of France.

Below: Iconoclasm in a Church, *painted by Dirck van Delen in 1630. A rare painting of a dark day in Dutch history, as Protestants destroy Catholic statues.*

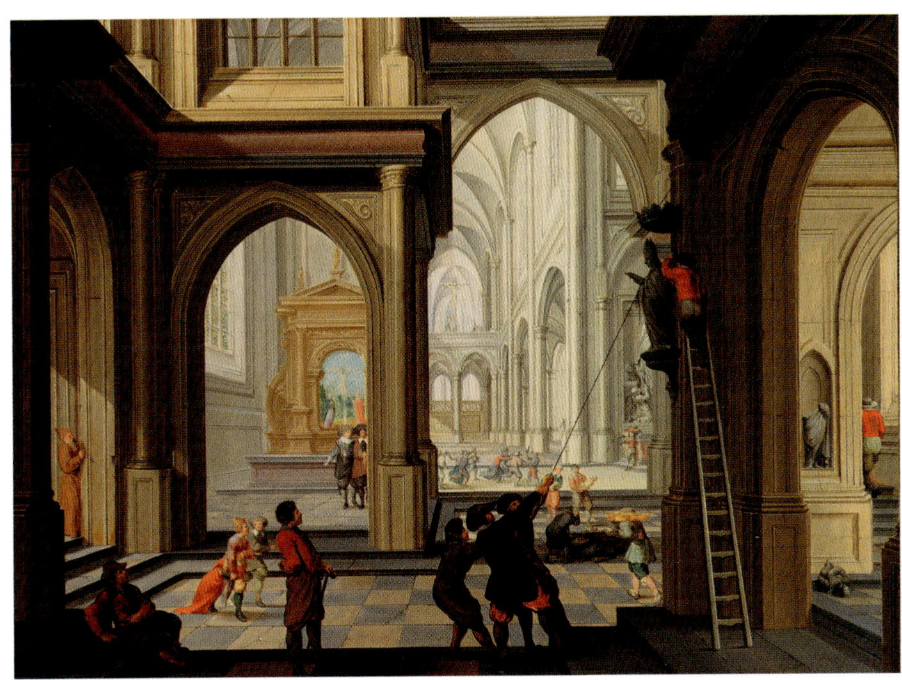

THE DUTCH REPUBLIC

The independent Republic soon became one of the wealthiest and most powerful nations in the world. Dutch explorers charted new territory; merchants forged new trade deals and routes; scientists, lawyers and educationalists developed new approaches; and Dutch artists expressed it all with remarkable skill.

After the wars, the whole of Europe was reshaped. With Hapsburg ambition now subdued, Bourbon France became stronger, and Sweden began rising as a great power. Dominating international trade, the new Dutch Republic created its own vast empire.

TOLERANCE AND OPENESS

The tolerance of individual belief in the Dutch Republic was unique and drew

Below: The Announcement of the Peace Treaty of Münster in 1648 from the Balcony of the Town Hall of Haarlem, *by Gillis Rombouts, marks the most important peace treaty of the 17th century in the Netherlands.*

religious refugees from all over Europe, particularly Jews, and later Huguenots. As a result, many successful industrialists, manufacturers and merchants included Protestants, Catholics and Jews. (It should be observed that this tolerance and understanding was limited; the slave trade remained part of the Republic's financial success.)

The climate of openness also attracted intellectuals and thinkers. By 1650, every province had at least one institution of higher education. In 1575, in gratitude for Leiden's staunch resistance against Spain during the war, William of Orange had established the University of Leiden and, along with the University of Utrecht, it became a gathering place

THE MIDDLE CLASS

Unlike other countries of the period, the urban merchant class dominated Dutch society. These confident and affluent people were usually Protestant, and typically wealthier, more worldly, better educated and healthier than their predecessors. They ate a more varied diet and they generally lived in towns, in tall, narrow townhouses, several storeys high. Together they shaped what was an entirely new form of social class, and they commissioned an original school of painting to reflect and celebrate it.

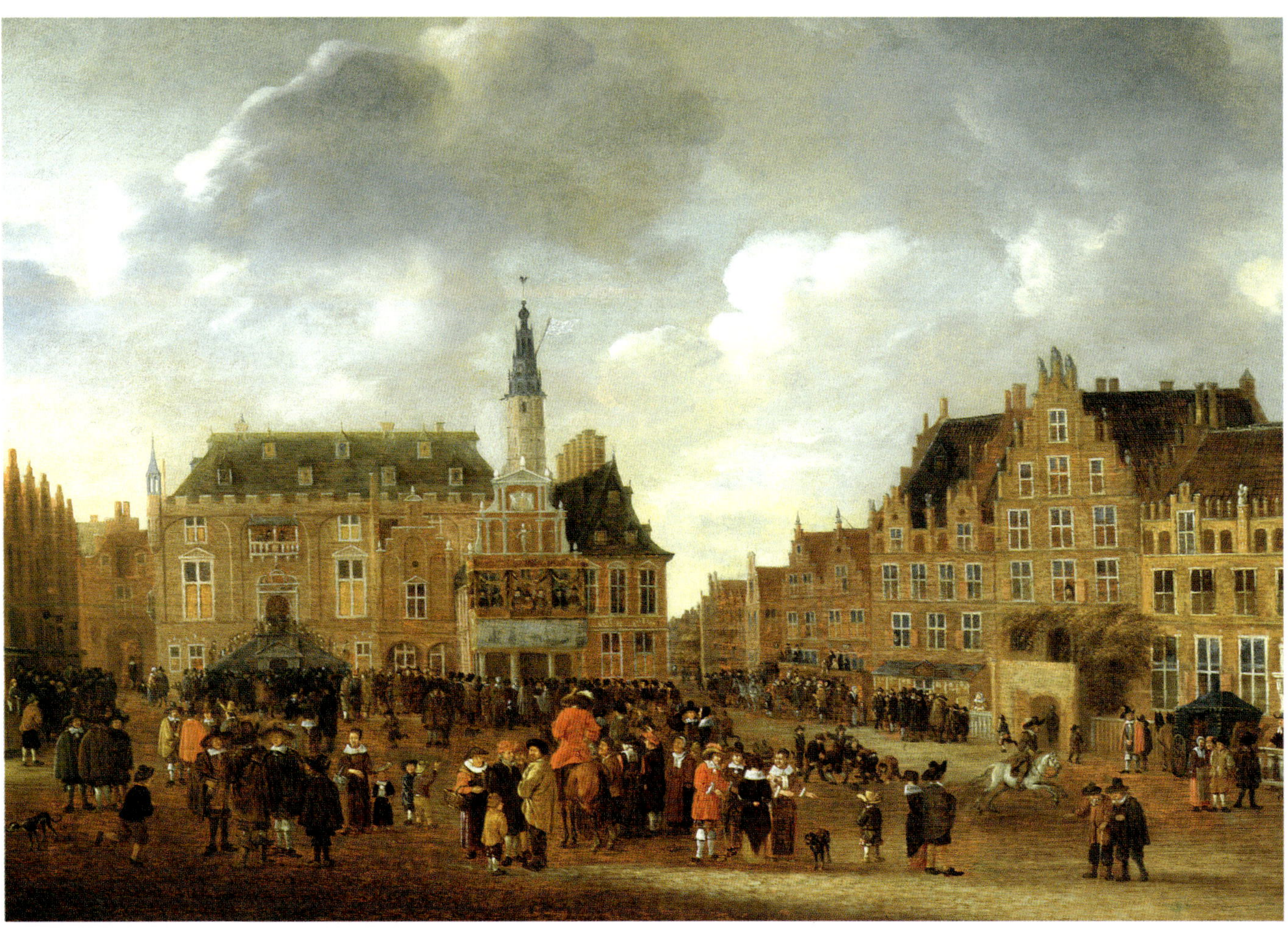

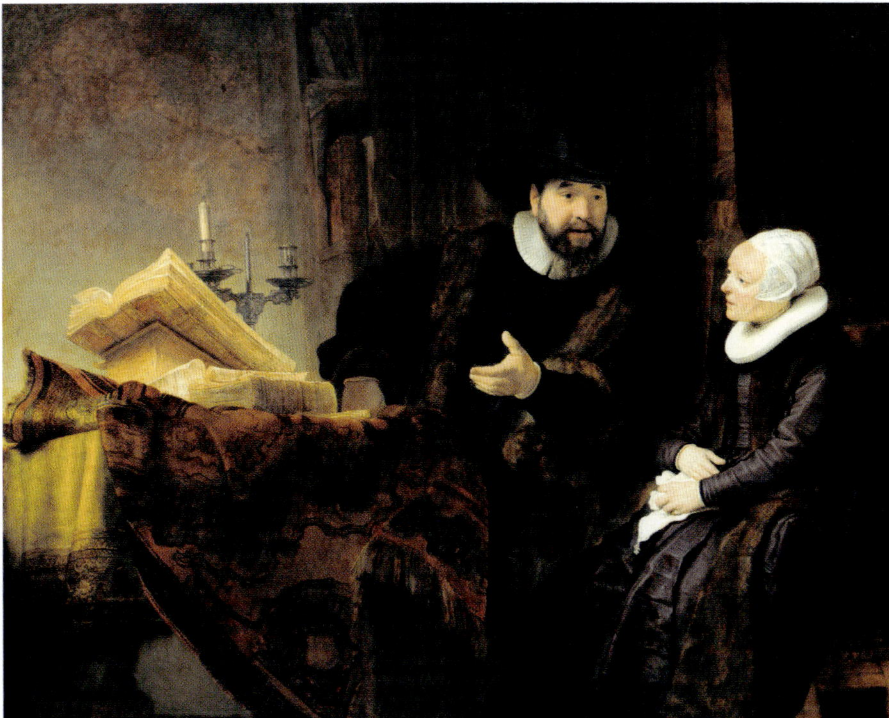

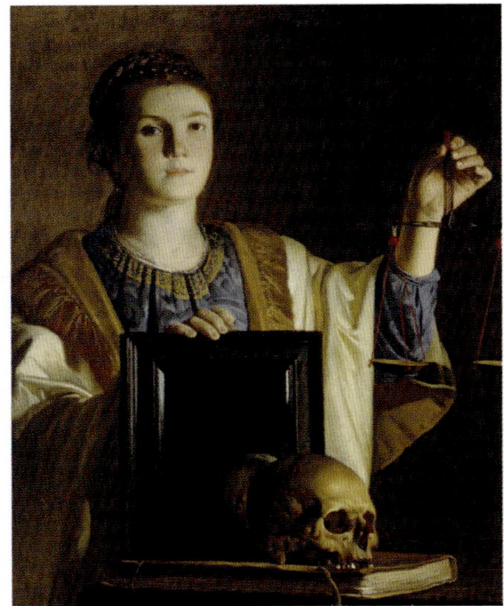

Above: Truth Presenting a Mirror to the Vanities of the World, *c.1625 (unknown artist) – in place of grand Christian scenes came smaller, moralistic paintings.*

for scientists, philosophers, theologians, lawyers and mathematicians. The French philosopher, mathematician and scientist René Descartes (1596–1650) lived in the Dutch Republic for 20 years, and

Below: A Trompe l'Oeil of Objects *is one of Samuel van Hoogstraten's remarkably realistic still lifes, reflecting his life and social standing.*

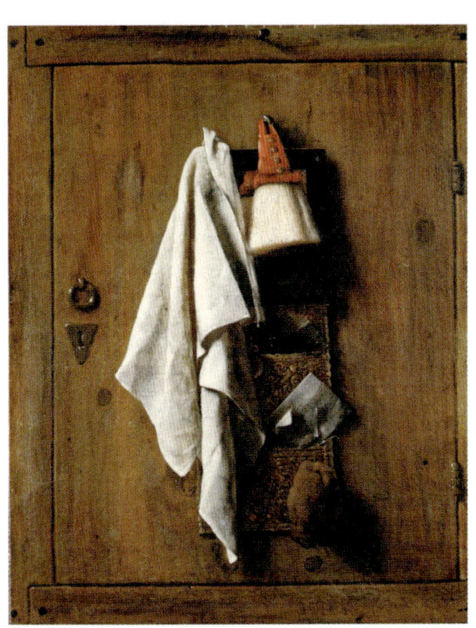

had his most important works published in Amsterdam and Leiden. Opposing his theories was Benedict Spinoza (1632–77), a Jewish Dutch philosopher of Portuguese origin. Lively debate was to be found in education, science and mathematics, while Dutch lawyers became famous for their knowledge of international and commercial laws.

Book publishing also flourished. For a large part of the 17th century, over one third of all books produced in Europe were published in Amsterdam. The open-mindedness and readiness to embrace new trends and ideas resulted in a wide range of books on numerous subjects.

NEW LANDS

Other factors contributed to the growth of trade, industry, the sciences and the arts. One was a proficiency in map-making, and another was the availability of cheap energy, from windmills and from the peat that was easily transported by canal to towns and cities. Fleets of fast ships with ample storage space for importing and exporting goods were built to the highest standards, using the latest methods.

As the Dutch began trading with the Far East, they gradually took over the dominant position in world trade. In 1602, the Dutch East India Company was formed. Financed by shares that established the first modern stock exchange, it was the first-ever multinational corporation. The Bank of Amsterdam was established soon after in 1609. In 1621, the Dutch West India Company was given a monopoly to trade in the West Indies, and founded colonies along the length of the American coast. Among other things, spices, sugar and exotic fruits were imported in bulk, and brought in huge profits.

Between 1607 and 1640, lakes were drained across the Republic to create large areas of new arable land, and between 1609 and 1672, the city of Amsterdam was restructured on a grid of canals. New villages and towns developed, and an efficient system of transportation was created along the rivers and canals, while horse-drawn boats connected large cities with smaller villages and towns.

The largest Dutch cities were Amsterdam, Rotterdam, Leiden, Alkmaar, The Hague, Delft, Dordrecht and Haarlem, all in the province of Holland, and eventually the dialect spoken in Holland became the standard Dutch language.

THE FLOWERING OF ART

With no commissions coming from powerful Catholic churches or royal courts, painters of the 17th-century Dutch Republic were independent but vulnerable. Although there were still some large civic commissions, on the whole paintings and prints – rarely sculpture – were bought to hang in homes.

The northern Netherlands that made up the new Dutch Republic had traditionally been less important artistically than the Flemish provinces in the south, but after the war this changed. The upheavals of conflict, the break with monarchy and with many

Below: A Girl Chopping Onions, 1646, by Gerrit Dou; the first and most important of the Leiden fijnschilders. The painting shows his meticulous brushwork, close observation of objects and high degree of finish.

Catholic traditions, and the increasingly wealthy Dutch citizens who were eagerly buying art for their homes, all led to artistic reinvention.

A BROADER MARKET

The relatively wide distribution of wealth in the Dutch Republic meant that more people of different social levels were buying art than had occurred previously. In just over a century, several million paintings were produced there. Apart from portraits, few of these were created to

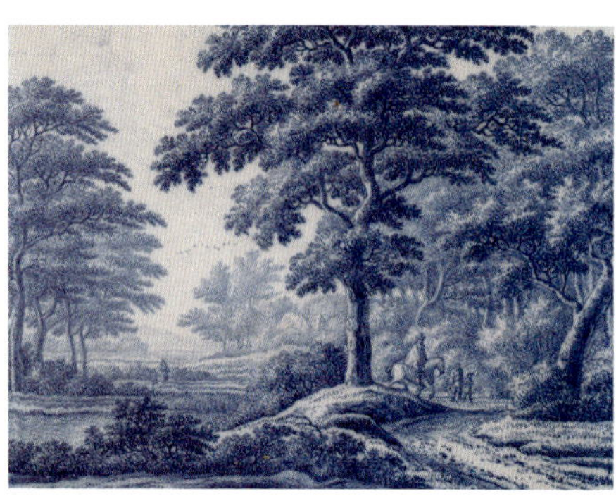

Above: A rare Dutch Delft blue and white tile, depicting wayfarers on a road in a wood, by Frederik van Frijtorn or Frytorn.

commission. So in another departure from European artistic tradition, many paintings were produced for the open market. Artists built on their strengths and became specialists in certain areas, and rather than production diminishing, there was a great surge in artistic creation. Although some artists such as Rembrandt van Rijn (1606–69) and Johannes Vermeer (1632–75) are now among the most famous, at the time, they were just two among many accomplished artists.

Unlike Flanders, which remained under the rule of the Spanish Habsburgs, the Dutch Republic was governed by an appointed stadhouder, or stadtholder, along with other officials from the States General, or Staten-Generaal. Although after the Dutch Revolt, stadholders were often the Princes of Orange, there was no royal court with a satellite class of nobles and aristocrats. Instead, the most powerful Dutch citizens were the new bourgeoisie, who sought new artistic subjects to celebrate their recently acquired eminence, experiences and aspirations.

TYPES OF PAINTINGS

Most Dutch paintings were fairly small – the few large paintings produced at the time were mainly group portraits,

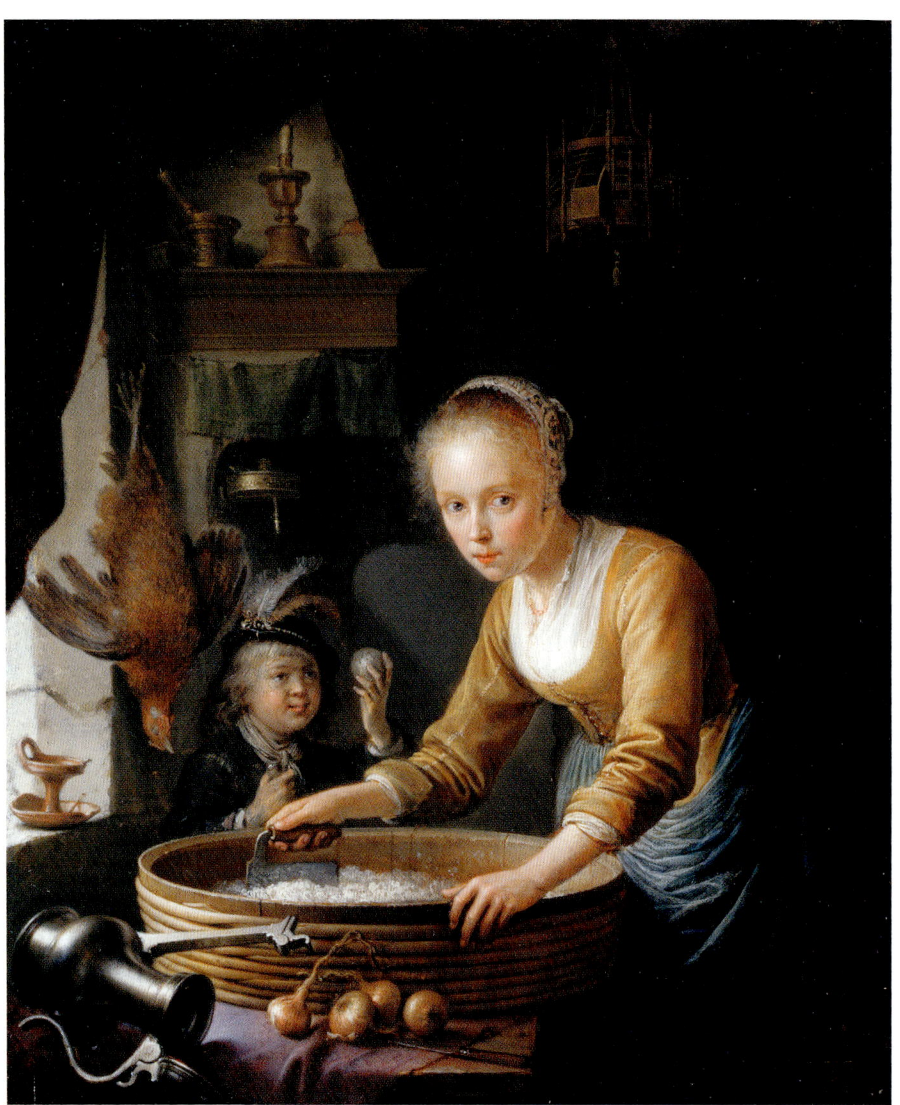

THE SCHOOL OF DELFT

Delft School artists mixed oil from locally-grown linseeds with their pigments to produce an especially fluid type of oil paint. Although they were not an official group, merely several skilful artists working in Delft during the period, they all created similarly-styled pictures. They became known for genre paintings, depicting interiors and exteriors of houses, internal church architecture, courtyards and local streets. There were several notable artists working in Delft at this time, among them Vermeer, Pieter de Hooch (1629–84), Carel Fabritius (1622–54), Gerard Houckgeest (c.1600–61), Emanuel de Witte (1617–92), Hendrick van der Burgh (1627–64), Adam Pynacker (1622–73) and Jan Steen (1626–79). Their calm, balanced paintings are structured on precise perspective and infused with light. Overall, the School of Delft only lasted from 1650–75. After that, many of the artists moved away in search of larger markets, usually to Amsterdam, and the prolific Delft period ended.

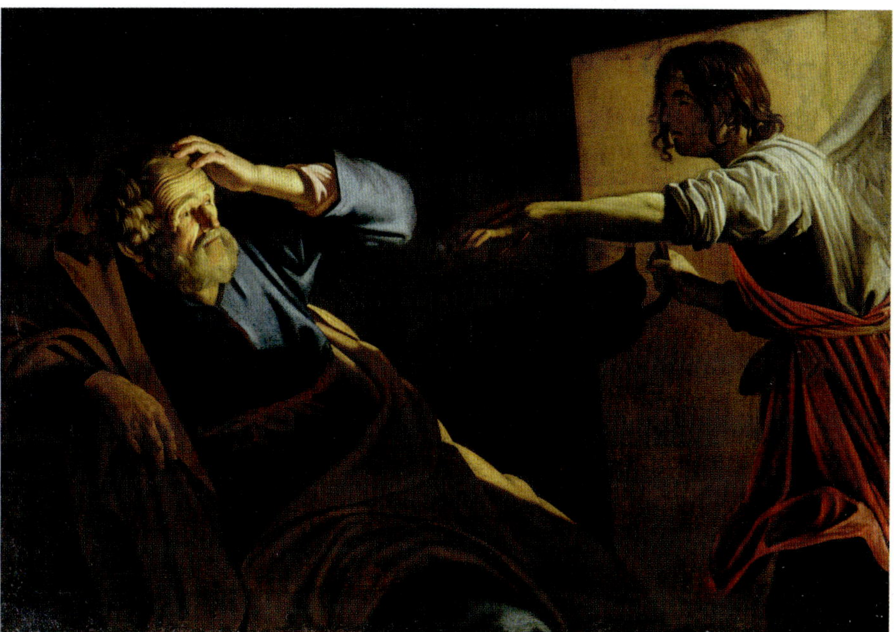

Above: Dramatic and animated, Saint Peter Released from Prison, *by Gerrit van Honthorst in 1618, shows that the Dutch Golden Age was clearly also part of the wider Baroque movement.*

Below: An Allegory of the Vanities of Human Life, *c.1640 – reflecting on worldly wealth, this is a vanitas painted by Harmen Steenwyck (1612–56).*

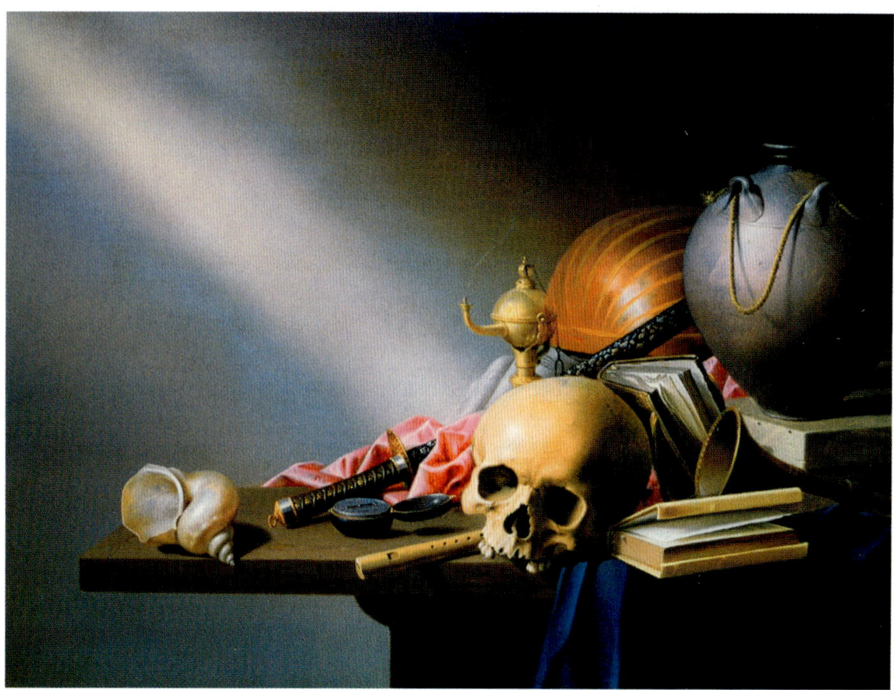

usually of civic militia companies or governing bodies of guilds or charitable organizations. The small pictures were placed on the walls of the homes of merchants, city officials, publishers, butchers, tailors and industrialists – anyone who could afford to buy art. The types of paintings they wanted celebrated the world around them. These included landscapes, seascapes and cityscapes of the country they were so proud of; still lifes of goods they produced or could afford to buy; and portraits and scenes of everyday life.

Although religious paintings were rarely commissioned, a fashion developed for small-scale works featuring Christian messages or moral lessons. Occasional religious paintings were produced, but in general, these were a few small-format biblical subjects.

Many artists became grouped under loose titles, such as 'fijnschilders' (fine-painters), who painted small-scale meticulous, natural-looking pictures. 'The Utrecht Caravaggisti' worked in Utrecht and produced paintings that were strongly influenced by Caravaggio (1571–1610), particularly his use of chiaroscuro. Other artists were labelled according to their location, such as 'the Haarlem School' or 'the School of Delft.'

Dutch Golden Age artists had various notable influences, including Pieter Bruegel the Elder (1525–69), the anonymous Flemish painter known as 'Master of the Small Landscapes', and Northern European Renaissance artists such as Jan van Eyck (c.1385/90–1441), Albrecht Dürer (1471–1528) and Hieronymus Bosch (1450–1516).

GUILDS AND TRAINING

While this book features many artists from the Dutch Golden Age, they are just a small proportion of the actual number. It has been estimated that there were possibly between 50,000 and 100,000 artists working at that time, producing between five and 10 million works of art between them.

APPRENTICESHIPS

In the early 17th century in Europe, artistic training generally followed the medieval system of apprenticeship in a workshop with a recognized master artist of a guild. In the Dutch Republic, guilds were established in each city and they usually limited workshops to only one or two apprentices at any time, so they were smaller than the workshops in Flanders and Italy. Apprenticeships usually began when the child (usually boys, rarely girls) was 10 to 12. The parents paid the master a fee. A young apprentice who remained living with his parents cost approximately between 20 and 50 guilders a year, more if he boarded. Famous artists such as Rembrandt or Gerrit Dou (1613–78) charged more. Compared with school education which generally cost between two and six guilders a year, it can be seen that apprenticeship to a workshop was expensive.

After between two and six years, an apprentice applied for membership in the guild by submitting a 'masterpiece,' showcasing all the skills he had learned. If he was judged to have reached the

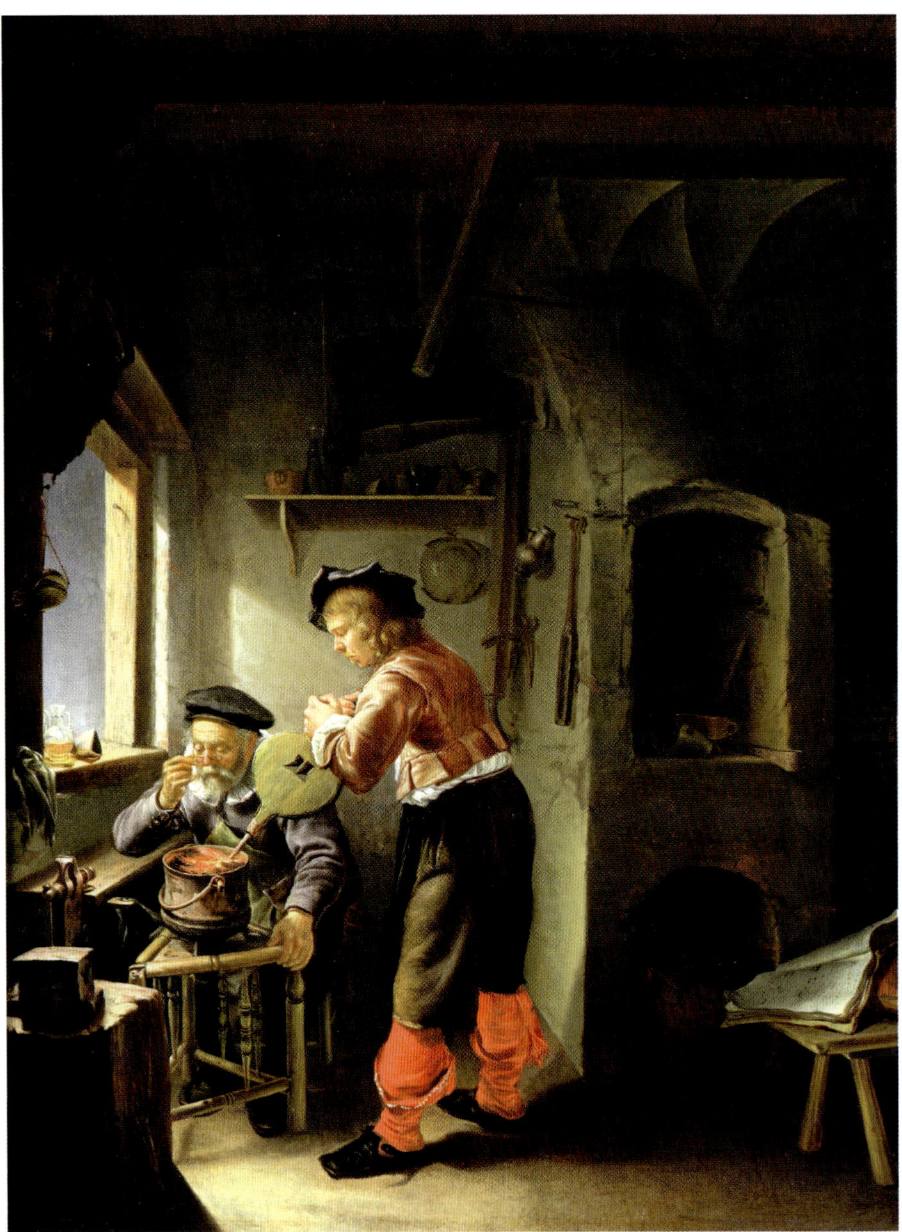

Above: An Old Alchemist and his Assistant *by Frans van Mieris shows an elderly alchemist intently watching an experiment performed by his young assistant.*

required standard, he was allowed to produce and sell his own work and take on his own apprentices.

Many apprentices worked in the same or a similar style as their masters, and some trained and then worked with their fathers, or married their master's daughters, and so dynasties of painters developed, often creating works of a similar style.

GUILDS

Since the medieval era, trades had been organized and protected by the guild system, and in the Dutch Republic, painters, printers, sculptors, bookbinders, glassmakers, embroiderers and art dealers usually joined the Guild of Saint Luke. As Saint Luke was the patron saint of artists, the Guild of Saint Luke was the name of all art guilds across Europe. It oversaw both the production and sale of art and the education of young artists.

Eventually there was a Guild of Saint Luke to be found in every Dutch town and city, each with its own rules and regulations. Each branch protected its members against competition and set rules to ensure quality and reasonable working conditions, including working hours, prices and quality standards. A large part of each guild's income was spent on helping poor members and their families.

However, as the status of artists rose in the Dutch Republic by the second half of the century, the influence of the guilds diminished, and new academies opened to train artists instead, which further reduced the power and influence of the guilds.

ADVICE FOR YOUNG PAINTERS

Karel (or Carel) van Mander (1548–1606), a Flemish painter, poet and art historian, believed that artists should display exemplary behaviour so that their profession would be taken seriously. In his *Painting Book* (*Schilder-Boeck* or *Schilderboek*), first published in 1604 in Haarlem, he urged artists: 'Do not waste time. Do not get drunk or fight. Do not draw attention by living an immoral life. Painters belong in the environment of princes and learned people. They must be polite to their fellow artists. Listen to criticism, even that of the common people. Do not become upset or angry because of adverse criticism... Thank God for your talent and do not be conceited. Do not fall in love too young and do not marry too soon... Keep away from prostitutes, for two reasons: It is a sin, and they make you sick... Show Italians how wrong they are in their belief that Flemish painters cannot paint human figures. At Rome, study drawing, at Venice, painting.'

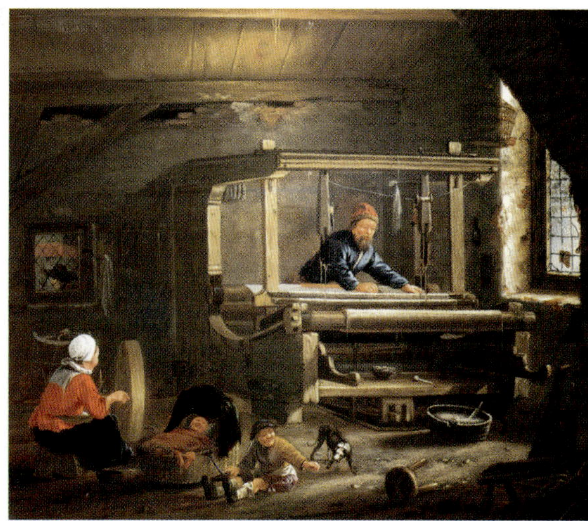

Above: This painting, The Workshop of a Weaver, *1656 by Gillis Rombouts, shows a craftsman – who would have been a member of the local guild – at his work. The general approach with a painting of an interior was to have one window lighting the scene from the left-hand side. With its illuminated window on the right-hand side, this painting was unusual.*

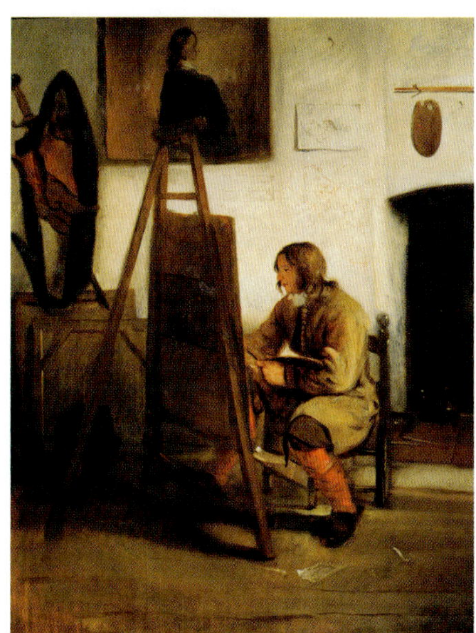

Above: It has been suggested that the model for Young Painter in his Studio *by Barent Fabritius may have been his brother Johannes (1636–1707).*

Right: The Painter in his Workshop, *c.1633, by Adriaen van Ostade shows an artist at work in his large studio. Strewn about is the clutter of artistic equipment; the atmosphere is one of hushed creativity.*

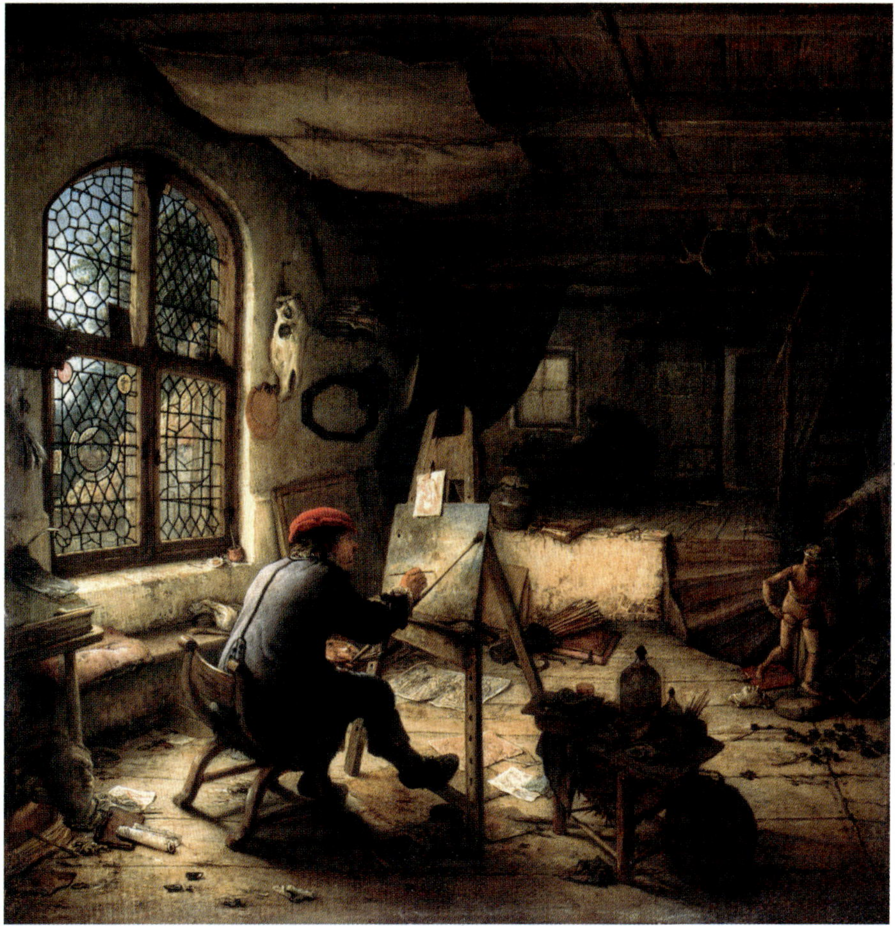

THE ART MARKET

From about 1600, the wealth of the northern Netherlands increased and the market for art rose correspondingly. People had much to celebrate, and buying and displaying art was a powerful way of doing this. Although richer citizens bought the most, even the less well-off adorned their homes with art.

Several factors contributed to the Republic's prosperity. More money was available to begin with, as the Dutch no longer paid the heavy taxes previously imposed by Spain. As part of the economic warfare against Spanish rule, in 1585, the Dutch navy had blockaded Antwerp, which ended its standing as Europe's busiest port. Within a short time, Amsterdam had taken over this position. Impressive Dutch ships navigated by accomplished sailors carried a wide range of imports and exports that were traded by proficient merchants. These faster, stronger ships, with skilful sailors, helped global exploration, which in turn opened up further opportunities for trade. Ultimately, the Dutch conducted trade in the Caribbean, East Indies, North America, Brazil and South Africa, and established colonies in all those locations. As the economy prospered,

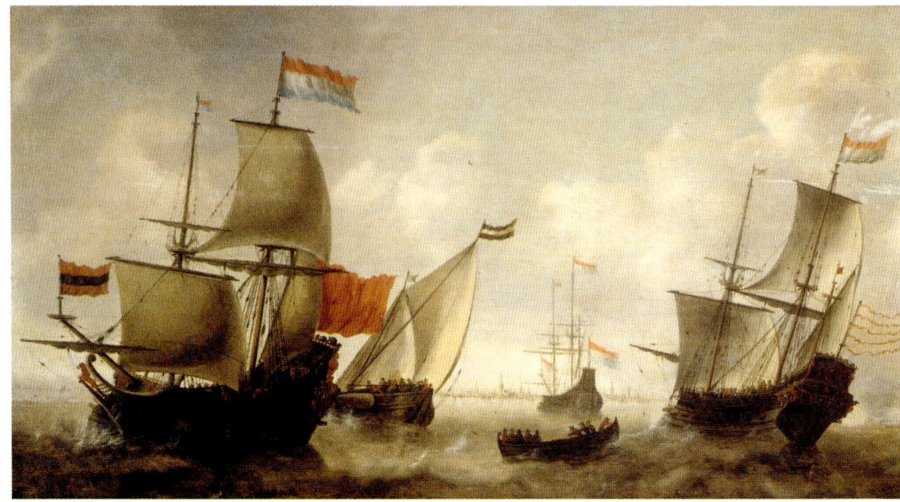

a society developed of great scientists, philosophers, engineers, writers, composers, architects and artists.

The production and sale of paintings and prints developed into a mass market. Thousands of artists produced tens of thousands of paintings and

Above: A Dutch Merchantman with a Wijdschip and other Shipping off Amsterdam, *by Jacob Adraensz Bellevois.*

Below: The Dutch Fleet of the Dutch East India Company, *by Ludolf Backhuysen (or Backhuisen).*

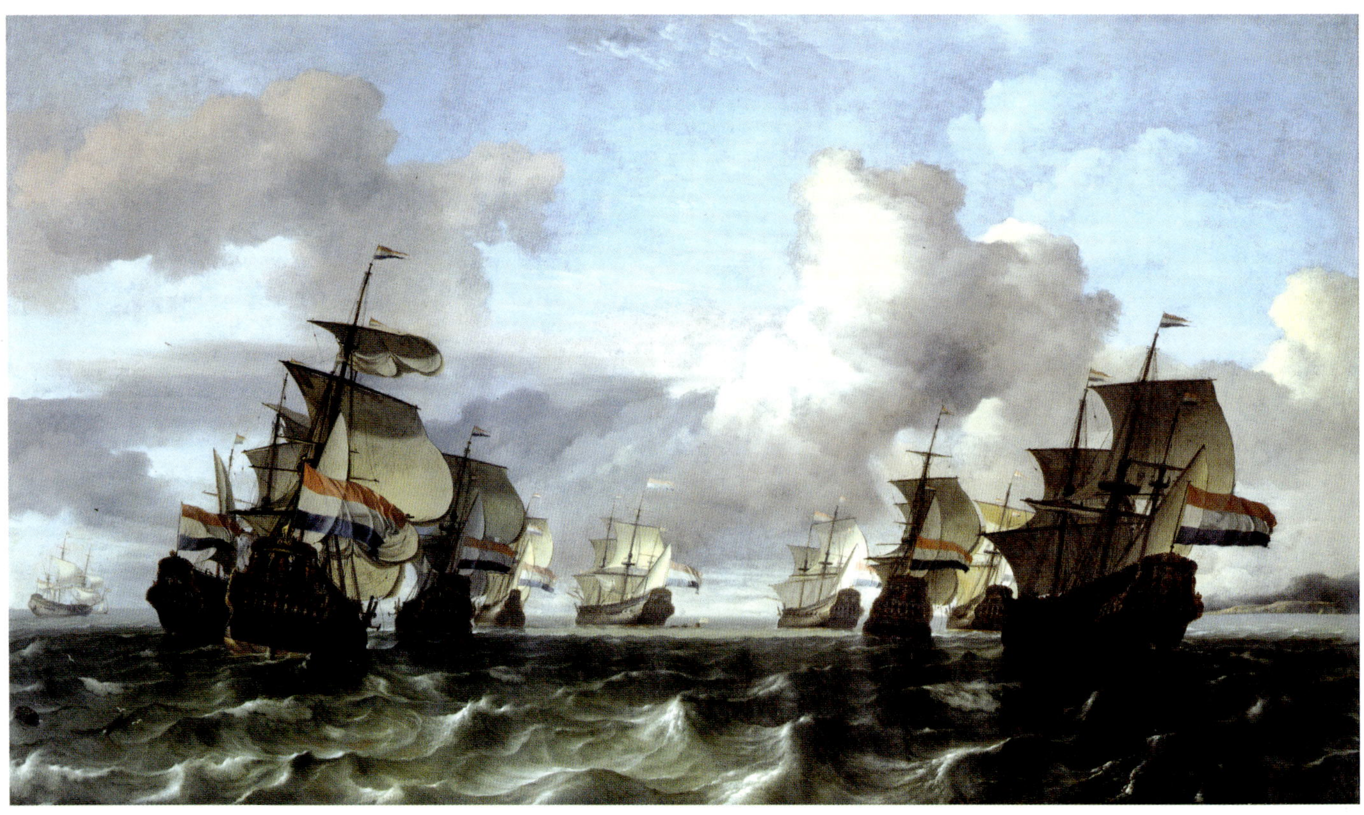

prints, and the Dutch bought and displayed them, especially on walls that faced the street, where passers-by could see them.

While members of the large Dutch middle class bought the majority of art, more modest citizens also displayed art in their homes, usually drawings and prints rather than paintings. It was not unusual in the early part of the century for a household to display on average ten pictures. As the century progressed, the number rose to approximately 50 to 100 pictures per household after 1648.

Professional art dealing burgeoned as a business. Several art dealers were also artists, such as Vermeer, Jan van Goyen (1596–1656) and Willem Kalf (1619–93). Rembrandt's dealer, Hendrick van Uylenburgh (c.1587–1661), and his son Gerrit van Uylenburgh (c.1625–79), became extremely important.

PRICING ART

There were huge differences in the quality and cost of paintings produced and sold. The few that were painted to commission were priced before they were painted, while many produced for the open market were painted quickly to meet demand. Only a small proportion were outstanding. The cheapest sold for a half or one guilder, which was the average daily wage of a skilled labourer. The most expensive sold for between 500 to 1,000 guilders. The small, highly-finished paintings or fijnschilders generally sold at the top end of the price range.

Some artists, such as Vermeer, sold only to one particular patron, but on the whole, most paintings were bought directly from artists' studios. A purchaser would visit and choose either a work in progress or a completed painting. Paintings were also bought from art dealers, booksellers and private collectors, or at annual fairs, auctions and lotteries, which became more popular over the period. Great competition developed among artists in efforts to appeal, and especially-popular artists' styles and subjects were copied.

Some printmakers specialized in reproductions of paintings and like the painters themselves, different

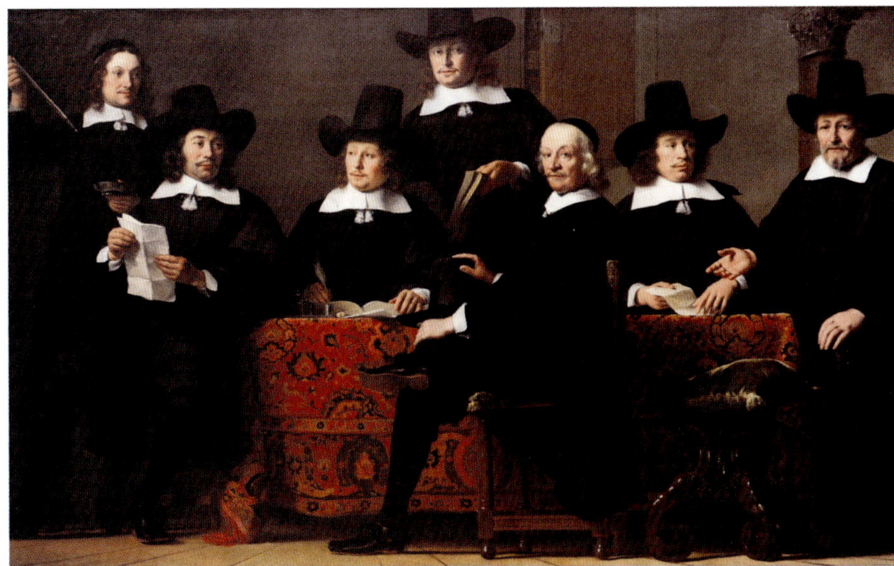

Above: Painted in the second half of the 17th century, Governors of the Wine Merchant's Guild *by Ferdinand Bol is an example of the highly popular group portraits of the Dutch Golden Age.*

Below: Abel Janszoon Tasman (1603–59) was a Dutch explorer and merchant for the Dutch East India Company. This portrait of him, his wife and daughter was painted in 1637, possibly by Jacob Cuyp.

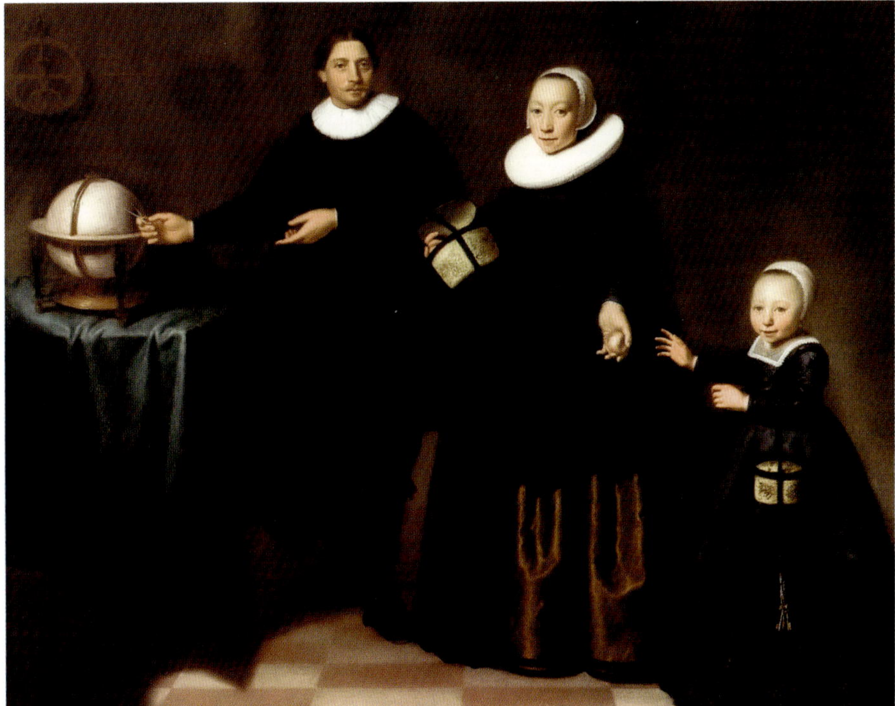

printmakers became specialists in printing different genres. Prints and drawings were always less expensive than paintings. An engraving, for example, could cost about a third of the price of a small painting, and far less than a medium-sized one.

Although painting production rose in the first half of the 17th century, when war broke out with England from 1665 to 1667, it had a negative effect on sales. Then came 1672, the 'Year of Disaster,' or Rampjaar (see page 80), when the Dutch Republic was simultaneously attacked by England, France and the bishoprics of Münster and Cologne. Subsequent defeats of part of the Dutch Republic brought a severe depression to the art market, which never quite recovered its earlier strengths.

ART GENRES

While Baroque art in Catholic countries was frequently dramatic and sensuous, Protestants advocated modesty, and so in general, themes that became popular in the Netherlands were restrained, expressing lifestyles and tastes of the contemporary world. These themes can be grouped into roughly five categories.

Genre is a French word meaning type or variety, and the genres that became established in the Dutch Republic were history and to a lesser extent religion, portraiture, landscape, still life, and paintings of everyday life. Somewhat confusingly, the paintings of everyday life are also known as genre.

After the Eighty Years' War, the Dutch were almost immediately confronted with two other powerful enemies: France and England, with whom they fought for the rest of the 17th century. Yet despite this constant backdrop of conflict, painting production continued, primarily of calm, tranquil themes.

Below: The Adoration of the Magi, *c.1622–24, is a large altarpiece by Abraham Bloemaert, a Catholic in the Protestant northern Netherlands who followed the exaggerated, elongated figures of Mannerism.*

THE HIERARCHY OF GENRES

The highly naturalistic approach to painting that developed focused on illusions of space and light, which suited all the genres. Elsewhere in Europe, the 'hierarchy of genres' placed history paintings and portraits as the most important genres, with landscape and still life the least, but in the Dutch Republic, landscapes, genre paintings and still lifes became equally popular. Several landscape painters began using techniques to speed up their output, such as applying looser, more painterly brushmarks. Ultimately, this meant that more landscapes were produced, but also that their prices fell.

History painting In his book *Schilder-Boeck* of 1604, Karel van Mander wrote that young artists should concentrate on painting figures and histories, with kitchen scenes, still lifes, animals and

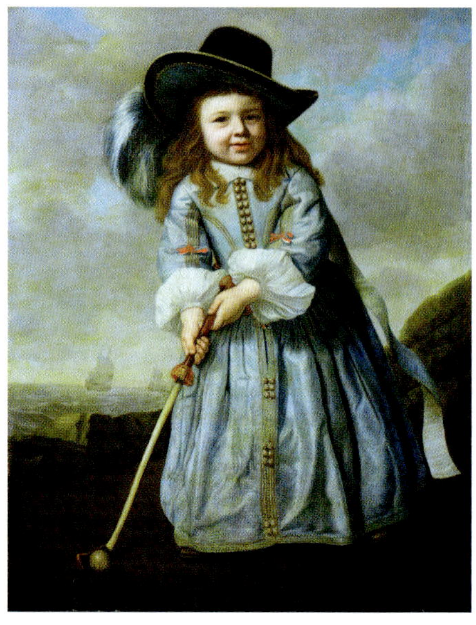

Above: Aelbert Cuyp was one of the leading landscape painters of the period, although this painting Child Playing Golf *shows his skills in another genre.*

landscapes taking second place. During the war, history paintings that included religious, mythological or literary themes were favoured, but although they remained respected, by 1650, portraits, landscapes, still lifes and genre scenes sold more readily. Dutch history paintings usually show an influence of Italian art, especially in the use of chiaroscuro.

Portrait painting Some estimates suggest that the number of portraits produced during the Dutch Golden Age was between 750,000 and over a million. Unlike the more flamboyant portraits produced in other European countries, Dutch sitters in sombre black clothing reflect the restraint of Calvinism where any suggestion of possessions would portray the sin of pride, although more adventurous artists gradually changed this. Group portraits became popular, with the cost often shared by the subjects. On some occasions, sitters for these paid

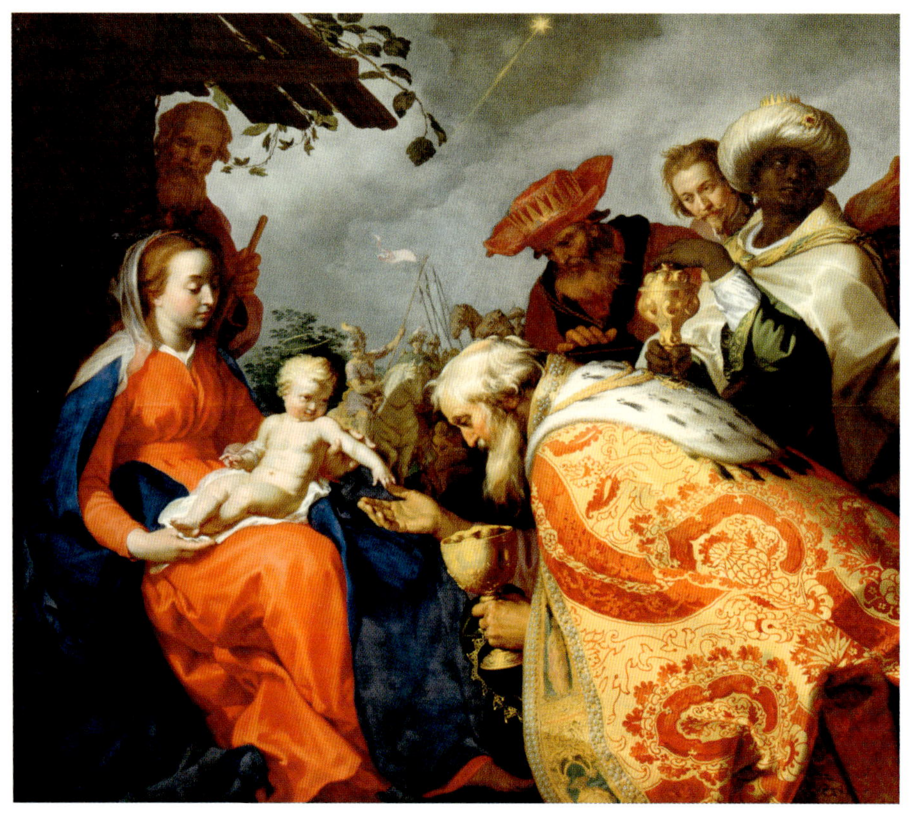

Right: With its typically low horizon, View of the Merwede off Dordrecht, *1660, is attributed to Jeronymus van Diest (1631–77).*

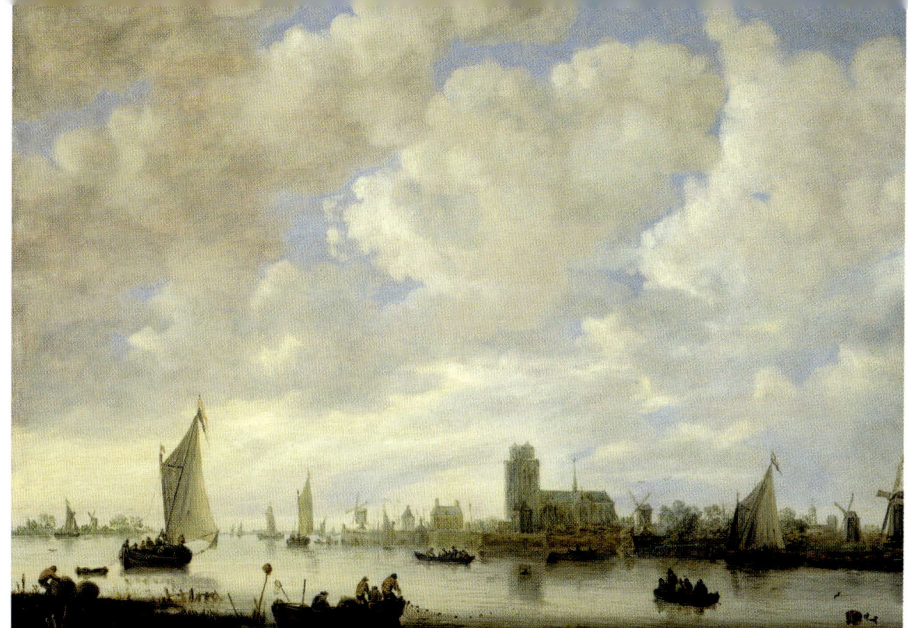

equally, while on other occasions, some paid more in order to be portrayed more prominently, although this did not always follow.

Landscape painting Usually portrayed from ground level as if viewers are actually in the scene, Dutch landscape paintings include scenes of the countryside, battles, cities, rivers and the sea. The low horizons enabled artists to focus on skies as well as the land, and they often evoke atmospheric effects. Some artists produced different types of scapes, including scenes of winter, Italianate style and city views.

Still life painting With an abundance of goods arriving from overseas, still life reminded Dutch viewers of their success and growing prosperity. Consisting solely of collections of inanimate objects, still life only emerged in the Dutch Golden Age, and the painters demonstrated remarkable skills in capturing realistic effects of light, surface textures and patterns. The paintings also often symbolized other meanings, such as the transience of life in rotting fruit, wilting flowers, shells, skulls or musical instruments with broken strings. These became known as 'vanitas' paintings. Flower paintings became another still life specialism, with many painted by the few female artists of the period.

Genre painting Often amusing or moral informal depictions of life, featuring figures to whom no specific identity can be attached, became to be called genre paintings in the late 18th century. They include single figures, peasant families, women working in the home, tavern, market or street scenes, winter scenes, parties, festivities, or scenes featuring animals. Evolving from some Early Netherlandish painting, particularly works by Hieronymus Bosch and Pieter Bruegel the Elder, the tradition developed in the Republic during the 17th century. Many genre paintings illustrate Dutch proverbs or convey moral messages.

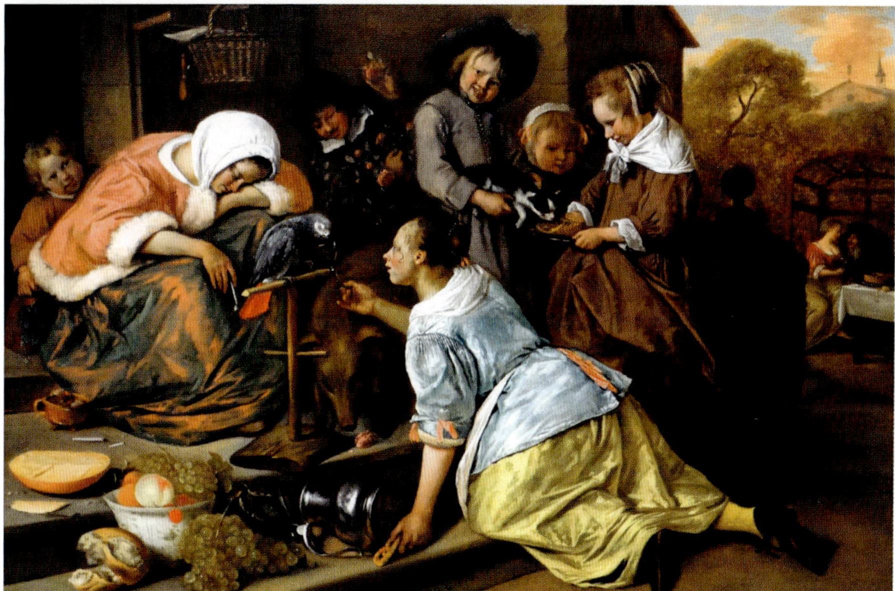

Above: Jan Steen became greatly admired for his genre paintings. Here, in The Effects of Intemperance, *a drunken woman's purse is being picked.*

Below: Still life started as a genre and became greatly admired. Pieter Claesz was one of several expert painters who rendered objects incredibly realistically.

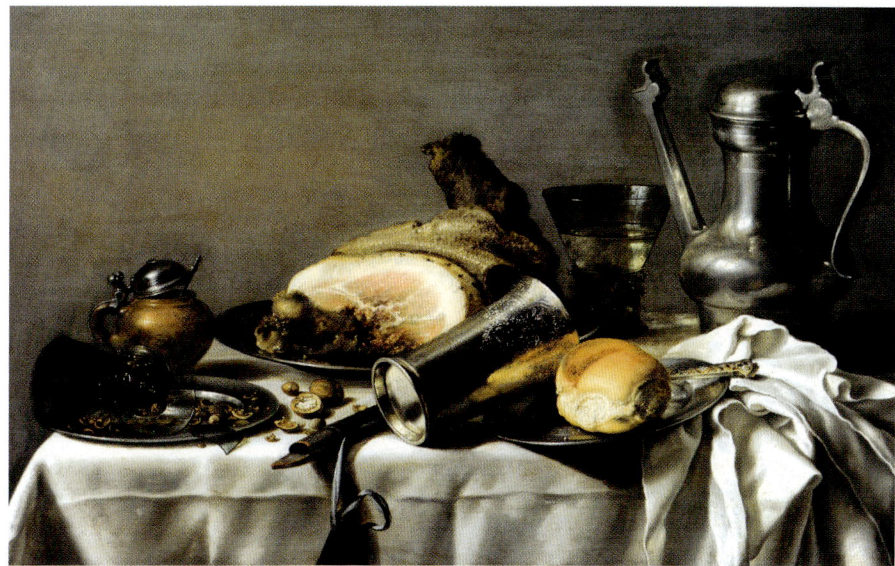

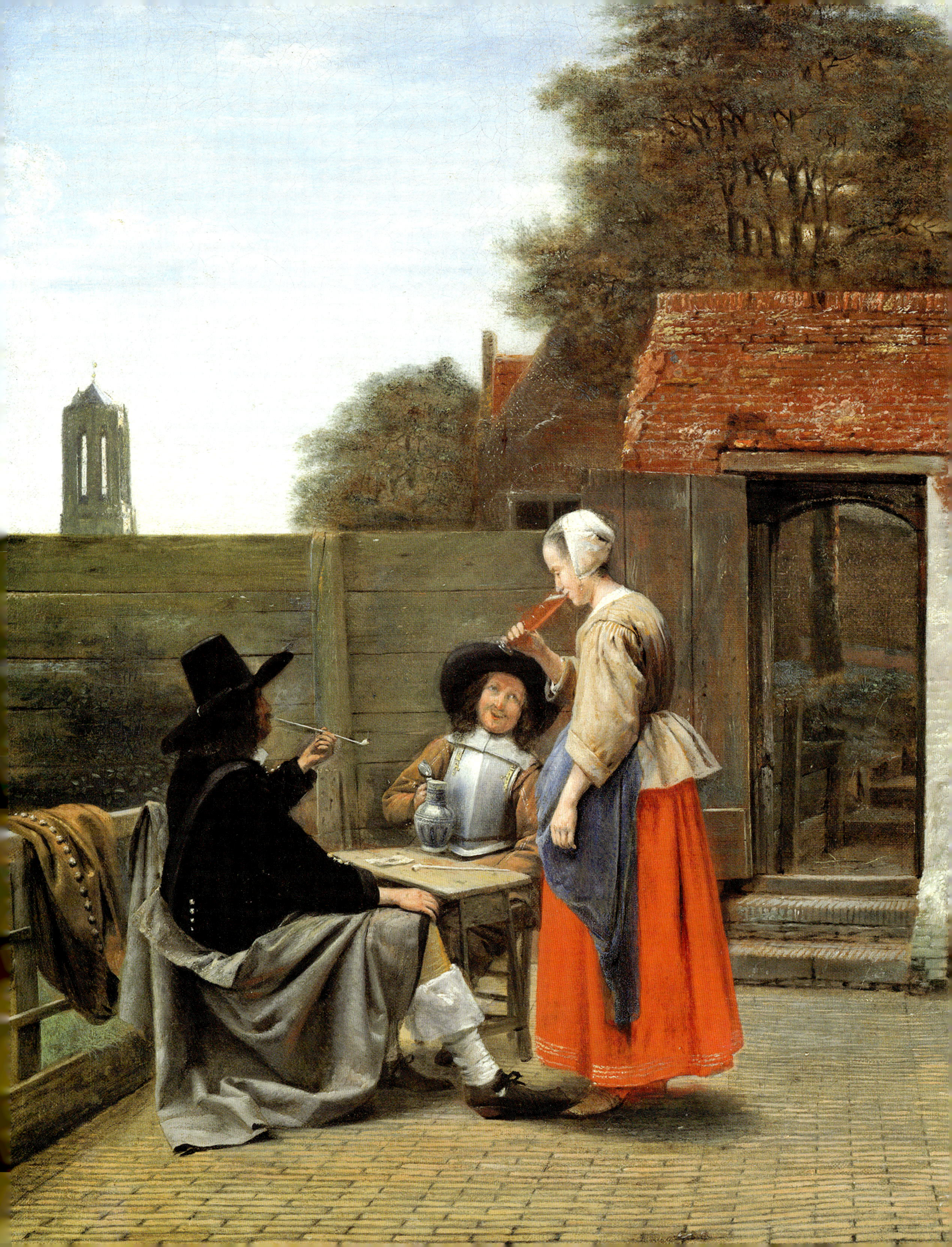

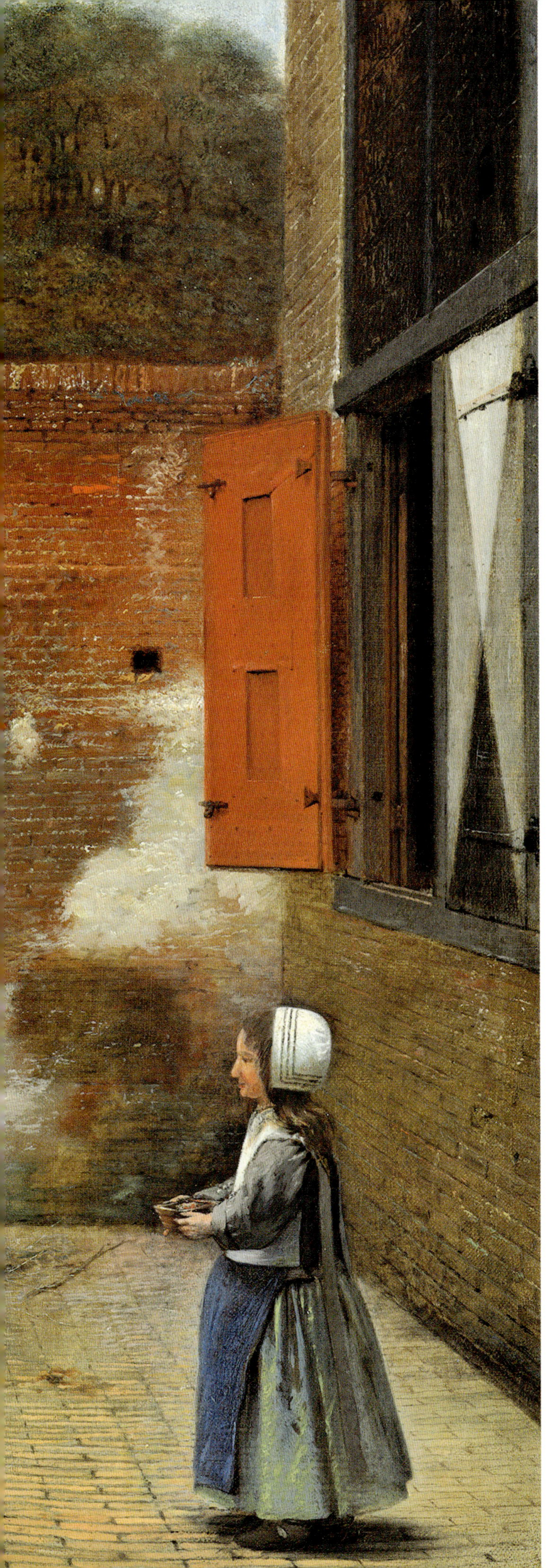

THE PAINTERS

The following section of the book is an introduction to some of the greatest Dutch Golden Age artists and their work. Roughly chronological, it explains who they were, where they came from, who they learned from and influenced, and why their work was often groundbreaking. Among others, included here are Frans Hals, Rembrandt, Jan Lievens, Judith Leyster, Gerrit Dou, Jan Steen, Jacob van Ruisdael, Pieter de Hooch, Johannes Vermeer and Rachel Ruysch. Yet the many artists explored here are just a small proportion of the exceptionally proficient painters of the period. Even in this book, there is room for only a fraction of them to be considered, which demonstrates how important art was at the time.

Left: Painted in the quiet city of Delft from 1658–60, Pieter de Hooch captured an everyday scene in A Dutch Courtyard, *conveying the clear natural light and emphasizing aspects of linear perspective (see also page 140).*

VAN DYCK · VAN DER AST · PEETERS

From the end of the 16th century, still life paintings began to increase in popularity in the Netherlands, reflecting the increasing urbanization of society, and emphasizing daily life. Three fairly early Dutch painters of the genre include van Dyck (1574/5–1651/4), van der Ast (1593/4–1657) and Peeters (1594–c.1657).

As well as vanitas, many still lifes had other symbolic meanings to remind viewers that earthly conceits should not divert their attention away from leading a moral life. These included such things as flowers representing God's wonder; grapes that suggested trade or purity; and shells that could symbolize exploration, power, wealth, scientific discovery, or time passing. As well as these underlying implications, the lush colours and balanced compositions of many Dutch still life paintings greatly appealed to the new buying public.

FLORIS VAN DYCK
After spending some years in Rome, in 1606 Delft-born Floris van Dyck (or Floris van Dijck) returned to Haarlem and became an assistant to Karel van Mander. Independently, he painted still lifes and in 1610, he joined the Haarlem Guild of Saint Luke, becoming dean there in 1637. He was particularly influenced by the Flemish painters Osias Beert (c.1580–1623/24) and Clara Peeters. Van Dyck's illusions of light and textures were astonishingly lifelike. His objects often appear haphazardly arranged and emerge from dark, shadowy backgrounds, projecting convincingly towards viewers, while fluid paint is applied with practically invisible brushstrokes. Dyck was first cousin of Pieter Cornelisz van Rijck (1567–c.1637) and second cousin of Claes van Heussen (1598–1633).

BALTHASAR VAN DER AST
Born in Middleburg, Balthasar van der Ast specialized in still lifes of flowers, fruit and shells. He was a pioneer of the still life paintings of shells, and also often included lizards in his paintings. Taught to paint by his elder sister Maria's husband, the painter Ambrosius Bosschaert the Elder (1573–1621), van der Ast subsequently taught Bosschaert's three sons: Ambrosius the Younger (1609–45), Johannes (c.1612/13–28 or later) and Abraham (1606–83/84) after Bosschaert's death. The five artists are often collectively referred to as the Bosschaert dynasty. Van der Ast moved with the Bosschaerts to Bergen op Zoom in 1615 and the following year to Utrecht where he entered the

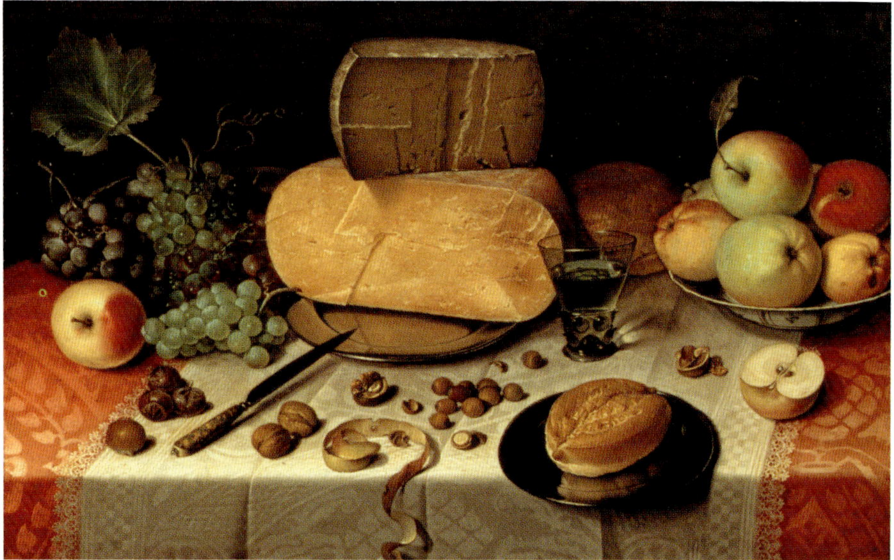

Left above: Known as a 'breakfast piece' or 'ontbijtjes,' this expensively laid table with cheeses, fruit, bread and nuts was painted by Floris van Dyck in 1613.

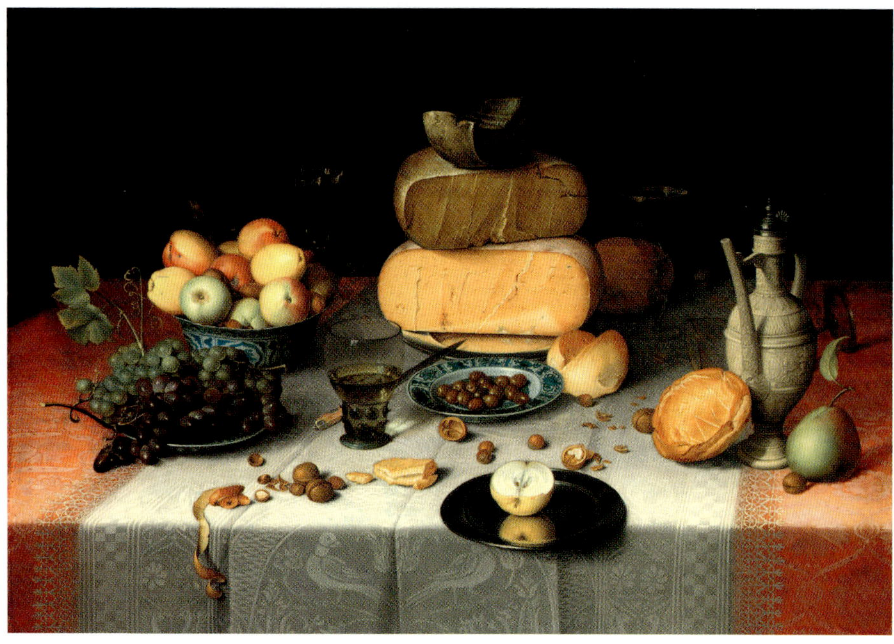

Left below: Still Life with Cheese, c.1615, by Floris van Dyck. Painted from a high viewpoint, all is symmetrical and rendered in exacting detail, appealing to those wealthy enough to afford such foods.

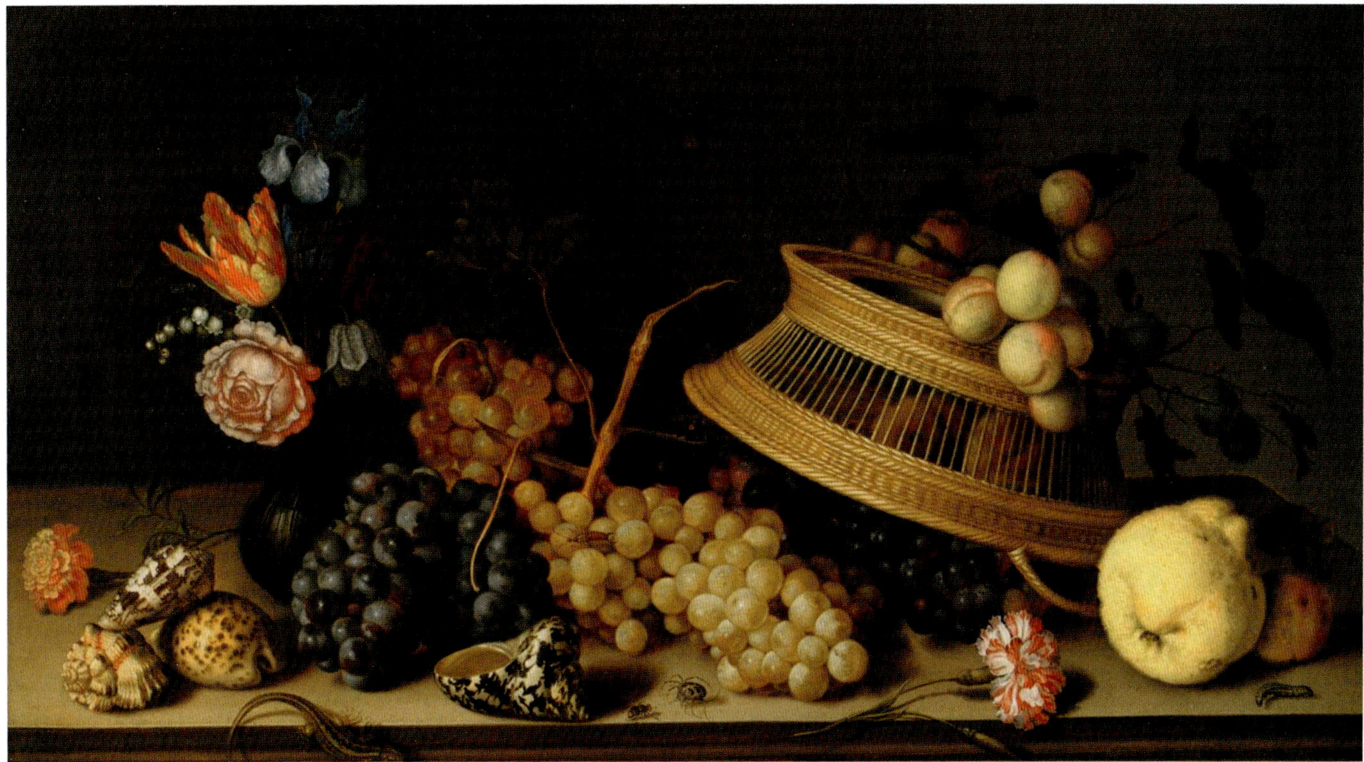

Above: Still Life of Flowers, Fruit, Shells and Insects, c.1629. At a time when such goods were rarely even seen, let alone afforded, Balthasar van der Ast made a name for himself painting them.

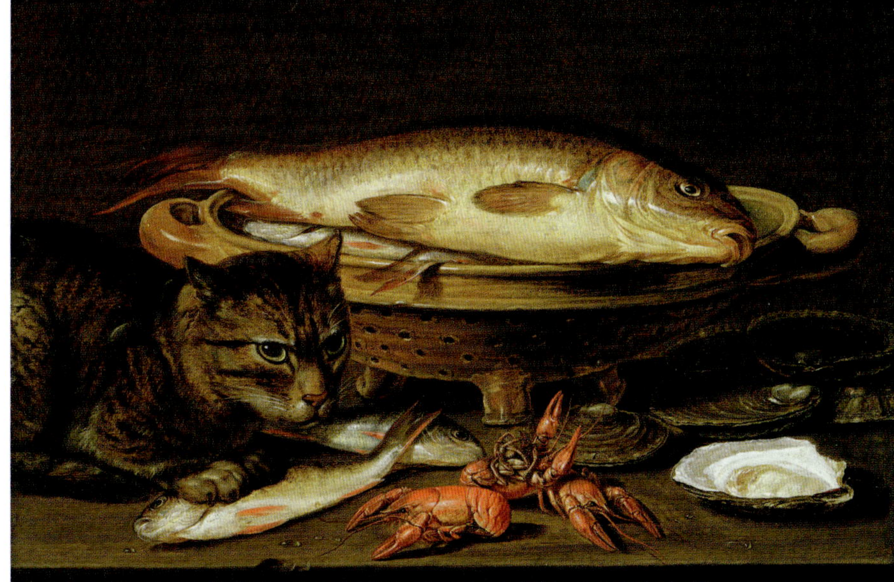

Right: Still Life with Fish and Cat. A painter of Flemish origin, Clara Peeters became highly respected for her realism.

Guild of Saint Luke. He also taught Jan Davidsz de Heem (1606–84) and was influenced by Roelandt Savery (1576–1639), whose work inspired his softer, more atmospheric approach. In 1632, he married and moved to Delft, and joined the Guild of Saint Luke there. His style of meticulously careful and balanced still lifes became more loosely painted in Delft.

CLARA PEETERS

Although born in Antwerp, Clara Peeters spent most of her career in the Dutch Republic. Little is known of her background, but her earliest oil paintings, created when she was 14 years old, are small-scale, detailed images of food and drink. Many art historians believe that she was a student of Osias Beert, but this has not been verified. She was established in Amsterdam by 1611 and is documented as being in The Hague in 1617. Unusual as a female painter at the time, she was among the earlier painters of still lifes and flowers, and she became prominent as one of the artists who moulded the traditions of Dutch 'ontbijtjes' or 'breakfast pieces' (see page 39) with plain food and simple vessels, and 'banketje', or 'banquet pieces,' featuring expensive cups and vessels made of precious metals. Peeters's influence on Dutch and Flemish artists is seen not only by her subject matter, but also in her use of a fairly monochrome palette, low viewpoints and compact compositions comprising just a few objects. Before 1620, she focused on painting textures and light and reflections on metal objects, often depicting herself in the reflections. After 1620, she began employing a more restricted palette and including more mundane objects such as cheeses, bread and plain jugs, which she painted in painstaking detail against dark backgrounds.

FRANS HALS

Distinguished by loose, painterly brushwork and a freer style than most Dutch Golden Age painters, Frans Hals the Elder (1580/3–1666) lived and worked in Haarlem. As well as specializing in lively portraits, he produced genre paintings, using colour and brushmarks in a manner that broke with painting conventions.

Frans Hals was born in Antwerp, the son of a Flemish cloth merchant, but worked for most of his life in Haarlem. Between 1600 and 1603, he studied under the artist and art historian Karel van Mander who was also a Flemish immigrant living in Haarlem.

In 1610, Hals became a member of the Haarlem Guild of Saint Luke, and he started work as an art restorer for the city council. He soon began to receive commissions to paint portraits of Haarlem citizens, and group portraits of families, members of the civic guard and regents of almshouses, widely considered to be his masterpieces, while privately he also painted a broader range of genre subjects.

MARRIAGES AND MONEY PROBLEMS

Hals married his first wife, Anneke, in 1610 and they had three children, but only one survived. Within five years, Anneke also died and two years later Hals married his second wife, Lysbeth Ryners, with whom he had eight more children.

Although he was successful during his lifetime, Hals also experienced financial difficulties because of the needs of his large family. In efforts to overcome his money problems, he also worked as a restorer, art dealer and art tax expert for the city councillors. Over his painting career, Hals produced about 300 paintings, which were predominantly large group portraits. His dynamic painting style soon spread throughout the Netherlands and influenced many artists during that time. With his paintings greatly in demand, Hals was able to command high prices for his work, but eventually, he went out of style as a painter. He experienced financial difficulties, and destitute, in 1664, he was given an annuity of 200 florins by the municipality.

VISIBLE BRUSHSTROKES

Contrasting with the approach of many of his contemporaries, Hals only painted what he considered to be essential, and in his portraits, those aspects that best captured their inner characters. His loose technique became increasingly free and he put his subjects into positions that conveyed their personalities, even within his group portraits, so that the individuals shone out, rather than the traditional objectively-portrayed Dutch group portraits with little differentiation between sitters.

Largely working with the 'alla prima' (at the first) method, with either no underdrawing or merely light drawing with chalk or paint over a grey or pink base, Hals painted in successive layers,

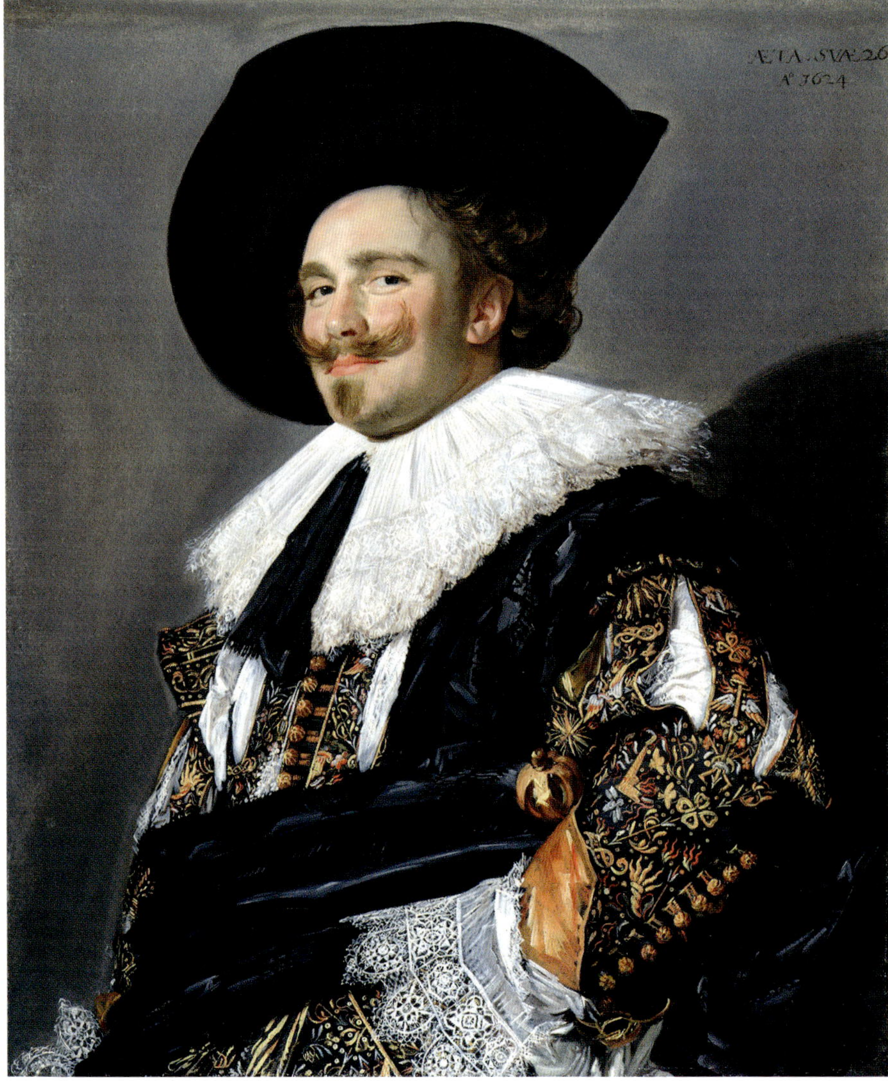

Left: The Laughing Cavalier, 1624. *With his loose painterly brushwork, Hals presents a courtly figure, the epitome of Baroque gallantry. Rakishly leaning back, he is smiling, not laughing, and is probably not a cavalier either.*

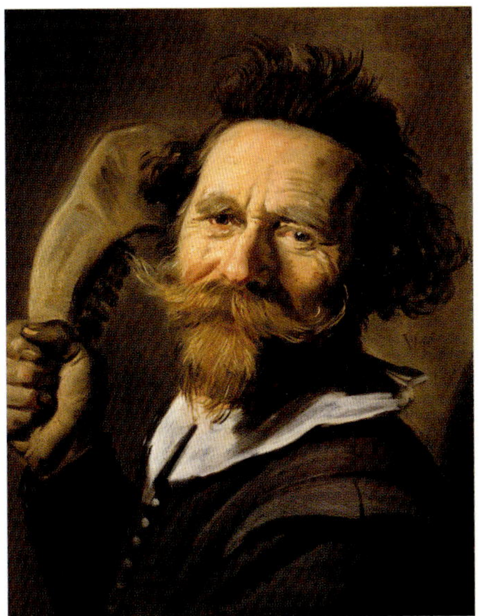

Above: This is Pieter Verdonck (c.1580–after 1636), a friend of Hals, modelling as the biblical figure Samson to help Hals with a composition c.1627.

building up colour and tone, using visible brushstrokes to emphasize surfaces and add movement. As he faced financial difficulties in the middle years of his career, Hals's palette became more limited, as coloured pigments were costlier than black and white, and after 1655, dark shadows dominated his works. His brushstrokes became looser, and fine detail became less important than the overall impression. Where

Below: Portrait of a Woman, c.1650, shows that despite the restrained clothing of the day Hals conveyed the friendliness of his sitter and a natural pose.

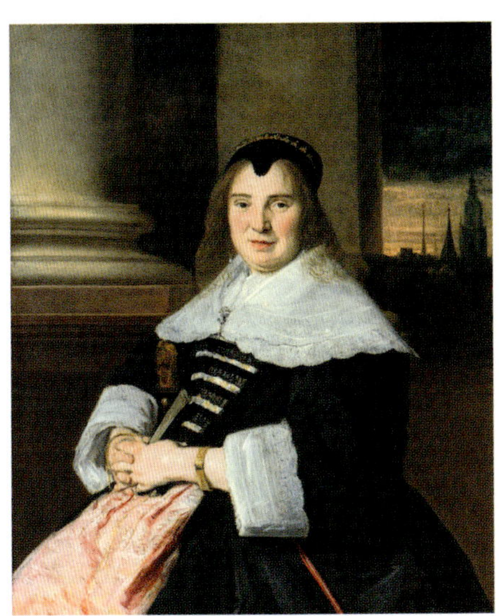

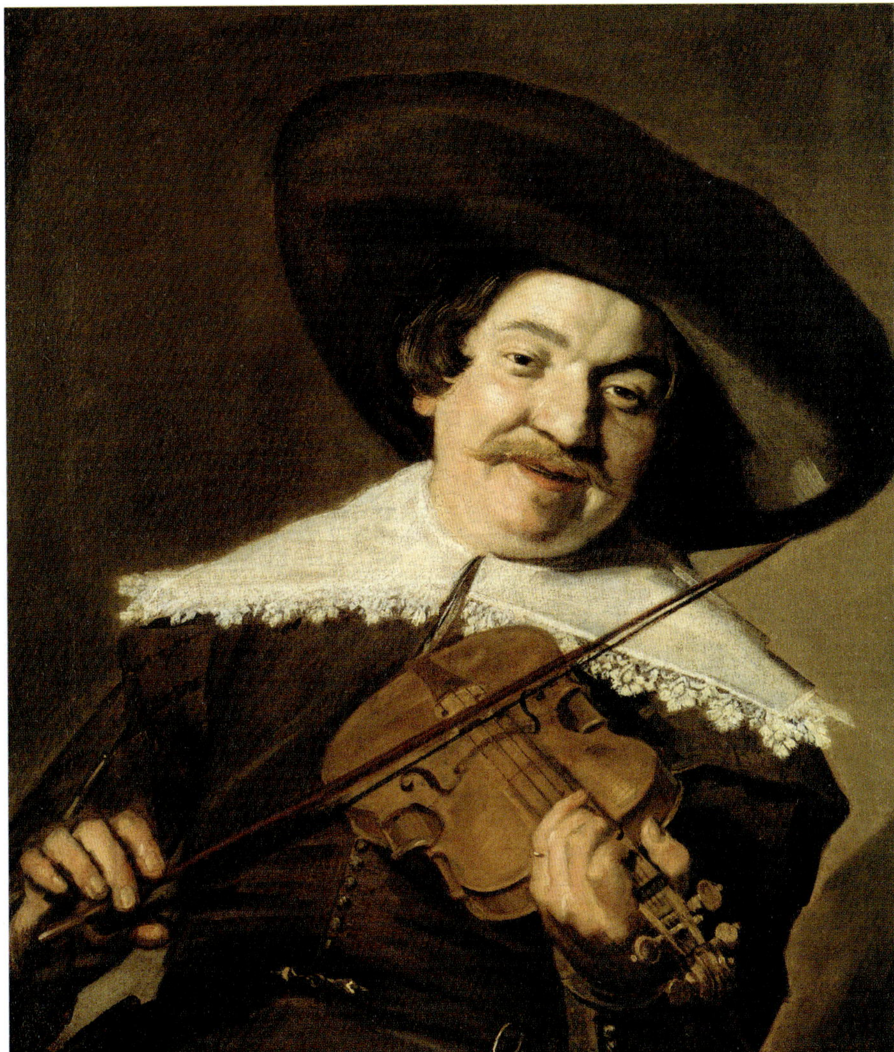

Above: Daniel van Aken Playing the Violin, c.1640, is a lively portrait by Frans Hals, showing how he captured spontaneity and created a sense of immediacy with loose, free brushwork – while the suggestion of music adds a rhythmic lilt to the image.

his earlier pieces radiated gaiety and liveliness, his later portraits emphasized the stature and dignity of his sitters.

Apart from portrait commissions, Hals painted genre scenes of working-class citizens of Haarlem. Unlike his upper and middle-class sitters, the lower classes were less limited in their expressions and more relaxed and open in their gestures.

EXTENSIVE INFLUENCE

Frans Hals had a large workshop in Haarlem and many students. His brother Dirck Hals (1591–1656) was also a painter and so were five of his sons: Harmen Hals (1611–69), Frans Hals Junior (1618–69), Jan Hals (1620–54), Reynier Hals (1627–72) and Nicolaes Hals (1628–86). Other contemporary painters who took inspiration from him were: Jan Miense Molenaer (1609/10–68), Judith Leyster (1609–60), Adriaen van Ostade (1610–85), Adriaen Brouwer (1605–38), Johannes Cornelisz Verspronck (1597–1662), Bartholomeus van der Helst (1613–70) and Cornelis de Bie (1621–64). Centuries later, Vincent van Gogh (1853–90) wrote to his brother Theo: 'What a joy it is to see a Frans Hals, how different it is from the paintings – so many of them – where everything is carefully smoothed out in the same manner.' The 19th-century Impressionist painters Monet and Manet were similarly inspired by Hals' fluid brushwork.

HENDRICK AVERCAMP

Although he is popularly believed to have been deaf and dumb because of his nickname De Stomme van Kampen (The Mute of Kampen), Hendrick Avercamp (1585–1634) may not have been. It could be that he was simply a shy or quiet man. He became widely admired for his winter landscape scenes.

Hendrick was born in Amsterdam, where in the early 17th century he probably studied with the Danish-born painter Pieter Isaacsz (1569–1625) and possibly also with with the Flemish-born artist David Vinckboons (c.1576–c.1632). The last quarter of the 16th century, when Avercamp was born, was one of the coldest periods of what became called The Little Ice Age. The long cold winters as well as

Right: Using bodycolour and ink, Avercamp captures fishermen working on a calm moonlit river with a fire glowing in the distance where boats are being repaired.

Below: Avercamp's winter scenes, such as this of the River Ijsel near Kampen, c.1615, fascinated and entertained viewers.

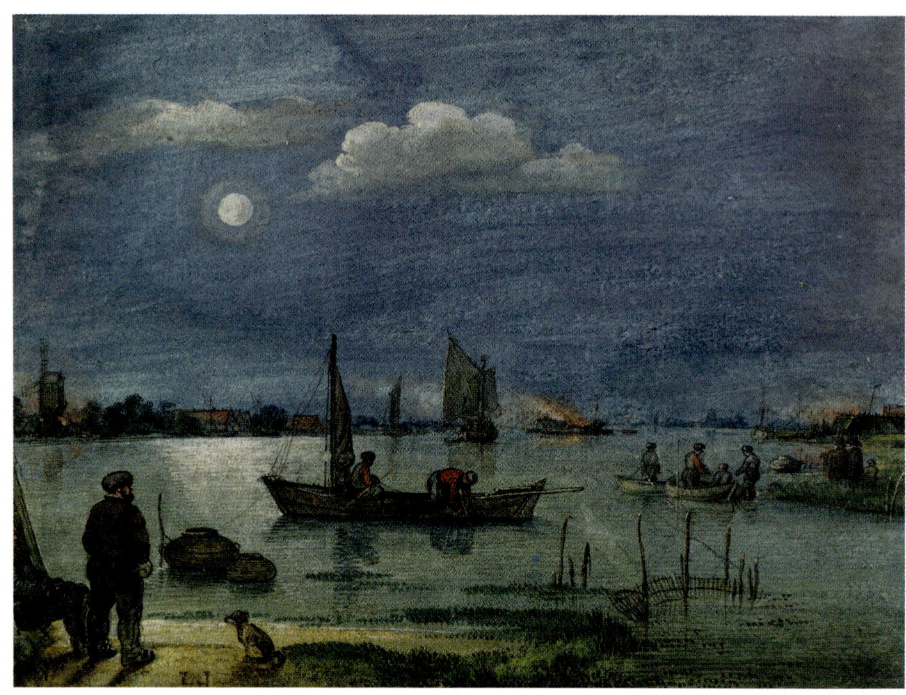

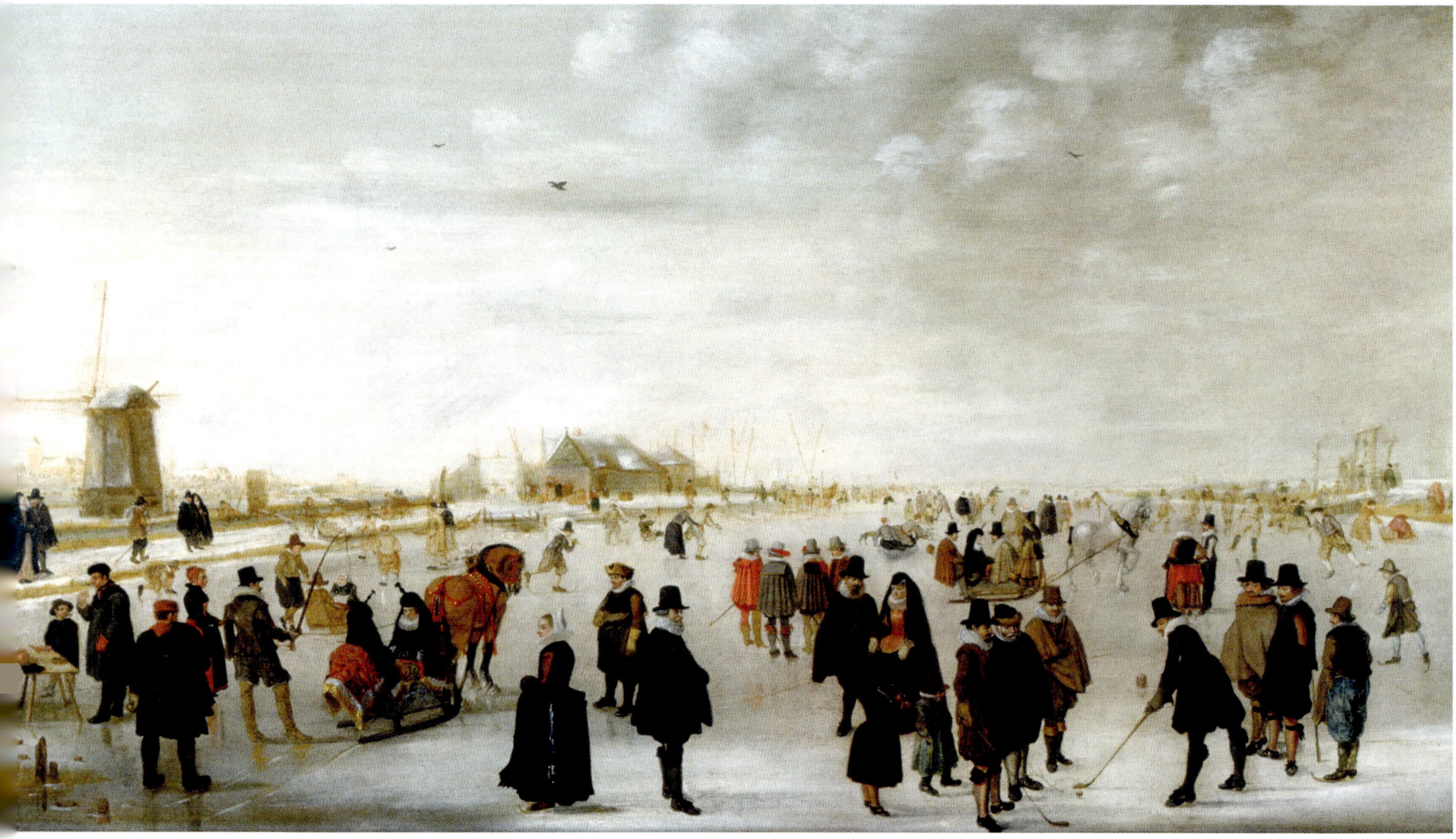

Right: Painted in c.1625, this winter scene captures a muffled, frozen river with skaters. Avercamp was a master at capturing the wintry atmosphere as well as the personalities enjoying it.

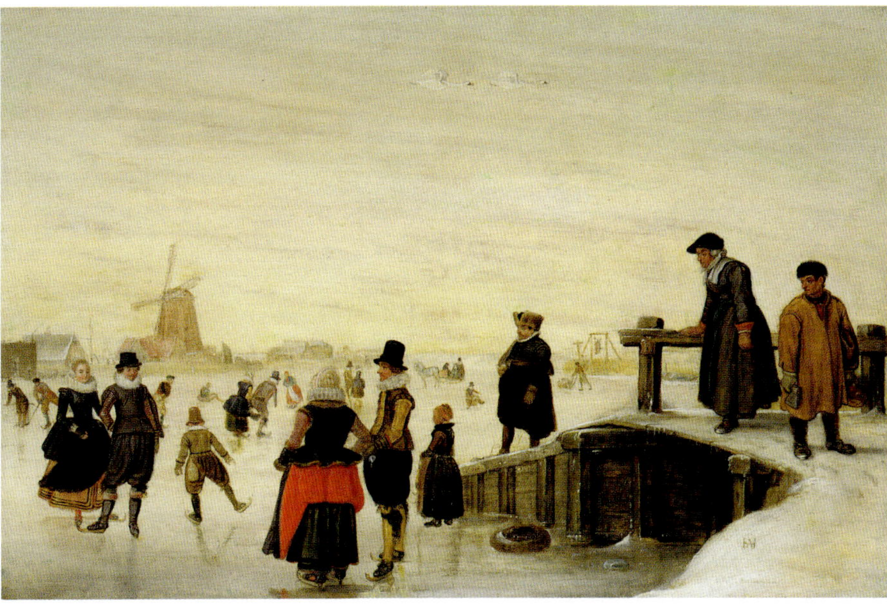

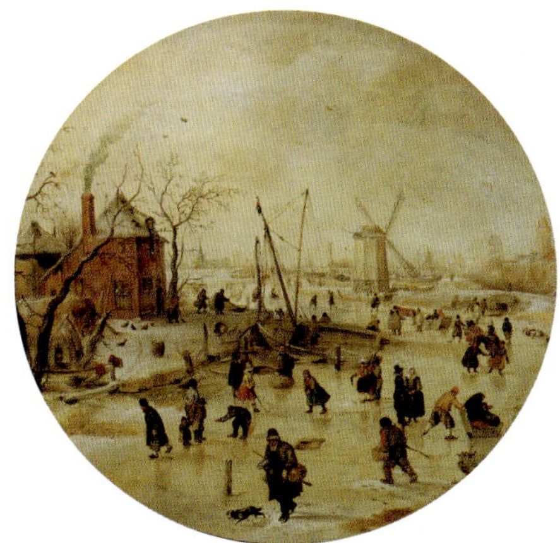

Above: Figures Skating in a Dutch Landscape, *c.1625. Avercamp painted this frozen river in the 1620s during a period of exceptionally harsh winters in the small town of Kampen where he spent most of his life.*

the paintings of Vinckboons and Pieter Bruegel the Elder seem to have inspired him to create his frozen scenes full of busy figures.

LIVELY WINTER SCENES

Details of Avercamp's life are quite sparse. Even the widely-held belief that he was deaf or mute or both has not been verified and it could be that he was simply a man of few words. In 1608, he moved from Amsterdam to Kampen where he lived for the rest of his life and became one of the first landscape painters of the Dutch Republic.

Kampen was not known for its artistic traditions, but Avercamp began painting his wintry surroundings almost immediately; the town's fortified walls can be seen in several of his paintings. He made many figure studies from life, and detailed, coloured drawings and paintings as well as sketches out of doors of the frozen landscapes. Back in his studio, he created his lively scenes.

These unique and often amusing paintings brought him widespread recognition. It is not easy to pick out where he became influenced, nor why

he chose and adhered to the winter theme. His colourful, vividly depicted landscapes are filled with people of all ages, abilities and classes, making the most of the severe winters that arrived early each autumn and continued into late spring. Carefully observed, the energetic figures are shown ice skating, tobogganing, walking, snowball-throwing, fortune-telling, dancing and participating in various other activities. Lavishly dressed middle-class figures mingle with poorly clad peasants, while gestures and activities convey strong personalities and a broad range of human situations, demonstrating Avercamp's astute powers of observation. Ultimately, the bustle of life in the freezing cold air portrays a great deal about 17th-century life in the Netherlands and the adaptability of the Dutch citizens.

ATMOSPHERIC PERSPECTIVE

Avercamp's earliest dated painting from 1608 came after an especially cold winter. His early landscapes have high horizons, so viewers focus on the figures and their activities; these narrative paintings are full of detail and anecdotes. Later in his career, Avercamp began to concentrate more on atmosphere and not just on his figures' antics, and gradually, his horizons lowered to incorporate greater expanses of sky. He was one of the earliest exponents of an extensive exploration of the effects of aerial

or atmospheric perspective, meaning that distant elements of his scenes became less detailed and more hazy, all the colours took on a bluish hue, and outlines were less distinct. One common feature in many of his scenes are the shadows of figures that he painted in at first and then, changing his mind, painted out. These are only becoming apparent in recent years as the paint becomes more translucent with age, which means that the lower layers of paint are now beginning to show through.

THE LITTLE ICE AGE

A period of cooling that lasted approximately from the 14th to the 19th centuries, and particularly from c.1300–c.1870, became known as the Little Ice Age. It was particularly cold during the two hundred years from c.1650–1850. Canals and rivers in the northern hemisphere frequently froze over in the bitterly cold winters, deeply enough to support ice skating and winter festivals. Pieter Bruegel the Elder was the first painter of the northern Netherlands to depict winter landscapes, followed by Avercamp, who like many of his contemporaries, often skated with his parents and friends during the extended frozen winters.

HENDRICK TER BRUGGHEN

Probably born in The Hague, Hendrick ter Brugghen (alternatively Terbrugghen or Ter Bruggen) (1588–1629) became profoundly influenced by the work of Caravaggio and is usually categorized as one of the 'Utrecht Caravaggisti', a small group of painters working in Utrecht.

In about 1591, ter Brugghen's middle-class family settled in Utrecht when his father, Jan Egbertsz ter Brugghen (c.1561–c.1626), a civil servant, was appointed secretary to the Court of Utrecht by the Prince of Orange, William the Silent.

By 1603 the family was living in Abcoude, a village between Utrecht and Amsterdam, and at that time, ter Brugghen may have been apprenticed to the painter Abraham Bloemaert (1566–1651).

IN ITALY

Definite dates have not been established, but it seems that Ter Brugghen left the Netherlands in about 1607, returning seven years later. He probably spent a large part of that time in Italy, including an extended period in Rome. While little of this has been securely verified, it is clear that he stayed in Milan during the summer of 1614 with fellow Utrecht artist Thyman van Galen (c.1590–1653). Although he was in Italy within Caravaggio's lifetime, in 1606 Caravaggio had fled Rome on a murder charge and so it is highly unlikely that the two artists met. However, ter Brugghen clearly studied Caravaggio's work that had caused a sensation in Italy, as well as the work of some of the Italian Caravaggisti, such as Orazio Gentileschi (1563–1639). Other Italian painters who influenced him during his stay there were Annibale Carracci (1560–1609), Domenichino (1581–1641) and Guido Reni (1575–1642). Once he was back in the Netherlands, ter Brugghen began using a highly personal painting style, of powerful tonal contrasts that evolved from the work of Caravaggio, blended with a soft handling of paint and pale vibrant colouring.

INFLUENCED AND INFLUENCER

Ter Brugghen was the first important painter to bring the influence of Caravaggio to the Dutch Republic. His style contrasted with the detailed realism of most Dutch painting of the

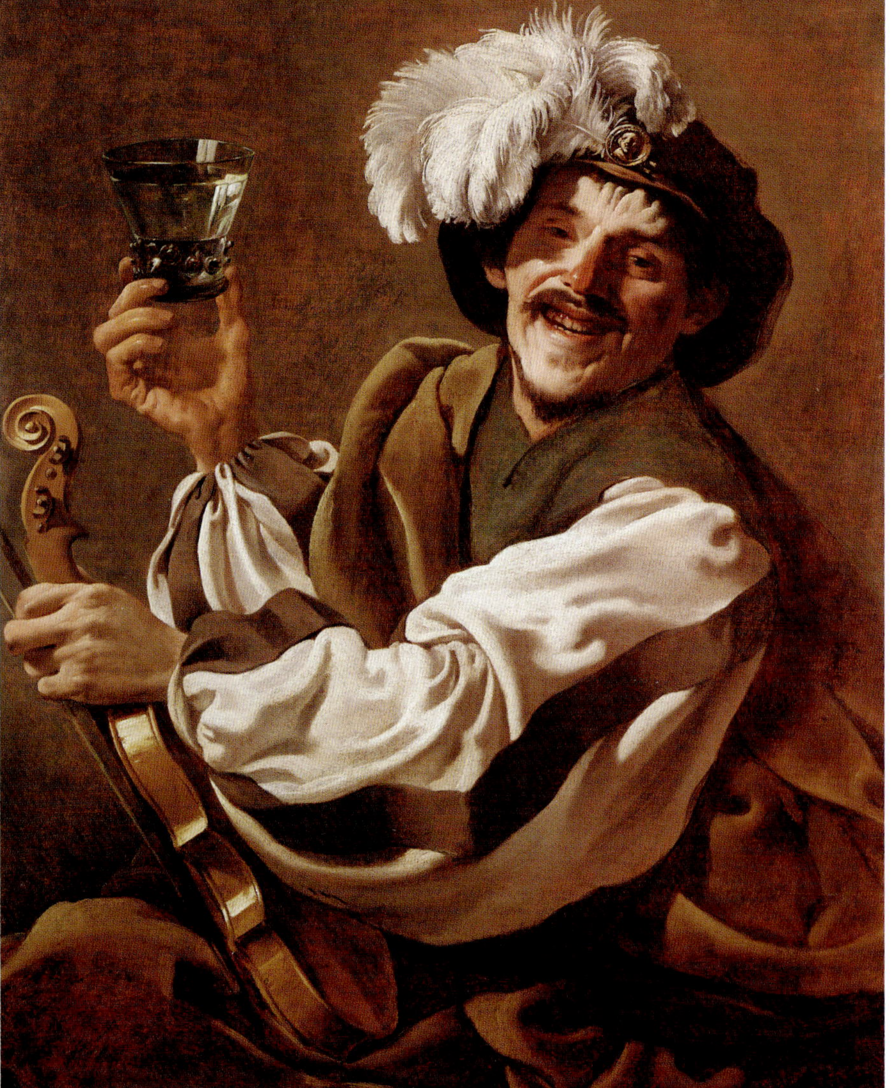

Left: A ruddy-nosed, drunken violinist grins out of the canvas. Hendrick ter Brugghen painted this lively, light-hearted A Violin Player with a Glass of Wine *in c.1623.*

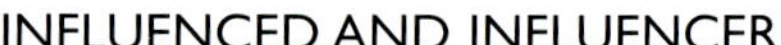

TENEBRISM AND CHIAROSCURO

Caravaggio's distinctive and dramatic painting technique of extremely dark shadows with vividly illuminated areas usually from a single source of light is called tenebrism, from the Italian word 'tenebroso', meaning murky. Caravaggio used a similar, slightly less dramatic, technique of strong tonal contrasts that made darkness the dominating feature of the image, known as chiaroscuro, from an Italian term meaning light-dark.

Right: Christ Crowned with Thorns, *c.1621–22, by Dirck van Baburen, another Utrecht Caravaggisti.*

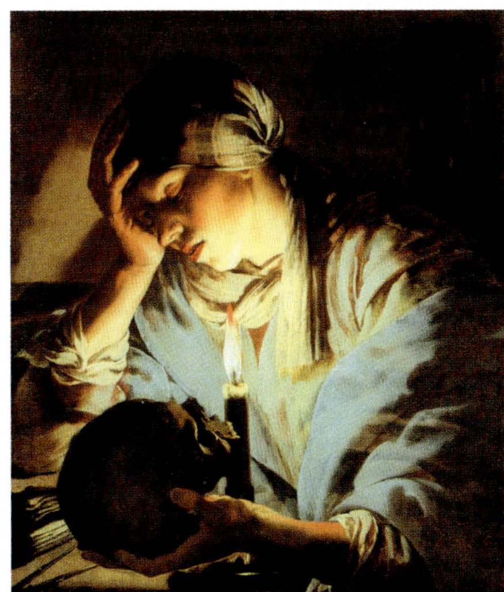

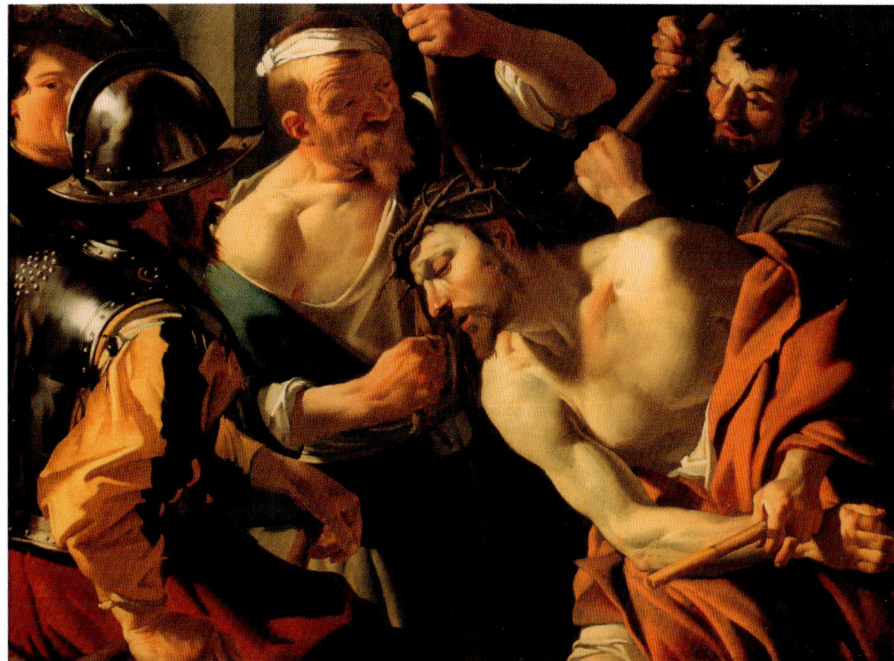

Above: A young woman gazes at a skull by candlelight. Ter Brugghen painted Melancholia *in c.1627; it may represent Mary Magdalene, an allegory of melancholy, or a demonstration of the artist's technical skill.*

Right: The Concert, *c.1626 – colourful costumes suggest travelling performers, while ter Brugghen has cropped the scene to create intimacy.*

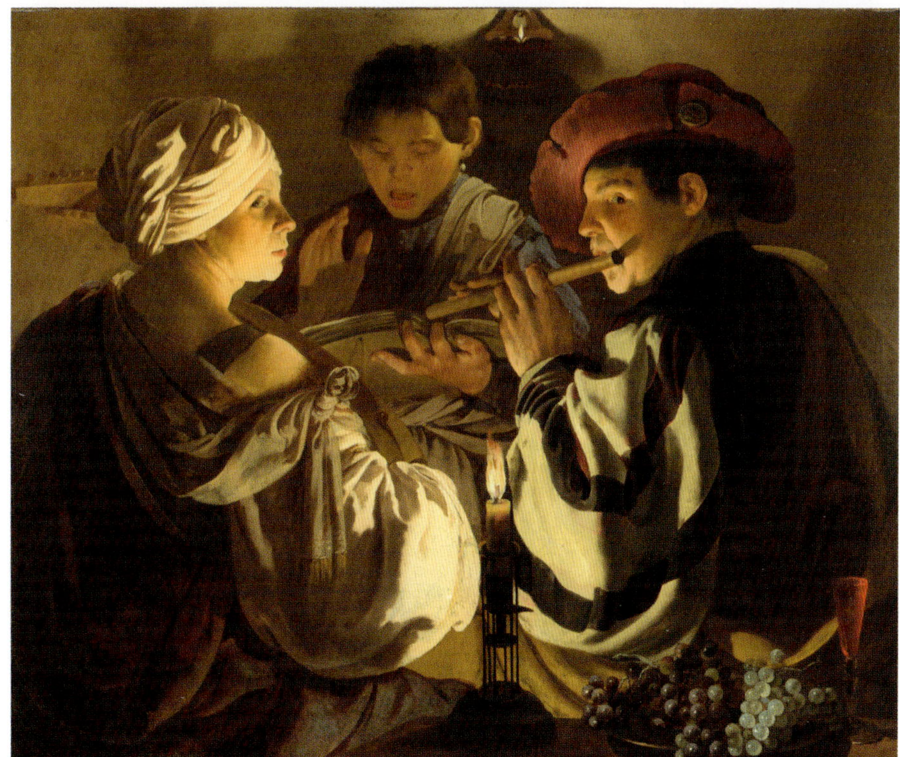

time, and he imbued his figures with a sense of dignity and grandeur. His subject matter comprised religious, mythological and literary themes, together with representations of figures, often in domestic settings. He also painted group portraits and became renowned for his bold images and subtle employment of tonal modelling.

As other artists in Utrecht, including Dirck van Baburen (*c.*1595–1624) and Gerrit van Honthorst, also painted with powerful chiaroscuro and tenebrism, they became classed collectively as the Utrecht Caravaggisti. Ter Brugghen's paintings of dark figures against light backgrounds subsequently influenced artists such as Vermeer, Fabritius, Hals and Rembrandt.

UTRECHT

By 1616, ter Brugghen was listed as a member of the Utrecht Guild of Saint Luke, and that same year he married

his elder brother Jan's stepdaughter, Jacomijna Verbeeck (date of birth unknown–1634). For the first ten years of their marriage, they rented a home in the Korte Lauwerstraat, and in 1626, they moved to the Snippevlucht, a narrow street near the centre of town, where they rented a large house from Johan Wtewael (1598–1652), brother of the painter Joachim Anthonisz Wtewael (*c.*1566–1638).

Unlike the rest of the Dutch Republic, about 40 percent of the Utrecht population in the 17th century was Roman Catholic, so there was a market for paintings of Christian themes. In 1627, the Flemish artist Peter Paul Rubens visited ter Brugghen and allegedly declared that he was the only 'real painter' he had met from the Republic and that his work was 'above that of all the other Utrecht artists.'

GERRIT VAN HONTHORST

Inspired by his Catholic faith as much as by his artistic pursuits, as a young man, Gerrit (or Gerard) van Honthorst (1592–1656) travelled to Rome. From that time, he became recognized for his depictions of artificially lit night scenes, and nicknamed Gherardo delle Notti – or Gerard of the Nights.

Reflecting the dramatic approach of Caravaggio, van Honthorst helped to popularize the use of strong chiaroscuro and tenebrism in the Dutch Republic after he had returned from Rome in 1620. He became one of the few 17th-century Dutch painters to achieve international fame.

WIDE RENOWN

Born in Utrecht to a large Catholic family, van Honthorst's father was a tapestry designer and a founding member of the Utrecht Guild of Saint Luke, and he initially trained his son. Gerrit van Honthorst and his brother Willem van Honthorst (1594–1666) then studied with Abraham Bloemaert in his busy workshop, probably along with the slightly younger ter Brugghen. Bloemaert was fascinated by Italian art and encouraged his pupils to follow contemporary Italian painting

Below: This Merry Group Behind a Balustrade with a Violin and a Lute Player, *painted by Honthorst in c.1623, is a typical example of the warmth and dynamism he bestowed on his characters.*

techniques, which included using colours in shadows and highlights. Once his artistic education had finished, van Honthorst travelled to Italy. He was in Rome in 1616 and stayed with the banker and art collector Marchese Vincenzo Giustiniani (1564–1637). Gustiniani was one of Caravaggio's great patrons, and van Honthorst became extremely influenced by Caravaggio's realism, strong colours, cropped compositions and dramatic chiaroscuro, as well as the work of other artists such as Carracci and Domenichino that were also in Gustiniani's collection. In response, van Honthorst began painting atmospheric, candlelit scenes which attracted the patronage of wealthy and powerful Italians including, as well as Giustiniani, Cardinal Scipione Borghese (1577–1633) and the Grand Duke of Tuscany, Cosimo II de' Medici (1590–1621). A contemporary art collector, dealer and critic Giulio Mancini (1559–1630) wrote of the high prices that van Honthorst was receiving for his work.

On his return to Utrecht in 1620, a great welcoming party was held for van Honthorst. He soon established a

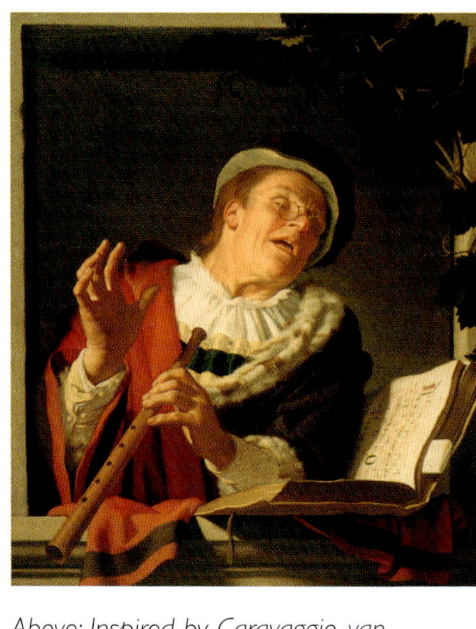

Above: Inspired by Caravaggio, van Honthorst painted several half-portraits of travelling entertainers, musicians and gypsies as with this Singing Cornett Player, *and created a new Dutch painting tradition.*

large workshop there and continued to build on the reputation he had started in Rome. Along with Dirck van Baburen, Hendrick ter Brugghen and Jan van Bijlert (1597/98–1671), he became known as one of the Utrecht Caravaggisti. In 1621, Dudley Carleton (1573–1632), an art collector and the British ambassador in The Hague, sent one of his paintings to Thomas Howard, Earl of Arundel (1586–1646) in Britain. Howard praised van Honthorst for his mastery of 'Caravagioes colouringe.' In 1622, he joined the Utrecht Guild of Saint Luke and served as its dean for several years. After marrying, van Honthorst and his wife lived near his close friend ter Brugghen.

COURT PAINTER

In 1627, Rubens spent a day visiting van Honthorst in his studio. Van Honthorst hosted a dinner for Rubens and also featured him in one of his paintings.

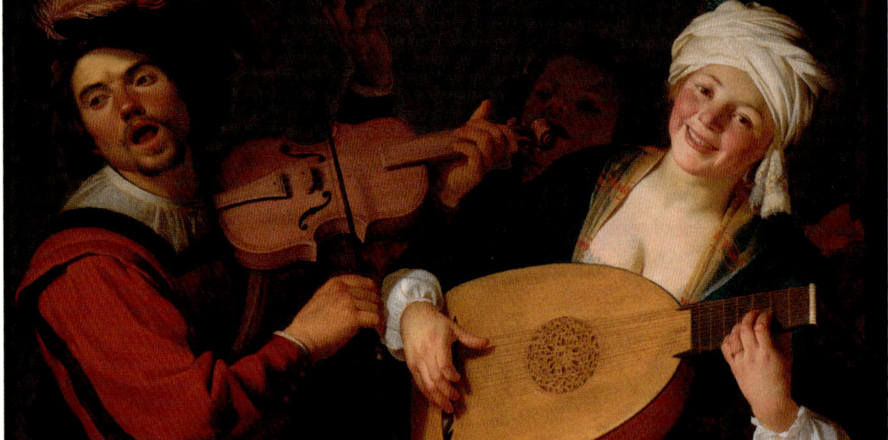

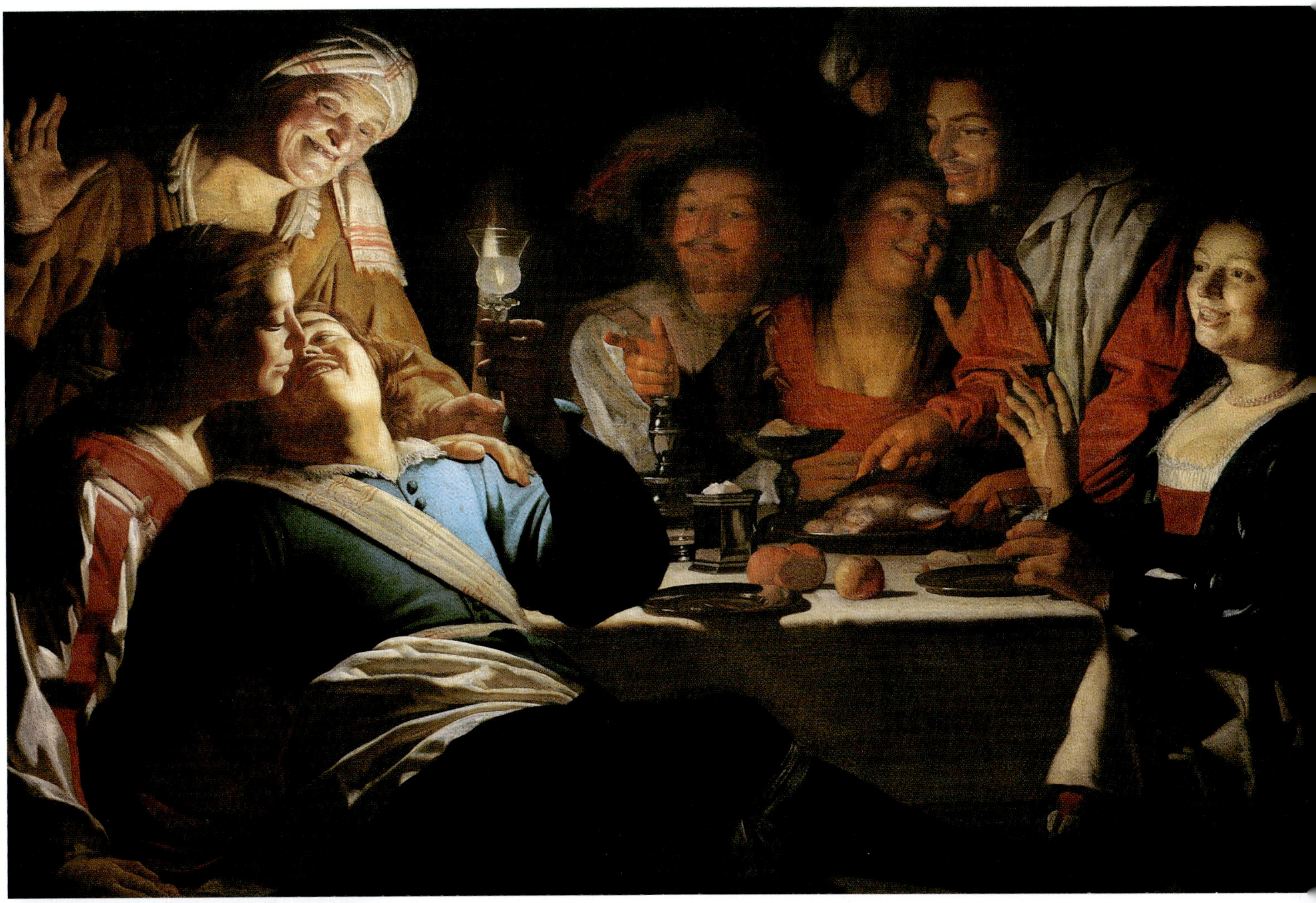

Above: During his lifetime, van Honthorst was celebrated and his work widely admired. He painted this flamboyant group Merry Company two years after returning to the Netherlands from Italy.

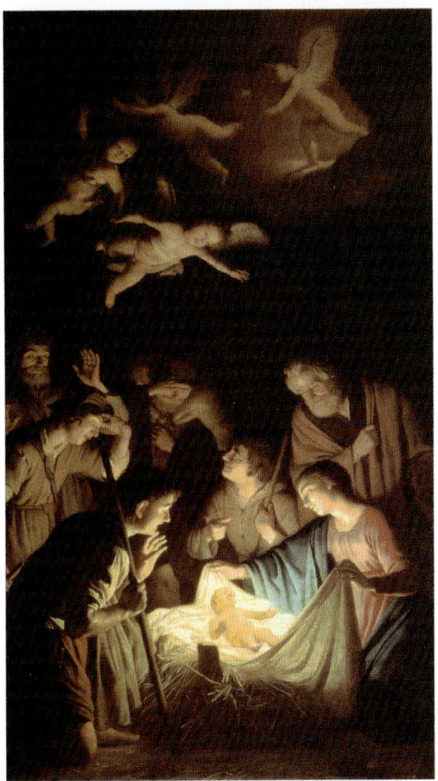

Left: Painted in 1620 while he was still in Italy, this Adoration of the Shepherds by van Honthorst clearly reveals the effect that Italy in general, and Caravaggio in particular, was having on him.

The two men may have met previously as van Honthorst may have visited Flanders to familiarize himself with the art there, particularly by the revered Rubens himself. At around the same time, the sister of Charles I of England, Queen Elizabeth of Bohemia and her husband King Frederick, who were in exile in the Netherlands, commissioned van Honthorst to paint for them and also employed him as a drawing teacher for their children. After Elizabeth praised his work to her brother King Charles I, van Honthorst was invited to England. He was at the English court from April to December 1628, where he painted several portraits and a huge allegory of the King and Queen as Apollo and Diana receiving the Duke of Buckingham as Mercury. Back in the Dutch Republic, van Honthorst moved to The Hague and continued working as a court painter for the exiled monarchs of Bohemia, for the stadtholder Frederick Hendrick of Orange and his wife, Princess Amalia van Solms, and for King Christian IV of Denmark. He bought a house in The Hague and joined the Guild of Saint Luke there in 1637. He remained in The Hague until 1652, when he returned to Utrecht until his death four years later. Many later painters, including Rembrandt and the French artist Georges de la Tour (1593–1652), were profoundly influenced by his work.

CLAESZOON HEDA • DIRCK HALS

Two friends from Haarlem, Willem Claeszoon Heda (1593/4–c.1680/2) and Dirck Hals (1591–1656) created detailed still lifes and genre paintings, focusing on a close depiction of light. They had a similar approach to composition and technical execution, although Heda's work appears slightly more controlled.

Not much is known about Heda's early life. Born in Haarlem, the son of a city architect and nephew of an artist, in 1616, at the age of 21, he became a member of the Saint George civic guard. He married in 1619, and taught at least one of his sons to paint. His earliest known painting is a vanitas of 1621, and he joined the Haarlem Guild of Saint Luke in 1631, later holding a series of posts within it, and also assisting Salomon de Bray (1597–1664) in the guild's reorganization. Although he painted some figure studies early in his career, he later concentrated exclusively on still lifes, especially focusing on the depiction of light reflected on smooth, shiny surfaces such as pewter, silver or brass candlesticks. In common with many other still life painters, he often featured the same objects in different paintings, and he became a master of 'ontbijtjes' or 'breakfast pieces' (page 39).

ORDERLY COMPOSITIONS

Although Heda's earliest known work was a vanitas, his later work comprised more sumptuous objects. His skill was recognized early on in his career by other notable figures in Haarlem, such as Samuel Ampzing (1591–1632), a Dutch minister and poet, who wrote in the *Beschryvinge ende lof der stad Haerlem in Holland* (Description and Praise of the City of Haarlem in Holland), published in 1628: '[I] ha[ve] to praise Heda with the banquet pieces of Salomon de Bray and Pieter Claesz, their skill deserves to be mentioned.'

By the 1630s, Heda was painting fine glass and elegant metalware, draped fabrics and various carefully placed foods. Unlike many of his contemporaries, Heda's compositions are relatively simple and ordered. His colouring, portrayal of light and fine brushwork convey an astonishing level of realism. His later still lifes feature

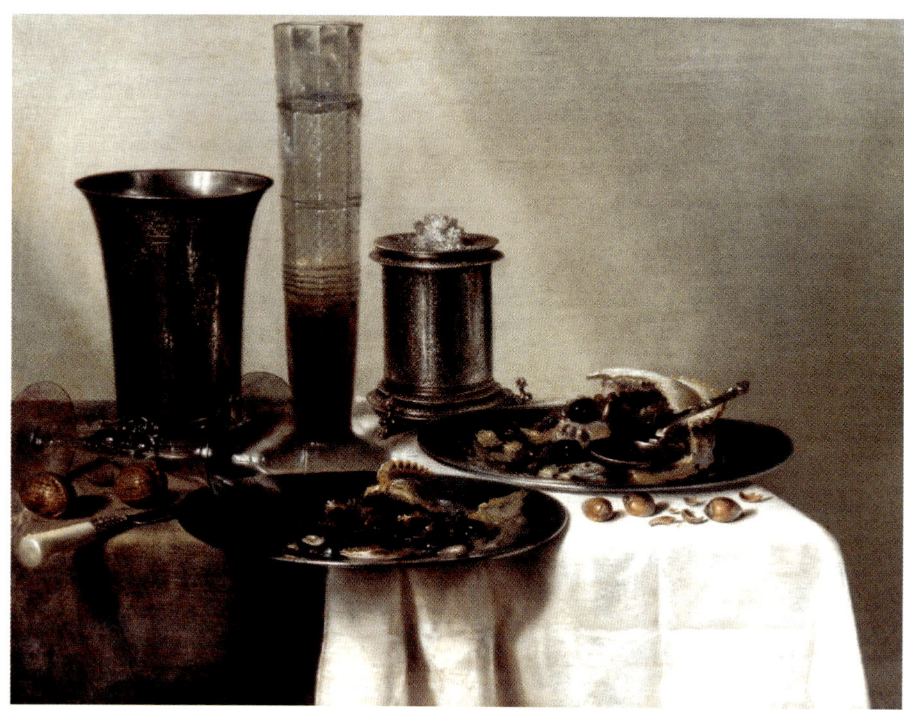

Above: Featuring drinking vessels and a gilt salt-cellar that reflects the light, a tall glass and plates with leftovers, Breakfast Still Life *was an early work by Heda.*

Below: An Elegant Party Making Music by an Ornamental Lake *is an oil on panel painting by Dirck Hals, showing the sumptuous fashions of the wealthy.*

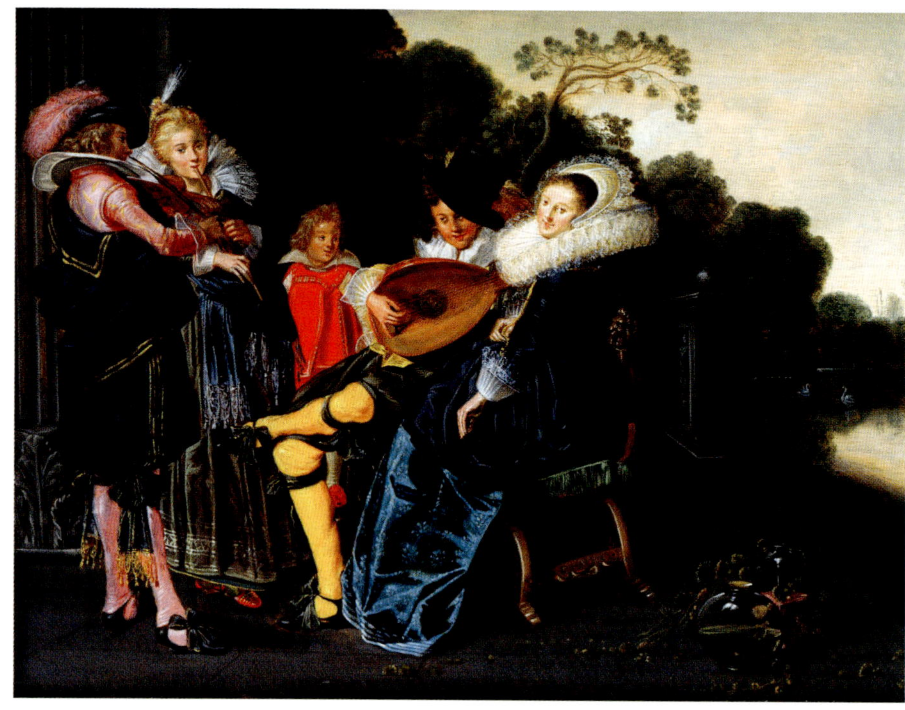

such things as crinkled napkins and fallen glasses or vases, and he began to include more objects and colours, which contrast with his earlier orderly compositions but are still carefully arranged.

After his death, Heda's work fell into obscurity, until it was rediscovered by the French art critic Théophile Thoré-Bürger (1807–69) in the 1860s. After seeing an example of his work at the Boijmans Museum in Rotterdam, Thoré-Bürger praised Heda's ability to make 'pétite nature into a splendid celebration of life.'

MERRY COMPANY SCENES

Dirck Hals, the younger brother of Frans Hals, was also born and worked in Haarlem. Hals the Elder influenced his younger brother with his painterly and colourful technique, but as with most of the painters of the Dutch Golden Age, much of his background is obscure. He probably trained with his brother and also with the genre painter Willem Pieterszoon Buytewech (1591/92–1624), and entered the Haarlem Guild of Saint Luke in 1627. In the early 1630s, he collaborated with the architectural painters Dirck van Delen (c.1605–71) and Bartholomeus van Bassen, usually providing the figure groups for lavish perspective interiors.

Dirck Hals is recorded as being in Leiden in 1641–42 and again in 1648–49. In his genre paintings that became known as 'conversation pieces' or 'merry company' scenes, he introduced a greater sense of space than other painters of the genre had presented, and applied quick and lively brushstrokes to convey the opulent and sophisticated costumes of the fashionable, as well as descriptive interiors and bucolic landscapes. One of his favourite themes was groups of people enjoying themselves, including festivals and ballroom scenes. In addition to Heda, Ampzing mentioned both the Hals brothers in his *Beschryvinge ende lof der stad Haerlem*, stating that both brothers were exceptional, and that Dirck painted his 'neat little figures... purely'. His influence spread far beyond Haarlem.

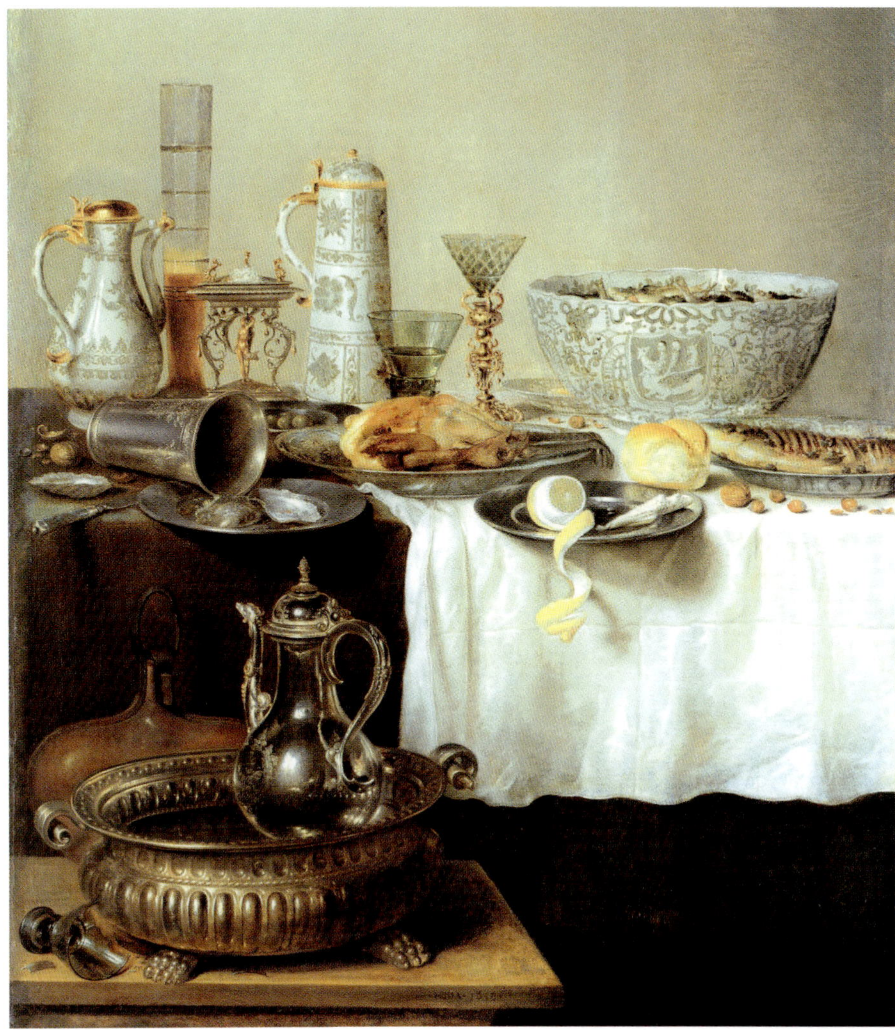

Above: Painted in 1638, this is a more complex ontbijt than many of Heda's other breakfast still lifes, including various delicately decorated objects.

Below: In this relatively simple Still Life with Gilt Beer Cup, *it can be seen that Heda was exceptionally skilled in depicting light reflected on shiny surfaces.*

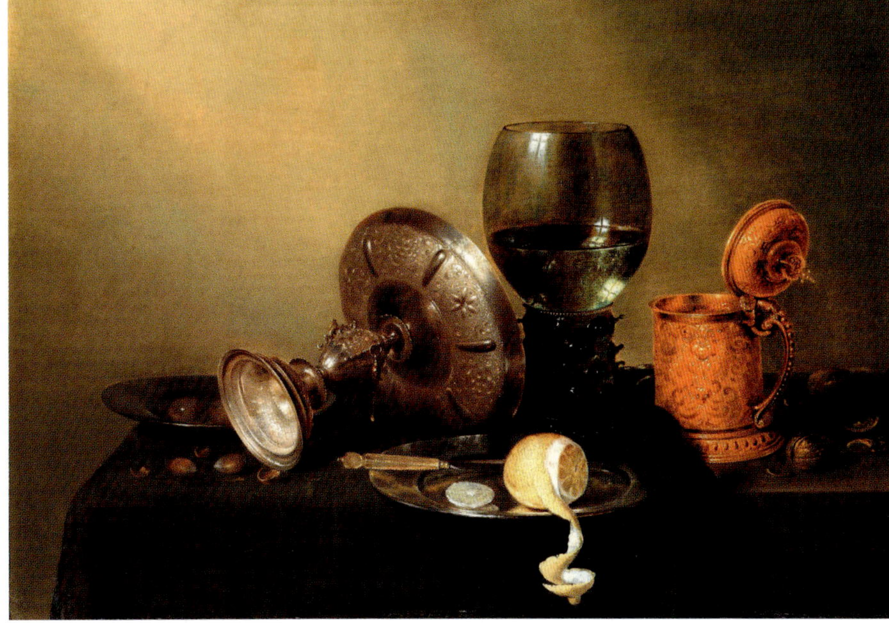

JAN VAN GOYEN

The son of a Catholic shoemaker, Jan van Goyen (1596–1656) was born in Leiden and first learned to paint there when he was 10 years old. Overall, he studied with six different masters in Leiden, Hoorn and Haarlem before moving to The Hague in 1631, where he stayed for the rest of his life.

Among van Goyen's tutors were Willem Gerritsz (before 1576–1628), Isaac van Swanenburg (1537–1614), and the glass painter Cornelis Cornelisz Clock (c.1561–1629). In about 1614, he returned to Leiden from Hoorn and then spent a year in France. He then moved to Haarlem and, from 1617, studied with the landscape painter Esaias van de Velde (1587–1630), whose characterful style initially deeply influenced him; some of his earliest paintings are virtually indistinguishable from his tutor's. He continued to sketch in the countryside and painted using deft brushstrokes, and he became one of the most prolific artists of his period, producing approximately 1,200 paintings and 800 drawings, which established his high reputation.

A SENSE OF SPACE

In 1618, van Goyen married in Leiden, and later bought a house there. He always painted landscapes, mainly of the Dutch Republic, with a few of France. Throughout the 1620s, his paintings,

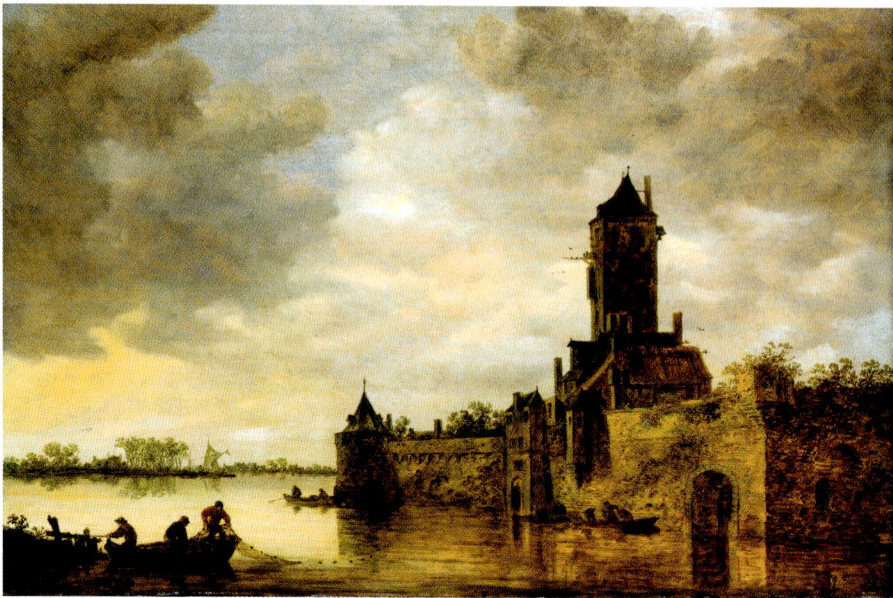
Above: Castle by a River; *painted in 1647, this scene of fishermen in front of a fortress below a moody sky is painted on a smooth oak panel, with several painterly effects evoking various textures.*

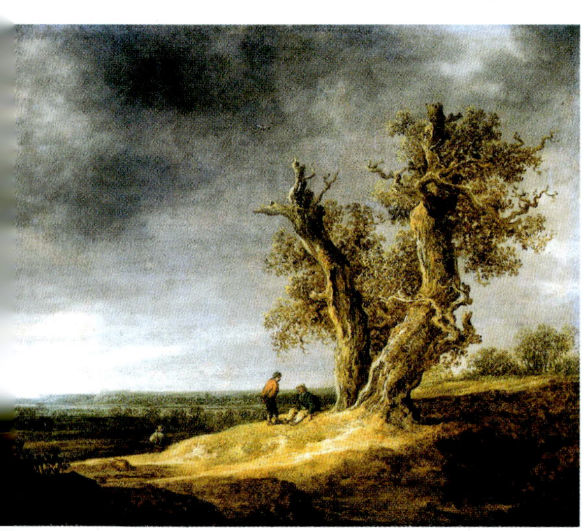
Below: Landscape with Two Oaks. *Illuminated by bright sunlight, the gnarled trees stand alone with two figures. Behind is the threatening, atmospheric sky.*

with their intense colours and intricate details, show the influence of Esaias van der Velde, but from about 1627, they began changing. He began lowering his horizons to convey a greater sense of space, and his rendering of light and atmospheric effects became subtler. Additionally, his palette became more monochrome and subdued, comprising mainly blues, browns, greens and greys.

Although he travelled widely across the Netherlands, van Goyen kept his family home in Leiden, but in 1631, he moved his family to The Hague, where he became a citizen in 1634 and was made head of the Hague Guild of Saint Luke in 1638. To support his family, as well as painting, he worked as an auctioneer, art critic and estate agent, and he speculated – and lost money – on tulip bulbs when the tulip market crashed in 1637.

SUBTLE AND VARIED EFFECTS

Van Goyen chiefly painted in oil on wood panels, using rich, fluid paint, and depicting atmospheric skies and water and especially calm scenes. He often represented tranquil rivers and

seas. He also excelled in scenes of Dutch cities, particularly Leiden and The Hague and in landscape etchings. By the 1640s, he focused his energies on capturing varied weather effects at various times of day, subtly changing his colours and brushmarks. In these later works, clouds take on an increasing importance, especially to evoke varying moods. By the 1650s, his colours became more luminous, but he never moved far from monochrome tonalities. This focus on natural light and weather and atmospheric effects was extremely popular amongst wealthy Dutch citizens, who enjoyed adorning their homes with such views of their own country.

In 1649, van Goyen's daughter married his pupil Jan Steen, the famous painter of genre scenes. Although he was an extremely popular painter, van Goyen never recouped his losses from Tulip Mania, and he died insolvent.

Right: Taking up most of the image is the cloudy Dutch sky, while below is a view of Leiden from the north-east via the river. Jan van Goyen painted it in 1650.

Centre right: Winter Landscape with Skaters Before S'Hertogenbosch. *Another painting that consists mainly of sky, this depicts a cold winter's day, when it seems that the whole town has come out to enjoy the ice.*

Bottom right: River Scene by a Fortified Shore, c.1640s. *A vast and atmospheric sense of aerial perspective provides the setting for hard-working figures, all meticulously recorded in great detail.*

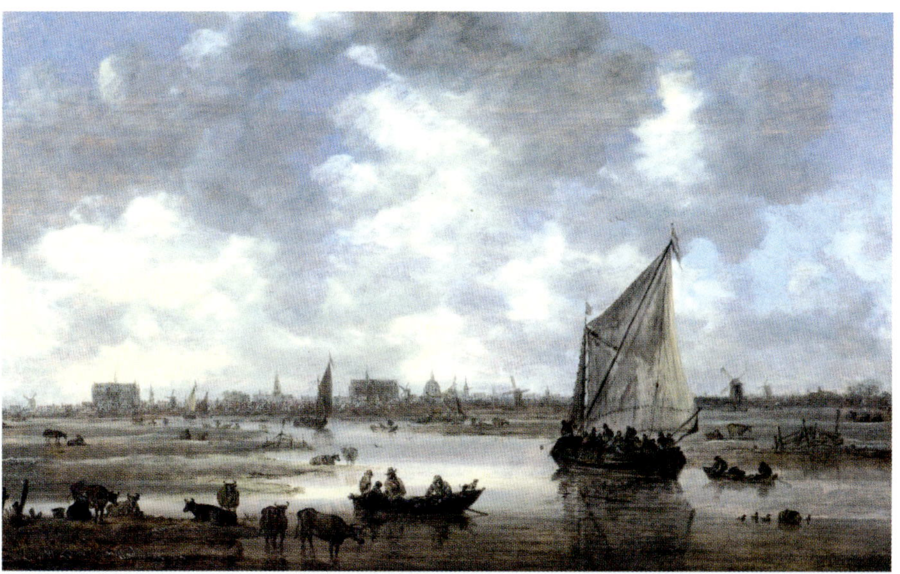

TULIP MANIA

Tulip Mania, Tulip Craze, or in Dutch, Tulpenwindhandel, was a fashion in the Dutch Republic over the sale of tulip bulbs. Soon after 1550, tulips had been introduced into Europe from Turkey, and the elegant, colourful flowers became both popular and astonishingly costly. The demand for differently coloured varieties soon exceeded the supply, and prices for unusual bulbs rose rapidly. By about 1610, a single bulb of some new varieties were so valuable that they were accepted as dowries for brides, and a French business was exchanged for one bulb of a particular type. The craze reached its height from 1633 to 1637. Before 1633, the Dutch tulip trade had been restricted to only expert growers and cultivators, but as prices rose, many ordinary middle and working class families began to speculate in the tulip market. As sales were made, properties were remortgaged and prices escalated in an unprecedented manner. It was clearly unsustainable, and early in 1637, the simmering doubts and concerns about the continuing price increases reached a crisis point. Almost instantly, the tulip price structure collapsed, leaving financial ruin in its wake for many, including Jan van Goyen.

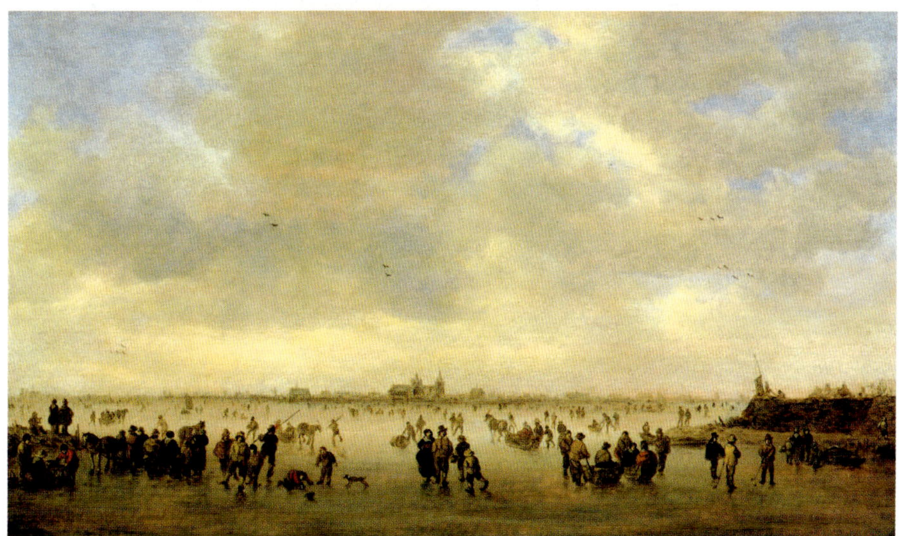

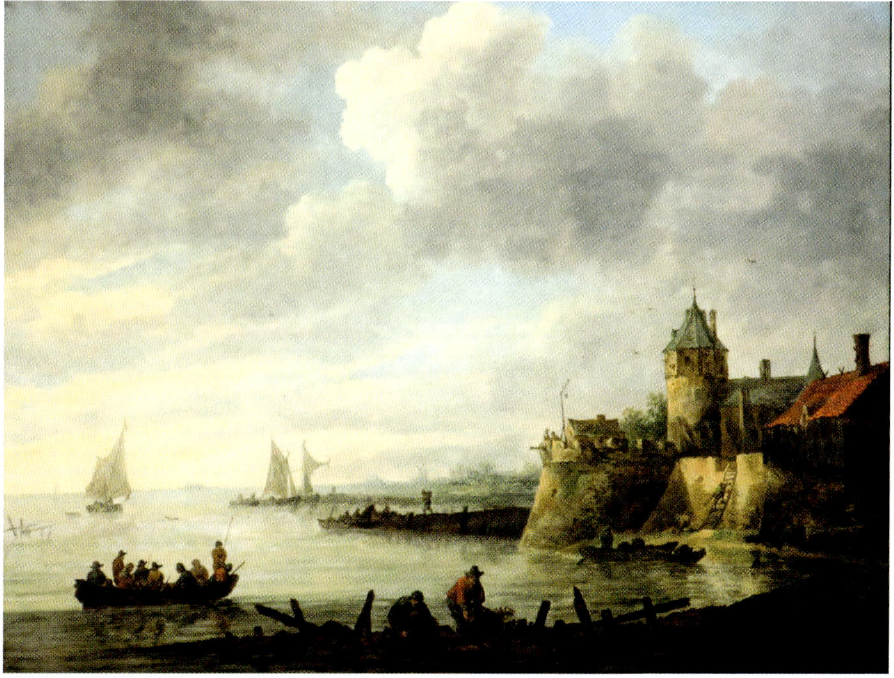

CLAESZ • BERCHEM

Both the still life painter Pieter Claesz (1596/7–1660) and his son Nicolaes Pieterszoon Berchem (1620–83), a landscape, allegorical and genre painter, were prolific and famous in their lifetimes. Despite their differences in subject matter, their elegant paintings feature strikingly atmospheric qualities.

With scant documentation, it is not clear exactly where Pieter Claesz was born. His parents were Dutch but he was born either in Berchem near Antwerp, or in Burgsteinfurt, Westphalia. It seems likely that it was Berchem as his son took the name of that location. In 1617, Claesz moved to Haarlem, where he married and his son Nicolaes Berchem was born three years later. In that same year, Claesz was admitted to the Antwerp Guild of Saint Luke, despite living in Haarlem. He also joined the Haarlem Guild of Saint Luke, and in 1634, he is registered in the Haarlem Guild as a master painter.

In 1635, after his first wife had died, Pieter Claesz married for a second time to a Flemish Catholic woman and the couple had two daughters, Lucia and Catharina.

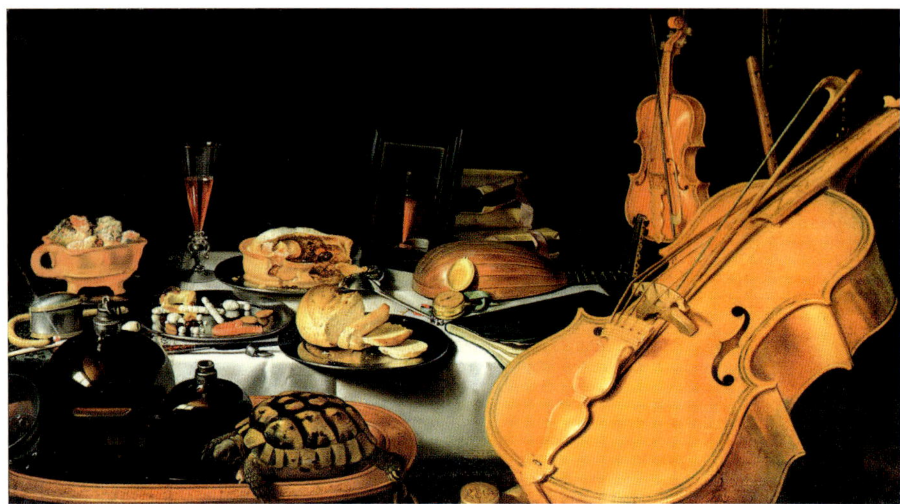

Above: Painted by Claesz in 1623, Still Life with Musical Instruments *conveys a wide range of textures in its variety of objects, including bread, a pie, instruments, books, a pocket watch and a tortoise.*

Below: Still Life of a Banquet. *Packed with items that almost completely cover the sharply ironed white tablecloth, this exacting work demonstrates the detail and precision that Claesz exerted.*

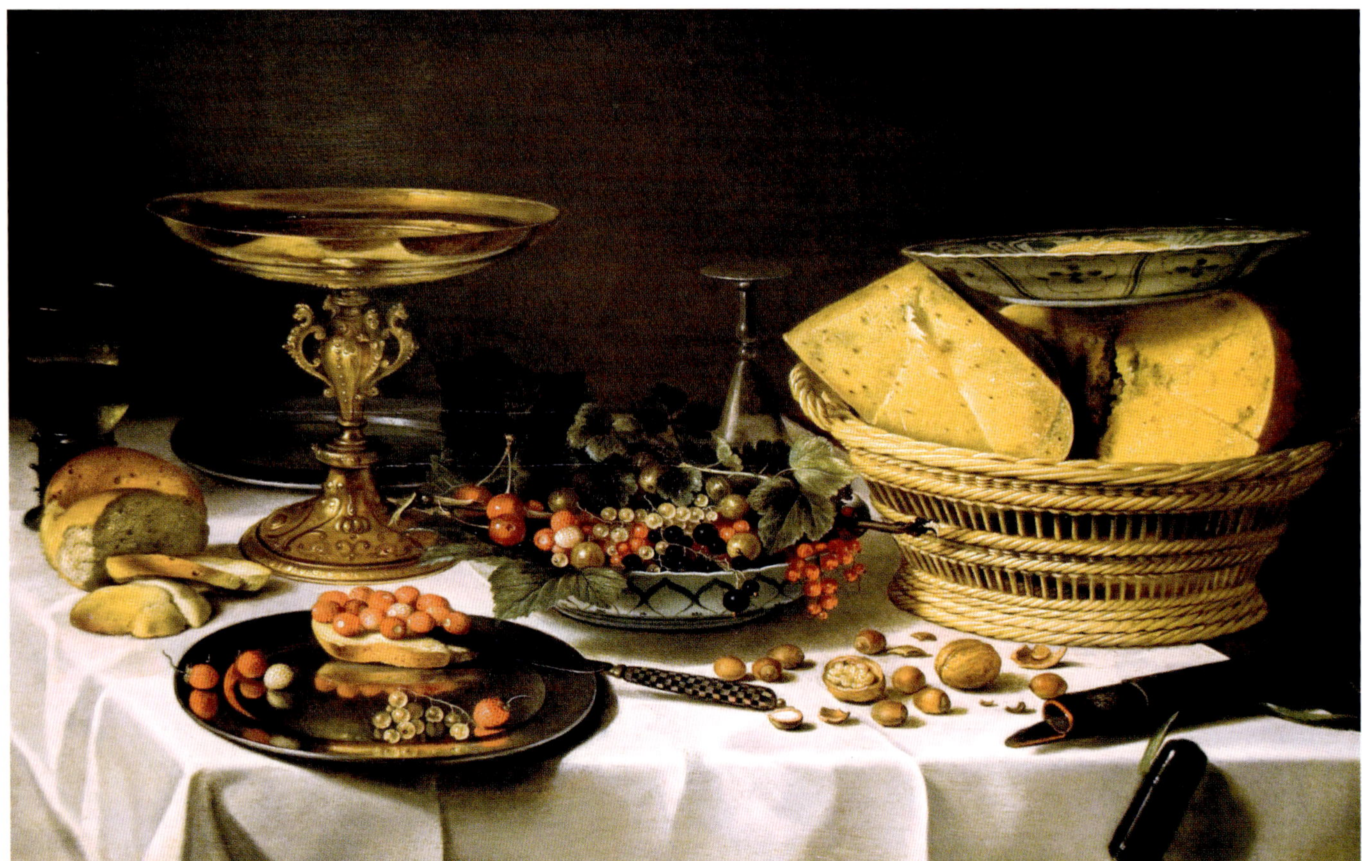

BREAKFAST PIECES

Claesz's education is not known, but his earliest works follow the style and themes of the Antwerp still life painters Osias Beert the Elder and Clara Peeters. Rather than specialize in common types of art, such as genre and portraits, Claesz continued to paint 'table-top' still lifes. These were arrangements of dining objects, including foods such as olives, herring, fruit, bread rolls and pastries, but with underlying moral messages, such as transience, time, impermanence or decay, and all painted with an extraordinary degree of naturalism, fine detail and carefully observed light effects.

Until about 1625, Claesz's still lifes were frequently of tables laid with crockery, silverware, drinking glasses, spices and fruit, executed in clear colours. After 1625, until about 1640, he began severely reducing the number of items in his compositions, rendering the materials and light as accurately as possible. He often included the edge of a table to give his paintings depth. Between 1630 and 1640, his palette became more subdued and restrained, and after 1640, he re-introduced more dramatic colours and more objects, including luxurious dishes, fine glass and boldly coloured fruits and flowers. He and Willem Claesz Heda were the most important exponents of the 'ontbijt' or 'breakfast piece', which is the depiction of a simple meal set near the corner of a table. Claesz and Heda captured their still lifes with a subtle handling of light and texture. Claesz's innovative compositions and ability to use the same objects in many unique arrangements influenced other Haarlem artists, and many far beyond, including the French still life painter Jean-Baptiste-Siméon Chardin (1699–1779).

GOLDEN SCENES

Claesz's son Nicolaes Pieterszoon Berchem was a highly esteemed and prolific painter of pastoral landscapes, populated with mythological or biblical figures. He also painted a number of allegories and genre pieces. Berchem's paintings, drawings and etchings are of idealized rural scenes, with hills,

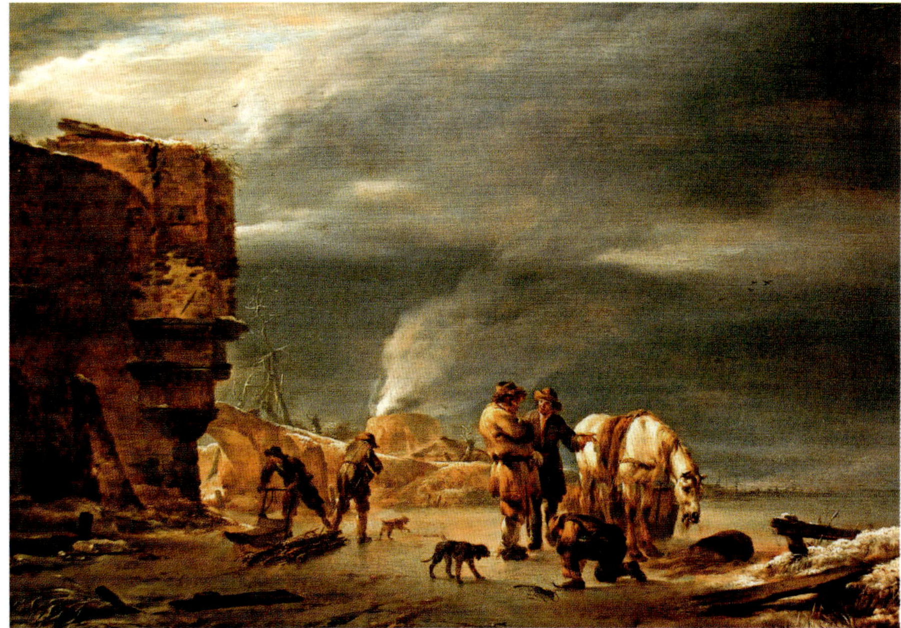

Above: Highly atmospheric, this winter scene, On the Ice Near a Town, *painted by Berchem in 1647, focuses on the effects of light as well as the activities of the figures, dogs and horse.*

Below: Landscape with a Hunting Party, *painted by Berchem in c.1660–65, is an idealized scene showing the Dutch landscape and wealthy people congregating for a hunt.*

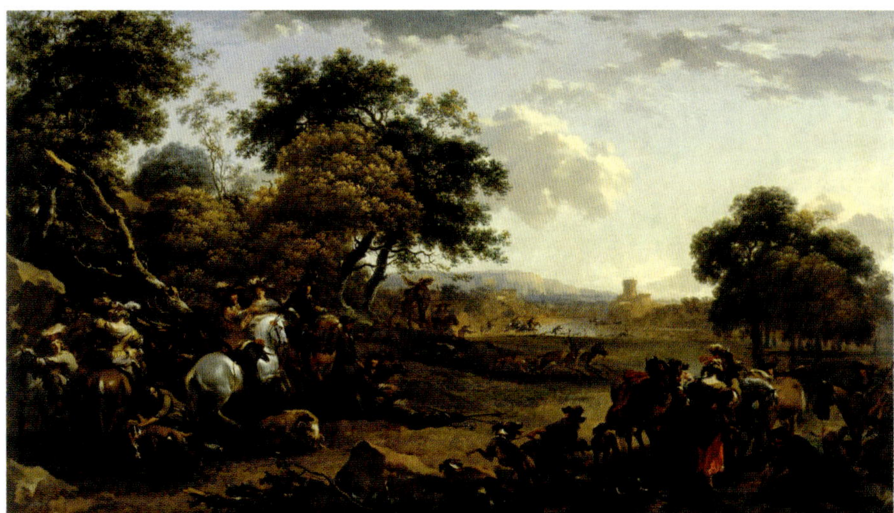

mountains, cliffs and trees bathed in golden light that contrasted with local Netherlandish landscapes, and they became greatly sought after. He also painted cityscapes and winter and pastoral scenes, all bathed in glowing Italianate light.

Berchem studied his craft from his father, and from Jan van Goyen, Pieter de Grebber (c.1600–52/3), Jan Baptist Weenix (1621–60), Jan Wils (1603–66) and Claes (Nicolaes) Cornelisz Moeyaert (1592–1655). In 1645, he became a member of the

Dutch Reformed Church and married the daughter of the painter Jan Wils. In about 1650 he travelled to Westphalia with Jacob van Ruisdael (1628–82). It has been speculated that he may have visited Italy but this is not verified. In about 1660, he worked for the engraver Jan de Visscher (1636–1712) designing an atlas. From 1661 he was registered as being in Amsterdam; in 1670 he moved back to Haarlem, but was living again in Amsterdam by 1677, where he died six years later. A popular teacher, Berchem influenced the work of many pupils.

BASSEN · SAENREDAM · HOUCKGEEST

Some Golden Age artists chose to paint buildings. With intricate perspective lines, angles and precise measures, this type of painting was a challenge for technical skills while it also celebrated the achievements and wealth of the Republic. As the buildings were often churches, it also conveyed the new Christianity.

BARTHOLOMEUS VAN BASSEN

The first Dutch architectural painters worked in the late 16th and early 17th centuries. Many of their buildings were imaginary, but they inspired younger artists to paint real buildings. Among the first of these was Bartholomeus Corneliszoon van Bassen (1590–1652) who was also an architect. While little is known of his youth, when he was 23, Bassen became a member of the Delft Guild of Saint Luke. Nine years later, he moved to The Hague, and became a prominent member of the Hague Guild of Saint Luke.

Some of Bassen's buildings are imaginary, but most are real, and for all, he made detailed, exact underdrawings, usually using sharp, single-point perspective. He also built up light effects, which together created convincing illusions of three-dimensional spaces. As well as dramatic church architecture,

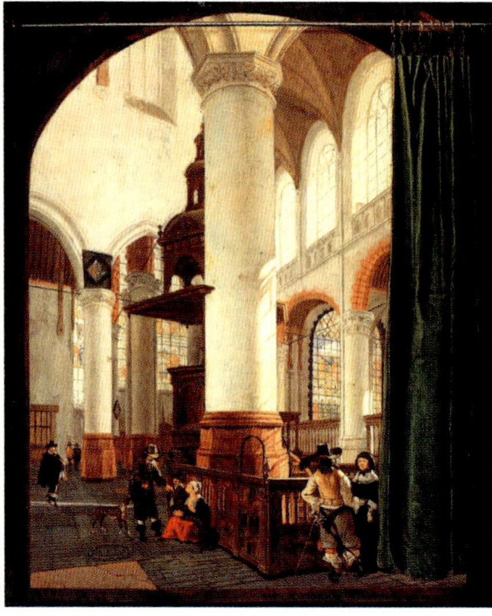

Above: Interior of the Oude Kerk Delft, *1648. Set around the pulpit in the Oude Kerk's nave, Houckgeest depicts various figures in the church, with sunlight streaming through the delicately coloured stained glass windows.*

he depicted lavishly decorated palace interiors with elegant figures.

In 1638, van Bassen was made city architect of the Hague and among other projects, he worked on the summer palace Huis Honselaarsdijk for Frederick Henry, the Prince of Orange (1584–1647). From 1649 until his death, he was involved with building the Nieuwe Kerk, one of the highlights of early Protestant Netherlandish church architecture. One of the most outstanding students in his busy workshop was Gerard Houckgeest.

PIETER JANSZ SAENREDAM

Pieter Saenredam (1597–1665) was born in Assendelft. His father, a Mannerist printmaker, died when Saenredam was 10, and from that year, he was apprenticed to Frans Pietersz de Grebber (1573–c.1649) in Haarlem for 11 years. He remained in Haarlem for the rest of his life, although he

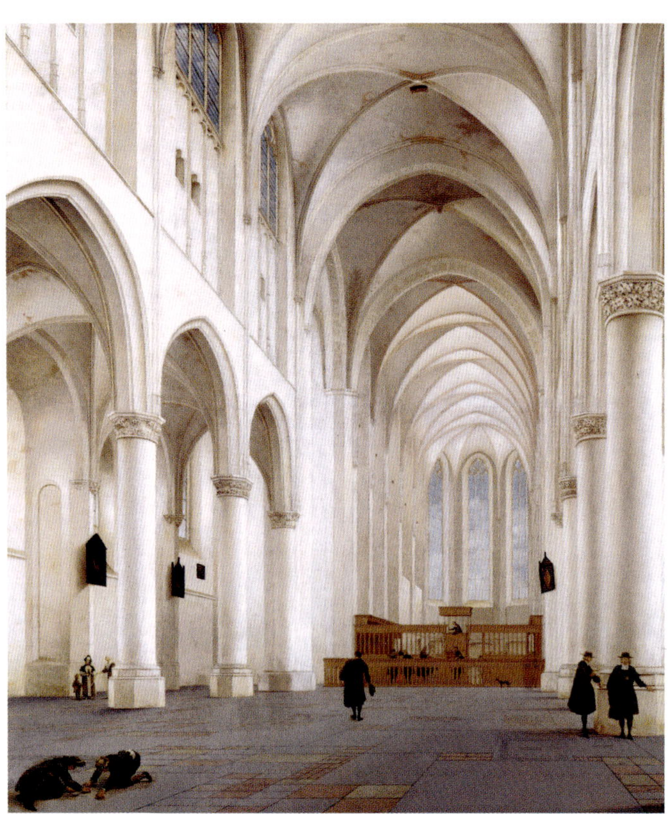

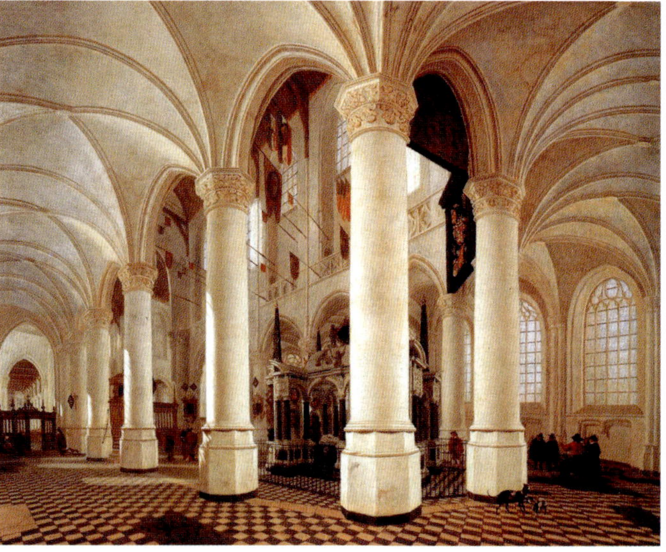

Above: The New Church in Delft with the Tomb of William the Silent, *by Houckgeest, 1650. He painted looking up and from an angle to create diagonal views across the church.*

Left: Saenredam painted the lofty St Katherine's Church in Utrecht from ground level to emphasize the white columns that extend up to the rib vault – and the tiny figures below.

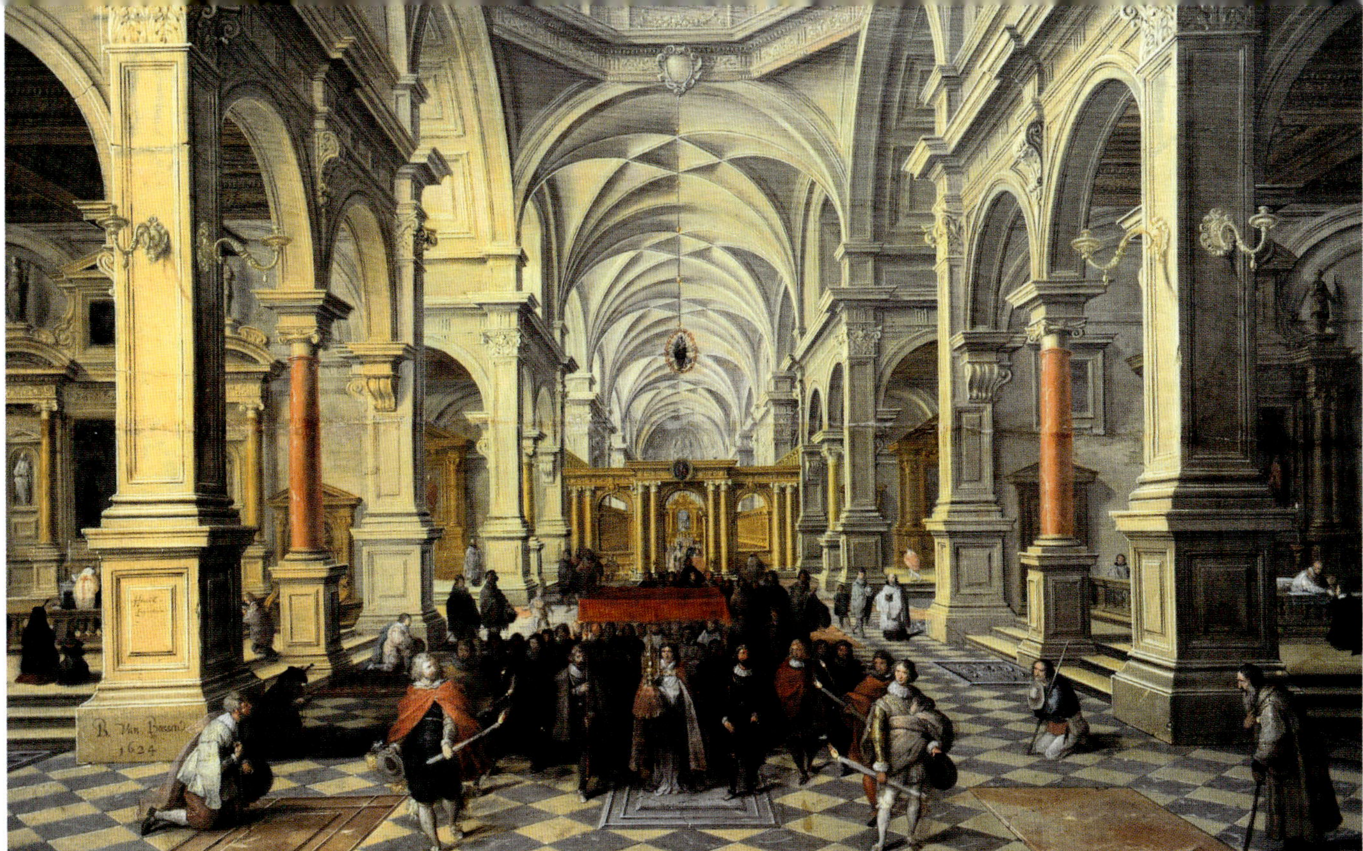

Above: Houckgeest was the first artist to depict spaces from a diagonal perspective, rather than directly from a straight angle. Here, visitors are looking at the tomb of William of Orange, painted in 1651.

often painted in other Dutch cities. His depictions of church interiors were meticulous, created from careful sketches made on site, in pencil, pen and chalk, with washes applied later. His final paintings, executed in his studio, emphasized calm light and geometry. When he was 26, Saenredam entered Haarlem's Guild of Saint Luke. Three years later, he was commissioned to produce illustrations for a history of Haarlem and he drew the interior of the church of Saint Bavo. From then on, he devoted himself almost exclusively to depicting Protestant church interiors. As a Catholic country, churches had been highly decorated, but in the Dutch Revolt many were 'cleaned' of Catholic influences and left bare. Working from low viewpoints and a pale palette, Saenredam painted few figures within the whitewashed interiors, stripped of their original decorations. His paintings are less to do with religion and more to do with perspective, following his fascination with the theories of proportion and balance of Andrea Palladio (1508–80).

GERARD HOUCKGEEST

Gerard Houckgeest (1600–1661) was probably born in The Hague. His uncle Joachim Houckgeest (1585–1644) was a portrait painter, and he learned to paint with Bartholomeus van Bassen. He worked in The Hague, Delft,

Below: One of the most important Dutch painters of church interiors during the 17th century, van Bassen produced imaginary scenes based on an amalgamation of actual interiors.

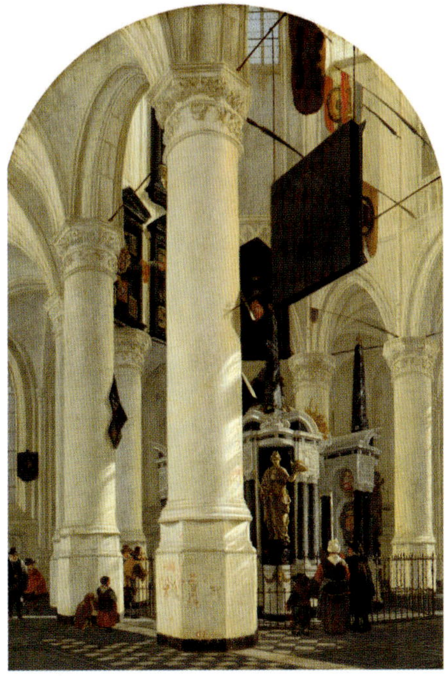

Steenbergen, Bergen op Zoom, and possibly also in England. King Charles I of England owned several of his paintings.

Following his teacher, Houckgeest initially specialized in painting church interiors and ornate Renaissance buildings, and using fairly sombre colours. After he moved to Delft in 1635, he adopted a lighter approach with his colours and brushwork, and began to use diagonal viewpoints in his compositions.

In Delft, Houckgeest also worked as an engraver and tapestry pattern-maker, and he married a young woman from a wealthy and influential family. In 1651, they moved to Bergen op Zoom. By then, Houckgeest had probably already worked at the court of the Princes of Orange and for the Staten Generaal, the national government in The Hague.

Houckgeest's innovative compositions that depicted interiors from oblique vantage points probably developed after he had seen other artists' work, such as Saenredam, Carel Fabritius, Emanuel de Witte or Hendrick Cornelisz van Vliet (1611–75). He made several other innovations including subtle nuances of daylight seeming to filter through high church windows, and obscuring some views with dramatic columns and pilasters in the foreground.

SALOMON VAN RUYSDAEL

The youngest of four sons and one daughter, born in Naarden, Salomon van Ruysdael (c.1600/03–70) painted landscapes and worked for most of his life in Haarlem. His brother Isaack van Ruisdael (1599–1677) was also a painter and the father of landscapist Jacob van Ruisdael.

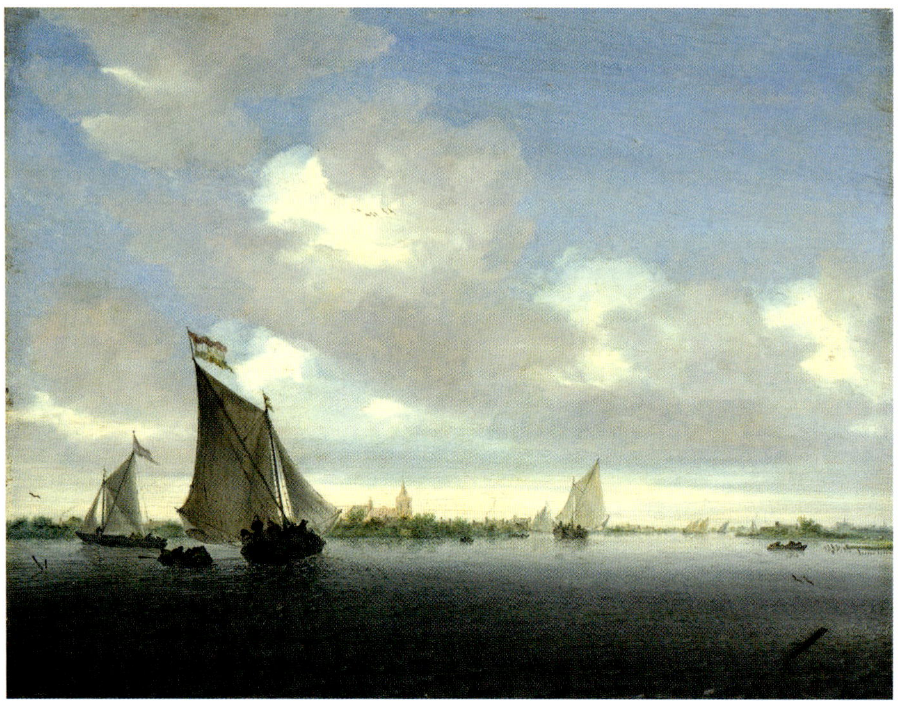

Left: Painted in 1650, this is one of a number of marine paintings that van Ruysdael painted in Haarlem. The boat flying the Dutch flag is a 'schouw' that was used to ship goods and occasionally carry passengers.

interpretations of the Haarlem countryside. He lived in Haarlem, but also painted views of Leiden, Utrecht, Amersfoort, Arnhem, Alkmaar and Rhenen. During the early 1630s, he restricted his palette to fairly subdued greys, greens, yellows, browns and blues, so the period is often referred to as his 'tonal phase'. From this decade, he began each painting with detailed charcoal underdrawings, then using paint to add elements such as figures and other details. Later, he abandoned the underdrawings, composing his paintings directly on to his panels or canvases,

Salomon van Ruysdael's father, Jacob Jansz de Goyer or Gooyer (c.1560–1616), was a moderately wealthy cabinetmaker, and although Salomon initially used his family name of 'de Gooyer', he soon followed his eldest brother and adopted the name 'van Ruysdael' (spelled Ruisdael by Salomon's brother's family) after a country estate near their father's home town Blaricum where the de Gooyer family may have been tenants. Shortly after their father's death, Salomon and Isaack moved to Haarlem, where Salomon entered the Guild of Saint Luke in 1623 (registering at the time as Salomon de Gooyer).

TONAL PHASE

Ruysdael specialized in river and estuary scenes. Although his training is unknown, his early paintings were influenced by Esaias van de Velde, Jan van Goyen and Pieter Molijn (1595–1661) – he may have studied with one, two or all three of these painters. In 1628, the Haarlem chronicler and poet Samuel Ampzing

praised Ruysdael's abilities in his book *Beschryvinge ende lof der stad Haerlem in Holland*.

Van Ruysdael's earliest paintings were winter scenes featuring low horizons and small figures, and he soon gained a reputation for his modest, unembellished

Below: Fishing Boats on a River, early 1600s. As a day draws to a close, Salomon van Ruysdael captures the changing light, focusing on the gliding silhouetted vessels on the still water, and the shining reflections.

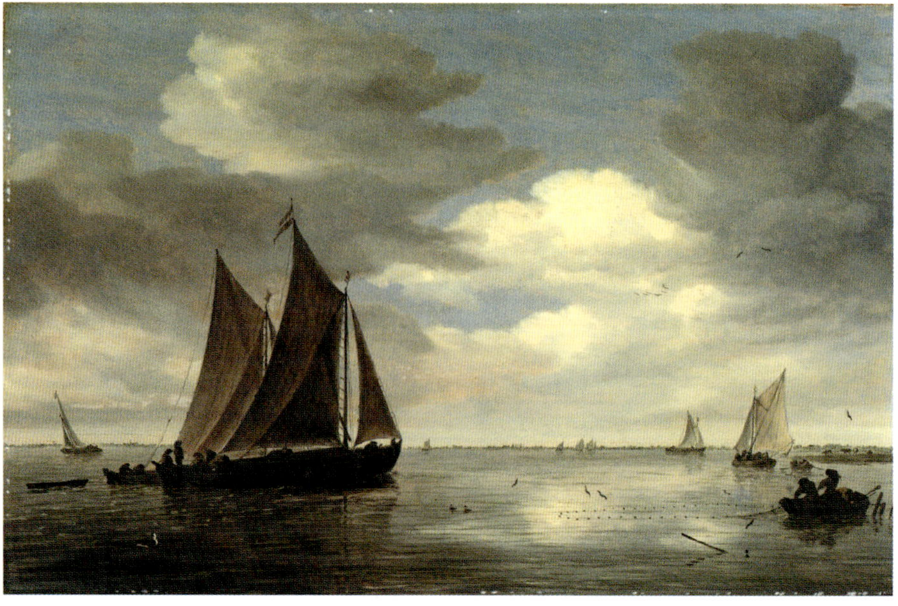

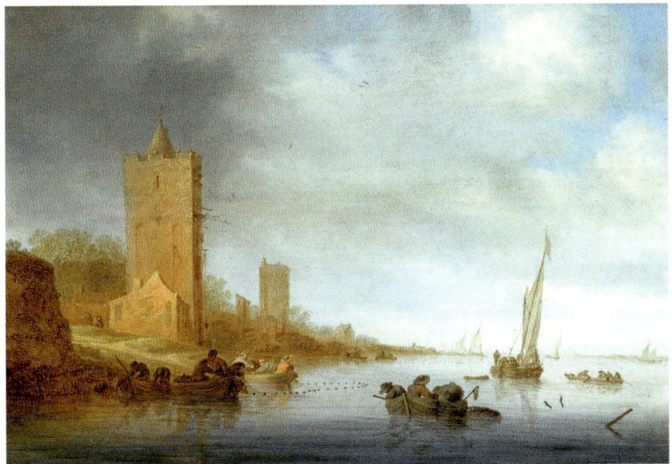

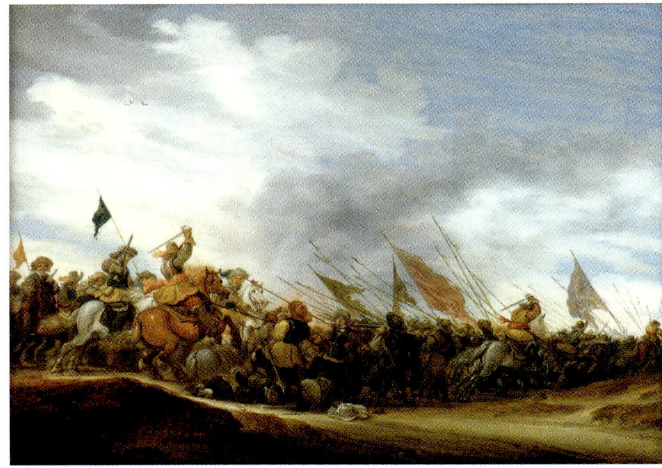

Above: River Landscape with Fishermen at Work. *A calm, still river scene with painterly effects used to capture crumbling brickwork, smooth, glassy water and soft shadows and reflections.*

Below: A Country Road, *1648. Following Karel van Mander's advice of painting small figures under tall trees, this scene leads the eye along the paths and into the distant low bridge where trees seem to sweep up to the clouds.*

Above: As with van Ruysdael's calmer landscapes, this more frenetic A Battle Scene, *featuring a fight with foot soldiers and cavalry, is painted from a low viewpoint; the sky takes up over half of the image.*

making changes and additions as he painted. In general, he painted thinly on light-coloured grounds, often allowing the grain of his wooden panels to show through in places.

A SENSE OF GRANDEUR

By the late 1630s, van Ruysdael's palette became more varied and after 1640, he reduced the number of trees in his compositions, instead making a small group of them, either in the centre or to one side. He made more of cloud formations and expanses of sky, and in place of his previous diagonal river views, he included broader expanses of water. This transformation was also part of a wider movement in Dutch landscape painting as more mundane, naturalistic views became 'classicized' or 'Italianate.' In response to this, van Ruysdael's landscapes also became grander. Increasingly, he used brighter colours and rendered greater atmospheric effects. In his seascapes, he created the illusion that viewers are on the water, watching the scene from a nearby craft. He also painted more winter landscapes and some still lifes, and from the mid-1630s, he created more than 30 paintings of horsemen and carriages, gathering in front of inns. His later landscapes reveal the influence of his more famous nephew Jacob van Ruisdael.

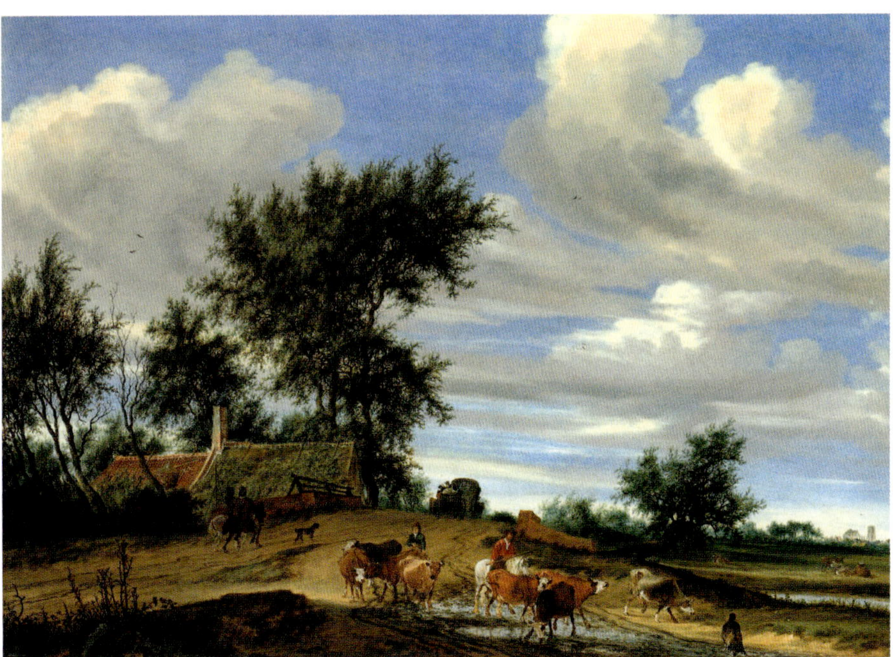

OTHER INCOMES

From 1647 until the end of his life, van Ruysdael took on several prominent positions within the Haarlem Guild of Saint Luke. Like many of his contemporaries, he did not earn his living exclusively from painting. In 1651 he was recorded as a merchant dealing in blue dye, and from 1658 to 1670, he was also a member of the Guild of Cloth Merchants. In addition, he invented a method of creating sculpted ornaments that when polished attained the appearance of shiny marble. These

became extremely popular, but when the secret of their manufacture was discovered, they were widely copied and sold, which reduced prices. However, along with his success as a painter, these varied activities brought Ruysdael considerable wealth, and he owned several houses in Haarlem. He and his wife had four children. One of Salomon's sons was the painter Jacob Salomonsz van Ruysdael (1629–81); there is sometimes confusion with his cousin of similar name, Jacob van Ruisdael, son of Salomon's brother Isaak.

AERT VAN DER NEER

Aert or Aernout van der Neer (1603/4–77) was a painter from Amsterdam who became known for his atmospheric landscapes, often bathed in moonlight or depicting dawn or dusk. He trained with the landscape painter Camphuysen (c.1597/98–1657), but was especially influenced by Flemish painting.

Van der Neer's father's name was Aegrom Aertsz van den Bosch, but he called himself van der Neer. He was born in Amsterdam, but spent his youth near Gorinchem in the south of the Netherlands. It was not until he was in his late 20s that he took up art. In 1629, he married his art teacher's younger sister, Lysbeth Goverts (dates unknown) with whom he had six children. One of his sons, Eglon van der Neer (1635–1703) later became a portrait painter, but little is known of the others. In 1632 van der Neer moved his family back to Amsterdam, where he produced his first known genre painting.

Van der Neer's brothers-in-law, Rafaël and Jochem Govertsz Camphuysen (1601–59) produced landscapes that are remarkably similar to van der Neer's, although his are more skilful. His main stylistic influence was the landscapes of the Frankenthal school.

TRANSLUCENT LIGHT

During the early years of his career, van der Neer painted realistic tonal landscapes and winter scenes inspired by Rafaël Camphuysen, Esaias van de Velde and Hendrick Avercamp. In 1643, he began specializing in nocturnes, or atmospherically illuminated outdoor scenes. The Dutch cities and villages he depicted seem realistic, but they were all created from his imagination and were never intended to be accurate renditions of real places. His focus was

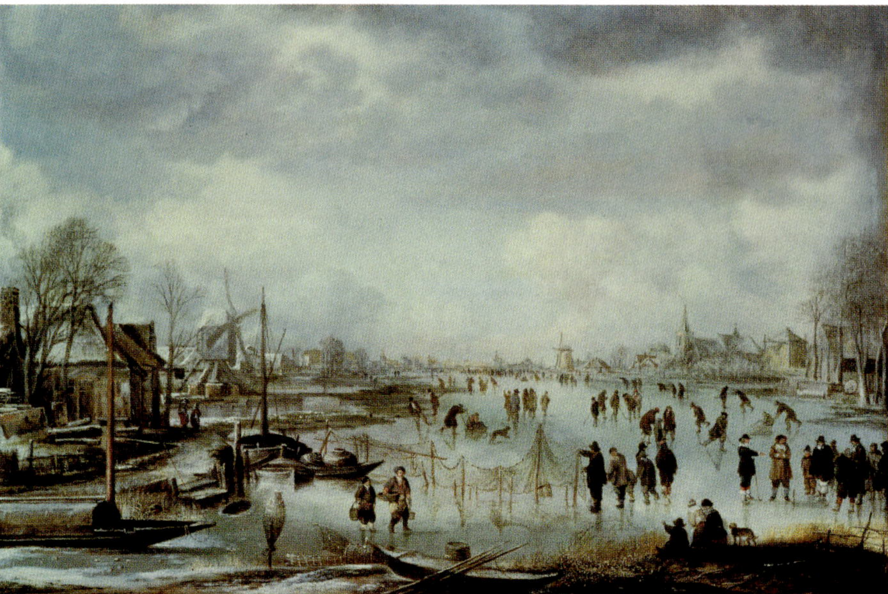

Above: Judging by the clothing in Winter Scene with Figures Skating, *this was painted in the early 1650s. The limited palette emphasizes the icy atmosphere.*

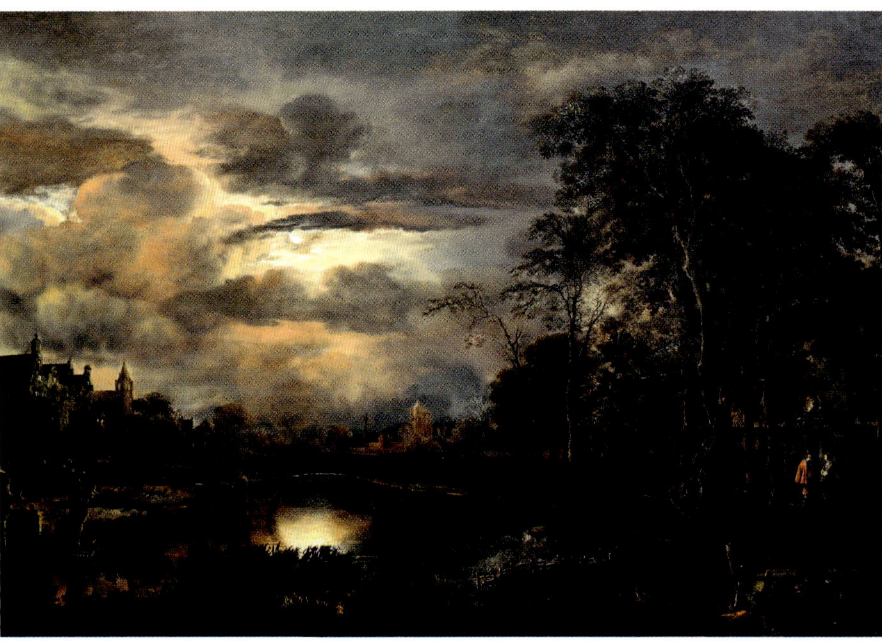

Left: Moonlit Landscape with Bridge. *By the late 1640s, van der Neer was painting nocturnes such as this, applying layers of translucent and opaque paint.*

THE FRANKENTHAL SCHOOL

From Antwerp, Gillis van Coninxloo (1544–1607) was one of a large family of landscape painters. In 1587, he emigrated to Frankenthal in south-western Germany, where he became the leader of a group of landscape painters who became known for their limited tonal palettes, luxuriant atmosphere created by evocative light, winding paths that lead the eye into the picture, and isolated figures. Van Coninxloo later settled in Amsterdam where his influence inspired Dutch artists, including van der Neer.

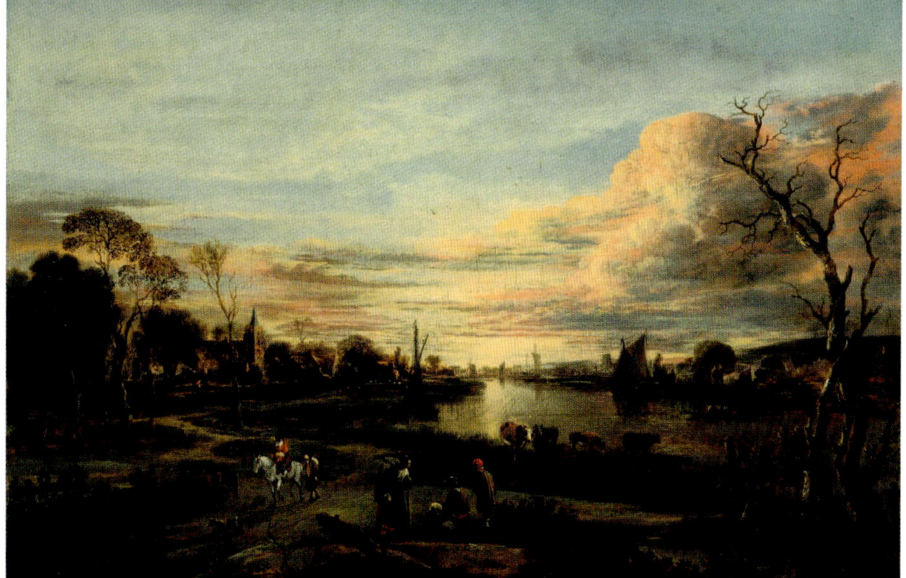

Above: Landscape at Sunset, *painted in the 1650s, focuses on the sun setting over a river, with pink and yellow tinting the clouds and the scene below.*

on evocative effects of light, and his scenes featured such things as radiant moons or rising suns, flames set against darkened backgrounds, and iridescent light on water or reflected against snow and ice. As well as night-time or early morning scenes, he also painted landscapes of ice filled with lively figures. He was one of several contemporary artists who were fascinated by the long icy winters of the Little Ice Age (see page 29) that brought so many out on to the ice to play and socialize in the frozen landscape, and he depicted their activities, such as sledging, skating and sliding or even picnicking or playing winter sports.

TRANSFORMING MOOD

As well as his canal and river landscapes bathed in the luminous glow of sunrise, sunset or moonlight, van der Neer painted flame-filled scenes after witnessing the burning of Amsterdam's town hall in 1652. He produced his most accomplished work between about 1645 and 1660, with his atmospheric effects of fire, dawn, dusk and winter skies. Restricting his palette to earthy colours, he applied thin layers of both translucent and opaque paint as he explored his fascination with the impact of light at different times of day and in different weather conditions. Like most artists of the time, he painted his exterior scenes in his studio using sketches made previously outside.

Yet, despite his productivity and skill, and although his work was much copied, van der Neer struggled to support his family; in about 1658 or 1659, he opened a wine tavern with his son Jan (1637–1712) in Kalverstraat, a busy street in Amsterdam. However, it failed and in 1662, he declared bankruptcy. He continued to paint, but lived in extreme poverty until his death 15 years later. With little attention during his lifetime, he died in obscurity, but more recently his work has received great praise.

Below: In Sports on a Frozen River, *probably painted c.1660, van der Neer amalgamated his passion for depicting light, winter landscapes and figures – here all bathed in the pink-gold glow of sunset.*

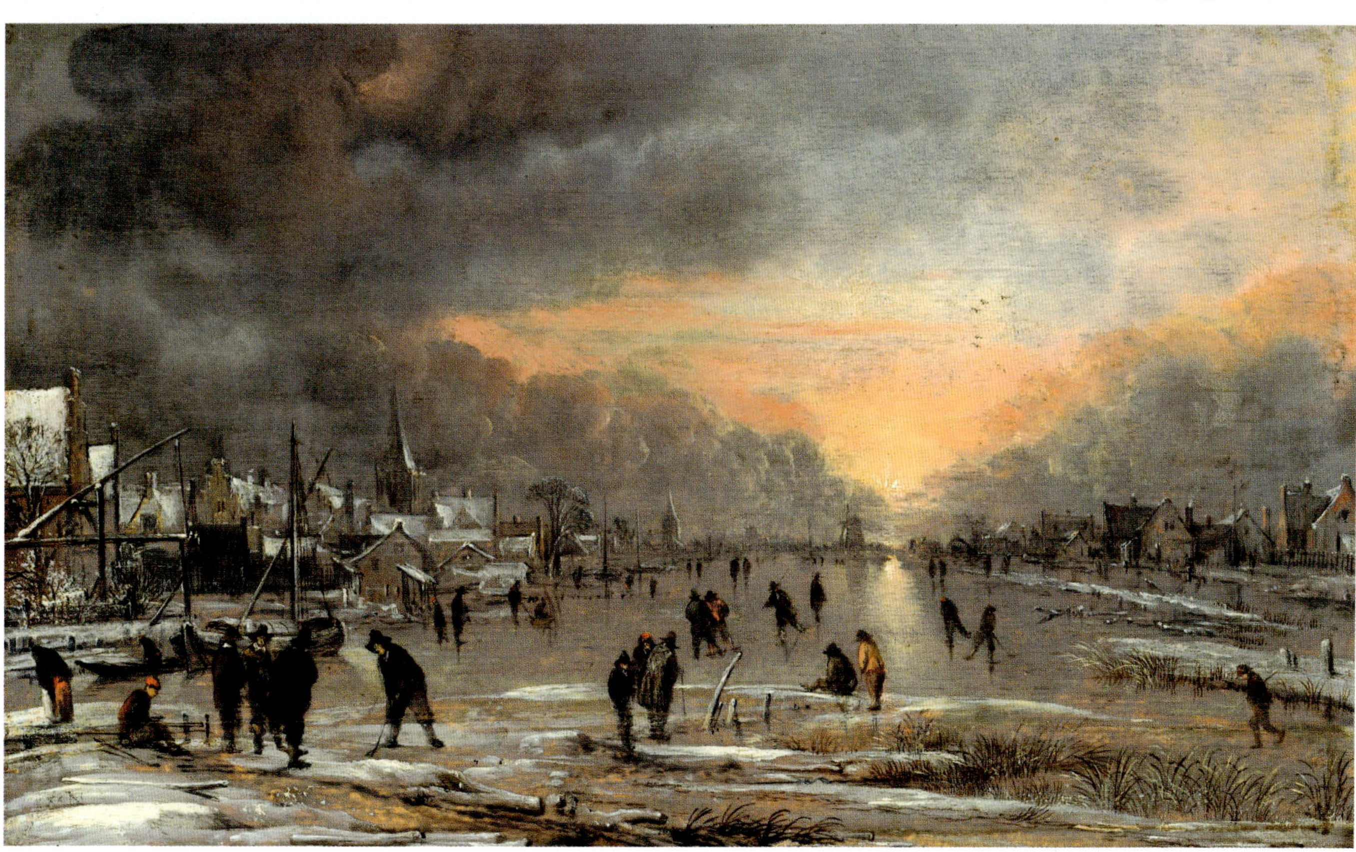

ADRIAEN BROUWER

Adriaen Brouwer (*c.*1605/6–38) was born Adriaen de Brouwer, or Brauwer, in Oudenaarde in Flanders. His father was a tapestry designer who died in poverty when his son was about 16. Soon after, Brouwer left Flanders for Amsterdam, where he initially stayed at an inn owned by the painter Barent van Someren.

Information about Brouwer's life is somewhat confused as early biographers made various claims that have since been disproved. Extremely sociable, he was also outspoken and a heavy drinker. He spent a great deal of time in taverns, smoking, drinking and making merry, and he accrued many debts – but he also observed the people around him and captured them vividly in his paintings. Although few of his paintings were signed and none dated, approximately 60 have been substantiated as his, all mainly small oil paintings on wooden panels that were highly influential to other artists across the Netherlands. Except for a small number of landscapes, he painted mainly genre themes drawn from everyday life and depicting such things as soldiers, amateur medical men, or peasants smoking, drinking or brawling in taverns. His figures are skilfully portrayed in vivid, often amusing and somewhat coarse scenes that contrast with his delicately applied brushstrokes.

Oudernaarde was a bustling city and the centre of Europe's tapestry trade, and as a child, Brouwer showed great promise as a draughtsman and colourist helping his father to design tapestries. But when his father died in 1622, Brouwer moved to Antwerp and began his career as an artist. Three years later, he moved to Amsterdam and in 1626 he was in Haarlem where he painted, socialized and joined the local Chamber of Rhetoric.

FIGURES AND TRONIES

Brouwer soon became well-known for his original ideas and approaches in both genre painting and in the development of tronies, which were studies of faces or figures. Unlike regular portraits, tronies were not intended to depict identifiable individuals, but were explorations of expression or

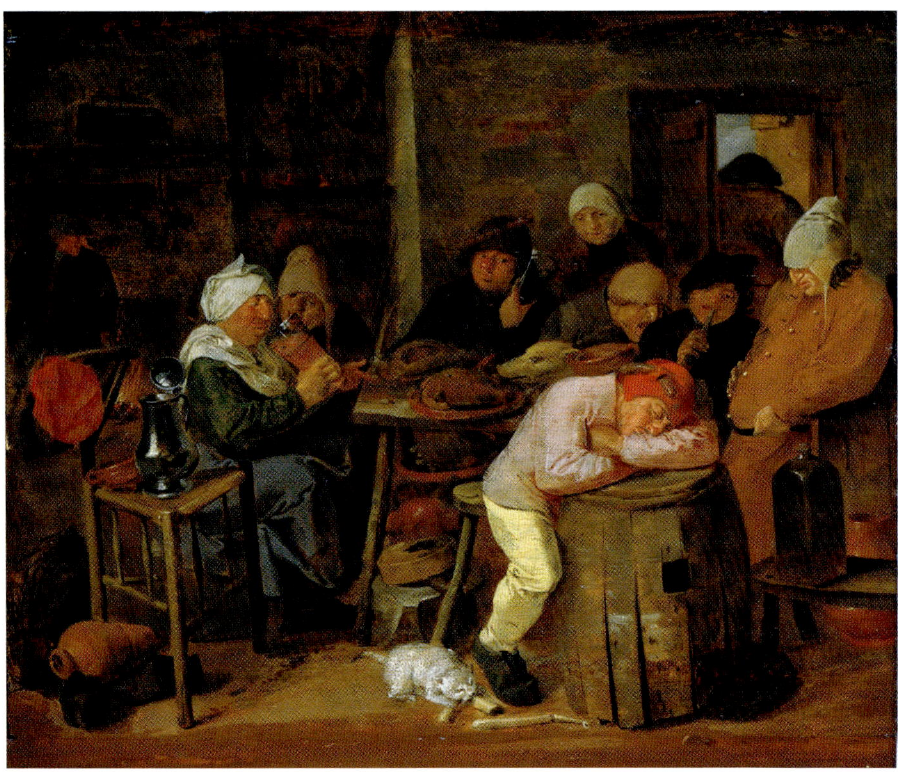

Above: Peasants *reveals Brouwer's humour along with his ability to capture a scene with a few strokes. Variously drunk, the characters are completely self-absorbed.*

Below: Playing Cards *was painted early in Brouwer's career and shows the influence of other Flemish artists. Typical humanizing details include the dog and fallen cards.*

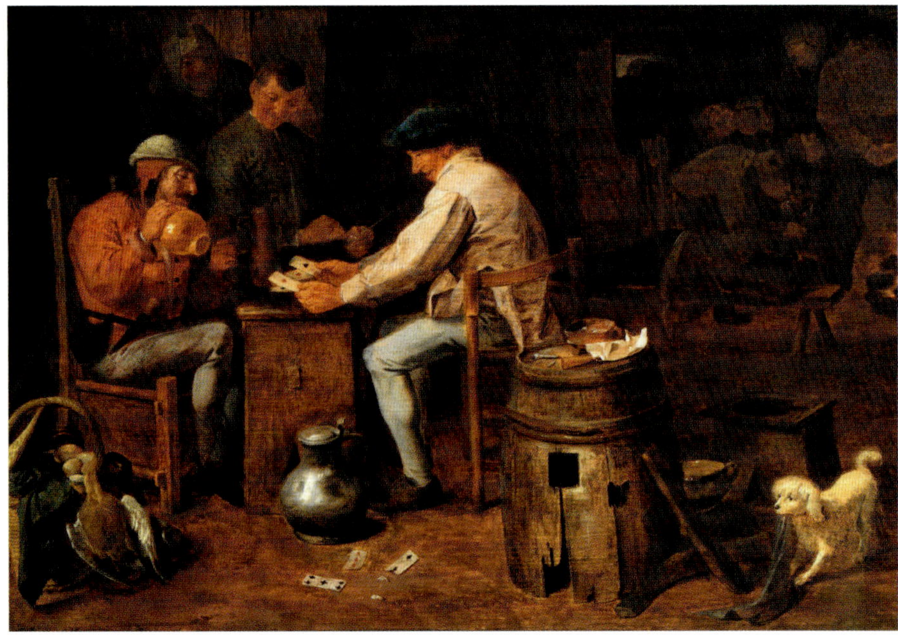

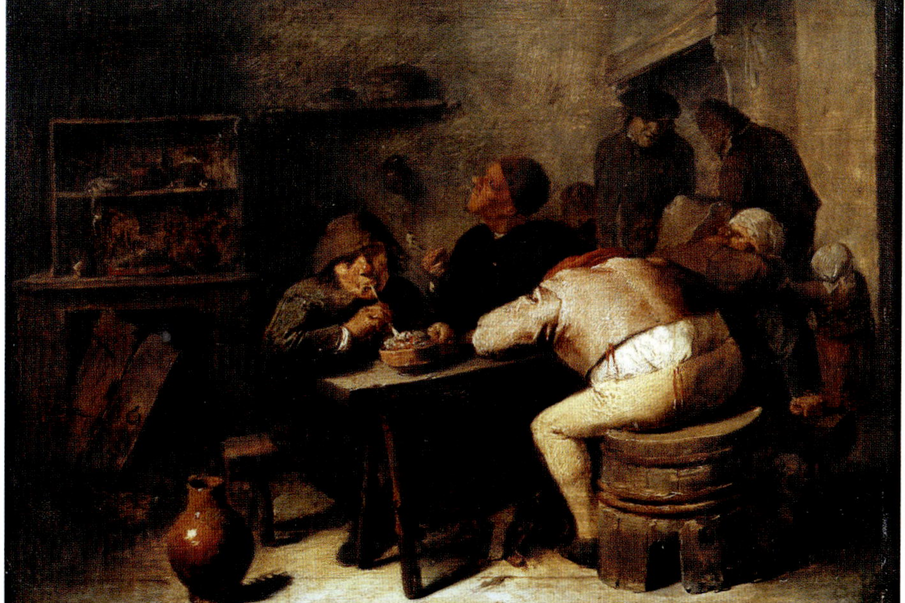

Above: Interior with Smokers, *1632. Brouwer's talent for capturing comical scenes attracted the esteem of Rubens and Rembrandt – for a time. In this murky interior, it seems that the slumped figure has passed out through over-indulgence.*

character. In general, Brouwer expressed emotions rather as human failings than as the moral messages more commonly emphasized in other Dutch genre paintings. For instance, he portrays anger as a lack of self-control rather than a Christian sin.

Right: Painted in c.1635–38, The Smokers *is a subject that Brouwer depicted more than once (there are other paintings with the same title) and he paints the scene as if the viewer has just happened upon these characters who are in a tavern. It is supposed he has used himself as the model for the main character..*

REDERIJKERSKAMERS

Rhetoric Rooms or Chambers of Rhetoric, known in Dutch as Rederijkerskamers (literally: practitioners of 'rhetoric' or the art of eloquence) were popular amateur literary societies in Dutch towns and cities where members – called Rederijkers – performed and read plays and poetry. In Antwerp, the Chamber of Rhetoric was called Violieren, and the Haarlem group was called De Wijngaertranken, which translates as Love Above All (In Liefde Boven Al).

RETURN TO FLANDERS

In 1631, Brouwer returned to Flanders where he was registered as a master in the Antwerp Guild of Saint Luke. Two years later, he was jailed there, but the reason for this is not clear; it could have been for tax evasion or because he was mistaken as a spy for the Dutch Republic. Although Jan-Baptist

Dandoy (active 1631–38) was his only officially registered pupil, it seems that his close friend Joos van Craesbeeck (c.1605/6–60) was taught by him, as van Craesbeeck's earliest paintings are almost identical to Brouwer's. In April 1634, Brouwer began lodging in the house of another friend, a respected engraver Paulus Pontius (1603–58). Together they joined Violieren, the local Chamber of Rhetoric. Brouwer also spent a lot of time with other artist friends drinking in local taverns. Yet despite being known for his regular drunkenness, his art was highly respected. At one point, Rubens owned 17 of his works, and Rembrandt, van Ostade and Teniers the Younger were also admirers. Rubens was so impressed by his skills that he invited him to work alongside him in his celebrated Antwerp studio, but after Brouwer turned up on several occasions either drunk or high on drugs, Rubens told him to leave.

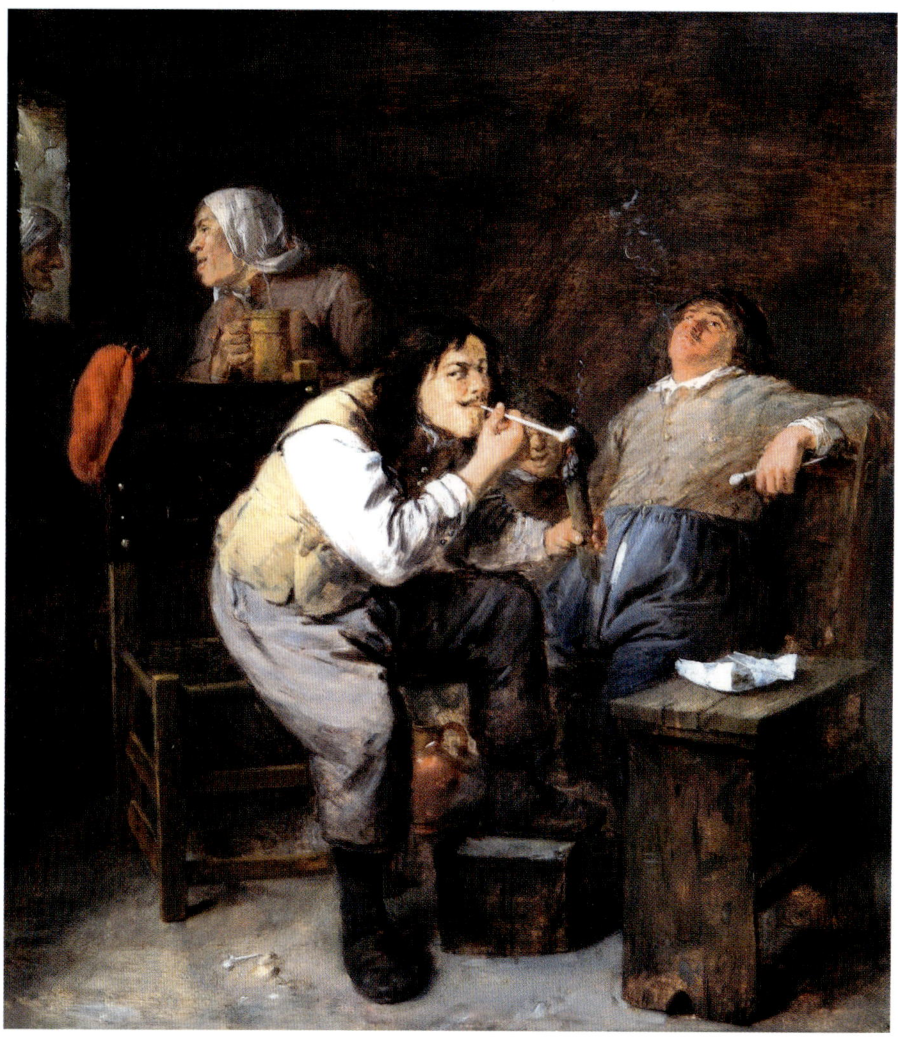

REMBRANDT VAN RIJN

By the time he was 19, Rembrandt Harmenszoon van Rijn (1606–69) was already a successful artist. In his paintings, etchings and drawings, he demonstrated a unique ability to depict light and a remarkable range of human emotions. World-famous during his lifetime, he became exceptionally wealthy – and then destitute.

The fourth of six surviving children out of ten, Rembrandt was born in Leiden. His father, Harmen Gerritszoon van Rijn (1568–1630) was a miller and wealthy enough to send Rembrandt to the town's Latin school. At 14, Rembrandt began studying at the University of Leiden, but within a few months he had left and was apprenticed to the artist Jacob Isaacz van Swanenburg (1571–1638) for approximately three years.

In 1624, Rembrandt moved to Amsterdam where he studied with the history painter Pieter Lastman (1583–1633) for six months, and then moved back to Leiden where he and Jan Lievens (1607–74) shared a successful workshop producing portraits and history paintings. When he was 22, he took on his first pupil: 14-year-old Gerrit Dou. By 1631 however, he moved back to Amsterdam. At the time, a master artist who moved towns had to serve an obligatory period of one or two years in a local workshop before being admitted to the local guild. So Rembrandt lodged in the house of the art dealer Hendrick van Uylenburgh and over approximately four years worked in his workshop, probably as head painter.

A RENOWNED PORTRAITIST

The most important families and organizations in Amsterdam were beginning to commission Rembrandt for portraits. His paintings were far livelier than those created by other portrait painters. By limiting the amount of detail, he led the eye directly to the face and suggested dynamism in his figures. He was also outstanding at convincingly rendering human skin. He began attracting many students, charging each a high annual tuition fee of 100 guilders.

As well as portraits, Rembrandt produced dramatic history paintings showing the influence of Caravaggio. As he never went to Italy, he probably

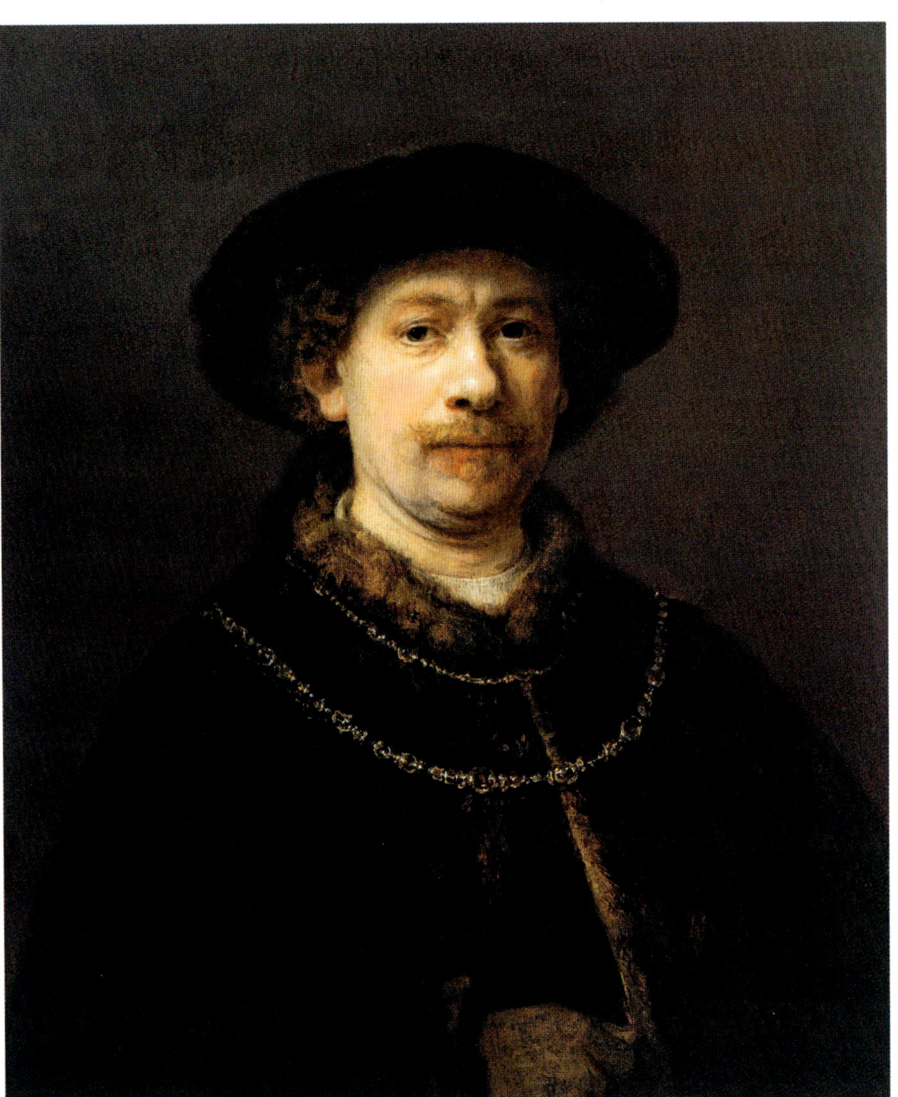

Left: Self-Portrait with Hat and Two Chains, *1642–43, demonstrates a skilful use of chiaroscuro, with strong contrasts of light and shade.*

Below: A Young Scholar and his Tutor: *a man in velvet instructs a boy wearing a lavish Eastern costume. This is a study in contrasts: mature and young, red and green, teaching and learning, light and dark.*

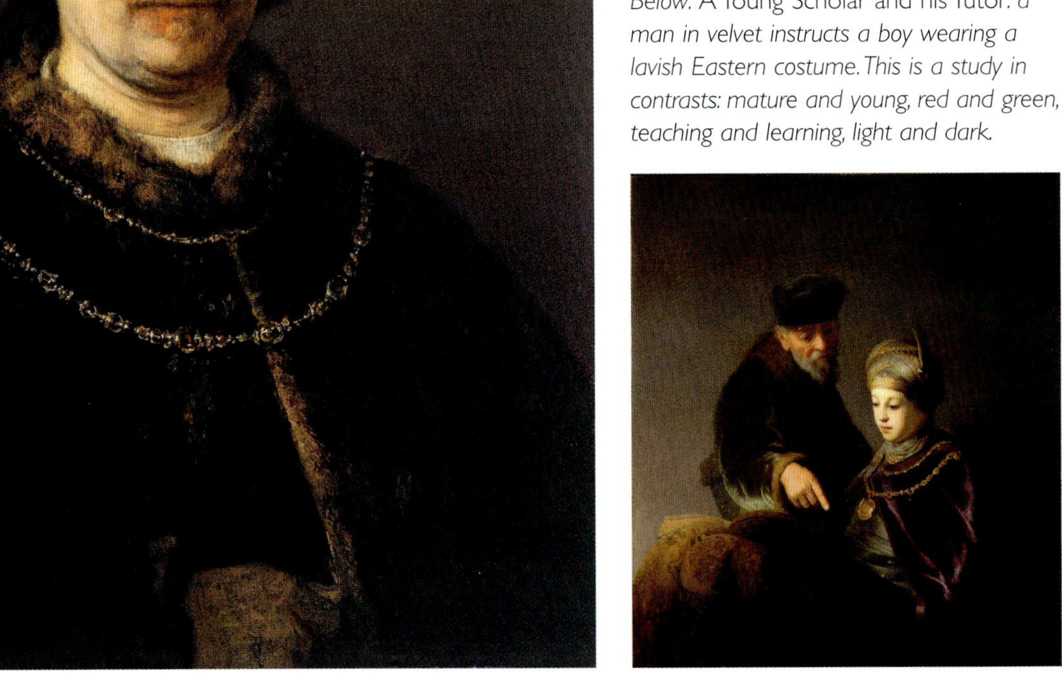

learned of his technique through Lastman or the Utrecht Caravaggisti.

ETCHINGS AND DRAWINGS

As well as his portraits and history paintings, Rembrandt's etchings attracted international renown, and his drawings were also avidly bought by collectors and admirers. He produced his first etchings in about 1628. Contemporary printmakers usually worked with a rather stylized application of lines and hatchings, but Rembrandt used a freer, more painterly technique, using various methods of hatching, creating an original and convincing sense of depth and texture. He sketched people on the streets of Amsterdam, applying lively marks to capture their expressions, and the drape and textures of their clothes.

LOVE LIFE

In 1634, he married Uylenburgh's wealthy young cousin, Saskia van Uylenburgh (1612–42). Despite earning good money and sharing Saskia's fortune, he often struggled financially, as he lived well and was a passionate collector of art and antiquities. In 1639, he and Saskia moved into a grand house near Uylenburgh's house. Saskia's family accused him of squandering her fortune, but by then, he was the most famous artist in Amsterdam.

Rembrandt and Saskia had four children, but only the fourth, Titus (1641–68) survived. Weakened after the births, Saskia made a will, leaving Rembrandt and Titus her fortune, but stating that if Rembrandt remarried, his share would be lost. She died soon after. Grief-stricken and alone with a baby, Rembrandt employed a nurse, Geertje Dircx (c.1610/15–c.56) who became his lover. Five years later, he took on a housekeeper, Hendrickje Stoffels (1625–63) and fell in love. His relationship with Dircx became acrimonious, with a lengthy court case after she accused him of breach of promise. It culminated in her imprisonment for unreasonable behaviour. Meanwhile, Hendrickje moved in with Rembrandt, unmarried, as the terms of Saskia's will meant that he could not afford to marry her. In 1654, they had a daughter, Cornelia.

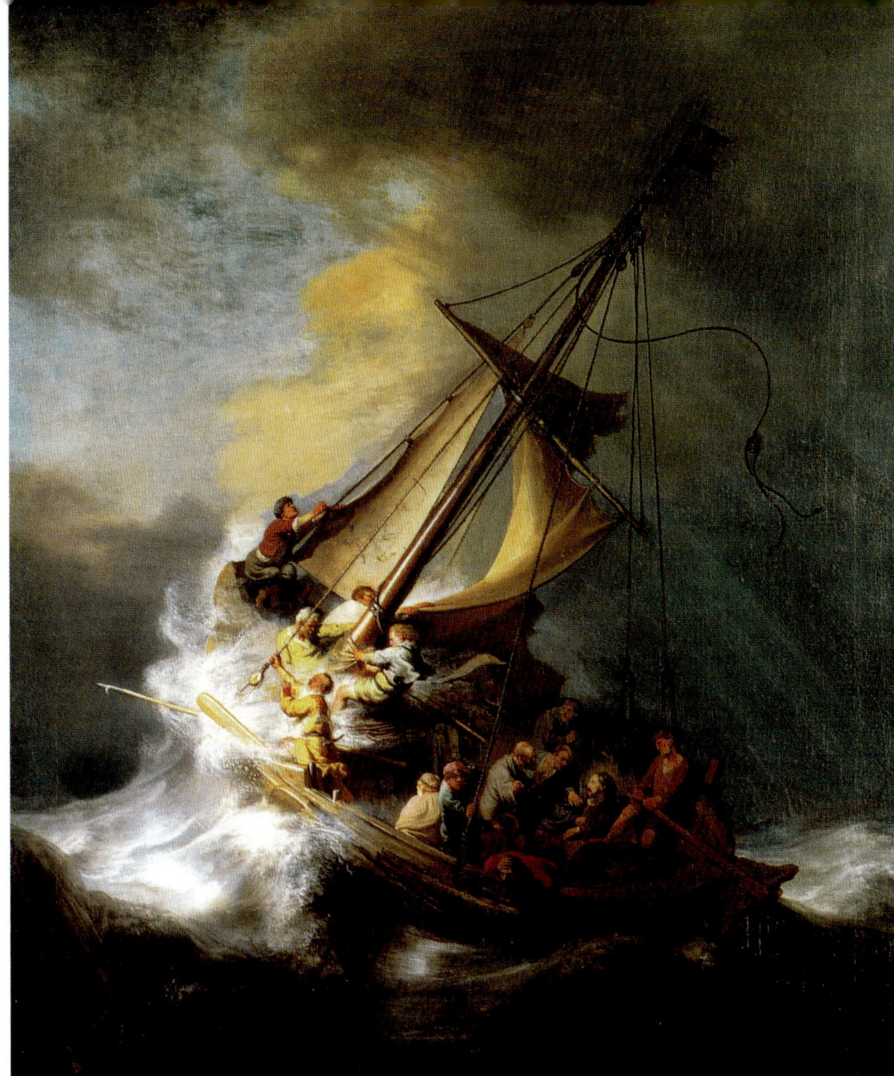

Above: Rembrandt's only painted seascape, The Storm on the Sea of Galilee, 1633, portrays the power of nature against human frailty, as Christ's apostles struggle against a sudden storm. Rembrandt painted it soon after moving to Amsterdam from his native Leiden.

Below: Rembrandt etched this image of a windmill in 1641. Known as Little Stink Mill because it was where tanned leather was softened by being treated, the mill stood along the western city wall. Rembrandt drew it in great detail on site, then created the print in his studio.

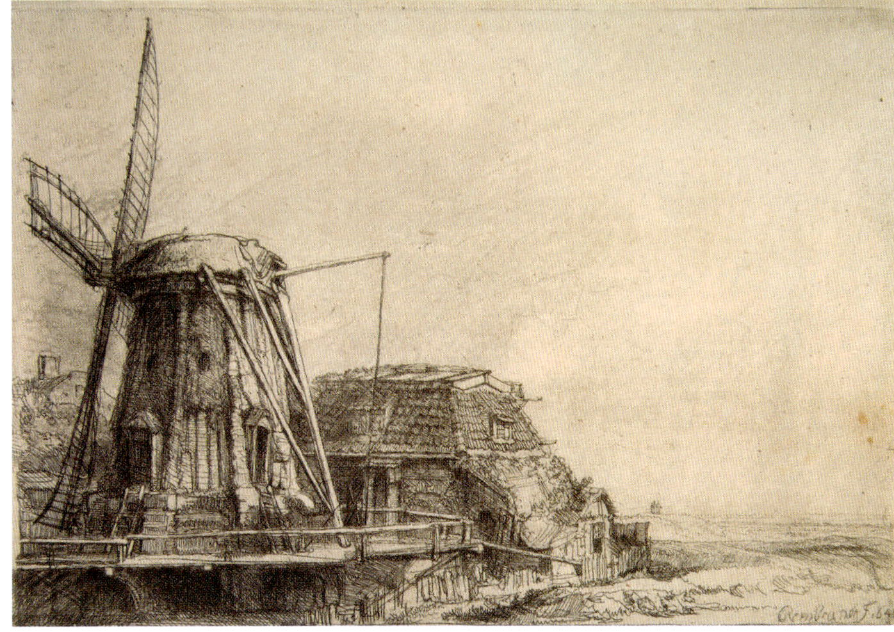

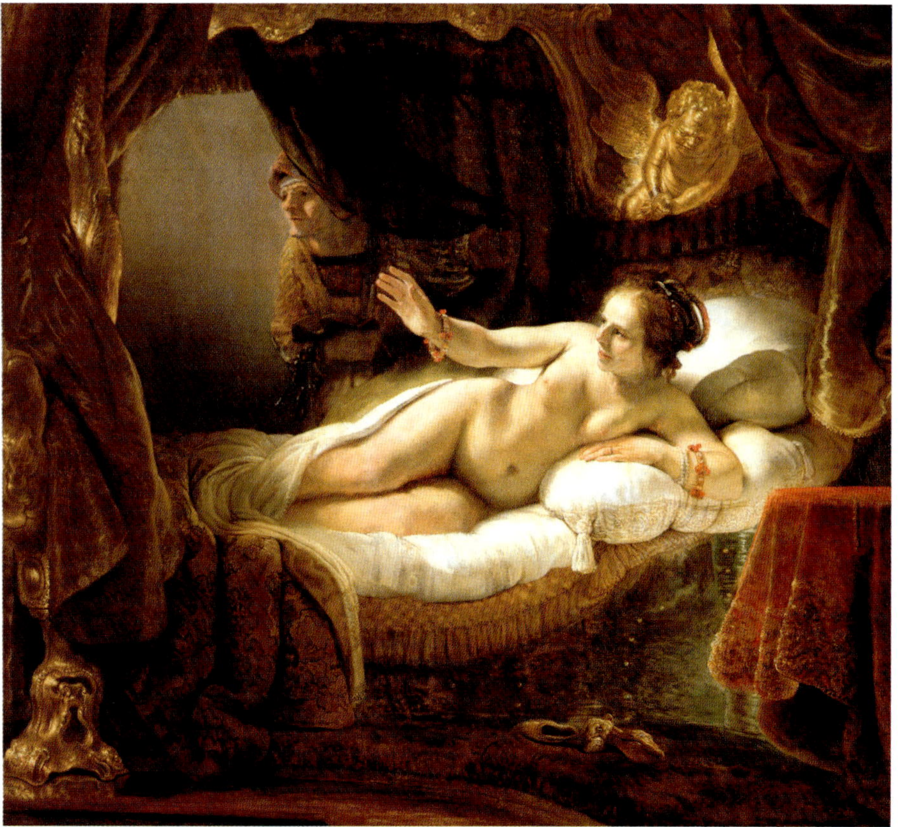

Above: Danaë, *a mythical character, is welcoming the god Zeus into her bed. Originally, Rembrandt used Saskia, his first wife as the model here, but later replaced her face with the face of his mistress Geertje Dircx.*

Below: Daniel and Cyrus before the Idol Bel, *1633. King Cyrus of Persia, at the centre, asks Daniel why he does not worship the deity Bel. Daniel replies that he worships a living god, not an idol.*

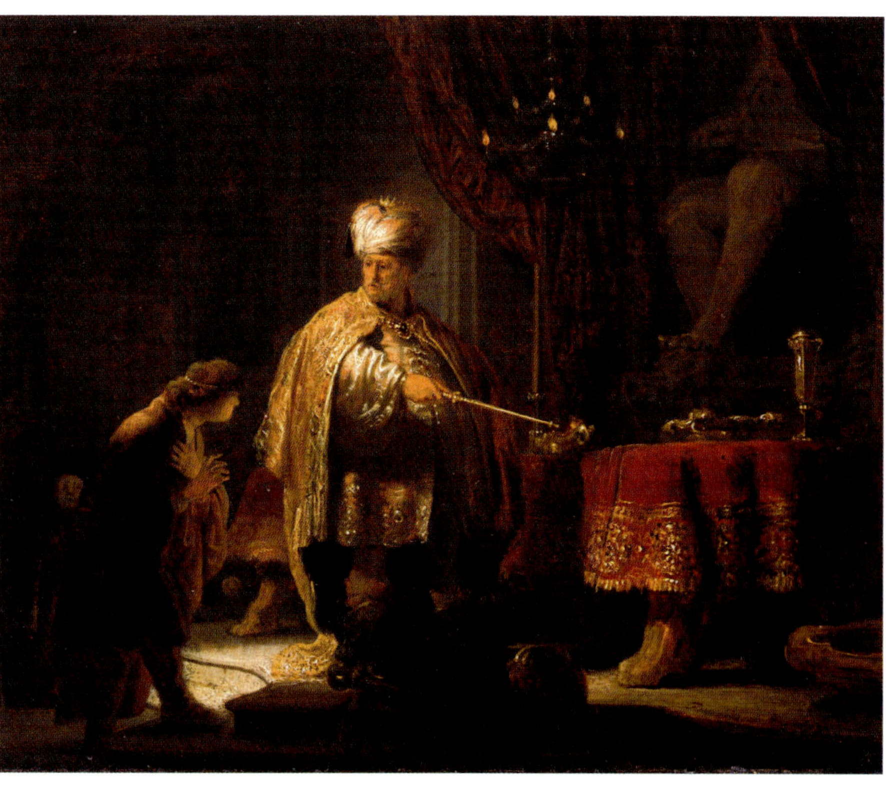

INFLUENCES AND MASTERPIECES

Most of Rembrandt's images were of portraits, self-portraits and biblical subjects, or sometimes of historical, mythological or allegorical themes. As he avidly experimented with different ideas and influences throughout his career, his approach to all aspects of image-making frequently changed. Yet his painting always comprised certain elements, including a range of colour, tones and brushmarks that all conveyed a broad variety of expressions, textures and surfaces.

Rembrandt's ambitions to be a great artist led him to explore and experiment widely, often through the study of other great artists' styles and techniques. Among these influences were Caravaggio, Raphael (1483–1520), Albrecht Dürer and Titian (c.1485/90–1576), and during the second half of the 1630s, he became especially preoccupied with Leonardo da Vinci (1452–1519). He owned a print of Leonardo's *Last Supper* (1495–98), and was particularly intrigued by the smoky 'sfumato' technique and balance of symmetry and asymmetry in the figure grouping.

Rembrandt produced many masterpieces throughout his career, including: *The Anatomy Lesson of Dr Nicolaes Tulp* (see page 200), *Belshazzar's Feast* (see page 231), *Self-Portrait Holding Brushes, Palette and Mahlstick* (see page 212) and *The Jewish Bride* (see page 236). In the early 1640s, he was occupied with a large group portrait of members of an Amsterdam civic militia company that has become known as *The Night Watch* (see page 197). The painting contains 34 figures; 18 are militia men from the company, and 16 others were added to create the impression of the large group. The work was painted in daylight, just before the company assembled for a parade; Rembrandt's strong tenebrism led to it appearing to many as a nocturnal scene. Rembrandt enhanced the light and dark effects by intensely illuminating a girl and a lieutenant in the foreground. Both shine out from the darkness in their yellow outfits. The painting is considered one of Rembrandt's greatest works.

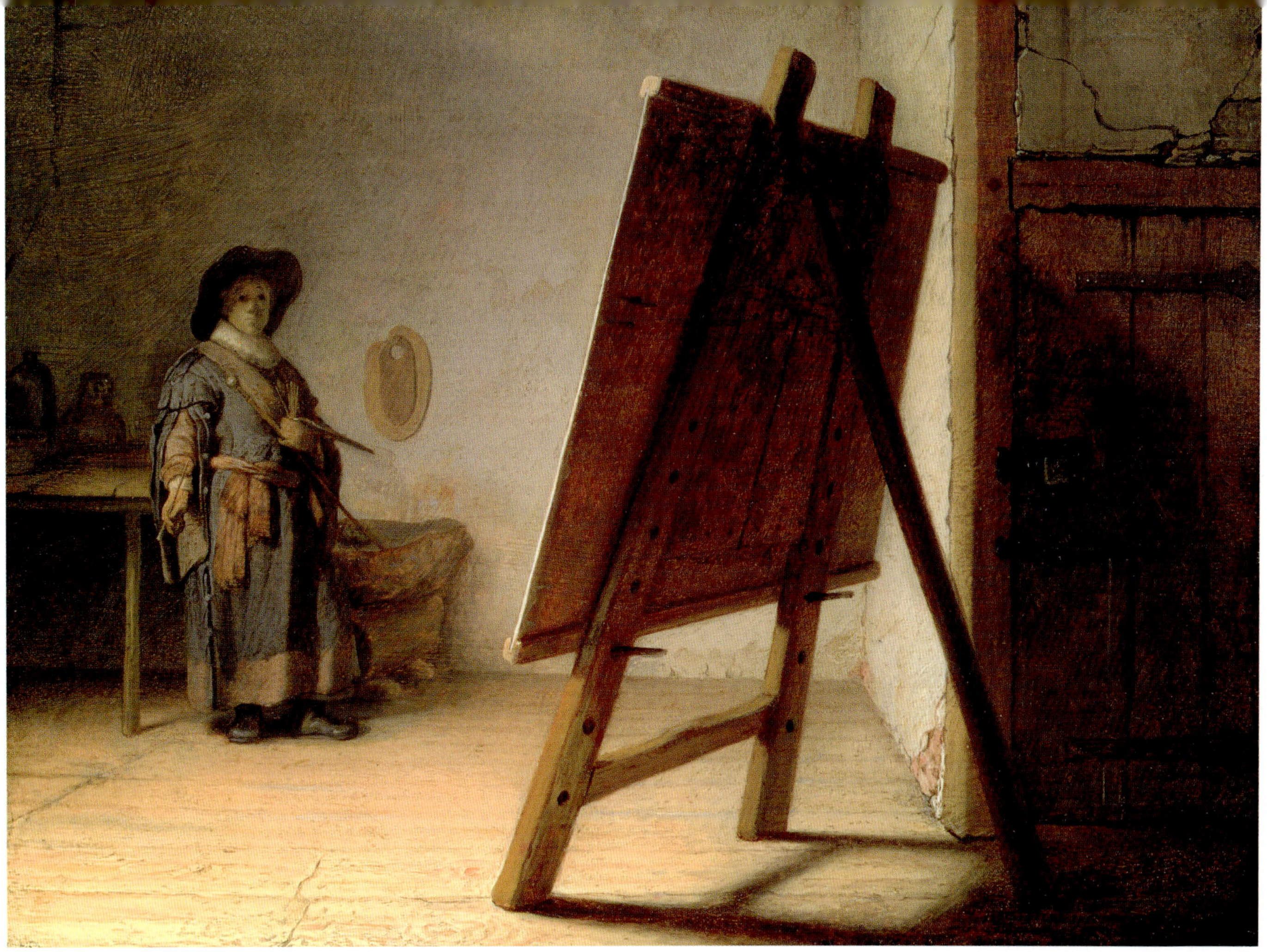

LAST YEARS

In the 1650s, Amsterdam was hit by a massive economic depression. Rembrandt was still paying for his house, and creditors began chasing him. Six years later, he successfully applied for 'cessio bonorum;' a respectable form of bankruptcy that avoided imprisonment. All his goods, including his valuable collection of paintings and antiquities were sold for a pittance. He, Titus and Hendrickje moved to poor area of Amsterdam, where he continued to paint. In the last 20 years of his life, he painted even more self-portraits. In 1663, after a long illness, Hendrickje died. Overwhelmed with heartbreak, Rembrandt was a broken man, and Titus, by then an elegant and comfortably-off young man, cared for his father, but in 1668, he married, and left Rembrandt with 14-year-old Cornelia. Delighted with his son's happiness and the impending birth of his first grandchild, Rembrandt's creative experimentation increased, but when Titus died of the plague six months before the birth of his daughter Titia, Rembrandt plummeted once more into grief. He died 13 months after Titus.

Although he died impoverished, Rembrandt's international reputation continued to rise. His many pupils included Dou, Govert Flinck, Ferdinand Bol, Nicolaes Maes and Carel Fabritius. Rembrandt inspired numerous 17th- and 18th-century European artists, such as Tiepolo and Fragonard. Seen as a forerunner of the Romantic movement, he became revered by many Romantic and Realist painters. He also profoundly influenced artists such as van Gogh and Francis Bacon.

Above: Artist in his Studio, *c.1628 – in a relatively empty studio, Rembrandt considers his canvas. At this early point in his career, Rembrandt painted with lighter colours and thinner paint than later on.*

Below: With its dramatic lighting, Rembrandt's interpretation of The Deposition *is complex, emphasizing Christ's twisting body.*

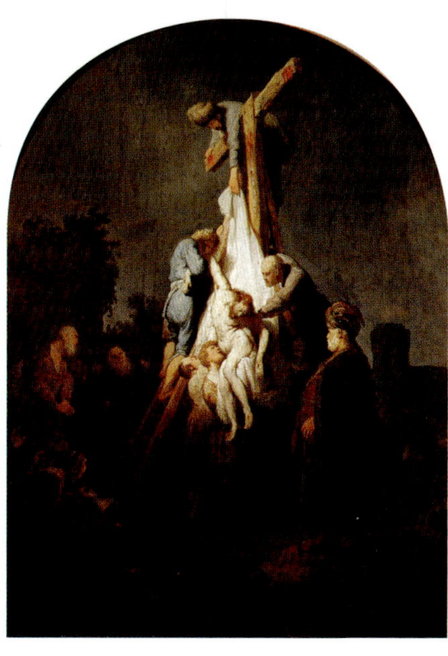

JAN LIEVENS

A painter of portraits and historical and biblical works, Jan Lievens (1607–1674) began his apprenticeship in his native Leiden at the age of eight. From 1617 to 1619, he studied in Pieter Lastman's studio in Amsterdam, where he met Rembrandt. In 1626, the two artists set up their own studio together.

The son of a tapestry worker, Jan Lievens initially trained under Joris Verschoten (alternatively van Schooten) (c.1587–1651), and then with history painter Pieter Lastman in Amsterdam from the age of 10. Two years later, he became quite a celebrity, working as an independent artist in Leiden, because of his young age and remarkable talent. Among others, he attracted the patronage of Maurice (or Maurits) of Nassau, Prince of Orange (1567–1625) who gave one of his paintings to the English ambassador in the Netherlands.

Below: Christ at the Column, c1625/7. This life-sized depiction of Christ is one of Lievens's earliest works. The painting was the type of work that inspired Rembrandt.

Eventually, the ambassador presented the painting to Charles I of England.

WORKING WITH REMBRANDT

When he was 19, Lievens set up a studio with Rembrandt in Leiden. The collaboration lasted until 1631 when Rembrandt moved to Amsterdam and Lievens to England. While they worked together, the two artists' work was extremely similar. Both styled their paintings after Lastman's bright colouring and dramatic tale-telling, and both became increasingly influenced by the work of the Utrecht Caravaggisti. Together they invented the exotic 'Oriental' portrait genre, and they painted on oak panels cut from the same tree.

THE HAGUE, LONDON AND ANTWERP

On first meeting Constantijn Huygens (1596–1687), secretary to three stadholders, Lievens asked to paint his portrait (see page 203). Subsequently Huygens invited him and Rembrandt to visit The Hague, then the Dutch capital. For years after, Huygens supported Lievens, recommending him to numerous courtly patrons, including probably the exiled King and Queen of Bohemia, Frederik and Elizabeth,

Below: Fire and Childhood, c.1668, one of a series of four paintings that depict the personification of the four elements and the four ages of man; this boy is blowing on an ember to light a torch.

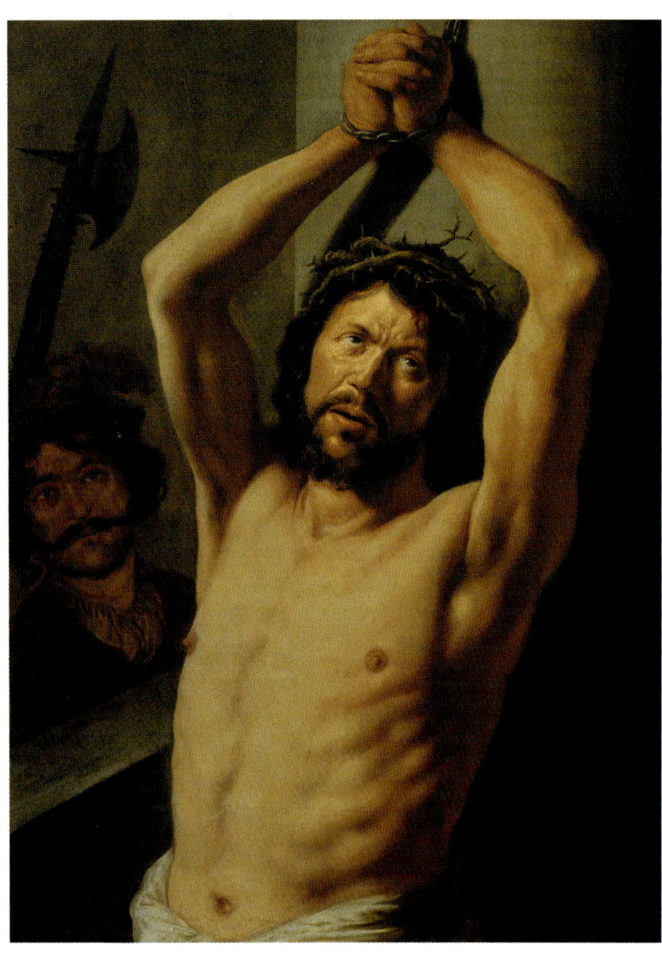

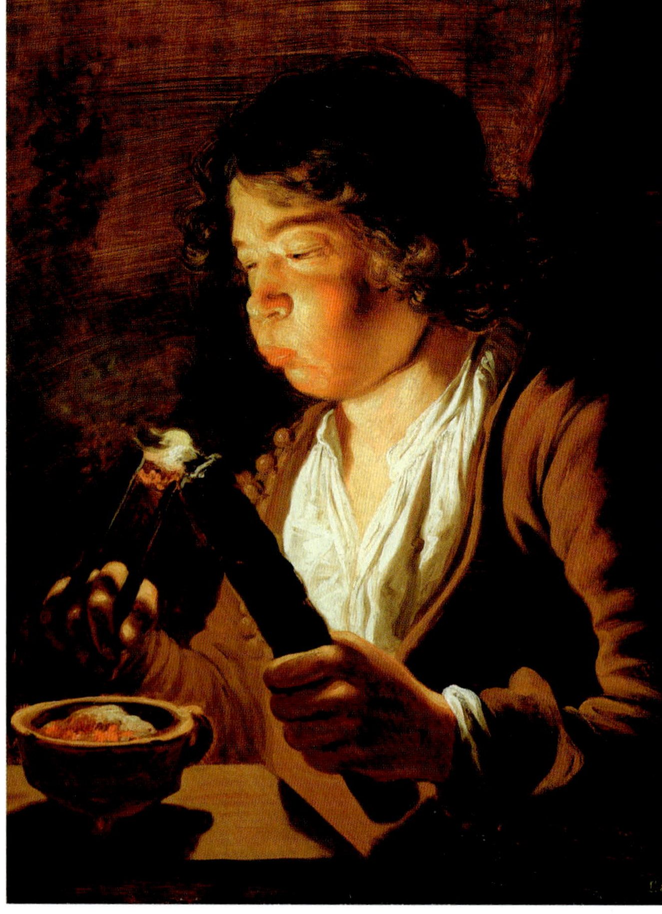

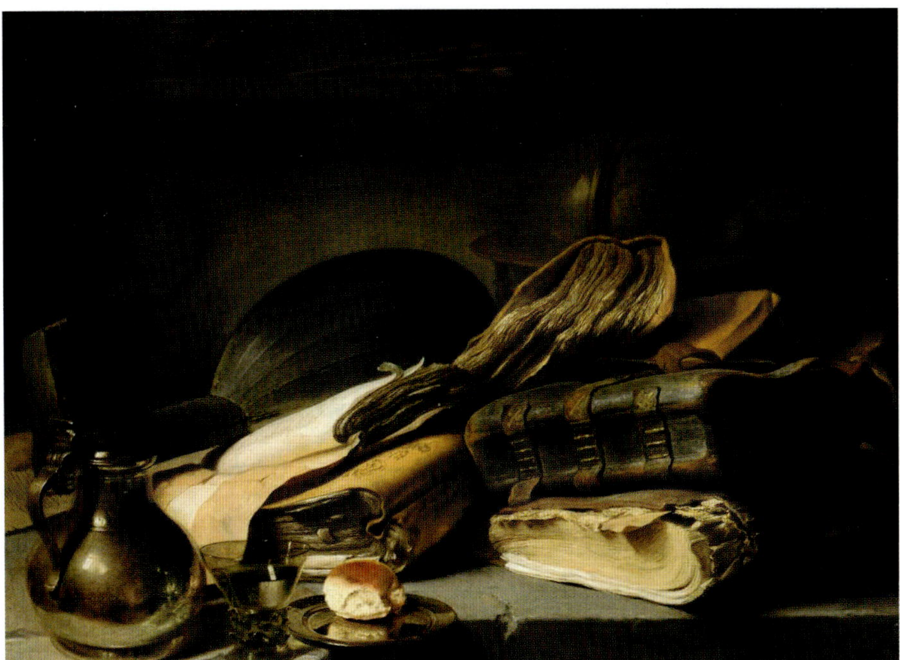

Above: Still Life with Books, *c.1630. Tatty old books and an overturned lute case, a pewter jug, bread, a glass and a globe: all seem to imply the transitory nature of life.*

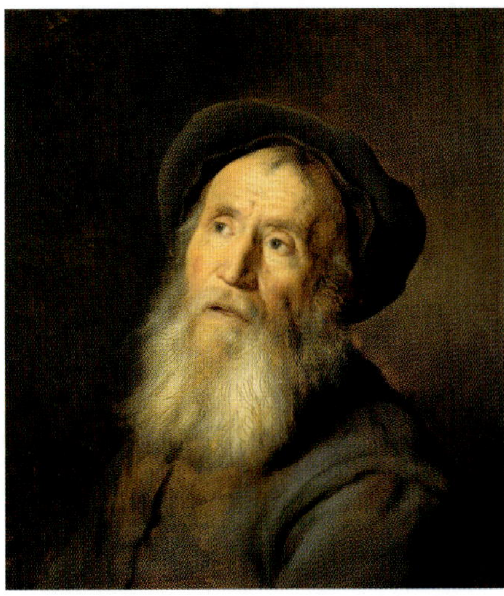

Above: Bearded Man with a Beret. *This is one of a series of tronies that Lievens made of elderly men and women quite early in his career. As a character study, this man was possibly intended to be a representation of a scholar.*

who was the sister of the English king Charles I; she commissioned Lievens to paint her eldest son. Huygens compared the two painters: 'Rembrandt is superior to Lievens in his sure touch and liveliness of emotions. Conversely, Lievens is the greater in inventiveness and audacious themes and forms. Everything his young spirit endeavours to capture must be magnificent and lofty... He has an acute and profound insight into all manner of things... My only objection is his stubbornness, which derives from an excess of self-confidence. He either roundly rejects all criticism or, if he acknowledges its validity, takes it in bad spirit.'

From 1632, Lievens lived in London for three years and his style, that had been becoming dated, began changing under the influence of the Flemish Baroque painter Anthony van Dyck (1599–1641) whom he had met previously in The Hague and who was King Charles I's leading court painter. After London, Lievens settled in Antwerp where he mixed with other artists, including the genre painters Adriaen Brouwer and David Teniers the Younger (1610–90), and the still life painter Jan Davidsz de Heem. In Antwerp, Lievens produced paintings, drawings and prints, taught himself to make woodcuts, worked with Adriaen Brouwer and studied Rubens's work, gradually assimilating elements of the great master's style. He married and had a son, Jan Andrea Lievens (1644–80), who also grew up to be a painter. In 1644 he moved to Amsterdam, where he remained for the rest of his life, only occasionally working in The Hague and Leiden. After being widowed, he remarried in 1648 and had six more children.

AN INNOVATIVE ARTIST

Always on a large-scale, Lievens's art was daring and original. He constantly absorbed new influences, often using thick impasto paint, bringing his figures close to the picture plane and dramatizing scenes with strong chiaroscuro, or conversely, applying fairly thin paint with elegant, small brushmarks. His paintings of genre scenes, landscapes, portraits and religious and allegorical images were highly sought after by many influential figures and his drawings and prints were also popular. However, he had a difficult personality, and lifelong problems in managing his affairs. In 1672, the invasion of the Netherlands by French and German forces ended the great patronage he had enjoyed, and he died in poverty.

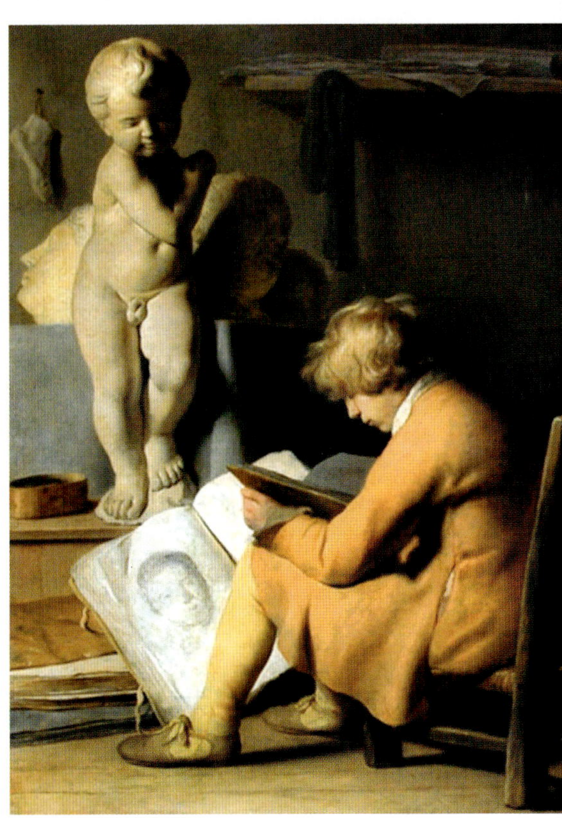

Right: Called The Young Artist *or* The Little Draughtsman, *using strong tonal contrasts, Lievens depicts the interior of an artist's workshop with a boy drawing from a plaster cast.*

JUDITH LEYSTER · JAN MOLENAER

Celebrated during her lifetime, Judith Leyster (1609–60) was one of the first women painters to be admitted to a Dutch painters' guild. She was described by a contemporary commentator as: 'The true leading star in art.' In 1636, she married fellow artist Jan Miense Molenaer (1609/10–68).

Although there were several other female Dutch artists at that time, Leyster was one of only two women to be accepted as a master in Haarlem's Guild of Saint Luke during the 17th century. Her lively brushstrokes captured expressive genre and still life themes that were greatly acclaimed, but after her death she was quickly forgotten, and her work became mistakenly attributed either to Frans Hals or to her husband Molenaer. It was not until 1893 that the error was discovered, and today approximately 35 of her works have been verified.

Born in Haarlem, the eighth child of a brewer and cloth maker, Leyster's artistic talents attracted positive attention from a young age. While the details of her training are uncertain, when she was 19, Samuel Ampzing praised her as a painter of 'good and keen insight,' in his 1628 book *Beschrijvinge ende lof der stadt Haerlem*. It is possible that she had been apprenticed to the Haarlem landscape and portrait painter Frans Pietersz de Grebber. She soon moved with her family to a town near Utrecht where she possibly met and became influenced by some of the Utrecht Caravaggisti. By 1633, she was a member of the Haarlem Guild of Saint Luke and she signed her works with a device of her initials with a star, which was a play on words as Leister means 'lead or lode star' in Dutch.

Below: Painted by Molenaer in 1630–32, Young Man Playing a Theorbo and Young Woman Playing a Cittern *shows a couple playing a duet, possibly symbolizing the harmony of true love.*

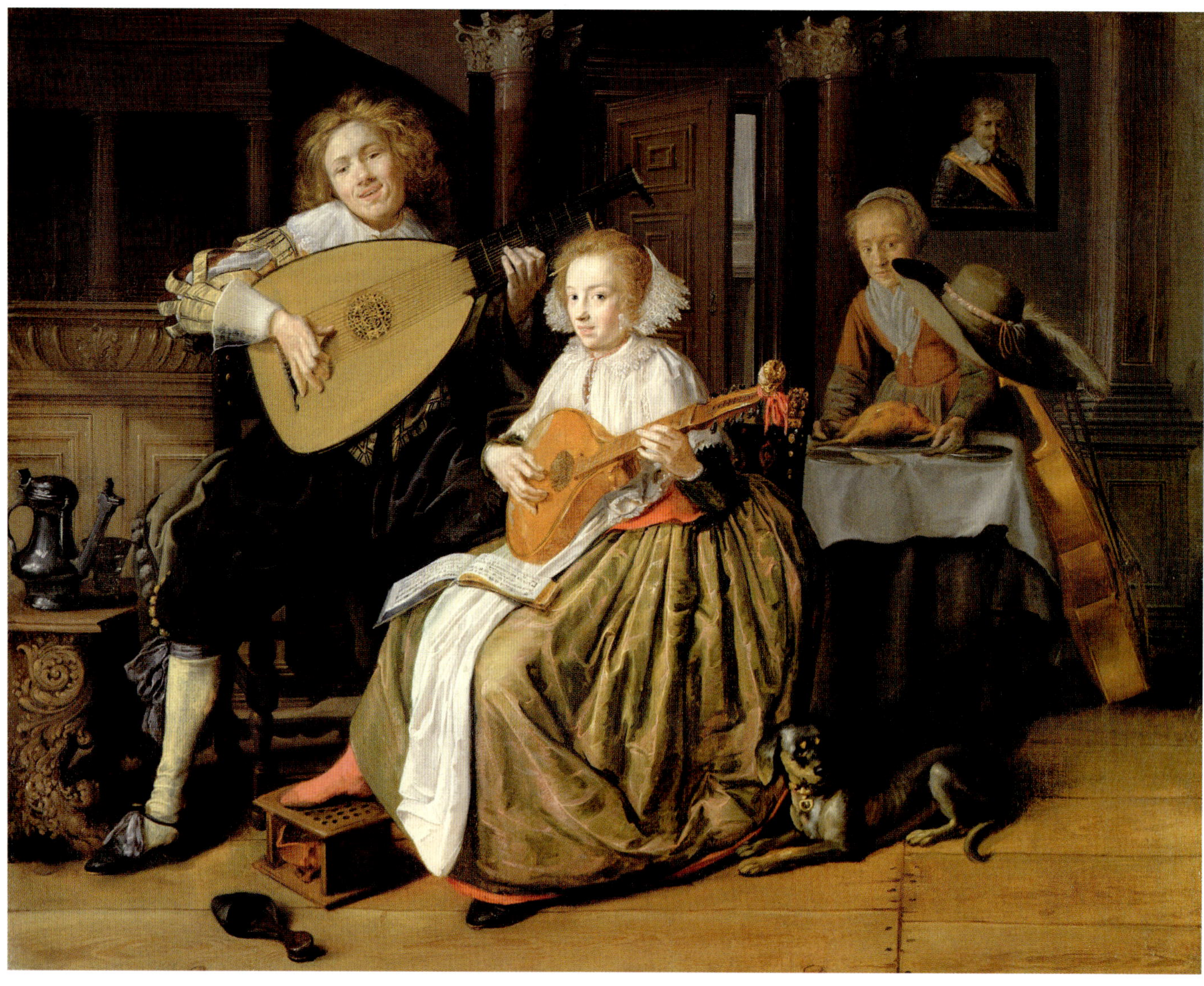

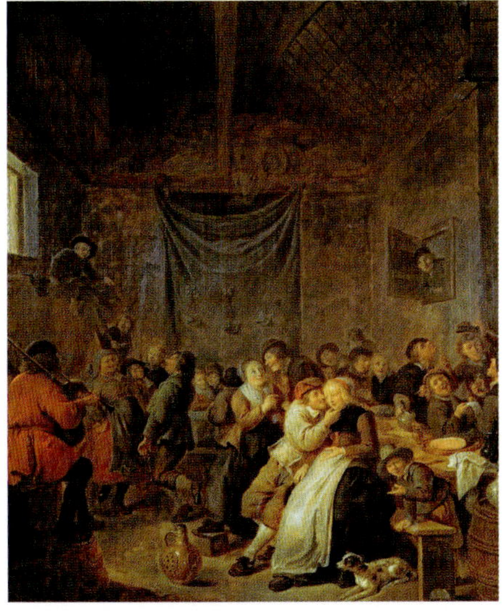

INFLUENCE OF HALS

From the start of her career, Leyster specialized in lifelike genre scenes, commonly featuring only a few figures within plain surroundings, or quiet scenes of women at home, often illuminated by candlelight. Although her images appear lifelike, the natural relaxed gestures and surroundings

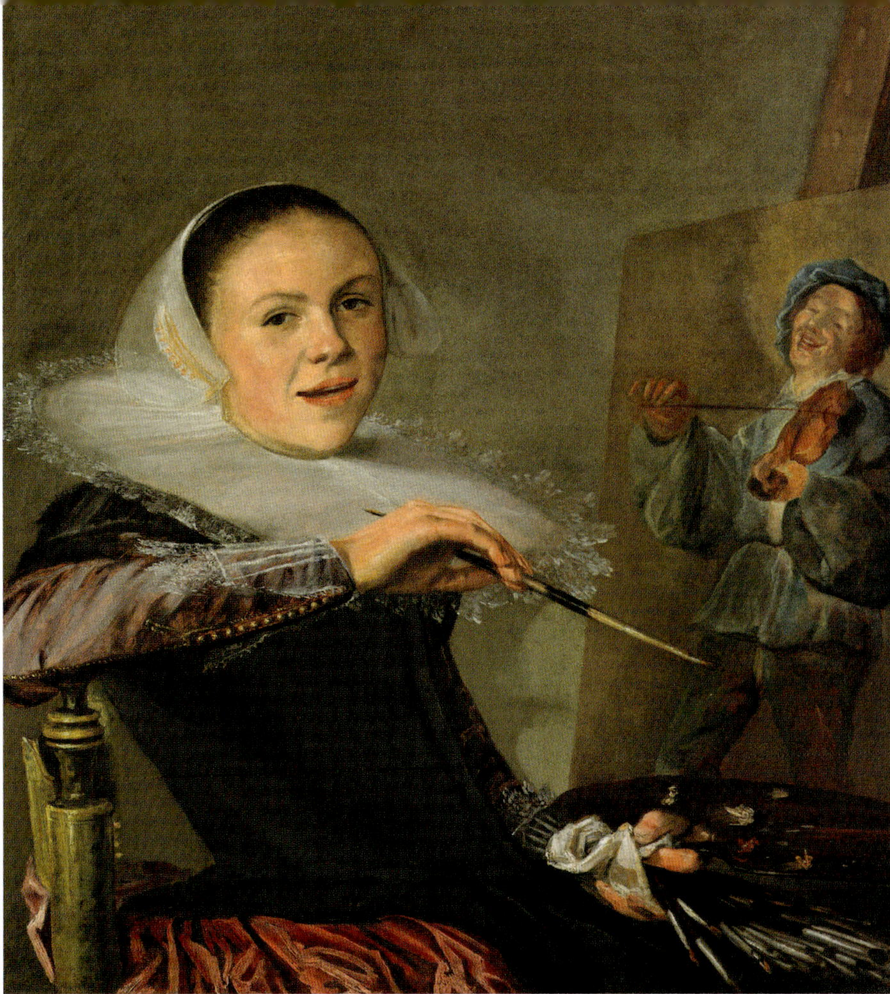

are created with loose, expressive brushwork following the innovations introduced by Hals in the 1620s. It is not known whether she was Hals's apprentice, apprenticed to his brother Dirck Hals, or whether they simply knew each other as friends and colleagues. The friendship did not last. Later in her career, she sued Frans Hals for accepting a student who had left her workshop and gone to his without the Guild's permission. Ultimately, the student's mother was ordered to pay Leyster four guilders in damages, which was only half of the amount that she had asked for, and Hals paid her three guilders as a fine. However, the apprentice did not return to her, and she was also fined for not originally registering him with the Guild.

EXUBERANT GENRE SCENES

Like Leyster, Molenaer was born in Haarlem and may have been a pupil of Frans or Dirck Hals, as the Hals bothers'

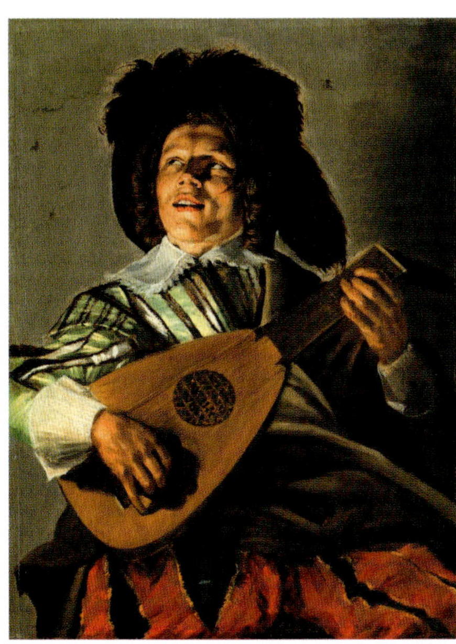

influence is apparent in his prolific and lively genre scenes. He and Leyster lived and worked together in Amsterdam for 11 years and then returned to Haarlem where they lived in a small house with a studio. They had five children, of which only two survived to adulthood.

More well-read than many of his contemporaries, Molenaer often chose to paint subjects inspired by the proverbs and poems of Jacob Cats (1577–1660) and Gerbrand Adriaenszoon Bredero (1585–1618). He painted numerous exuberant 'merry company' scenes (geselschapje or vrolijk gezelschap in Dutch), describing paintings of a small group of people enjoying themselves, often drinking and making music, some inside taverns, some depicting the five senses, and some portraying weddings, as well as family portraits and biblical scenes set in contemporary places. Many of his works have allegorical meanings. His painting style was quite varied, sometimes using precise and refined brushmarks, occasionally loose and free. Many early pictures seem to anticipate Jan Steen's work, while his later style seems closer to the look of Adriaen van Ostade.

ADRIAEN VAN OSTADE

Best known for his paintings of everyday scenes, often of interiors featuring peasants, Haarlem-born Adriaen van Ostade (1610–1685) was trained by Frans Hals, and possibly studied alongside Adriaen Brouwer. By 1632, he was a successful artist and by 1634, had joined the Guild of Saint Luke in Haarlem.

The eldest son and the third of eight children of a weaver from the town of Ostade near Eindhoven, Adriaen van Ostade became a pupil of Frans Hals when he was 17 in 1627. He may have also been apprenticed to Salomon van Ruysdael, and whether or not he met and studied with Adriaen Brouwer is not clear, but Brouwer's influence is apparent in van Ostade's early works, reflected in his paintings of rustic life and carousing peasants, set in shadowy interiors, often with a single source of light illuminating a specific group.

By 1632, van Ostade was registered in Utrecht, but two years later, he had returned to Haarlem where he joined the Haarlem Guild of Saint Luke. At 26, he also joined a company of the civic guard at Haarlem, and soon after he married, but was widowed within two years. In 1657, he married again, to a wealthy Catholic woman from Amsterdam, for whom he converted to Catholicism, and the couple had one daughter. In 1655 he became the guardian of his sister's five children, and from 1668, he also took on responsibility for the children of his brother Jan. After the death of his second wife in 1666, he inherited a considerable legacy from her and her father, and by 1670 he was living comfortably in a wealthy area of Haarlem. However, just before the French invasion of the Netherlands in 1672, he fled to Amsterdam.

PEASANT SCENES

A prolific artist, van Ostade produced over 800 paintings and many more prints, working with oil paint and pen

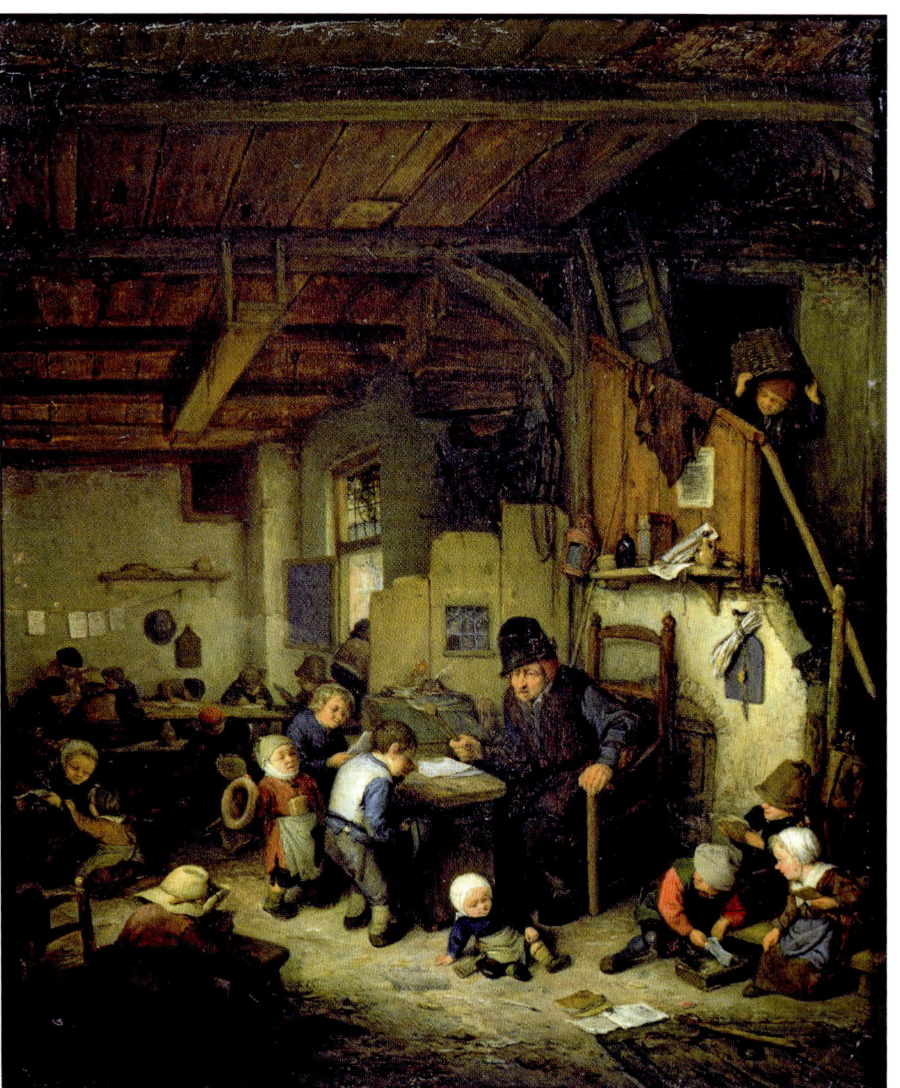

Left: Little children have been carefully observed for the creation of this painting The Schoolmaster, *1662, depicting the interior of a village school with one teacher and children of different ages.*

DEVELOPMENTS IN PAINTINGS OF EVERYDAY LIFE

In the first half of the 17th century, paintings of everyday life were usually directly-executed pictures of figures indoors or outdoors, eating, drinking, dancing or singing. Later, the subjects became more complex and the paint application thinner. Brouwer was the first to depict peasants in interiors, and van Ostade built on this, sometimes setting his figures in spacious, but shabby-looking rooms. Van Ostade was also one of the first to paint single figures, or just two or three, which became popular, especially his scenes featuring women and children. Later in the century, as the Dutch became wealthier, the settings became more comfortable and opulent, compositions more complex or intimate, and painting techniques and effects more refined.

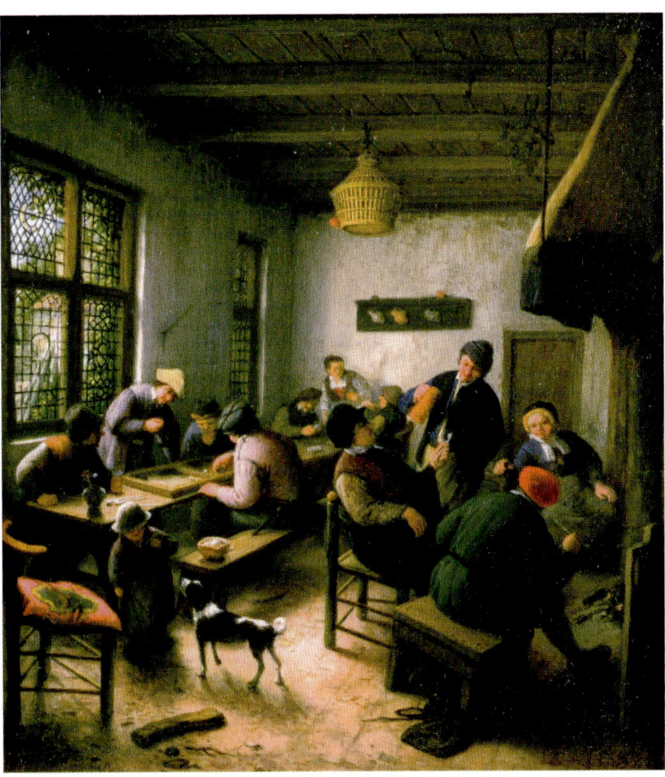

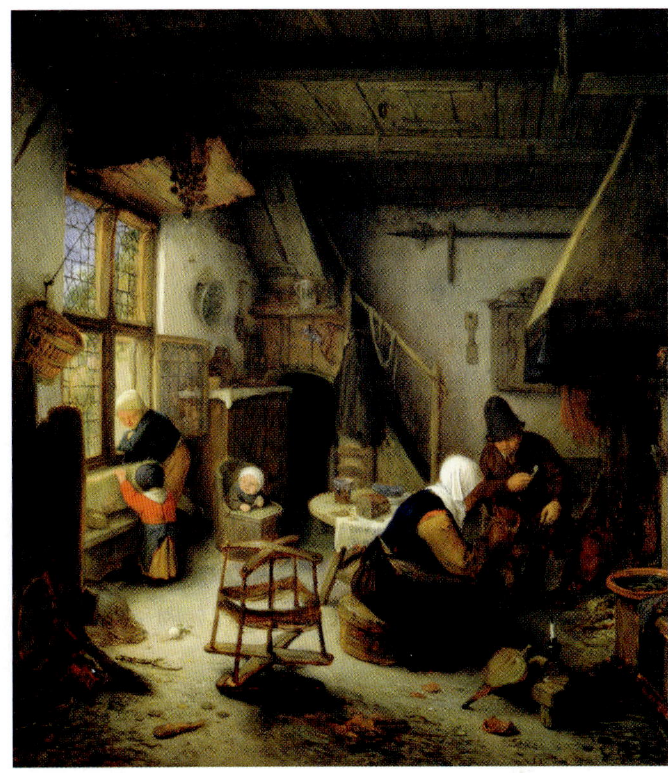

Above: Van Ostade painted Village Inn with Backgammon and Card Players *in 1674/75. His composition, light and details are compelling, leading the eye around the image.*

and ink, and in later life, watercolours. Through the distribution of his prints, he became extremely well known, and imitated by other artists, and his lively, and humorous images of village fairs, inn scenes, family life, and all kinds of workers, including domestic, agricultural and tradespeople, earned him the reputation of the leading Dutch painter of genre scenes. He also painted portraits and still lifes, and was often employed to add figures to other artists' paintings. His brushwork was always vigorous. During the 1630s, his palette was fairly subdued, sometimes animated by a single bright colour. From the 1640s however, his palette became brighter overall, and his peasants became slightly more refined and less bawdy. During that decade as well, Rembrandt's influence seems to appear in his use of chiaroscuro.

In 1662 van Ostade was selected as president of the Haarlem Guild of Saint Luke. Among his many pupils were his younger brother Isack van Ostade

(1621–49), Jan Steen and Cornelis Dusart (1660–1704).). Initially, Isack followed his elder brother Adriaen's style and choice of subject matter, though just before his early death at 28, he had started to paint landscapes in a different style. Jan Steen was also profoundly influenced by Adriaen van Ostade. After van Ostade's death in 1684, Johannes Vermeer directed the sale of the vast contents of his studio.

Above: Details in A Peasant Family at Home *of 1661, including the baby in the high chair, bellows for the fire, bread on the table, the man with his clay pipe and children at the window, gave contemporary viewers much to enjoy.*

Below: An Alchemist, 1611. In a messy room, a man stokes a fire. Around him tools are strewn; he has been studying De Re Metallica (On the Nature of Metals).

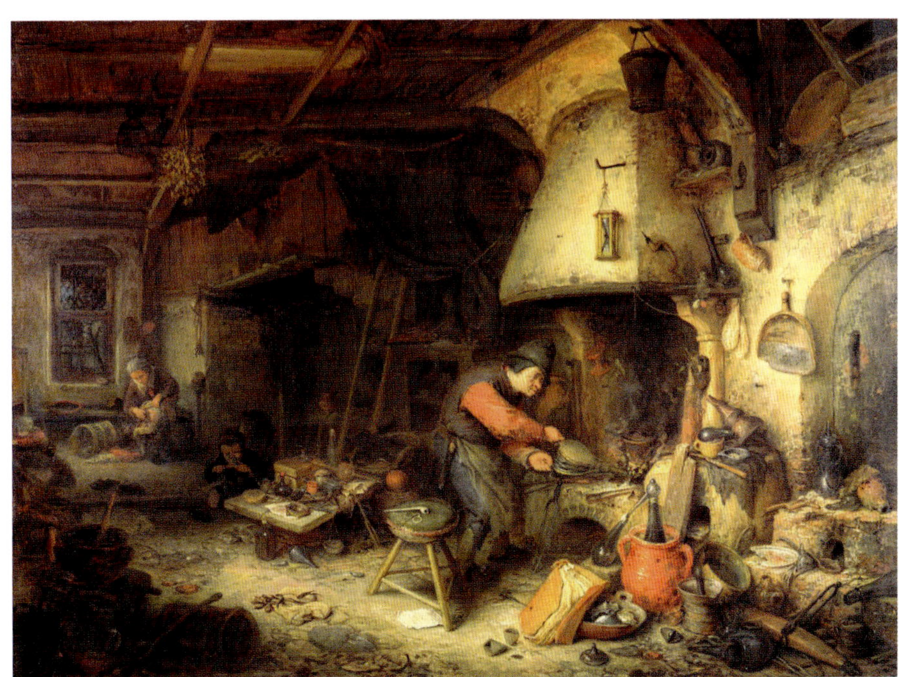

VAN DE VELDE

Descending from a Flemish seaman, the van de Velde family became a dynasty of Dutch marine and landscape painters, beginning with Willem van de Velde the Elder (c.1611–93) and followed by his sons, Willem van de Velde the Younger (1633–1707) and Adriaen van de Velde (1636–72).

WILLEM VAN DE VELDE THE ELDER

Willem van de Velde, who later became called the Elder, was born in Leiden, and possibly accompanied his father on sea expeditions as a boy. While there, he discovered a love of drawing and painting ships. Many of his pictures are detailed grisailles of ships, focusing on tonal effects. For a while he was employed as an official artist for the Dutch fleet and several of his works are of contemporary naval battles. To capture detail and authenticity, he regularly accompanied the Dutch navy on voyages and assignments to observe events and battles directly. On board, he made detailed drawings and sketches that he developed back in his studio into meticulously detailed pen paintings – *penschilderijen* – and later into oil paintings. His representation of

Below: A Hoeker Alongside a Kaag at Anchor, *painted by Willem van de Velde the Elder, c.1660, shows his skill at conveying both atmosphere and accuracy of detail.*

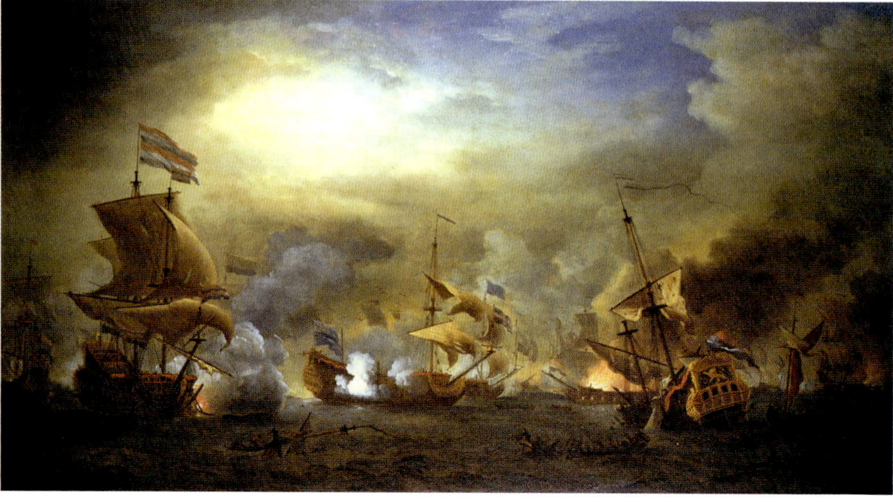

Above: Painted from a high viewpoint, The Battle of Texel, Kijduin *by Willem van de Velde the Younger depicts the last great battle of the Anglo-Dutch War in 1673.*

sea battles continued during the Second Anglo-Dutch War that began in 1665.

In the mid-1630s, van de Velde moved to Amsterdam. He and his wife had three children: a daughter, Magdalena, and Willem and Adriaen, but the marriage was stormy and he was divorced in 1662. A decade later, in the winter of 1672, when he was in his 60s and although the Netherlands and England were again at war, he travelled to London to join his son Willem, and entered the service of Charles II. The king gave him a salary of 100 per annum for 'taking and making draughts of sea fights,' while his son Willem was responsible for 'putting the said draughts into colours.' He also received an annual allowance of 50 from James, the Duke of York. He and his son established a studio in the Queen's House in Greenwich where they carried out royal commissions, including a series of designs for a suite of tapestries. His painstaking, detailed depictions and keen observation attracted several more commissions from other prominent patrons.

WILLEM VAN DE VELDE THE YOUNGER

Probably trained by his father and also by the marine painter Simon de Vlieger (c.1601–53), Willem van de Velde the Younger produced accurate images of ships, rigging and weather conditions at sea. His paintings were delicate and vibrant, with exact and realistic detailing.

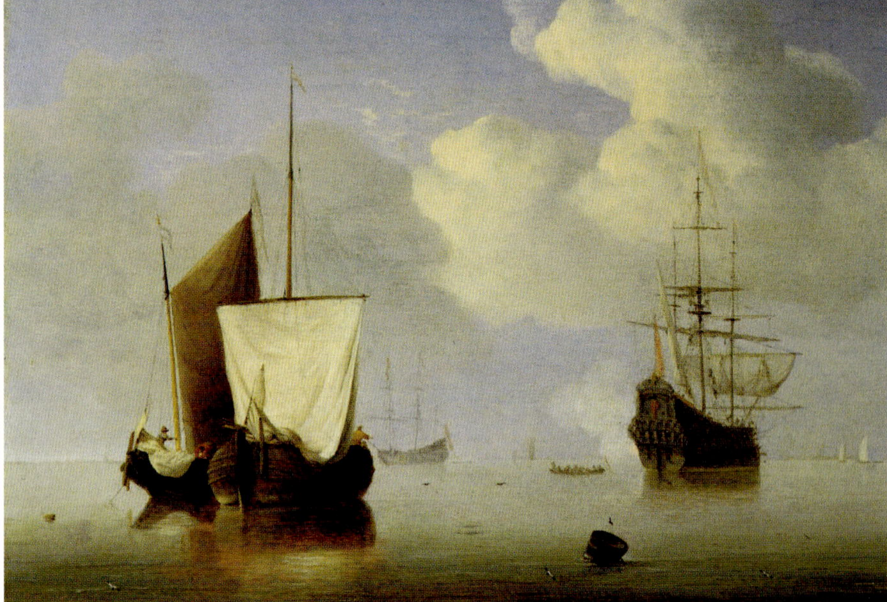

Born in Leiden, as was his father before him, Willem van de Velde the Younger first worked in Amsterdam, but in 1672, he moved to England and within two years, he and then his father had entered the service of Charles II at the royal court. They worked together in a studio in the Queen's House at Greenwich, for both Charles II and James II, then two years after the accession of William and Mary in 1689, they were compelled to move to Westminster.

Van de Velde the Younger's paintings became highly influential on the development of seascape painting in Britain. Yet most of his finest works represent views of his homeland, of Dutch shipping off the coast of Holland.

ADRIAEN VAN DE VELDE

Willem the Younger's younger brother Adriaen painted prolifically from a young age. As a child, he drew or painted on any surface he could, and he regularly stole his older brother's brushes and paints to explore his own creativity. Taught by his father and Jan Wijnants (1632–84), Adriaen was also influenced by Philips Wouwerman (1619–68), which compelled him to break away from the family tradition

Below: Portrait of a Couple with Two Children and a Nurse in a Landscape, *1667, reveals Adriaen van de Velde's skill in country scenes, which contrasted with his father and brother's marine paintings.*

of marine painting. As well as various types of landscapes, he also produced religious and mythological works, portraits, animal paintings and etchings, and he painted figures in other artists' landscapes, such as those of Meindert Hobbema (1638–1709) and Jacob van Ruisdael. His style blended Dutch landscapes with mythological pastoral scenes in Italian settings. Tragically however, he died at the age of 35, just before his father and brother emigrated to England.

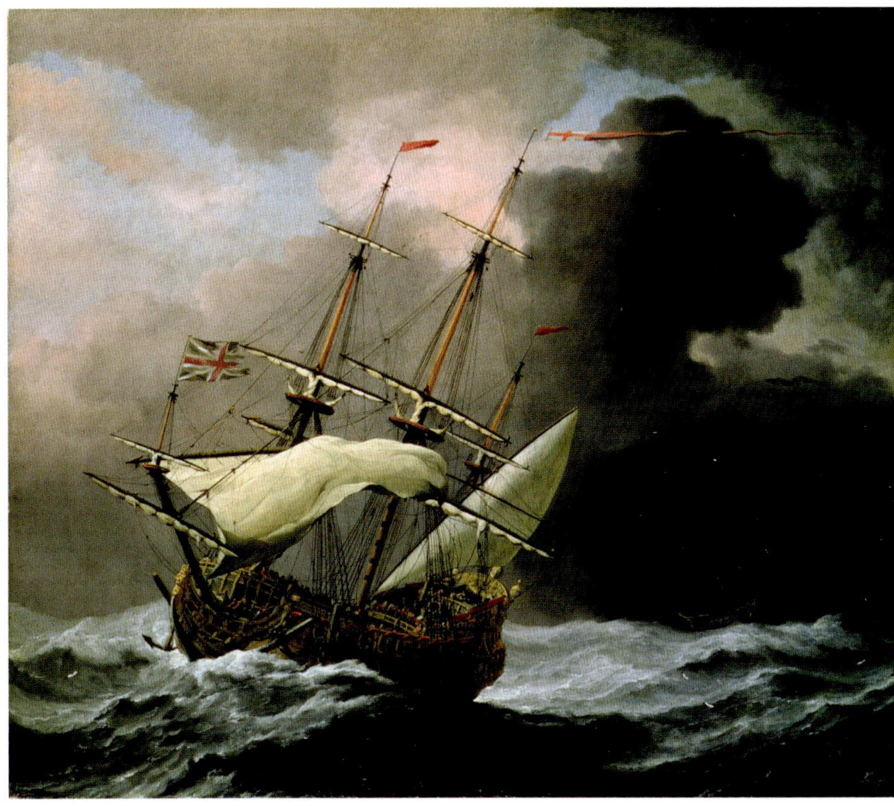

Above: This powerful painting by Willem van de Velde the Younger represents the ship the Hampton Court *in a storm. Both Willem and his father were renowned as the greatest Dutch marine painters of their day.*

Below: Haymakers Resting in a Field *by Adriaen van de Velde. A light-filled scene of farmworkers in a field on a late summer's day anticipates elements of Realism and Impressionism that developed in France nearly 200 years later.*

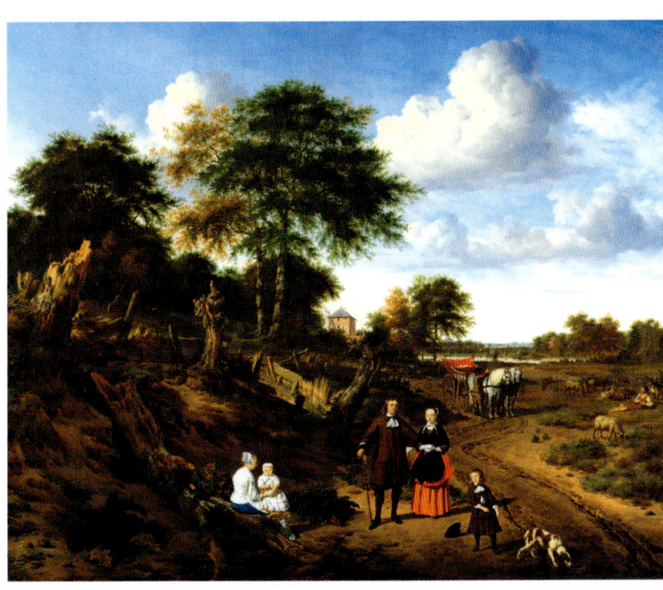

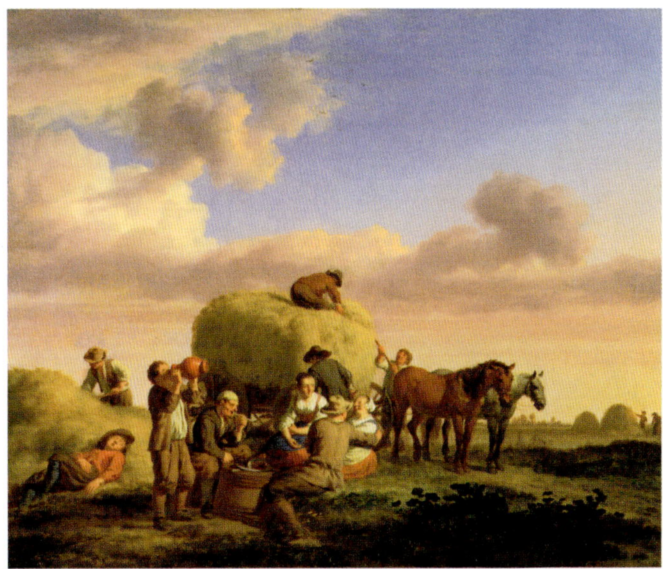

BARTHOLEMEUS VAN DER HELST

From a young age, Haarlem-born Bartholomeus van der Helst (1613–70) became recognized for his remarkable talent in composing large, often life-sized, naturally composed groups of lifelike figures. By the mid-1640s, he had succeeded Rembrandt as the most fashionable portrait painter in Amsterdam.

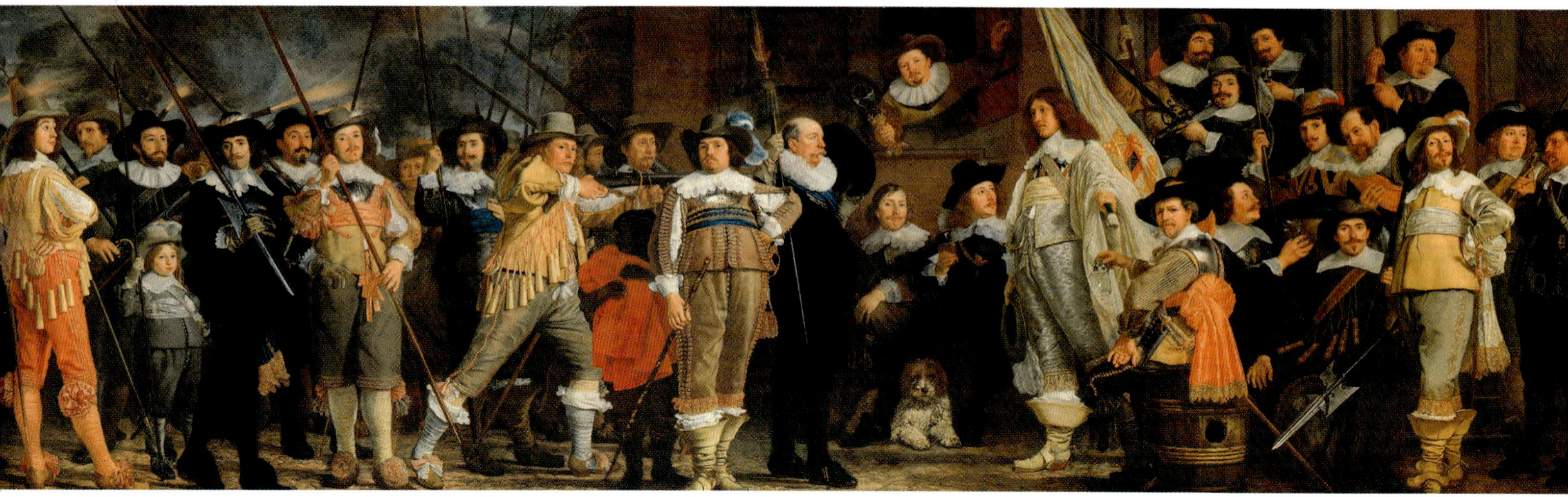

Although his earliest years are not known, when he was 14, Helst moved from Haarlem to Amsterdam where he probably trained in the workshop of Nicolaes Eliasz Pickenoy (1588–1653/6), as much of Pickenoy's style is apparent in Helst's early paintings. In 1639, he was commissioned to paint a large group portrait of *Militia Company of District VIII under the Command of Captain Roelof Bicker and Lieutenant Jan Michielsz Blaeuw* for the same series as Rembrandt's *The Night Watch* (see page 202). When he completed the large and prestigious work in 1643, his reputation soared and he received even more commissions for esteemed civic guard and individual portraits. His painting technique became smoother with small, almost imperceptible brushmarks and his details of clothes and accessories became even more exacting and meticulous. His second group portrait, *Banquet of the Amsterdam Civic Guard in Celebration of the Peace of Münster of 1648* (see p.207), demonstrates the peak of his development, with a smooth paint application and intensely detailed modelling of figures. He began receiving important commissions from patrons both within and beyond Amsterdam, and from the upper and middle classes. For instance, he painted the Amsterdam burgomaster Andries Bicker and his wife and son in 1642, the animal painter Paulus Potter in 1654, the official portrait of Maria Henrietta Stuart, widow of William II

Below: Portrait of a Lady in Black Satin with a Fan. Although the sitter is unknown, she is clearly a wealthy woman of status, with a confident gaze. Van der Helst's skills are apparent, and it is clear why he was one of the most successful portrait painters in Amsterdam.

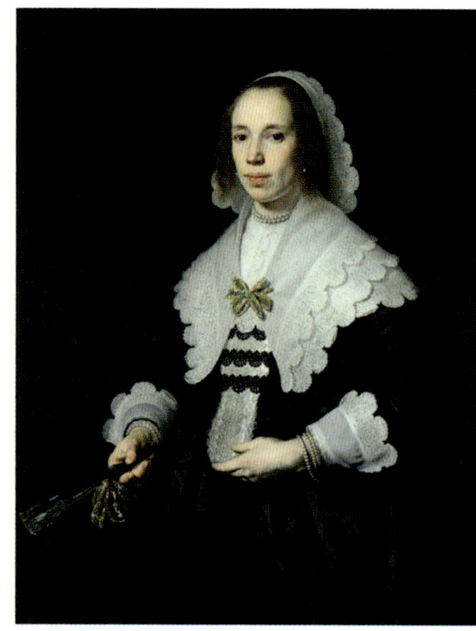

Above: Militia Company of District VIII under the Command of Captain Roelof Bicker, c.1640–c.43. This creative group portrait of 30 militiamen by van der Helst established his reputation.

DEMOCRATIC PORTRAITS

Compared with other European societies, Dutch portraits were more democratic. Beyond the Netherlands it was extremely rare for middle-class sitters to be represented in large scale and full length, yet Dutch artists portrayed their middle-class patrons in this way, imitating upper-class portraits and so raising their perceived status. Bourgeois members of society were delighted to celebrate their wealth and paid artists such as Helst to portray this new-found prosperity and prestige. Helst complied and often introduced elements to emphasize wealth and status in Dutch society, such as large properties owned by the sitters, references to aristocratic pursuits such as hunting, and sumptuous fabrics and jewels.

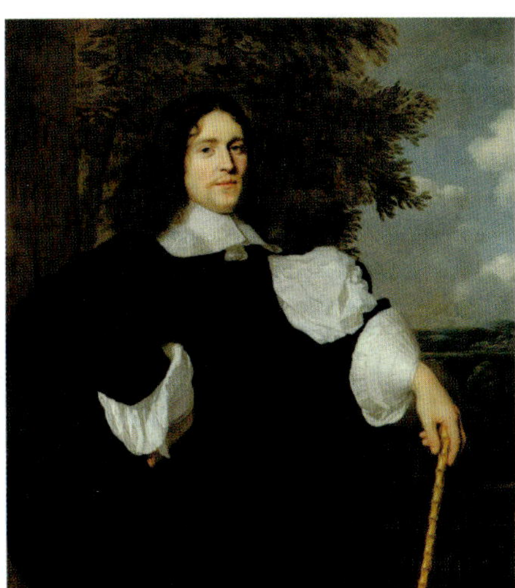

Above: Jacobus Trip (1627–70), Armanents Dealer of Amsterdam and Dordrecht. *Standing in front of a balustrade with a Dutch landscape in the background, the weapons dealer places one hand on his hip and the other on a walking cane.*

Right: A Young Woman Celebrating Wine. *Painted in 1665, this brightly coloured, animated and realistic-looking portrait of a young woman was the type of image that made van der Helst more popular than Rembrandt as a portraitist at the time.*

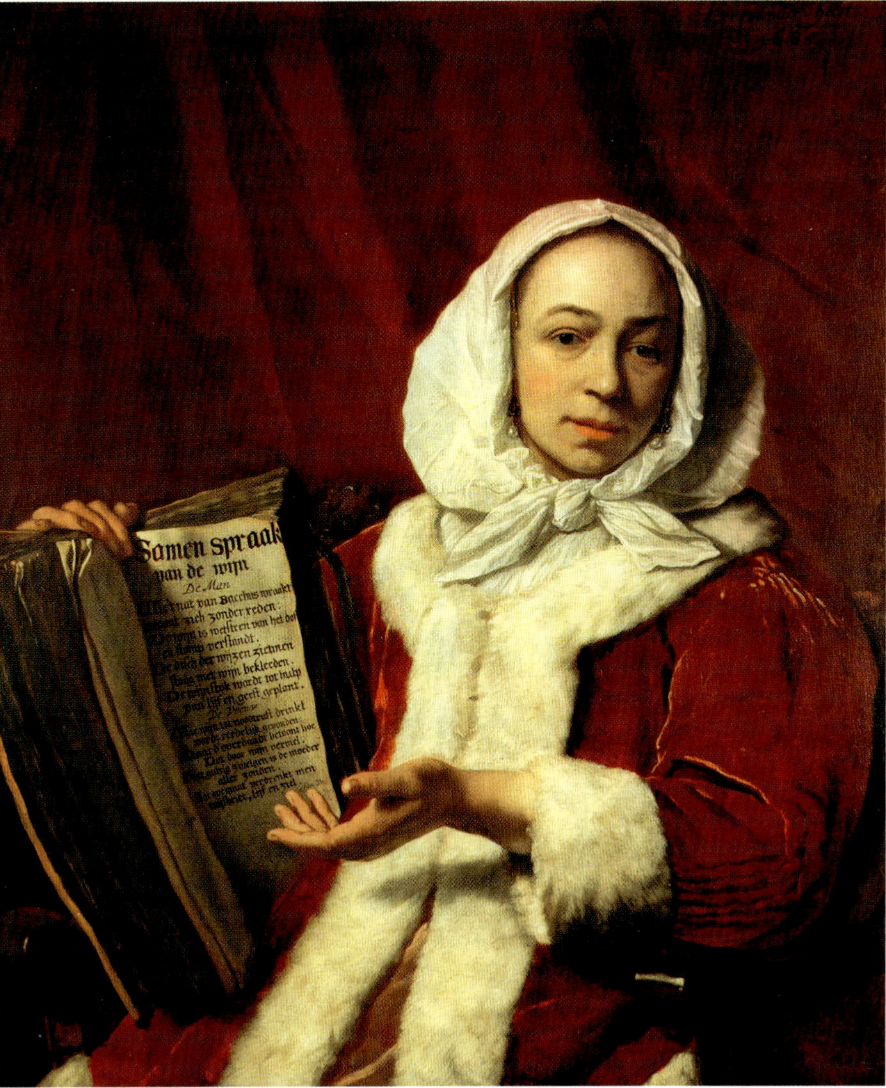

of Orange Nassau and a family portrait for Pieter van de Venne, a wealthy burgher of Amsterdam, both in 1652. Helst's commissions included individual portraits, family portraits, double portraits and pendant portraits.

METICULOUS FINERY

Helst remained the leading portrait painter of Amsterdam's nobility for the rest of his life and his style had a significant influence on numerous contemporary artists. His popularity occurred mainly because tastes in general were changing at the time. Rembrandt's style was becoming more personal, more broadly painted and darker, when the buyer's preference was for more elegant portraits that echoed the work of French painters and of the Flemish painter Anthony van Dyck.

As well as his smooth finish, van der Helst's painting style was boldly coloured with meticulous renderings of finery, sophisticated depictions of light, and realistic likenesses rather than idealizations. He preferred balanced compositions that project naturalism rather than formal arrangements. His palette included a dazzling array of colours, including light, clear and deep reds, brilliant whites and blues, and soft and intense greens, yellows and browns. Amsterdam's elite and middle classes loved his style, and he was astute enough to adhere to their tastes. The appeal of his work was enduring. When the celebrated British portraitist Sir Joshua Reynolds (1723–92) visited Amsterdam in 1781, he praised the group painting of Captain Bicker's Company: '[It] is, perhaps, the first picture of portraits in the world, comprehending more of those qualities which make a perfect portrait than any other I have ever seen.'

OTHER WORKS

In addition to his celebrated portraits, Helst painted many genre, biblical and mythological subjects. In these, he often combined elements of still life, buildings and figures. He also regularly collaborated with other artists, such as Ludolf Bakhuizen or Backhuysen (1630–1708), who was a prominent marine and landscape painter. Bakhuizen painted the backgrounds for Helst's portraits of the Dutch naval heroes Vice-Admiral Johan de Liefde and Lieutenant-Admiral Aert van Nes. In some other works, van Helst collaborated with more than one other painter, producing images that were extremely popular as much for their subject and execution as for the additional prestige of owning a painting that had been produced by several of the most fashionable artists of the time.

GERRIT DOU

As the son of a glass engraver, Gerrit, or Gerard, Dou (1613–1675) first learned how to engrave and paint glass, and later learned to paint as Rembrandt's first pupil. As an established artist, he became recognized and in demand for his small, meticulously painted genre scenes often conveying dramatic effects of light.

Gerrit Dou became particularly noted for his chiaroscuro candlelit scenes and trompe l'oeil 'niche' paintings, which were greatly sought after and sold for high prices; he was the most admired Dutch painter of the time, and for the next century. In 1648, he became one of the founders of the Leiden Guild of Saint Luke. Despite offers of appointments to royal courts abroad, including to King Charles II of England, he did not leave his birthplace of Leiden for his entire career.

INTRICATE DETAILS

Dou developed an exacting style that evolved from his early training in the stained-glass workshops of his father and then in the workshop of the distinguished printmaker and glass painter Pieter Couwenhorn (1599–1654) as well as some additional artistic

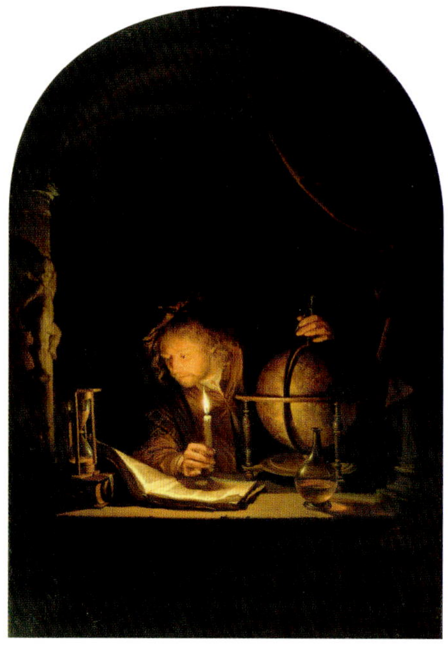

Above: Astronomer by Candlelight, *late 1650s. Through a window-like arch, an astronomer works late into the night. His candle is the only source of illumination.*

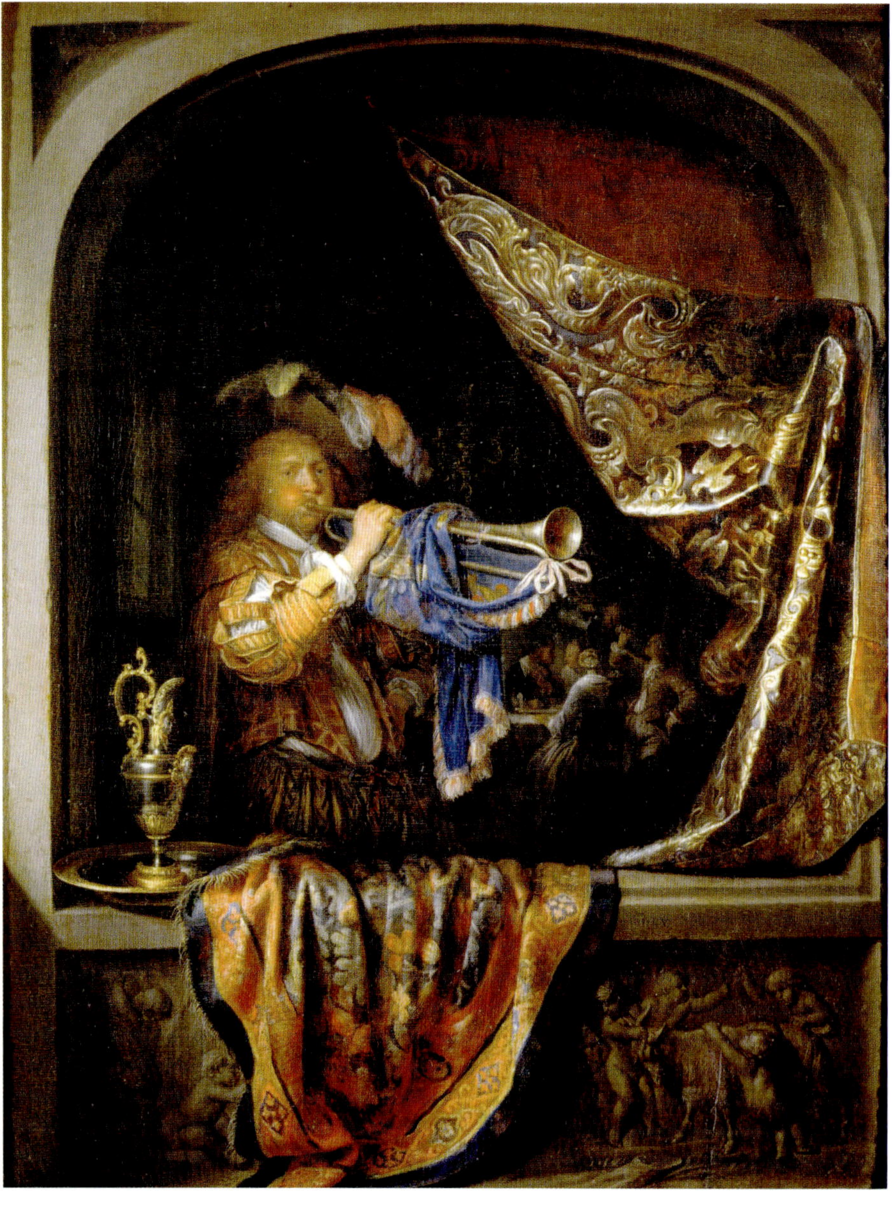

Left: Trumpet Player in Front of a Banquet. *Swathes of embellished draped fabric, fringing and feathers, a shiny trumpet, and ornate jug on a tray. In the midst of it all, a man blows the trumpet. Almost obscured are figures at a banquet.*

LEIDEN FIJNSCHILDERS

Also called simply fijnschilders meaning fine-painters, the Leiden fijnschilders were Dutch Golden Age painters who lived and worked in Leiden from approximately 1630 to 1710 and were masters of the art of illusion through paint. The name refers to a specific type of small-scale painting, with extremely credible rendering of textures and details, and strong tonal contrasts. Gerrit Dou was one of the first and most admired Leiden fijnschilders.

training from the Leiden glaziers' guild. In February 1628 when he was 14, his father sent him to study in Rembrandt's studio. Rembrandt was then aged 22 and he taught Dou a range of skills, including careful draughtsmanship, dramatic light and colour effects, the use of impasto paint, and the creation of original compositions. Dou stayed in Rembrandt's studio for approximately three years until Rembrandt moved to Amsterdam in 1631 or 1632, and soon after that, Dou's art began to lose evidence of Rembrandt's influence as his work developed a more refined, distinctive style, with a cooler palette, the rendering of minute details, and the application of smooth, glossy paint. He became exceptionally fastidious about his tools and working conditions, and began using his own handmade brushes, and often painted using a magnifying glass in order to create especially precise and exacting details. In 1637, the German painter and art historian Joachim von Sandrart (1606–88) visited him and reported that Dou spent so

Right: Anne and Tobias, or Reading the Bible, 1645. Bathed in glowing light, a contemporary Dutch couple represent the biblical Tobias, who was blind, and his wife Anne, who reads the Bible to him.

Below: Self-Portrait, c.1665. Dou was inspired by Rembrandt to paint self-portraits, sometimes as here in a theatrical costume. Dou became famous for his jewel-bright colours and detail.

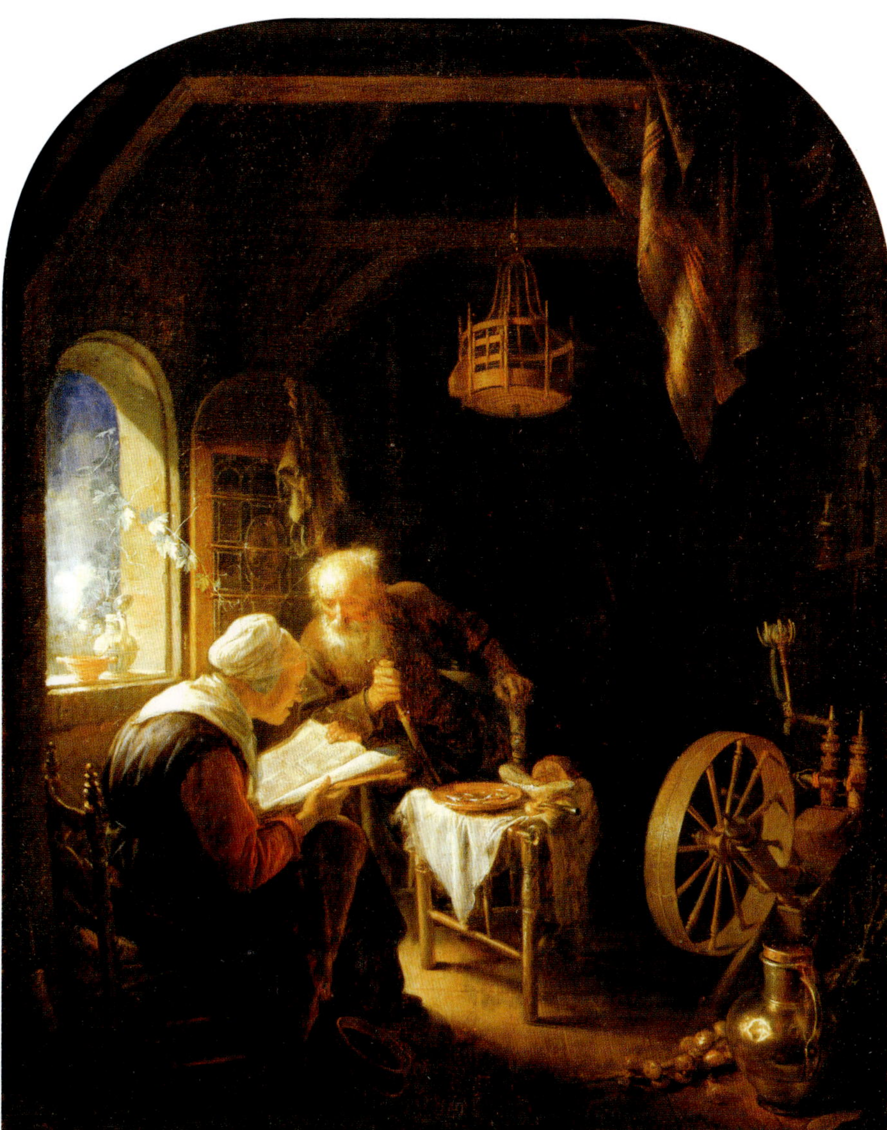

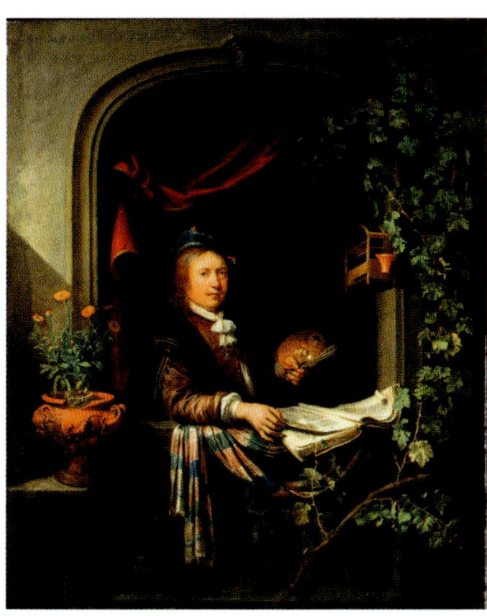

much time painting intricate details that it could take him five days just to paint a hand. Von Sandrart also praised many aspects of Dou's style, including 'the care that he had lavished on painting a broomstick no larger than a fingernail.'

Dou became best known for painting domestic interiors, usually containing one or two figures, and surrounded by books, musical instruments, or household equipment. In many works he included detailed still lifes, such as kitchen scenes crowded with vegetables, poultry and utensils. After 1650, he also became known for his dramatically-lit night scenes. At first he painted portraits, but commissions for these gradually declined because he took so long to complete them. His paintings were always small and generally oil on wood, often enclosed in specially made cases which he also decorated, and his most characteristic device was the painted 'frame within a frame;' pictures of domestic interiors surrounded by a painted window, a draping curtain, or an arched stone opening.

PROSPEROUS AND CELEBRATED

Unlike Jan Steen, Dou was respected throughout his life and became one of the highest paid artists in the Netherlands. Among his exalted international patrons were Charles II of England, Queen Christina of Sweden, Pieter Spiering, the Swedish Ambassador in The Hague, and probably Cosimo III de' Medici (1642–1723). His most noted pupils included Frans van Mieris the Elder (1635–81) and possibly Gabriel Metsu (1629–67) who followed his painstaking approach.

GOVERT FLINCK · FERDINAND BOL

Two of Rembrandt's favourite pupils, Govert Flinck (1615–1660) and Ferdinand Bol (1616–1680), originally modelled their styles on his, but Flinck later developed a more flamboyant approach, while Bol's paintings became more colourful and elegant. Both artists painted portraits, and narrative and historical subjects.

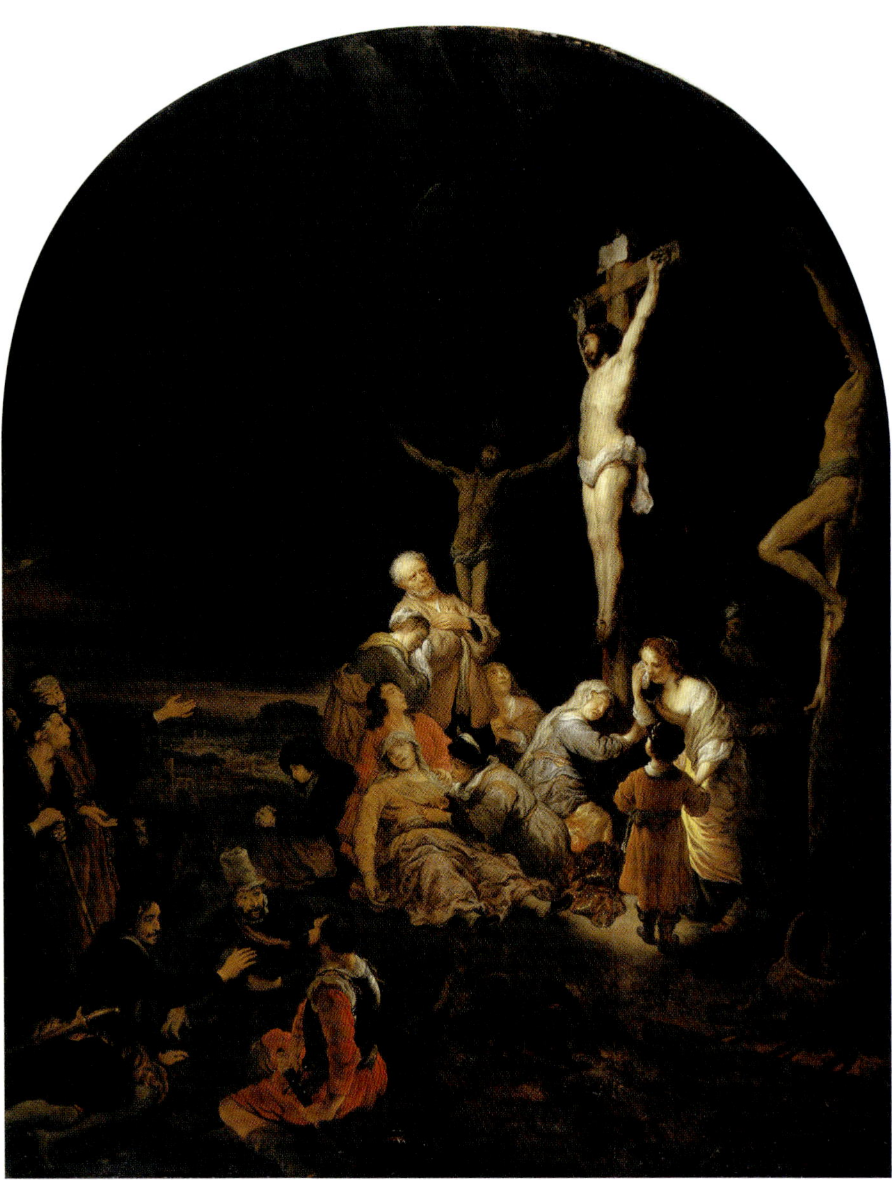

Left: Calvary, or Golgotha, *by Govert Flinck, 1649. A dramatic depiction of the crucifixion, painted from a mid-height side angle, showing Jesus and the two thieves, with the Virgin Mary swooning at the foot of the cross; it reveals the powerful influence of Rembrandt's chiaroscuro.*

DUTCH CLASSICAL ARCHITECTURE

Flourishing at the same time as Dutch Golden Age painting, Dutch Baroque, or Dutch Classical architecture began with Utrecht-born Hendrick de Keyser (1565–1621) who introduced a Venetian-influenced style in early 17th century Dutch architecture in buildings such as Noorderkerk (Northern Church, 1620–23) and Westerkerk (Western Church, 1620–31) in Amsterdam. After beginning his career as a painter, Haarlem-born Jacob van Campen (1596–1657) also created a restrained architectural style that suited the social and political climate, became known as 'Dutch Classicism' and was internationally influential. While he was living in Italy between 1616–24, Jacob van Campen studied the work of Italian architects who favoured a Classical style, such as Andrea Palladio (1508–80), and on his return to the Netherlands, he began designing buildings based on Palladio's ideas and the theories of Vitruvius. In the 1630s, van Campen and Pieter Post (1608–69) designed the Mauritshuis (now the Royal Picture Gallery) in The Hague, and in c.1645 van Campen designed the Nieuwe Kerk in Haarlem, a church that influenced Christopher Wren. In 1648, he began the large Town Hall of Amsterdam that Bol helped to decorate.

GOVERT FLINCK

Govert Flinck was born at Cleves in north-western Germany near the Dutch border, which was then under the control of the Dutch Republic. Although initially apprenticed by his father to a silk mercer, Flinck asked to train as an artist, and he was sent to Leeuwarden where he boarded with Lambert Jacobszoon (1598–1636) who was a preacher as well as a painter. Later, Flinck entered Rembrandt's studio in Amsterdam, and he began producing mainly biblical and allegorical subjects, showing a strong influence of Rembrandt's methods and style. When Joachim von Sandrart visited Holland in 1637, he found that Flinck was acknowledged as one of Rembrandt's best pupils. After 1648 however, Flinck moved away from Rembrandt's influence, instead showing a greater inclination towards the more extravagant approach of Peter

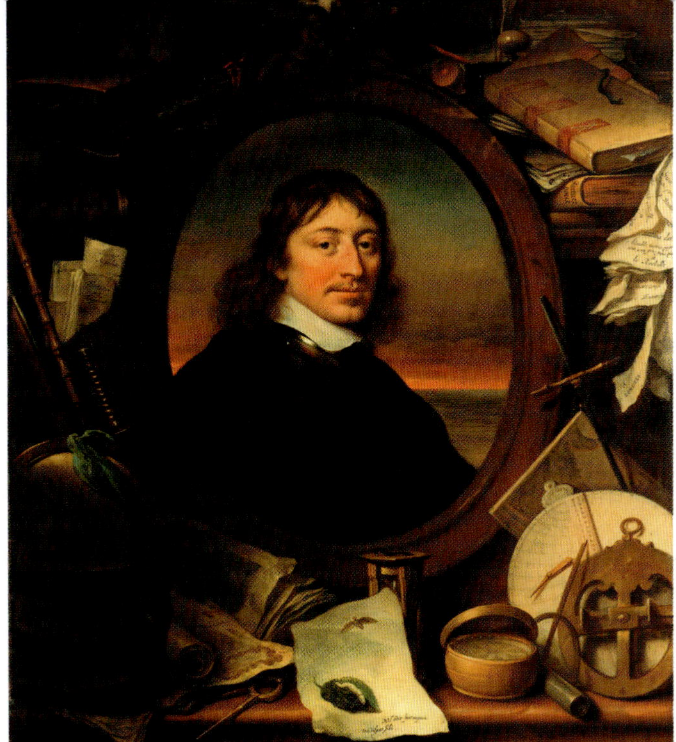

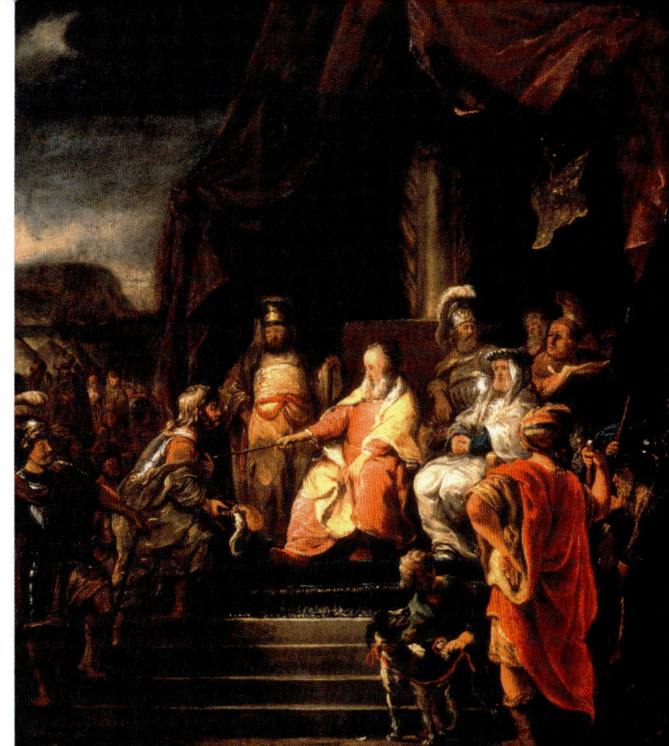

Above: Painted by Flinck in 1654, this is the portrait of the First Councillor and Director-General of the Dutch East India Company.

Paul Rubens, which led to him being commissioned to paint many official and diplomatic works for important patrons, including those at the court of the Great Elector, Friedrich Wilhelm I of Brandenburg, and the Stadtholder of Cleves, John Maurice of Nassau. His most successful works were portraits, particularly of groups.

FERDINAND BOL

Having grown up in Dordrecht, Ferdinand Bol, the son of a prosperous surgeon, later became known for his portraits and history paintings. He learned to paint either in Dordrecht under Jacob Gerritsz Cuyp (1594–1651), the father of the landscape painter Aelbert Cuyp, or in Utrecht under the painter Abraham Bloemaert. Later, rather than travelling to Italy at the age of about 20, which was expected of most young artists learning their profession, he moved to Amsterdam and became apprenticed to Rembrandt between 1635 and 1641. During that time, he imitated

Right: Six Regents and the Beadle of the Nieuw Zijds Institute for the Outdoor Relief of the Poor, Amsterdam, *painted in 1657 by Ferdinand Bol.*

Rembrandt's style so closely that for centuries afterwards, some of Bol's works were mistaken for Rembrandt's. In 1642, he set up as an independent artist, and although his style changed, his subjects continued to follow Rembrandt's, as he painted histories, portraits – often with sitters posed by a window – and figures wearing exotic costumes. His palette lightened and brightened, his brushstrokes became longer, his paint consistency thinner and his figures more refined. Assisted by his marriage to a woman from an influential family, he received many official commissions and became a burgher

Above: The eyes are led around the red-cloaked figure, then the boy and dog, and up the steps, as Bol depicts Moses and Jethro. *In the Bible, Jethro was Moses's father-in-law.*

of Amsterdam. By 1655, he was head of the Wine Merchants Guild and was one of the painters commissioned to decorate the new Town Hall designed by Jacob van Campen. In 1660, he was widowed. Nine years later, he married for a second time to a wealthy woman and gave up painting. His last work was probably a self-portrait that he executed in the late 1660s.

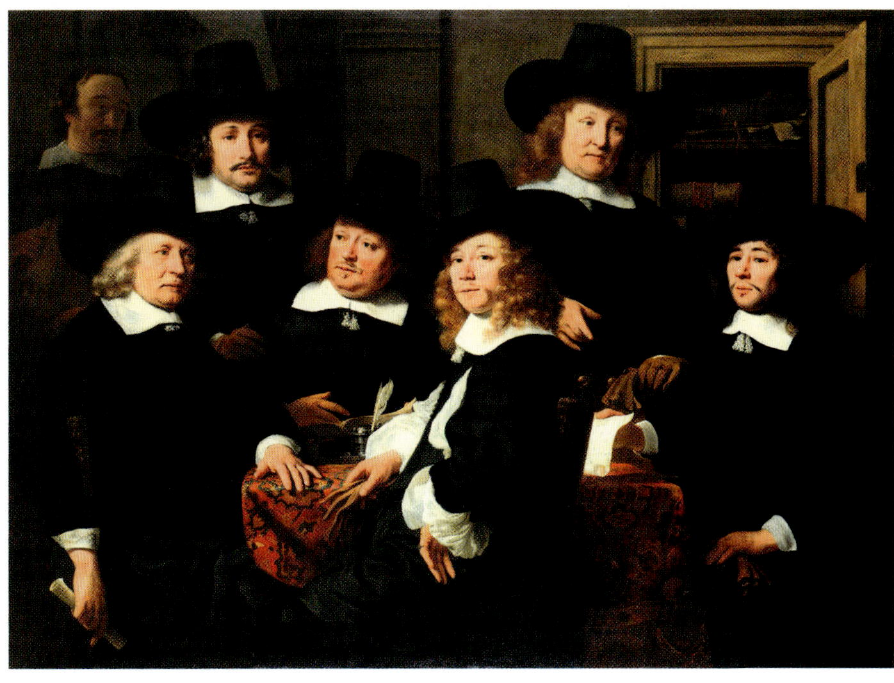

DE WITTE • DE JONGH

Emanuel de Witte (1617–1692) and Ludolf Leendertsz de Jongh (1616–79) became known for their paintings of interiors, often of public buildings. De Witte became a specialist in painting both real and imaginary church interiors, while de Jongh painted interiors along with several other subjects.

EMANUEL DE WITTE

Born in Alkmaar in north Holland, Emanuel de Witte learned to paint in Delft with the still life painter Evert van Aelst (1602–57). In 1642, he joined the local Guild of Saint Luke and began his career painting historical subjects and portraits, but influenced by Gerard Houckgeest, Hendrick Cornelisz van Vliet and Carel Fabritius, he soon became more interested in depicting interior architecture. By 1652 he moved to Amsterdam, where he remained for the rest of his life. From that time, his most frequent subjects were the interiors of public buildings of Amsterdam, often places of worship such as the Nieuwe Kerk (New Church), the Oude Kerk (Old Church)

Below: Built between 1671–75 for the Spanish and Portuguese Jews in Amsterdam, this synagogue appealed to de Witte for its architecture and light.

CHURCH INTERIORS

As Dutch Calvinism forbade religious paintings in churches, interior walls were whitewashed and plain, but the buildings, with their Gothic arches and heavy columns, were grand and dignified. Numerous artists of the period painted church exteriors, using precise linear perspective to convey details of architecture, but gradually an interest emerged in painting the interiors of these grand buildings too, and over the 17th century, greater realism evolved, with artists creating ever more credible images from their imaginations. Among the most prominent of the Dutch Golden Age artists who specialized in visualizing church interiors were de Witte, Houckgeest, Vliet and Saenredam.

and the Portuguese Synagogue. He had first learned the theories of linear perspective from his schoolteacher father, and he continued to use it often quite elaborately. However, although many of his interiors appear to have been made from direct observation, a large number were created from his imagination. For extra theatrical effect, he often painted large hanging screens or curtains in front of his scenes to give viewers the impression of peering within. De Witte also created the idea of light filtering through windows, illuminating walls, columns and floors, and throwing shadows to suggest depth, space and volume. His interiors are usually busy with figures, sometimes

Below: De Witte's interiors always include figures, and in this church there are many people, of different ages, but he contrasts their stature with the tall columns and other aspects of the lofty building.

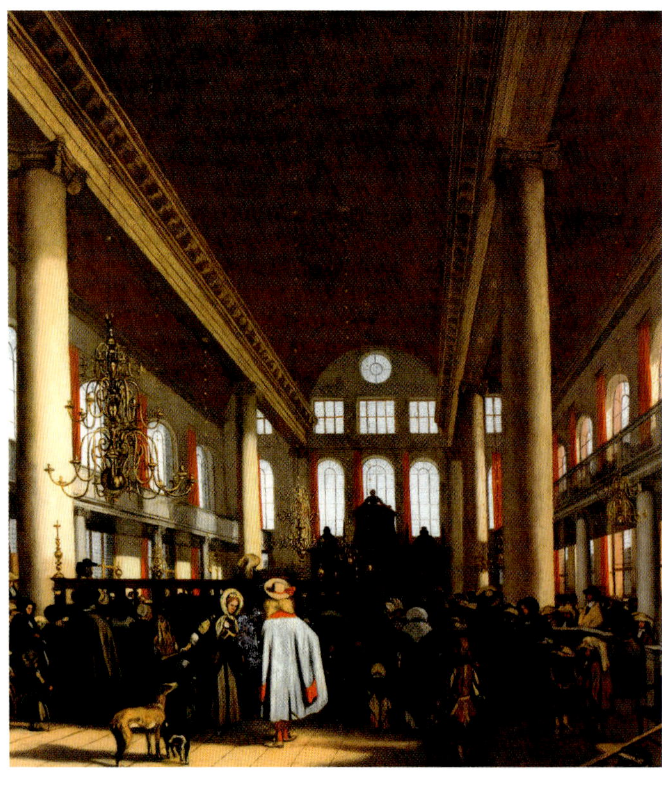

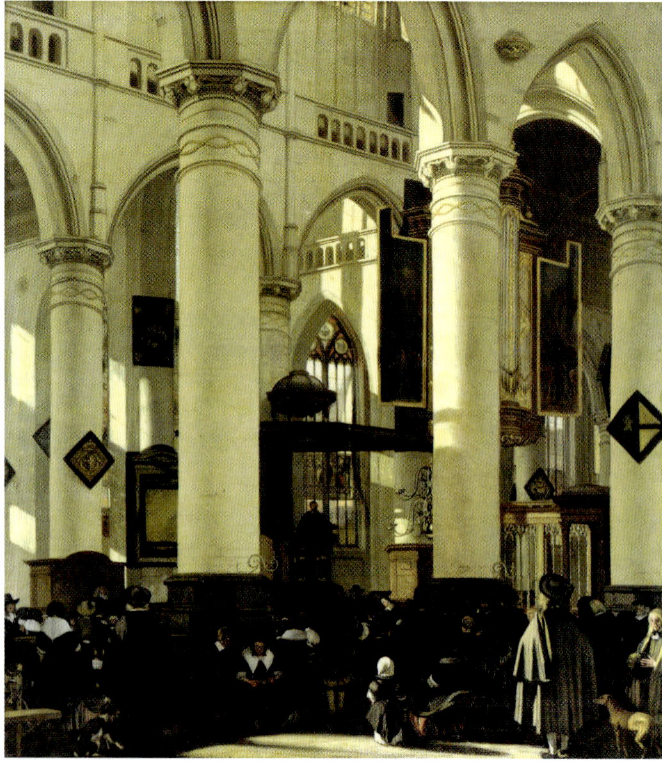

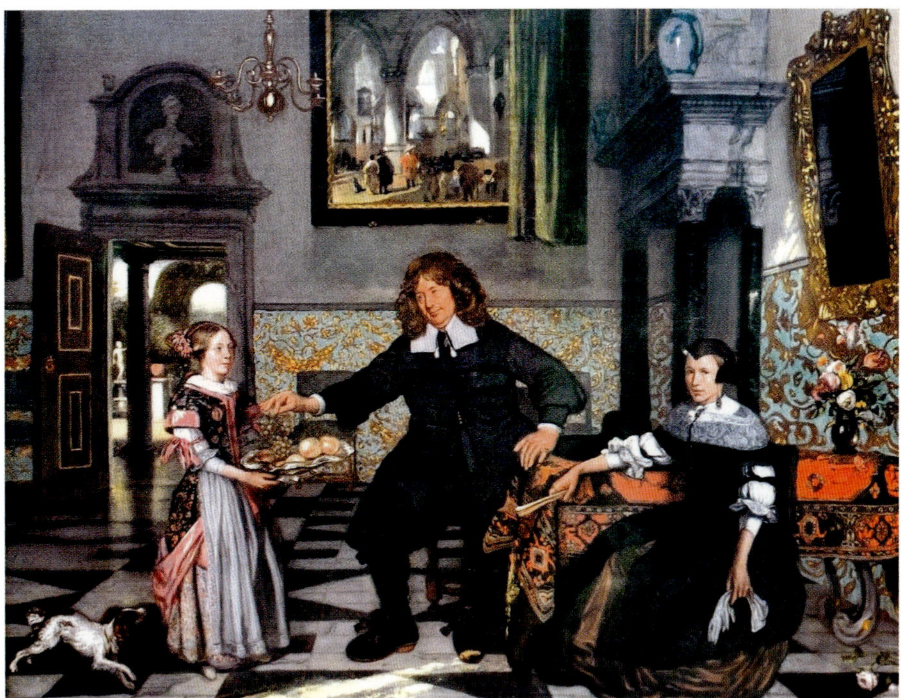

Above: Captured with clarity and precision, de Witte painted this Portrait of a Family in an Interior *in 1678. The family and richly appointed interior are unidentified, however.*

Below: Paying the Hostess. *This genre painting by Ludolf de Jongh portrays a man paying the landlady for a night at her inn. Another man leads his horse from the stable, while another smokes, smiling.*

Cornelis Saftleven (1607–81) who was especially influenced by the drama and chiaroscuro of Caravaggio's art. De Jongh also studied under the portrait painter Anthonie Palamedes (1601–73) in Delft and then with the genre painter Jan Hermansz van Bijlert (1597/8–1671) in Utrecht.

Ludolf Leendertsz de Jongh left the Netherlands for France in 1635 and only returned in 1642 because his mother was ill. Soon after returning home, he opened a shop in Rotterdam and began selling his paintings that comprised a wide variety of subject matter, including portraits, interiors, genre paintings, landscapes and historical subjects. Like his first teacher, de Jongh was strongly influenced by the Utrecht Caravaggisti and he experimented with various painting methods and palettes to express brilliant light and dramatically dark tones in his interiors and portraits, also conveying the more psychological aspects of life through his sitters' individualistic facial expressions, poses and gestures.

lone individuals, and also often dogs. The scenes are frequently seen from oblique angles, making the perspective quite intricate, offset by a fairly neutral, muted palette with the occasional addition of a soft or bright red or green.

Despite his meticulous elements, unlike many of his contemporaries de Witte aimed to create an immediate overall impact rather than dwell on minute details and so his brushstrokes are frequently loose. In addition, rather than the dramatic chiaroscuro that was so fashionable in Dutch painting of the time, his tonal contrasts are generally softer and more gradual.

LUDOLF LEENDERTSZ DE JONGH

Although he is less well-known now, de Jongh was one of the most fashionable painters of Rotterdam during the 1650s. Born in the village of Overschie, he grew up to become a respected member of Rotterdam town council – the vroedschap. Rebelling against his strict shoemaker father's wishes, he chose to study art, and he entered the Rotterdam workshop of

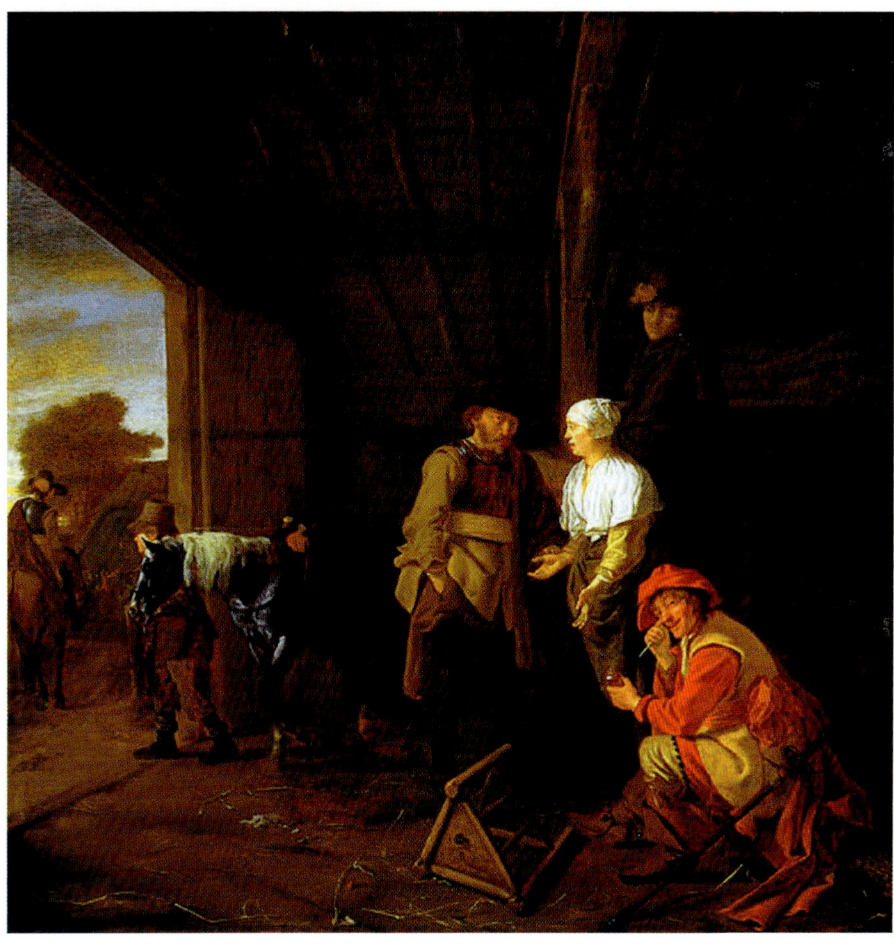

GERARD TER BORCH

Known variously as Terburg or Terborch, Gerard ter Borch (1617–81) was the son of an artist who became a tax collector. Ter Borch himself grew up to become celebrated as a painter of small, delicate portraits and tranquil genre scenes. Although mainly living and working in the Dutch Republic, he also spent time abroad.

Gerard ter Borch was the most accomplished of a family of artists, born in Zwolle, in the province of Overijssel. His mother died soon after his birth, and in 1621, when he was four years old, his father married again. His step-uncle from this marriage was the well-known engraver Robert van Voerst (1597–1636). In 1628 his father married for a third time and ter Borch had three more half-siblings: Gesina, Harmen and Moses. Gesina (1633–90) and Moses (1645–67) also became artists. Gesina worked predominantly in watercolour and during his short life, Moses was an outstanding draughtsman. Although neither became as renowned as their older half-brother, they were both accomplished. Gesina wrote poetry as well as painting observations of family life, topical events and fashionable figures.

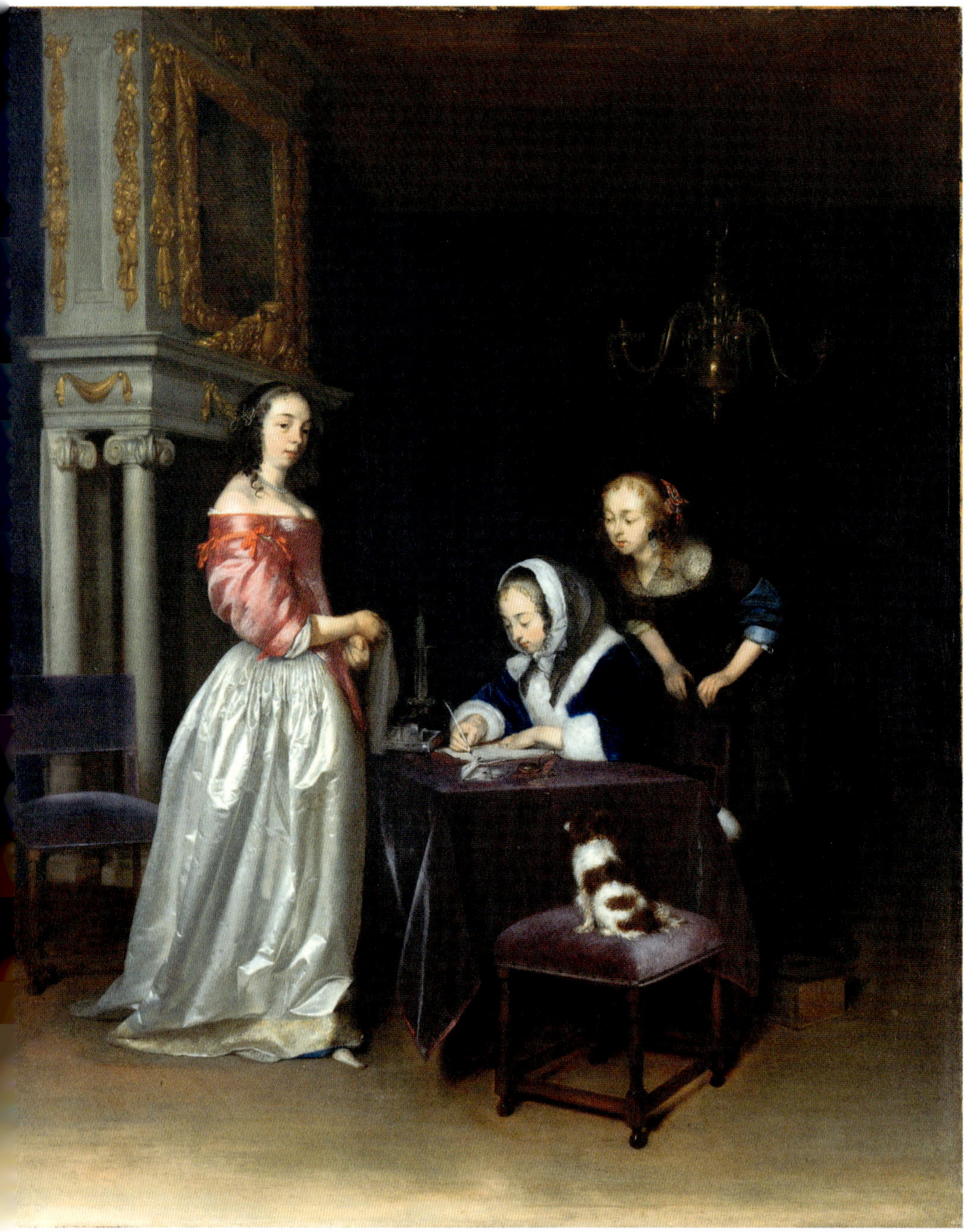

TRAVELLING ARTIST

After receiving his first instruction from his father, ter Borch became known as Gerard the Younger, while his father is usually called Gerard ter Borch the Elder (1583–1662). In 1632, at the age of 15, Gerard the Younger was in Amsterdam, where he possibly studied

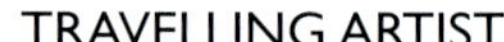

Left: Called Curiosity, *this painting by ter Borch from 1660/2 shows three women in a luxurious interior. The eldest writes a letter, the youngest looks over her shoulder and the woman on the left observes, slightly anxiously. A little dog also watches on intently.*

Below: Woman Writing a Letter. *Most of ter Borch's paintings depict people absorbed in situations that viewers are not necessarily meant to fully understand.*

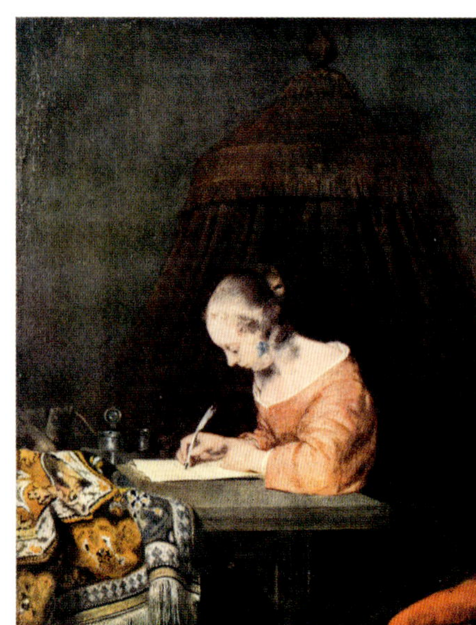

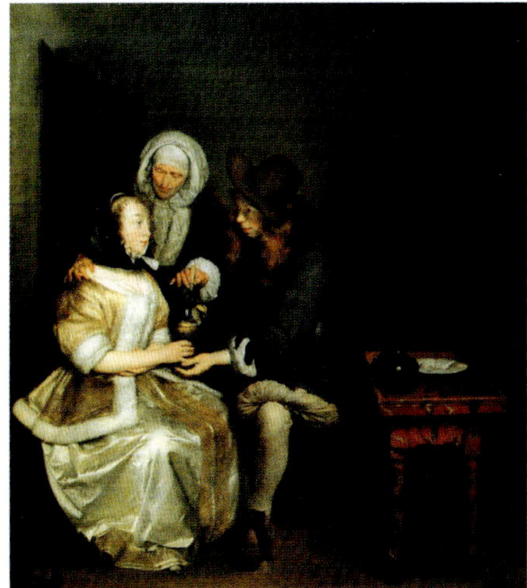

Above: The Glass of Lemonade. *A wealthy young woman appears to have become faint. She is sitting down, taking a glass of lemonade from an attentive young man. The maid has apparently not noticed the looks passing between them.*

Right: The Letter. *Three figures are in an opulent room. A dog is curled up and a young woman in a lavish outfit reads a letter. A boy and another young woman watch her, but all is ambiguous.*

with Willem Cornelisz Duyster (1599–1635) or Pieter Codde (1599–1678), but by 1633 he had returned to Zwolle. The following year he went to Haarlem to study with the landscape painter Pieter Molijn or Molyn (1595–1661) and entered the Haarlem Guild of Saint Luke there in 1635. That summer he travelled to London to work with his step-uncle Robert van Voerst, who had recently been appointed as engraver to Charles I. After that, ter Borch probably visited Italy, Spain, France and Flanders. In Spain he worked at the royal court in Madrid, and was so highly esteemed that King Philip IV sat for him, although the portrait no longer exists. Whether he actually met Diego Velázquez (1599–1660) while he was there is not clear, but from that time, his work shows a strong influence of Velázquez's style. Neither is it clear how long he remained in Spain, but he was probably back in the Dutch Republic by around 1640, and then in Rome in 1641 when he painted some small portraits on copper. By 1648 he was living in

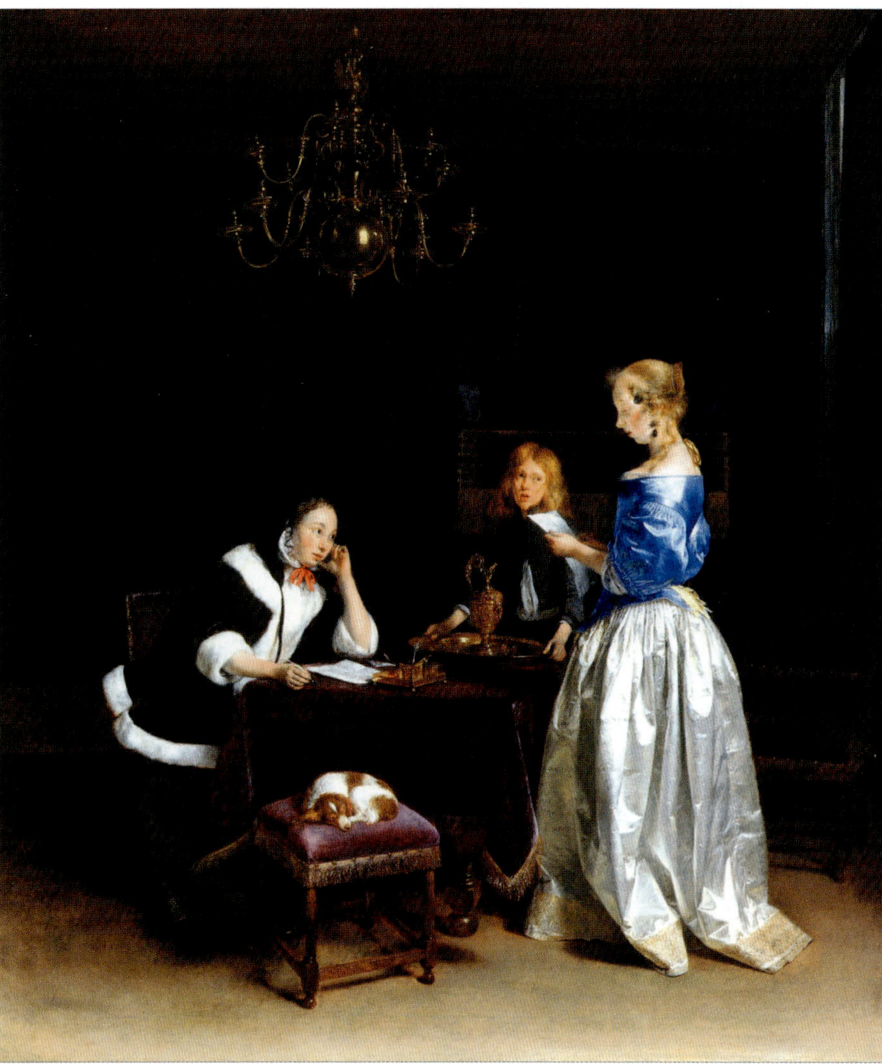

the German city of Münster, where the Treaty of Münster was signed in October 1648, which ended the Thirty Years' War. There, ter Borch painted what became a famous group portrait: *The Swearing of the Oath of Ratification of the Treaty of Münster* (see page 11) depicting the meeting of the congress that ratified the peace treaty between the Spanish and the Dutch. Next, he possibly visited Brussels, as it seems likely that he was knighted and received a gold chain and medal from Philip of Spain while there. In February 1654, he married and moved to Deventer in the province of Overijssel where he lived for the rest of his life, becoming a city councillor (gemeensman) in 1666.

INDEPENDENT STYLE

On his return from Münster, ter Borch typically painted scenes of ordinary citizens, such as soldiers at rest or playing cards, demonstrating the influence of Willem Duyster and Pieter Codde, but after moving to Deventer, he evolved a different style, replacing his figures with elegantly dressed characters set against shadowy backgrounds, engaged in genteel activities such as letter writing or music making, or else he painted full-length portraits, but always using his sensitive and delicate brushwork, and frequently conveying elements of the psychology of his sitters. His colours are rich but subdued, his tonal gradations subtle, and his rendering of textures, such as wood, velvet and satin, are sophisticated,. Ter Borch was the first Dutch painter to develop this particular kind or style of depiction, which significantly influenced the work of other leading genre painters of the time such as Metsu, de Hooch, van Mieris and Johannes Vermeer.

PHILIPS WOUWERMAN

One of the most prolific artists of the Dutch Golden Age, Haarlem painter Philips Wouwerman (or Wouwermans) (1619–68) initially produced simple depictions of everyday life, but he gradually developed an individual style and expanded his range, painting landscapes featuring figures and, especially, horses.

Although approximately 1200 paintings were accredited to Wouwerman, many of these have now been established as probably painted by either his brothers Pieter (1623–82) and Jan (1629–66) or by his numerous followers and imitators. It is now established that approximately 570 of these were actually by Wouwerman. Initially trained by his father the painter Pouwels (or Paulus) Joosten Wouwerman (c.1580–1642), little else is verified about the rest of Philips Wouwerman's training. Suggestions have been made of other teachers, including Pieter Cornelisz van Rijck, Pieter Cornelisz Verbeeck (1610–54) and Frans Hals, but none of these have been verified and

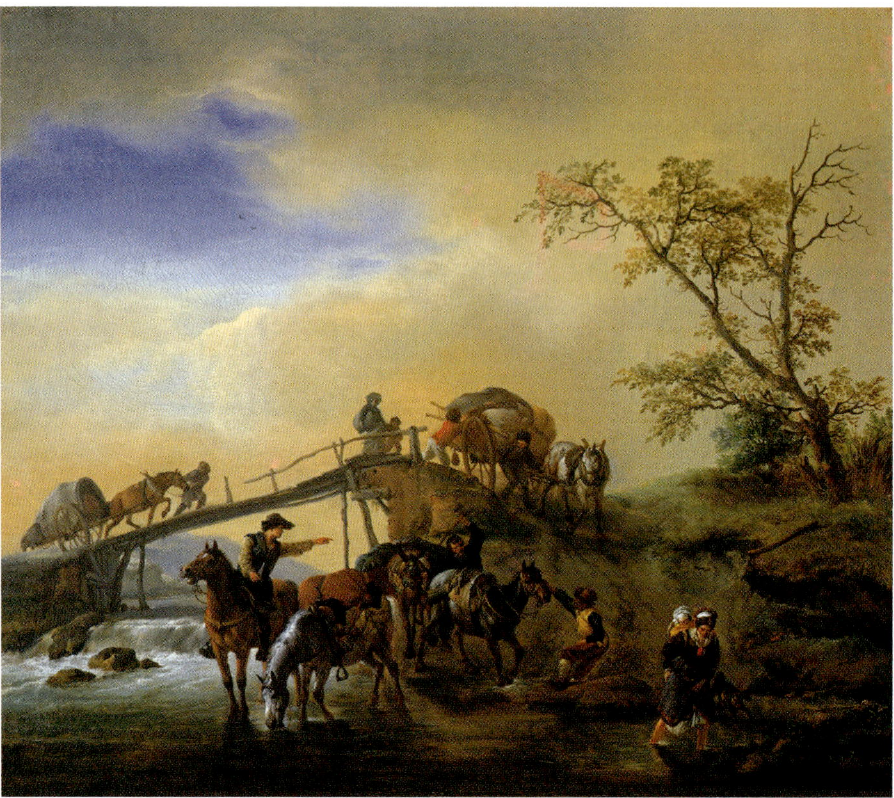

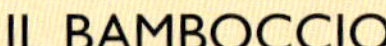

IL BAMBOCCIO

Like Wouwerman, Pieter Bodding van Laer was from Haarlem, but he spent over ten years in Rome, and his paintings became known and influential across much of northern Europe. His subject matter included genre scenes, animal paintings and landscapes set in and around Rome. Van Laer was an active member of the association of mostly Dutch and Flemish artists in Rome that lasted from about 1620 to 1720, known as the Bentvueghels (Dutch for 'Birds of a Feather') or the Schildersbent ('Painters' Clique'). As it was customary for the Bentvueghels to adopt an appealing nickname, van Laer became called Il Bamboccio (meaning roughly: chubby child, ugly doll or puppet). His followers became known as the Bamboccianti. The first Bamboccianti included Andries Both (1612/3–42), Jan Both (c.1615–52), Karel Dujardin (1622–78), Jan Miel (1599–1656) and Johannes Lingelbach (1622–74).

Wouwerman's painting style does not show any particular influence of these artists. However, his work does seem to draw on aspects of the style of Pieter Bodding van Laer (c.1599–c.1641/2), and he is often described as a Bamboccianti (see box).

CHANGING STYLES

Wouwerman's early paintings can be described as Bamboccianti, but his style and subjects later evolved to something far more unique and personal, often including horses – in battles and encampments and on hunts, usually with figures and often in everyday situations of the time, such as at an inn or the blacksmith. As with the majority of Dutch Golden Age artists, Wouwerman rarely painted large pictures, mainly painting small-scale works. With his fairly subdued palette, he often includes vignettes of human details that are

Above: Travellers with Pack Horses and Wagons near a Wooden Bridge *uses soft brushmarks and a glowing palette.*

Below: The Grey Horse, *1646. Viewed from behind, we look slightly upwardly at the scene set against a cloudy sky.*

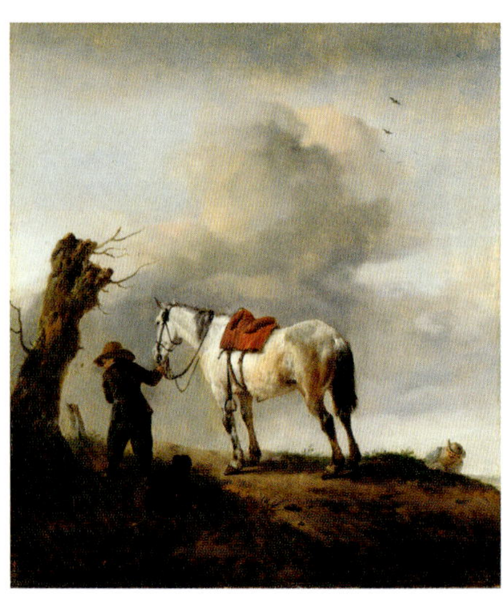

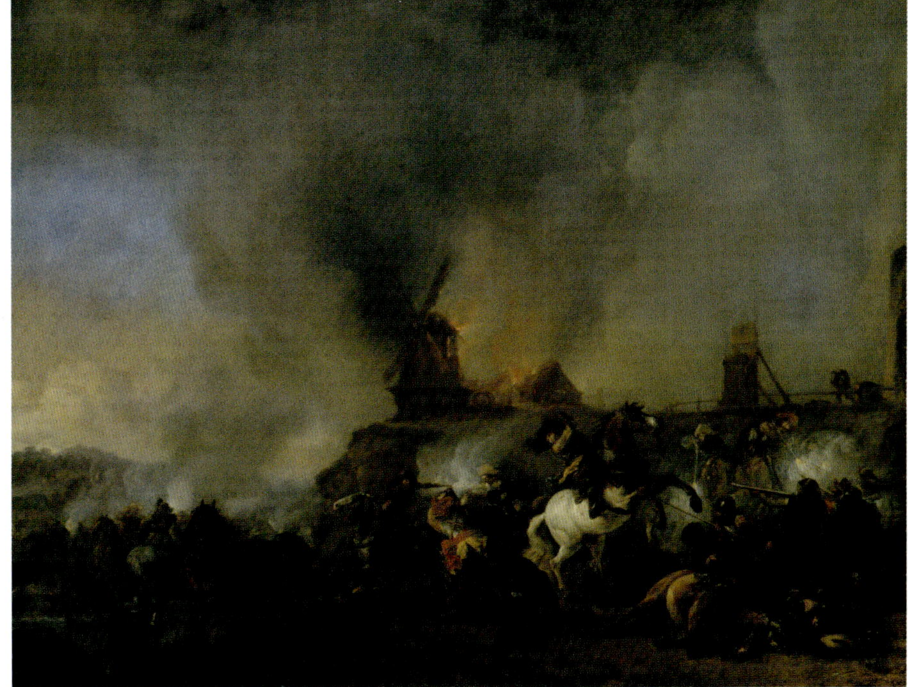

Above: Wouwerman was the most successful painter of horses during his lifetime. He was also prolific. He painted Cavalry Battle in Front of a Burning Mill *in the 1660s.*

Below: A dynamic composition, here Wouwerman has depicted Riders Watering their Horses, *creating a soft background with the horses in clear focus. He painted many similar scenes.*

silvery-grey light and atmosphere of Haarlem. By the end of his life, his painting skills were exceptional; his skies were soft and light, and his portrayals of texture convincing. Particularly noted for his skilful depictions of horses of all breeds, either alone or in large groups, often in motion, he has become accepted by many as the most successful Dutch painter of horses. His paintings *Travellers with Pack Horses near a Wooden Bridge* and *Cavalry Battle in Front of a Burning Mill* are good examples of his later style.

IN GREAT DEMAND

As well as an artist, Wouwerman worked as an estate agent in Haarlem. Apart from a short stay in Hamburg at the end of the 1630s, he appears to have lived in Haarlem for his entire life, and his work was in great demand. In 1640, he joined the Haarlem Guild of Saint Luke. After his death, especially during the 18th century, his work became even more sought after and was often bought for art collections across Europe. He died at just 48.

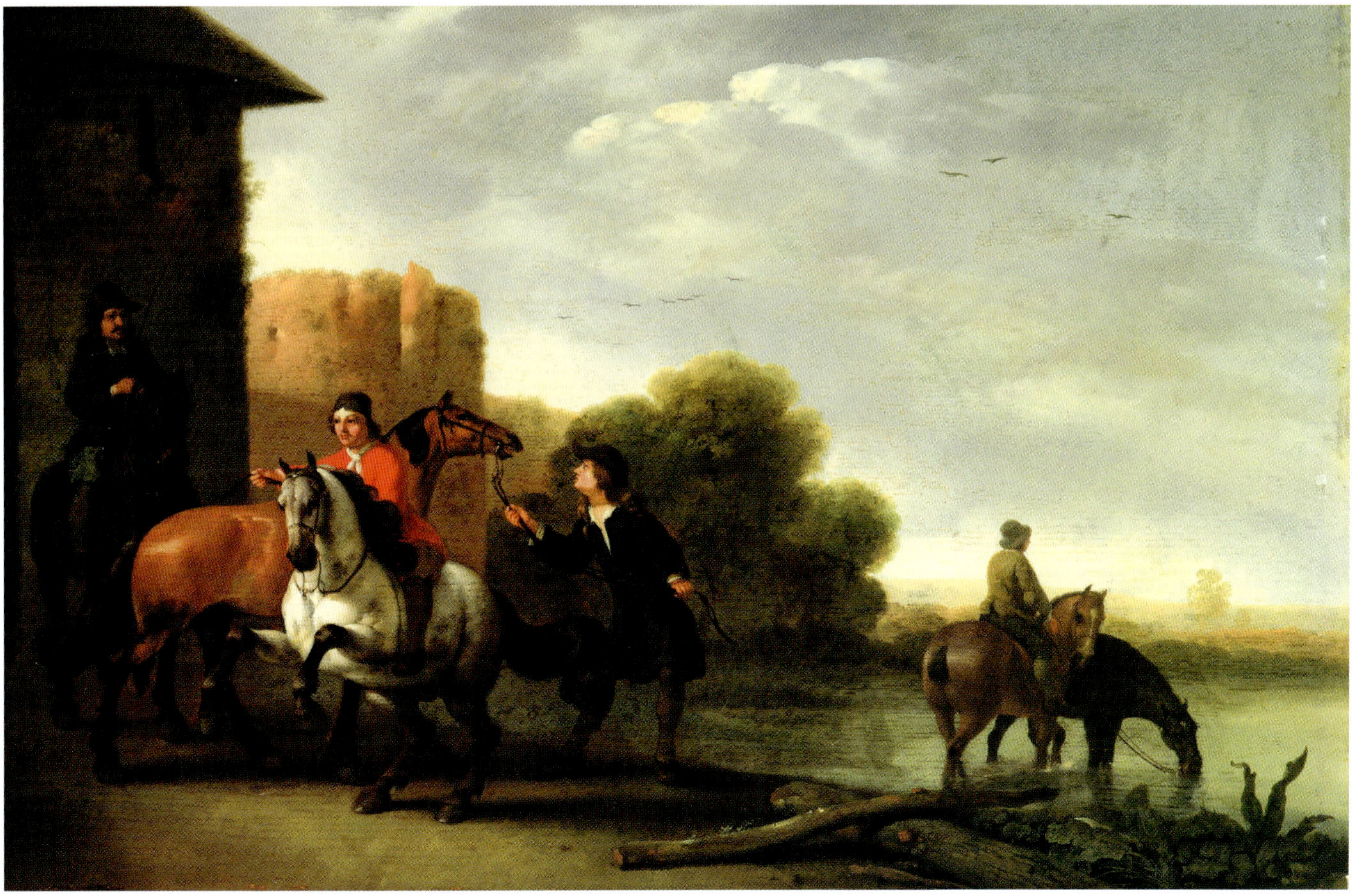

characterful, light-hearted or humorous and always realistic. During his early period, from approximately 1634 to 1640, he generally used a palette in which browns dominate, while during his middle period, approximately from 1640 to 1650, his palette was brighter and clearer; during his last period, from about 1650 onwards, he often featured scenes that amalgamated imaginary southern landscapes with the cooler

AELBERT CUYP

One of the leading landscape painters of the Dutch Golden Age and the most famous member of a family of painters, Aelbert Cuyp (1620–91) lived and worked in Dordrecht, and became especially known for his large landscapes of tranquil Dutch countryside bathed in atmospheric early morning or late afternoon light.

Aelbert Cuyp's uncle and grandfather were stained-glass designers and his father was the portrait and landscape painter Jacob Gerritsz Cuyp. As his influence is visible in both the style and subject matter of several of Aelbert's works, Jacob probably first taught his son to paint.

EXTERNAL INFLUENCES

Little is known about Cuyp's life in detail. His period of activity as a painter is usually considered to be the years between 1639 and 1665 and he remained in Dordrecht throughout his life, although he travelled around the Netherlands sketching for paintings. As well as with his father, Cuyp may have studied under Jan van Goyen, as his early style has much in common with van Goyen's approach. Some of his later

Below: A mix of seascape and history painting, this is The Maas at Dordrecht, *painted by Cuyp in c.1650, depicting a large Dutch transport fleet carrying soldiers and their equipment, a scene that occurred in 1646.*

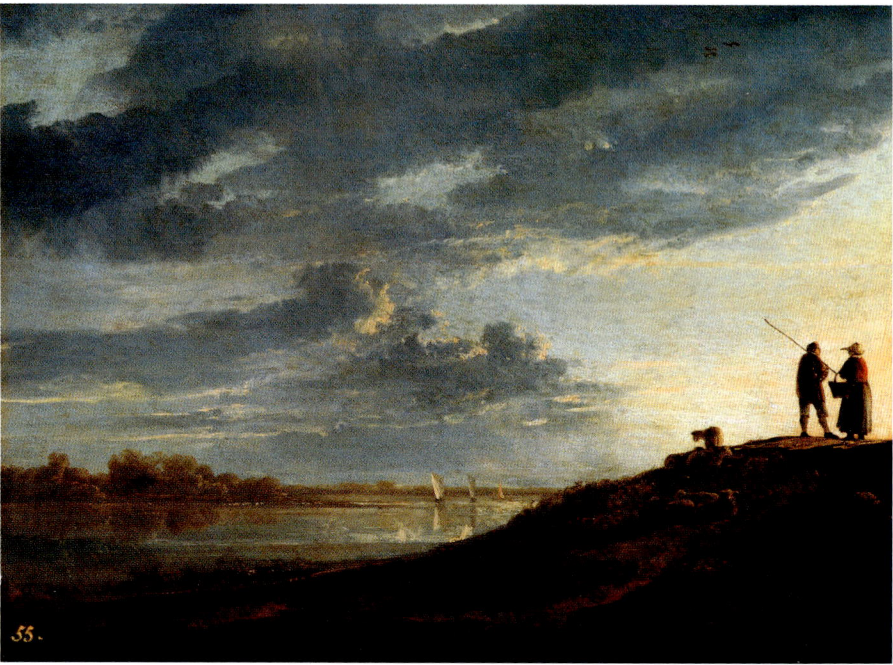

Above: Painted on a calm summer evening in the 1650s, Cuyp depicted Sunset over the River, *using a limited palette and a dramatic composition.*

paintings also show a strong influence of the painter Jan Both who spent time in Rome but was based mainly in Utrecht. In 1637 or 1638, Jan Both had stayed in Rome where he collaborated with and became influenced by the French landscapist Claude Lorrain

(c.1604–82). Lorrain's indirect influence in his rendition of light and Italian-style elements can be distinguished in many of Cuyp's river scenes.

THREE STYLISTIC PHASES

Cuyp's landscapes were based both on reality and scenes of his own invention. Although always finely painted and atmospheric, his painting style seems to have evolved through three phases. Until the early 1640s, in his first phase, he produced small-scale, precisely painted landscapes featuring cattle and figures, executed with firm brushwork and recalling the style and methods of van Goyen. He also began using a similar palette to van Goyen, including more ochres, and adopted van Goyen's broken brush technique, using short brushstrokes and barely blending colours.

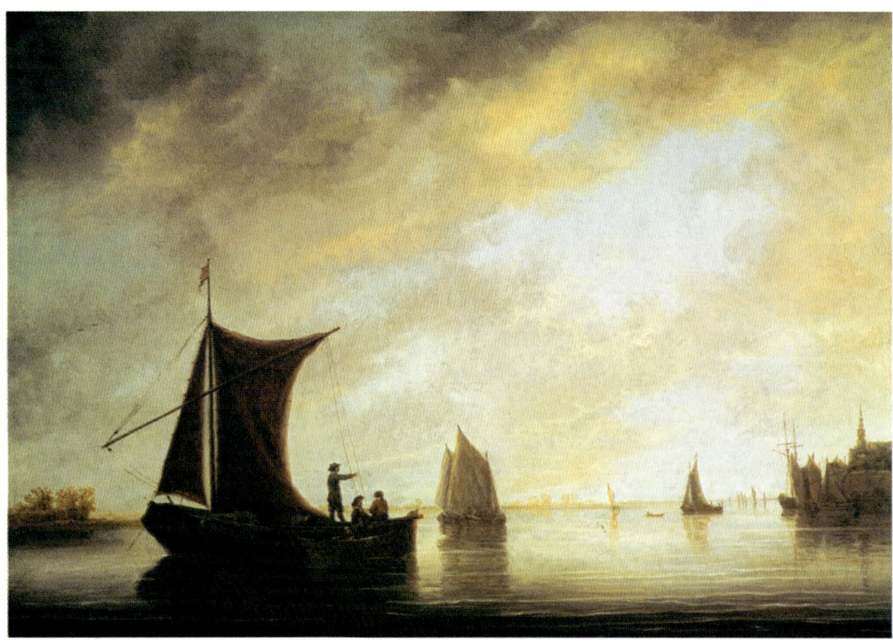

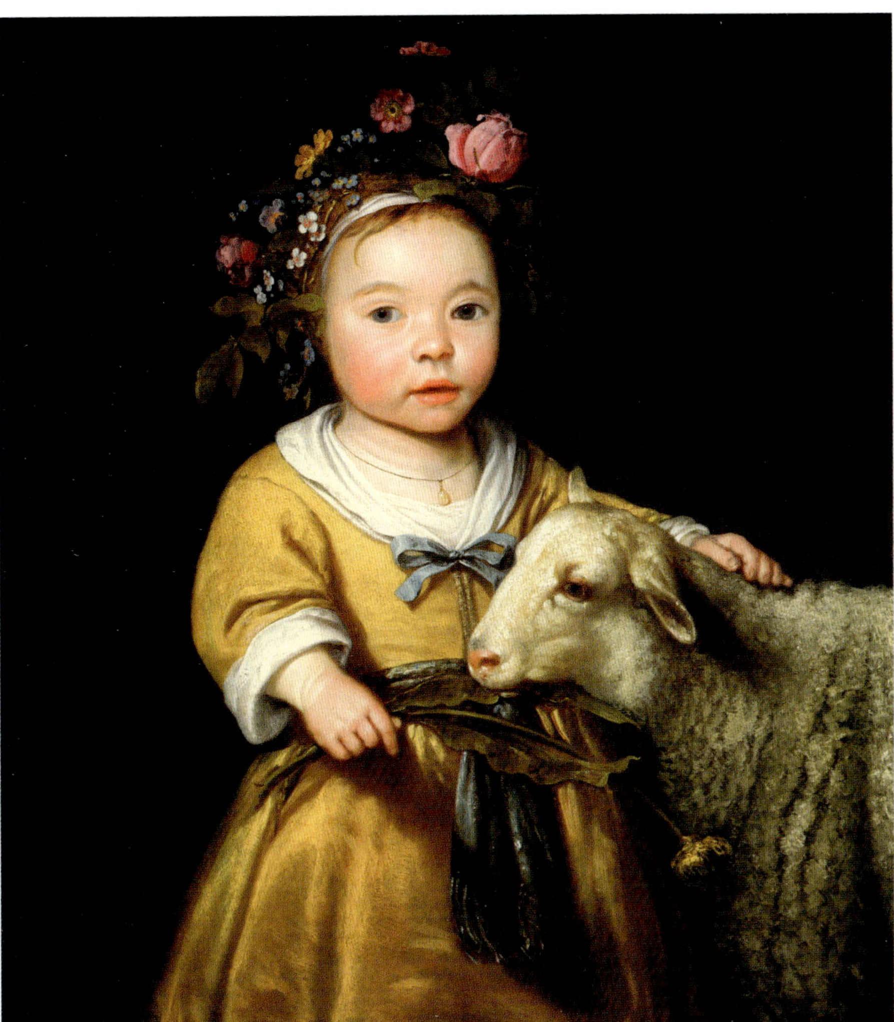

Above: An unusual digression from his usual landscapes and water scenes, Cuyp here paints a little girl and a sheep. The painting, of 1655, is entitled Flora *and shows his detailed brushwork.*

In the mid-1640s, after Jan Both had returned to Utrecht from Rome, Cuyp's style changed to his second phase, adopting Both's back-lit landscapes. Contrasting with traditionally side-lit landscapes, this new viewpoint created a sense of drama, shadows and silhouette.

By the late 1640s, Cuyp moved into his third stylistic phase, painting serene views of the Maas and Waal near Dordrecht, featuring ships on calm, still water; resting cattle silhouetted against evening skies, highlighted with small touches of pale gold; and landscapes featuring groups of horsemen or peasants, all bathed in subtly glowing light. This third phase shows his father's influence, and as they often worked in collaboration, it is not always clear which elements were painted by which Cuyp. However, Aelbert began depicting distinctive, large-scale elements in his work, often including animals as the focus, and with highlights of pale gold. All his paintings are hazy and atmospheric, with colourful figures standing out crisply, and his drawings are skilfully created with washes of golden brown ink.

CONTENTIOUS SIGNATURES

It is difficult to attribute many of Cuyp's paintings as it is not clear which were collaborations with his father, nor which were painted by his follower Abraham van Calraet (1642–1722), who closely emulated Cuyp's style. Although Cuyp signed many of his paintings, he did not sign or date them all. A signature that resembles Cuyp's was added later to some works, possibly by their owners, and some are merely initialled 'A. C.,' which suggest that the work may have been completed by one of his assistants; the initials could indicate Cuyp's approval but not necessarily that he had a hand in the production.

RETIREMENT

By 1654, after his parents died, Cuyp came into property. Soon after, he married Cornelia Boschman (1617–87), a wealthy widow with three children, with whom he had one daughter. By 1665, he stopped painting as he served in administrative and ecclesiastical posts, eventually becoming a deacon and elder of the Reformed Church.

Below: A Herdsman with Five Cows. Probably painted in the 1650s, this scene glows from the left by a warm low sun that glitters on the water.

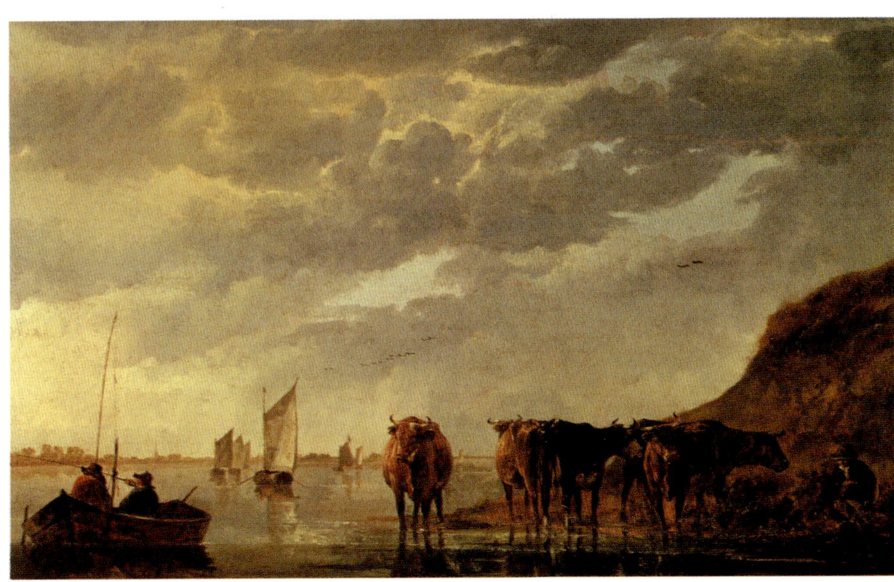

FABRITIUS • VAN HOOGSTRATEN

Carel Fabritius (1622–1654) was one of the most significant and successful of Rembrandt's pupils, who went on to develop his own personal artistic style, experimenting with perspective and lighting. Samuel van Hoogstraten (1627–1678) was also a pupil of Rembrandt who developed a distinctively individual approach.

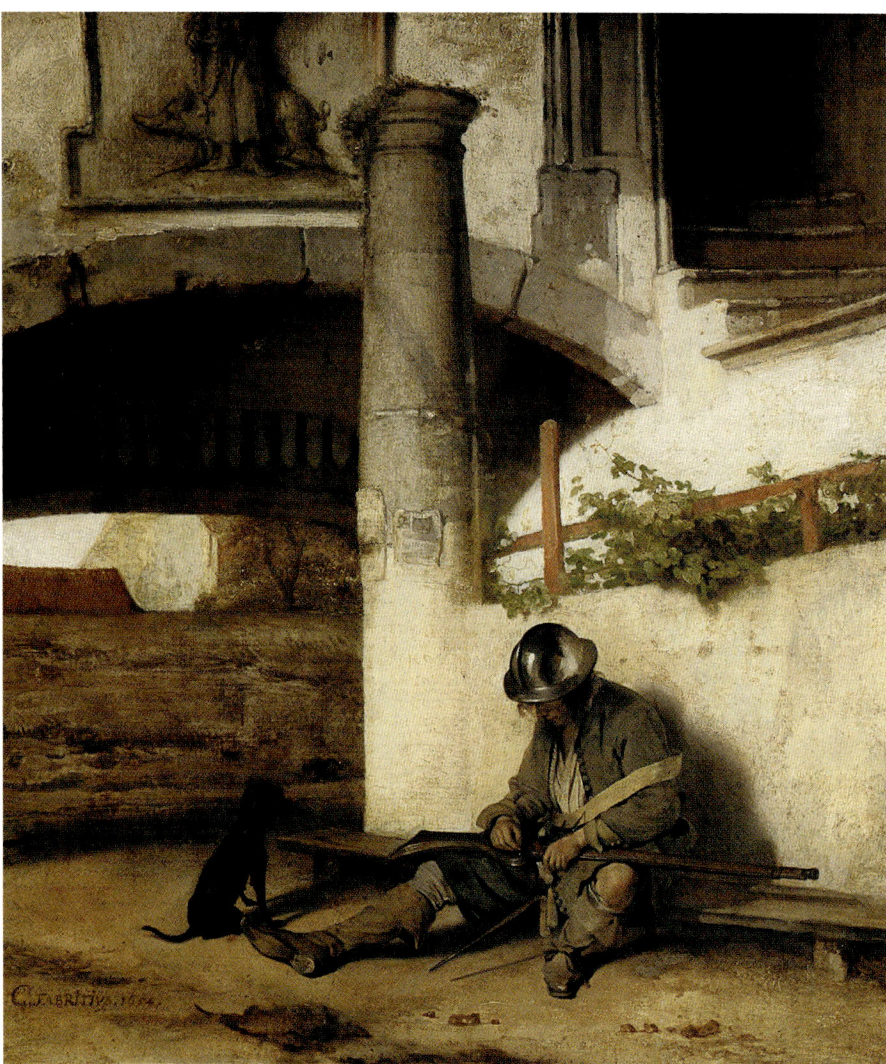

In 1641, Fabritius married, but sadly, his wife died two years later. He moved back in with his parents in Middenbeemster. In 1650 he married again and moved to Delft. Once there, he joined the Delft Guild of Saint Luke and established his own studio. He was probably working in his studio in October 1654 when a gunpowder magazine exploded. Over 100 people were killed, thousands were wounded and approximately a quarter of the city was destroyed. Fabritius, who was only 32 years old, was among the dead. The explosion – later called The Delft Thunderclap (or the Delft Donderslag) destroyed his studio and many paintings.

Left: The Sentry, c.1654, by Fabritius. In a quiet corner of a street, a sentry has fallen asleep while on duty; dog watches him with the attention he should be showing.

Below: One of the most renowned of the few works left by Fabritius, painted in 1654, The Goldfinch conveys sharp realism, similar to trompe l'oeil.

CAREL PIETERSZ FABRITIUS

Not much is known about Fabritius's life. Sons of a schoolmaster, sexton and part-time painter, Carel and his brother Barent (1624–73) were both painters. They probably grew up in Middenbeemster, a village just north of Amsterdam. In the early 1640s, Fabritius studied in Rembrandt's Amsterdam studio. Fabritius initially worked as a carpenter, then changed to study painting and from the start used brushwork to show different textures, tones and nuances of light. Although influenced by Rembrandt, contrastingly he often painted delicately lit subjects set against light, textured backgrounds. Particularly interested in the technical aspects of painting, he used cool colour harmonies, complex spatial effects and exaggerated perspective. He became especially admired for his illusionistic architectural views.

Although only about a dozen paintings by Fabritius survive, they show great dexterity. He developed his own personal style showing sensitivity towards colour and tonal contrasts, combining thin glazes with areas of impasto to create depth and texture.

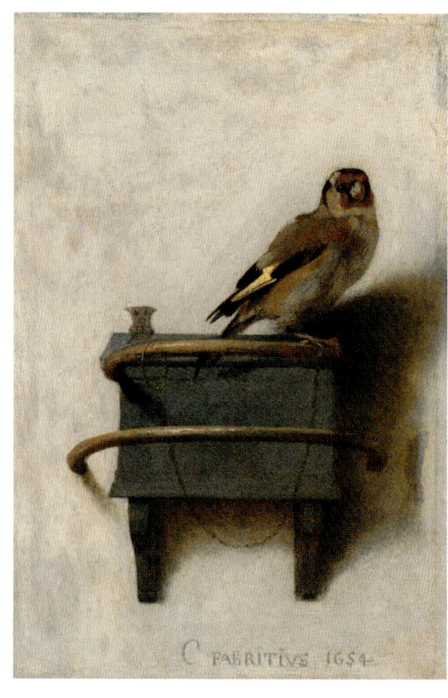

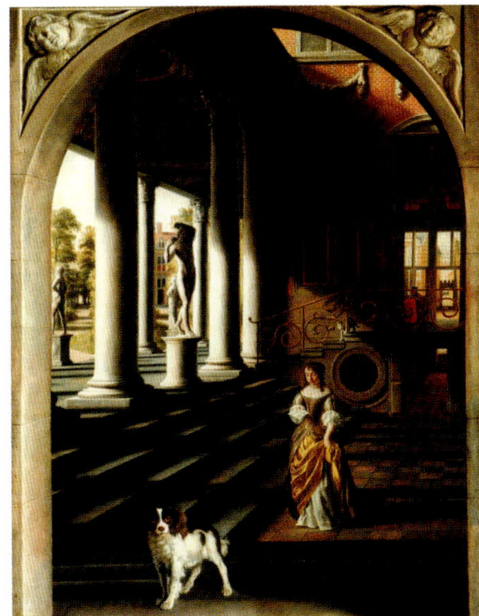

Above: Perspective View with a Woman Reading a Letter, *c.1670. Van Hoogstraten was best known for his peep boxes and architectural interiors that emphasize perspective.*

Right:: The Beheading of John the Baptist *is an early work by Fabritius, painted in c.1648. The drama and naturalism of Rembrandt's influence is apparent.*

SAMUEL VAN HOOGSTRATEN

Van Hoogstraten lived in Vienna, Rome and London, but returned to settle in his native town of Dordrecht. He first trained in Dordrecht with his father Dirk van Hoogstraten (1596–1640), but when his father died, Samuel moved to Amsterdam and entered Rembrandt's studio. There he befriended Fabritius. Over his career, van Hoogstraten worked in different styles, including emulating Rembrandt, painting architectural interiors and, from 1654, detailed trompe-l'oeil still lifes, or 'cheaters' as they were called. Fascinated by perspective, he created several 'perspective boxes', also called peep boxes or 'peep shows'. Acknowledged as one of the great advocators of Dutch Realism, he used strong contrasts of light and dark like Rembrandt, but unlike Rembrandt, small, precise brushmarks and sharp details. He also produced etchings and wrote poetry and in 1678, published his treatise: *Introduction to the Advanced School of Painting: The Visible World.*

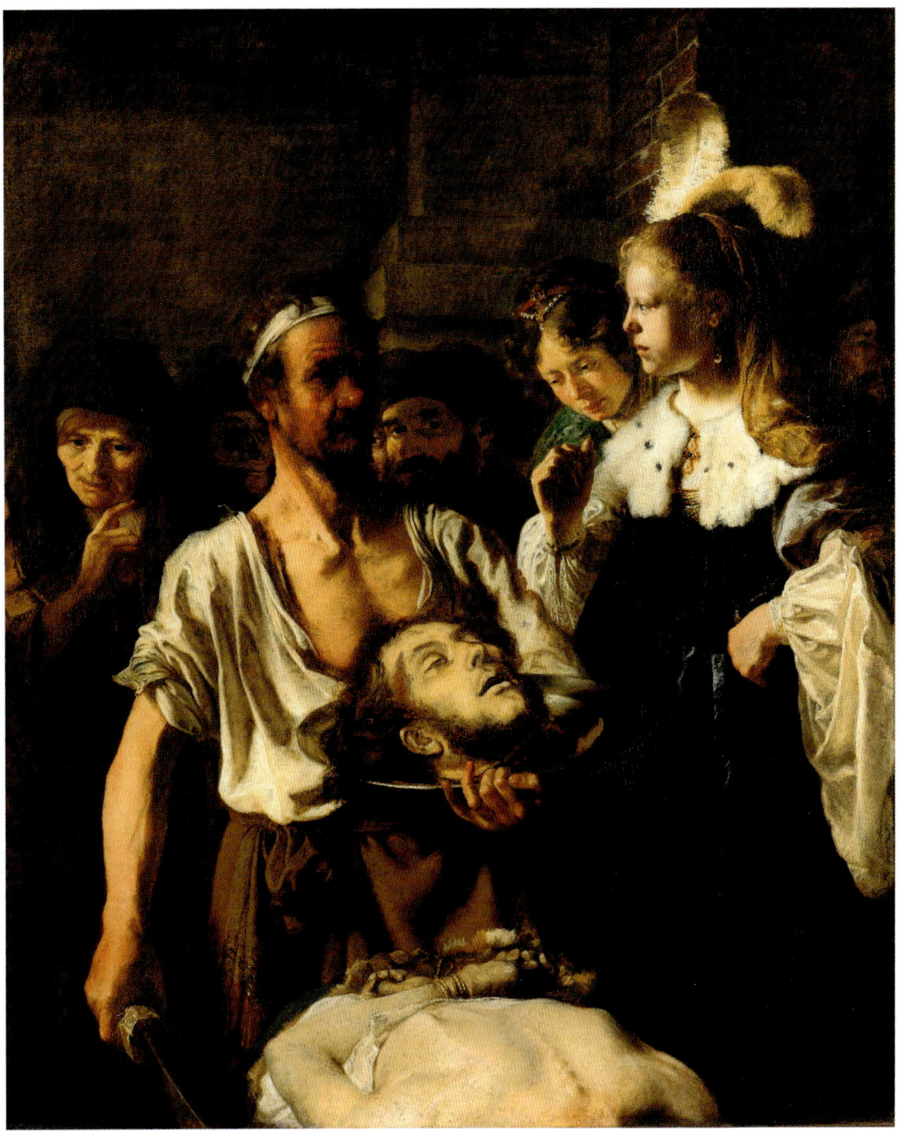

TROMPE L'OEIL

Trompe l'oeil translates as 'fool the eye' and the term was first used in the 17th century, even though ancient Roman artists had created illusions of reality centuries earlier. By the medieval and later Renaissance periods, artists were often employed to create realistic-looking columns or other architectural elements inside churches, and once the application of linear perspective had been mastered, these illusions became more convincing. Donato Bramante (1444–1514), for instance, was commissioned to create an illusion of space inside the Santa Maria presso San Satiro in Milan. He painted a false apse, making the church appear far larger than it really is.

The Venetian painters Vittorio Carpaccio (1460–1525) and Jacopo de Barbari (c.1440–1516) began including small trompe-l'oeil features in their paintings, and by the High Renaissance, this type of painted illusion became even more popular. In the 17th century, Caravaggio, the hero of many Dutch Golden Age painters, was highly accomplished at illusionistic painting, and painters of the Dutch Golden Age expanded on the tradition with trompe l'oeil reaching new heights of illusionism. For instance, van Hoogstraten and Evert Collier (1640–1708) were noted for their incredibly lifelike paintings of letter racks (see pages 252 and 253 for examples).

PAULUS POTTER

Paulus Potter, or Paulus Pieterszoon Potter (1625–54) became celebrated for his lifelike renditions of animals that he incorporated in his paintings. These animals are usually depicted on their own or in groups, often silhouetted against the sky and often in landscapes that also include peasants and rural buildings.

Potter came from a family of artists. His father, Pieter Simonsz Potter (c.1600–52), was a painter and so was his uncle Willem Bartsius (c.1612–after 1639). When he was six years old, the family moved from the city of Enkhuizen to Amsterdam, where Potter studied painting under his father and possibly also with the painters Claes (Nicolaes) Cornelisz Moeyaert and Jacob de Wet (1610–c.75). Showing a precocious talent, he created and dated his first highly competent painting when he was just 15. In 1646, the family was living in Delft, and Potter joined the Delft Guild of Saint Luke, but by 1649, he had moved to The Hague. The following year, he married the daughter of a city architect and the couple rented a house owned by Jan van Goyen. During that time, Potter began receiving prestigious commissions from the widow of the Prince of Orange, Amalia of Solms-Braunfels (1602–75). However, it seems that he did not fulfil all his commitments, as in 1651 he was sued by the royal court for failure to deliver a painting. By the spring of 1652, he returned to Amsterdam, persuaded by the surgeon professor Nicolaes Tulp (1593–1674) who had spotted Rembrandt's genius 20 years earlier, and who became his mentor. During the following year, Potter painted a life-sized equestrian portrait of Tulp's son, Dirck Tulp (1624–82).

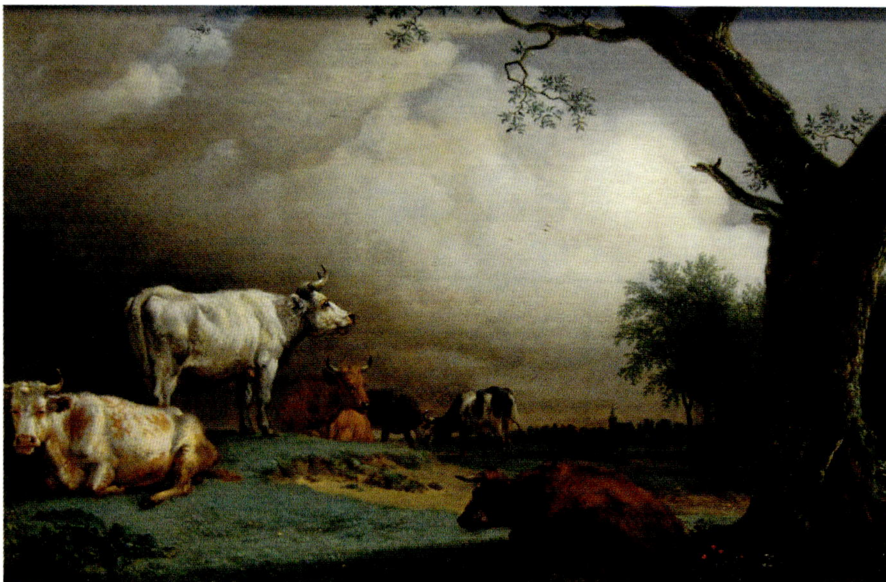

Above: Painted in 1652, Cattle in a Field also includes travellers in a wagon and a church tower in the distance, with a rain storm approaching.

Below: Commissioned by Princess Amalia van Solms, The Farmyard *features cows, goats, chickens and horses, illuminated by sunlight through the trees.*

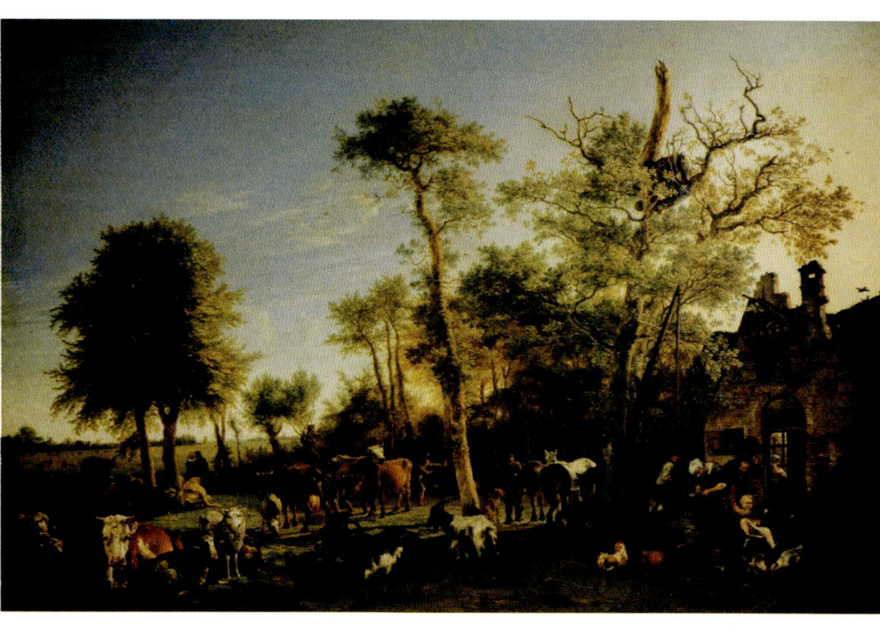

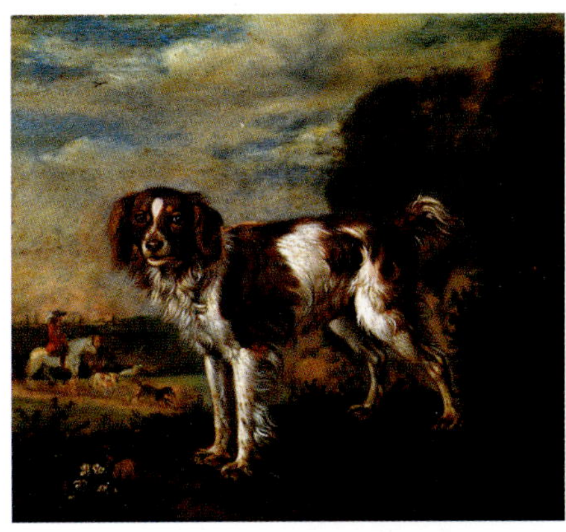

Above: A Spaniel, c.1653. *Rendering the fur with sweeping, feather-light brushstrokes, Potter painted this spaniel with the dog's owner in the distance.*

Right: Punishment of a Hunter (detail) *shows the triumph of justice over the human who killed animals without penalty.*

Below: Proud and noble, The Piebald Horse *is set against darkening, gathering clouds, its head alert.*

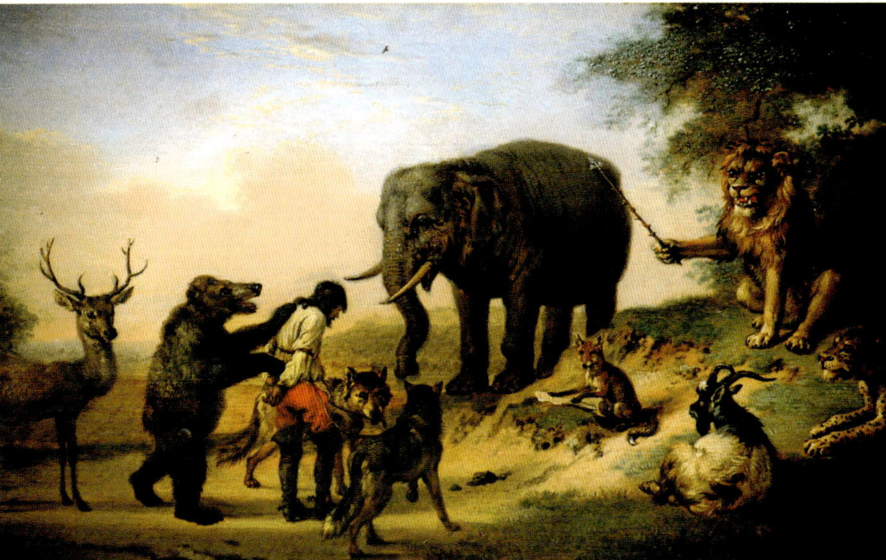

ANIMALS AND WEATHER

Although Potter died at just 28 from tuberculosis, his paintings and etchings were original and influential. His wife recalled that he often sketched in the countryside around The Hague, capturing farm animals at various times of day and in different weather conditions. From the start of his career he gave the animals prominence, depicting them as subjects in their own right rather than in the background as other artists did. Even in his relatively small paintings, he became an expert in creating compelling compositions, grouping forms and using silhouettes in dramatic ways, and being particularly sensitive towards animals' characteristics, movements and behaviour. Potter was also one of the first Dutch artists to paint inclement weather rather than calm, still conditions. In some of his paintings, winds batter trees, while dark clouds gather menacingly, and animals are silhouetted against bright breaks in the sky. An example of this can be seen in *The Piebald* (left), where in scrupulous detail, a grey spotted horse stands alert and striking against stormy, darkening clouds. These closely observed compositions had a great impact on the development of Dutch animal and landscape painting, as well as reflecting the importance of animals in the Netherlands at the time.

He had no documented pupils, but Potter may have taught and certainly influenced Karel Dujardin; although Dujardin is also described as a Bamboccianti (see page 70), several of his landscapes resemble Potter's. Additionally, along with Wouwerman, Potter seems to have influenced the Amsterdam painter Adriaen van de Velde (see pages 58–59).

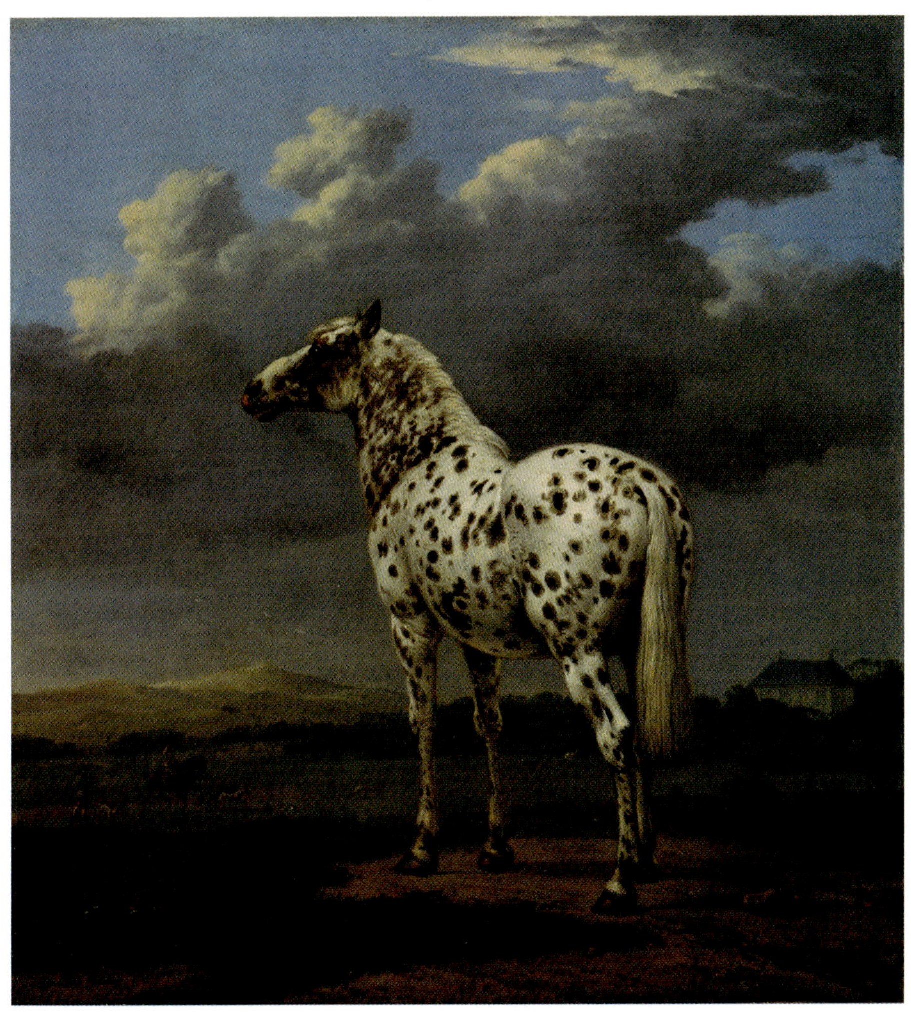

JAN STEEN

One of the most famous painters of the 17th century, Jan Havicksz Steen (*c*.1626–79) mainly painted genre scenes, often of interiors with people, showing aspects of life that were widely admired for their psychological insights. Steen became famous for his skilful brushwork, allusions to proverbs – and wit.

The eldest son of a wealthy Catholic couple, Jan Steen was born in Leiden. His father worked in the family-owned brewery, the Red Halberd, and his paternal uncle, Pieter Dircksz Steen (1561–after 1593) was a painter and goldsmith. At the age of 20, Steen enrolled at the University of Leiden and two years later, with Gabriel Metsu and some other local painters, he helped to found the Leiden Guild of Saint Luke. It is probable that he was taught by the historical painter Nicolaus Knupfer (*c*.1603–55) in Utrecht, Adriaen van Ostade in Haarlem, and Jan van Goyen in The Hague. In 1649, he became van Goyen's assistant, and lived in van Goyen's house in The Hague. In that

Below: Peasant Family at Meal Time, *c.1665 – a little girl on the right of the table is saying grace while her mother prepares a meal.*

same year, he married van Goyen's daughter Margriet (or Margaret) Grietje Jans van Goyen (*c*.1624–69), with whom he had eight children.

DELFT THEN HAARLEM
Steen worked with his father-in-law until 1654 when he moved to Delft. That was the year of the Delft Thunderclap (see page 74), which caused deaths, destruction – and economic depression. Steen nonetheless remained in Delft for two years, running a brewery called De Roscam (The Curry Comb) or De Slang (The Snake). Unfortunately, both the art market and the brewing industry were suffering in the financial climate, and Steen was soon in serious financial difficulties. Van Goyen died in 1656, leaving his estate heavily in debt after he had lost money in the tulip market crash in 1637. This added to Steen's financial straits.

That year, 1637, Steen and his family moved to Warmond, a village in the western Netherlands. From 1661–70 they lived in Haarlem, where Steen joined the Haarlem Guild of Saint Luke and after adopting some of the methods of the Haarlem school of painting, he produced some of his most accomplished works.

Contrasting with many of his friends and fellow citizens, Steen remained a Catholic all his life, which influenced some of the religious content of several of his paintings.

ASTUTE OBSERVER
Steen became known for his rendering of intricate details, complex

Below: Grace Before Meat, *painted in the 1660s. Steen's sharp gaze and skilful painting style conveyed the comic side of family life.*

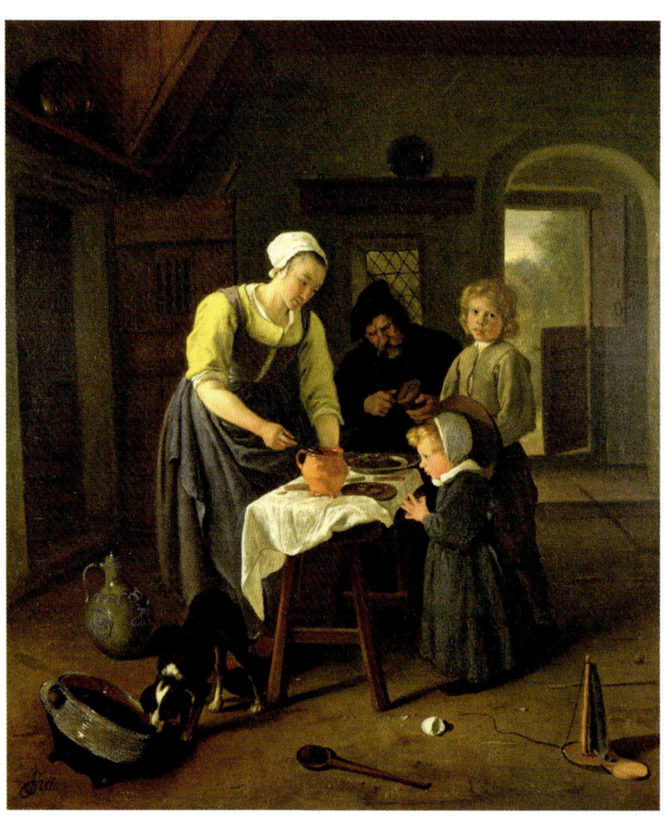

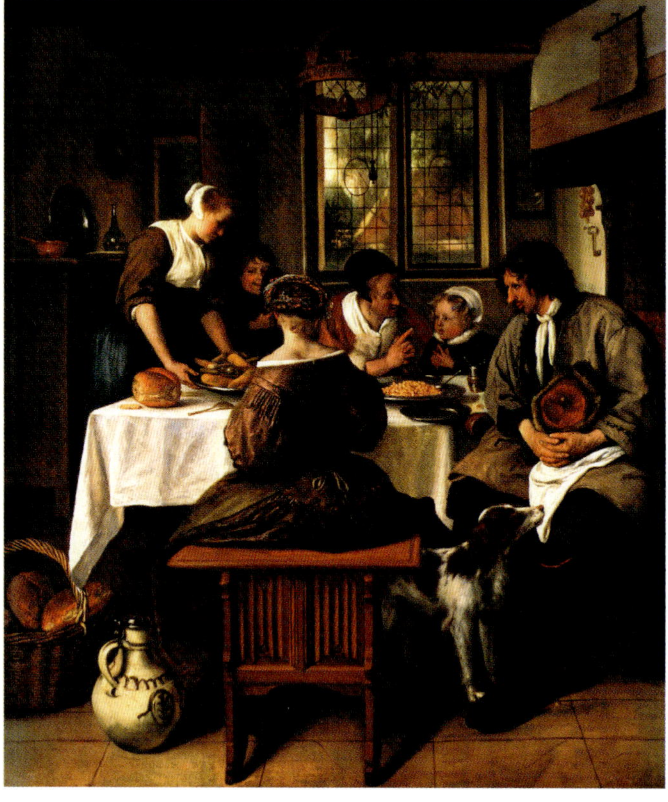

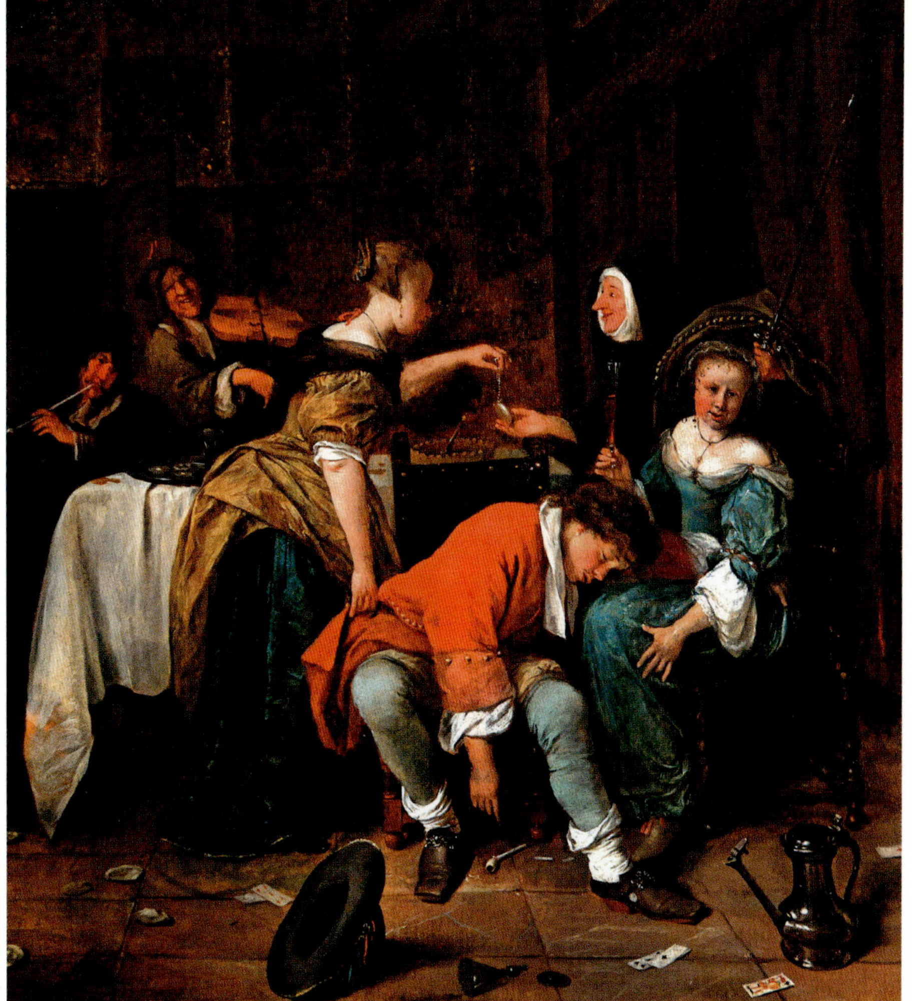

Above: The Bad Company. *A drunken man reaches to pick up his pipe from the floor, while on either side of him, prostitutes pick his pockets.*

REDERIJKERSKAMERS

Modelled on contemporary French dramatic societies, the Dutch Rederijkerskamers (see also page 47) had individual names, slogans and emblems, and were run like guilds or confraternities. Rederijkers met regularly to rehearse plays, read poetry, and discuss current political and religious ideas. On market days, public holidays and other festivals, they staged performances for the public, and as well as holding regular meetings and providing entertainment for all, they looked after each other, for instance attending members' funerals and holding collections for sick or poor members. Steen's uncle belonged to the Leiden Rederijkerskamer and Steen painted several scenes featuring Rederijkers, conveying them as ebullient, warm and earnest characters, with fun and positive outlooks on life.

Below: Revelry (Merrymaking) at an Inn, 1674 – *a large, ambitious painting showing Steen's combination of direct observation and fantasy to create jovial, vivacious and at times mocking scenes, but conveying a good-natured sense of the working classes drinking and enjoying life.*

compositions, rich colours and sense of humour conveyed through busy narratives. Paying particular attention to the minutiae of life, he presented the world as he observed it, with charm and without guile, presenting the faults and foibles of humanity amusingly, and allowing viewers to make up their own minds about what they saw. As well as genre subjects, he also painted portraits and a number of mythological, historical and religious works, especially during the 1660s and 1670s.

Steen's detailed still lifes and careful finish suggest that he probably had contact with the work of the Leiden fijnschilders and learned from their painstaking processes. On initial viewing, his genre paintings often appear to have been created simply for amusement, but within them are subtle warnings about human folly. Many of his paintings are large, complex scenes of families and merrymakers, often illustrating proverbs and other moral messages. Some exploit contemporary literature and popular theatre, depicting characters from both the Italian Commedia dell'Arte and the Dutch Rederijkerskamers.

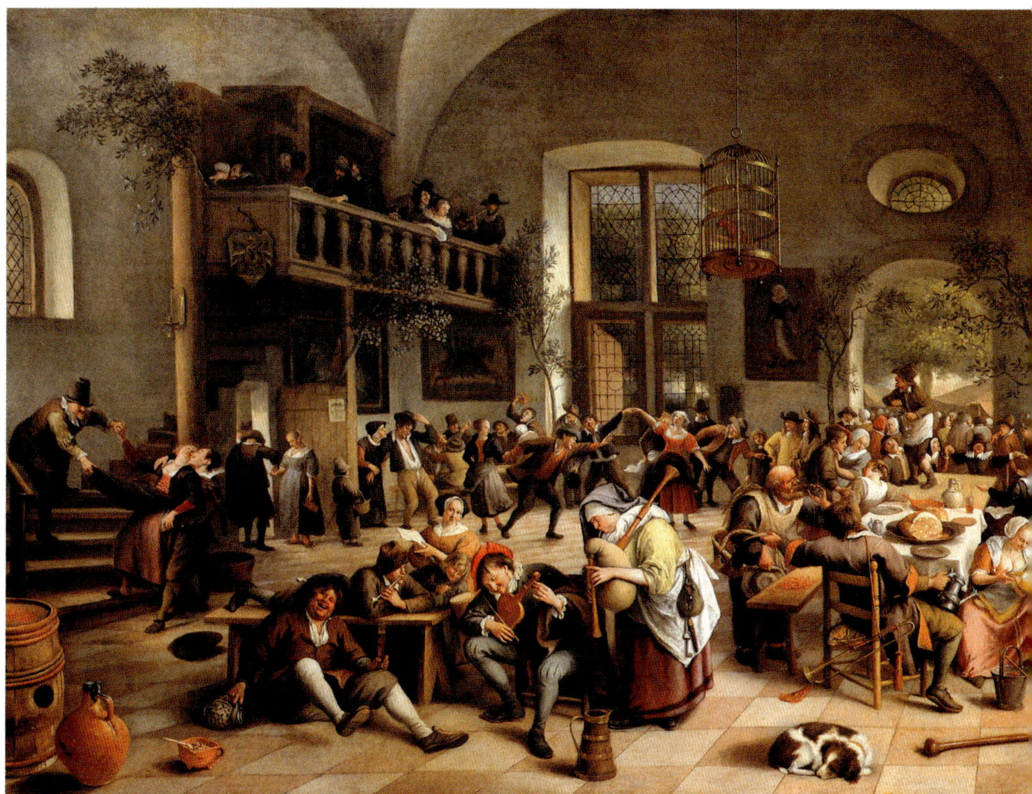

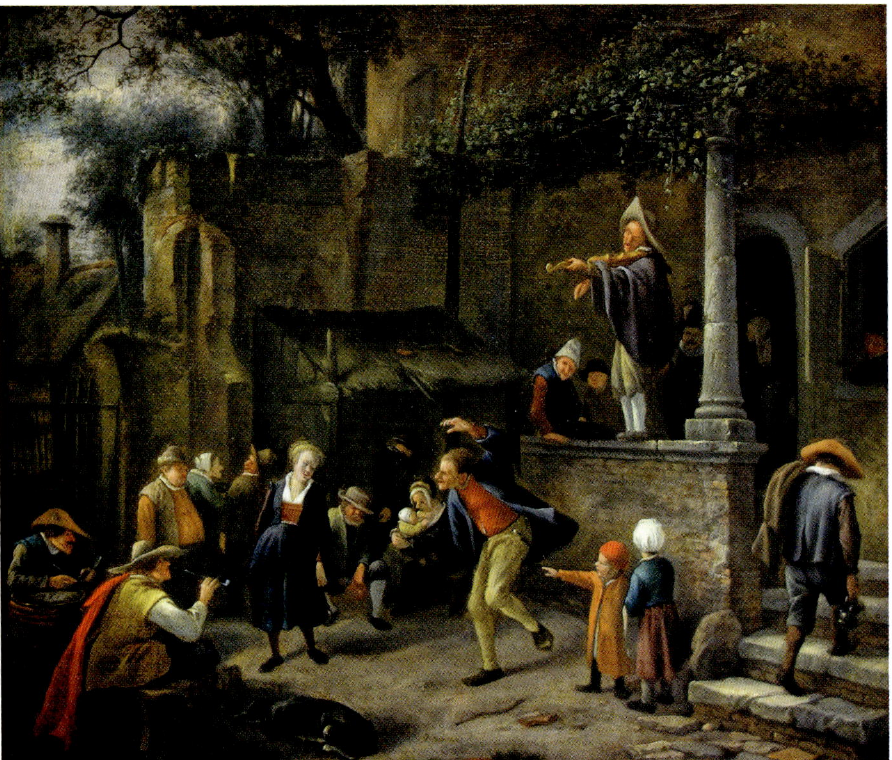

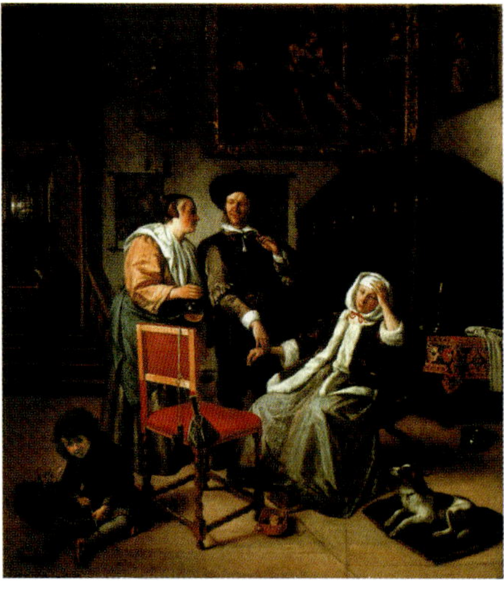

Above: The Doctor's Visit. *This young woman is lovesick. The doctor takes her pulse and looks at the maid, who holds a bottle of the patient's urine which will confirm that she is pregnant.*

Left: Steen produced many genre scenes with musical themes, including village festivals, weddings and dances. In The Village Fiddler, *a man on a wall plays the violin and a couple improvises a dance.*

RETURN TO LEIDEN

Steen moved back to Leiden in 1670, after the death of his wife and then his father. Now an established and respected artist, he rejoined the painters' guild. He was appointed headman three times and then dean of the guild, but these positions were unpaid and his financial problems continued. The year 1672 was named the Rampjaar, or Year of Disaster, when a number of disastrous events occurred. Among other things, the art market became particularly depressed. Few had money to spend on art then or for several years after, so alongside painting, Steen followed his father's career and in 1672, he became licensed as a tavern keeper and opened an inn called The Peace (De Vreede). From that time in particular, his paintings began including drunken figures, showing evidence of the consequences of drinking too much. Although it was reported that Steen often drank at his inn with good friends such as Frans van Mieris the Elder, there is no definitive proof that he was a drunkard as has often been suggested. Nonetheless, his paintings suggest that he was comfortable with the effects of drinking alcohol, conveying that it was a weakness but not a sin, and his frequent incorporation of people merrymaking at inns probably reflects his own background as an innkeeper and the son of a brewer.

In April 1673, Steen married Maria van Egmond or Marije Herculens van Egmont (unknown–1687), with whom he had another child. The following year, he became president of the Guild of Saint Luke in Leiden that he had helped to found in 1648. At this time, he also became close friends with Frans van Mieris the Elder.

A PROLIFIC LEGACY

During his career, Steen produced over 800 paintings. Out of those, probably 350 have survived. His diligence, technical skills, handling of colour and talent for visual storytelling were his greatest assets, and his most popular works are his genre scenes of domestic uproar showing human follies that frequently illustrate the proverbs that he and his contemporaries loved, with no obtrusive moralizing. None of his interiors were idealized or romanticized, and the mess that he so often portrayed gave rise to a Dutch expression, 'een huishouden van Jan Steen' ('It's a Jan Steen household'), describing a chaotic and messy home that is nonetheless full of life.

Acutely observant, Steen studied people, their behaviour, their

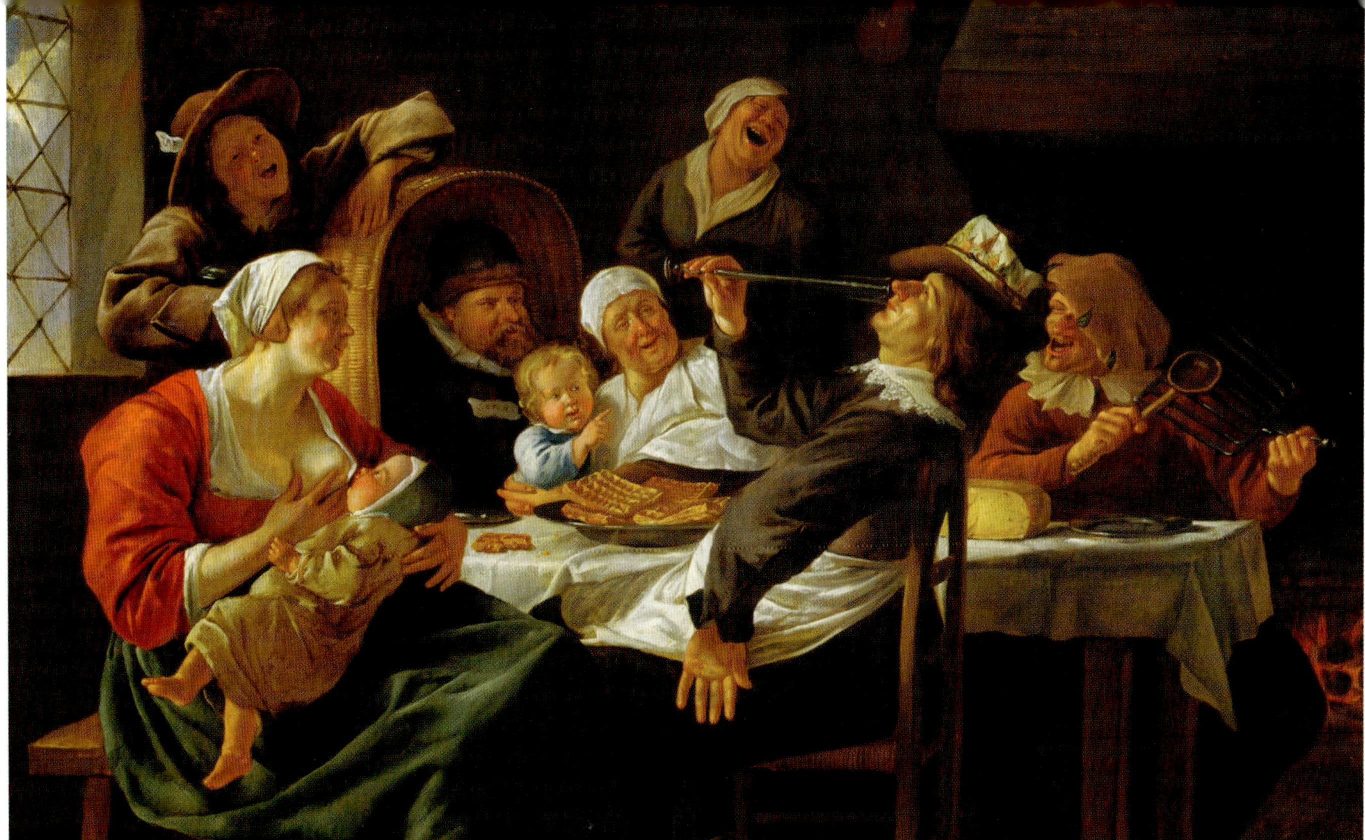

Above: Twelfth Night Feast. *Marking the start of Epiphany, Twelfth Night is observed on 6th January. In Holland the feast is known as Driekoningenaroud and here Steen depicts the jovial atmosphere of a Dutch family's celebrations.*

Below right: In The Merry Family, c.1668, *Steen paints a lively, noisy domestic scene. The father, mother and grandmother sing and the children either blow into a wind instrument or smoke a long pipe.*

Below: Skittle Players Outside an Inn. *Eating, drinking and playing skittles and bowls in country inns was a popular pastime, captured in Steen's painting.*

mannerisms and their relationships, from babies and children to young, middle-aged and older adults; he painted people of all types and backgrounds, conveying great insight and charm. Unaware of his gaze, the people are animated and natural, arguing, drinking, working, playing, eating, sleeping and more.

Steen is also well known for his mastery of light and attention to detail, most notably in Persian rugs and other textiles. He was a master at capturing subtleties of facial expression, especially in children. As time passed, Steen's figures became fewer, larger and more individually characterized. During his last years his depictions became increasingly elegant and less energetic. However, although his paintings were enjoyed and admired during his lifetime, they were not taken seriously and sold for relatively little. It was only in the 18th century and after, that Steen's reputation as an artist rose.

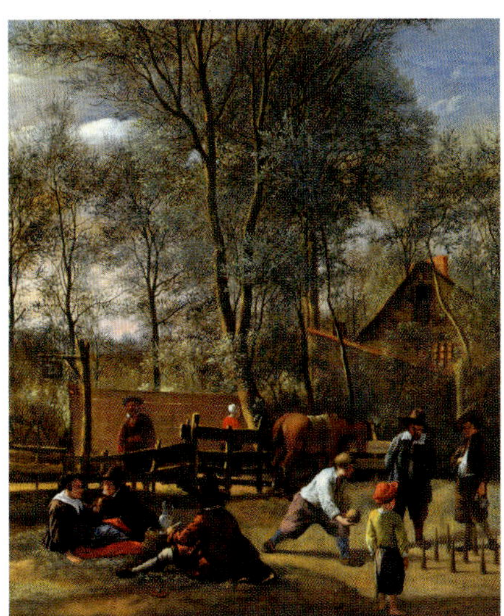

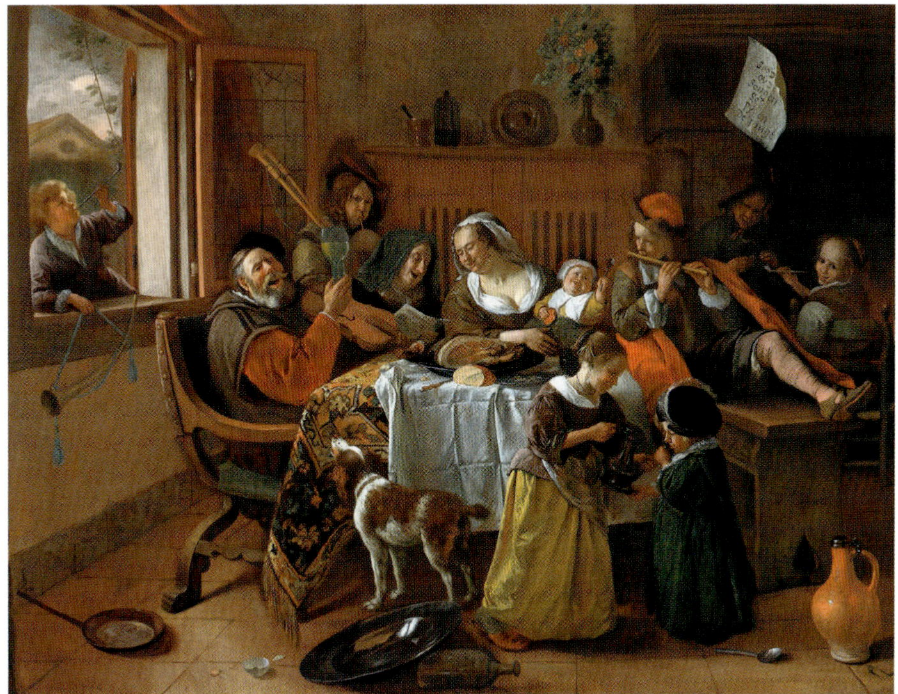

JAN VAN DE CAPPELLE

A painter of beach and estuary scenes, rivers and harbours, and landscapes bathed in early morning or evening light, Jan van de Cappelle (1626–79) painted lifelike cloud formations, ships, reflections and wintery scapes. He spent most of his time however, running his father's large and successful dyeing business.

Jan van de Cappelle lived in Amsterdam for the whole of his life. He only painted in between running his father's dye works that specialized in producing the expensive dye carmine and which he and his brother inherited in 1674. A wealthy man, he also owned several properties and was an avid art collector.

Although he did not rely on selling his paintings to earn a living, van de Cappelle is generally perceived as one of the most important 17th-century Dutch marine painters. Yet his education and artistic development are not clear. A contemporary wrote that he had 'learnt painting for his own pleasure.' It seems that he did not join Amsterdam's Guild of Saint Luke as most professional artists living there would have done, but he may have been involved with the separate 'brotherhood of painters' that was founded in Amsterdam in 1653. It is possible that he received some training from the marine painter Simon de Vlieger, as Vlieger's influence is apparent in his early paintings. For similar reasons, he also possibly had some tuition from

Below: An early work, A Small Vessel in Light Airs and Another Ashore *was painted in c.1650. The serene atmosphere is enhanced by the low viewpoint.*

an artist such as Willem van de Velde the Elder. However he learned his craft, because he was independently wealthy, he could please himself in terms of his choices of subject matter and the style of painting he used.

PAINTING LIGHT

With a passion for boats and sailing, van de Cappelle often sailed along local rivers and around the coast in his own boat, making sketches and drawings from different viewpoints. Most of his paintings feature low horizons, and his waterways are calm and smooth, reflecting clouds and ships. Vessels are often cut off at the edges of several of his paintings and only partially seen, which was innovative for the time. Although few of his paintings are dated, judging from the evolution of his style, the majority of his works seem to have been made between 1652 and 1654. A cool, muted palette dominates his early works, while after 1650, his colours became warmer, but all his paintings convey softly glowing luminous light.

Although he did not sign them all, van de Cappelle also made a small number of etchings. Overall, even without participating in the usual commercial art of the day, he exerted a considerable

influence on other painters, including Willem van de Velde the Younger, Jan van Kessel (1641–80) and Hendrick Dubbels (1621–1707).

FRIEND OF REMBRANDT

In February 1653, van de Cappelle married Annetje Jansdr Grotingh (c.1605–63) with whom he had seven children. That July, he received the prestigious honorary citizenship of Amsterdam. Friends with a large circle of artists, scholars and poets, he was the only person to have his portrait painted by both Rembrandt and Frans Hals, although both portraits have been lost. Additionally, he had portraits painted by Gerbrand van den Eeckhout (1621–74) and Jan van Noordt (1623–81), but they too are now lost. Probably Rembrandt's friend, he collected several of Rembrandt's drawings and paintings and it is likely that he used his business contacts to secure Rembrandt's last group portrait commission in 1662.

After his death, an inventory of van de Cappelle's art collection was made.

Below: A Small Dutch Vessel Before a Light Breeze. *The wind is apparent with the tilt of the two vessels. The shadowed foreground draws the eye in.*

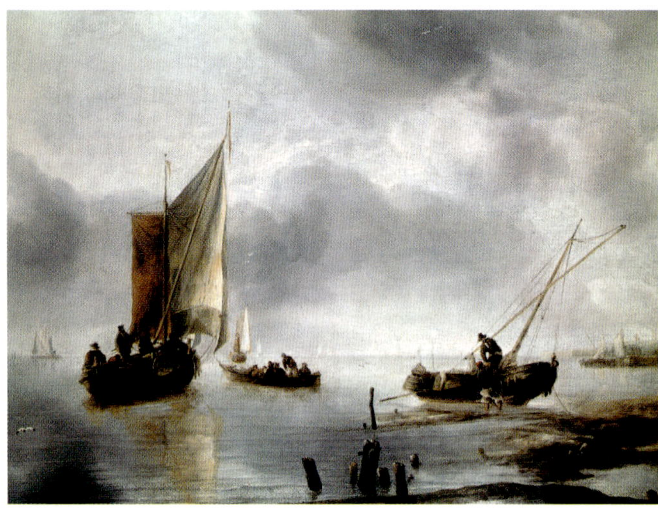

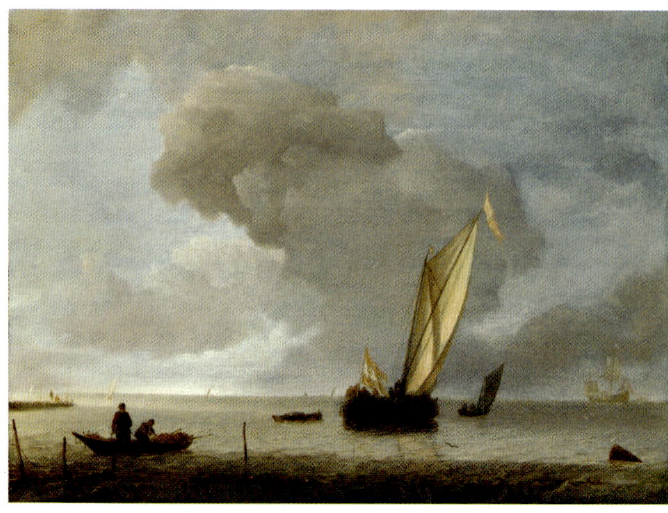

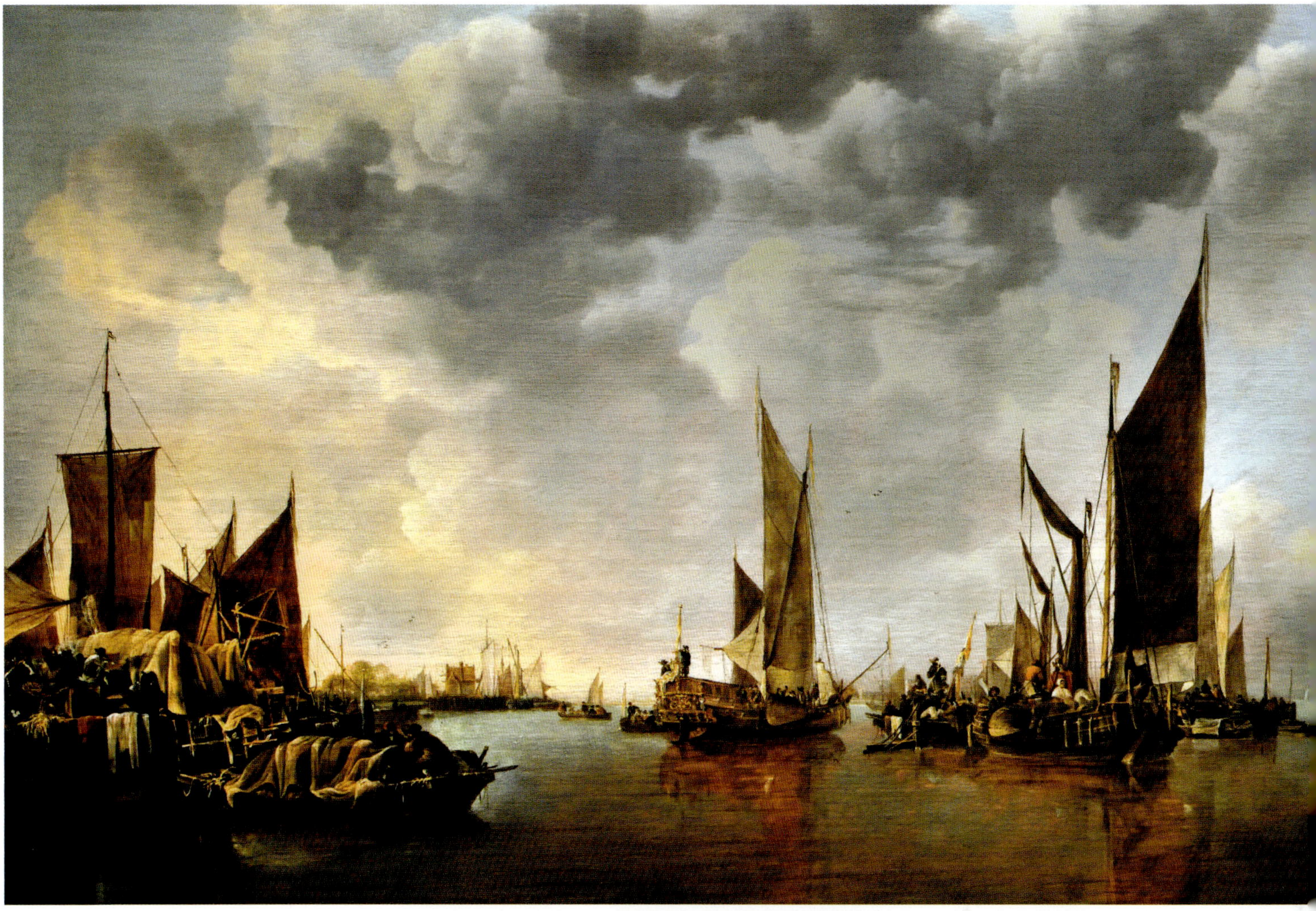

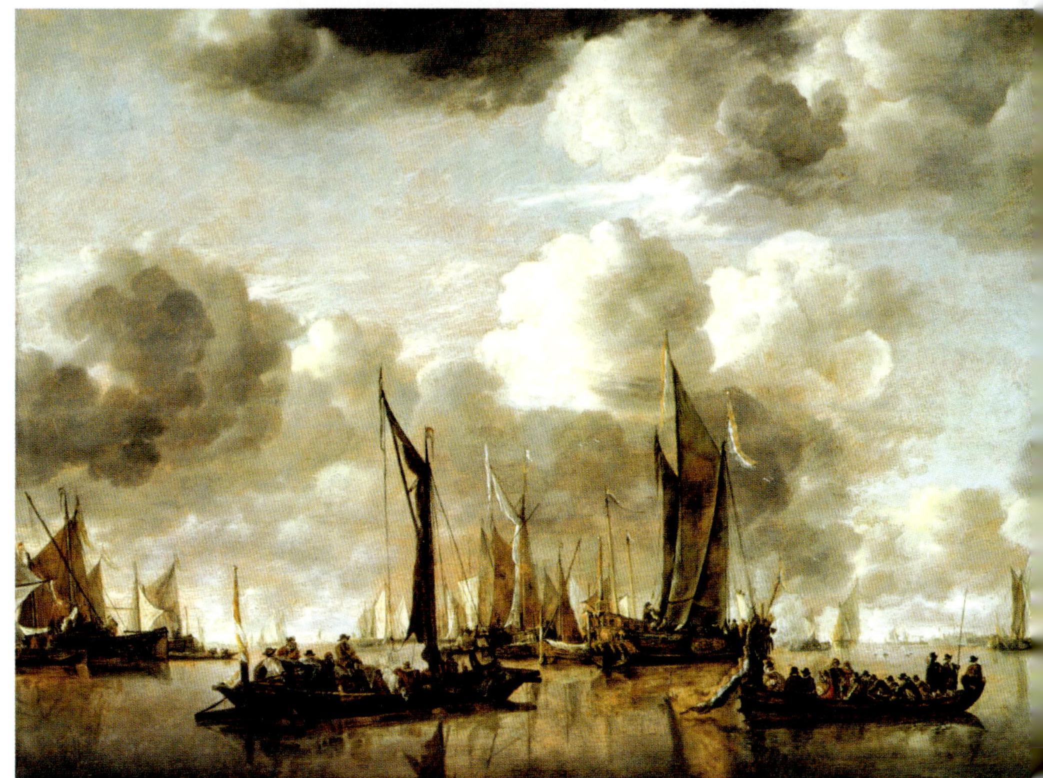

Above: A Shipping Scene with a Dutch Yacht firing a Salute, *1650; the pattern of the clouds complements the calm reflective water and grouping of vessels.*

Right: Illuminated from the back left, this Seascape with Ships *shows van de Cappelle's expertise with sea vessels and skill in portraying reflections and light.*

It was one of the largest of the time, listing 200 paintings and thousands of prints and drawings, including works by Hendrick Avercamp, Rembrandt, Simon de Vlieger, Frans Hals, Jan Lievens, Jan van Goyen, Adam Elsheimer and Rubens. He also left his children houses, a yacht and other bequests that together was valued at more than 90,000 guilders (equivalent now of approximately £4,795,549 or $6,159,218). Of his own drawings, almost 750 were listed in the inventory, but fewer than 20 of those have survived and been identified.

SALOMON AND JAN DE BRAY

Salomon de Bray (1597–1664) and his sons Jan (c.1627–97), Dirck (c.1635–94) and Joseph (1630–64) were all artists. Their surname is sometimes spelled 'de Braij'. Salomon was also a designer of silverwork, a poet, an architect and a town planner. Of his sons, Jan became the most celebrated.

SALOMON DE BRAY

Although born in Amsterdam, Salomon de Bray spent almost his entire life in Haarlem. He possibly studied drawing and painting with Jan Pynas (1582–1631), Claes (or Nicolaes) Cornelisz Moeyaert, and Pieter Lastman, and he served an apprenticeship with Cornelis van Haarlem (1562–1638) and Hendrick Goltzius (1558–1617). In 1630, he became a member of the Haarlem Guild of Saint Luke. Other concurrent members included Jan van Goyen, Salomon van Ruysdael, Willem Claeszoon Heda, Judith Leyster and Adriaen van Ostade.

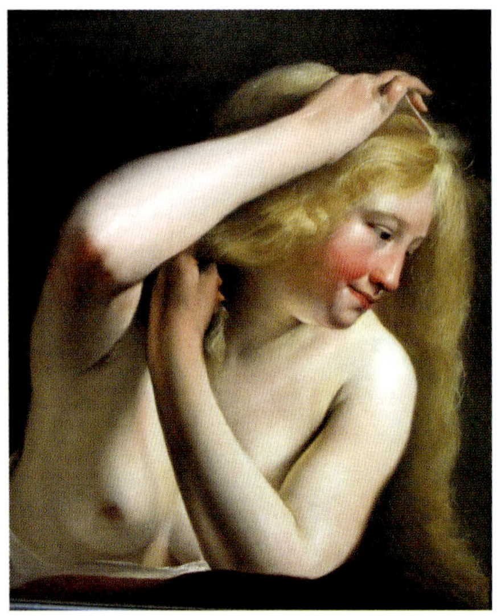

Above: Salomon de Bray's distinctive half-length figure, Young Woman Combing her Hair, painted in 1635, is vibrantly lit and shows an influence of Rembrandt's chiaroscuro.

As a poet, de Bray was also a member of the rhetoric chamber De Wijngaertrancken, which was probably where he met his wife Anna Westerbaen (c.1605–63), the sister of the painter Jan Westerbaen (1631–after 1669) and the poet Jacob Westerbaen (1599–1670), who were all also members of De Wijngaertrancken. Salomon also worked as an architect and was involved in several projects in Haarlem, including the Zijlpoort city gate, a castle in Warmond and an orphanage in Nijmegen.

As a Roman Catholic, as well as history paintings, portraits and

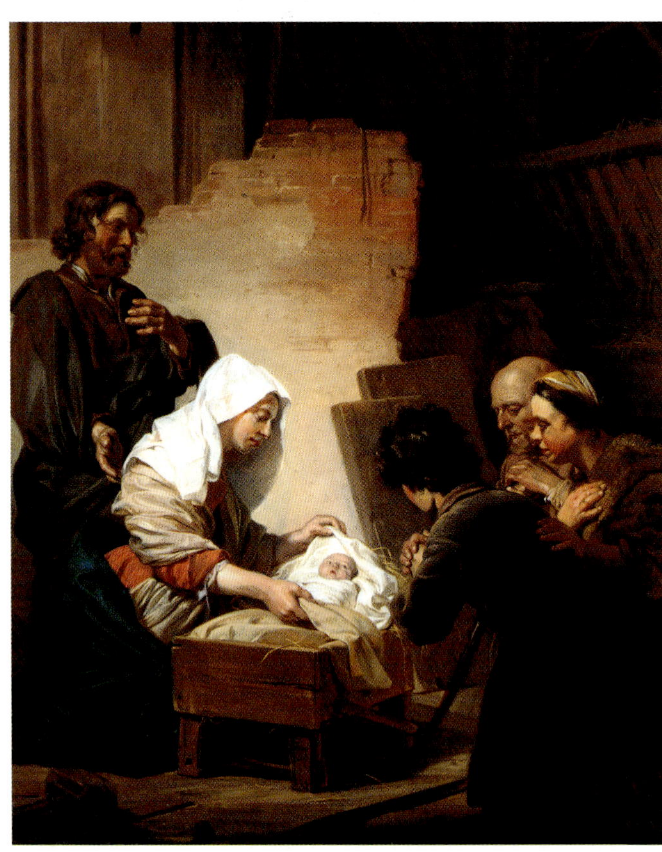

Below: The Adoration of the Shepherds, 1665. Jan de Bray uses warm light and muted colours to create an intimate atmosphere as three shepherds kneel to the newborn baby in the stable.

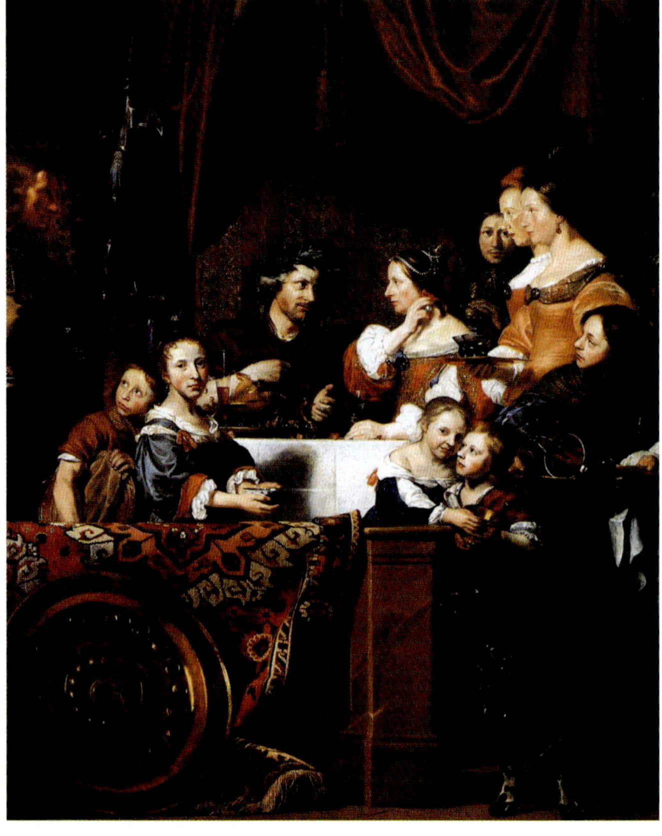

Below: In this portrait all members of the de Bray family participate in a legendary ancient banquet. The artist, Jan, is probably in shadowed profile on the left. His parents represent Antony and Cleopatra.

THE SCHUTTERIJ

In the Netherlands, the schutterij were a voluntary, defensive city guard set up to protect towns or cities from attack or other dangers. Members were called schuttersgilde, and each town or city used weapons of their choice, usually a bow, a crossbow or a gun. Schuttersgilde trained regularly and rose up the ranks according to individual prowess or length of membership. Each night, in shifts, two schuttersgildes guarded their district, also closing and opening the city gates. Members of the Haarlem schutterij had to buy their own weapon and uniform. The term 'Cloveniers' refers to the weapon used, as it means 'musket bearers.'

landscapes, Salomon made several altarpieces for underground Catholic churches known as mission stations, or staties. In general, his painting style shows an influence of Rembrandt's chiaroscuro. He helped to reorganize the Guild of Saint Luke, becoming headman in 1631, and he published a collection of love poems and a book on contemporary architecture, *Architectura Moderna*. He was also a member of the schutterij in the St Adrian's Cloveniers.

Below: Entitled Still Life in Praise of the Pickled Herring, *this was painted by Joseph de Bray in 1656. Still lifes featuring fish became almost as popular as flowers.*

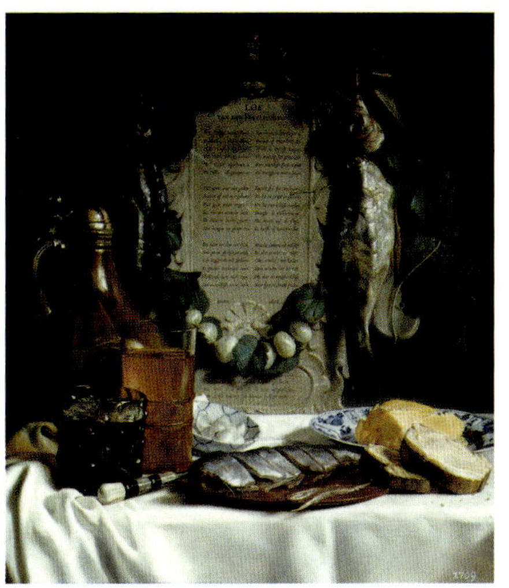

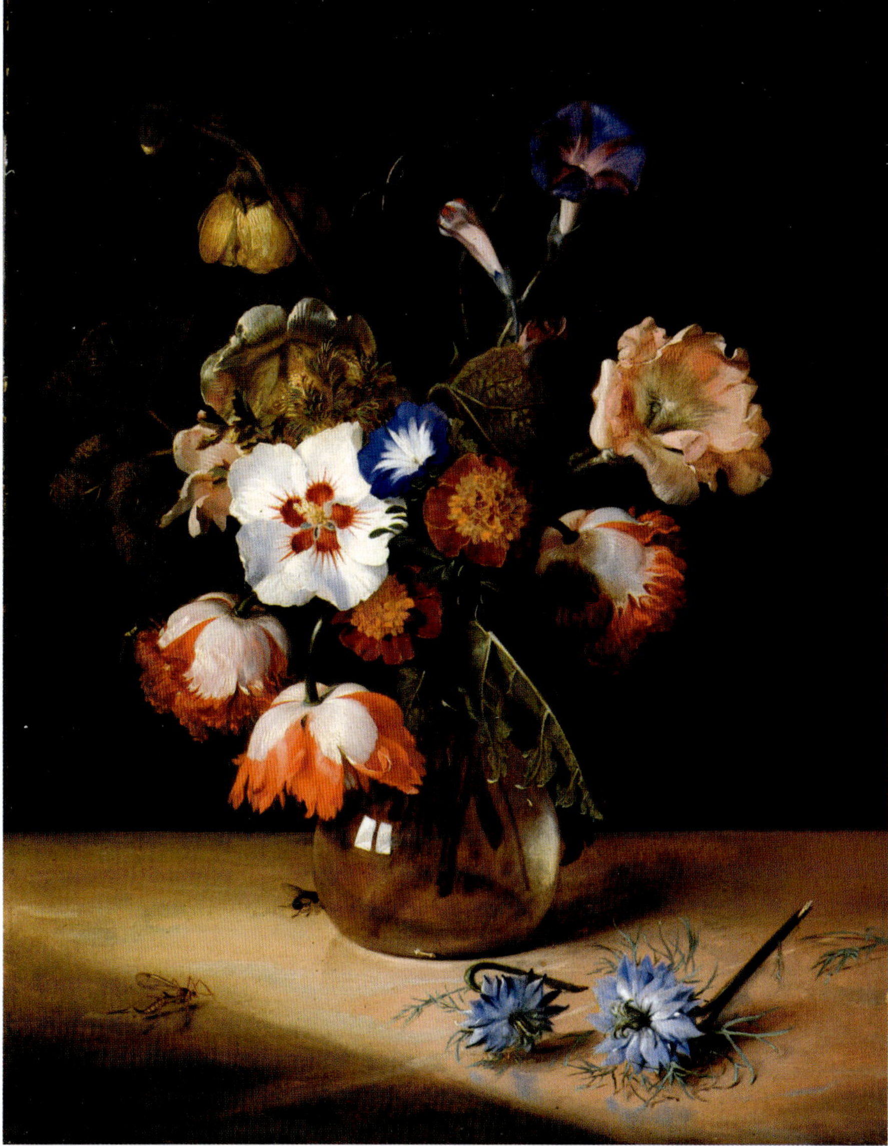

Above: Flowers in a Glass Vase. *With exceptional skill, Dirck de Bray depicts the delicate petals in a shiny glass vase. The flowers are past their first bloom and the insects also represent a memento mori.*

JAN DE BRAY

In 1663–64, plague struck the de Bray family, killing both Salomon and Anna and four of their ten children. Salomon had taught three of their sons, Jan, Dirck and Joseph to paint. Dirck was a flower painter who later became a monk, and Joseph painted still lifes, but died of the plague four days after his father.

Like his father, Jan lived in Haarlem for most of his life, working as a painter, draughtsman and etcher, and for years he was dean of the Haarlem Guild of Saint Luke. He was influenced by Bartholomeus van der Helst and Frans Hals as well as his father; unlike Hals, however, he worked with small, neat brushstrokes, and with less pronounced contrasts of light and dark.

Jan mainly produced portraits and history paintings. He specialized in the type of portrait that depicted contemporary people as historical figures, and which became known by the French term 'portrait historié' (literally 'historicized portrait'). Among the most famous of these were two versions of *The Banquet of Cleopatra* that Jan painted in 1669, in which he included his own family and himself (see opposite). The story, told in *The Natural History* of Pliny the Elder (61–113) had been popular with previous artists, and was translated into Dutch in 1660. In Jan's painting, the two main characters are modelled by his parents Salomon and Anna. He also painted a few religious, mythological and genre subjects and some prints and architectural designs.

Despite Jan's popularity, however, in 1689 he was declared bankrupt and moved to Amsterdam from 1686–88. He married three times, each wife predeceasing him.

JACOB VAN RUISDAEL

Generally perceived as the leading Dutch Golden Age landscape painter, Jacob Isaackszoon van Ruisdael (*c.*1629–82) depicted a wide variety of landscapes, influencing the work of his fellow Dutch artists, the later English landscapists, the Barbizon School in France, and the Hudson River School in America.

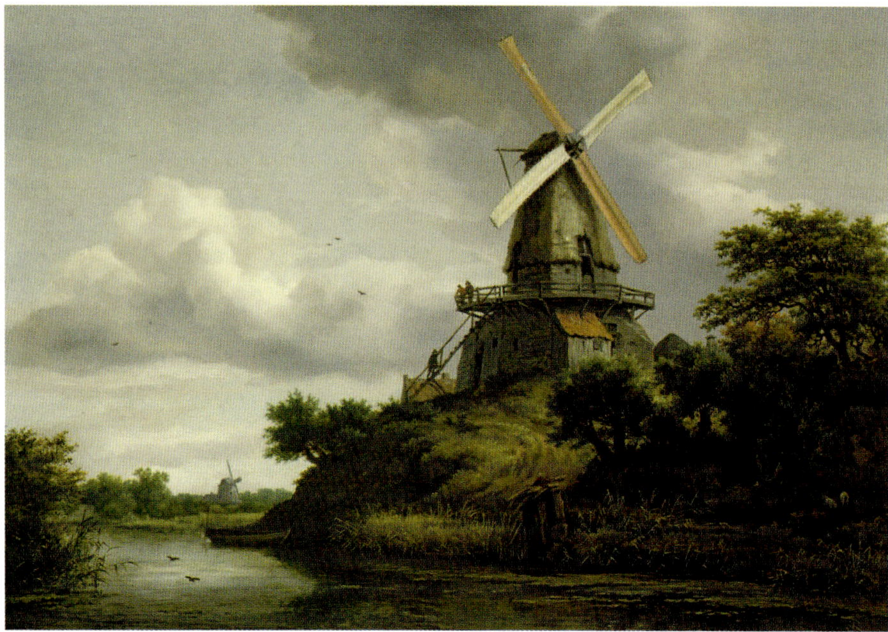

Above: Windmill on the Banks of a River *is a sunny summer scene. Van Ruisdael draws viewers into the landscape through the curving river, grassy bank and large windmill placed to the right.*

The leading practitioner of the classical period of Dutch landscape painting, Jacob van Ruisdael conveyed atmosphere through his scenery. His father, uncle and cousin were also painters, although they used two spellings for their family name. His father was Isaack (or Isaac) van Ruisdael, his uncle was Salomon van Ruysdael (see pages 42–43), and his cousin was Jacob Salomonsz van Ruysdael. Because of their similarities in name and subject matter, much confusion has since arisen over the correct attribution of their paintings.

Van Ruisdael was born in Haarlem. His earliest signed and dated paintings and etchings were made in 1646. It is not known whether he was taught by his father and uncle, but from a young age, he demonstrated outstanding skills. Other influences seem to have been the landscapists Cornelis Vroom (1591–1661) and Allaert van Everdingen (1621–75). In 1648, when he was 19 or 20, he became a member of the Haarlem Guild of Saint Luke.

GATHERING MATERIAL

Despite painting a wide range of landscapes, van Ruisdael did not travel too far to gather material. During the 1640s, he went to Rhenen, Blaricum and Egmond aan Zee in the Netherlands, then in the 1650s, he travelled with fellow Haarlem artist Nicolaes Berchem (see pages 38–39) to Bentheim and Steinfurt in Germany. In 1661, he also probably journeyed with Meindert Hobbema (see pages 108–109) across the German border again. Hobbema was his only registered pupil and their paintings have often been confused. After seeing watermills in Germany, some appeared in a few of van Ruisdael's paintings; an element that no other painter had featured before.

Van Ruisdael painted a broad range of landscapes in different seasons. After moving to Amsterdam in 1657, he added city panoramas and seascapes to his usual range. In all his landscapes, the sky often takes up two-thirds of his compositions, and his clouds, skies and trees are particularly skilfully painted. His work in Haarlem, from c.1646 to the early 1650s, features dunes, woods and atmospheric effects. Building up rich textures, he applied fairly heavy paint, but created overall a sense of spaciousness and luminosity.

The word haerlempjes became used for landscape paintings that included a view of Haarlem, and referred most often to van Ruisdael's panoramic views of the city.

PANORAMIC DUTCH LANDSCAPES

In the early 17th century, history painting, which included religious and mythological as well as historical themes, was the most popular genre in the Dutch Republic, but after 1650, landscape painting exceeded them in reputation and demand. Until then, landscapes as a genre had only been recognized in China. Italianate landscapes became popular among Dutch artists who travelled in Italy and who began incorporating several Classical elements into their paintings. One of the most distinctive changes was the painting of wide panoramic views. These were characterized by low horizons and expansive vistas and skies. Even winter or ice-skating scenes were often portrayed from these panoramic angles. Van Ruisdael was one of the most accomplished practitioners of this kind of landscape, which profoundly influenced the subsequent history of landscape painting.

MYSTERIES

There are several mysteries about van Ruisdael's life. For instance, although he painted more than 150 Scandinavian views featuring waterfalls, there is no evidence that he actually visited Scandinavia. For unknown reasons, he more or less stopped dating his work from 1653, and it is not clear who taught him the art of etching, but 13 etchings produced by him are known and there may of course, be more. There is also some speculation that he became a doctor, travelling to Caen in France in 1676 to study medicine, and then performing surgery in Amsterdam. While this is possible, it could alternatively have been a case of mistaken identity.

Right: With its strong contrasts of light and the built and natural environment, this atmospheric winter scene is View of the Hekelveld, Amsterdam, in Winter, looking South.

Right: Dramatic light, high viewpoint and torrential water make up this image of A Watermill. *Van Ruisdael's use of the bushes in the extreme right foreground is an example of 'repoussoir' that draws the eye into the scene.*

Below: Van Ruisdael painted Landscape with a Stream *during the summer. Several of his characteristic elements are featured, including a cottage on a hill bathed in sunlight, gathering clouds, and a waterfall.*

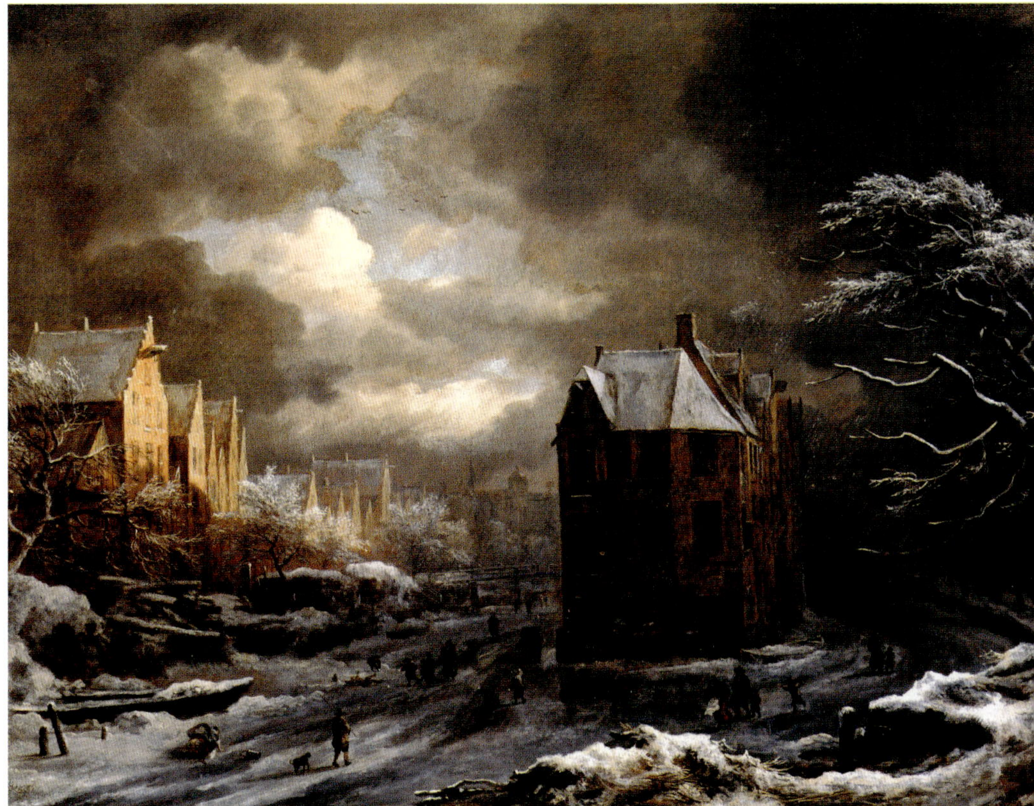

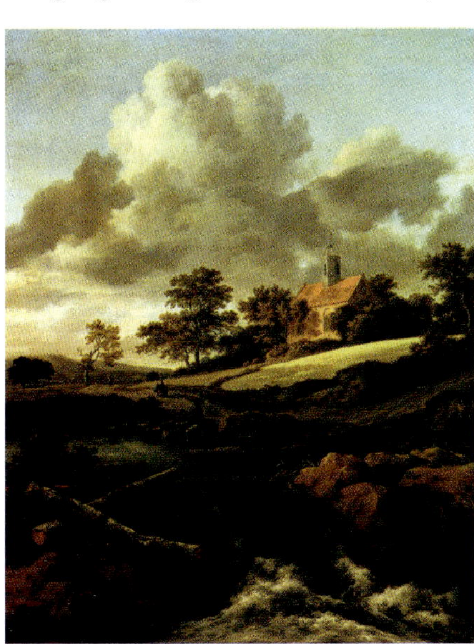

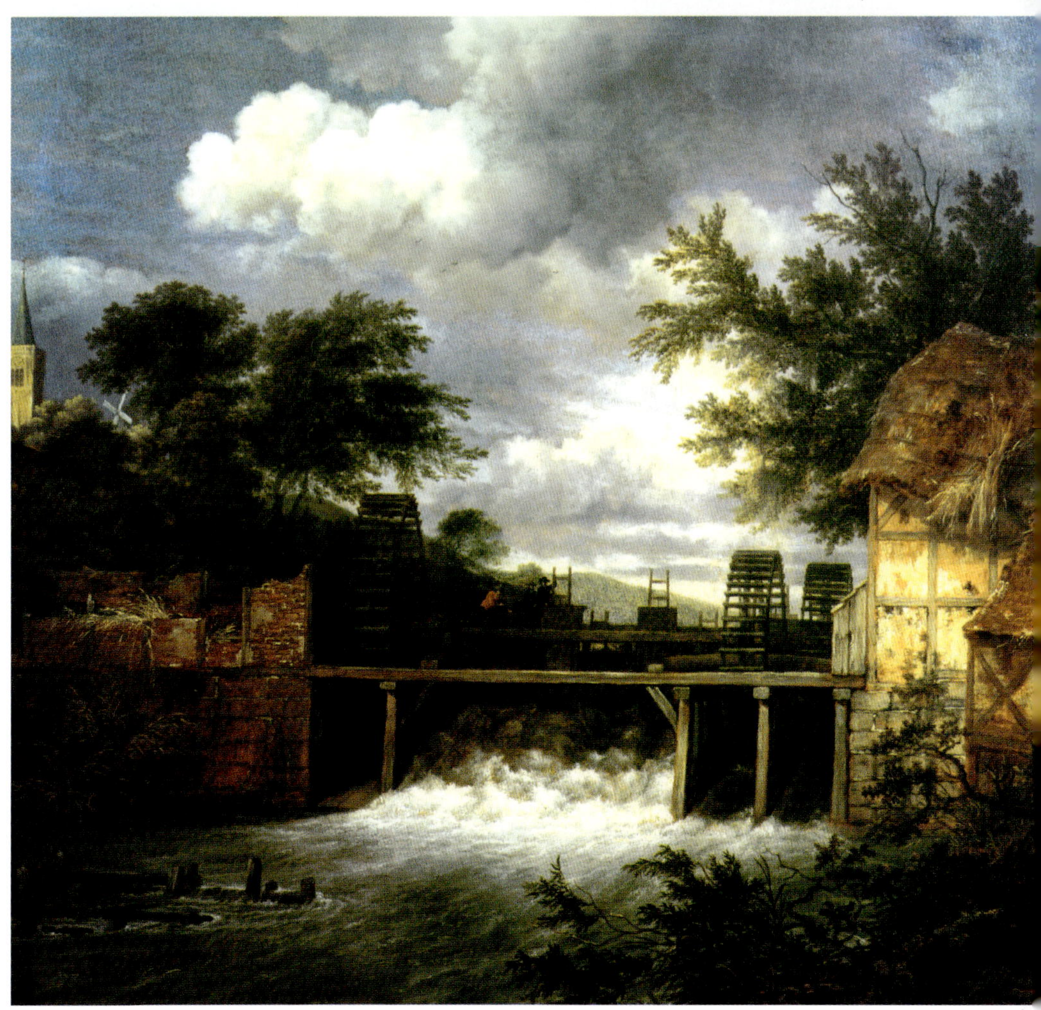

GABRIEL METSU

The son of a painter and tapestry designer who died before his son was born, Gabriel Metsu (1629–67) created still lifes, portraits and genre paintings, changing his style and technique over the course of his life, although customarily painting 'through the window' type compositions.

One of the leading genre painters of the Dutch Golden Age, Gabriel Metsu excelled in conveying gripping visual stories, evoking human emotions and dramatic effects, using harmonious colours, fluid brushwork and detailed rendering of surfaces and materials. His scenes of daily life seem spontaneous and almost timeless. Using a wide range of artistic techniques and styles over the course of his 22-year painting career, Metsu consistently evoked the emotions of his characters as he visually narrated their stories.

As with so many of the Dutch Golden Age painters, information about Metsu's background and artistic training is somewhat vague. He was born in Leiden, several months after the death of his father Jacques Metsu (c.1588–1629), and he was raised as a Catholic by his mother, Jacquemijntje Garniers (c.1590–1651) who was a midwife and possibly also an amateur painter; she had three children already from a previous marriage. From 1636, a stepfather (a skipper by trade) also contributed to Metsu's upbringing.

EDUCATION

Partly because of his late father's occupation and partly because of the thriving art market in the Dutch Republic at the time, Metsu became an artist, probably serving an apprenticeship with Frans Pietersz de Grebber from the age of 14. Four years later in 1648, he became a founding member of Leiden's Guild of Saint Luke (though he ceased to subscribe in 1650). To begin with, as a young artist, he created mainly history paintings and biblical scenes. An early biographer of many Dutch Golden Age painters, the painter and writer Arnold Houbraken (1660–1719) wrote that Metsu was taught by Gerrit Dou, although this has not been verified.

Left: Probably painted c.1665, A Man and Woman Seated by a Virginal *features several ambiguous ideas to imply a story, including a painting of a Twelfth Night Feast partially behind a curtain and a landscape.*

Below: The Vegetable Market *was painted in c.1660–61. It depicts the market by the Prinsengracht canal in Amsterdam, using vivid colours, bright light and a sense of fun.*

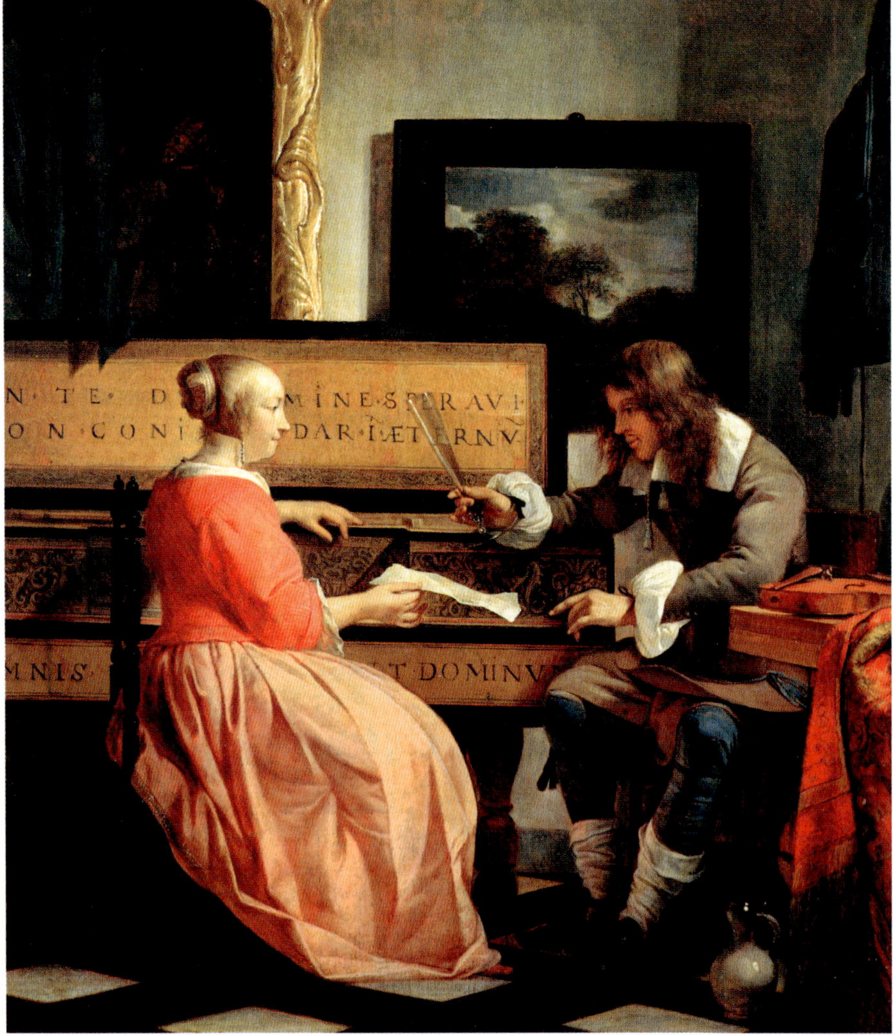

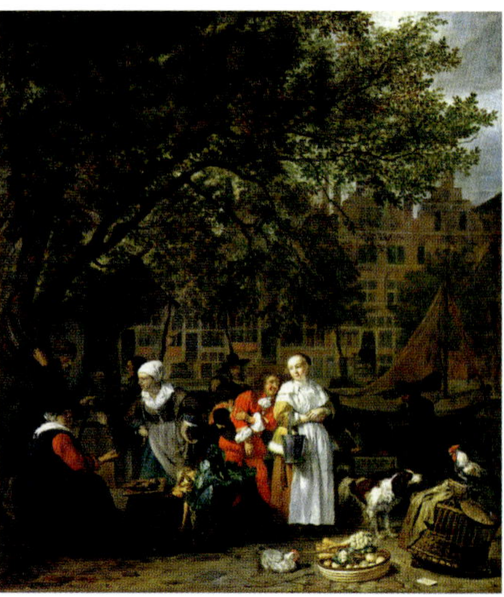

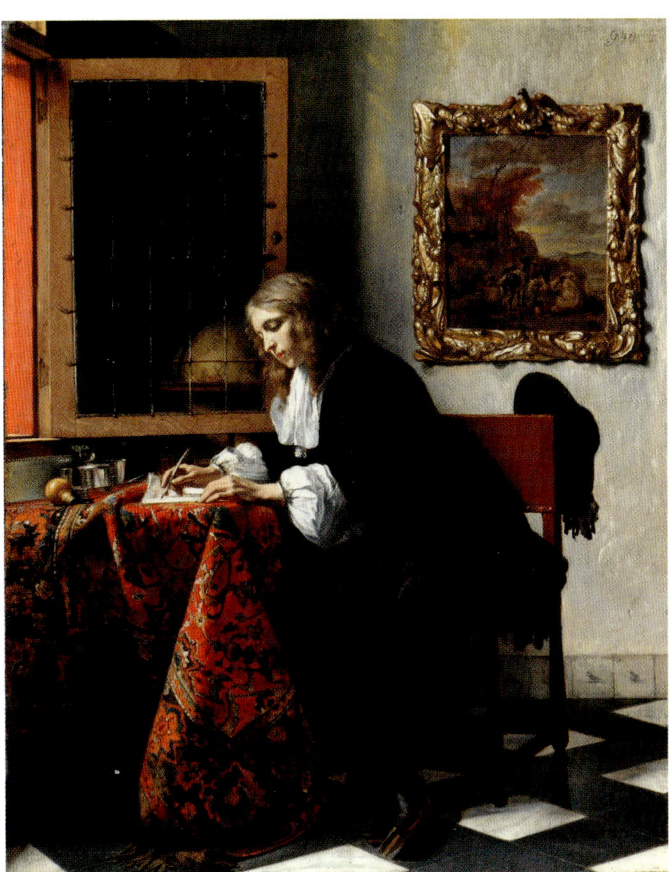 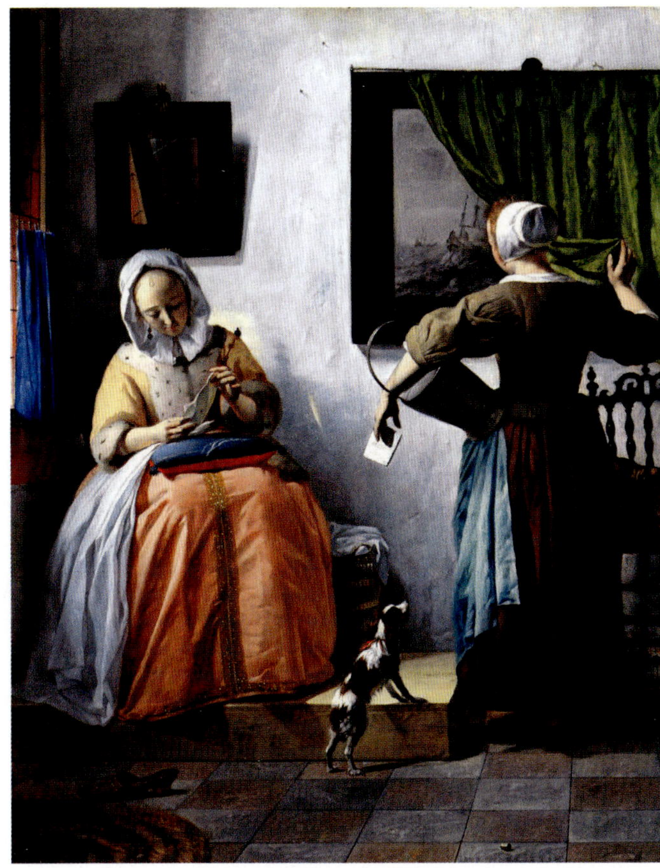

Above and right: Produced as companion pieces, these paintings are both touched by silvery daylight and tell a story between them. In one, a man writes a letter, while in the other, the recipient reads it by the light of a window. Letter writing and reading in Dutch Golden Age art are usually associated with love. The rough seascape seen behind the curtain that is pulled aside by the woman's maid suggests that the path of true love can be hazardous.

In about 1650, Metsu left Leiden and moved to Utrecht where he probably studied with the history painter Nicolaus Knupfer (who probably also taught Jan Steen) and he also became influenced there by Jan Baptist Weenix, with his Italianate landscapes, still lifes, and harbour and beach scenes. Other influences during his career included Jan Steen and Jan Lievens. On his return to Leiden two years later, Metsu began painting interiors using precise linear perspective and depicting natural light effects, but by 1655, he left Leiden once more and moved permanently to Amsterdam, probably because the city of Amsterdam had far more opportunities for an artist than the smaller town of Leiden.

In 1658 he married Isabella de Wolff (1631–1718). Her grandfather, uncle and brother were artists, her father was a potter and her mother Maria de Grebber (1602–80) was also a painter. As his favourite subjects became young women engaged in domestic work or in taverns drinking with clients, he frequently used Isabella as his model.

METICULOUS FINISH

Once in Amsterdam, Metsu realised that small-scale genre scenes were far more popular with art buyers than large-scale religious works, and he abandoned the historical and biblical subjects completely, instead often painting market scenes, emphasizing bustling activities of everyday life, using careful and meticulous brushwork.

When he saw the popularity of (and the high prices being paid for) the intricate paintings of the fijnschilders from his native Leiden, especially Gerrit Dou and Frans van Mieris the Elder, Metsu began painting in a similar style. He painted with dramatic chiaroscuro, creating exacting, lifelike details of objects such as silks, velvets, patterned rugs, translucent glass and liquids. He often used tiny brushes to produce his nearly invisible strokes, and Metsu became the most famous of the Amsterdam fijnschilders.

SYMBOLISM

At first glance Metsu's genre paintings might appear to be simple depictions of daily life, but many have underlying symbolic meanings that contemporary viewers understood, such as certain Christian ideas, probably inspired by his Catholic upbringing, and other messages. At the same time as his genre paintings, he also painted several self-portraits, and once again began emphasizing more religious subjects, particularly those with a Catholic inclination, using his highly finished techniques and sense of drama.

Metsu died at the height of his career, when he was 38 years old. From that time his reputation fluctuated until the 18th century when his paintings became revered once more.

PIETER DE HOOCH

Part of the School of Delft along with Johannes Vermeer and Carel Fabritius at the height of that city's artistic prosperity, de Hooch (1629–1684) became famous for his genre paintings of figures in quiet, light-filled domestic settings, such as a room or a courtyard, frequently seen through an open door or a window.

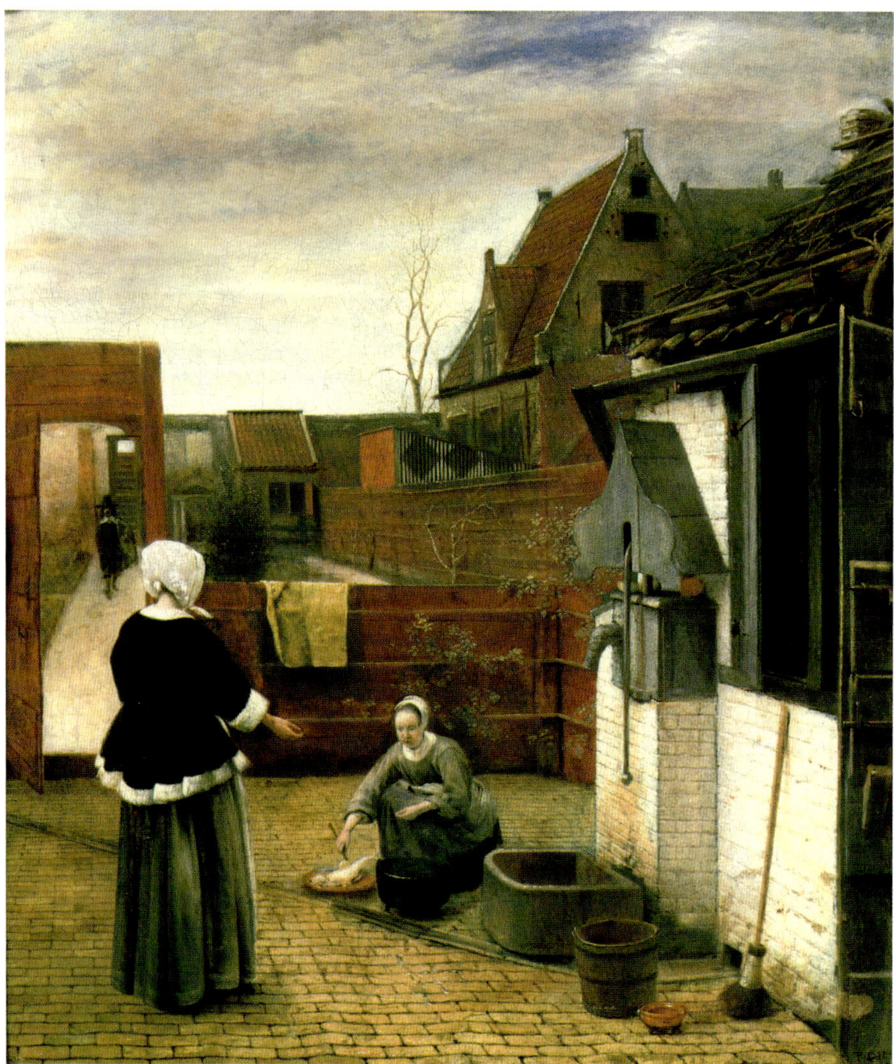

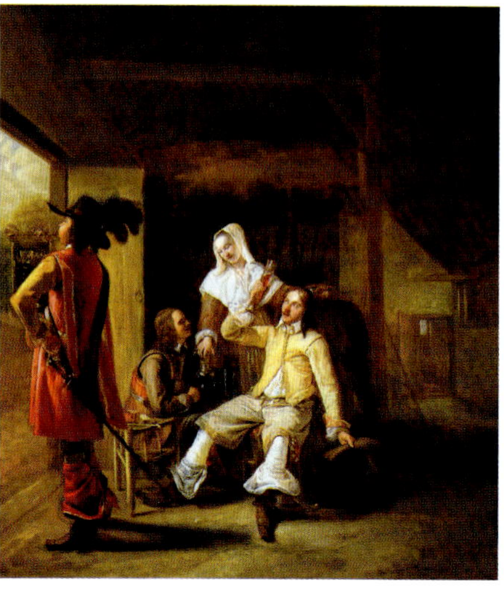

Above: De Hooch painted Two Soldiers and a Serving Woman with a Trumpeter *in c.1654–55, a scene of flirtation and drunkenness in strong chiaroscuro.*

Left: Woman and Maid in a Courtyard. *Unlike many other Golden Age artists who painted from direct observation, de Hooch depicted imaginary scenes.*

DOMESTIC LIFE

In 1654, the year of the Delft Thunderclap, de Hooch married Jannetje van der Burch (unknown–1667) who was probably the sister of his friend genre painter Hendrick van der Burgh (1627–64). The couple had seven children, and after starting his family, de Hooch changed his focus to domestic scenes. His painting style for these seem to have evolved from the influence of fellow Delft painters, Fabritius who had recently died, and Vermeer, especially in his depictions of daily life, renditions of light, linear perspective and spatial illusions. De Hooch's scenes of this period mainly feature one, two or three figures, often women and children, in interiors and courtyards, occupied with domestic activities or in some restrained form of entertainment or merrymaking.

Born in Rotterdam to a builder (Hendrick Hendricksz de Hooch) and a midwife, Pieter de Hooch (also spelled Hoogh or Hooghe) was the eldest of five children. Although little is known of his early life, he seems to have served his apprenticeship under Ludolf Leendertsz de Jongh in Rotterdam and later under the landscape painter Nicolaes Pietersz Berchem in Haarlem. Berchem's landscapes seem to have had little effect on his apprentice however, as de Hooch began his career painting 'koortegardje' (from the French expression 'corps de garde' or 'guard house'); scenes of soldiers and peasants in stables and taverns. He painted such scenes to develop greater skills in portraying light, colour and perspective, and his style for these recall the paintings of Adriaen van Ostade.

In 1650, de Hooch worked as a painter and servant for a linen-merchant and art collector named Justus de la Grange (or Oranje) (dates unknown) in The Hague, Leiden and Delft, but by 1655–56, de la Grange had lost all his money and within a few years, emigrated to America. De Hooch moved to Delft in 1652.

These light-filled paintings convey a sense of stillness, illuminated powerfully by outdoor light pouring in and changing as it falls through de Hooch's complex architectural constructions. This type of painting was known as 'gezelschappen,' which translates as 'companies' or 'parties.' As often occurs in Dutch genre painting, although these everyday interiors seem peaceful and mundane, they were also used to convey moral messages. Like Vermeer's, de Hooch's paintings are all fairly small and precisely painted, displaying careful finish and refined compositions. De Hooch produced them between about 1655 and 1663 while he lived in Delft. Considered his best works, they show his preoccupation with linear perspective and how light falls on different surfaces and how its intensity changes inside rooms, in enclosed courtyards and beyond. In several of his works, he probably used his own family members as models, but his paintings of women breastfeeding and caring for children suggest that he also found models through his mother in her work as a midwife.

In 1655, de Hooch registered with the Delft Guild of Saint Luke as an independent painter. He became part of the School of Delft (see page 15) along with Vermeer, Emanuel de Witte, Hendrick van der Burgh, Adam Pynacker,

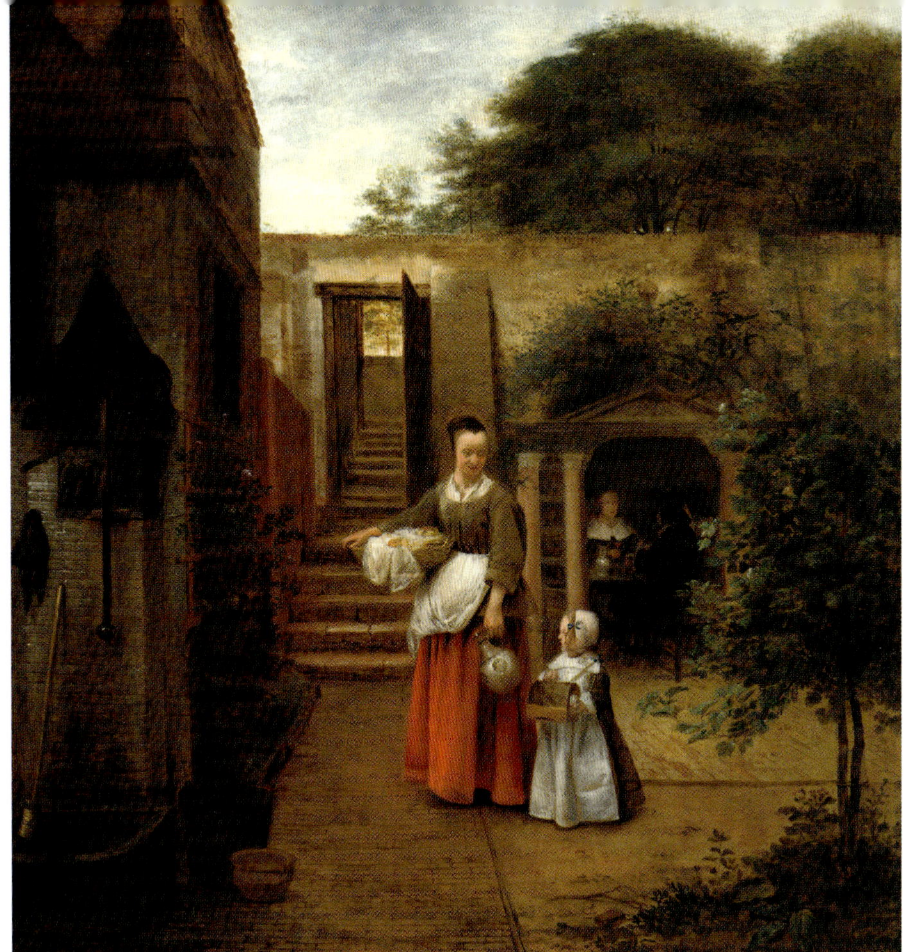

Above: Woman and Child in a Courtyard, *1658/60 – the old town wall of Delft is the rear of this courtyard where a maid, carrying a jug and a laundry basket, and a child go to a water pump.*

Below: Woman with a Child in a Pantry, *c.1656–60, features two doorkijkjes: one into the cellar, the other into the entrance hall. Daylight is conveyed through de Hooch's use of white paint.*

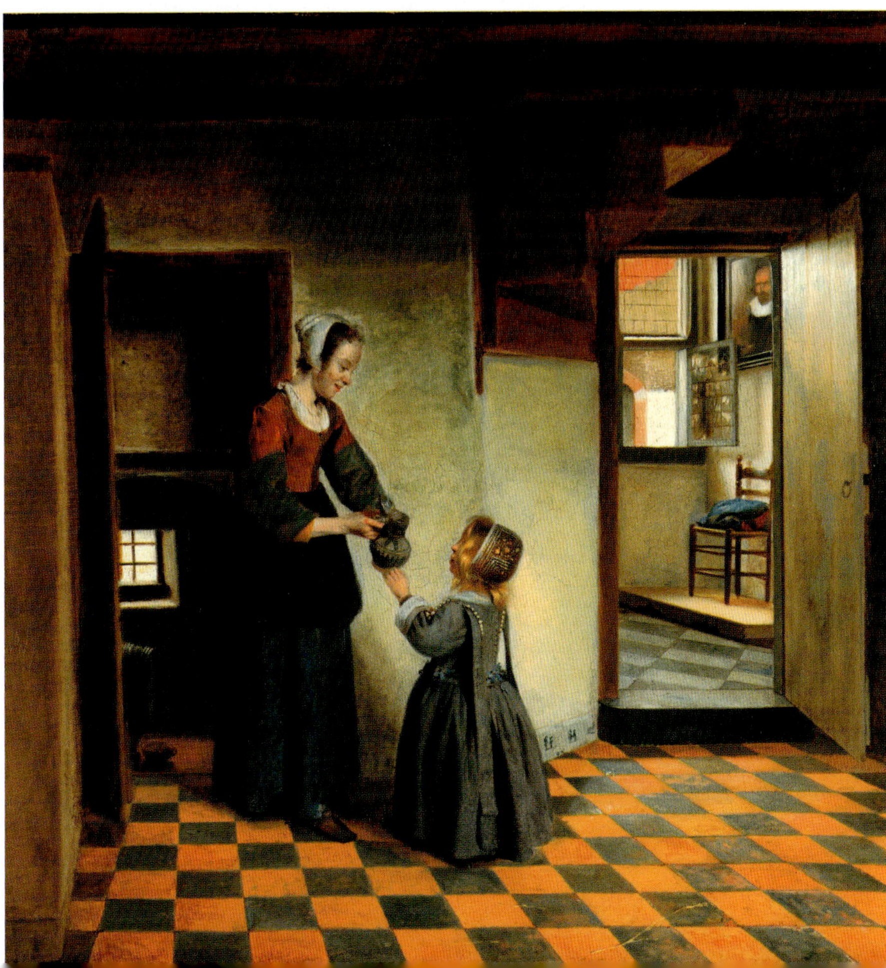

Jan Steen, Carel Fabritius, Pieter Saenredam, Paulus Potter, Nicolaes Maes, Leonaert Bramer (1596–1674), Christiaen van Couwenbergh (1604–67) and Gerrit Houckgeest.

LIGHT EFFECTS

In 1661, Pieter de Hooch moved from Delft to Amsterdam. There he was commissioned by wealthier patrons, and his domestic groups and figures became more elegant and expensively dressed, and the settings more bourgeois, including such things as exotic tapestries and marble fireplaces. De Hooch had become known by the 1660s for his refined paintings of details of everyday life that are often ignored. His treatment of light was sophisticated, his perspective complex, while his compositions and grouping of figures appear natural and uncontrived.

Throughout his life, de Hooch demonstrated his enjoyment of painting complex light sources and effects. Traditional Dutch interior views are lit from left to right, and although he often used this treatment, he also tried out other approaches. Unlike his contemporaries, he often created backlit scenes. In *The Bedroom*, for example, the scene is lit from both the back and the left hand side, so light falls on the shoulders of the child, the woman's face, the tabletop and the floor, and also on the polished wood and the small ceramic pot. *A Boy Bringing Bread* is almost completely backlit, but the light is staggered as it filters through the complex arrangement of doors and arches. Once he was established in Amsterdam, de Hooch began changing his style as can be seen in *Man Reading a Letter to a Woman*. His rendering of

light became more diffused, built up with both small and sweeping strokes. Also painted in Amsterdam, *Interior with a Woman Knitting, a Serving Woman and a Child* depicts light streaming through a door at the back and also falling diagonally from a window, so the woman on the left is illuminated brilliantly, while the maid, child and cat are in shadow.

TEXTURES, COLOURS, PERSPECTIVE

During his early career when he painted koortegardjes, or soliders relaxing, de Hooch's palette was browns and ochres. For his interiors, courtyards and gezelschappens in Delft, his palette lightened and brightened. Later, by the 1670s, it became darker and richer.

In his Delft period, de Hooch built up his images with complex lines and angles. Rooms opened on to antechambers which led to other rooms or courtyards, each with their own sense of atmosphere and light. Through his complex use of perspective, different places are glimpsed through open doors or windows. In common with other artists of the period, he marked in

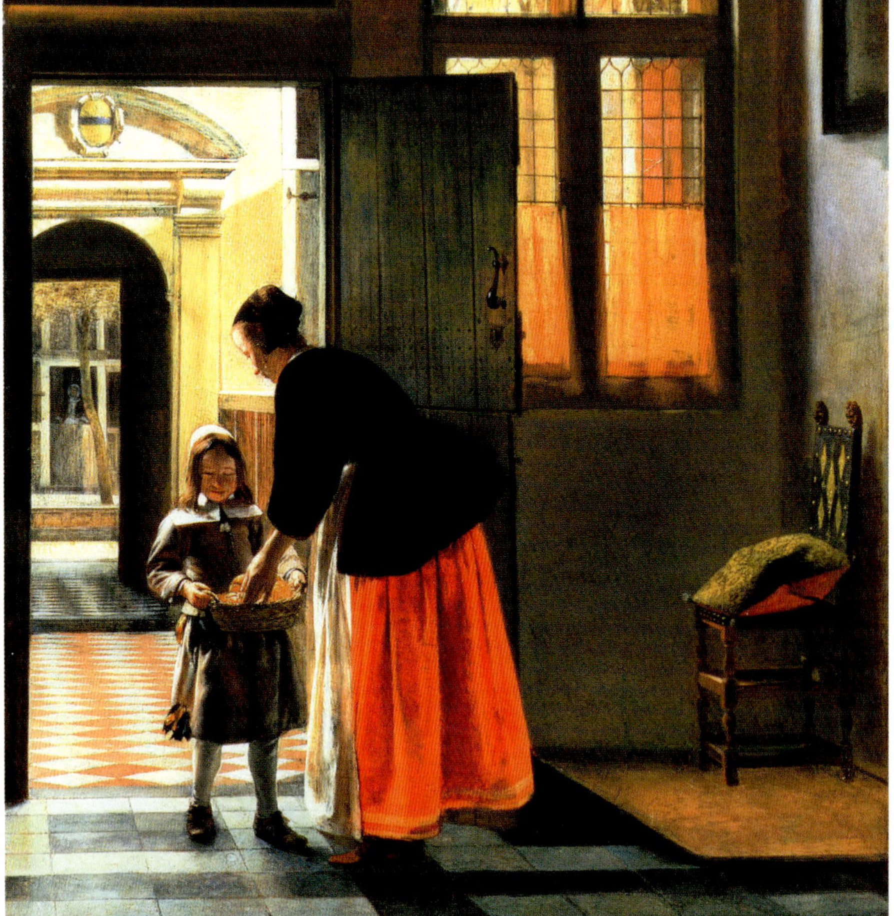

Left: A Boy Bringing Bread, 1663. A woman chooses some bread from a tray held by a small boy. Behind him is a courtyard, then another doorway on to the street and perhaps a canal.

Below: Man Reading a Letter to a Woman, 1670–74. The man reading the letter, the paintings on the wall, and the fireplace and furniture are in shadow, while the woman is illuminated.

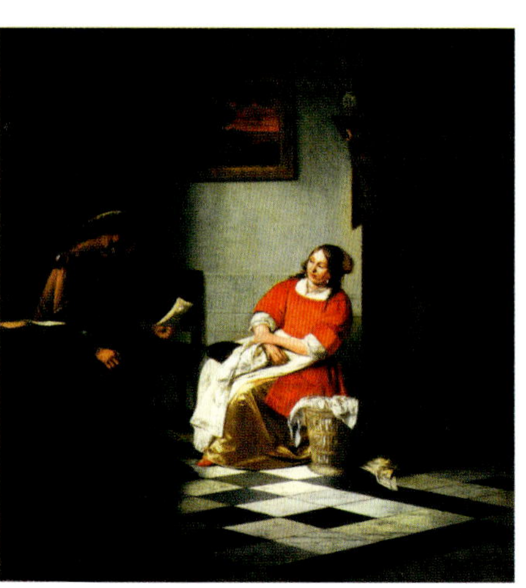

perspective lines with a piece of string pinned in the canvas at the vanishing point to establish the orthogonal lines.

After 1667, when de Hooch's wife Jannetje died, his work changed. He still showed his remarkable skill for rendering textures and light, but his compositions became more staged and grander, with larger, more opulent figures. These changes reflect the prosperity of Amsterdam. His rooms became more lavishly decorated, with bare wooden floors replaced by patterned marble tiles, tables covered with Turkish carpets, and mantelpieces adorned with Oriental ceramics. Previously simple clothing was exchanged for the latest fashions, made of luxurious fabrics such as velvet, silk, satin and taffeta.

VERMEER AND DE HOOCH

Much has been written about the relationship between de Hooch and Vermeer, but no conclusions have been drawn. It seems that they were mutually influential, and were possibly in friendly competition with each other while both were members of the Delft Guild of Saint Luke. Both demonstrate a masterly control of light, colour and complex composition. After Vermeer died, de Hooch's reputation rose while Vermeer's declined and de Hooch's signature was added to various works painted by Vermeer in order to increase their commercial value. Many of their subjects and scenes are similar, comprising Delft interiors featuring ordinary people undertaking everyday activities, but while Vermeer bathed his interiors with a single source of golden light from the left, de Hooch depicted light falling from multiple sources.

Above right: Interior with a Woman Knitting, a Serving Woman and a Child, *1673. The richly dressed lady is being offered a pie by a child. Her house is neat and clean and she is undertaking a respected feminine activity of knitting.*

Right: The Bedroom, *1658–60. Infused with soft light, this scene shows a woman preparing the room used as a bedroom at night, as a sitting room for the day.*

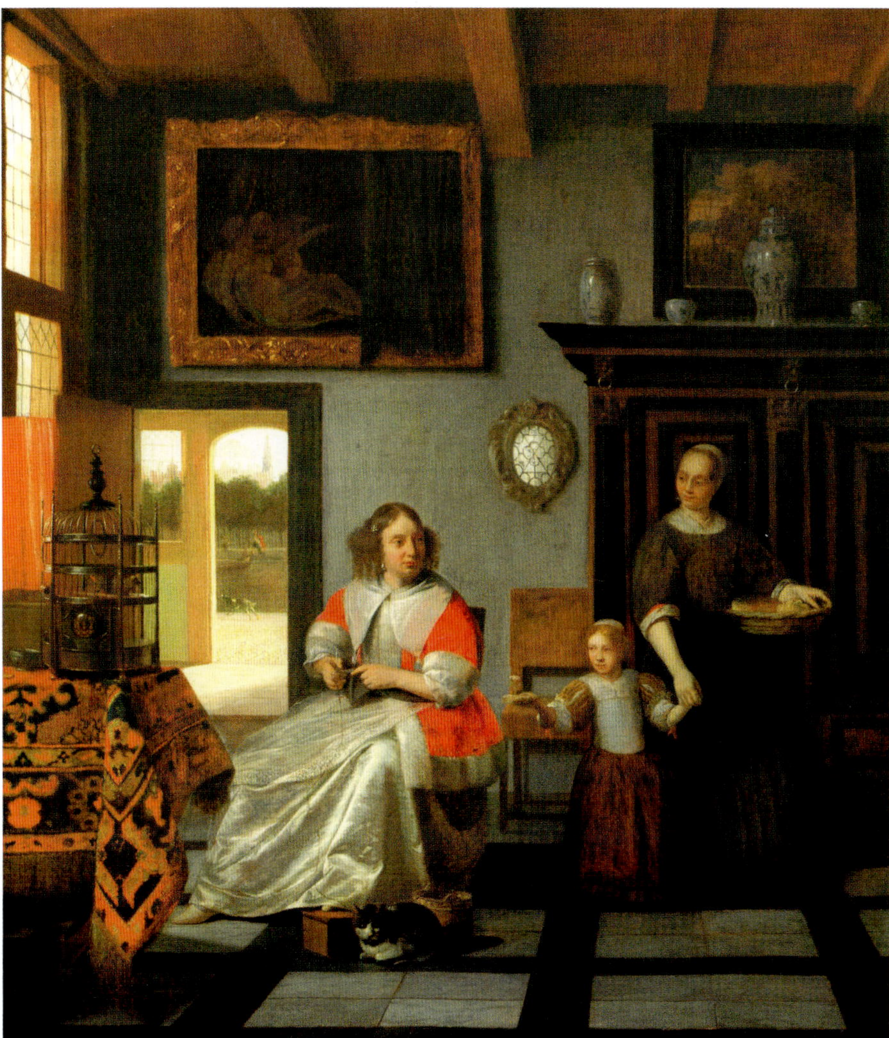

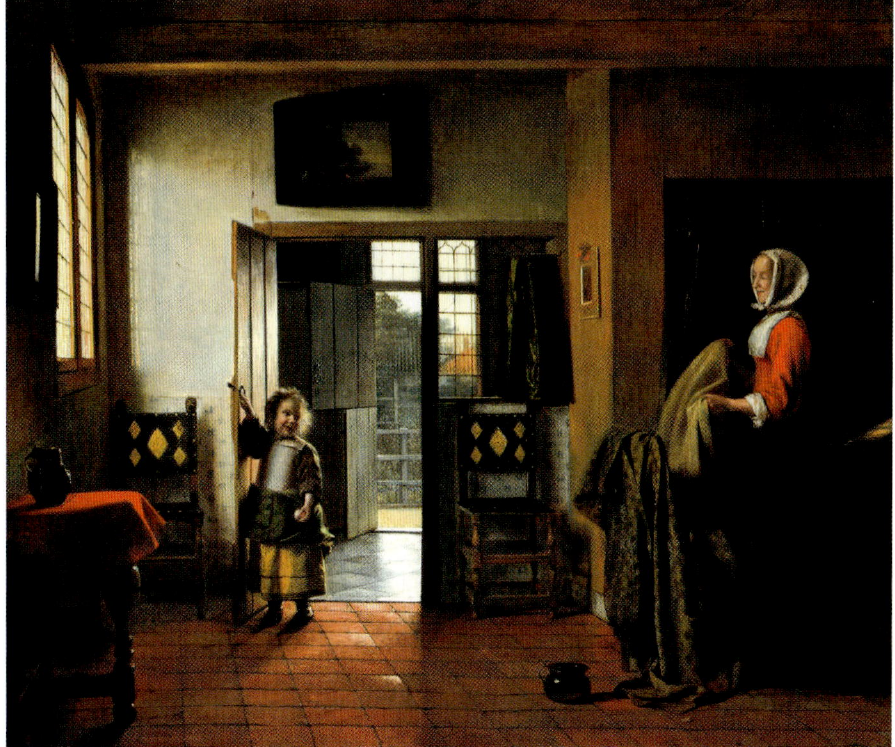

KALF · VAN OOSTERWIJCK

Traditionally, still life was the lowliest genre in the hierarchy of painting, but during the Dutch Golden Age, several extremely skilful artists raised its status. Notable among those painters of the later generation that continued this trend were Willem Kalf (1619–1693) and Maria van Oosterwijck (1630–93).

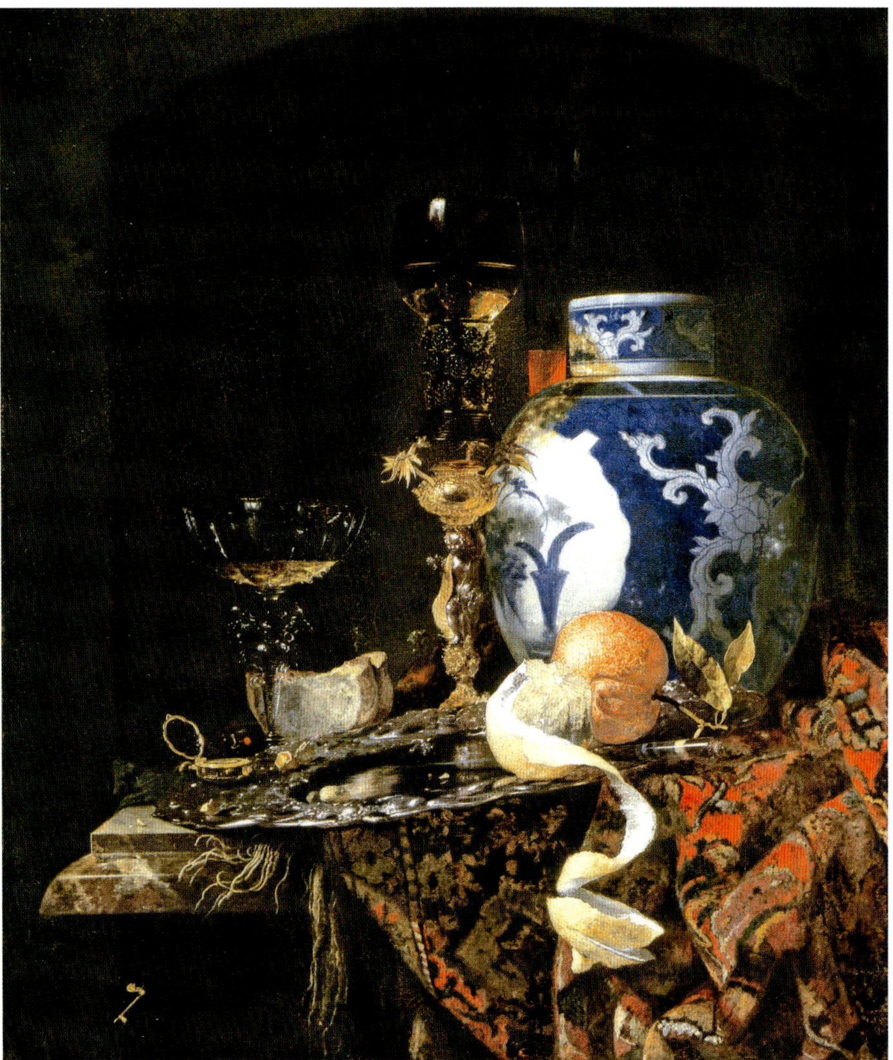

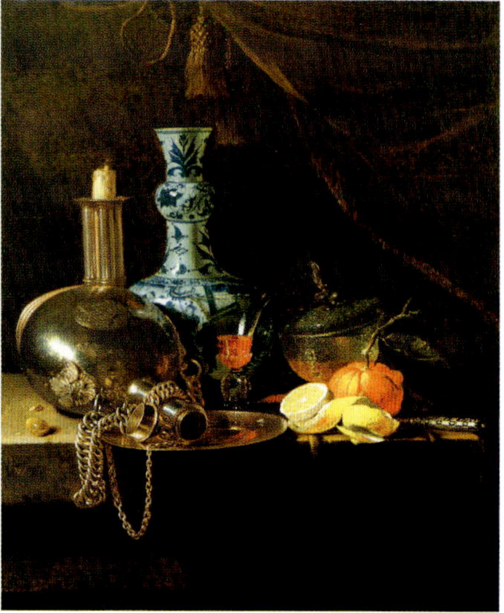

Above: Featuring highly expensive man-made objects, Still Life with a Pilgrim Flask, Candlestick, Porcelain Vase and Fruit *by Willem Kalf is a pronkstilleven nonetheless: as much as the objects depicted may have been highly desirable, the message of the painting was that materialism is futile.*

Left: Another pronkstilleven by Kalf, Still Life with a Chinese Bowl, *1669, is a dynamic composition of luxury goods, including a large porcelain Ming jar, a lemon with spiralling peel, a delicate Venetian glass vase, an ornamented silver tray and a wine glass.*

WILLEM KALF

One of the most celebrated of all still life painters, Willem Kalf was born in Rotterdam to a wealthy family and may have trained in Dordrecht, although few details about his life are known. He was a student of Hendrik Gerritsz Pot (c.1580–1657), a painter of historical subjects, and probably also of Cornelis Saftleven at the same time as Ludolf de Jongh. In the late 1630s, Kalf went to Paris where he lived among the Flemish artists who had emigrated to St-Germain-des-Prés. He remained working in Paris between

PRONKSTILLEVEN

Describing painted groups of ornate man-made objects, often with complex compositions, the term pronkstilleven was first used in Antwerp in the 1640s, and soon after also in the Dutch Republic. The expensive items portrayed the aspirations of the paintings' owners, and Willem Kalf and Jan Davidsz de Heem were the main Dutch painters of this type of still life. As well as being aspirational in subject, pronkstillevens were also often interpreted as a form of vanitas, symbolizing the transience of life and the ultimate worthlessness of wealth and possessions. Hourglasses for instance, suggest time passing, and empty glasses or vases allude to the shallowness of material things. In Dutch paintings, pronkstillevens often evolved from the banketjes or 'little banquet pieces' painted by artists such as Pieter Claesz, Willem Claesz Heda, Clara Peeters and Kalf, that also featured such things as cups and vessels made of precious metals.

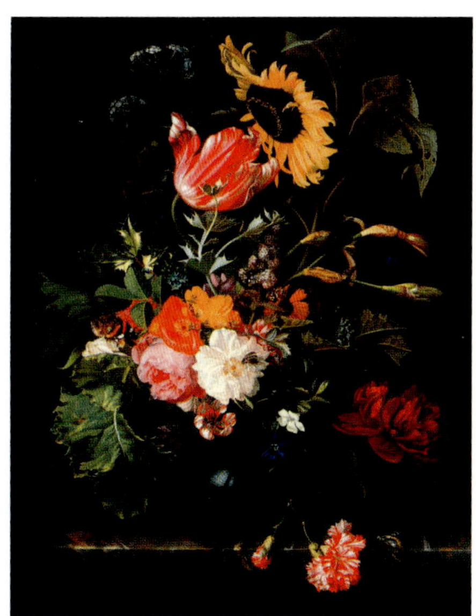

Above: It would have been impossible to create this Bouquet of Flowers in a Vase *using real flowers as a model, as they bloom in different seasons. Typical of her work, Maria van Oosterwijck painted this in c.1670.*

1642 and 1646, painting small-format interiors of farmhouses and kitchens featuring groups of vegetables, buckets, pots and pans arranged as still lifes in the foreground. These rustic interior paintings especially influenced French art of the time.

In 1646, Kalf returned to Rotterdam, and in 1653 he moved to Amsterdam where his style evolved and became closer to Vermeer's in terms of his handling of paint and treatment of light. His mature works are mainly still lifes, of a type called 'pronkstilleven' in Dutch, which means 'ostentatious or showy still life.' These paintings often feature the same objects, usually a draped damask cloth or tapestry over a table that is laden with vessels made of gold, silver, pewter and Venetian glass, usually along with a Chinese porcelain bowl containing fruit. Luxury goods such as this in paintings made the works themselves highly esteemed. His backgrounds are predominantly dark, while his objects are accented with small, brilliant highlights. Because of their realism and the aspirational content depicted, Kalf's paintings were in great demand among the wealthy inhabitants of Amsterdam.

MARIA VAN OOSTERWIJCK

Van Oosterwijck (or Oosterwyck) was born in Nootdorp, a small town near Delft. In 1658, she moved to Leiden and to Utrecht in 1660, where she was apprenticed to Jan Davidsz de Heem who encouraged her skills in still life and floral paintings. Six years later, she settled in Amsterdam, and began working as an assistant to the still life and flower painter Willem van Aelst (1627–c.1683). Through Aelst, she gained her first international recognition when in 1669 the Grand Duke of Tuscany, Cosimo III de' Medici bought one of her still lifes. At the time, fresh flowers were rare and expensive, and in conjunction with Tulpenwindhandel (see page 37) van Oosterwiijck's floral paintings sold for high prices.

Van Oosterwijck was exceptionally unusual, even in terms of the relative freedom of Dutch Golden Age female artists. Most had artist fathers or husbands, but she remained single throughout her life. She was also able to travel at a time when it was not easy to do so as a single woman, and even more unusually, she became a woman of independent means. Her paintings that helped to popularize the genre of floral still life were small-scale still lifes and works with allegorical themes featuring precise details, rich colours and dramatic chiaroscuro. She was a philanthropist, and a shrewd businesswoman, using an agent to market her paintings abroad. Her patrons included Louis XIV of France, the Holy Roman Emperor Leopold I, Augustus II, William III of England, and the King of Poland.

Below: A Floral Still Life with Yellow and White Lilies, *painted by van Oosterwijck in 1675, this large selection of flowers are set against her characteristic dark background. The almost robust, colourful lilies contrast with the delicate butterfly.*

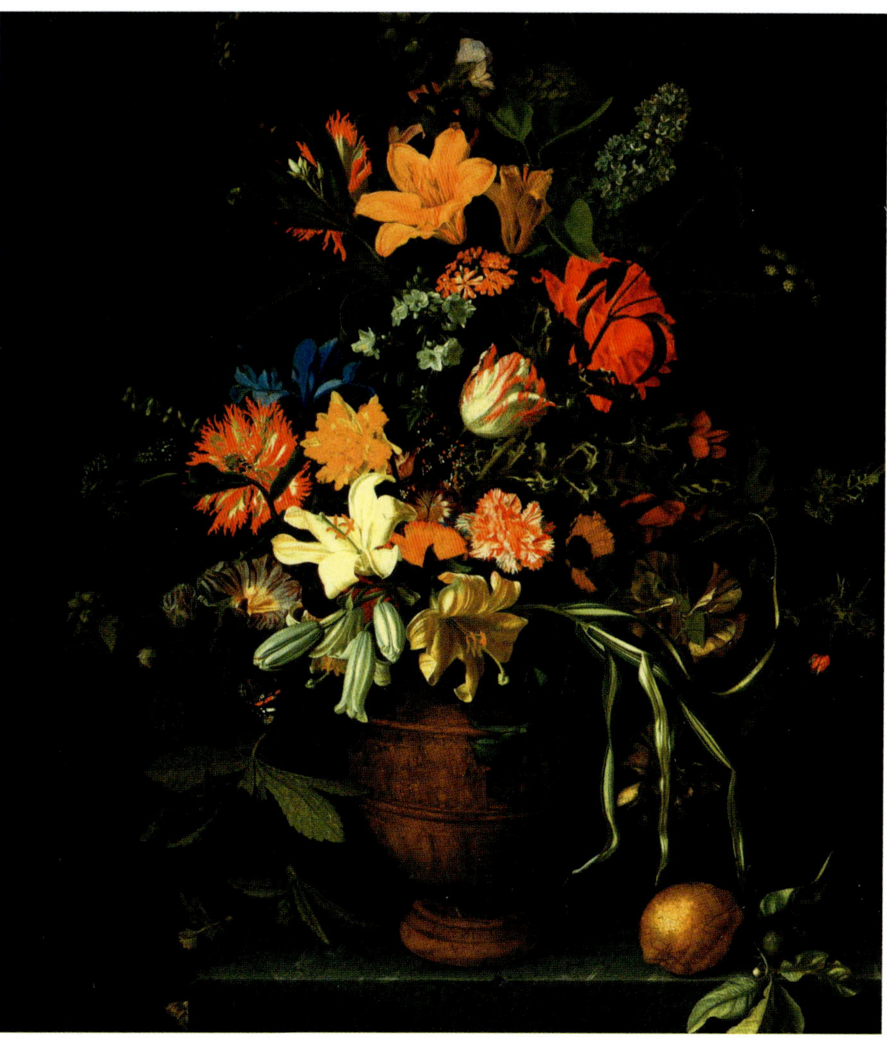

JAN WYNANTS

Depicting scudding clouds, shifting sand dunes and undulating hills around Haarlem and Amsterdam, Johannes Jansz Wynants (1631/2–84) was a prolific landscape painter who captured transitory effects in nature. Although many of his landscapes also feature figures, it is likely that others added them later.

Jan Wynants (alternatively Wijnants) was born in Haarlem, the son of a Catholic art dealer with the same name. After his mother's death, his father remarried and the painter Egbert Jaspersz van Heemskerck (1634–1704) became Wynants's stepbrother. There is sparse information about his early life and training, but it seems that he began painting during or just after 1650. In 1653, he was in Rotterdam, where the painters Ludolf de Jongh and Adam Pynacker were active. Probably the most important early influence on Wynants was de Jongh's brother-in-law, Dirck Wijntrack or Wyntrack (1615–78), as his first works depict brick farm buildings and country cottages that have clear similarities to Wyntrack's work. Wynants and Wyntrack frequently collaborated, with Wyntrack painting the wildlife in some of Wynants's landscapes. In 1659, Wynants was back in Haarlem, and his work then began to show the influences of Philips Wouwerman and Jacob van Ruisdael, although his palette

Below: Wooded River Landscape with Peasants on a Path *demonstrates a favourite composition: a raised area and tree, a winding path, and panoramic view.*

was lighter and brighter. By December 1660, he was in Amsterdam, where he married Catharina van der Veer (1632–1720). He remained in Amsterdam for the rest of his life.

SENSE OF SPACE

Wynants became known for landscapes created with soft brushstrokes, clear light, meandering ribbon-like paths and rivers, and a sense of harmony and space. Natural sunlight appears to fall on most of his scenes that include fields, dunes, sandy roads, trees, distant hills and streams. Inspired initially by the

Below: A Dune Landscape with Figures *– sand dunes were among Wynants's primary motifs, but his figures were painted by others.*

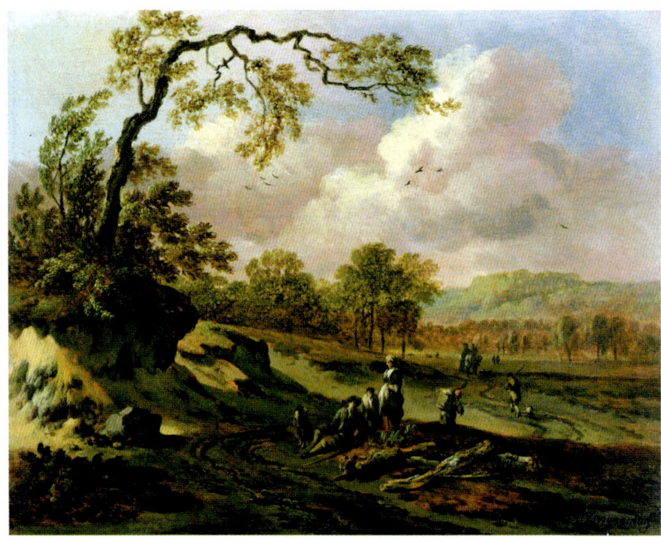

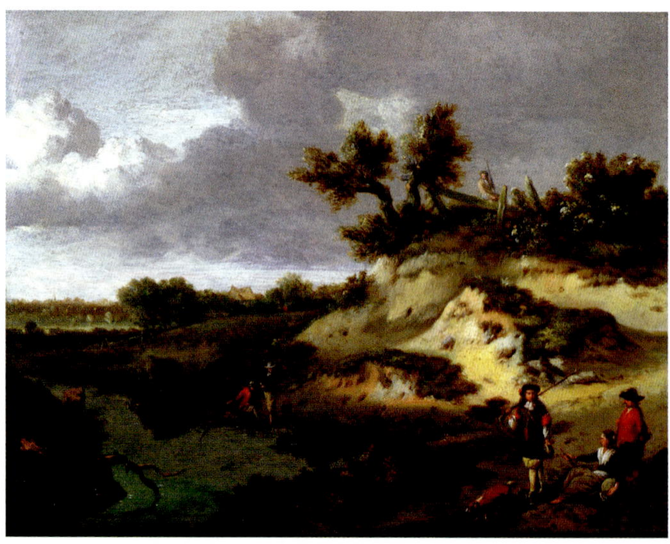

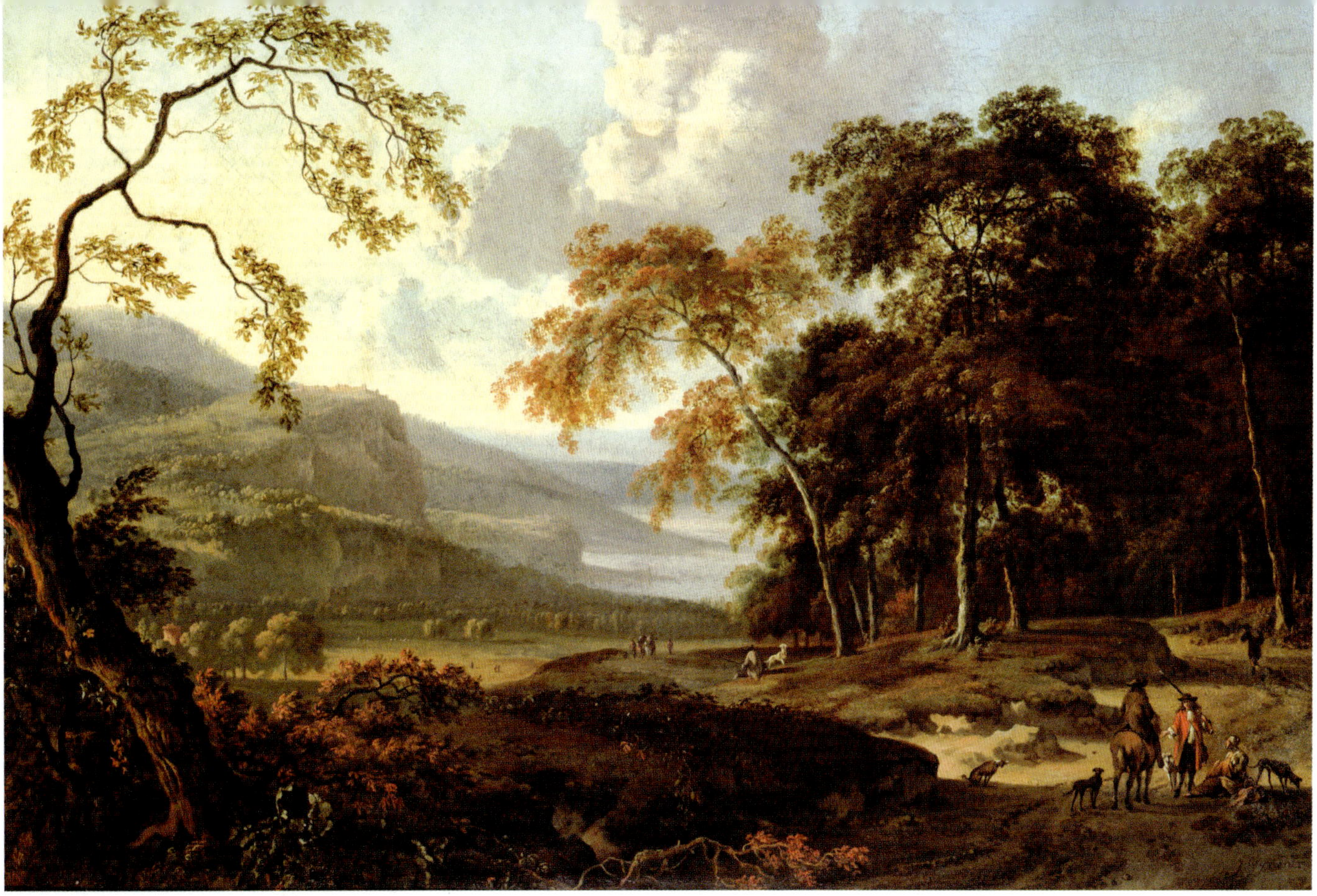

Above: A Hunting Party in a Classical Landscape, c.1672–77. Jan Wynants *was one of the most important Dutch landscape painters of the second half of the 17th century.*

countryside around Haarlem and then, from 1660, of the landscape around Amsterdam, he produced unpretentious, naturalistic views that became favourites with collectors across Europe for the rest of the 17th and the whole of the 18th centuries. Although he never travelled to Italy, his later paintings became more golden and Italianate, often featuring an elm or oak tree dominating the foregrounds. Many of his landscapes feature shepherds, hunters and travellers resting, and these were usually painted in by other artists such as Wouwerman, Johannes Lingelbach and Adriaen van de Velde.

Van de Velde was one of his pupils, and Wynants also influenced other artists beyond the Netherlands, including François Boucher (1703–70) in France, Thomas Gainsborough (1727–

88) and John Crome (1768–1821) in England, and Wilhelm von Kobell (1766–1853) in Germany.

SUPPLEMENTING HIS INCOME

Despite his success, Wynants constantly fell into debt. In common with several other artists of the period, he had a second career. Like Barent van Someren and Jan Steen, Wynants also kept an inn to supplement his income. Unfortunately he still experienced financial problems and numerous creditors chased him for money.

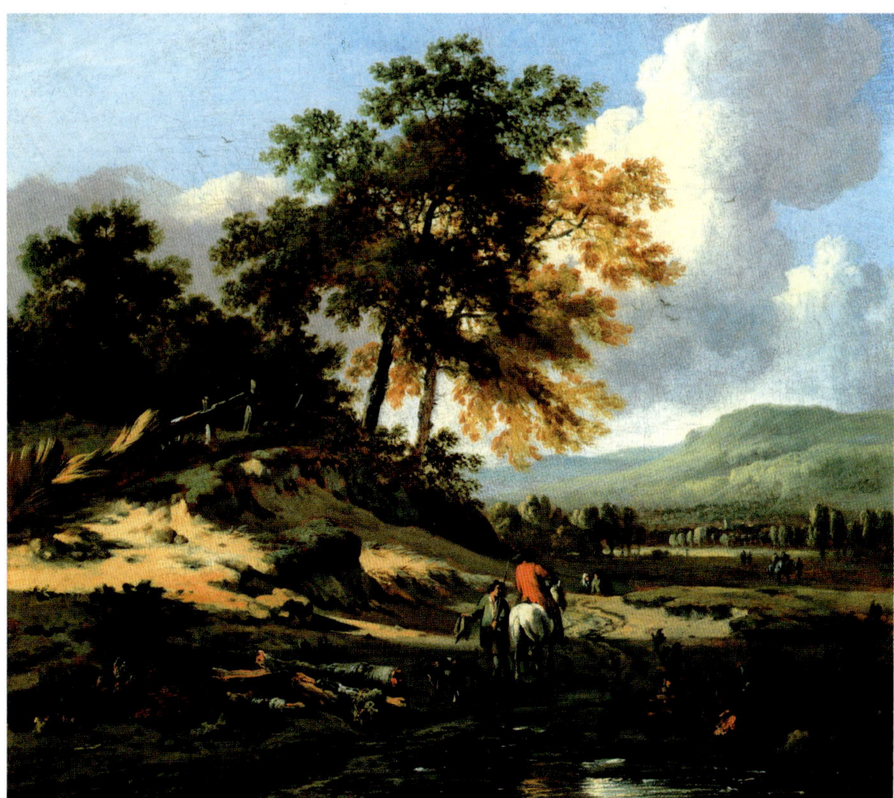

Right: Landscape with Figures *was painted by Wynants in 1679. Natural light filters through the clouds and vegetation in patches.*

JOHANNES VERMEER

Despite his brief career and the fact that only 36 works are attributed to him, Johannes (Jan) Vermeer (1632–1675) is now revered as one of the greatest artists in history. Yet he died in debt at just 43 years old, and he and his work were soon forgotten, not to be rediscovered until the 19th century.

Although during his life Vermeer was recognized in Delft and The Hague and commanded large sums of money for his work, soon after his death he fell into obscurity. It is not clear where and with whom he studied, but many art historians speculate that he was apprenticed to Leonaert Bramer or Carel Fabritius. Others believe that he taught himself, and a third suggestion is that he trained with Abraham Bloemaert.

Vermeer's father, Reijnier (or Reynier) Jansz Vos (1591–1652) was an art dealer, a worker of silk or caffa (a mixture of silk and cotton or wool), and from 1625 to 1629, also an innkeeper near Delft's busy marketplace. He displayed paintings for sale on the inn walls and lived upstairs with his family. When he died in 1652, Vermeer took over the art dealing business and a year later, at the age of 21, he married a Catholic girl, Catharina Bolnes (1631–87) who had recently moved to Delft from Gouda with her wealthy mother Maria Thins (c.1593–1680). Before marrying her

Below: Girl with a Pearl Earring, painted by Vermeer in c.1665 is based on a model, but is a tronie (see page 46) rather than a portrait.

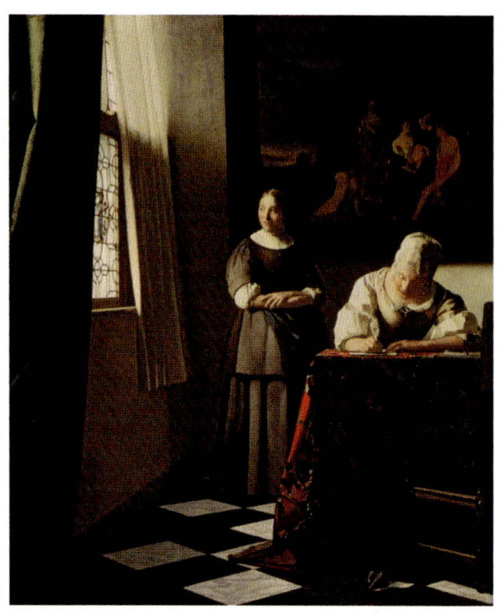

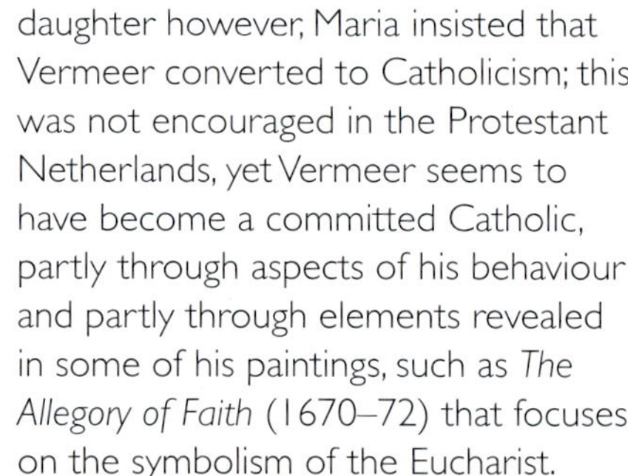

Above: Lady Writing a Letter with her Maid, 1670–71, shows a middle-class woman writing, while her maid waits to take the letter to the lady's lover.

daughter however, Maria insisted that Vermeer converted to Catholicism; this was not encouraged in the Protestant Netherlands, yet Vermeer seems to have become a committed Catholic, partly through aspects of his behaviour and partly through elements revealed in some of his paintings, such as *The Allegory of Faith* (1670–72) that focuses on the symbolism of the Eucharist.

In December of 1653, Vermeer became a member of the Delft Guild of Saint Luke, and later acted as headman and Chairman of the Board, highly respected as a master painter. Meanwhile in 1654, the Delft Thunderclap occurred (see page 74), which depressed the economy and adversely affected his art dealing.

In 1660, Vermeer and Catharina moved in with Maria, to her large house at Oude Langendijk in the centre of Delft's Catholic community. Vermeer remained there for the rest of his life, using a large second floor room as his studio. Over the course of their

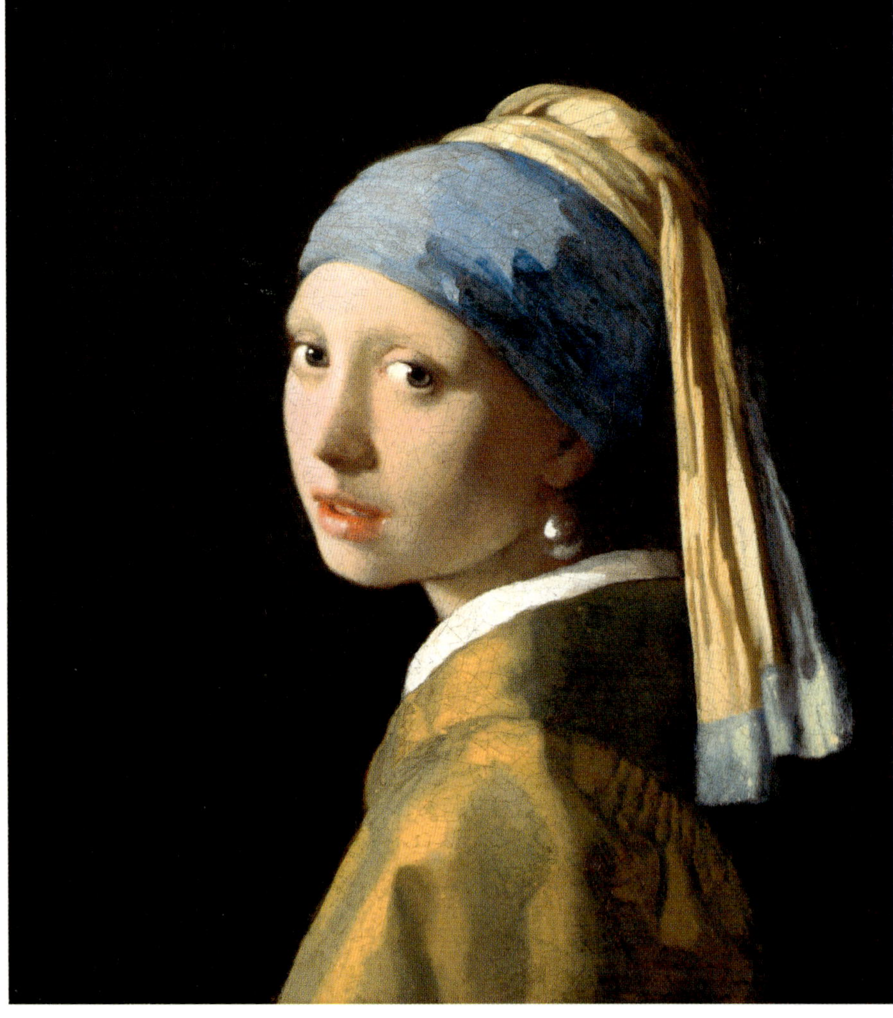

marriage, Catharina gave birth to 15 children of whom 11 survived.

WEALTHY PATRONS

Rather than painting speculatively for the public art market, Vermeer painted for a few wealthy local patrons, including the baker Hendrick van Buyten (1632–1701), typographer and printer Jacob Abrahamsz Dissius (1653–95) and Pieter van Ruijven (1624–74), who inherited money from his family's brewery business and probably bought 21 of Vermeer's works.

Vermeer's first works were large-scale biblical and mythological scenes, but his later paintings – for which he is most famous – were mainly scenes of daily life, set in middle-class interiors, featuring radiant light, vivid depictions of textures and a sense of calm.

Vermeer enjoyed a high reputation as a painter of quality and an art expert. In 1672, he was invited to The Hague with other artists to authenticate paintings bought by Frederick-William, the Elector of Brandenburg (1620–88).

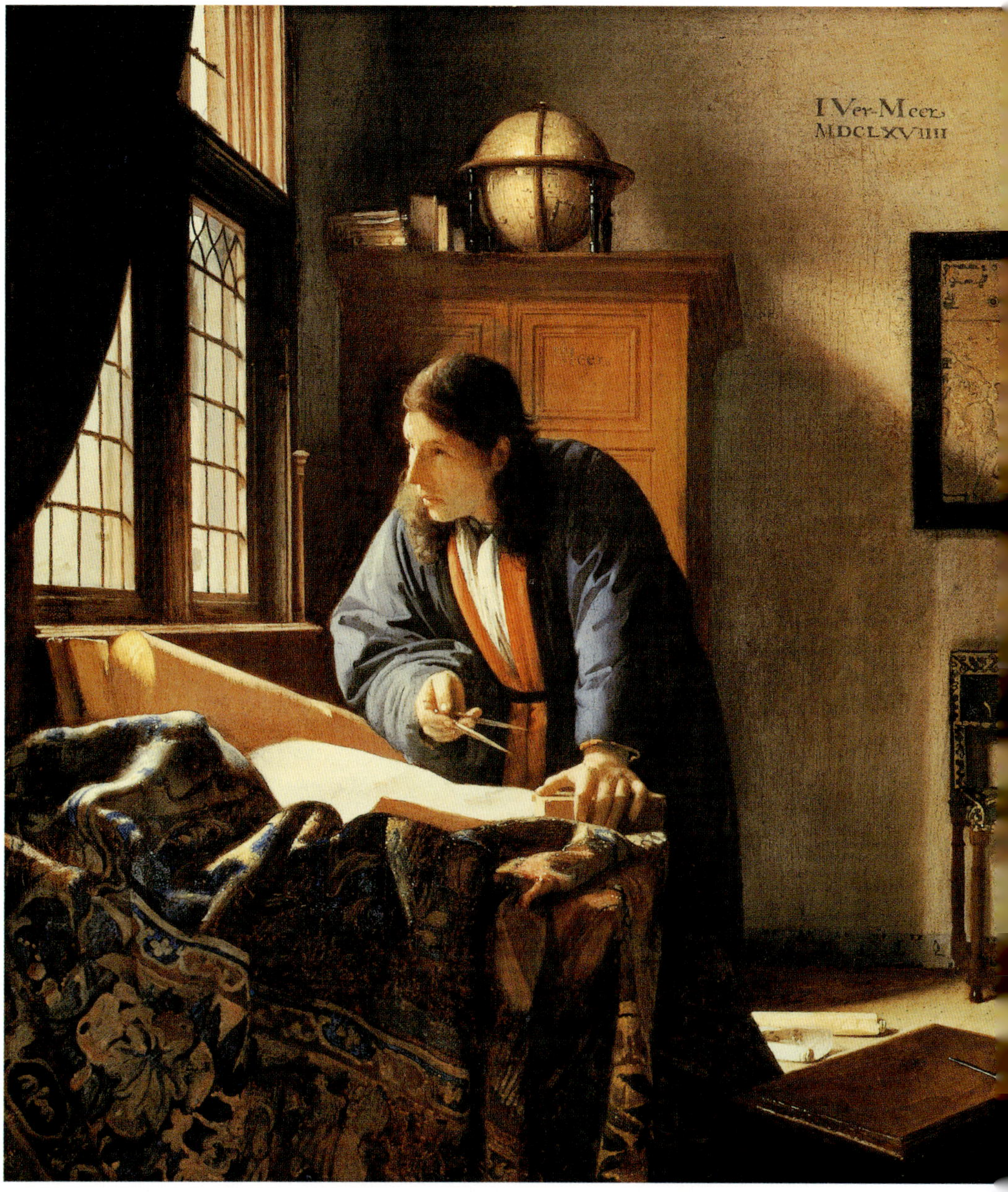

Right: Painted in 1669, The Geographer *depicts a man measuring distances on a map with his compass. The globe and map on the wall represent the pioneering developments of cartography in the Netherlands.*

Below: Woman with a Lute *c.1662–63 – looking out of a window while tuning her lute, is a young woman. Behind her, a huge map is displayed on the wall, conveying the Dutch pride in their achievements.*

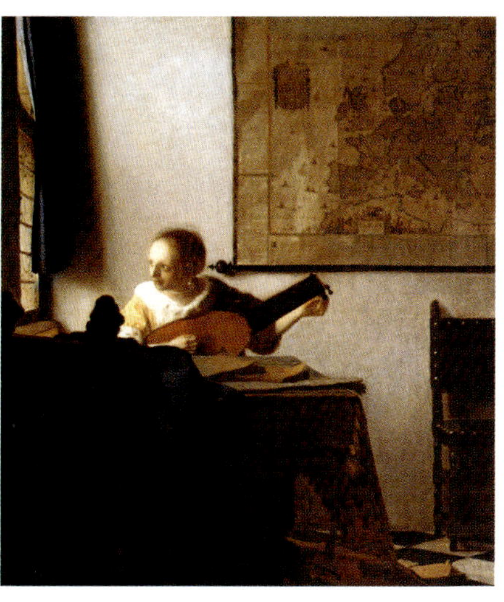

VERMEER'S PALETTE

Unlike most other Dutch painters, Vermeer regularly used some of the most expensive pigments available, including natural ultramarine, which he used in almost all of his paintings. He used it for blue-coloured objects, but also in the shadows of other coloured objects. A bright blue pigment, natural ultramarine was made from the extremely costly semi-precious stone lapis lazuli, that was mined in Afghanistan and shipped to the Netherlands via Venice. To turn it into paint, the stone was ground into a fine powder and mixed with walnut oil. As well as expensive, it was also difficult to grind. In general, though considered a master of colouristic effects, Vermeer only used between 10 and 20 pigments in any one painting. Among these were: green earth, verdigris, indigo, smalt, vermilion, madder lake, red ochre, lead-tin yellow, yellow ochre, weld, azurite, carmine, bone black, charcoal black and lead white. As with other artists of the time, he had to make up all his own paint by grinding the pigments and then mixing the powders with oil. Unused paint could be kept for a while in pigs' bladders, but these soon dried up so Vermeer only made up small batches at a time.

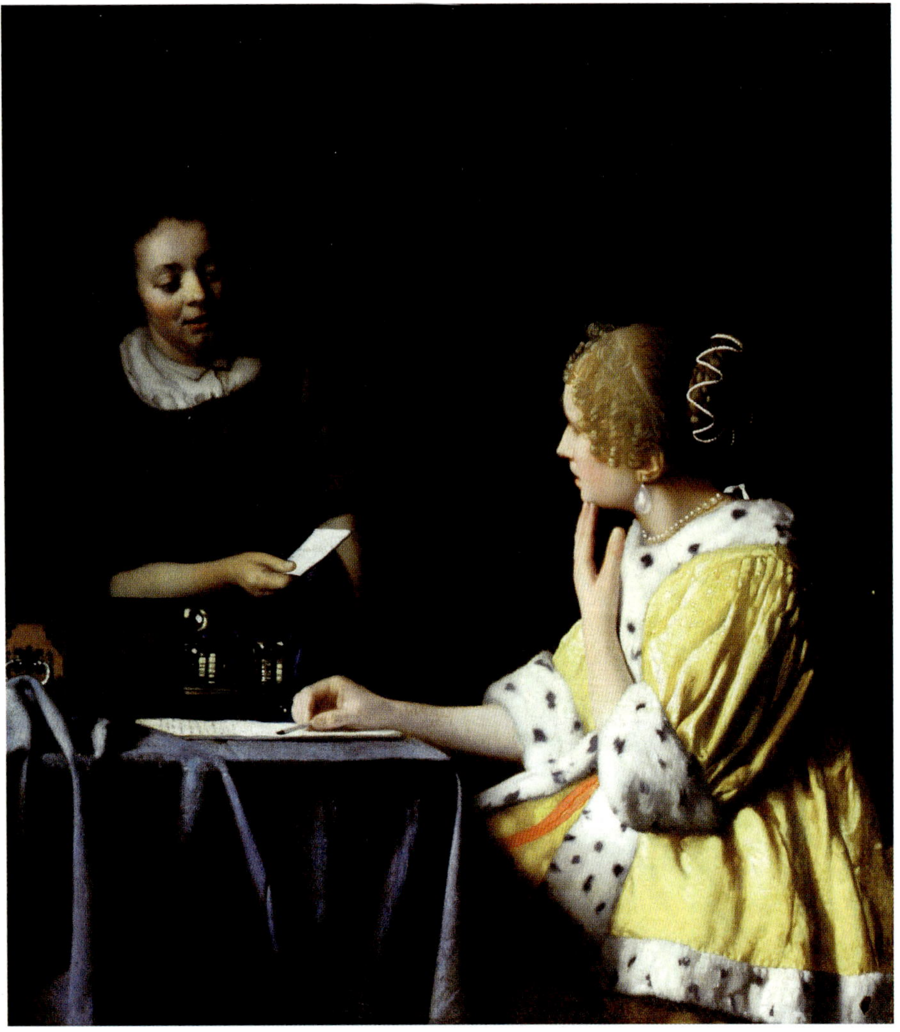

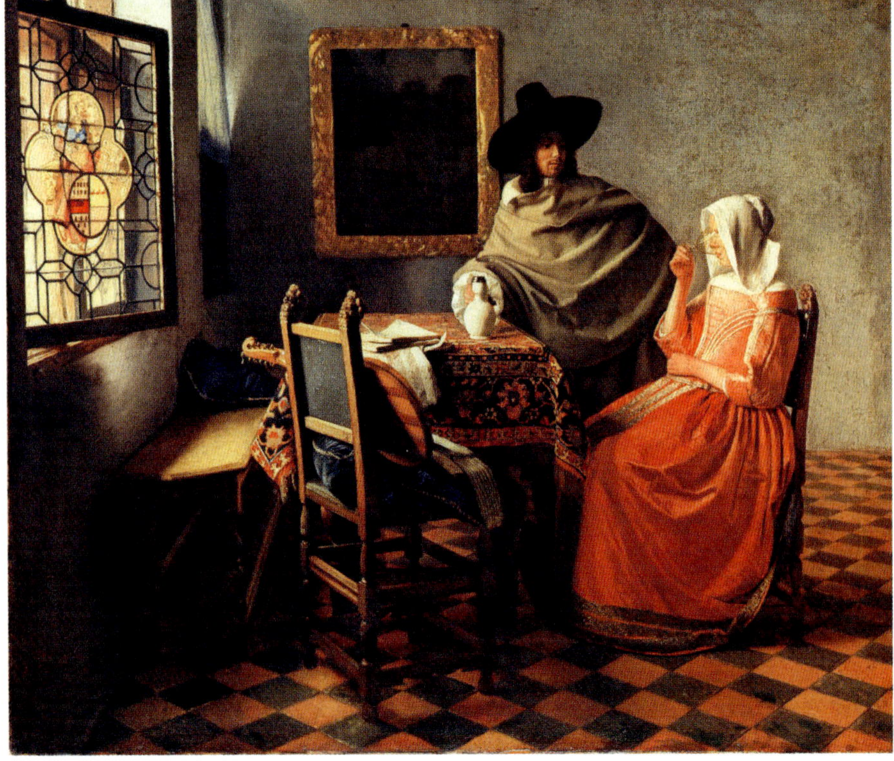

SLOW AND CAREFUL WORK

Vermeer's uniqueness lies in his choice of subject matter and the individual spaces he created with striking perspective and vivid colours, seemingly lit by clear, bright or diffused light. With the exception of two cityscapes and two allegories, he mainly produced views of domestic interiors and portraits in which his characters' inner lives are implied, and the tactile qualities of textures are clearly conveyed. Almost all of the interiors seem to be set in two fairly small rooms in his house in Delft, as the same furniture and decorations are depicted. Most of these paintings allude to some sort of story, each of which remains enigmatic.

Among Vermeer's influences were Jacob van Loo (1614–70), Carel Fabritius, the Leiden fijnschilders, Pieter de Hooch, Caravaggio and the Utrecht Caravaggisti (some of Vermeer's paintings feature works by the Utrecht Caravaggisti in the backgrounds).

Each painting by Vermeer portrays a tranquil and often ambiguous moment in time, although his method was far from spontaneous. He worked slowly and carefully, producing far fewer paintings than other Dutch painters; approximately two, three or four finished works a year.

No drawings, sketches or other preparatory works by Vermeer survive, which has given rise to a great deal of speculation about his methods. Two of Vermeer's paintings feature scientists at work, which aligns with his interest in scientific and technological developments, but it has also often been speculated that he used instruments to assist his painting as he never drew preparatory lines. Among the tools it is suggested that he used were a compass

Above left: Mistress and Maid, *1666–67, portrays a wealthy young woman writing a letter and her maid bringing her a letter. Letter writing and receiving was a popular subject during the period.*

Left: Painted in c.1658–60, The Glass of Wine *demonstrates Vermeer's skill in portraying textures and light as well as an enigmatic narrative.*

for drawing circumferences and a camera obscura for projecting and then tracing images.

FINANCIAL BREAKDOWN

In 1672, the year of the Rampjaar (see page 80), a severe economic downturn occurred in the Netherlands. Panic ensued and the following five years remained depressed. This damaged Vermeer's businesses as a painter and an art dealer and he suddenly faced financial ruin.

Nonetheless, he carried on painting, still using costly natural ultramarine, which suggests that at least one of his patrons was continuing to commission him, and in 1674, he joined the local civic guard, demonstrating the continuance of his involvement in Delft's communal life. In the summer of 1675, he borrowed 1,000 guilders from an Amsterdam silk trader using his mother-in-law's property as security, and then suddenly, at the end of the year, completely unexpectedly after a short illness, he died. Left with 11

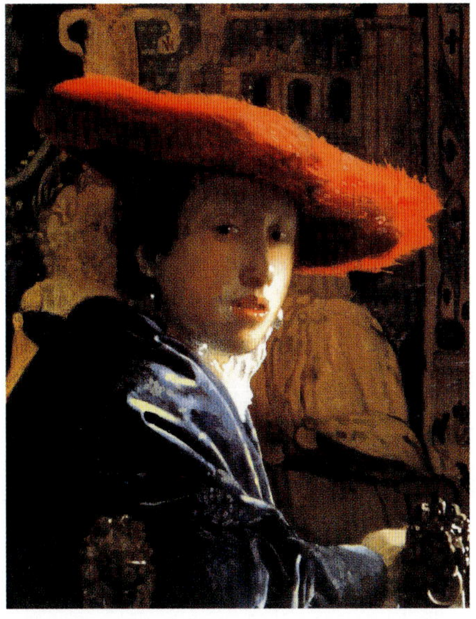

Above: Painted in c.1665, Girl with a Red Hat *is the only known painting by Vermeer on panel. The girl has turned in her chair to look directly at viewers.*

children and debts, Catharina attributed her husband's early death to money worries. She applied to the High Court in The Hague, and relinquished all her rights of inheritance; Vermeer's creditors therefore inherited the paintings he had not sold during his lifetime.

Vermeer and his art were soon forgotten, and it was not until the 19th century that it was rediscovered by Gustav Friedrich Waagen (1794–1868) and Théophile Thoré-Bürger (1807–69) and became internationally admired. Despite not having any pupils, Vermeer was influential to other Dutch painters, including de Hooch, Metsu and van Hoogstraten.

Below: View of the Houses in Delft, *or* The Little Street, *c.1658 – full of textural detail, the painting shows an area of Delft where Vermeer's aunt lived.*

CAMERA OBSCURA

Since Vermeer's rediscovery in the 1860s, aspects of his art have mystified many who have wondered whether his incredibly accurate perspective and foreshortening, and almost photo-realistic paintings, could be the result of his use of a camera obscura; a box or cupboard into which an image is projected. While there is no physical evidence or documentation, the theory has persisted, and various art historians have performed experiments to try to establish the truth. The conclusion remains divided. No one aims to minimize Vermeer's achievements, but many in Delft in the mid-17th century were fascinated by lenses and optics, and those who believe that he used the instrument maintain that he was in accord with the spirit of his time. Those who believe that he did not, assert that his exceptional skills eliminated any need for mechanical devices.

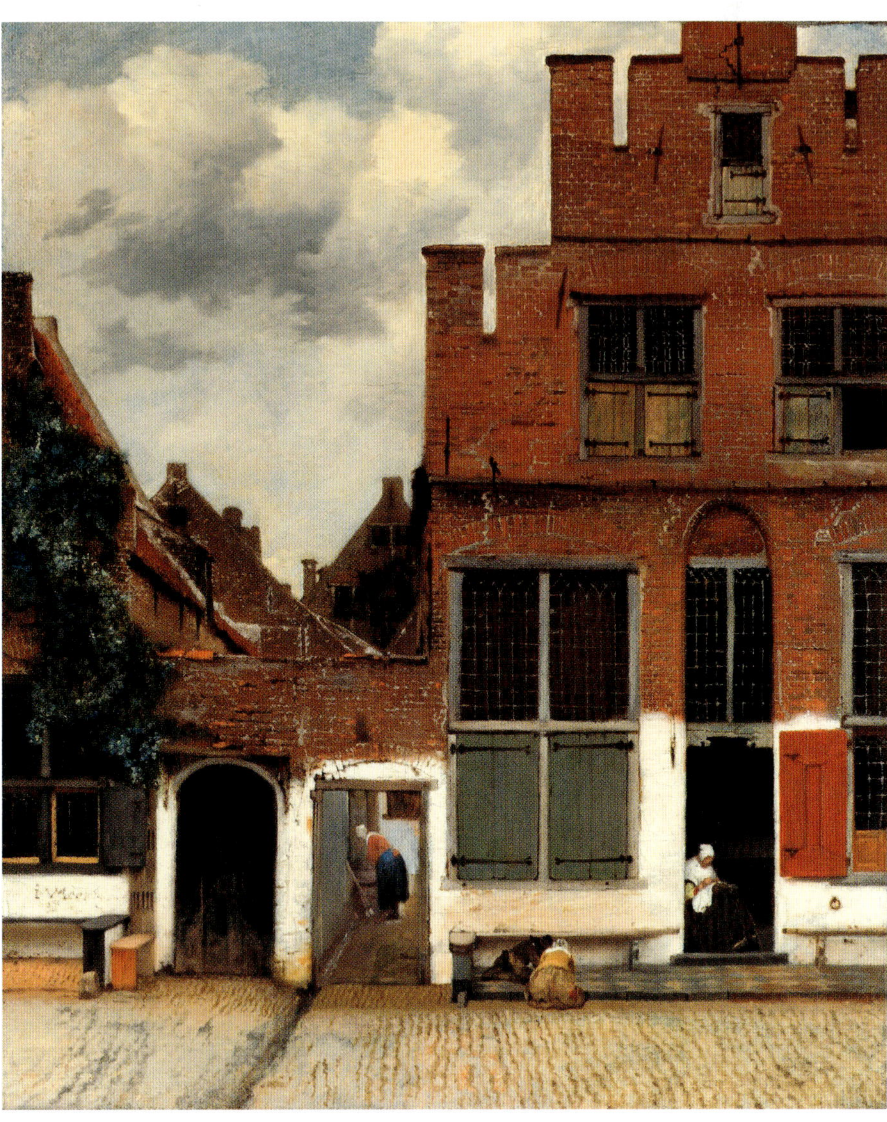

NICOLAES MAES

One of the most accomplished of Rembrandt's pupils, Nicolaes Maes (1634–1693), also spelled Nicolaas Maas, initially painted large-scale biblical scenes, but between 1654 and 1660 he concentrated on domestic views with few figures. Eventually, he devoted himself to portraiture which brought the most success of all.

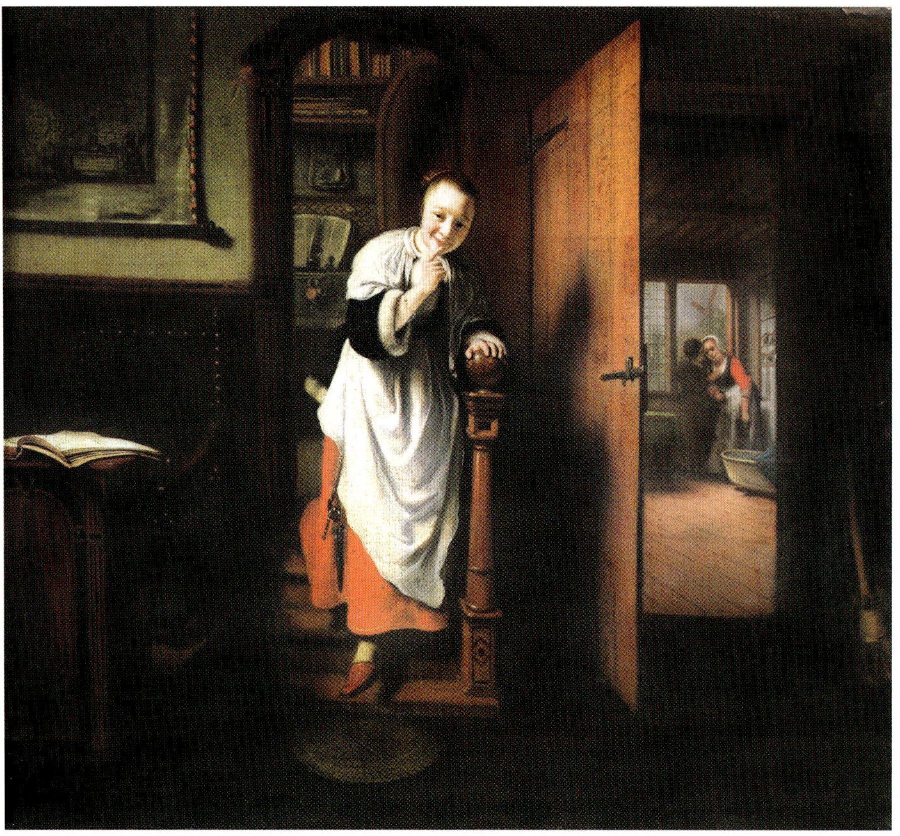

Left: Lovers with a Woman Listening. *Engaging viewers with her direct gaze, expression of collusion and gesture to be silent, this woman invites viewers to notice the lovers in another room.*

Below: In The Idle Servant, *a housewife invites viewers to witness the laziness of the sleeping servant who has left her dishes unwashed and has allowed the cat to snatch a fowl.*

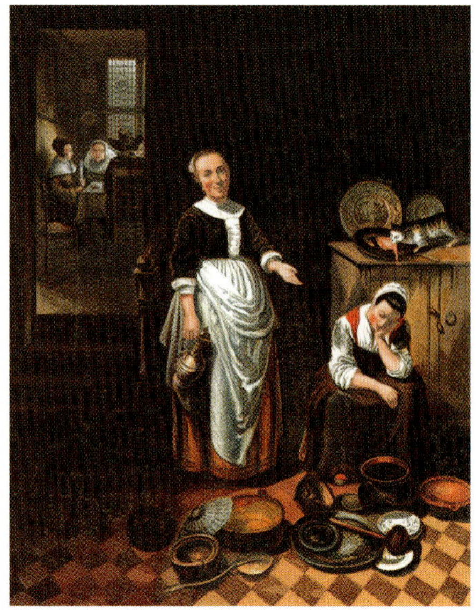

The second son of a cloth merchant, Nicolaes Maes was born in Dordrecht where he learned to draw with an unidentified artist. In 1648, when he was about 15, his father died, and Maes moved to Amsterdam where he entered Rembrandt's workshop. He remained with Rembrandt until 1653, learning all he could from the master, including the use of a rich, glowing palette, chiaroscuro and methods of portraying atmosphere. His first works as a professional artist were fairly large-scale history scenes, although he also painted some smaller genre works, and it is for these that he has become most recognized.

SHARING SECRETS

One of the most individual elements of Maes's genre paintings is his frequent inclusion of one character who looks directly at viewers and appears to invite them to share a secret. These paintings are generally set in domestic interiors with partial views into other rooms, giving viewers the opportunity to see things happening elsewhere. This is what the main figure is inviting viewers to notice, which creates the idea of a viewer participation and a sense of intimacy. Among Maes's favourite subjects for his genre scenes were women spinning or lace-making, eavesdropping, standing on stairs, reading the Bible or preparing meals, such as peeling apples.

A CHANGE OF STYLE

After leaving Rembrandt's workshop, in 1653, Maes returned to Dordrecht, where he produced almost all of his small-scale genre paintings. Soon however, Rembrandt's influence began to diminish, and Maes abandoned his warm-toned palette for a lighter and cooler range of colours, including blacks and greys in shadows rather than browns, although he continued to utilize the drama of chiaroscuro.

Mainly in order to earn more money, by the end of the 1650s, Maes turned to portraiture, and from about 1660 he worked exclusively in this genre. At this time, as well as his changing painting style, he also altered his signature from block letters to a more elegant script.

As he concentrated on portraits, Mae's style became closer to the Flemish painter Anthony van Dyck than Rembrandt, with his use of smoother paint and inclusion of finer details. At some point between 1660 and 1670, he travelled to Antwerp to study the work of Flemish masters including van Dyck and Rubens, and there he also met Jacob Jordaens (1593–1678). Back in Dordrecht, his portraits became extremely sought after.

At the beginning of 1654, Maes married a young widow with whom he had three children (although one died at a young age), and in 1658, he bought a house on the prestigious Steegoversloot in Dordrecht. He paid for the house in part with a family portrait of the previous owner and his family.

The money Maes earned for his portraits was fairly good at a time when the Dutch economy was struggling, and he was well-regarded in Dordrecht. A member of the local civic guard, he rose to the rank of lieutenant. However, in 1673, following the Rampjaar, he and his family left Dordrecht for Amsterdam where his portraits became greatly in demand among the large and wealthy population. Considered the leading portrait painter of the time, he ended up with too many commissions and could not finish all the portraits he agreed to. Prosperous and successful, Maes died a few years after his wife and was buried in the Oude Kerk.

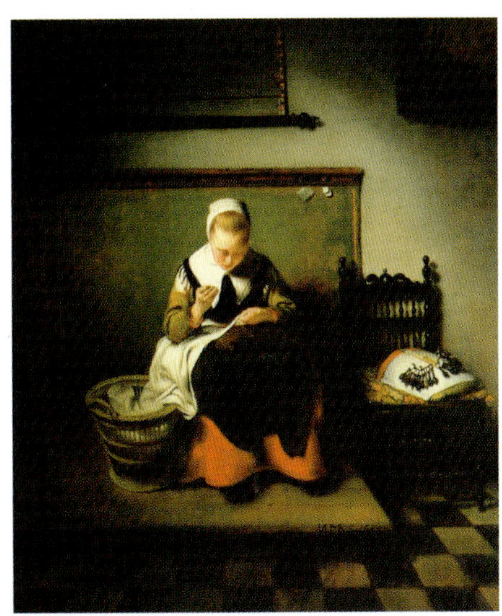

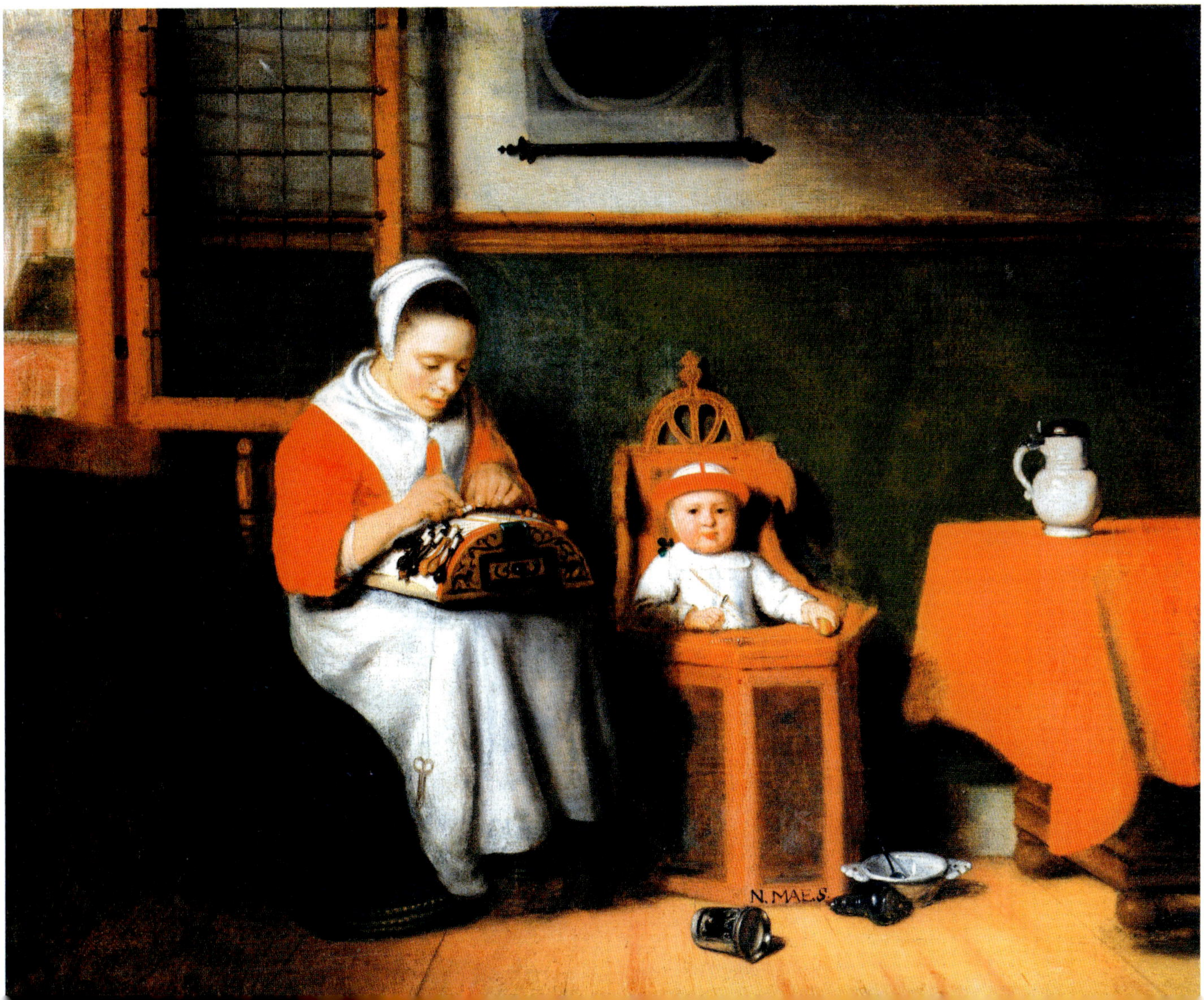

Above: With meticulous attention to detail, A Young Woman Sewing, *painted in 1655, reveals dignity in a mundane task.*

Below: The Lacemaker. *With wonderful realism, Maes portrays an interior scene where a woman concentrates on her work and a baby gazes directly at viewers.*

FRANS VAN MIERIS THE ELDER

With his polished, detailed domestic scenes, Frans van Mieris the Elder (1635–1681) was one of Gerrit Dou's most accomplished pupils and the most distinguished member of a family of artists. Depicting both the lives of working-class figures and those of the wealthy, his paintings were in great demand.

Born into a family of gold- and silversmiths and painters, Frans van Mieris the Elder grew up in Leiden and as his father Jan Bastiaans van Mieris (1586–1650) wanted him to join the family profession, he was first apprenticed to his cousin Willem Fransz van Mieris (c.1600–56) for six years. However, the boy's outstanding drawing skills soon became apparent, and his father sent him to the drawing master and glass engraver Abraham Toorenvliet (c.1610–92) in 1650.

'PRINCE OF MY PUPILS'

Van Mieris developed so well under Toorenvliet that he was next sent to Gerrit Dou, one of the most highly respected local artists and the most important of the Leiden fijnschilders. Within a short time, Dou nicknamed van Mieris the 'prince of my pupils.' For a period, van Mieris also trained with the Leiden history painter and portraitist Abraham van den Tempel (1622/3–72) before returning again to Dou's studio.

Below left: After van Mieris painted Woman at a Harpsichord, *1658, Vermeer, Jan Steen and others painted their own versions of it.*

Below: The Doctor's Visit, *1667, shows a young woman with a dreamy look in her eyes. The doctor is checking her pulse; this is no illness, the woman is lovesick.*

Bottom: A patron is visiting an artist and discussing various artefacts around the room in The Painter's Studio, *c.1659.*

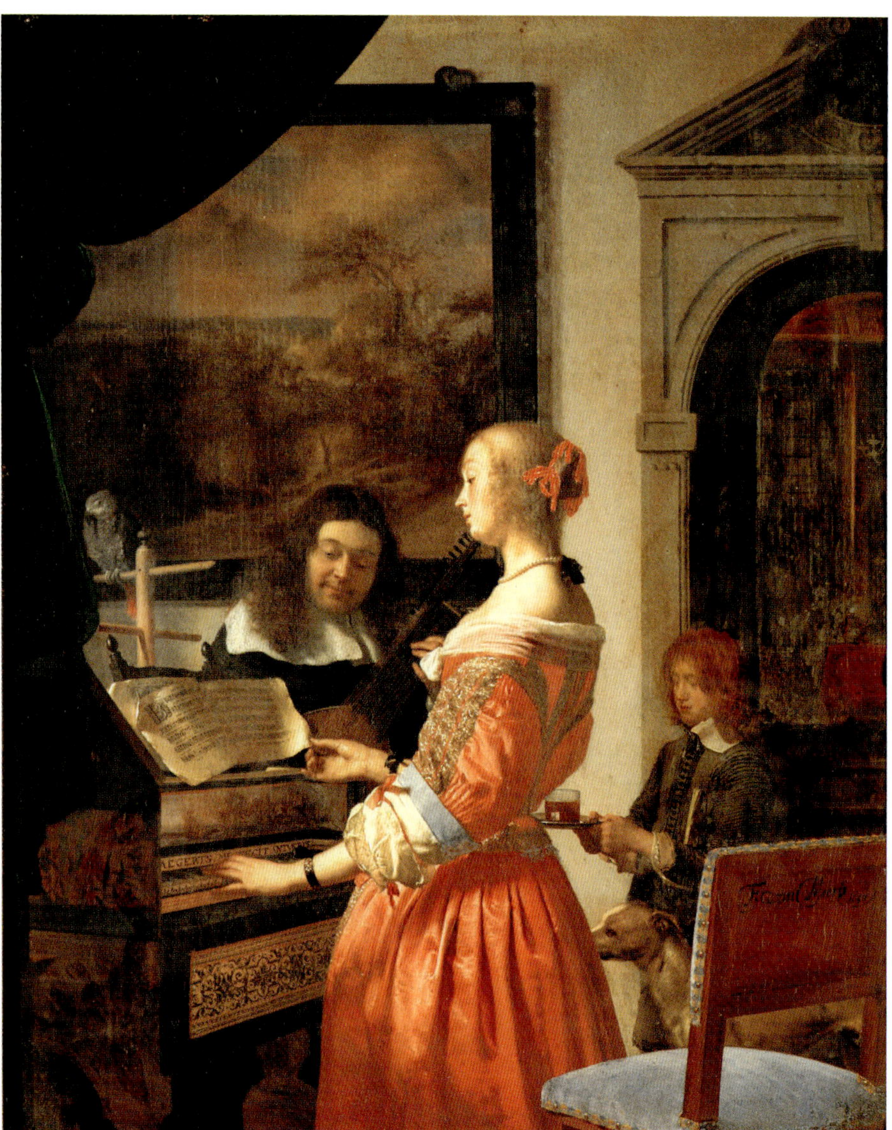

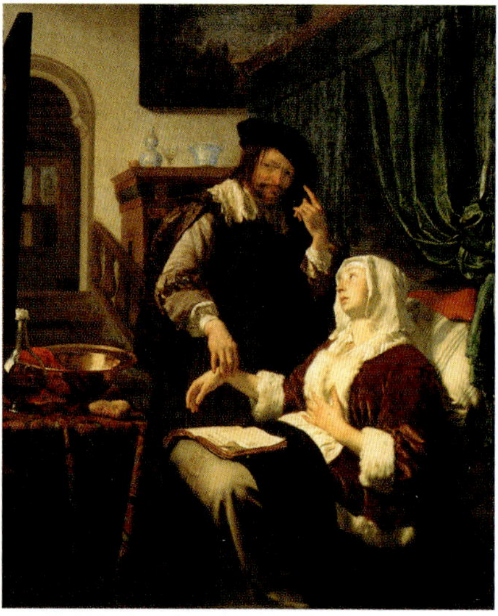

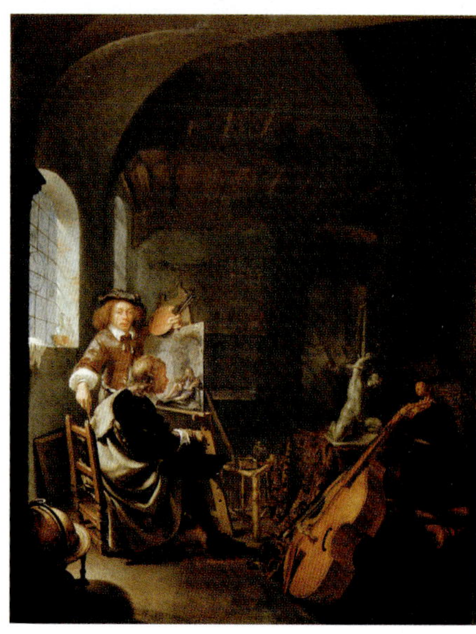

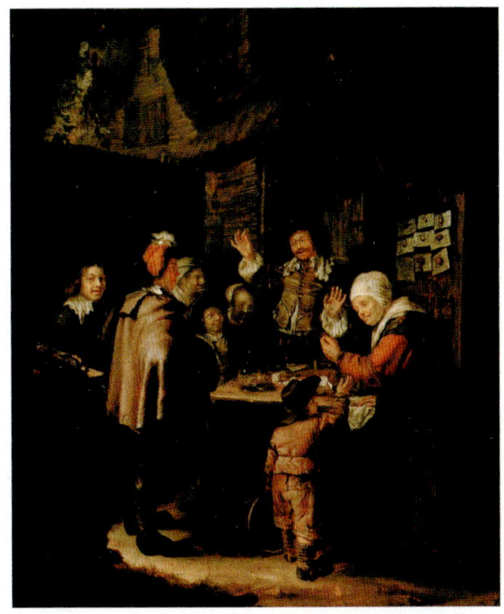

Above: Painted between 1653–55, The Dutch Charlatan *shows a conman at work, enthralling all who are gathered around him, except for the young child.*

Right: One of several paintings of a similar theme, Lady at her Toilet, c. 1659–60, *shows the skills that made van Mieris so admired.*

From the start of his career, van Mieris followed the approach of the Leiden fijnschilders, initially emulating Dou's style, with carefully proportioned subjects, bright colours, and an astute attention to detail, but after joining the Leiden Guild of Saint Luke in 1658, his individual style began to emerge. He still often derived subjects from Dou, but also began drawing inspiration from Adriaen van Ostade and Gerard ter Borch. He abandoned the extreme detailing so typical of Dou, instead focusing more on the interaction between figures, creating a sense of liveliness. His style became extremely popular, and eventually, he was one of the highest-paid painters in the Dutch Republic.

Part of the reason for his change from Dou's approach was the influence of his good friend Jan Steen, who had returned to Leiden from Delft in 1657. From that time, the two men mutually influenced each other. Also in 1657, van Mieris married Cunera van der Cock (1629/30–1700), six days after the birth of their first daughter, Christina (1657–85). The couple had four more children,

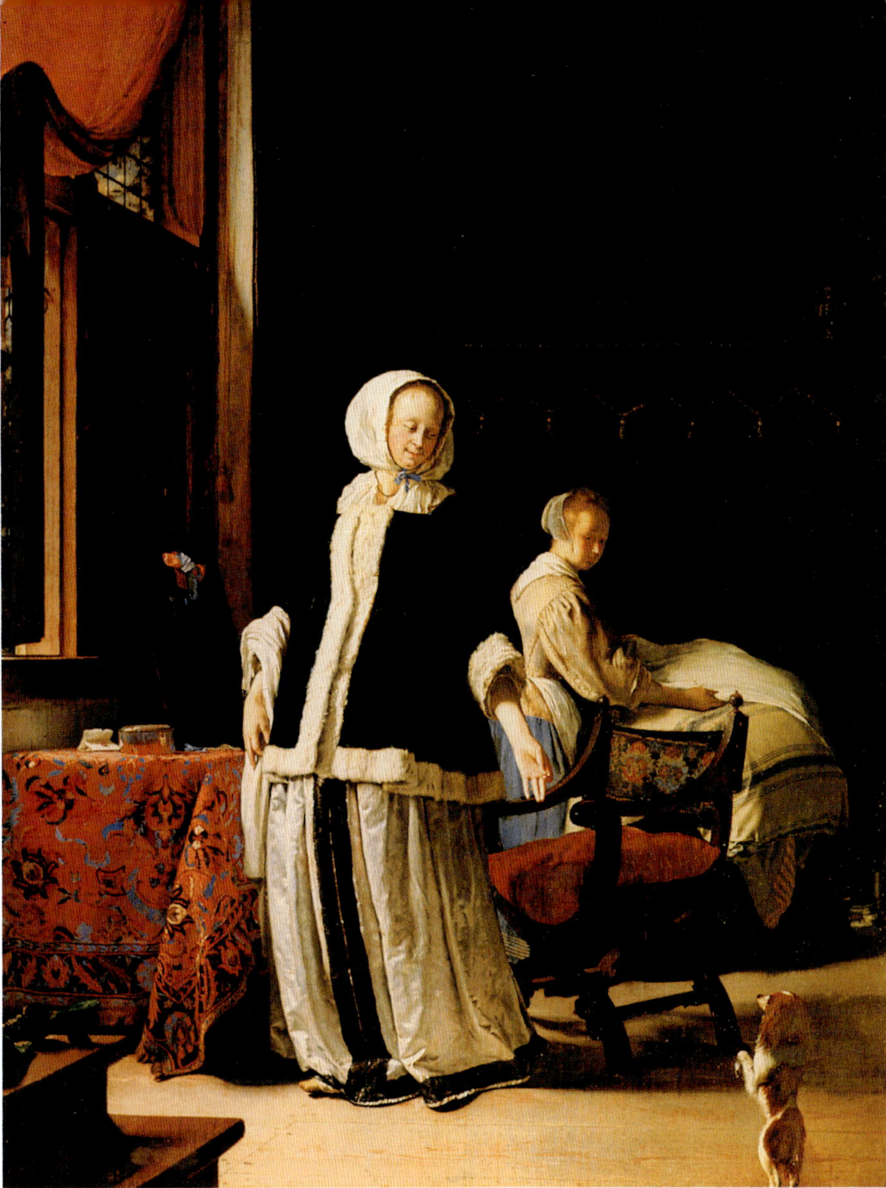

including his sons Jan (1660–90) and Willem (1662–1747), who also became artists – as did, later, his grandson Frans II (1689–1763).

PATRONS

Held in great esteem, van Mieris was patronized by a number of Leiden's wealthiest and most prominent citizens and by foreign nobility. Among his patrons were Isaac Gerard (1616–94), Franciscus de le Boë Sylvius (1614–72), Cornelis Paets (1636–94) and someone who has only been identified as 'Vredenburg.' The most important of these was Sylvius who owned a large art collection and who also acted as an agent for van Mieris, for instance, obtaining him a commission from the Archduke Leopold Wilhelm (1614–62) in Vienna. The Archduke subsequently tried to persuade van Mieris to work at the court in Vienna for a huge remuneration, but he declined the offer.

Sylvius also introduced van Mieris to Cosimo III de' Medici, Grand Duke of Tuscany when he visited Leiden in 1667 and 1669. Cosimo engaged van Mieris to paint five pictures, including a self-portrait for his gallery in Florence.

Despite having so many patrons who paid high prices for his work, van Mieris was almost constantly in debt. Records of unpaid bills at taverns and letters complaining of late delivery of paintings tend to corroborate Houbraken's claim that he was a drunkard. He is reported to have turned up drunk for at least one appointment, having left the painting he was supposed to be delivering at the tavern he had just been in. With regards to the payment for this painting, his wife insisted that the money be given to her, otherwise she said, it would evaporate 'like acid on an etching plate.' Houbraken documented that he was often with his friend Jan Steen and that 'our Mieris tended to have one too many.'

JAN VAN DER HEYDEN

One of the first Dutch artists to specialize in town- and cityscapes and a leading architectural painter, Jan van der Heyden (1637–1712) worked as a draughtsman, painter, glass painter and printmaker, while also working as an engineer and inventor, and making significant contributions to firefighting technology.

Born in Gorinchem, the third of eight children, Jan van der Heyden was about eight years old when he moved to Amsterdam with his family, and he remained there for the rest of his life. It is unclear what artistic training he received if any, although it is likely that he was initially apprenticed to his eldest brother, Goris van der Heyden (c.1607–67) who made and sold mirrors, and he may also have received drawing instruction from the glass painter Jacob van der Ulft (1621–89).

LANDSCAPES

At the start and end of his career, van der Heyden painted still lifes. In addition, early on he painted on glass using a skilled technique that later became known as verre eglomisé. He also painted landscapes, both on canvas and

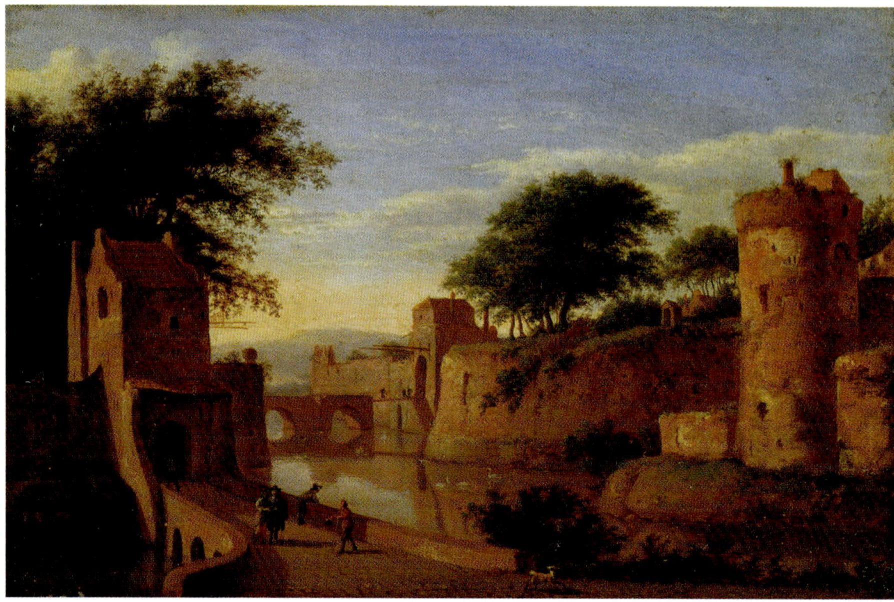

Above: Van der Heyden painted A Fortified Moat or Canal *in c.1670 using oil on copper. As well as the imagined, Italianate surroundings and light, he creates a narrative with the figures.*

on glass. Any figures in his landscapes however were painted by Adriaen van de Velde, and after van de Velde's death in 1672, by Johannes Lingelbach and Eglon van der Neer.

Although he was not a full-time artist, from early in his career, van der Heyden

commanded large sums of money for his paintings. Meanwhile he was also working as a civil engineer, inventor and municipal official, and he bought a house on Herengracht, along the most fashionable canal in Amsterdam. In 1661, he married Sara ter Hiel (c.1631–1712).

As well as some still lifes and landscapes, most of van der Heyden's paintings are of town- and cityscapes and views of groups of buildings such as country houses. He mainly painted views of Amsterdam, but occasionally painted other towns and cities, and it seems that he probably visited Brussels, Cologne and London. While many of his views are depictions of actual locations, others are imaginary, of the type known as capricci (or capriccio in singular), a term meaning architectural fantasies that first emerged in Italy in the 16th century. Characterized by precise attention to detail, all van der Heyden's paintings

Below: Painted with sharp, one-point perspective in c.1653, this is van der Heyden's View of the Boterbrug with the Tower of the Stadhuis, Delft.

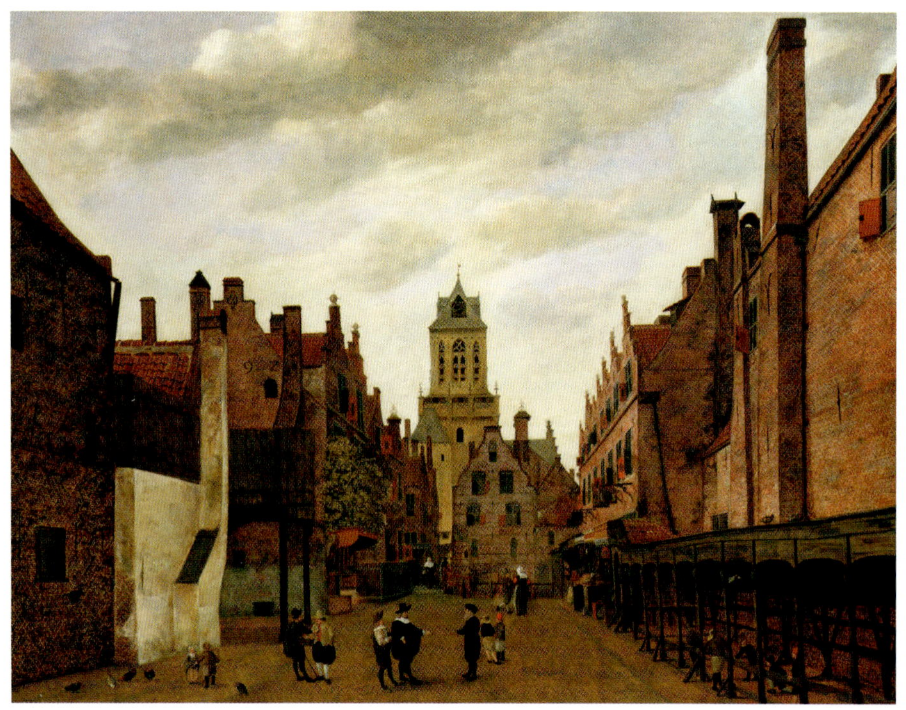

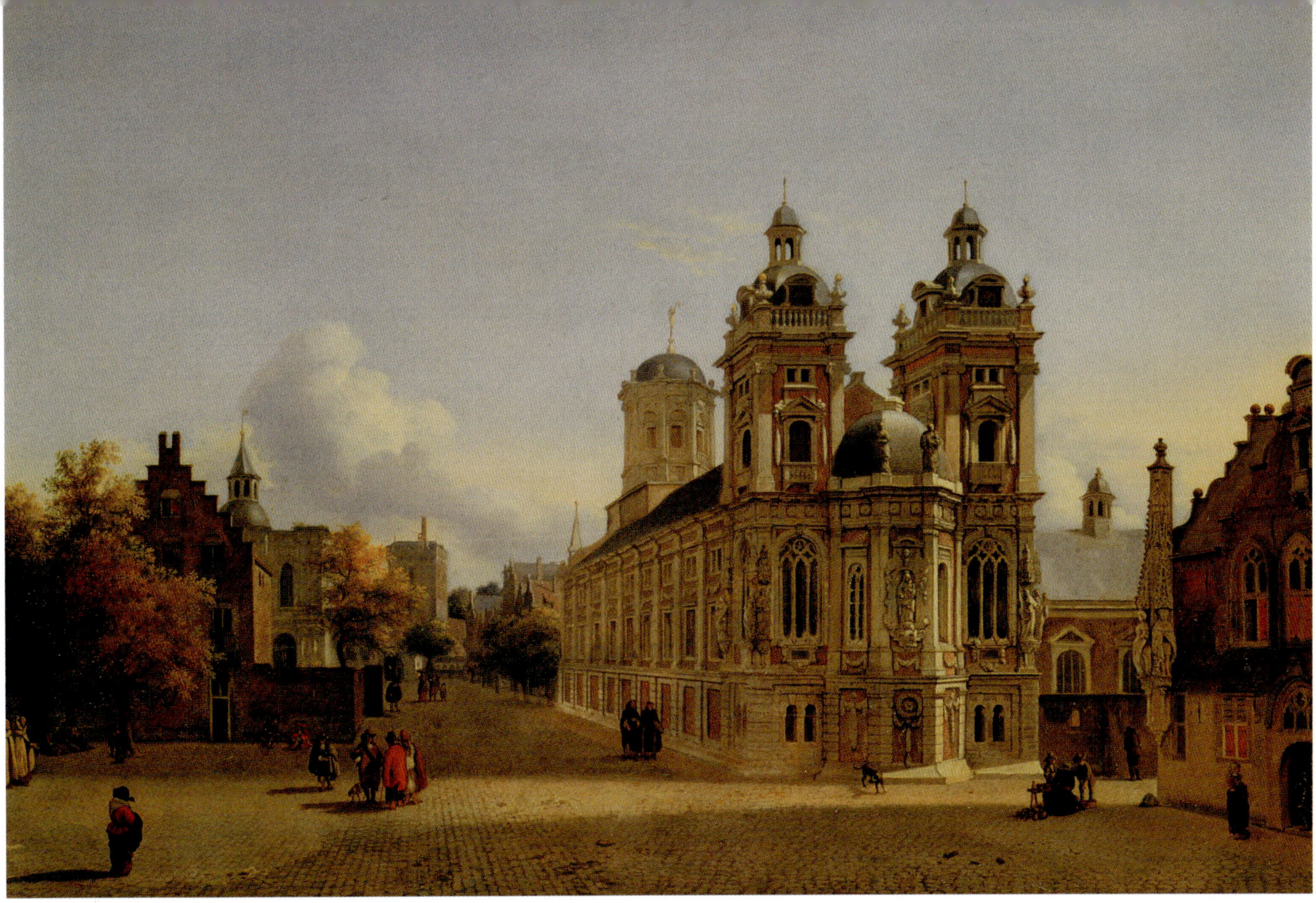

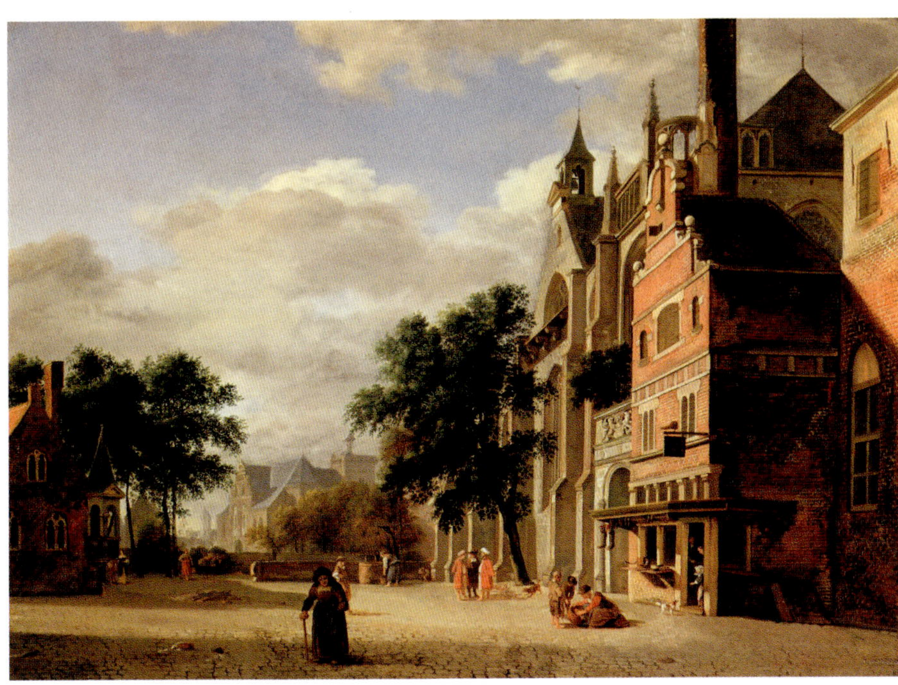

Above: Cityscape with a Church and a Square *is a view of Düsseldorf, painted c.1666–69 by van der Heyden. It was a collaborative painting; Adriaen van de Velde painted the figures.*

Below: With warm Italian light and carefully composed buildings, A Capriccio of a Town Square *is an example of van der Heyden's imaginative, but realistic-looking scenes.*

are bathed in a bright, crisp light, with balanced and harmoniously coloured compositions, each rendered with remarkable detail and realism, created with various methods. For instance, to create the texture of bricks, he pressed a metal plate into his paint while it was still wet. Similarly, he used moss or a sponge to create leaves on trees. Overall, his cityscapes became influential in the development of architectural

painting in northern Europe during the 18th century.

Although his painting output was considerable, van der Heyden remained busy with his other occupations. Among his other achievements were the design and implementation of a street-lighting system for Amsterdam that remained in operation from 1669 until 1840 and was adopted as a model by many other towns in the Netherlands and abroad.

THE FIRE BRIGADE

From 1688 to 1671, van der Heyden and his brother Nicolaes, who was a hydraulic engineer, worked on the invention of a new water pumping mechanism for the fire brigade. In 1672, the brothers produced an improved fire hose. Preoccupied with effective methods for fighting fires, in 1679 he bought land on the Koestraat in order to build a house and fire-engine factory. He modified the manual fire engine, reorganized the volunteer brigade and wrote and illustrated (with his own etchings) the first ever firefighting manual, *The Fire Engine Book* (*Brandspuiten-boek*) that was published in 1690.

MEINDERT HOBBEMA

First a pupil and then a friend of Jacob van Ruisdael, Meindert (or Meyndert) Hobbema (1638–1709) lived all his life in Amsterdam. During his life he had little success, but after his death, he became one of the most highly respected landscapists of the Dutch Golden Age.

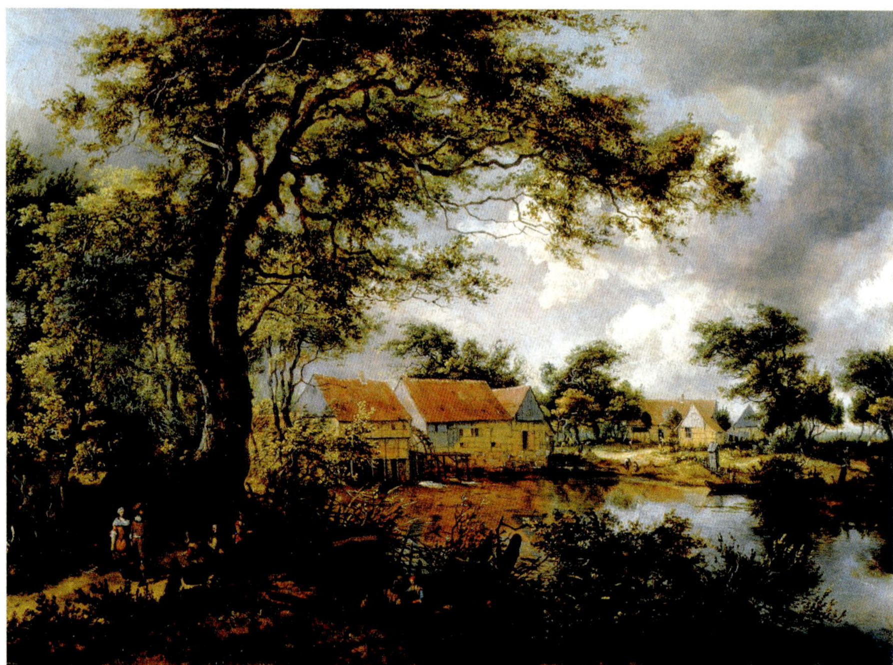

Above: Wooded Landscape with Water Mill, *c.1660s – Hobbema painted different scenes, but often used recognizable and similar elements in each..*

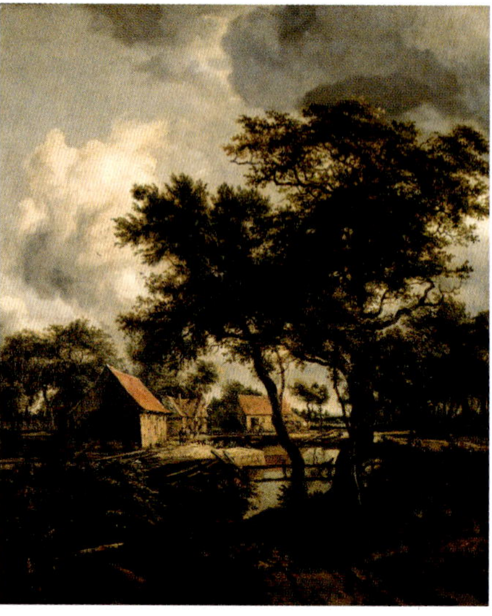

Above: Painted in the 1660s, The Watermill *features precisely painted trees and a path leading the eye.*

Meindert Lubbertsz changed his surname to Hobbema quite early in his life, although it is not clear why, although it was his grandmother's surname. At the age of 15, he and his younger brother and sister entered an orphanage and two years later, in 1655, he became apprenticed to the eminent landscape painter Jacob van Ruisdael. Hobbema was in fact van Ruisdael's only documented pupil.

Although Hobbema's earliest works from the late 1650s were mostly river scenes that seem to follow the styles of Cornelis Vroom and Salomon van Ruysdael, from around 1662, his work began to show more of his master's influence. However, for various reasons, he was not as successful as van Ruisdael during his career and it was only long after his death that his work became sought after. One of the main reasons for his lack of patronage and success was that he was working at the end of the Dutch Golden Age, when the general demand for painting had severely declined.

SUN-DAPPLED SCENES

From around 1662, Hobbema began painting wooded landscapes, often featuring ponds, roads and one or two buildings. Even in a period when specialization was the norm, this was quite a narrow subject area. He and van Ruisdael went on sketching tours together and regularly painted the same views, but van Ruisdael also painted other types of landscape. While van Ruisdael frequently captured weather effects and wilder scenes, Hobbema focused on restrained, gentle views of the sun-dappled countryside, with thick groupings of trees, meticulous depictions of foliage, an occasional stream and a few scattered buildings such as a watermill. Although these carefully composed paintings are not as dramatic as van Ruisdael's, during the 1660s, Hobbema produced most

HOUDING

A Dutch term that was used to describe a painting's 'pleasing and effective evocation of space' is 'houding.' All Dutch Golden Age paintings were expected to convey a realistic sense of the space and depth, light, harmonious colouring and include lifelike elements. The word 'houding' conveys the artist's success in creating an illusionistic space and in giving viewers the notion or impression that they can enter a picture and walk around it, or that they can perceive distances and spaces between the objects in a painting. The painters were expected to combine several techniques in the pursuit of this effect, including use of colour, chiaroscuro and atmospheric perspective, which together create a sense of depth and illusion. If the houding is to be considered successful, the painting will look like a piece of real life.

of his best works, increasing their size and the amount of detail included and conveying a varied range of the effects of natural light. His use of perspective was complex and compelling and his paths or roads usually wind diagonally across his compositions through abundant vegetation, with the few buildings generally placed in the near distance. No drawings by him survive even though his complex compositions appear to have been painted in the studio from preparatory works. For an unknown reason, after the late 1660s, he stopped signing his works, which caused later confusion.

In 1668, when he was 30, Hobbema married Eeltje Pieters Vinck (1634–1704) from Gorcum, who was cook to the burgomaster of Amsterdam. Van Ruisdael acted as one of the witnesses to their marriage in the Oude Kerk in Amsterdam.

Through his wife's influence, Hobbema obtained a minor municipal appointment as an exciseman, or wine-gauger, where his duties comprised checking weights and measures of imported wines.

After his marriage and employment, Hobbema painted less, but even so, he was never well known and died a pauper, a few years after the death of his wife. A victim of changing artistic fashions during his lifetime, his landscapes became much admired in the late 18th century.

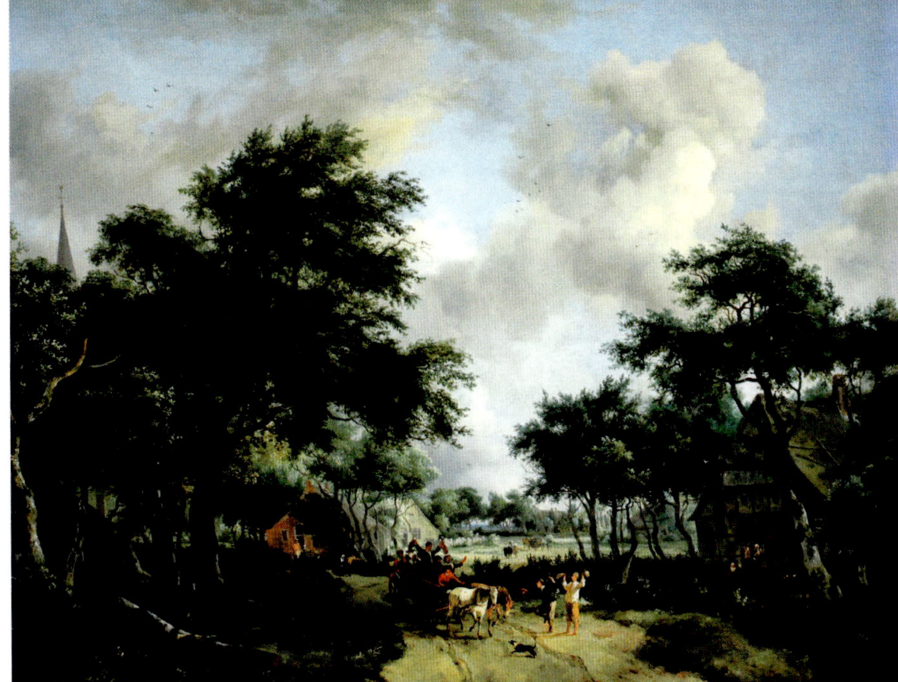

Above: Wooded Landscape with Merrymakers in a Cart, c.1665. *Lively travellers are enjoying themselves in a horse-drawn wagon as they drive through trees along a country road.*

Below: The Avenue at Middelharnis, *1689, is Hobbema's most famous work and generally regarded as the last great landscape of the Dutch Golden Age.*

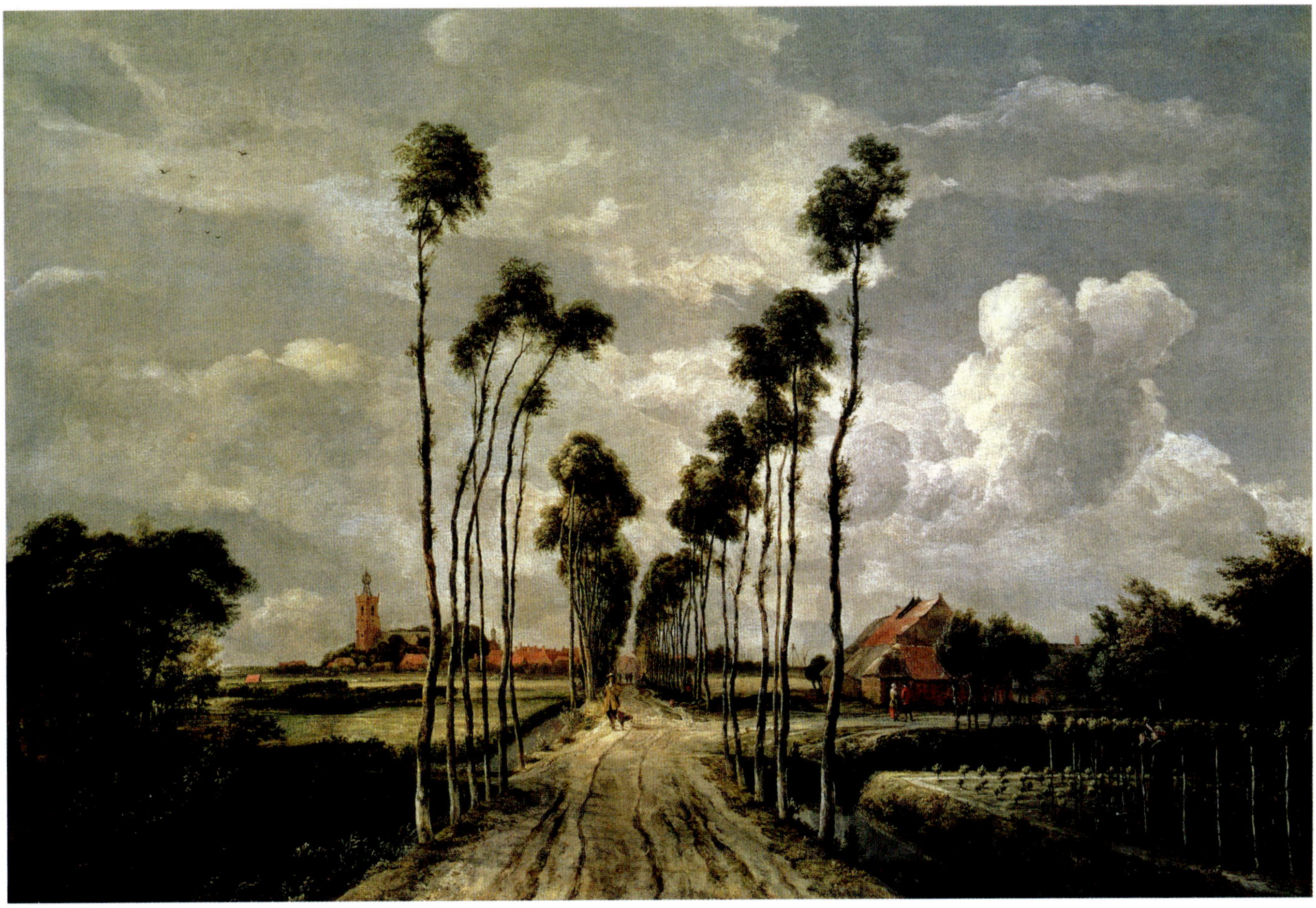

RACHEL RUYSCH

One of the most celebrated flower painters, who invented her own style, Rachel Ruysch (1664–1750) achieved international fame during her long career that spanned over six decades. Using both vibrant and delicate colours in dramatic chiaroscuro, she became the most documented female painter of the period.

Rachel Ruysch was born in The Hague, the daughter of an eminent botanist, physician and anatomist, Frederik Ruysch (1638–1731) and granddaughter of the architect, painter and printmaker Pieter Post (1608–69). As a child she drew her father's large collection of flower and insect samples, learning from his scientific approach and developing an ability to depict nature with great accuracy.

Ruysch moved to Amsterdam with her family and from 1679, when she was 15, she was apprenticed to the still life and prominent flower painter Willem van Aelst, with whom Maria van Oosterwijck had also worked. (his studio overlooked hers). Ruysch studied with van Aelst for four years until his death in 1683.

PLANTS, INSECTS AND LIZARDS

Along with the essentials of drawing and painting, van Aelst taught Ruysch ways to arrange flowers in a vase so that they appeared unplanned and casual, though from the start of her career, she painted flowers that did not

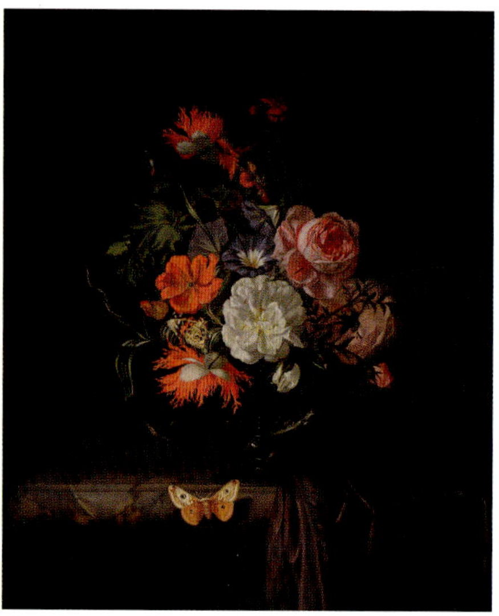

Above: A Still Life of Flowers in a Vase on a Ledge. *At a time when flowers were exceptionally costly to buy, realistic paintings of them meant that Ruysch must have earned well throughout her life.*

Left: A Still Life on a Marble Ledge. *Continuing the traditions of her fellow Golden Age painters, Ruysch created natural-looking compositions. Her lifelong career was unusual for a woman at that time, while she was simultaneously a wife and a mother of 10 children.*

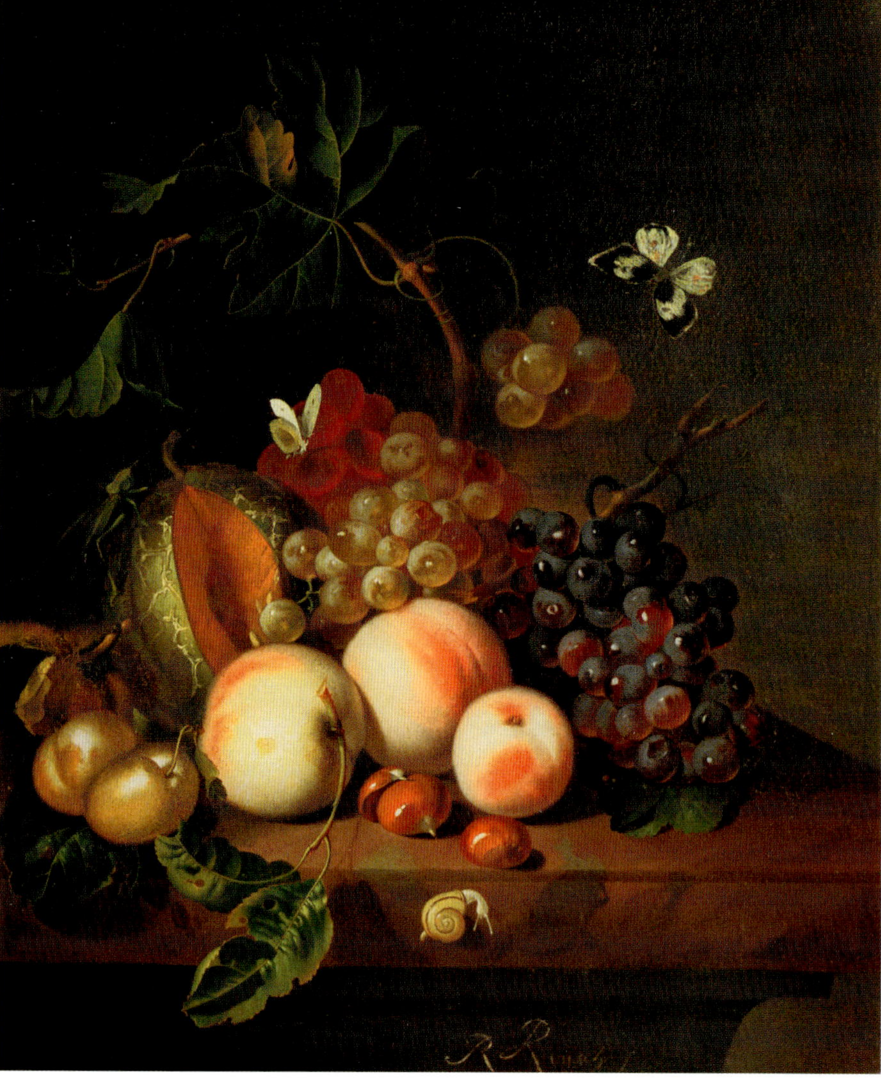

necessarily bloom at the same time. By the time she was 18, she was working as an independent artist, painting still lifes, flower paintings and woodland scenes, but it is unknown whether she ever joined the Amsterdam Guild of Saint Luke. As well as van Aelst's influence, her early paintings show the influence of the still life painter Otto Marseus van Schrieck (1620–78), who was known for his depictions of forest plants with insects and lizards.

WORKING MOTHER

In 1693, Ruysch married the Amsterdam portrait painter Juriaen Pool (1665–1745), with whom she had

10 children. Yet this did not prevent her from also maintaining her prolific career. By 1699, she and her husband moved to The Hague where they both joined the Guild of Saint Luke and in 1701, she became the first female member of the artist's society, Confrerie Pictura. Seven years later, she was invited to Düsseldorf to serve as court painter to the Elector Palatine in Düsseldorf, Johann Wilhelm II (1658–1716). She remained working there from that time working for the prince and his wife until 1716. Just before he died, Johann Wilhelm sent her 1711 painting *Still life with Fruit and Insects* and one other to his father-in-law Cosimo III de' Medici, the Grand Duke of Tuscany.

After returning to the Netherlands, Ruysch continued painting fruit and flower images in her precise and lifelike way for a prominent circle of wealthy patrons, and her richly detailed and delicate still lifes with fruit, flowers

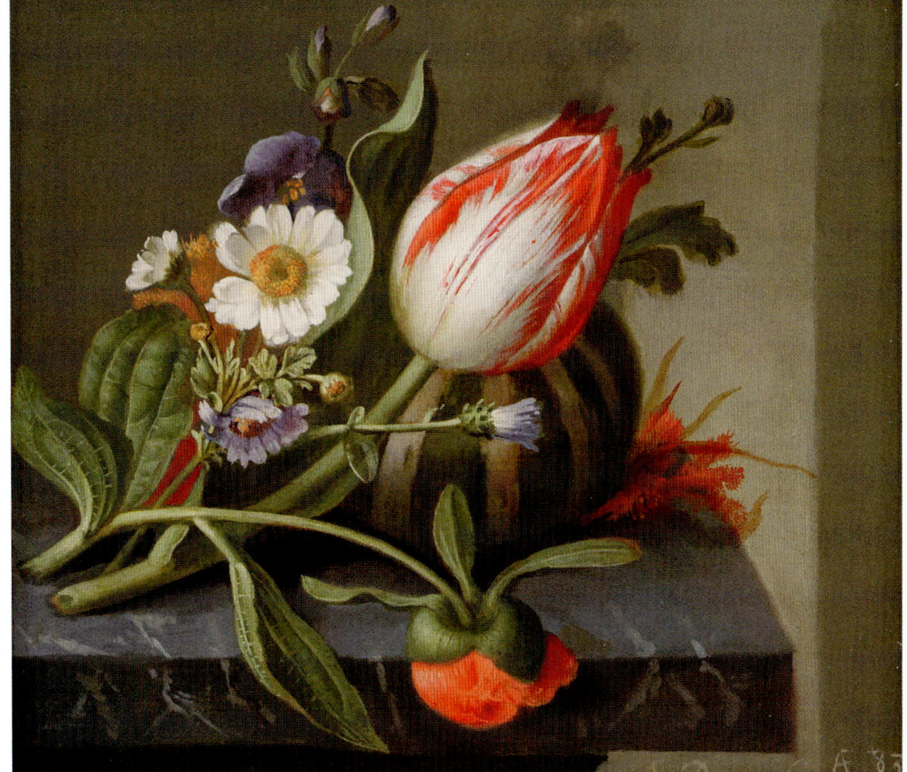

Above: Still Life of a Tulip, a Melon and Flowers on a Ledge. *A later painting, this conveys the bright colours and exoticism of the flowers that were so admired, but always with the underlying awareness of death's inevitability.*

and woodlands, set against dark backgrounds, commanded high prices. Although not particularly innovative, her work was exceptionally skilful. The bright colours she used effectively propelled her flowers forward in the painting. As well as her father's scientific drawings, her later works were in some ways inspired by Jan Davidsz de Heem and Abraham Mignon (1640–79).

Having painted hundreds of works over 70 years, Ruysch died at 86. Throughout her career, until her last work at the age of 83, she signed and wrote her age on her paintings. Her reputation remained high through her life, and it has never waned.

Below: Painted in 1711, Flowers and Insects *is one of the two paintings that was given to Cosimo de' Medici.*

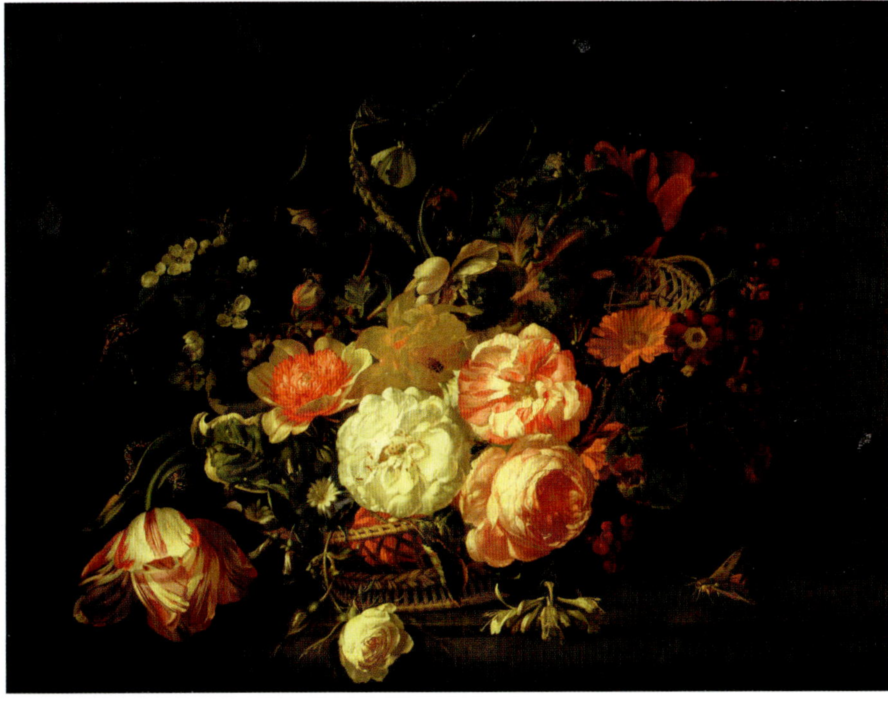

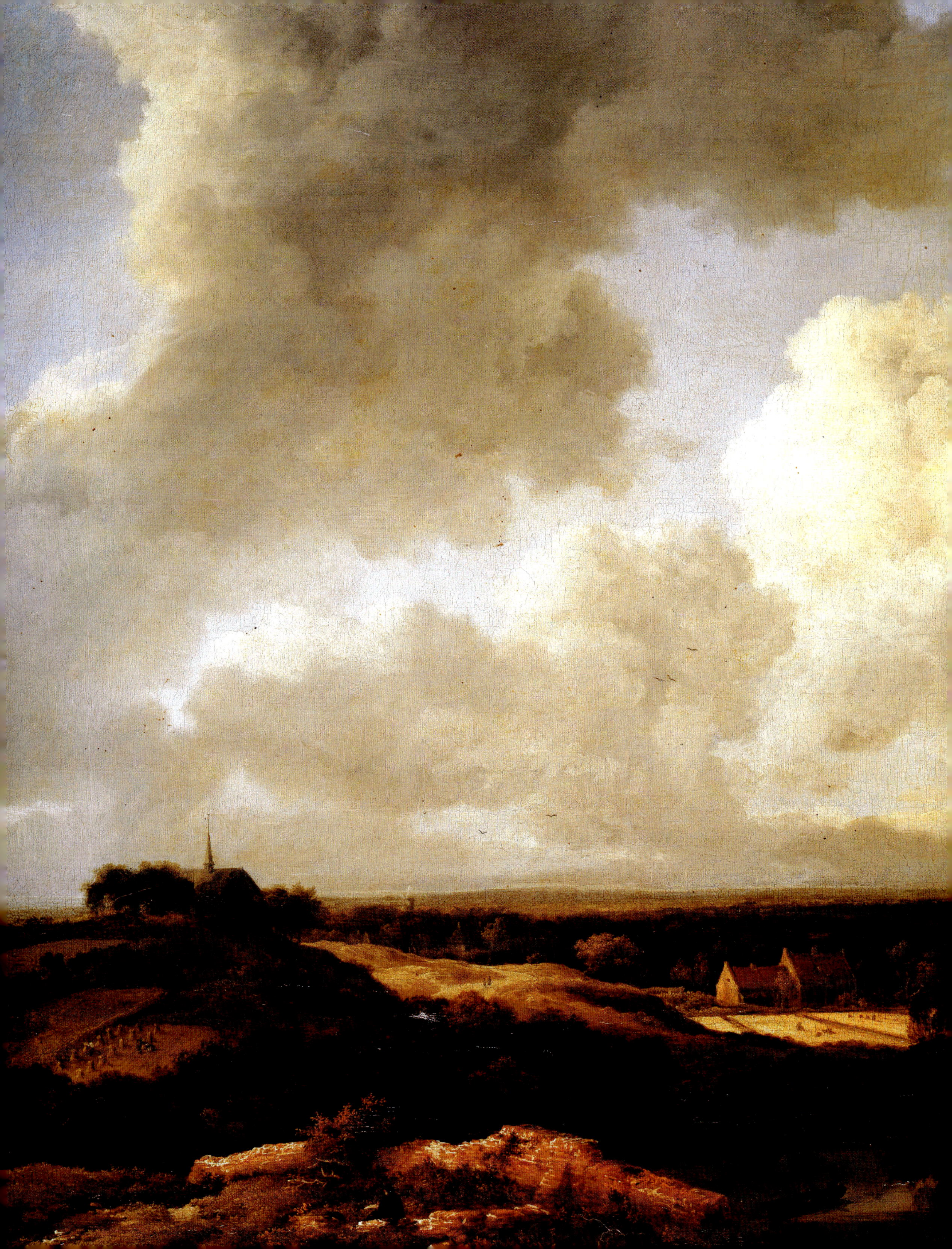

THE GALLERY

As has been seen, a number of factors including religious, political, intellectual, social and economic, facilitated the extraordinary flowering of art during the Dutch Golden Age. The artists painted life as never seen before; often their technical skills were outstanding and the art was distinctive in its use of lifelike people, objects and places. Yet these realistic-looking elements were often an amalgamation of truth and imagination, created with incredible powers of observation and a sharp visual memory. This section features an approximately chronological gallery of works by many outstanding artists, divided into the themes of landscape (which can include towns, the sea and so on); portraits; genre (in its more specific interpretation of scenes of everyday life); history and religion; and still life, giving an overview of what constituted the art of the Dutch Golden Age.

Left: An Extensive Landscape in Summer, *c.1665–70, by Jacob van Ruisdael. The low viewpoint adopted in this painting only allows a narrow strip of land to be depicted. Yet much is conveyed. Through the towering clouds, the slanting sun lights up patches of the fields below. Within the scene are a ruin, a farmhouse and a church that lead the eye around. Van Ruisdael's meticulous draughtsmanship and naturalistic colour inspired many artists after him, including the English landscapists in the 18th century and the French Barbizon School in the 19th.*

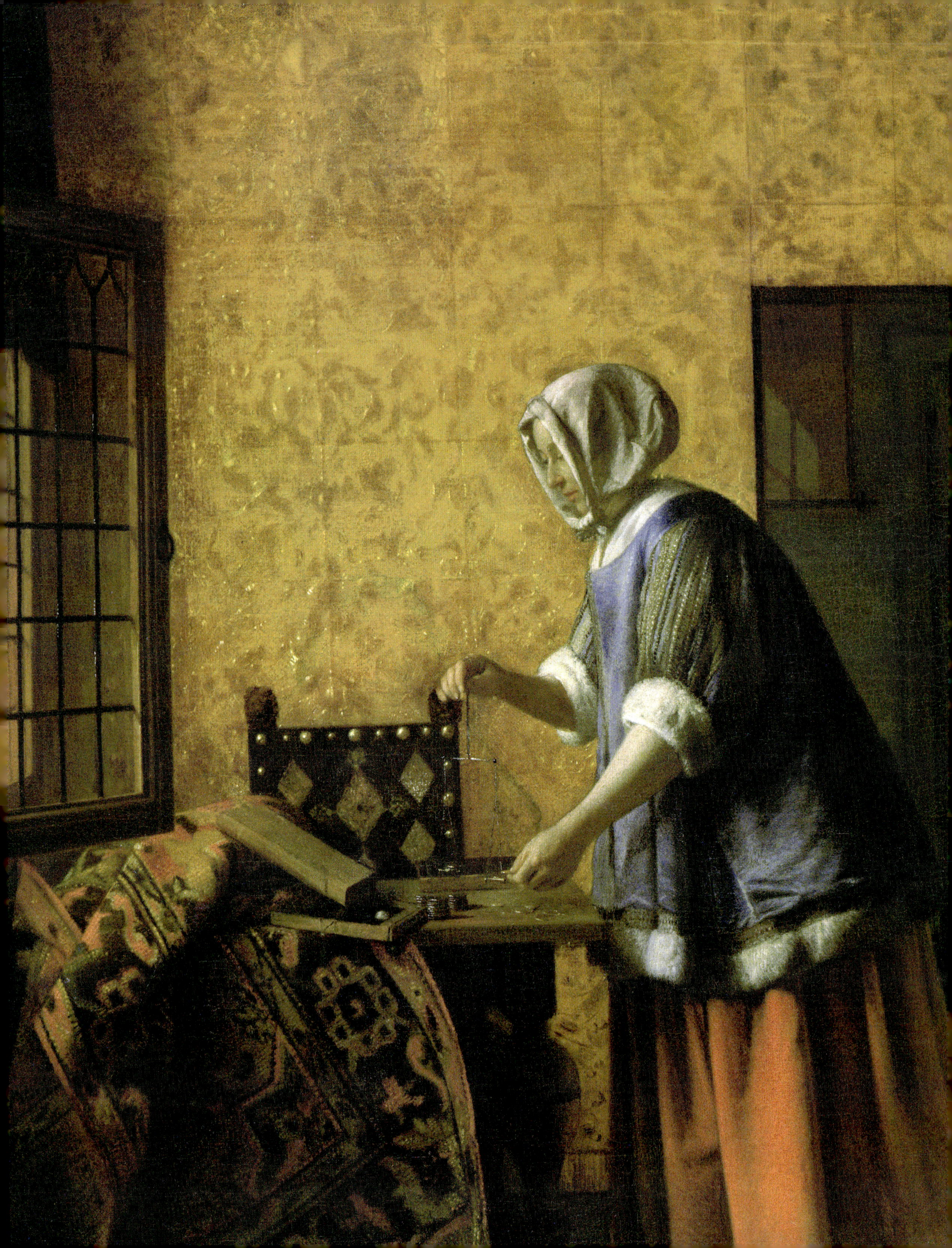

GENRE

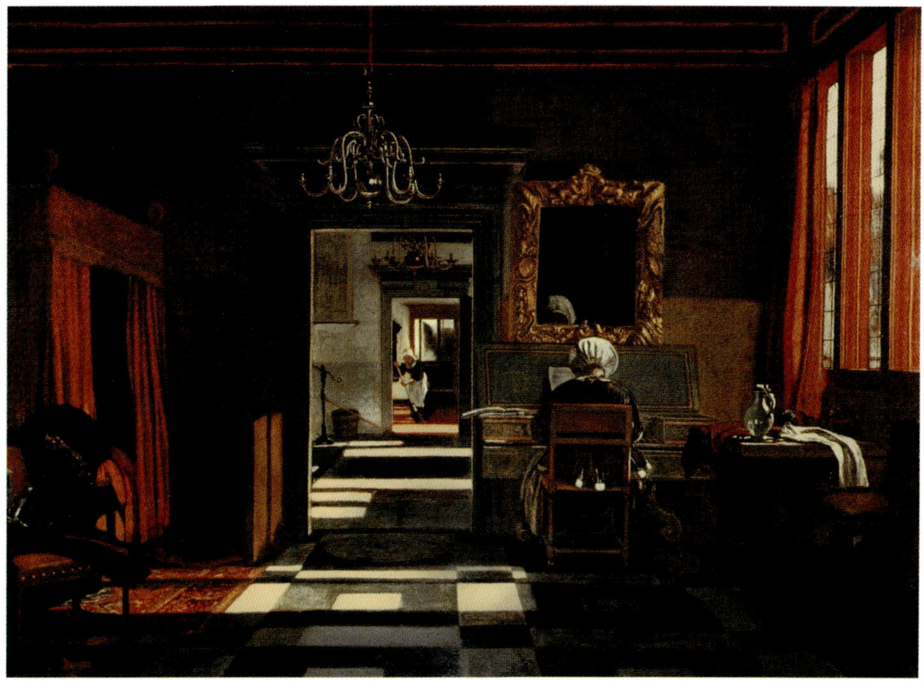

A fight in a tavern, a maid peeling apples, people playing games, the delivery of a secret love letter, a family playing musical instruments, a busy classroom; presenting a widely varying range of subjects from everyday life, both high and low – genre paintings are quintessential to the art of the Dutch Golden Age. Genre painting was particularly popular among Dutch citizens, and the many artists who specialized in the area made it one of the most highly respected of themes, after being dominated for so long by history paintings and portraits. Even though so many of the underlying moralizing elements are no longer recognized, the qualities of these paintings continue to have strong and widespread appeal.

Merrymakers at Shrovetide, Frans Hals, *c.*1616–17, oil on canvas, 131.4 x 99.7cm (51¾ x 39¼ in), The Metropolitan Museum of Art, New York, USA

Among Christians, Shrovetide is the traditional period of feasting and merrymaking before the abstinence of Lent. At this time, plays and performances were often put on by members of the Guilds of Saint Luke and Rederijkers. Here, Hals portrays two well-known figures from these traditional plays: Hans Worst, with a sausage dangling from his cap, and Pekelharing (or Peeckelhaering, see page 128), wearing a garland of salted fish and eggs. They flank a girl in costume, with still life objects in the foreground.

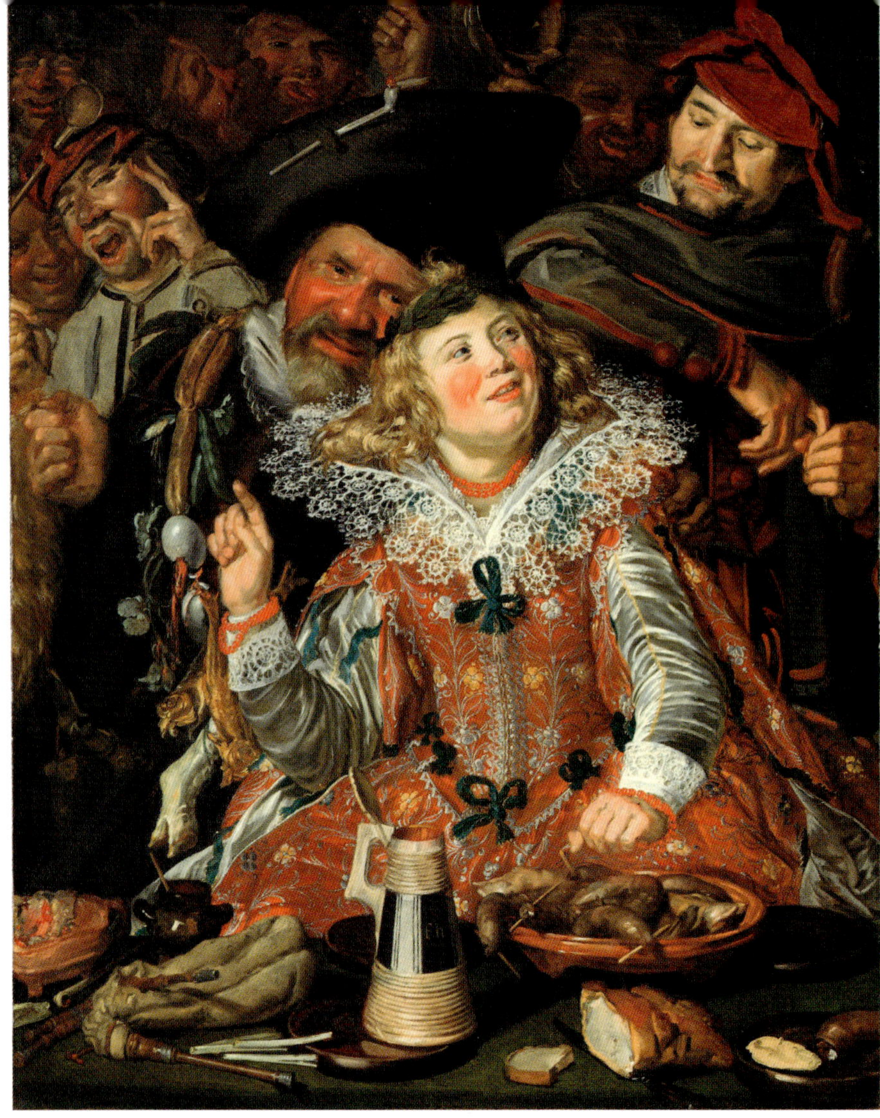

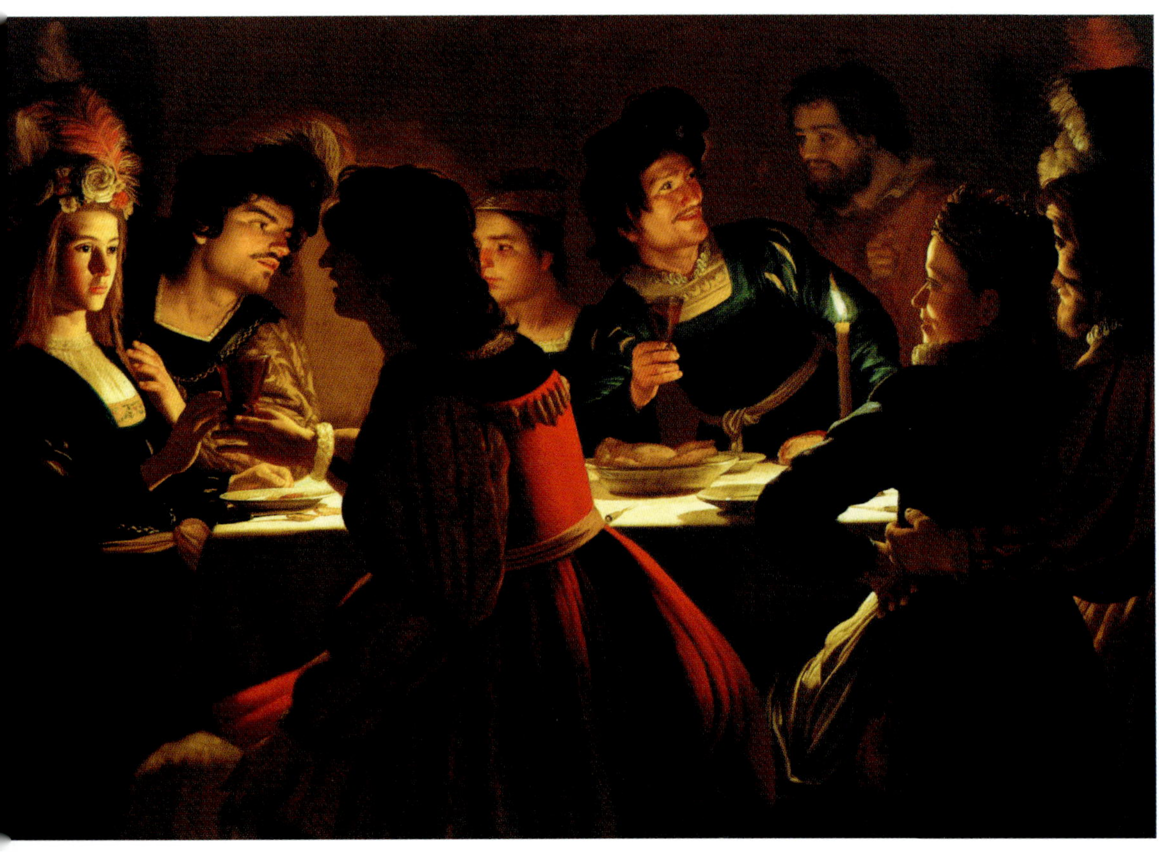

Feast Scene with a Young Married Couple or *The Wedding Supper*, Gerrit van Honthorst, c.1617, oil on canvas, 138 x 203cm (54⅓ x 80in), Galleria degli Uffizi, Florence, Italy

In his use of chiaroscuro inspired by Caravaggio, van Honthorst became internationally famous. When he painted this, he was living in Italy, but he returned to the Netherlands three years later. Candlelit night scenes with lifelike figures became fashionable through his example. At a table, people are having a meal: light bathes the faces of a couple at one end; although they are both talking to others, the husband places his hand protectively on his new wife.

Dinner with a Lute Player,
Gerrit van Honthorst,
c.1619–20, oil on canvas,
138 x 203cm (54⅓ x
80in), Galleria degli Uffizi,
Florence, Italy

Painted during the artist's
time in Italy, this image
shows a candlelit supper.
One entertains the others
with some lute playing,
while another is about to
have his tooth pulled. Using
a range of warm colours,
van Honthorst became
extremely skilled in rendering
such atmospheric night
scenes, often incorporating
odd events and incongruities
of life. His adroit rendering of
light enhances the sense of
warmth and illusion of depth.

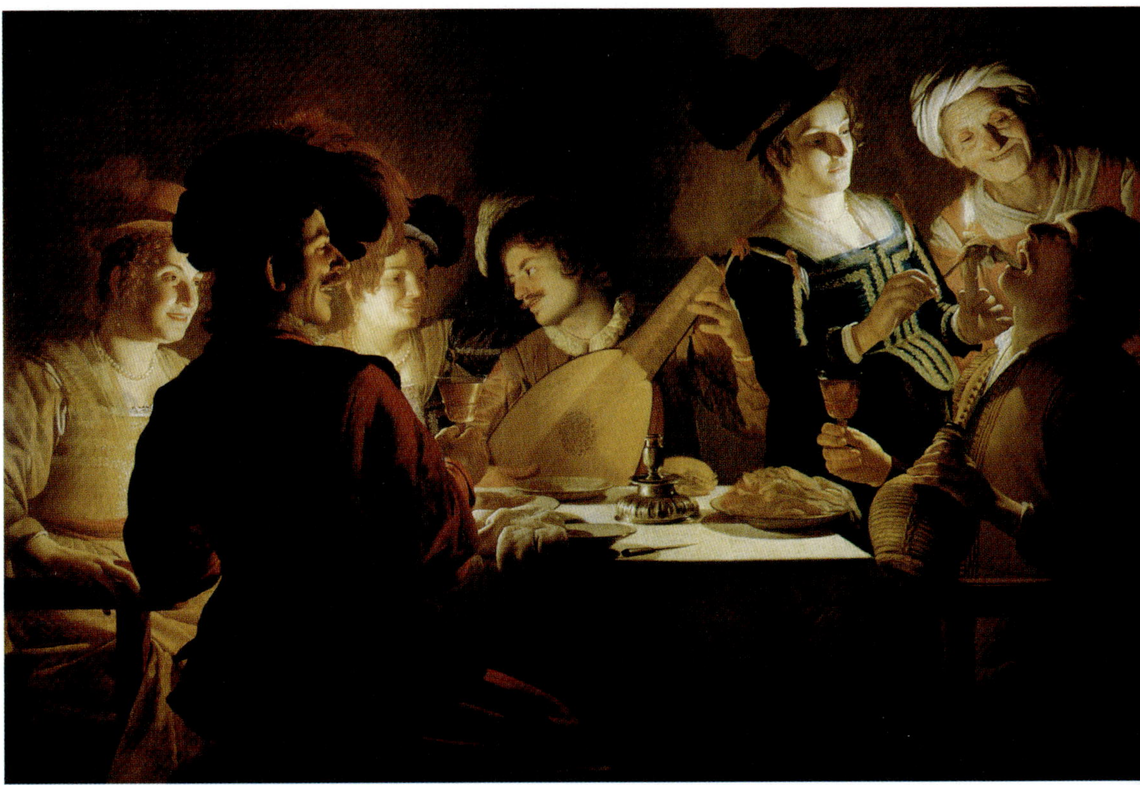

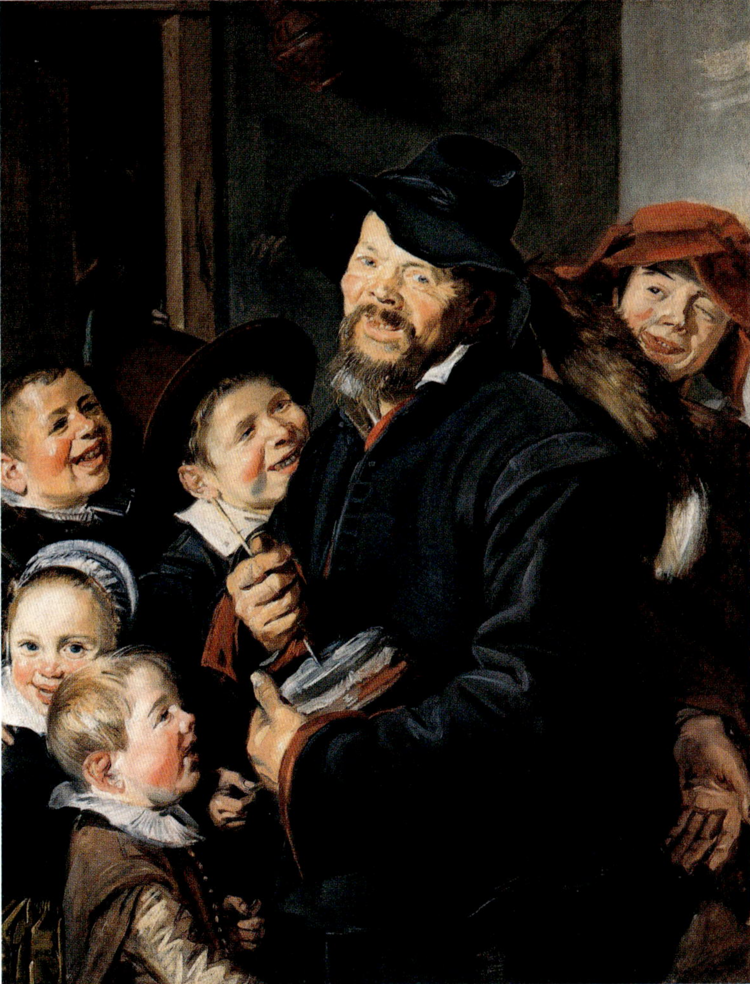

The Rommel Pot Player,
Frans Hals, 1618, oil on
canvas, 106 x 80.3cm (41¾
x 31⅝in), Kimbell Art
Museum, Fort Worth, USA

Frans Hals captures a
beaming man playing a
rommel pot, surrounded by
grinning children enjoying
the strange sounds emitting
from the instrument. A
rommel pot was made of a
pig's bladder stretched over
an earthenware jug half-
filled with water. Bound in a
small pocket in the middle
of the bladder was a reed
that moved up and down to
produce a rumbling sound.

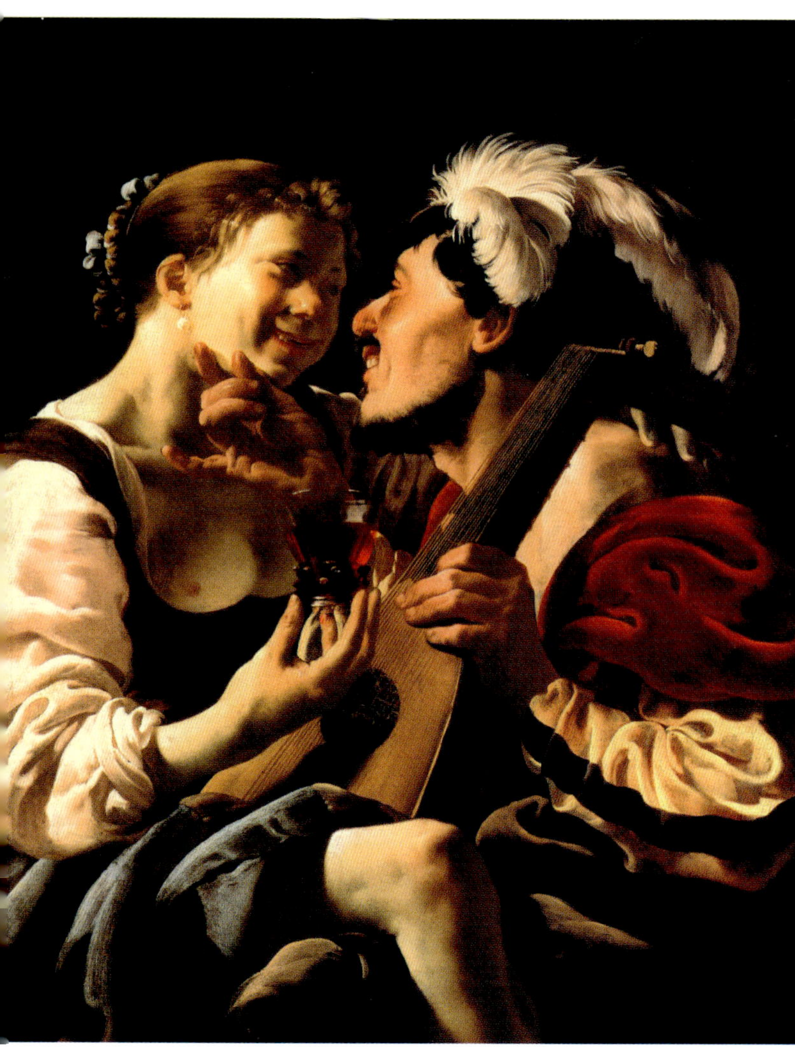

A Lute Player Carousing with a Young Woman, Hendrick ter Brugghen, 1621, oil on canvas, 105.5 x 86.4cm (41½ x 34in), Private Collection

While he spent ten years in Italy, ter Brugghen became deeply influenced by Caravaggio, and he and van Honthorst became the most important artists of the Utrecht Caravaggisti (see page 15). Here, a flamboyantly dressed man and woman flirt with each other. The man is holding his lute and the woman's breasts are exposed. Overt sexual connotations, musical instruments and strong chiaroscuro were all elements that many viewers admired.

Musical Group on a Balcony, Gerrit van Honthorst, 1622, fresco, 308.9 x 114cm (121⅔ x 44⅞in), Private Collection

Singing and playing musical instruments, some people gather around a balcony, along with a parrot and a dog, looking down at viewers below as if inviting them to join in the merriment. Van Honthorst painted this ceiling two years after his return from Italy; it was the earliest example of this type of illusionistic ceiling fresco in the Netherlands and reflects ideas he had seen abroad, including skilful foreshortening.

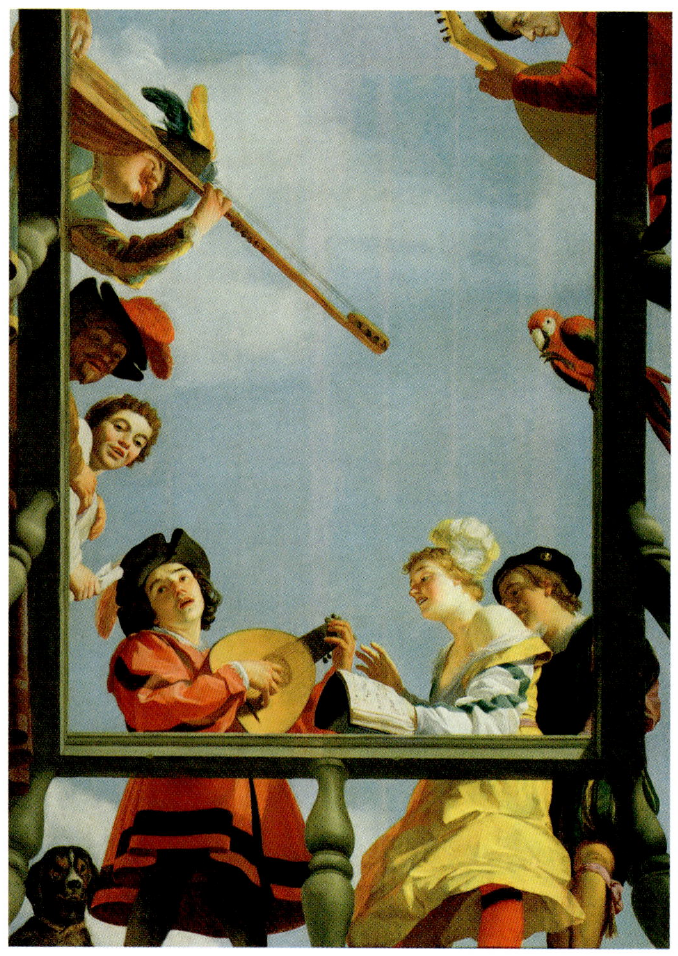

Musical Group by Candlelight, Gerrit van Honthorst, 1623, oil on canvas, 117 x 146cm (46 x 57½in), Statens Museum for Kunst, Copenhagen, Denmark

Glowing light illuminates the faces of four figures sitting around a table enjoying a merry evening of music. Three are singing from a sheet of music while the fourth plays a lute. The candle cannot be seen behind the sheet music, but the silver candlestick tells viewers where it is. Although he was not alone in emulating Caravaggio's style, van Honthorst was one of the most skilled at conveying dramatic nocturnal lighting, which earned him the nickname 'Gherardo delle Notti' (Gerard of the Nights).

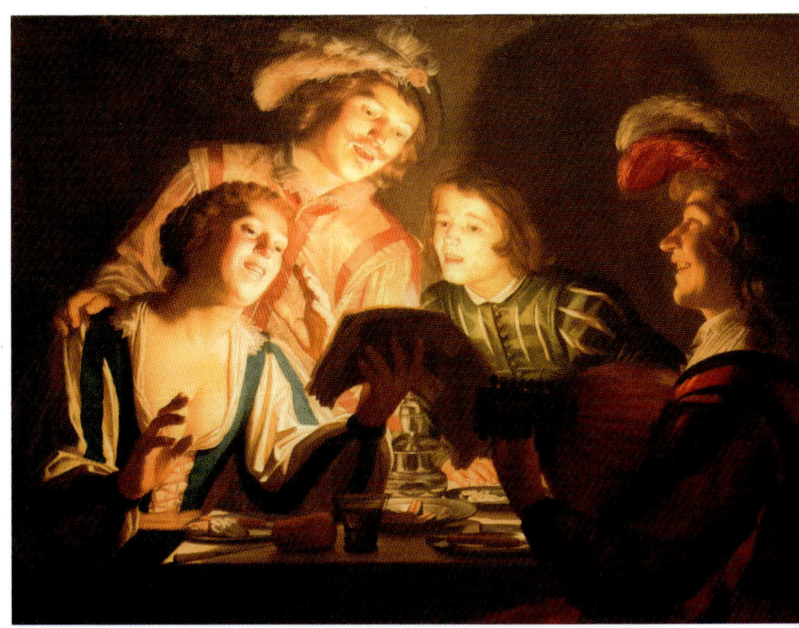

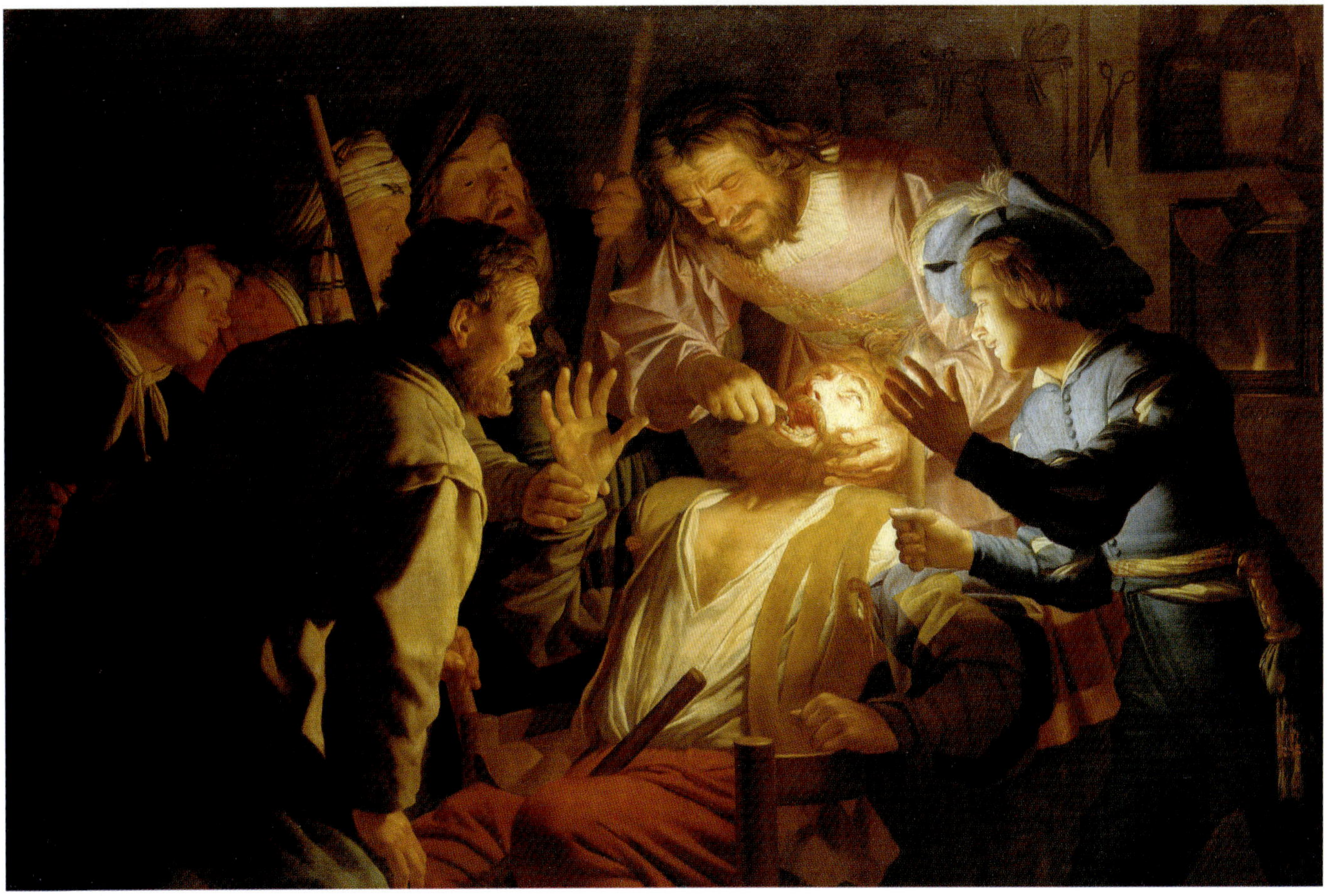

The Dentist, Gerrit van Honthorst, 1622, oil on canvas, 147 x 219cm (57⅞ x 86¼in), Gemäldegalerie Alte Meister, Dresden, Germany

After his return from Rome van Honthorst interpreted Caravaggio's style in his own Dutch manner. Here he depicts a dental operation dramatically, as if it is being acted out on stage. Figures group around the man having his tooth pulled. One holds up a candle, another holds the patient's wrist. Leaning over him is the smiling dentist, while fascinated and horrified onlookers watch, and the terrified patient cannot escape.

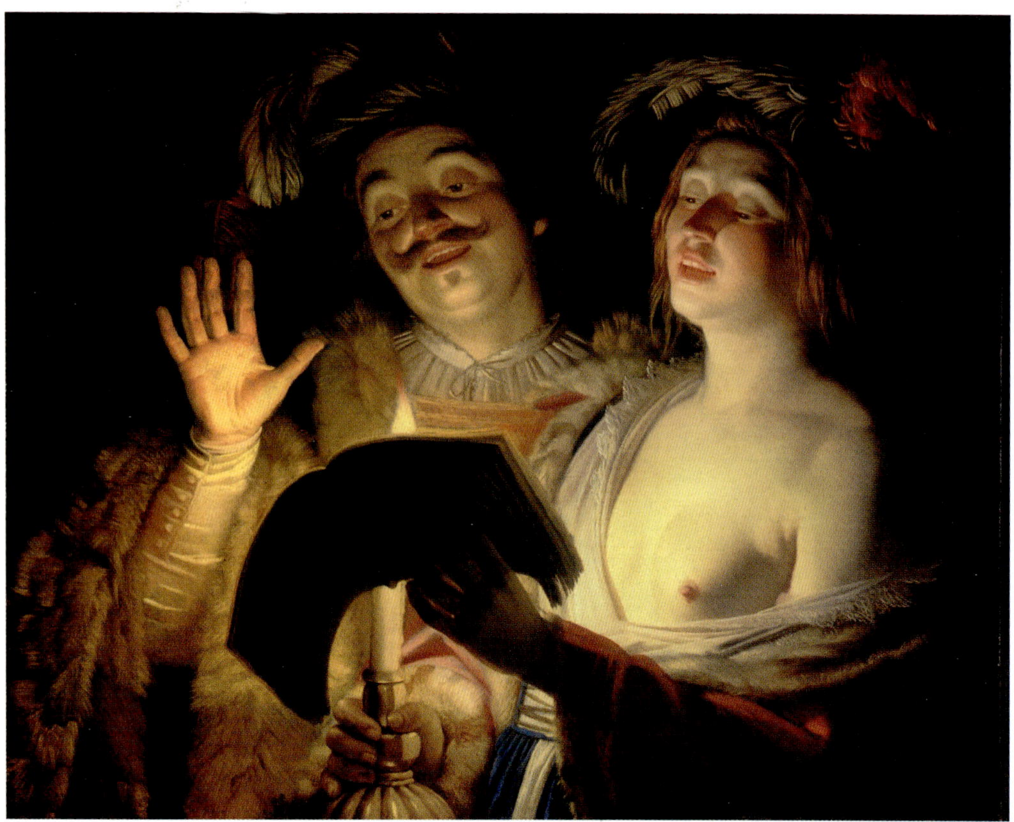

The Duet, Gerrit van Honthorst, 1624, oil on canvas, 78 x 94.5cm (30¾ x 37¼in), Private Collection

In dramatic light, a couple sing together over an open book. Both wear plumed hats and the man wears sumptuous clothing, while the woman is barely covered – her left breast is exposed. The only light comes from the flame of a partially obscured candle, which allows van Honthorst to demonstrate his skill in painting textures, including fur, silk, satin and skin.

The Merry Fiddler, Gerrit van Honthorst, 1623, oil on canvas, 107.2 x 88.3cm (42¼ x 34¾in), Rijksmuseum, Amsterdam, Netherlands

A man in expensive, Italian-style clothing appears from behind a tapestry and leans out over a balustrade. Protruding into the viewers' space, he seems to be gesturing as if trying to propose a toast. As so often in Dutch paintings of this time, this does not convey what it might seem. The underlying message is that there is more to life than just partying and drinking.

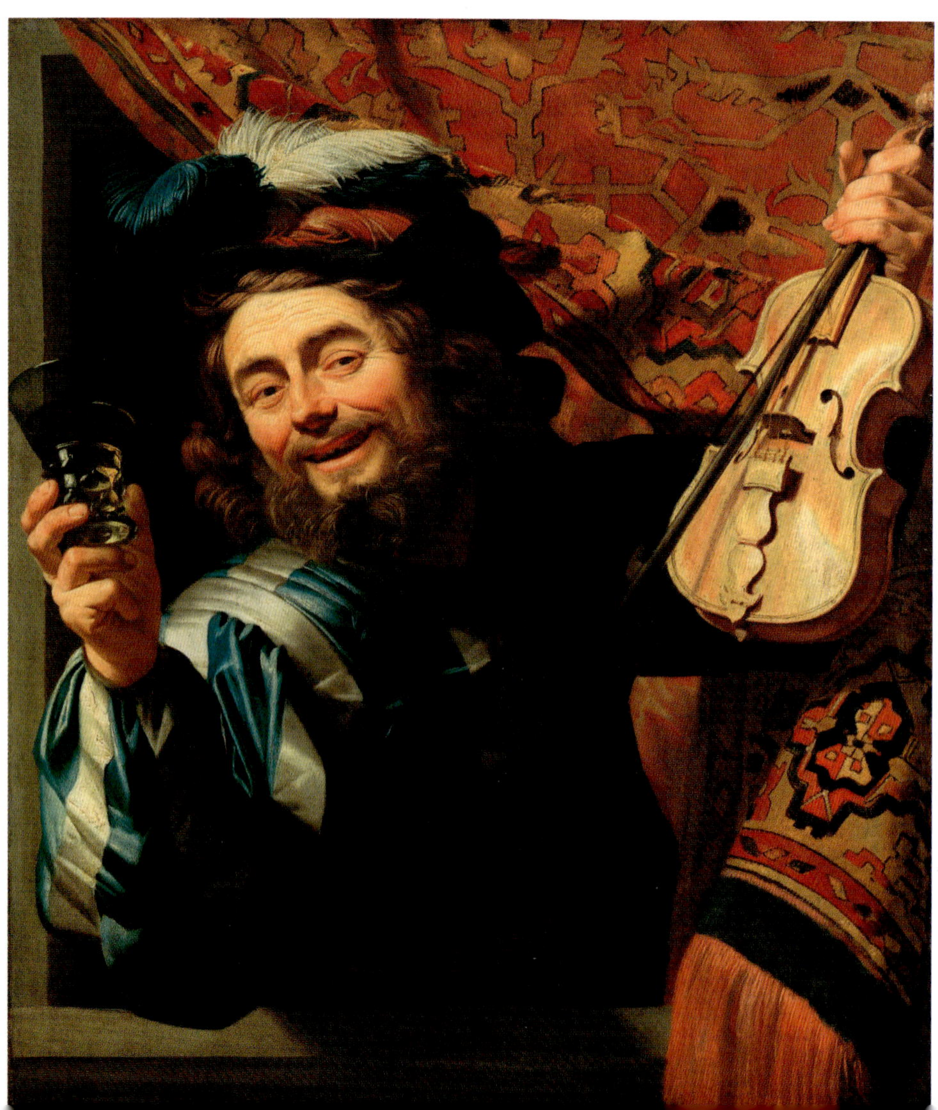

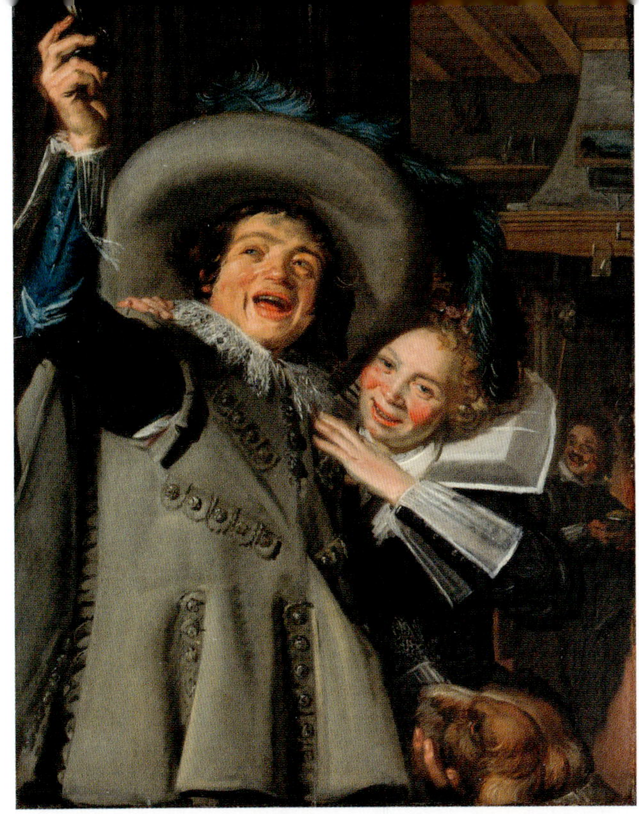

Young Man and Woman in an Inn, Frans Hals, 1623, 105.4 x 79.4cm (41½ x 31¼ in), The Metropolitan Museum of Art, New York, USA

Applying the bold brushwork that he learned from Flemish painting, Frans Hals depicts a young couple singing in a curtained doorway. Their rosy cheeks and the glass in the man's hand suggest that they are drinking and that their behaviour clashes with contemporary ideals of propriety. The man strokes his dog's head and beyond the pulled-back curtain behind them is a room with a fireplace and a man carrying a dish.

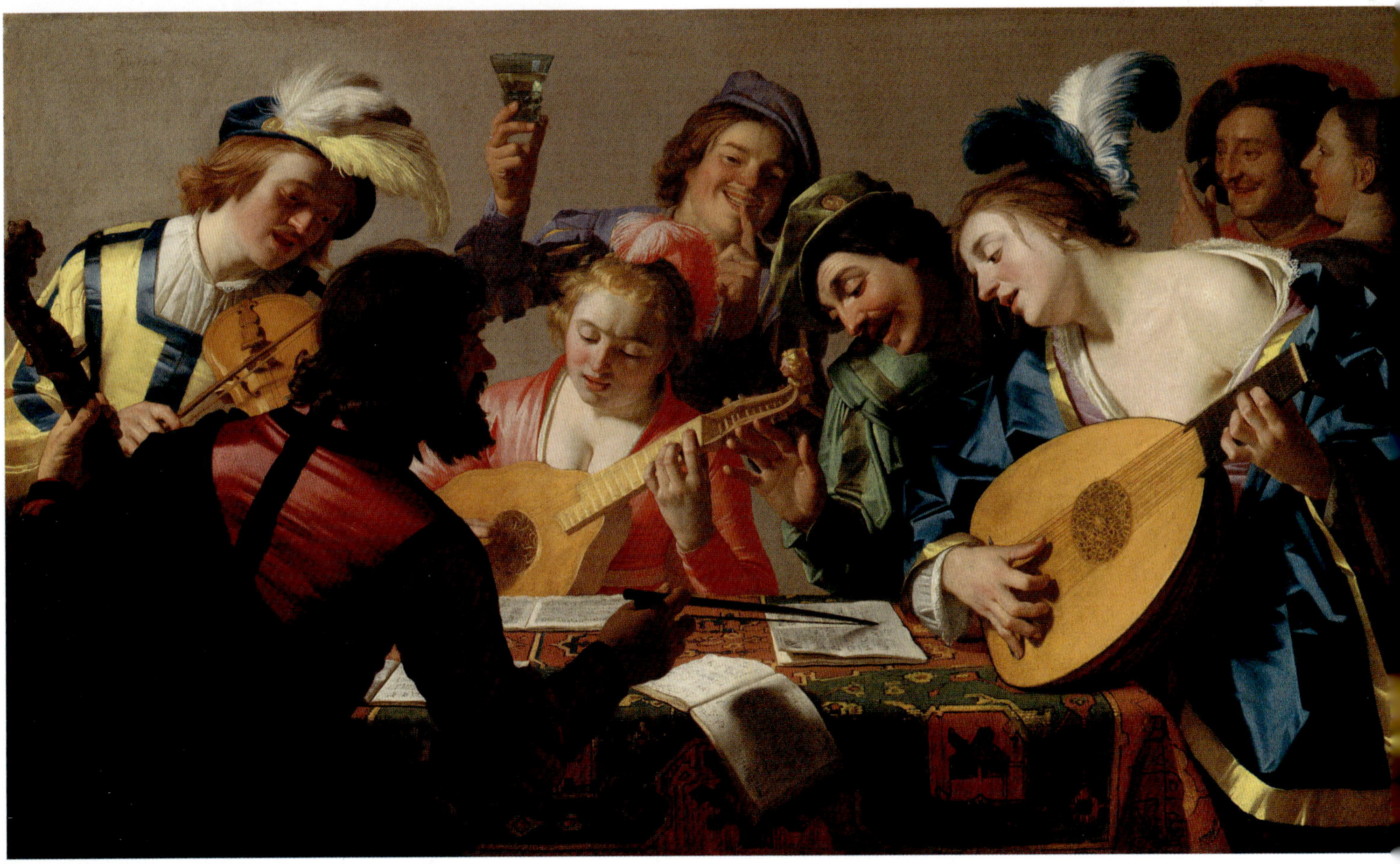

The Concert, Gerrit van Honthorst, 1623, oil on canvas, 123.5 x 205cm (48⅝ x 80⅝in), National Gallery of Art, Washington DC, USA

Using a broad range of brilliant colours and strong chiaroscuro, van Honthorst has painted life-sized figures dressed in exotic costumes enjoying their own concert. Probably painted for Maurits, the Prince of Orange, this symbolizes love and harmony, conveying that everyone is 'singing from the same song sheet.' It was a positive sentiment during a period of strife in the Netherlands.

The Concert Group, Gerrit van Honthorst, 1624, oil on canvas, 168 x 178cm (66 x 70in), Musée du Louvre, Paris, France

Painted for Frederick Henry, Prince of Orange, this work was created to be hung above a mantelpiece, which is why the figures are shown on a balcony. Red damask curtains are drawn back to reveal cherubs and musicians.

Five women are giving a concert. Their brightly coloured, old-fashioned clothes add to the sense of exuberance. Three singers read from sheet music, while the two musicians accompany them. One musician plays a lute and the other plays an archilute or bass lute. The singers are closely following their lyrics, while the musicians smile at the viewers.

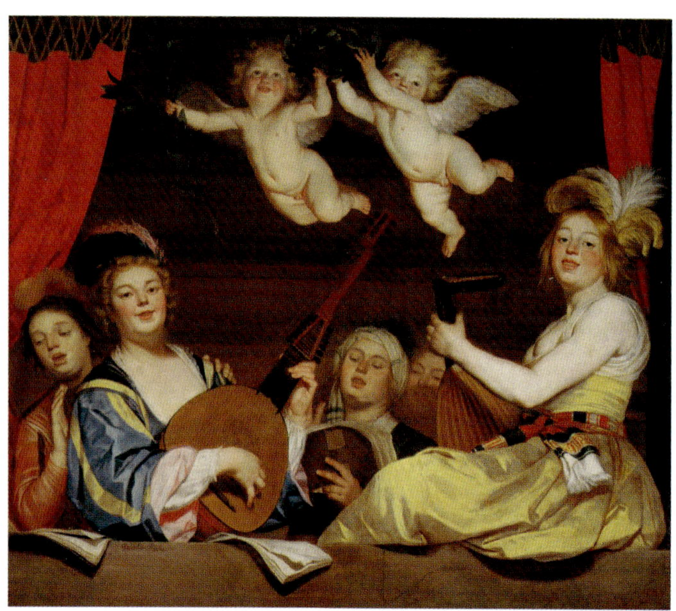

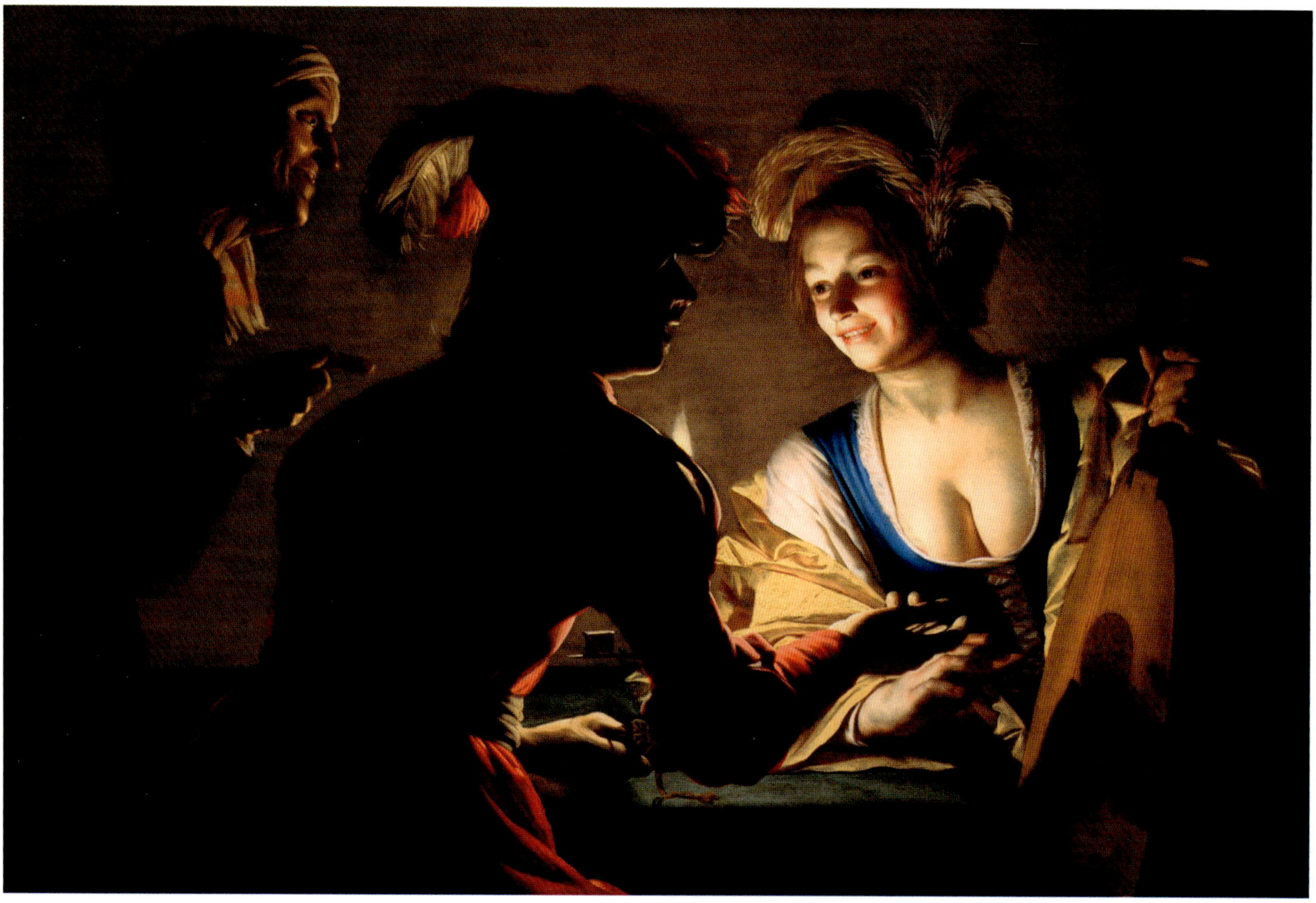

The Procuress, Gerrit van Honthorst, 1625, oil on panel, 71 x 104cm (28 x 41in), Centraal Museum, Utrecht, Netherlands

Leaning forward to tempt the man opposite with her exposed cleavage, this smiling young woman is a prostitute. The lute that she holds had sexual significance at the time. The old woman in the shadows is the procuress, whose job was to introduce prostitutes to men and take their money. Silhouetted in the foreground, the young man holds his wallet ready.

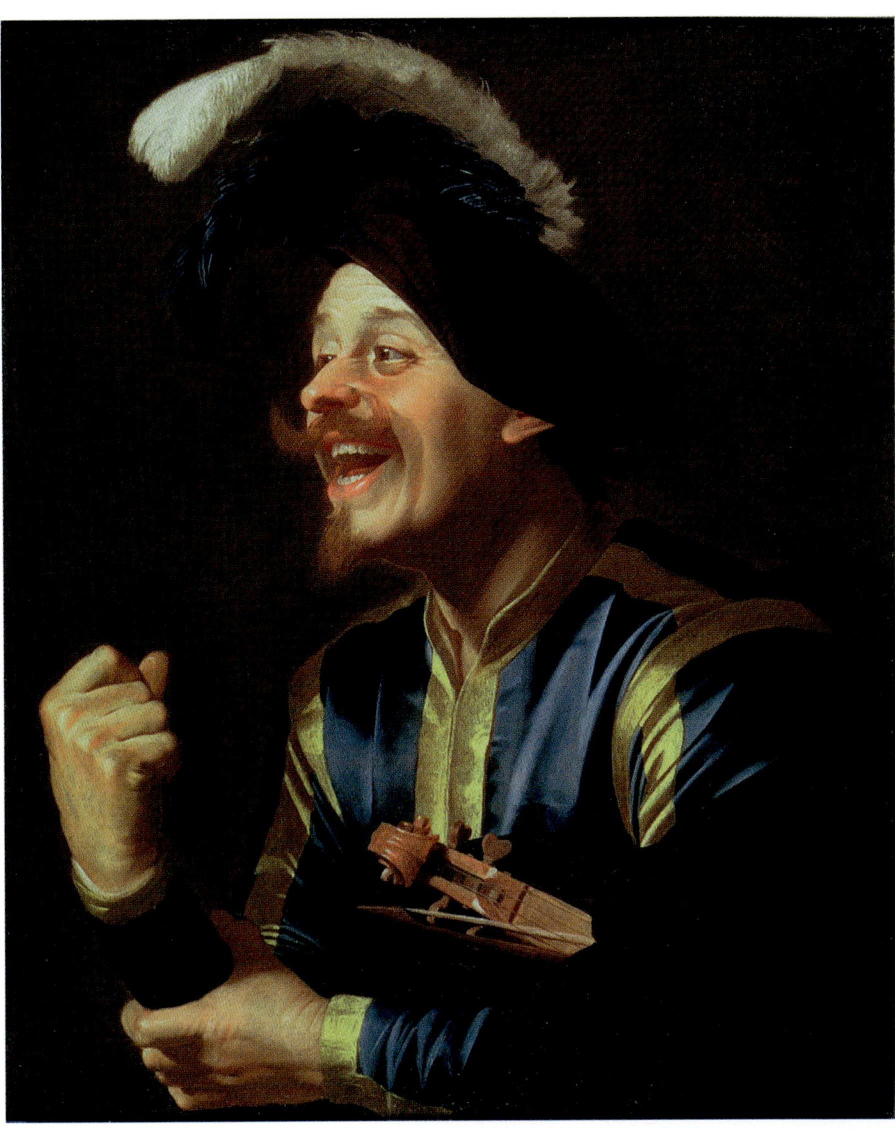

The Laughing Violinist, Gerrit van Honthorst, c.1624, oil on canvas, 81 x 64.2cm (31¾ x 25¼ in), Private Collection

With his violin under his arm, a man in a blue and yellow striped doublet and plumed cap laughs. Music was a common theme in Dutch Golden Age paintings, partly for their symbolism and partly to reflect elegant middle-class pursuits. Van Honthorst creates the effects of bright light shining from one side, which makes the man's skin and eyes appear to glow and his satin doublet shine.

The Debauched Student or *Merry Company*, Gerrit van Honthorst, 1623–25, oil on canvas, 125 x 156cm (49¼ x 61⅓in), Alte Pinakothek, Munich, Germany

This depicts a young man (a student) in the company of two prostitutes and in the shadows, a procuress carrying a baby. A large open book on the table is powerfully lit by candlelight, revealing a moralizing image. The man is grinning and drinking, even though the potential consequences of his behaviour can be seen in the shadows.

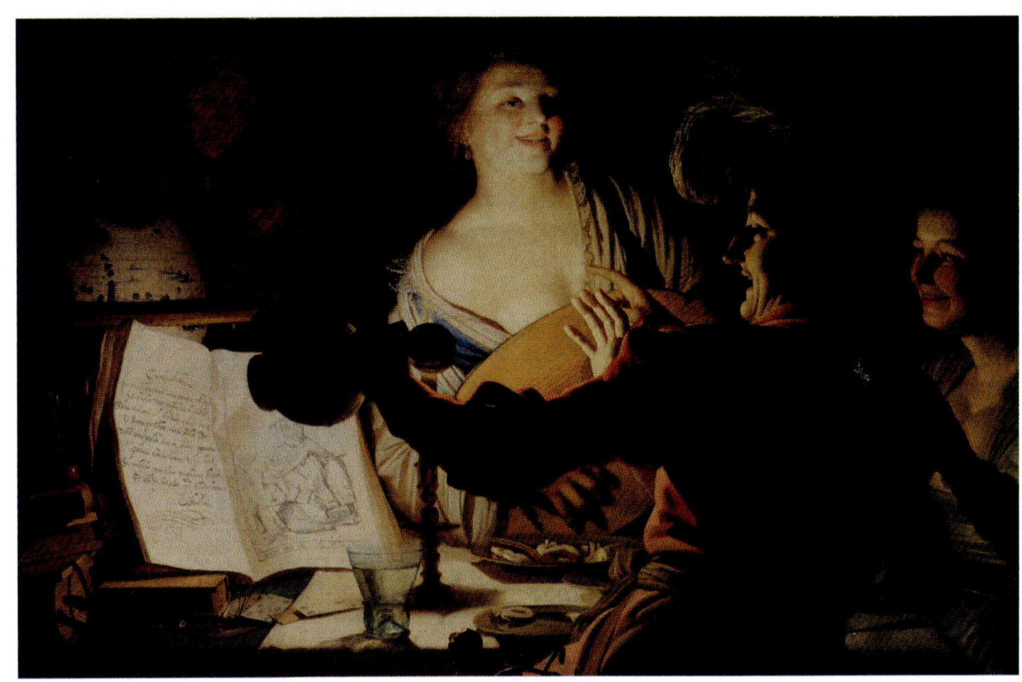

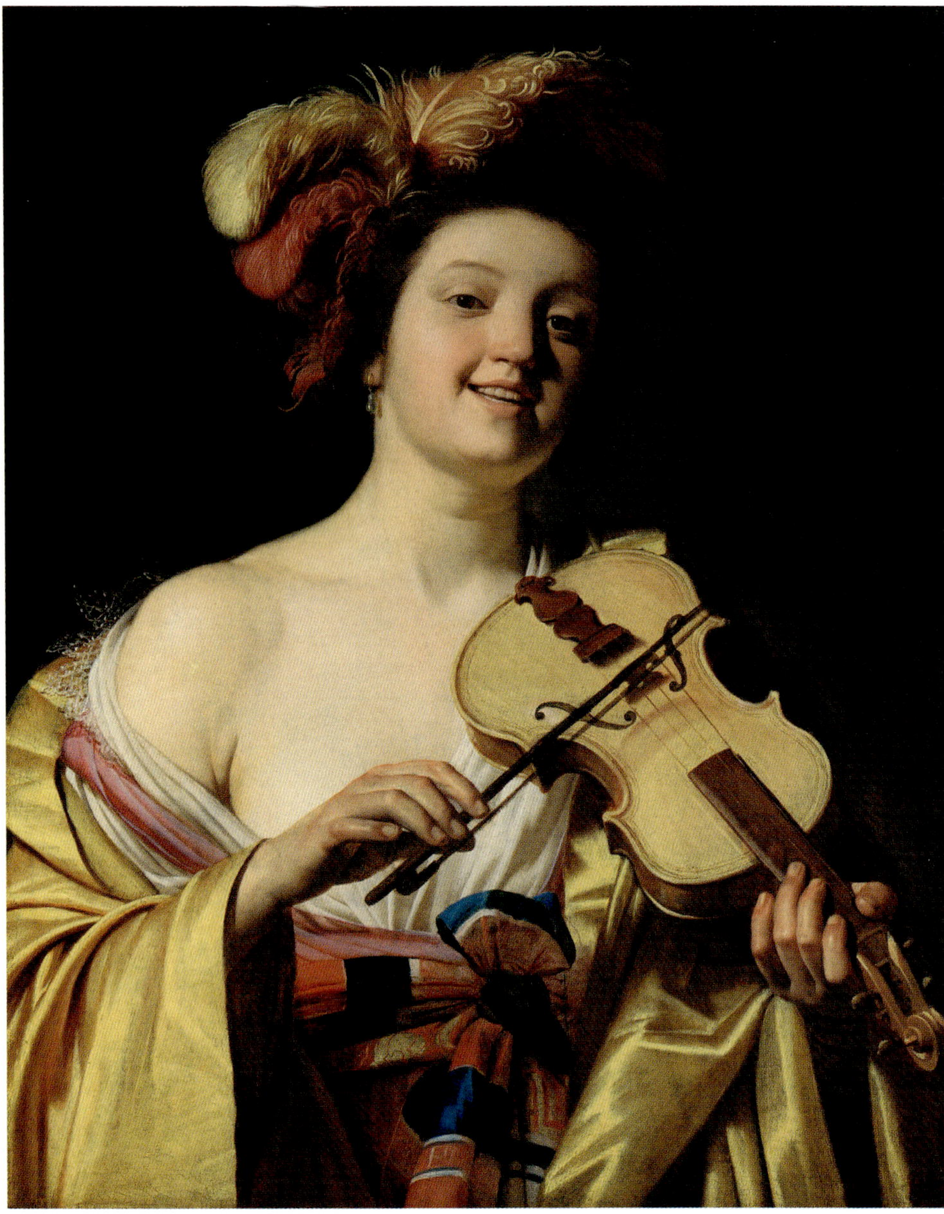

The Violin Player, Gerrit van Honthorst, 1626, oil on canvas, 84.5 x 66.1cm (33¼ x 26in), Mauritshuis, The Hague, Netherlands

With fine brushmarks and soft colours, van Honthorst creates a sense of intimacy. It seems as if we have interrupted the young woman as she plays her violin – and made her laugh; she shows her white teeth and her pearl earring trembles. Light falls on her violin, her hair dressed with feathers, the lace around her shoulders, and the silky scarf tied as a belt.

Drunken Peasants at an Inn, Adriaen Brouwer, c.1625–26, oil on panel, 18.6 x 26cm (7⅓ x 10¼ in), Mauritshuis, The Hague, Netherlands

Although he originated in Flanders, sociable Adriaen Brouwer lived for some time in the Dutch Republic and he introduced the genre of peasant painting there. His caricatures of peasants with their rustic, unsophisticated behaviour were intended to appeal to the wealthier middle-class citizens. Everyone in this inn is inebriated. They are laughing, sleeping and falling over. The woman in the foreground has passed out and fallen off her stool.

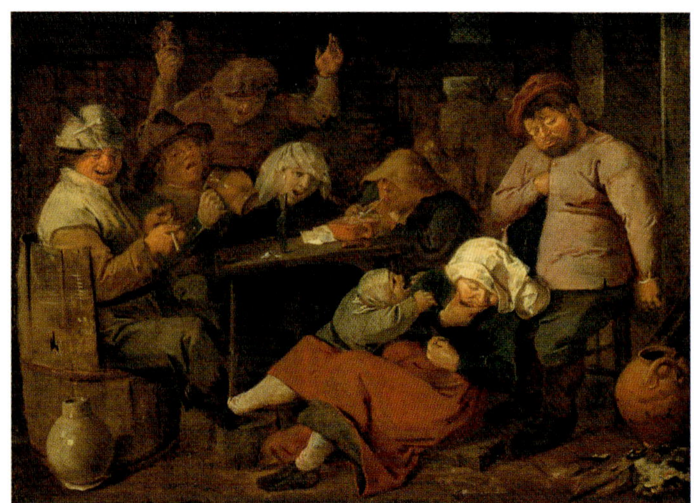

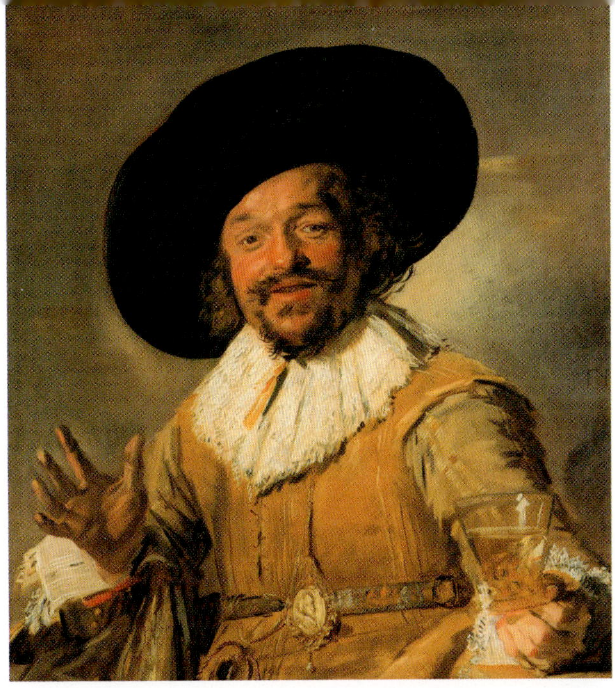

A Militiaman Holding a Berkemeyer, or *The Merry Drinker*, Frans Hals, c.1628–30, oil on canvas, 81 x 66.5cm (31¾ x 26¼ in), Rijksmuseum, Amsterdam, Netherlands

This militiaman merrily raises his glass, inviting all to join him. His animated gesture and relaxed expression are matched by the free brushstrokes and seemingly swift, spontaneous application of paint made by Hals. Although the fashion then was for intricate, detailed paintings, Hals worked with loose, confident brushstrokes, giving his subject a sense of movement and warmth, which broke with tradition but for which he was greatly admired.

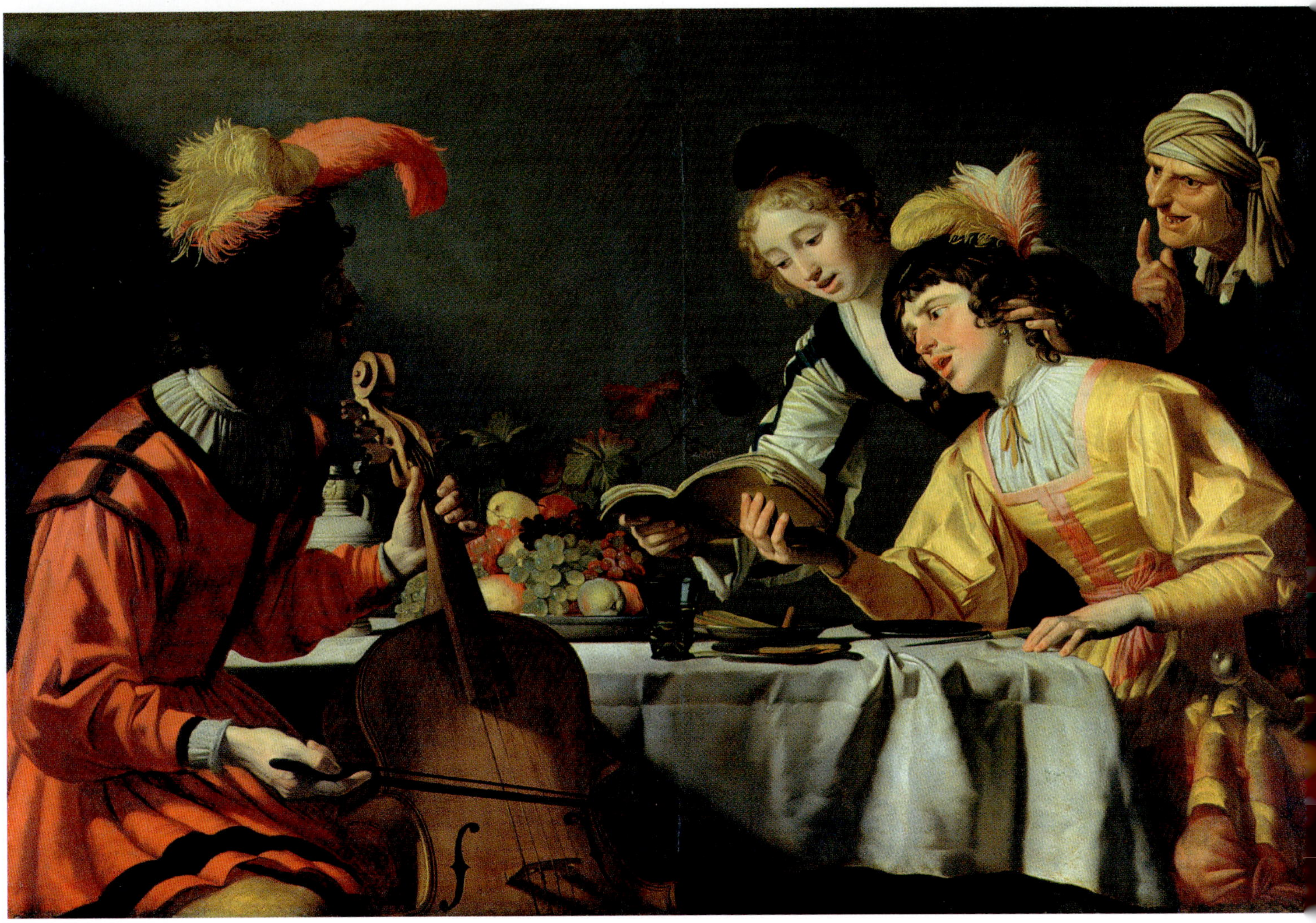

The Concert, Gerrit van Honthorst, 1626–30, oil on canvas, 168 x 202cm (66 x 79½ in), Galleria Borghese, Rome, Italy

While the man on the right concentrates on his singing, he has not noticed that the girl standing next to him is about to steal his earring, The old woman seems to be indicating to the musician playing the bass viol opposite not to say anything., which implies that three of the four figures here are complicit. The comparison of the young and old women with the splendid dress of their unsuspecting victim can also be viewed as an allegory of vanity.

Old Woman Reading, Gerrit Dou, oil on panel, 71.2 x 55.2cm (28 x 21¾in), Rijksmuseum, Amsterdam, Netherlands

The book is rendered in such detail that it is easy to see what the woman is reading: the beginning of chapter 19 of the Gospel of Luke. The passage tells of the entry of Jesus into Jericho and states that those who wish to do good must give away half of all they own to the poor. The old woman's expensive clothing contrasts sharply with this message: evidently she is still attached to worldly possessions.

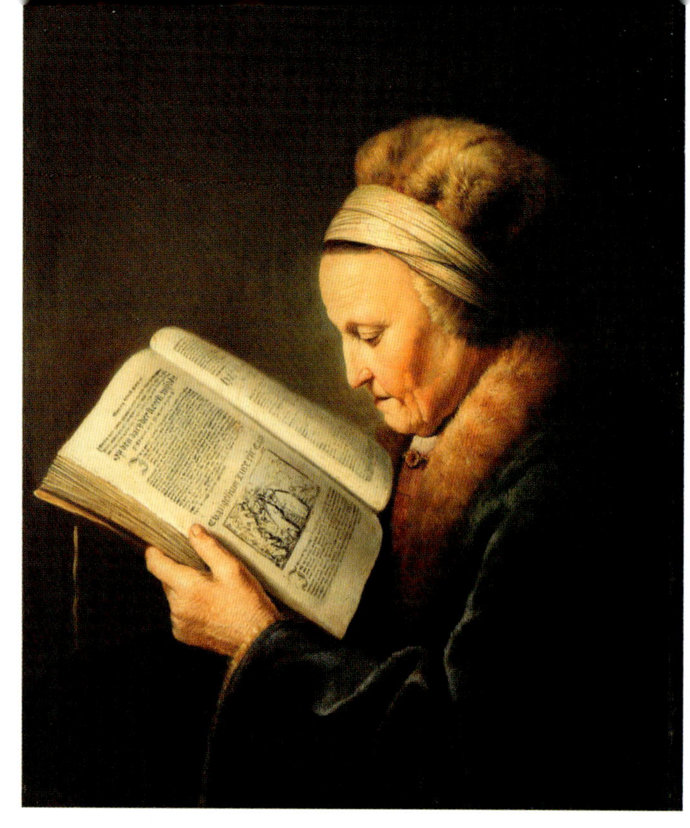

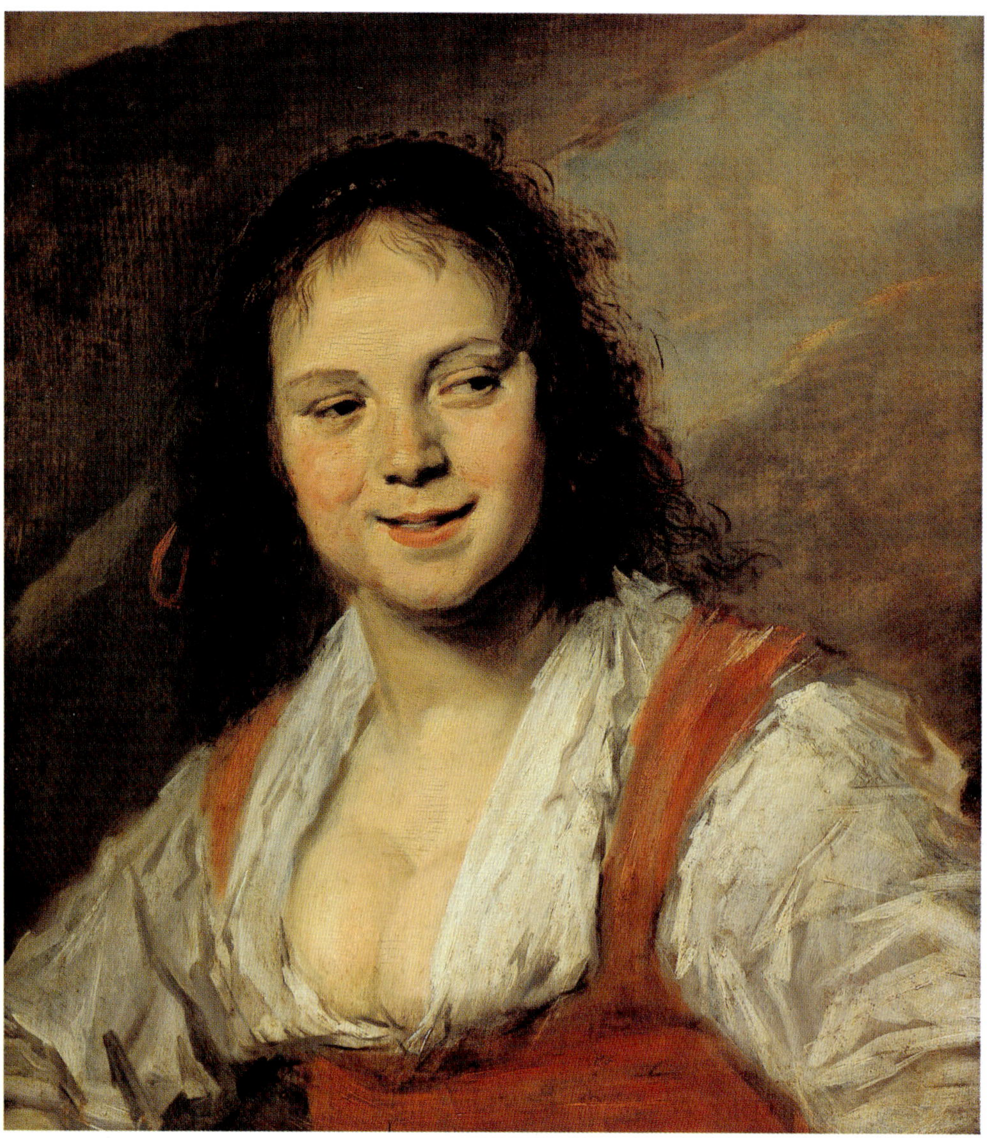

The Gypsy Girl, Frans Hals, 1628, oil on wood, 57.8 x 52.1cm (22.8 x 20.5in), Musée du Louvre, Paris, France

Although this painting was named *The Gypsy Girl*, the sitter was in fact a courtesan from Haarlem. She often modelled for Frans Hals, and in this painting, he shows the influence of van Honthorst and the Utrecht Caravaggisti. The girl's unkempt clothing, messy hair and laughing face are conveyed with spontaneity and rapid, loose brushstrokes. This type of expressiveness contrasted with the more precise work of the Leiden fijnschilders.

Peasants Brawling at Cards,
Adriaen Brouwer, c.1630, oil
on oak, 26.5 x 34.5cm (10⅓
x 13½in), Gemäldegalerie
Alte Meister, Dresden,
Germany

Partly because it made
them feel superior, Adriaen
Brouwer's scenes of peasants
showing dissolute behaviour
became extremely popular
among wealthy citizens
during the mid-17th century.
As well as heavy drinking,
card playing was perceived
as depraved in the Dutch
Republic as many were falling
into debt through gambling.
Brouwer deliberately
depicted these figures with
large limbs and plain features
so that the middle and
upper classes who bought
these works would feel
complacent.

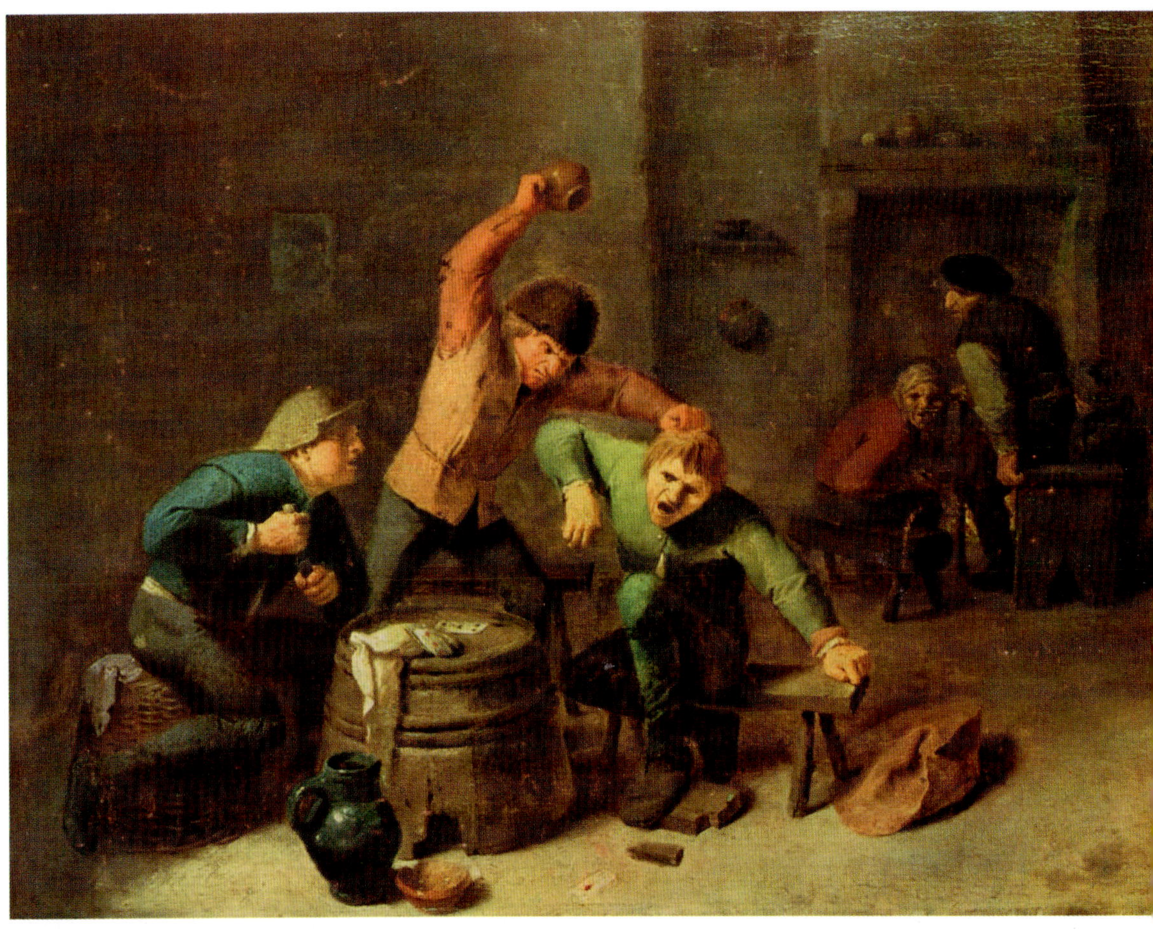

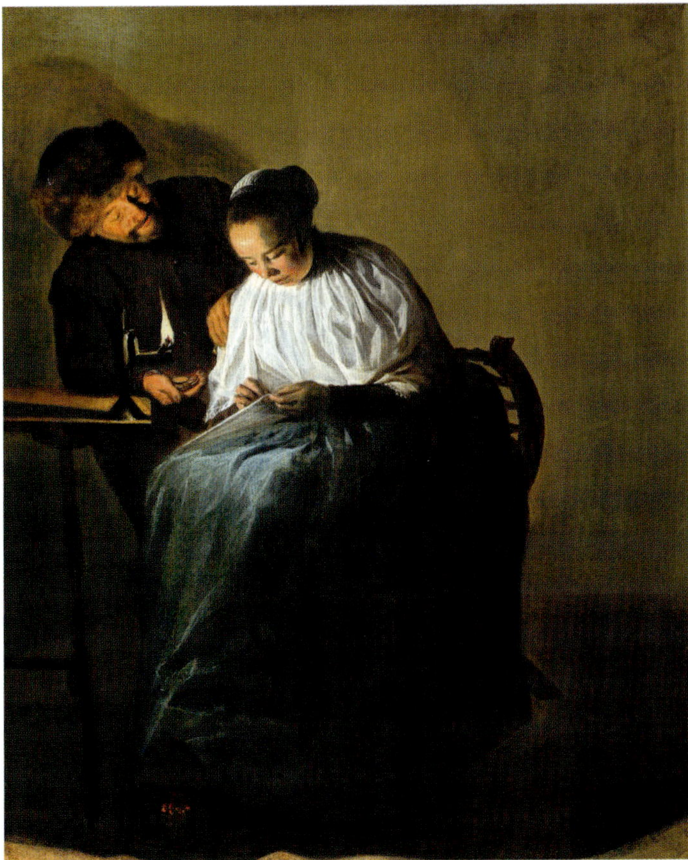

*Man Offering Money to
a Young Woman*, Judith
Leyster, 1631, oil on panel,
30.8 x 24.2cm (11¼ x
9½in), Mauritshuis, The
Hague, Netherlands

An early work by Judith
Leyster, this depicts
a woman sewing by
candlelight with a man
leaning over her, touching
her shoulder. Although
he offers her coins,
she is ignoring him and
concentrating on her
sewing. Engaged in a
simple everyday domestic
chore, dressed plainly and
demurely, she is clearly
not keen on the man's
proposition. She hopes that
by ignoring him, he will go
away.

Peeckelhaering, Frans Hals, early 1640s, oil on canvas, 75 x 61.5cm (29½ x 24¼in), Schloss Wilhelmshöhe, Kassel, Germany

Peeckelhaering, or Pekelharing, is an old Dutch word for pickled herring, but it was also the name of a comic character in European theatre during the 17th century, and this is an actor playing the role. Peeckelhaering was always drunk, and as a comical figure, usually wore a brightly coloured costume. With a tankard in his hand, the tipsy man looks back at viewers, tilting his head. Make-up on his face implies that he is ready for his stage performance.

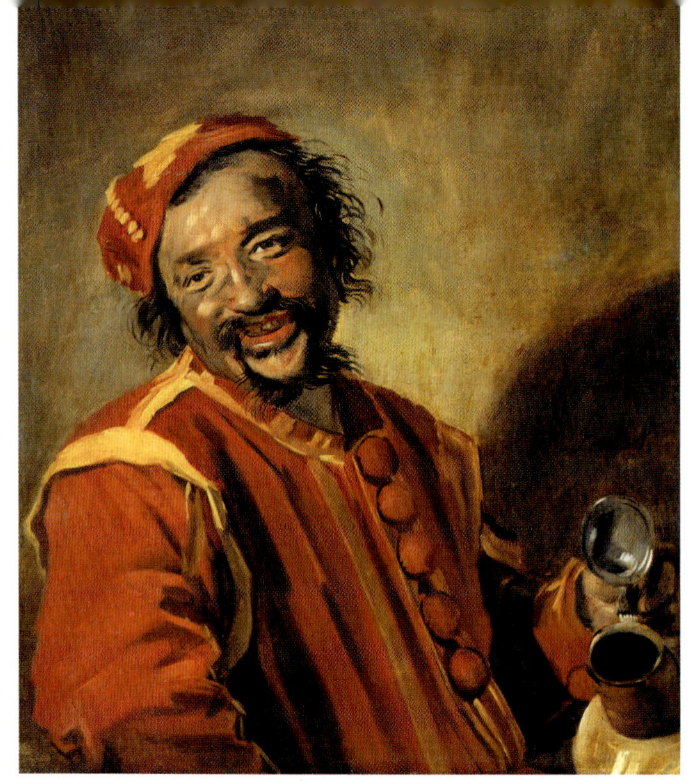

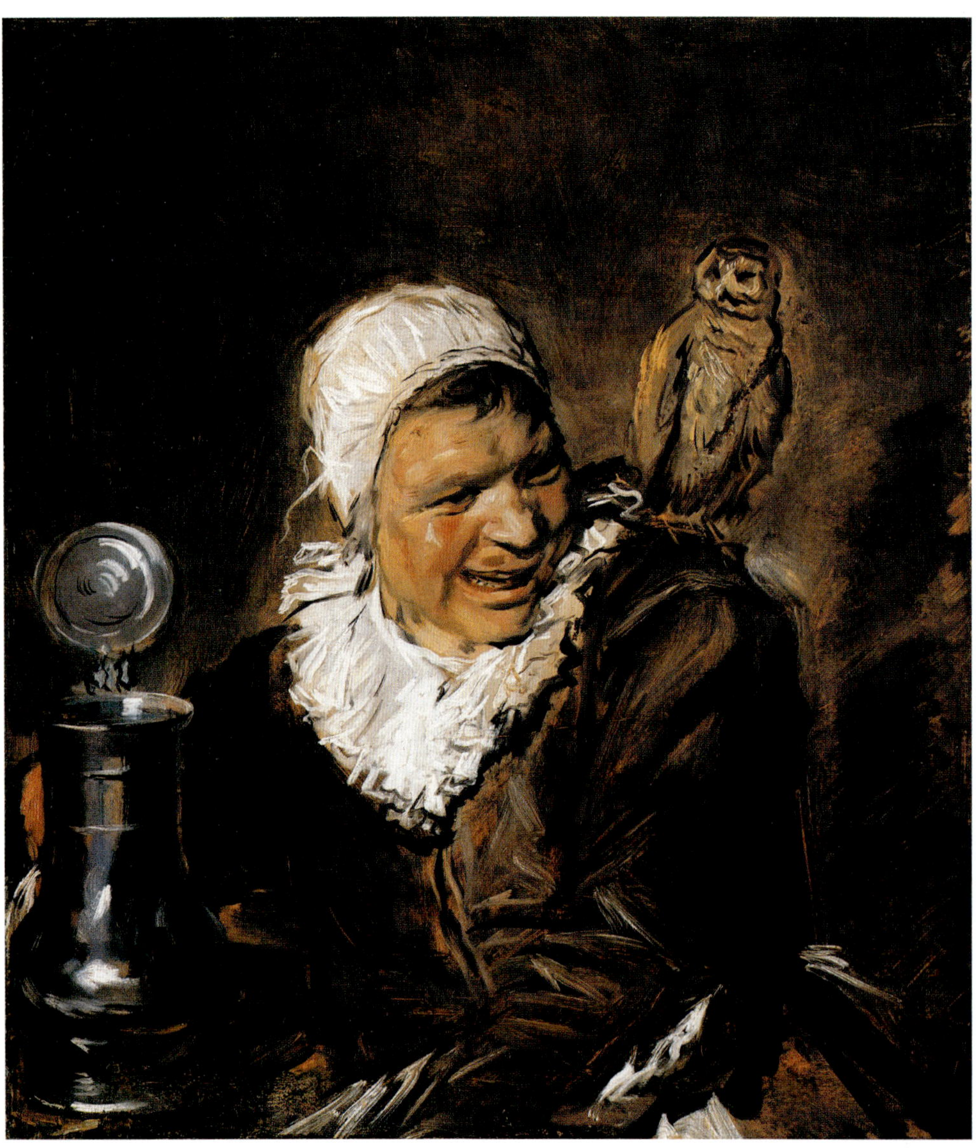

Malle Babbe, the Witch of Haarlem, Frans Hals, 1633, oil on canvas, 75 x 64cm (30 x 25in), Gemäldegalerie, Berlin, Germany

A genre-style portrait of Malle (Mad or Crazy) Babbe; a woman who spent 15 years in a shelter in Haarlem for mentally ill people. She may have been an alcoholic as the owl on her shoulder alludes to the contemporary saying 'zoo beschonken as een uil' (as drunk as an owl). With her right hand, she grabs the handle of a pewter jug that probably contains alcohol. The twisting movement and sketchy brushstrokes convey spontaneity.

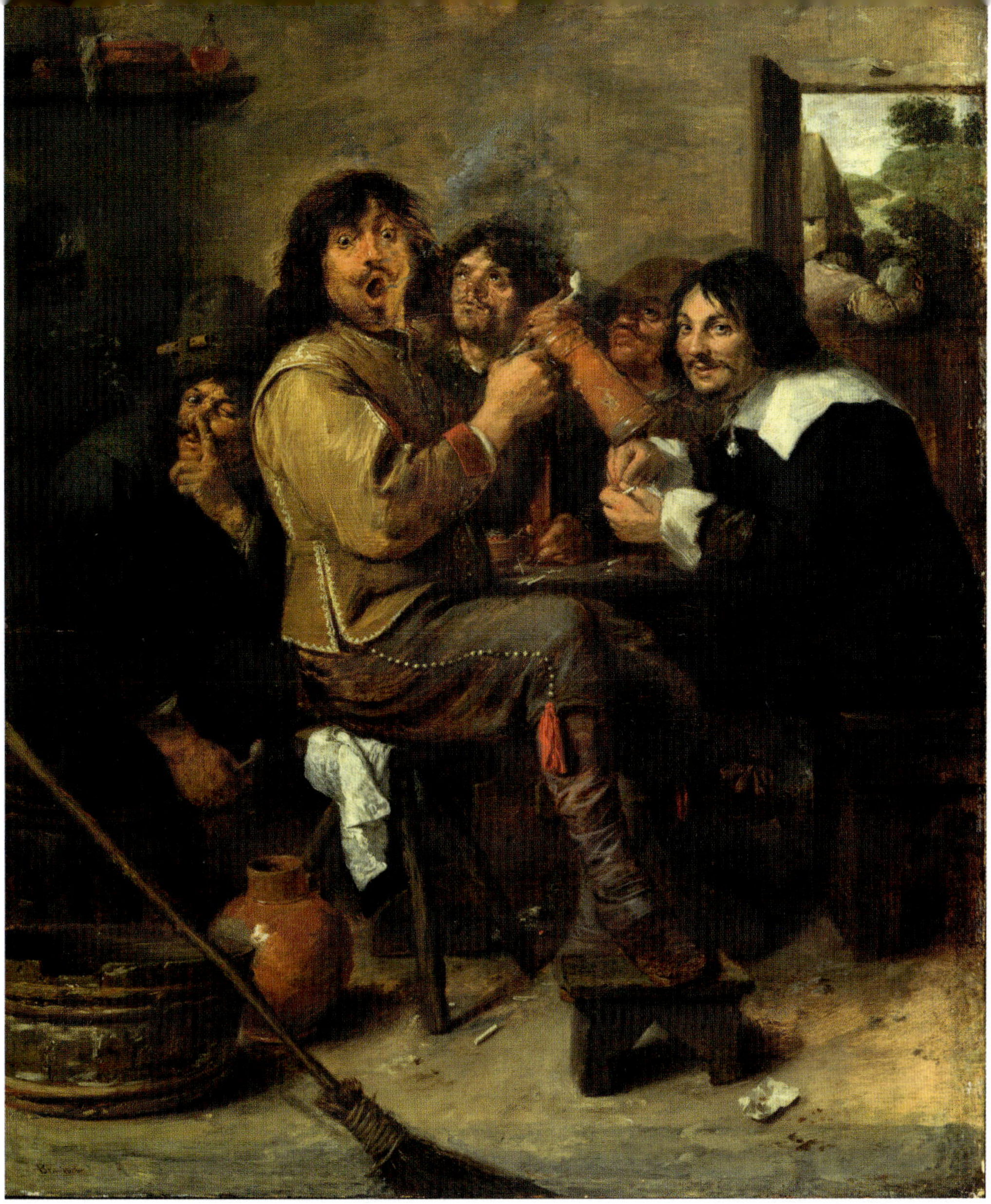

The Smokers, Adriaen Brouwer, c.1636, oil on wood, 46.4 x 36.8cm (18¼ x 14½in), The Metropolitan Museum of Art, New York, USA

Brouwer has painted himself in the centre foreground, sitting in an inn with his friend and fellow painter Jan de Heem and a group of other men, all smoking and relaxing. Brouwer was among the first to create amusing genre images of the working classes in taverns. Even here with this self-portrait, he conveys the liveliness and a sense that he has captured the men unwittingly.

Innkeeper Singing, Adriaen Brouwer, after 1633, oil on 31.5 x 34.5cm (12½ x 13½in), The State Hermitage Museum, Saint Petersburg, Russia

These intoxicated peasants are simple people, singing in a squalid interior. Brouwer's depictions of comical characters such as these were extremely popular in the Dutch Republic, and artists admired his delicate brushwork and refined style. Here the innkeeper throws up his arms as he sings, another man near to him turns to look at viewers, and another slumps on the table in a drunken stupor.

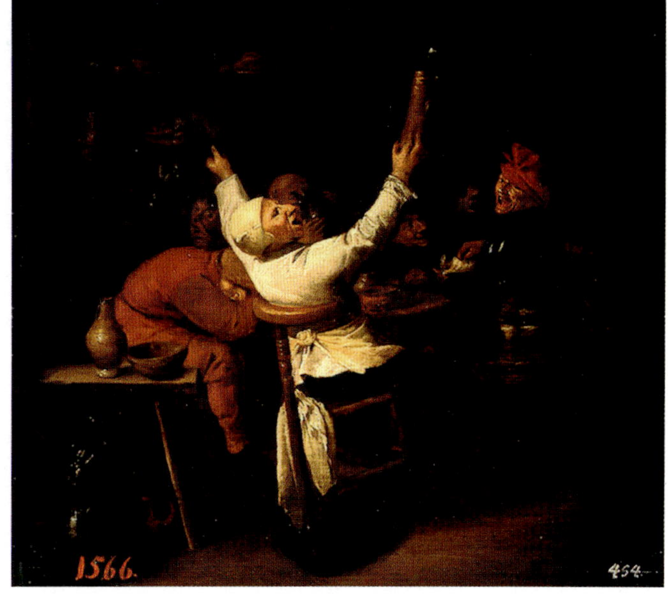

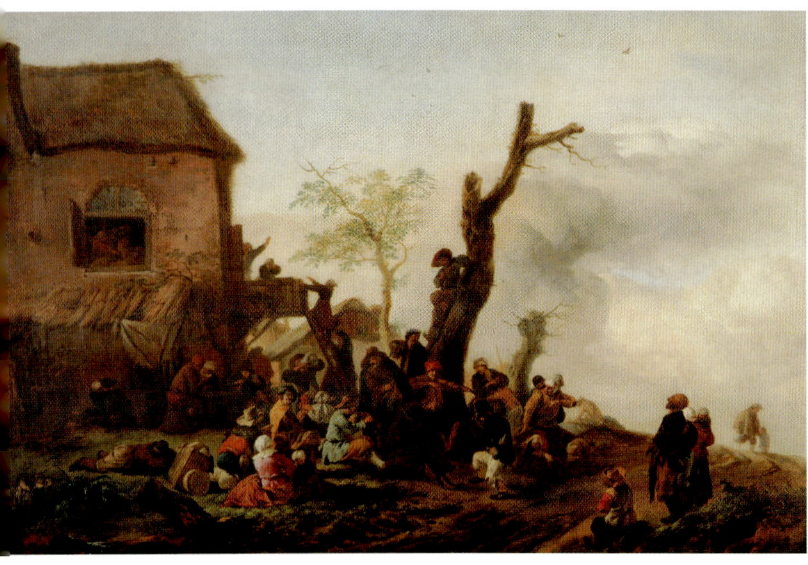

Landscape with a Large Number of Peasants Merrymaking in Front of a Cottage, Philips Wouwerman, 1646, oil on canvas, 52.5 x 75.1cm (20½ x 29½in), Manchester Art Gallery, Manchester, UK

A cross between a genre work and a landscape, this composition is dominated by a large dead tree that draws the eyes towards the group of cheerful, colourfully dressed peasants at its base. The figures laugh and dance to the music of a lyre, flute, fiddle and bagpipes. Their close grouping was inspired by Il Bamboccio, Pieter van Laer (see page 72), and overall, this work combines Italian and Dutch styles.

The Doctor, Gerrit Dou, 1653, oil on oak, 49.3 x 36.6 cm (19⅓ x 14⅓ in), Kunsthistorisches Museum, Vienna, Austria

The arched window framing this scene, the balcony with the still life of objects and the relief beneath it have all been painted to create an illusion of another world. Meanwhile, a physician is also looking into a flagon containing urine; he is probably checking to see whether a woman is pregnant. Characterized by fine details, Dou's paintings feature well-dressed figures in niches or windows performing mundane activities. He painted on wood because it had a smoother, firmer surface than canvas.

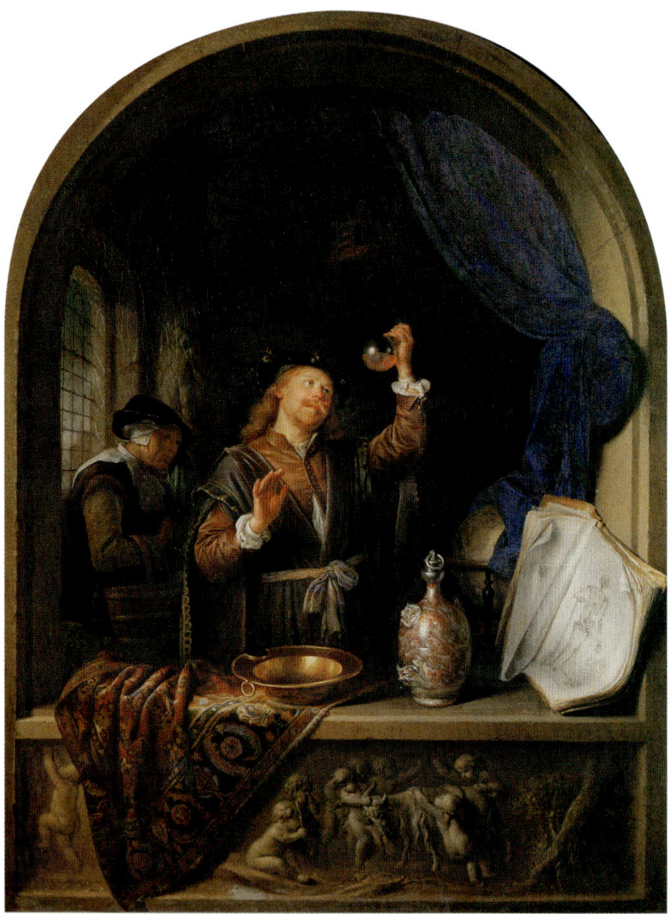

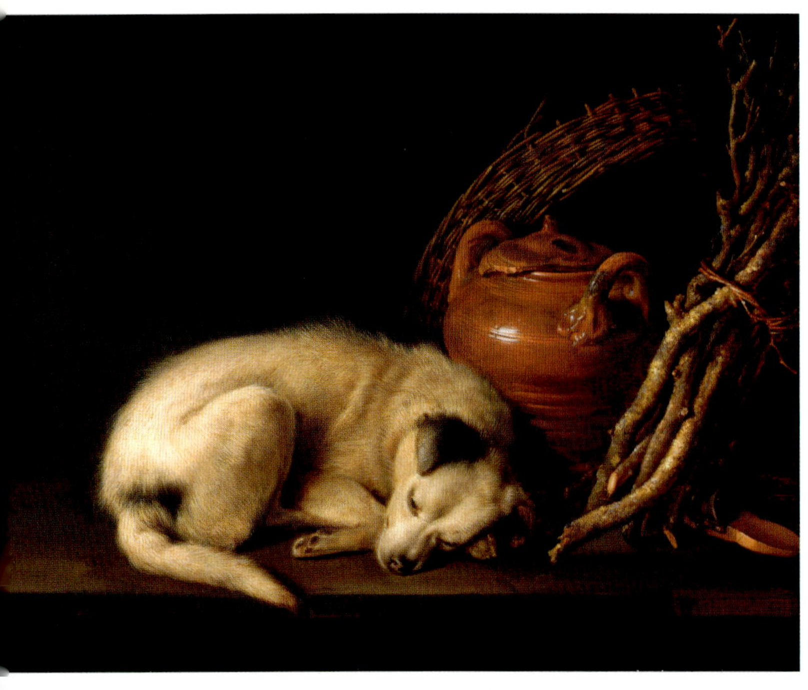

A Sleeping Dog with a Terracotta Pot, Gerrit Dou, 1650, oil on panel, 16.5 x 21.6cm (6½ x 8½in), Private Collection

The most famous member of the Leiden fijnschilders, Gerrit Dou painted this sleeping dog beside a terracotta jug, a basket, a pair of clogs and a pile of kindling wood, using his meticulously rendered brushmarks, thinly glazed paints and astute observations of life to render the image as realistically as possible. The small format was also his specialism, as were his depictions of artificial light. His paintings sold for extortionate prices and he became internationally famous.

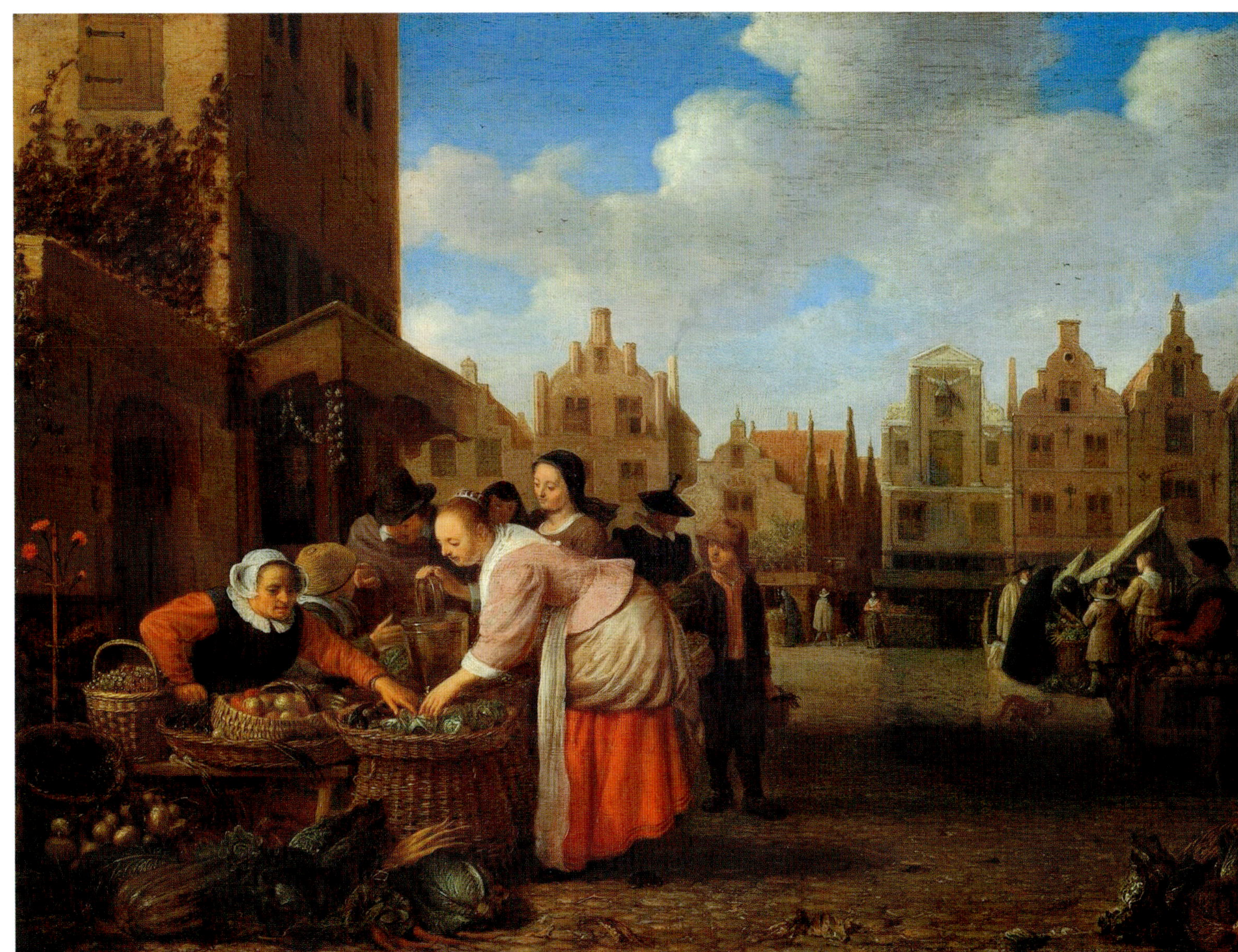

View of the Great Market in Rotterdam, Hendrik Sorgh, 1654, oil on panel, 30.5 x 40cm (12 x 15¾in), Museum Boijmans van Beuningen, Rotterdam, Netherlands

Hendrik Martenszoon Sorgh (c.1610–70) mainly painted interiors with peasants, but also, as here, market scenes, which were popular during the Dutch Golden Age as they gave artists scope to depict brightly coloured fruit and vegetables as well as cobbled streets, skies, baskets and people as well as a narrative – quite a range to demonstrate skills. Here, large cabbages, a pumpkin, onions and carrots are on the ground while in the baskets are small cabbages, apples and grapes.

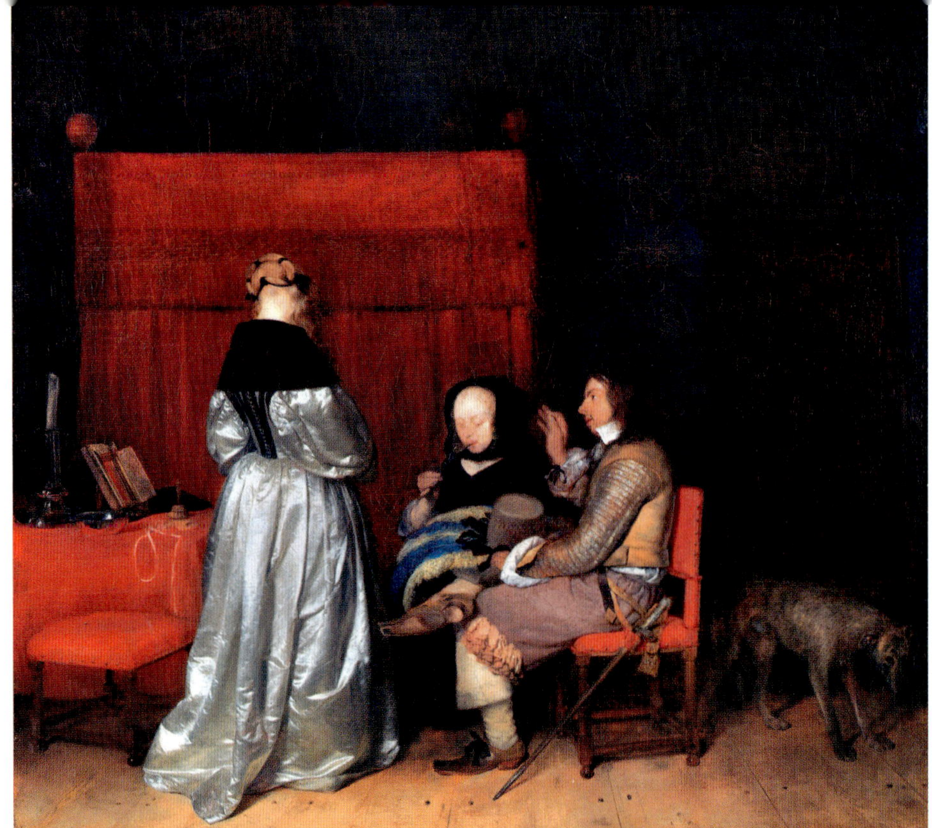

The Parental Admonition, Gerard ter Borch, c.1655, oil on canvas, 70 x 60cm (27½ x 23½in), Staatliche Museen, Berlin, Germany

Although the title that has been given to this painting suggests one thing, the ambiguity of the content suggests another. Set in a bedroom, probably a brothel, we cannot see the girl's face and it is not clear quite what is happening. The seated man is a soldier who is offering her a coin. The older woman sipping wine is probably her procuress and she is a prostitute.

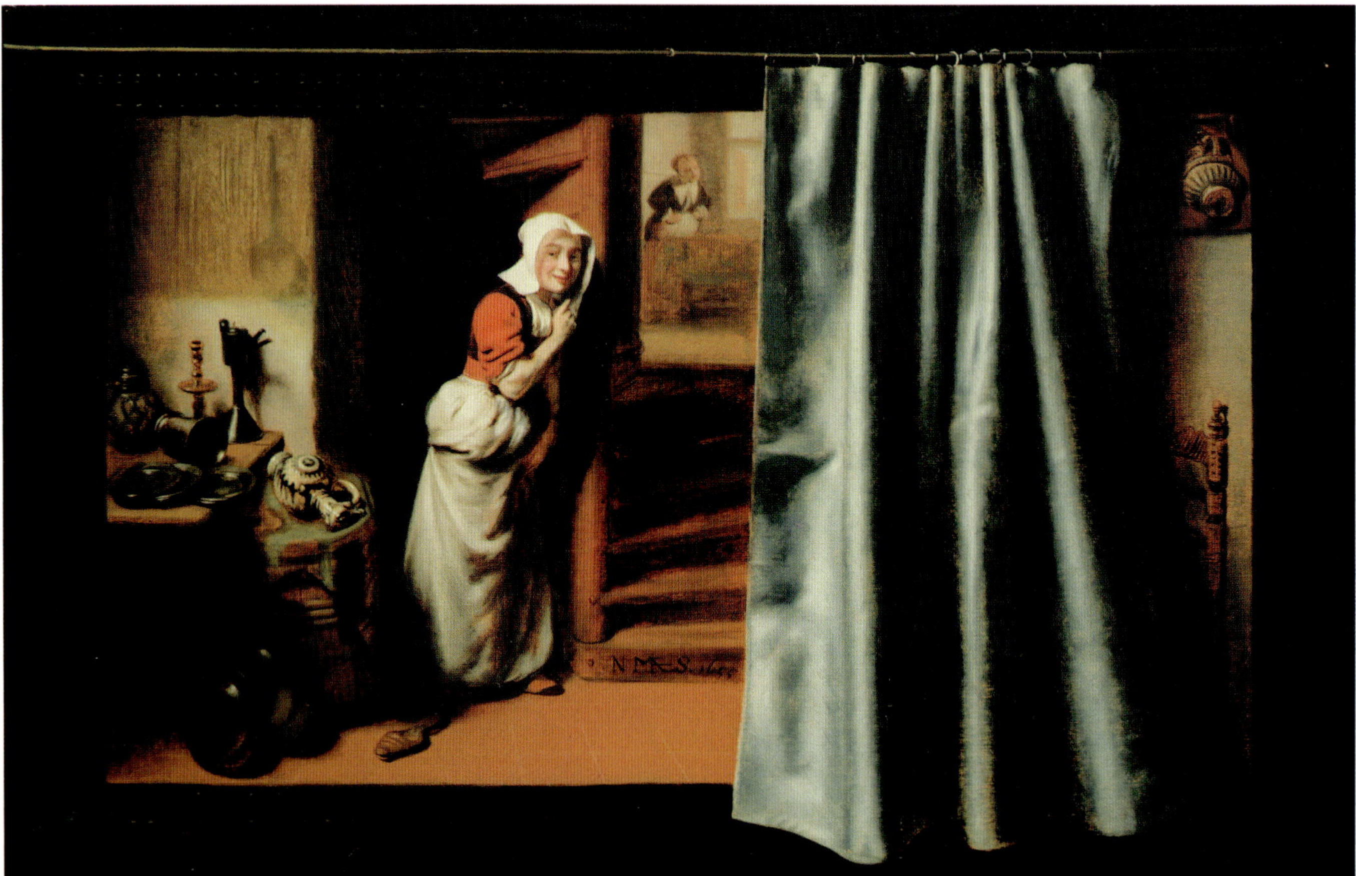

Eavesdropper with a Scolding Woman, Nicolaes Maes, 1655, oil on panel, 46.3 x 72.2cm (18¼ x 28⅓in), Private Collection

Famous for his genre paintings of women and children in domestic interiors, Nicolaes Maes here depicts a maid smiling covertly at viewers and pointing upstairs, so we listen in on a mistress scolding someone. A curtain obscures the focus of the woman's anger, so viewers are not as informed as the maid. The messy utensils on the left show that she should be working and not eavesdropping.

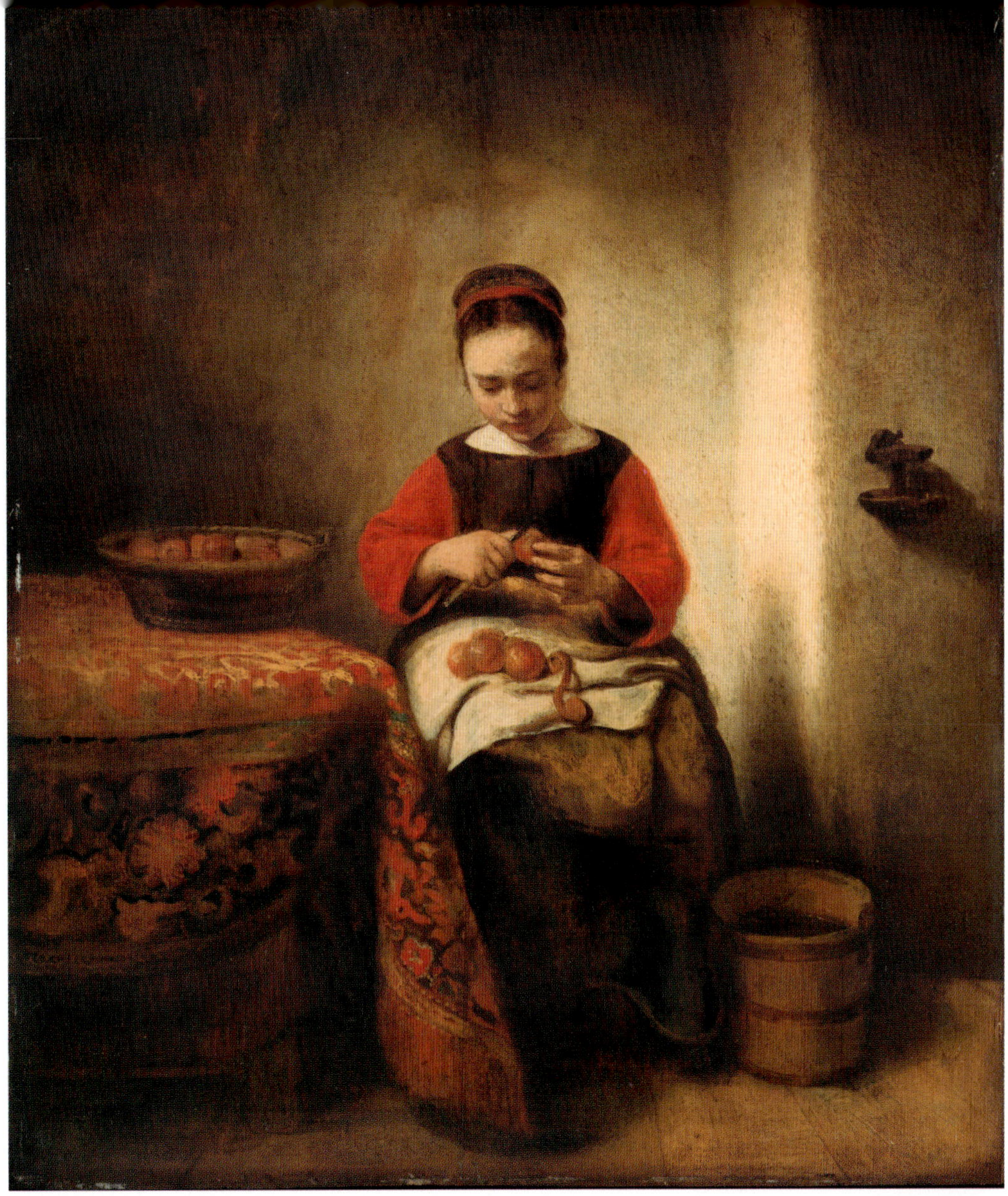

Young Woman Peeling Apples, Nicolaes Maes, *c.*1655, oil on wood, 54.6 x 45.7cm (21½ x 18in), The Metropolitan Museum of Art, New York, USA

After leaving Rembrandt's studio in 1653, Maes began painting mainly domestic interior scenes. Here, softly diffused light effects, muted shadows and facial features show Rembrandt's influence. The subject and its treatment also contrasts with previous Dutch paintings of female servants, who were usually either mocked or treated as sexual objects. The charm, sensitivity and dignity with which Maes depicted such workers created a significant precedent.

An Evening School, Gerrit Dou, *c.*1655–57, oil on wood, 25.4 x 22.9cm (10 x 9in), The Metropolitan Museum of Art, New York, USA

Children gather around a table illuminated by one candle. The teacher sharpens his pen. Gerrit Dou painted this in Leiden, which was home to a famous university and a centre of learning, so the work would have appealed to the local inhabitants. The candle is a metaphor for knowledge, and the lighting of the second candle alludes to the idea of learning passed on from teacher to pupil.

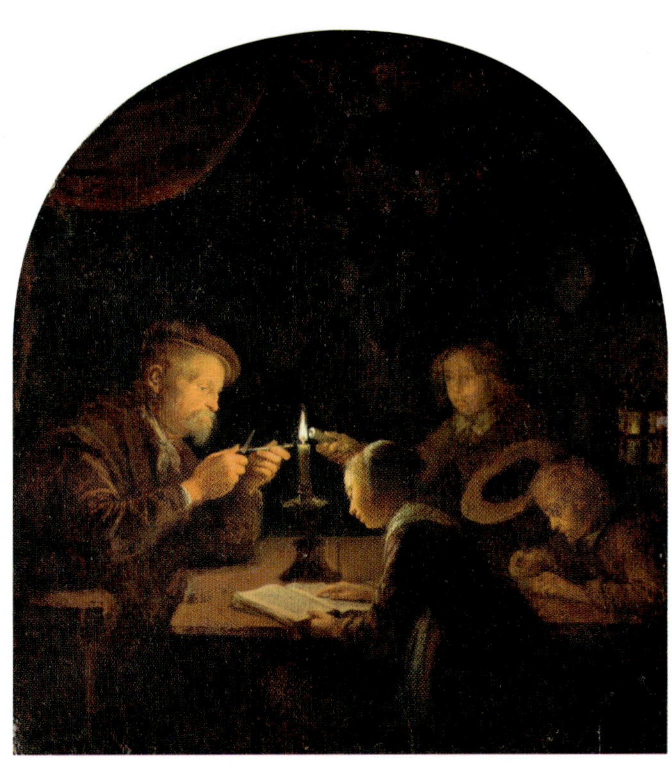

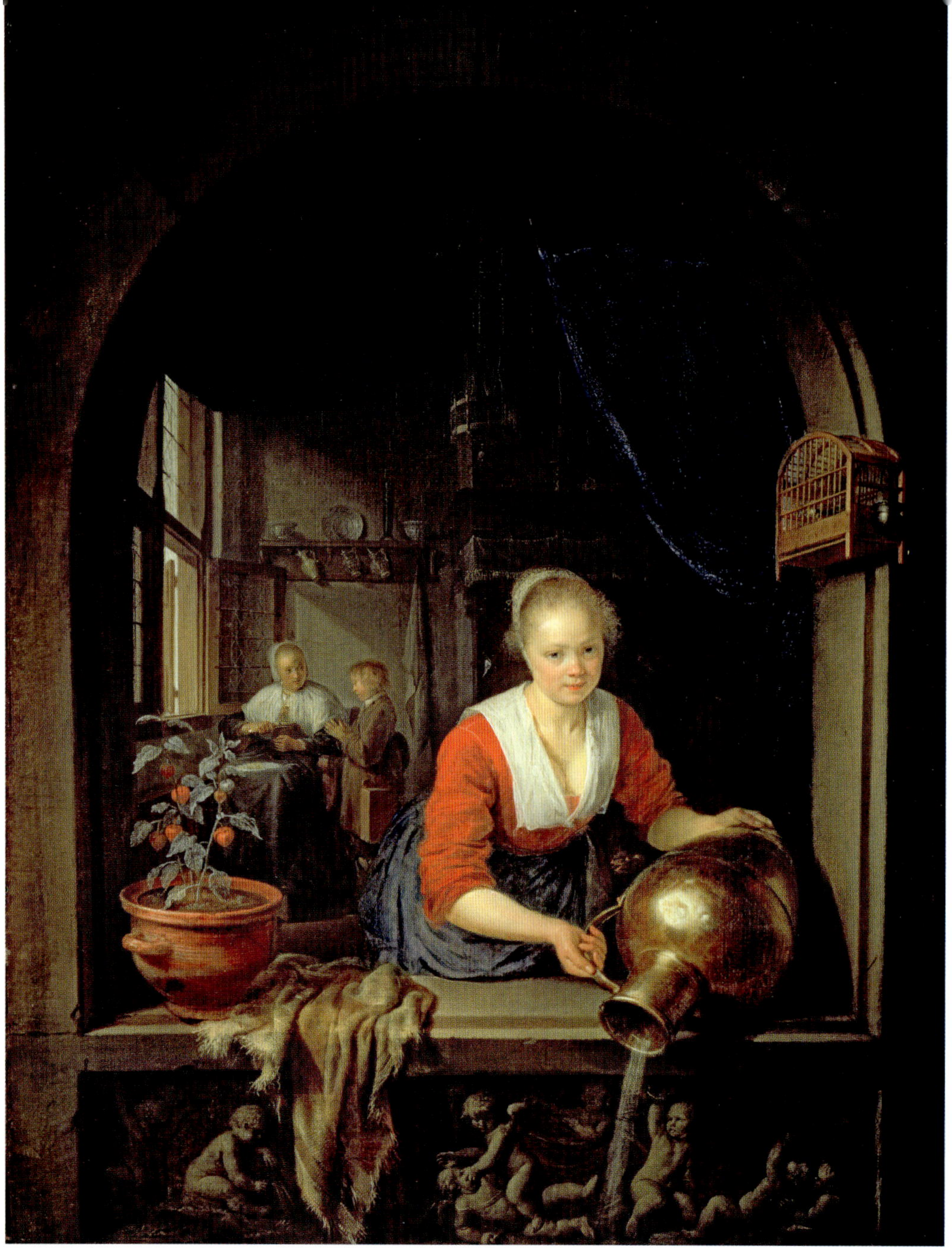

Maid at the Window, Gerrit Dou, c.1660, 280 x 380cm (110¼ x 149½in), Museum Boijmans van Beuningen, Rotterdam, Netherlands

Symbolizing the victory of divine love over worldly love, this seemingly ordinary scene would have been understood on both its levels by Dou's contemporaries. Below the window where the maid is pouring water from an urn is a relief of fighting putti. Behind her, a mother and son are praying. The heavy draped curtain pulled to the side was another of Dou's specialisms.

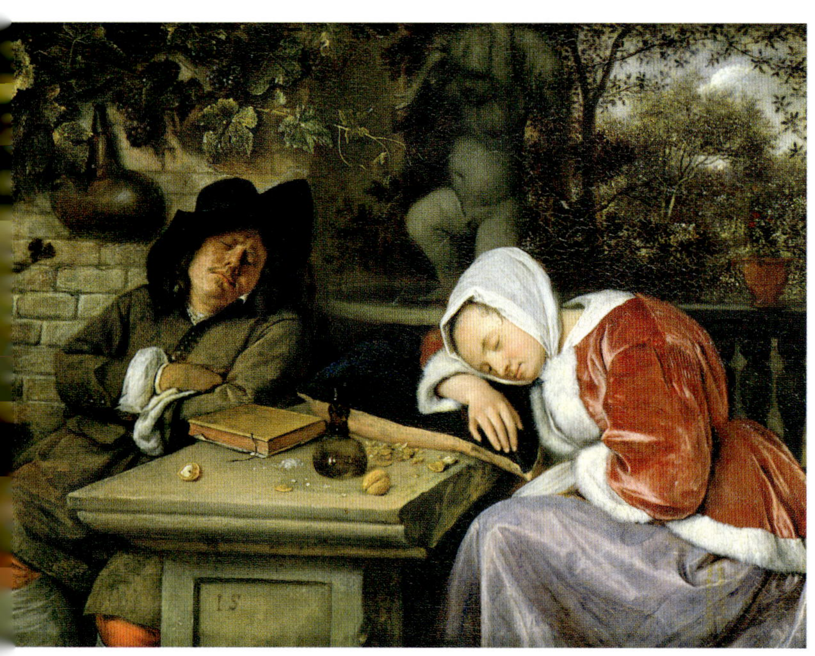

The Sleeping Couple, Jan Steen, c.1658–60, oil on copper, 18.7 x 24.5cm (7⅓ x 9⅔in), The Harold Samuel Collection, London, UK

Best known for his humorous genre scenes, Jan Steen was not as popular when he was alive as he became in later centuries. His animated paintings convey his warm-heartedness and empathy with human weaknesses. Painted on copper, this is one of his most famous works. Although superficially the painting depicts a couple dozing after eating bread and drinking wine, to the Protestants of the Dutch Republic, it represented laziness.

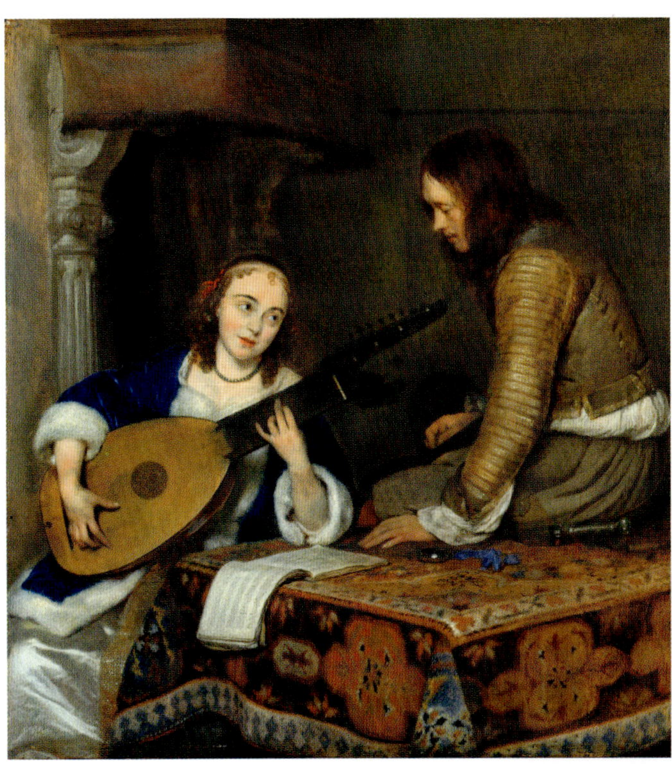

A Woman Playing the Theorbo-Lute and a Cavalier, Gerard ter Borch the Younger, c.1658, oil on wood, 36.8 x 32.4cm (14½ x 12¾in), The Metropolitan Museum of Art, New York, USA

A wealthy, well-dressed young couple are together in an expensively-furnished room. The woman plays a lute while her suitor sits close and listens. She is singing to him from a song book, which he has probably given her as a lover's present. The silver watch on a blue ribbon next to the song book symbolizes time passing, suggesting several aspects about this couple, including perhaps the fleetingness of the affair.

The Account Keeper, Nicolaes Maes, 1656, oil on canvas, 66 x 53.7pcm (26 x 21in), St Louis Museum of Art, Missouri, USA

A middle-aged, modestly-dressed woman is sitting at a desk, working. The large map on the wall behind her reminds viewers of the importance of the Dutch Republic within the world. Beside her on a ring are several large keys; these are for the safe, cash box and drawers which hold her important files. Maes frequently painted women at work, depicting them with respect. This woman is significant in the world of work and commerce.

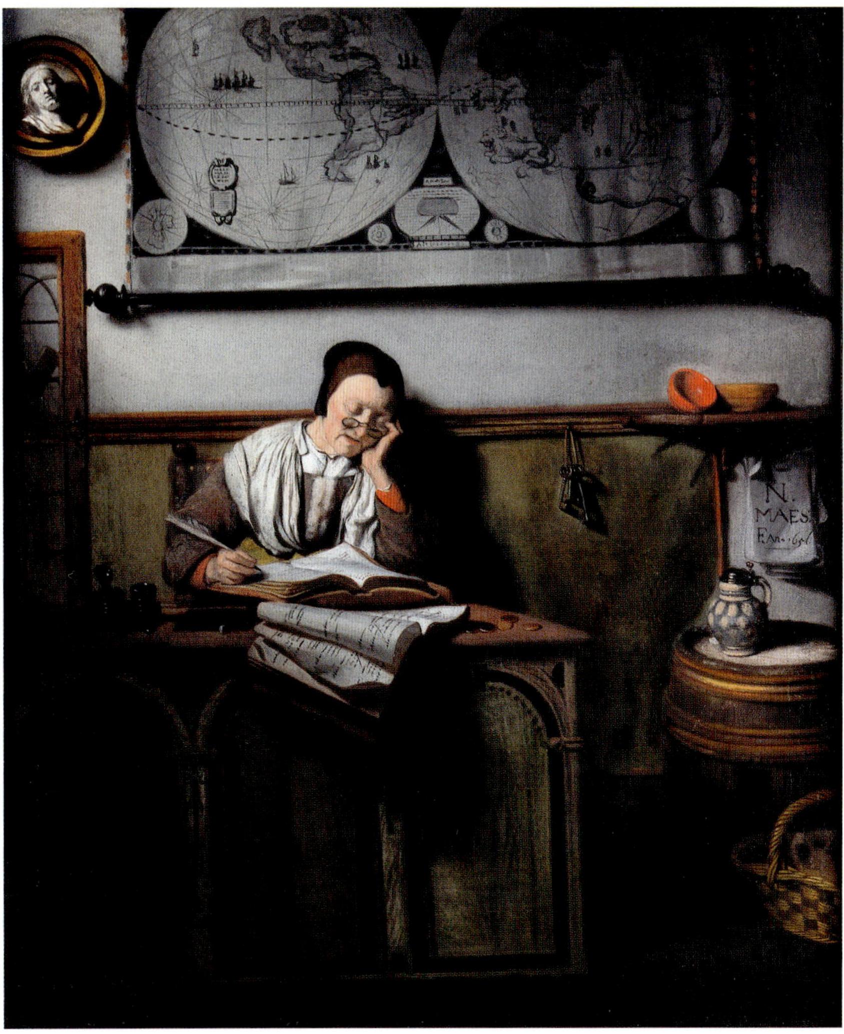

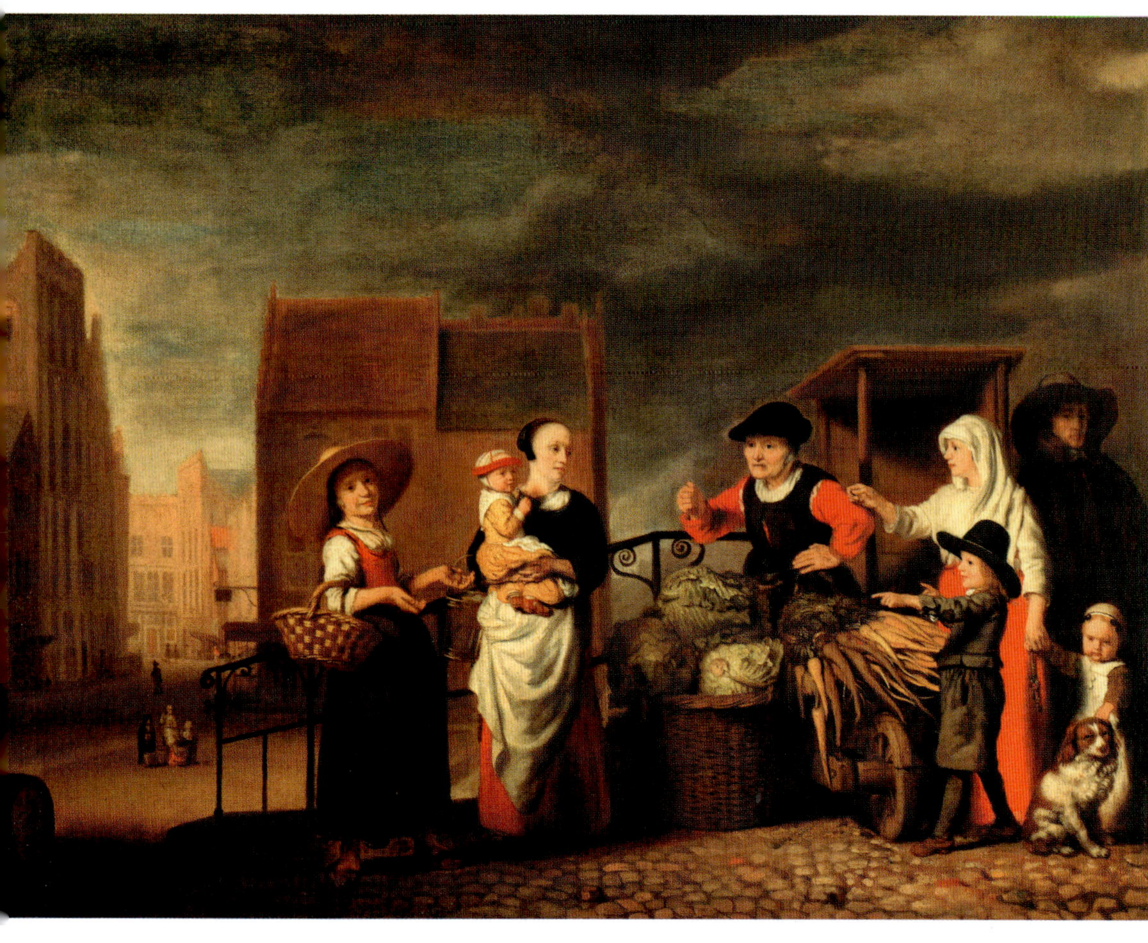

Vegetable Market, Nicolaes Maes, 1655–65, oil on canvas, 71 x 91cm (28 x 36in), Rijksmuseum, Amsterdam, Netherlands

An innovative painter, Nicolaes Maes adapted Rembrandt's brushwork and chiaroscuro; restricting his palette to blacks, browns, whites and reds, he applied both meticulously fine marks and looser impasto paint to create a range of textures. In this vegetable market, a group gather around a stall on a bridge where an old woman is selling vegetables. All are trying to attract the seller's attention, except for a maid with a basket who looks directly at viewers.

The Spinner, a Niddy-Noddy Hanging on the Wall, Nicolaes Maes, 1652–62, oil on panel, 41.5 x 33.5cm (16⅓ x 13in), Rijksmuseum, Amsterdam, Netherlands

A niddy-noddy is a tool used to make skeins from yarn, and here, it forms part of the elderly woman's work. The woman sits in the corner of a room and spins. She peers through spectacles at her yarn on the spinning wheel as she concentrates on the task she is undertaking. Maes always portrayed working people, especially women, with respect.

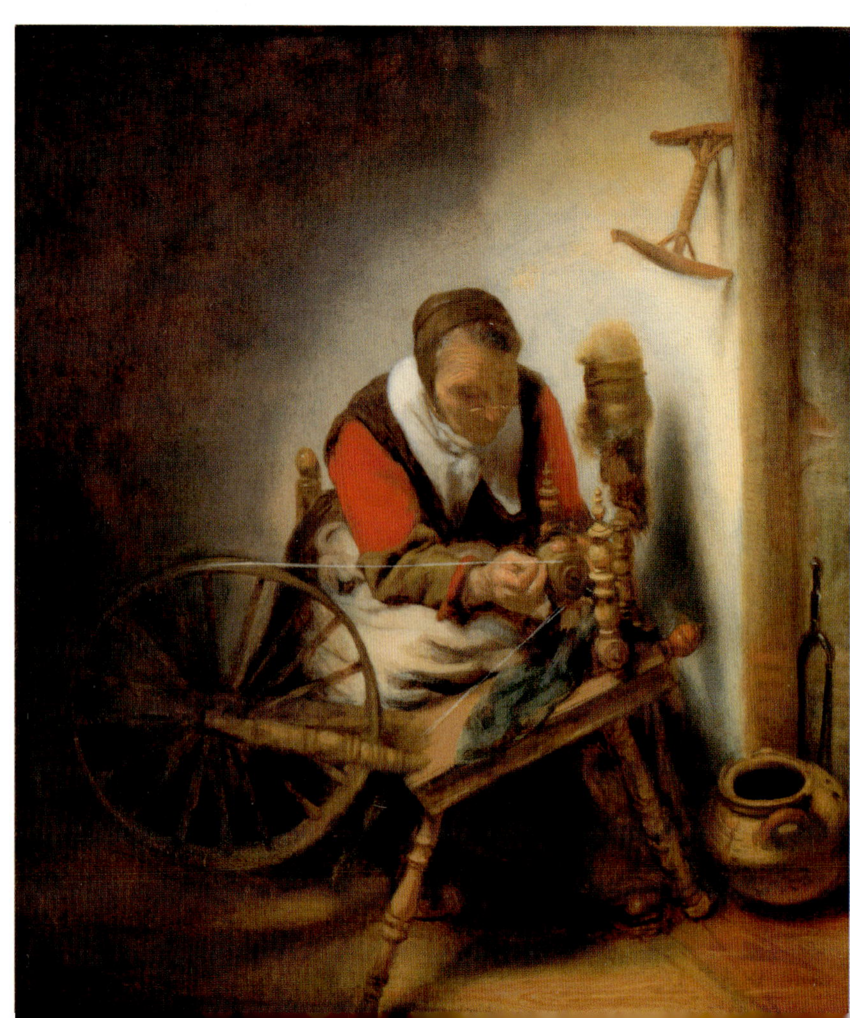

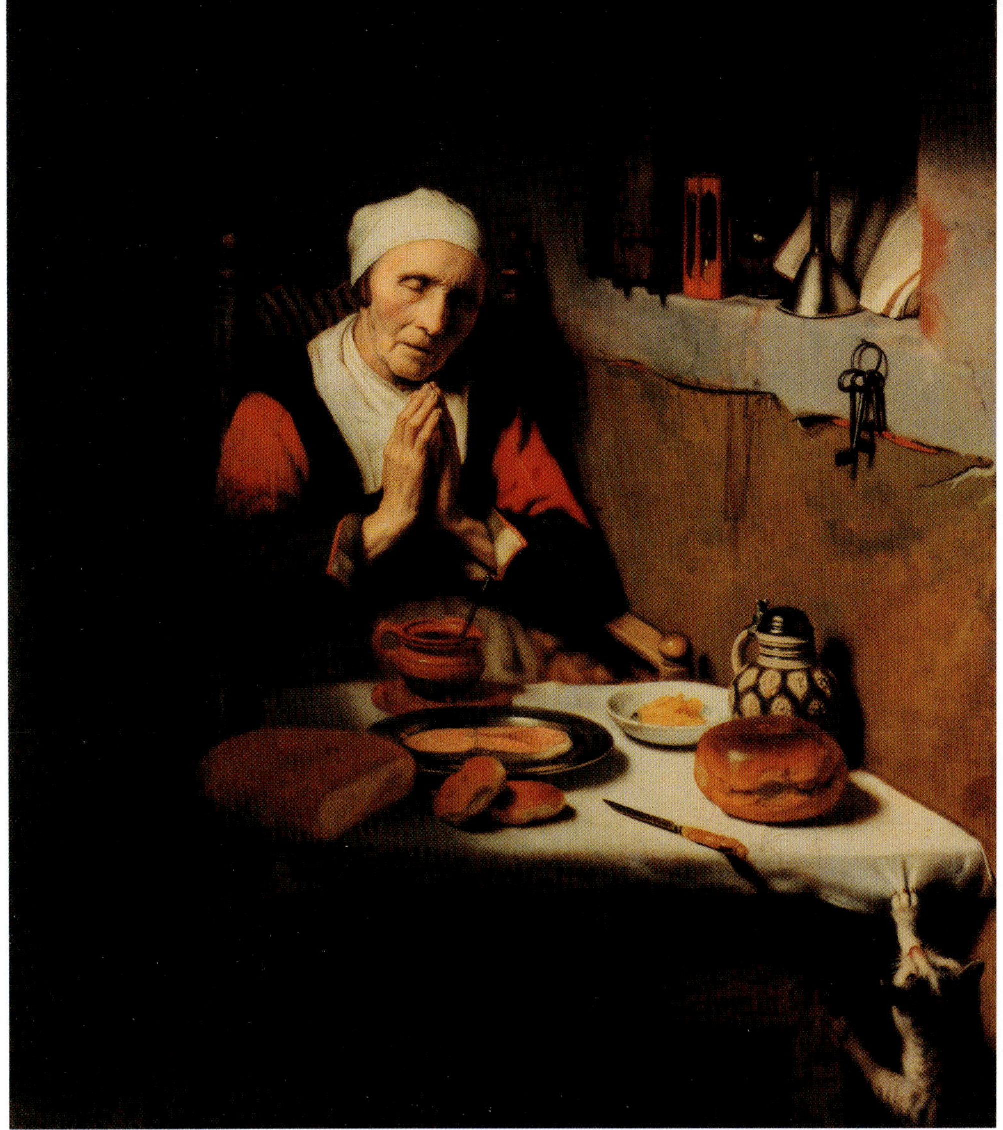

Old Woman Saying Grace, or *The Prayer without End,* Nicolaes Maes, *c.*1656, oil on canvas, 134 x 113cm (52¾ x 44½in), Rijksmuseum, Amsterdam, Netherlands

In a semi-darkened room, an old woman prays fervently before eating her meal that is in front of her. She must have been praying for some time as her cat is tugging on the tablecloth, trying to attract her attention. Maes was conveying the old woman's virtue as she is presumably as hungry as the cat, but she shows constraint and puts God before her own needs. In the predominantly Protestant Dutch Republic, this was greatly esteemed.

The Listening Housewife, Nicolaes Maes, 1656, oil on canvas, 84.7 x 70.6cm (33⅓ x 27¾in), The Wallace Collection, London, UK

One of Maes's most innovative motifs was the interior with an eavesdropper who invites viewers to join with her and secretly spy on other members of the household.

Here a housewife invites viewers to witness two servants below stairs flirting, and ignoring their duties to the people upstairs waiting for their services. Additionally, while they are preoccupied, a cat is licking plates on the floor. Viewers will appreciate that the main character should also be working, but is wasting time.

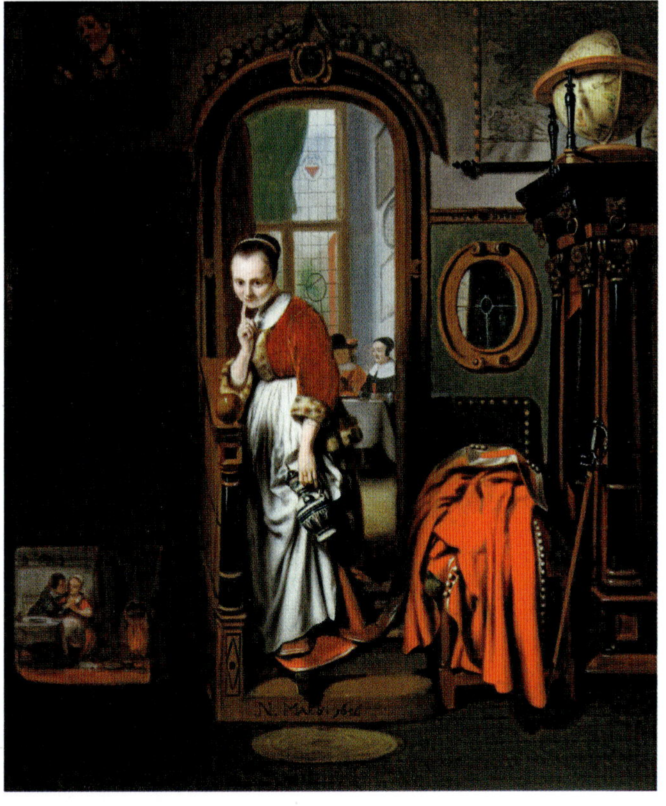

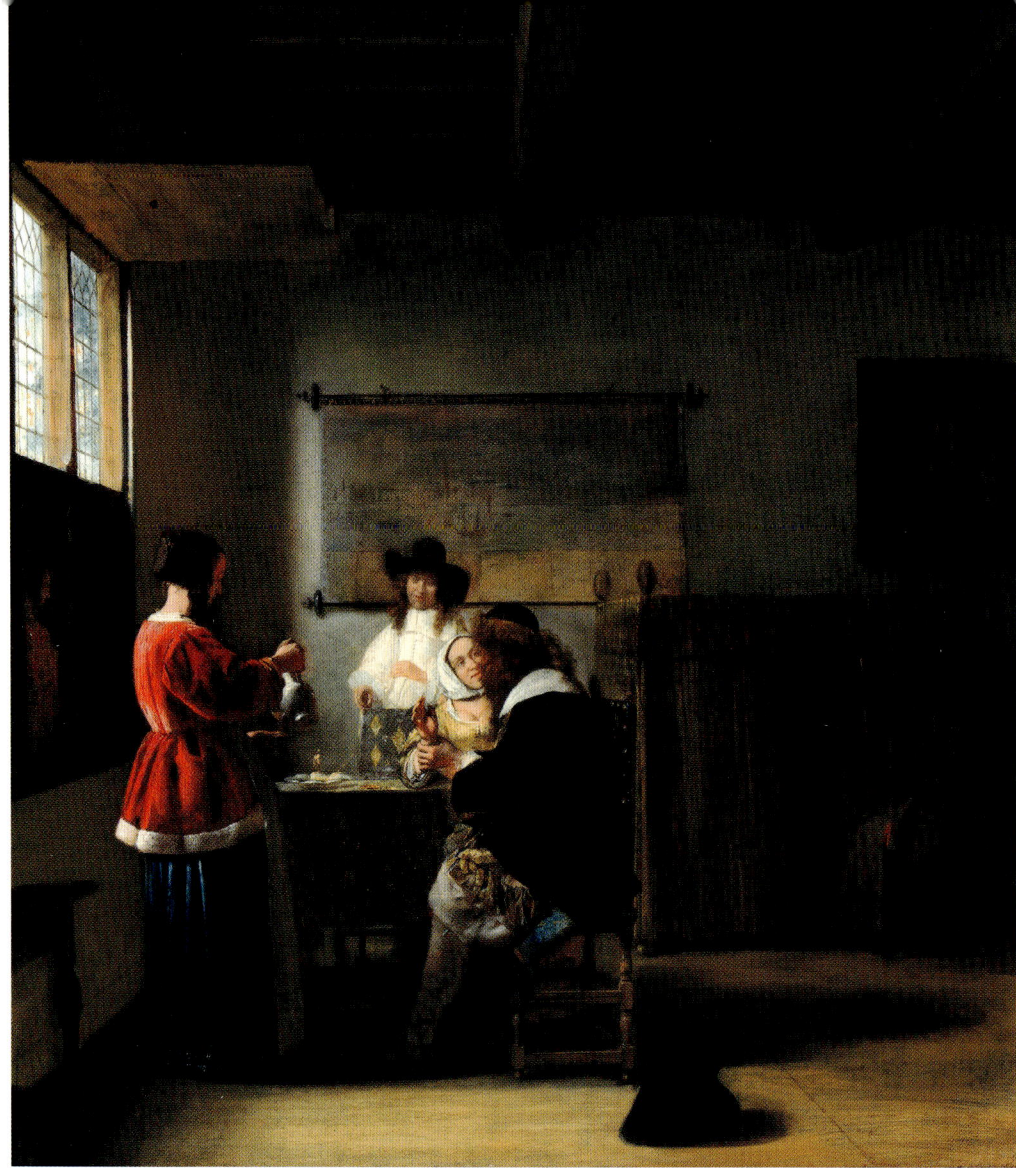

The Visit, Pieter de Hooch, c.1657, oil on wood, 67.9 x 58.4cm (26¾ x 23in), The Metropolitan Museum of Art, New York, USA

Light filtering through the window conveys a sense of space and atmosphere. On the table, the oysters are in a Delftware bowl alongside a silver fork and a slice of lemon. Elements such as the plate of oysters and the canopied bed imply that this is a brothel. It is likely that the men are paying for the women's services rather that this being a scene of courtship.

Young Woman Drinking, Pieter de Hooch, 1658, oil on canvas, 60 x 69cm (23⅔ x 27in), Musée du Louvre, Paris, France

Using subtle plays of light and a nuanced palette, Pieter de Hooch conveys a moment in time. A woman in a red dress and silver jacket sits in the centre of the room, raising a glass that has been filled by a man standing nearby, while an older woman seems to be asking him to stop. Another man smokes a pipe and in the foreground a small dog sleeps. An image of Amsterdam hangs on the back wall, and a painting depicting Christ and the adulteress.

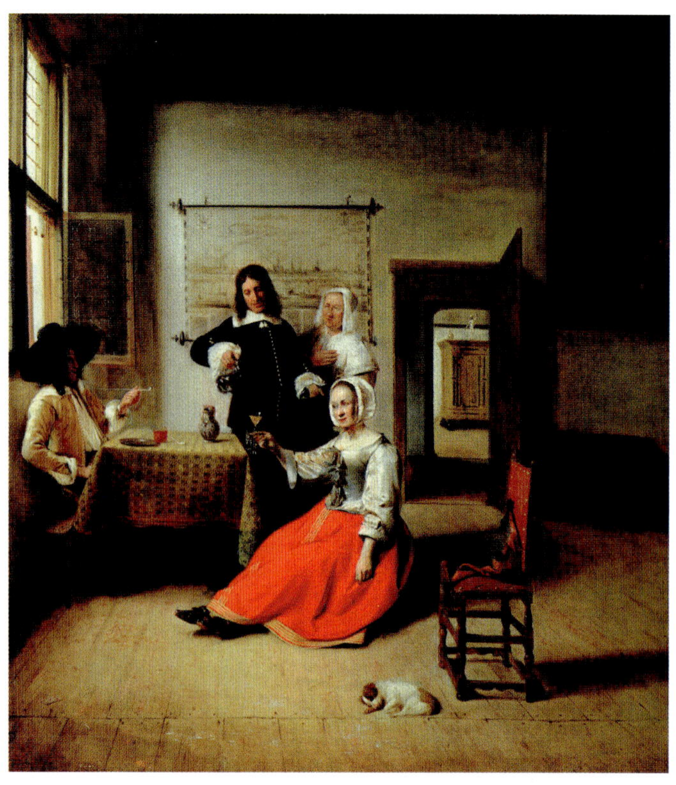

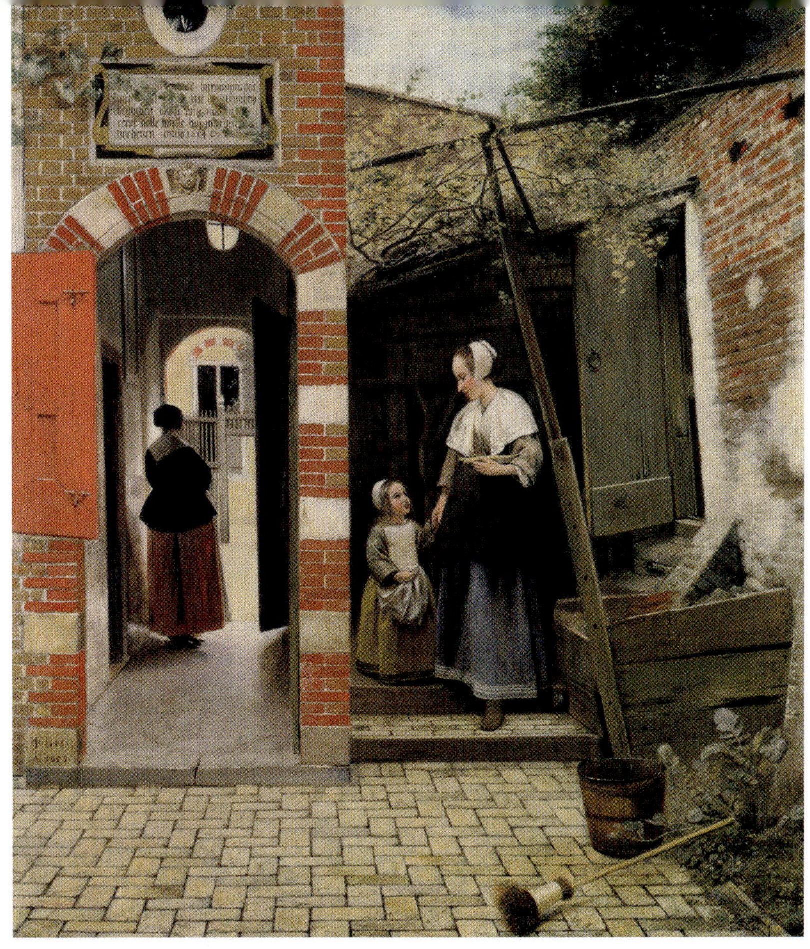

The Courtyard of a House in Delft, Pieter de Hooch, 1658, oil on canvas, 73.5 x 60cm (29 x 23⅔in), The National Gallery, London, UK

Using small, precise brushmarks, Pieter de Hooch depicts a neat building, a decayed garden wall and a passage leading to the street beyond. A woman and a child hold hands outside an outbuilding, looking as if they have just collected something for dinner. The woman carries a bowl, and the child carries something in her pinafore. All around is tidy; a broom leans by the freshly swept cobbles. In the alleyway, another woman watches the street.

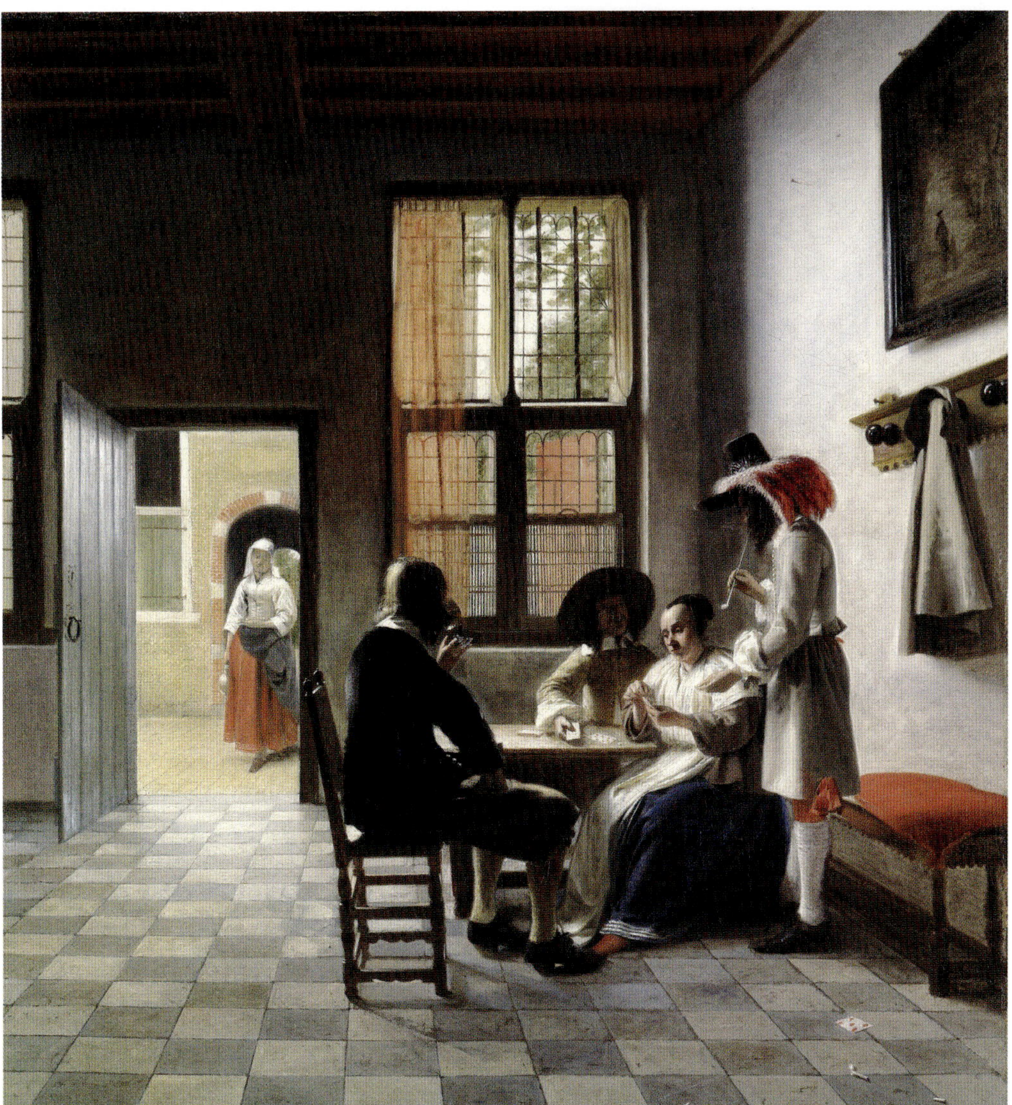

Card Players in a Sunlit Room, Pieter de Hooch, 1658, oil on canvas, 77.2 x 67.4cm (30⅓ x 26½in), Royal Collection Trust, London, UK

Exploring the fall of light and the way in which it appears to change textures and colours, de Hooch has painted an interior scene with figures around a table playing cards. Two men flanking the woman are a cheating partnership. The room itself is painted in great detail, meticulously conveying the light falling on surfaces, and viewers' eyes are drawn towards the figures so that they can decide on the enigmatic story for themselves.

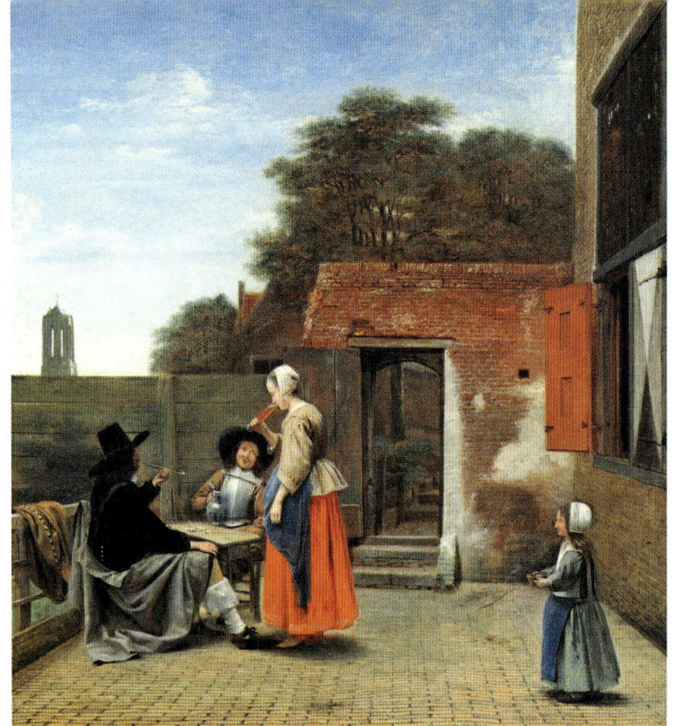

A maid has been entreated to join two soldiers in playing a drinking game. Contemporary viewers would have recognized that she is drinking from a 'pass-glass' used in drinking games. Players took turns to drink from the pass-glass, each time trying to drink the correct amount in order to match the level of liquid with a mark on the glass. A little girl carries a brazier of hot coals from which the two soldiers will light their long-stemmed pipes.

Girl Eating Oysters, Jan Steen, c.1658/60, oil on panel, 20.5 x 15cm (8 x 6in), Mauritshuis, The Hague, Netherlands

Smugly looking at viewers, this sumptuously dressed young woman sprinkles salt on an oyster in her hand. At the time, oysters were widely believed to have aphrodisiac properties. Nearby on the table is a jug with a silver lid, a glass of wine, a silver dish containing a bread roll, a knife, some salt and a bag of peppercorns. In the kitchen in the background, more oysters are being prepared.

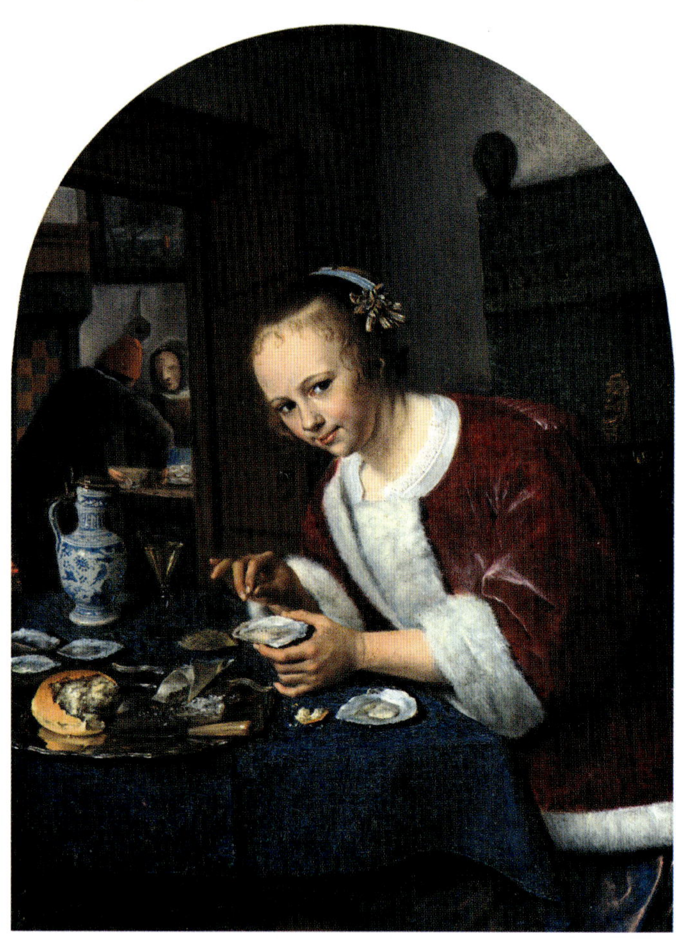

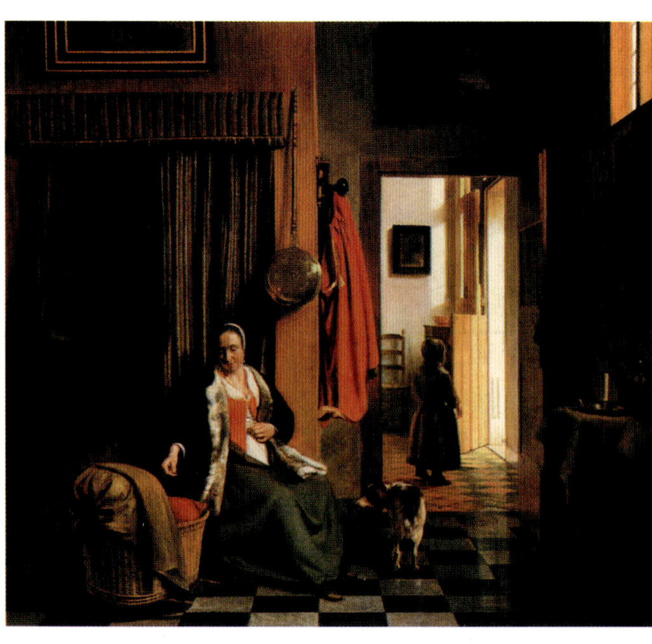

Mother Lacing Her Bodice Beside a Cradle, Pieter de Hooch, 1659–60, oil on canvas, 92 x 100cm (36¼ x 39¼in), Staatliche Museen, Berlin, Germany

A mother sits by a cot, having just breastfed her baby, while her dog – a traditional symbol of fidelity – stands close by. In the background, a toddler looks out of an open door that represents the world beyond the intimate interior. The elaborate perspective and effects of light emphasize the space and solidity of the house. This painting, and others like it, express Dutch ideals of caring for children and the home.

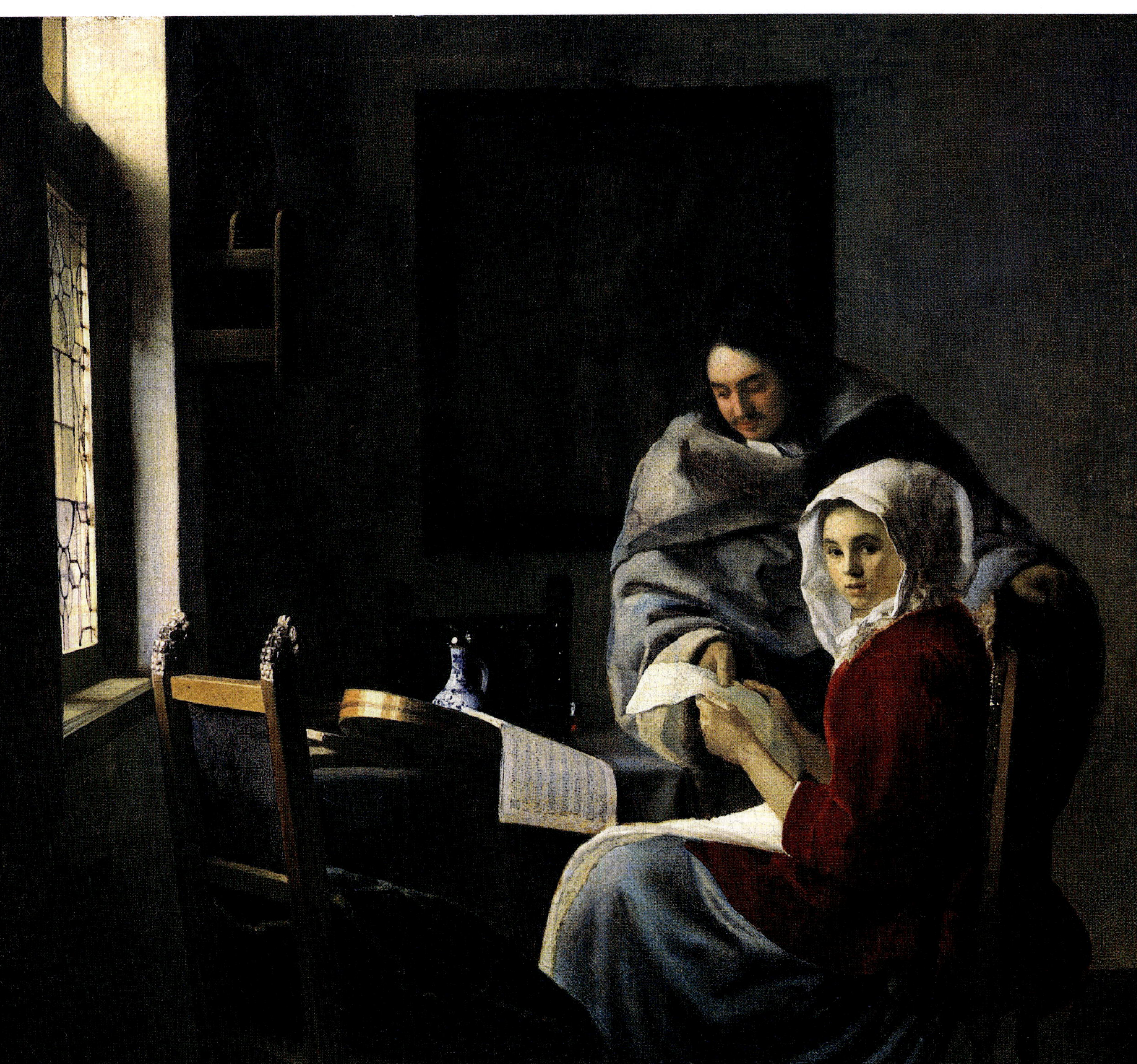

Girl Interrupted in her Music, Johannes Vermeer, c.1658–61, oil on canvas, 39.4 x 44.5 cm (15½ x 17½ in), Frick Collection, New York, USA.

By being interrupted, this girl has moved her head, which allowed Vermeer to suggest movement while still presenting his usual calm type of composition. The music teacher still concentrates on the lesson, but the girl has turned to look directly at us, the viewer. Light falls on the enigmatic scene from a window on the left-hand side of the room.

The Milkmaid, Johannes Vermeer, *c.*1660, oil on canvas, 45.5 x 41cm (18 x 16in), Rijksmuseum, Amsterdam, Netherlands

Wearing a white headdress, yellow bodice with green sleeves and a blue apron, the milkmaid of the title watches with silent concentration as she pours milk from a jug into a cooking pot. Light from a window on the left-hand side falls on her forehead, bodice and forearms. On the table is a basket of bread and some rolls, all lit by the sunlight that picks out details of textures and colours.

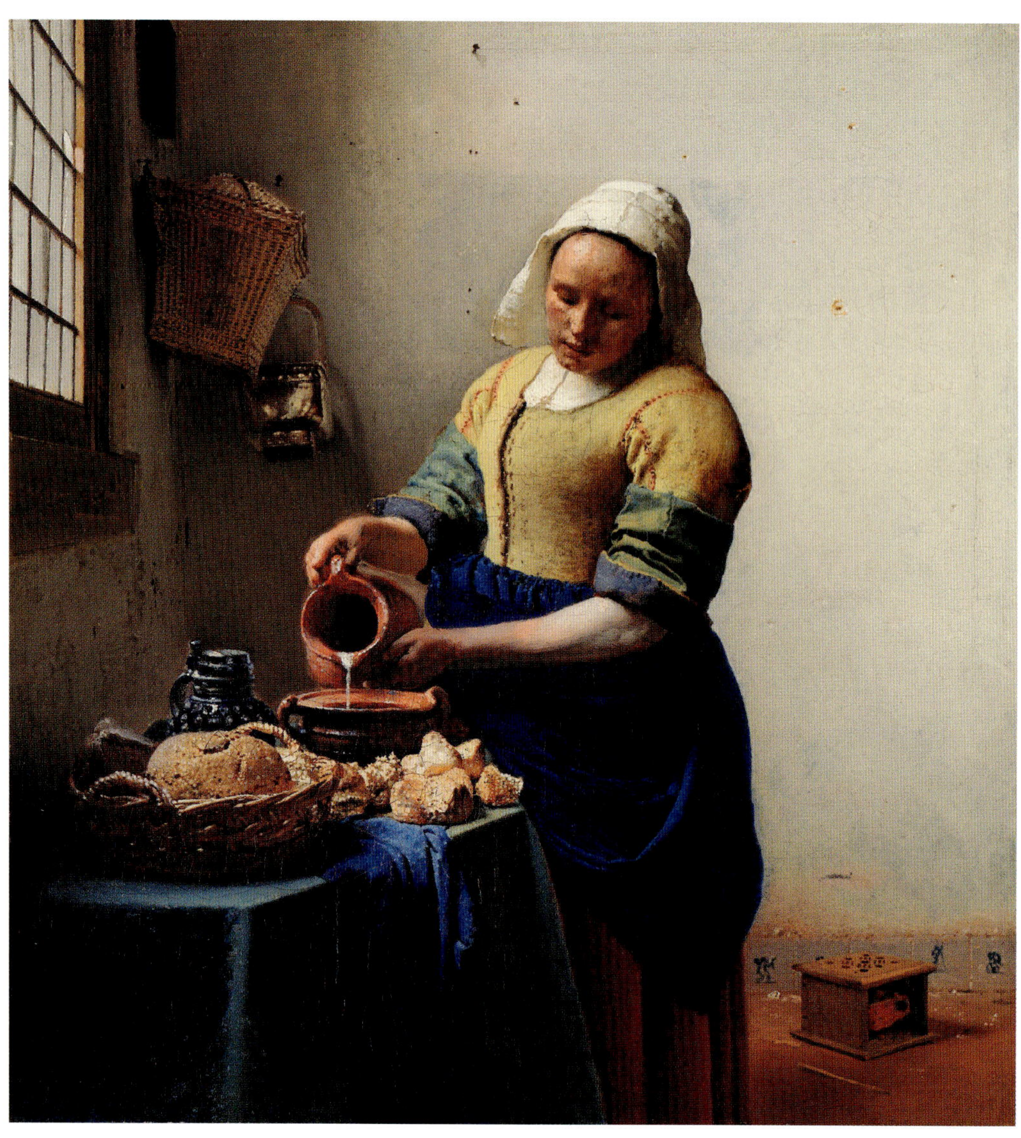

Easy Come, Easy Go, Jan Steen, 1661, oil on canvas, 104 x 79cm (41 x 31in), Museum Boijmans van Beuningen, Rotterdam, Netherlands

Jan Steen painted himself as the man laughing at the table. This is a doorkijkje (see page 91), and in the room beyond, two men are gambling. The inscription on the fireplace is a Dutch saying meaning 'easy come, easy go,' that is conveyed throughout the room. The warning is that fortunes won easily through gambling can soon be lost.

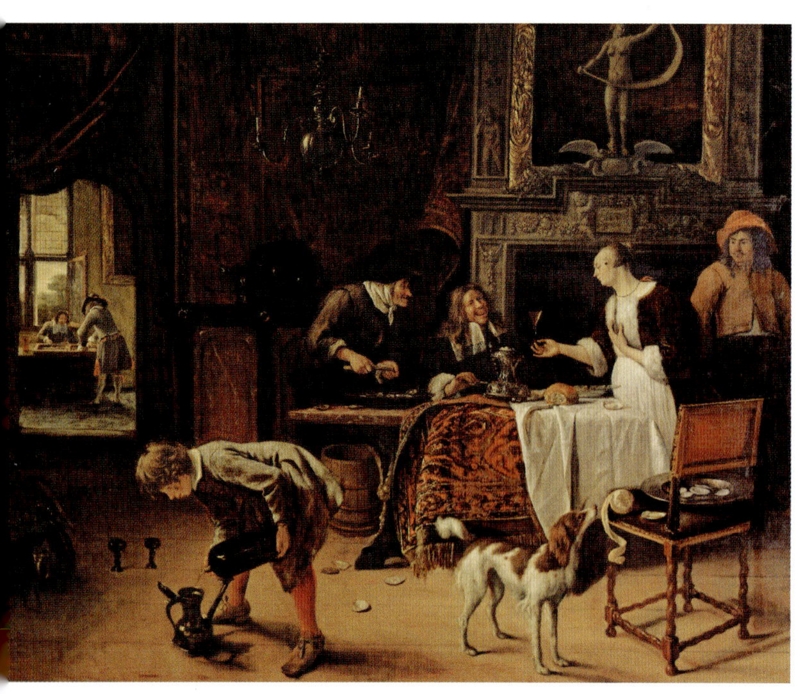

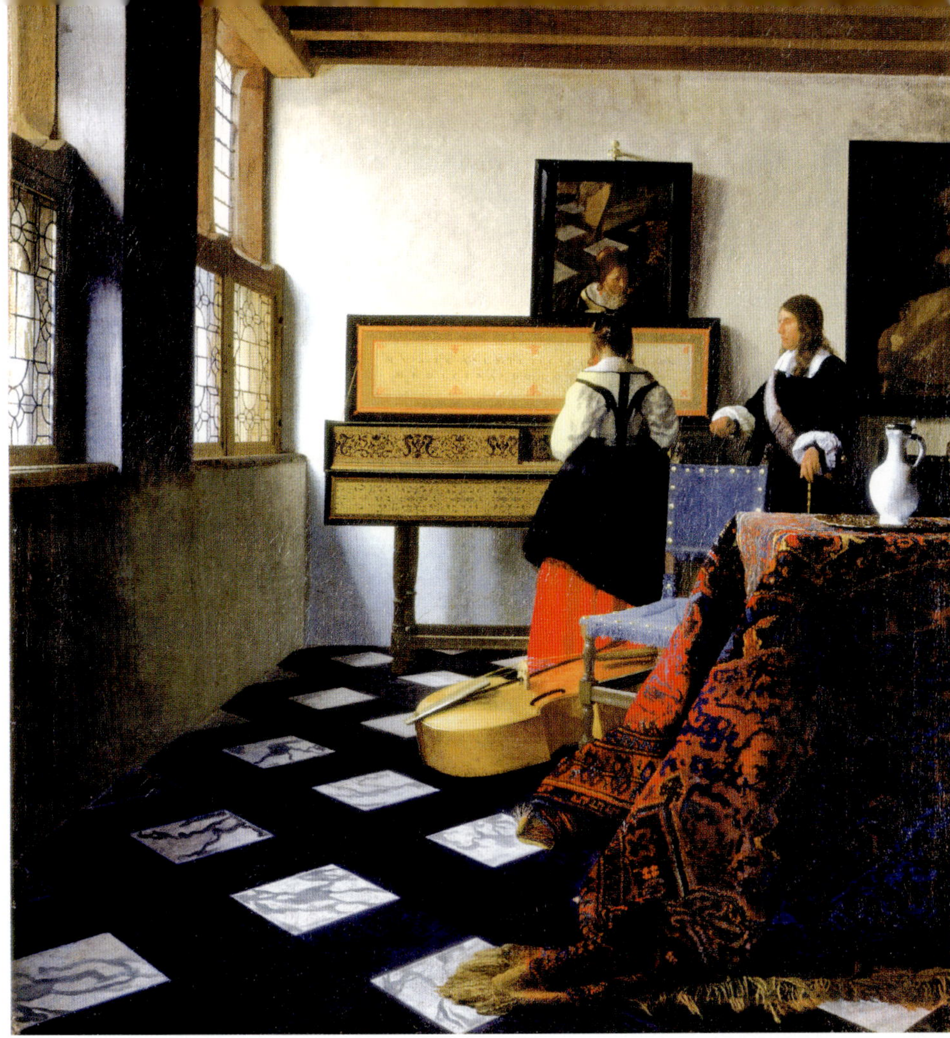

The Music Lesson, Johannes Vermeer, *c.*1662–65, oil on canvas, 74.1 x 64.5cm (29 x 25¼ in), Royal Collection Trust, London, UK

Characterized by its precise use of perspective that draws the eye towards the figures at the back of the room, this is another of Vermeer's ambiguous paintings suggesting that we are intruding on a private moment. With her back to viewers, the young woman is playing the virginal, watched by her music teacher at the side. Light shines through the windows on the left, illuminating the room and casting soft shadows.

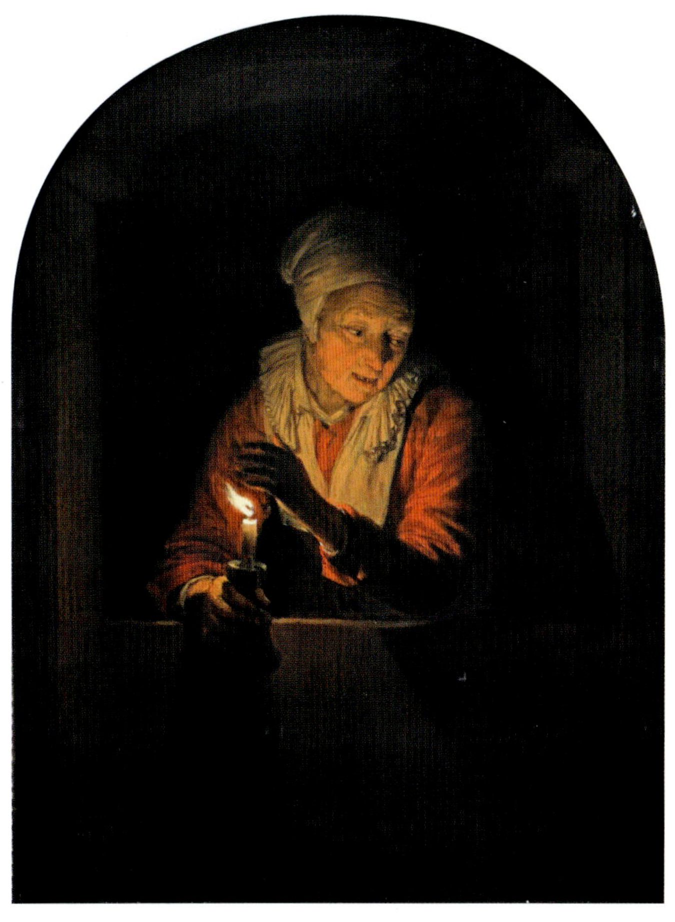

Old Woman with Candle, Gerrit Dou, 1661, oil on oak, 31 x 23cm (12¼ x 9in), Wallraf–Richartz Museum, Cologne, Germany

Gerrit Dou captures a seemingly spontaneous moment. On hearing a noise from outside, an old woman leans out of her arched, stone window and peers into the darkness. She is illuminated by the flickering flame of her candle that she shields from any breeze with one hand. Dou demonstrates his skill at projecting the figure forward, and in creating a mysterious atmosphere.

The Urine Doctor, Gerrit Dou, 1663, oil on wood, 56 x 42cm (22 x 16½in), Musée des Beaux-Arts, Angers, France

Dou uses his characteristic device of a window with a parted curtain revealing a scene. A doctor is looking at a patient's urine, surrounded by various vanitas objects, including a Bible, a skull, an extinguished candle and a globe. Standing next to him is the patient, an elderly peasant woman. Admired for his refined painting technique and for the realism and naturalness he conveyed, Dou became extremely popular.

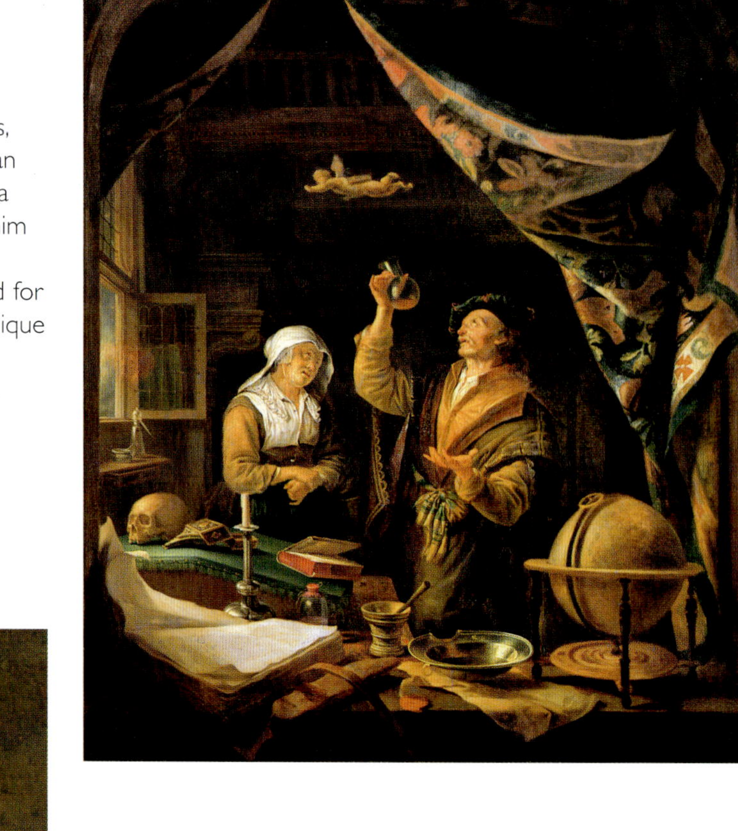

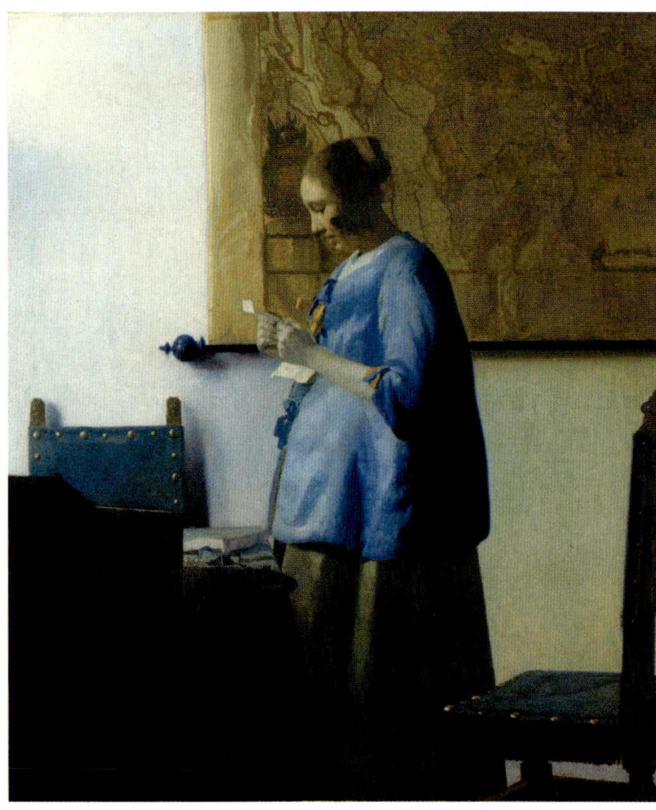

Woman Reading a Letter, Johannes Vermeer, 1663, oil on canvas, 46.5 x 39cm (18¼ x 15¼in), Rijksmuseum, Amsterdam, Netherlands

Standing in profile and facing left, this woman dressed in blue is reading a letter. As usual with Vermeer, the narrative is ambiguous. Her mouth is slightly parted and her expression could be one of shock, sorrow or simply concentration, so viewers are left wondering about the content of the letter. Behind her on the wall is a large map – conveying the pride the Dutch felt about their country at the time.

Interior with Women Beside a Linen Cupboard, Pieter de Hooch, 1663, oil on canvas, 70 x 75.5cm (27½ x 30in), Rijksmuseum, Amsterdam, Netherlands

In a middle-class home, a maid hands freshly laundered linen to her mistress. Everywhere is clean and polished. Across the hall, a child plays while nearby a statue of Mercury, the god of commerce, can be seen, holding a money bag, conveying the increasing wealth of many citizens such as these. De Hooch specialized in painting precise details, with exacting perspective and soft light, here creating an intimate scene highlighted by the women's colourful clothing.

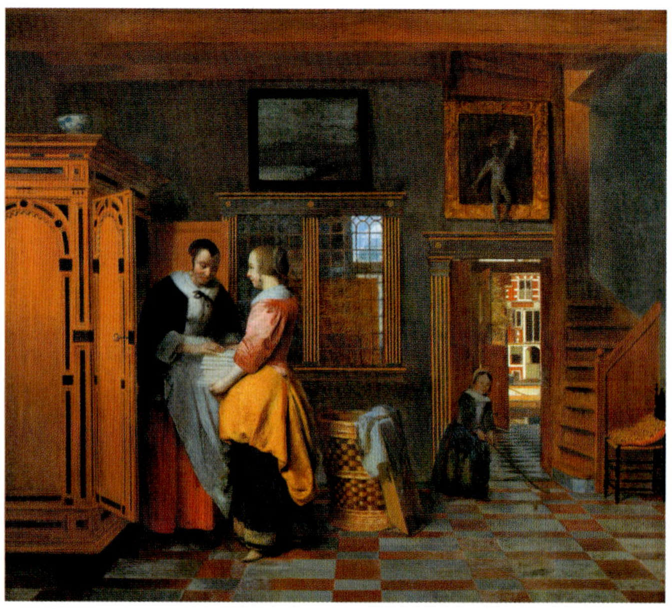

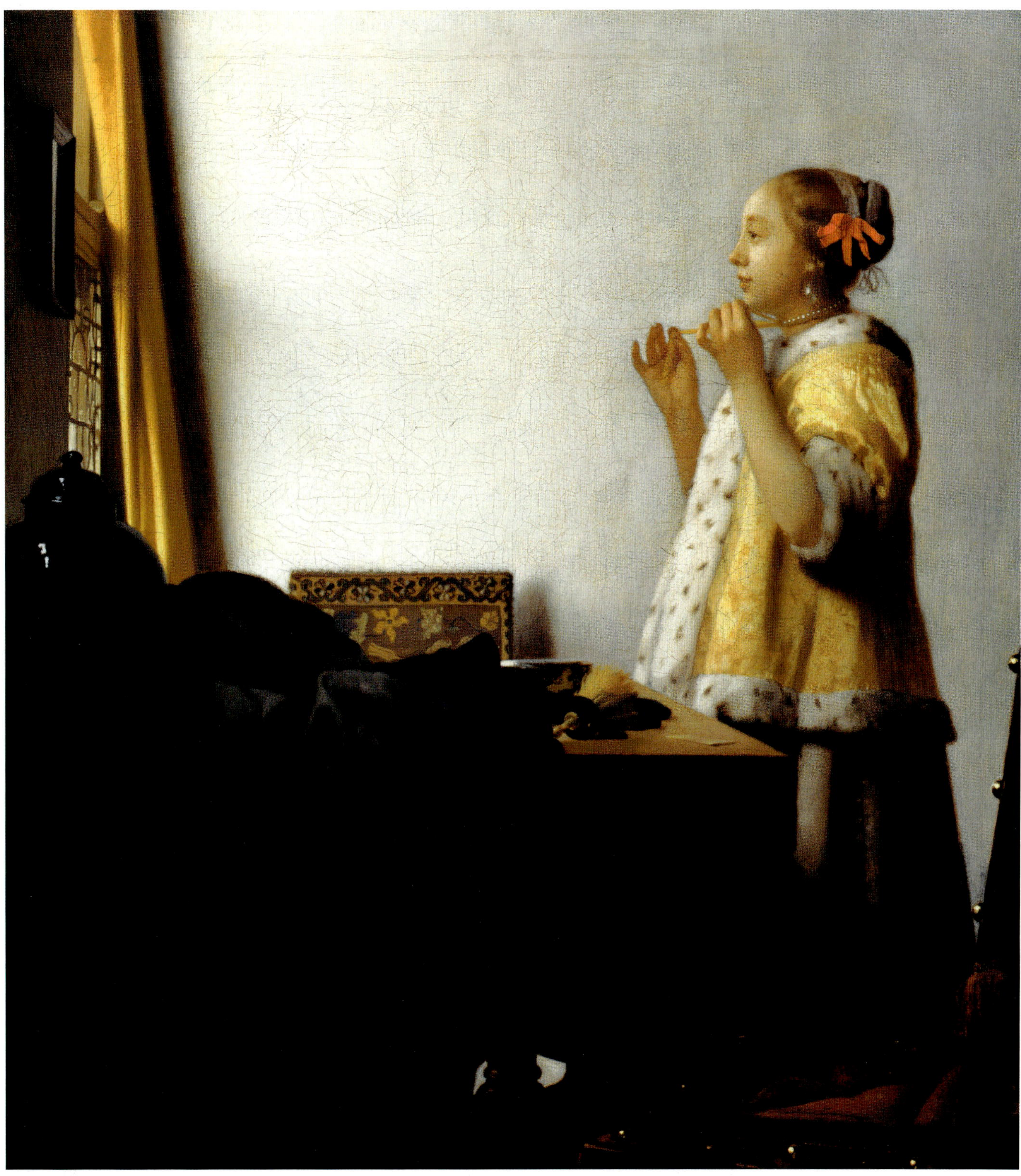

Young Woman with a Pearl Necklace, Johannes Vermeer, c.1662, oil on canvas, 56.1 x 47.4cm (22 x 18½in), Gemäldegalerie, Berlin, Germany

Standing by a table in front of a mirror, a young woman arranges her pearl necklace. Soft light filters through the leaded window behind the mirror, illuminating the young woman's face. Soft grey-white on the wall serves to create a sense of space between the deep yellow of the curtains and the paler yellow of her clothing. As usual, Vermeer's perspective is created to draw the eye into the scene.

The Dissolute Household, Jan Steen, 1660s, oil on canvas, 80.5 x 89cm (31⅔ x 35in), Apsley House, London, UK

Portraying the effects of intemperance, the master of the house (modelled by Steen himself) is too busy flirting to notice the chaos around him. His wife's pocket is being picked while she flops in a drunken stupor, the dog eats from a silver platter on the floor, and a maid steals a necklace. On the mantelpiece, a monkey has stopped the clock and cards on the floor symbolize misfortune.

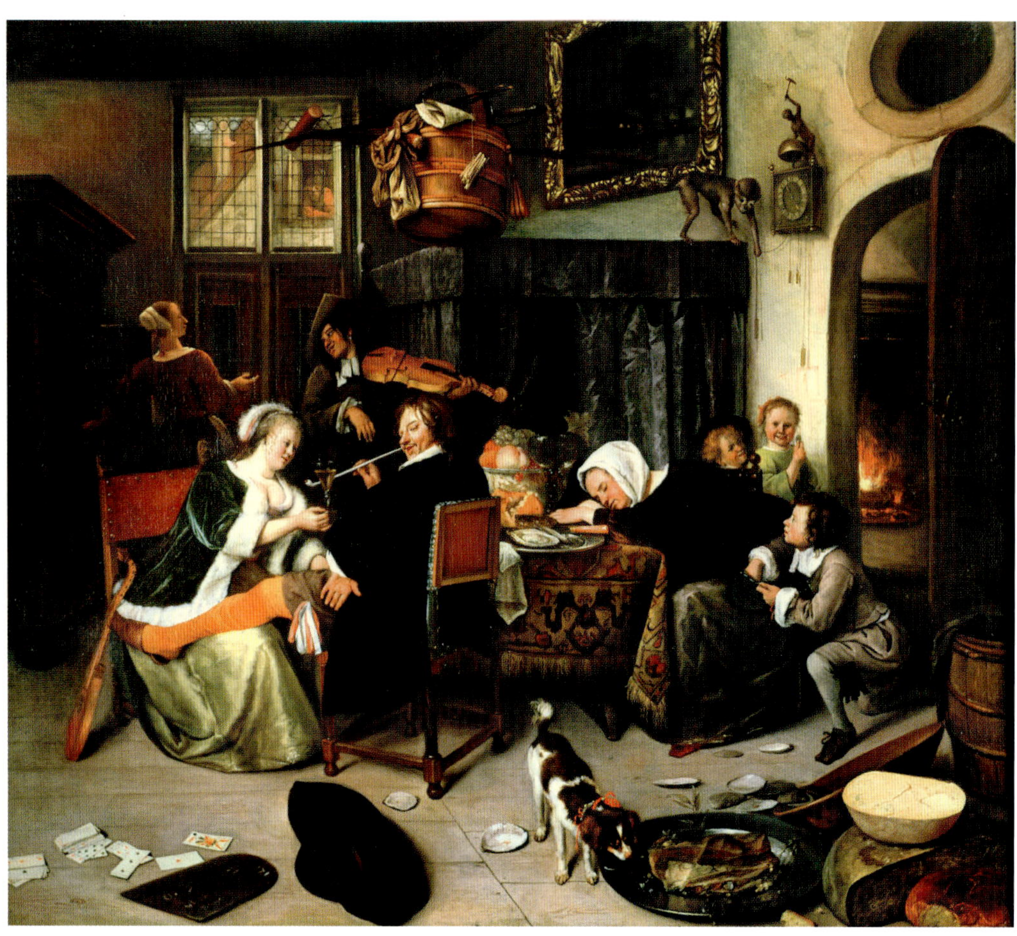

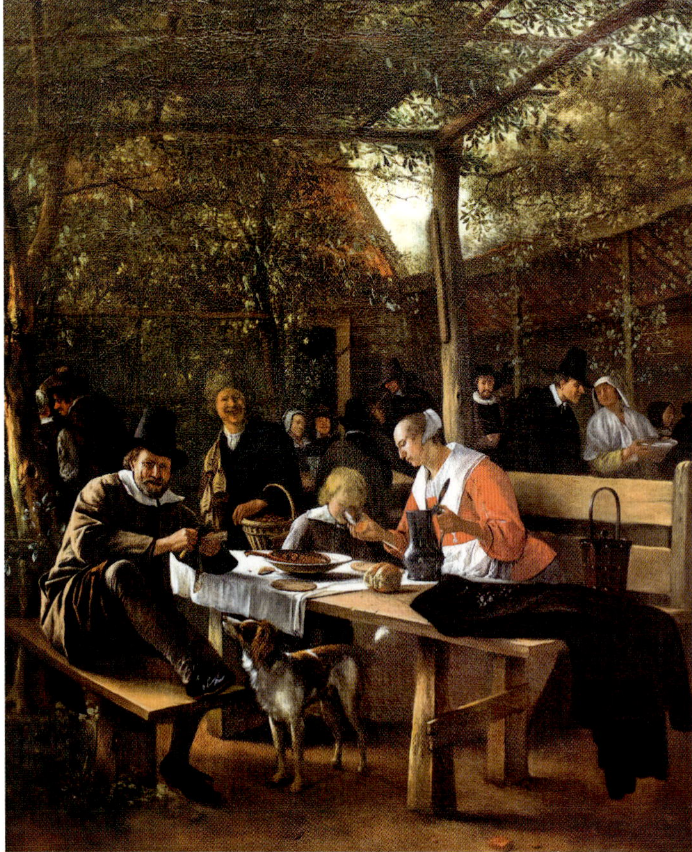

The Tavern Garden, Jan Steen, 1663, oil on canvas, 69.7 x 58.6cm (27½ x 23in), Gemäldegalerie, Berlin, Germany

Jan Steen depicts a moment on a late summer's day. At a wooden bench covered with a white cloth, a mother gives her child a drink from a pewter jug. The man opposite, possibly the father of the child, skins a herring, while a dog watches him. Further back is a fishmonger with a basket of crabs and dried fish slung over his shoulder.

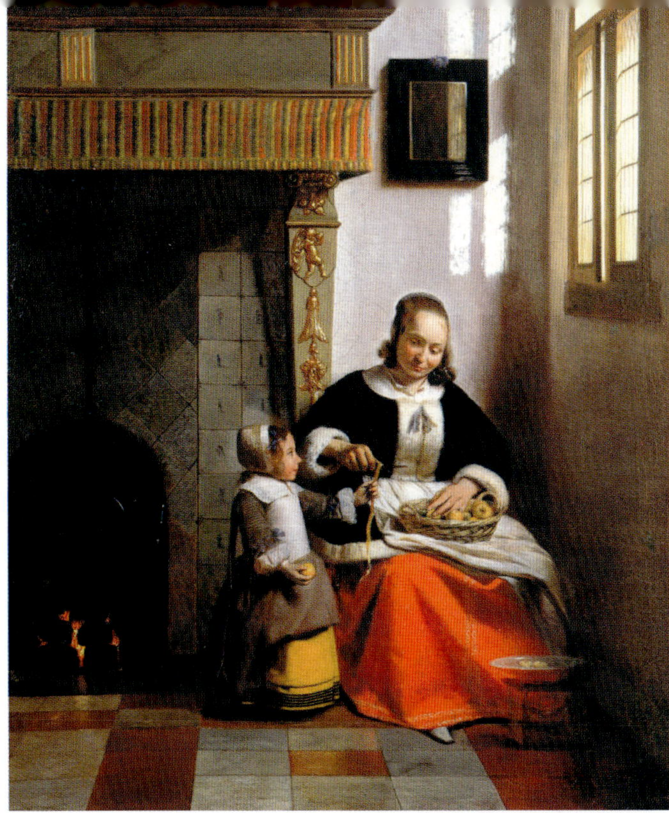

A Woman Peeling Apples, Pieter de Hooch, 1663, oil on canvas, 67 x 55 cm (26 x 22 in), Wallace Collection, London, UK

An ornate fireplace and costly clothing reveal this to be a prosperous household. The cupid on the fireplace conveys love. A woman in a black fur-trimmed jacket, red skirt and white apron peels an apple from a basket, and holds out a long piece of apple skin to a little girl standing by her. Sunlight filters through a window and this, along with other details, show the influence of Vermeer.

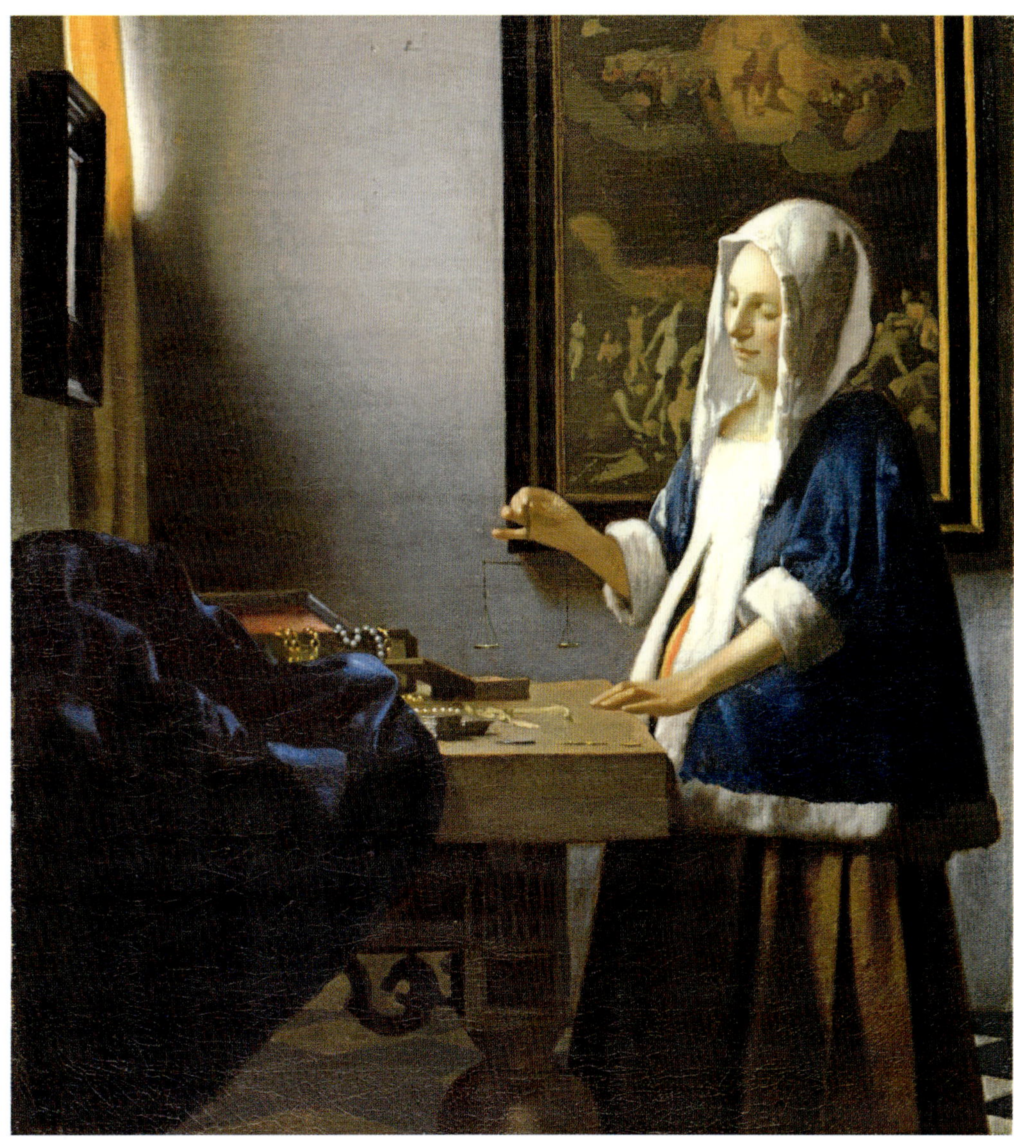

Woman Holding a Balance, Johannes Vermeer, 1662–64, oil on canvas, 40.3 x 35.6 cm (16 x 14 in), National Gallery of Art, Washington DC, USA

A young woman holds an empty balance over a table upon which there is an open jewellery box, with pearls and gold spilling out of it and a crumpled blue cloth by the side of it. Behind the woman on the wall is a painting of the Last Judgement. One interpretation of the work is that the woman weighing valuables should be living a more pious life.

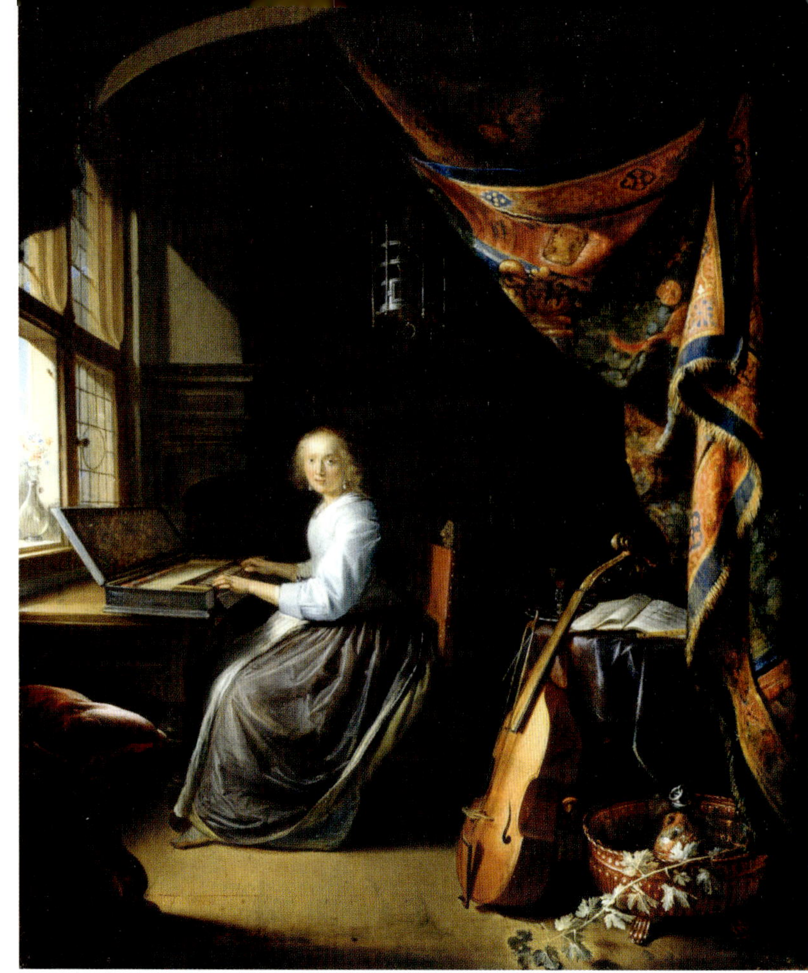

A Woman Playing a Clavichord, Gerrit Dou, c.1665, oil on panel, 37.7 x 29.9cm (15 x 11¾in), Dulwich Picture Gallery, London, UK

Behind a tapestry, a young woman sits alone playing a clavichord. Sunlight shines on her from an open window. As she looks towards viewers, light catches her dangling pearl earrings. Light also touches objects around the room, and above her, an empty birdcage is suspended from the ceiling. This suggests that someone has left – perhaps her husband or lover.

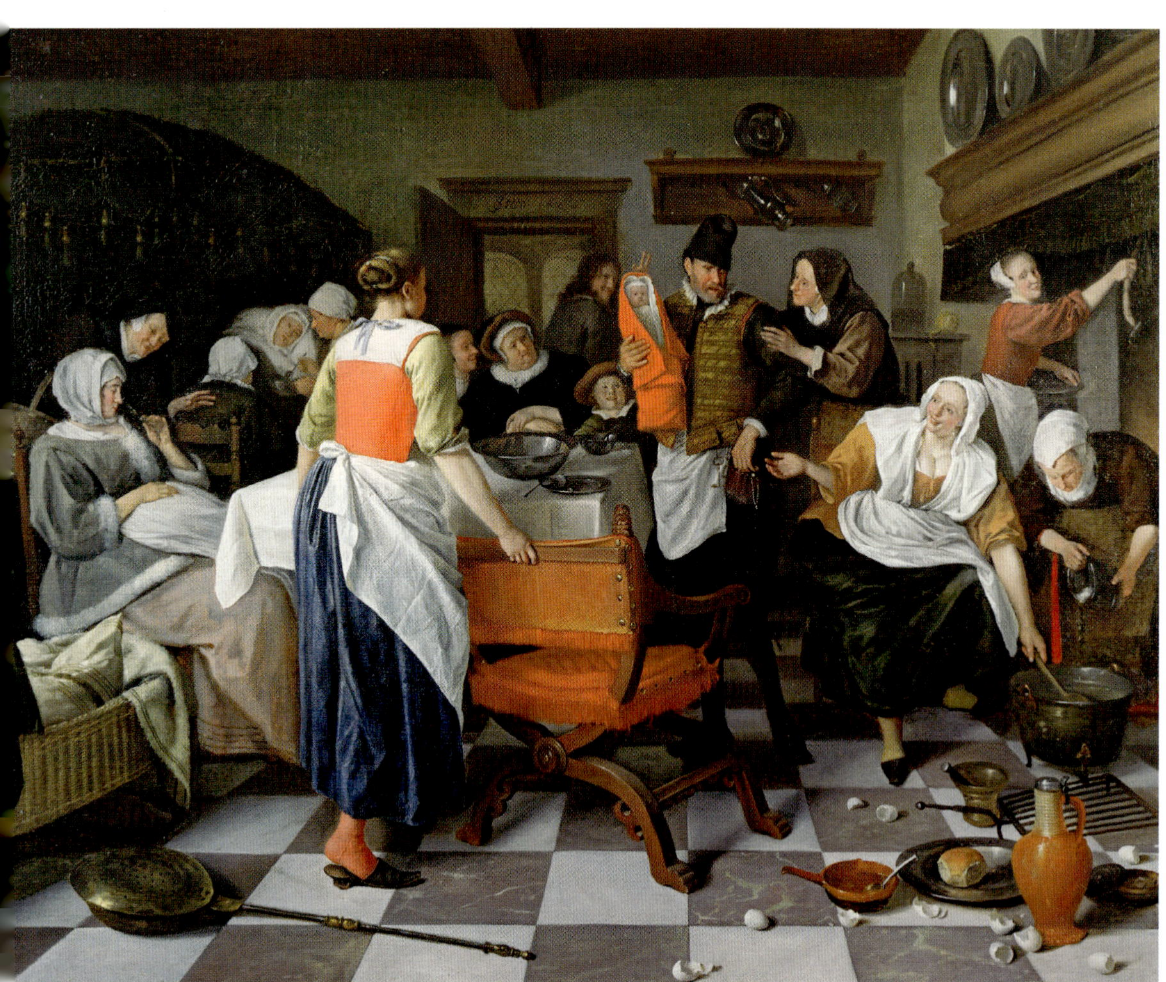

Celebration of the Birth, Jan Steen, 1664, oil on canvas, 87.7 x 107cm (34½ x 42in), Wallace Collection, London, UK

A proud father holds his newborn baby. Around him, people celebrate. In the background, the new mother is in bed, and leaving by the door, a man holds up two fingers, revealing that he is really the baby's father. The warming pan on the floor tells of a cold marriage bed and the limp sausage held by a servant represents the husband's impotence.

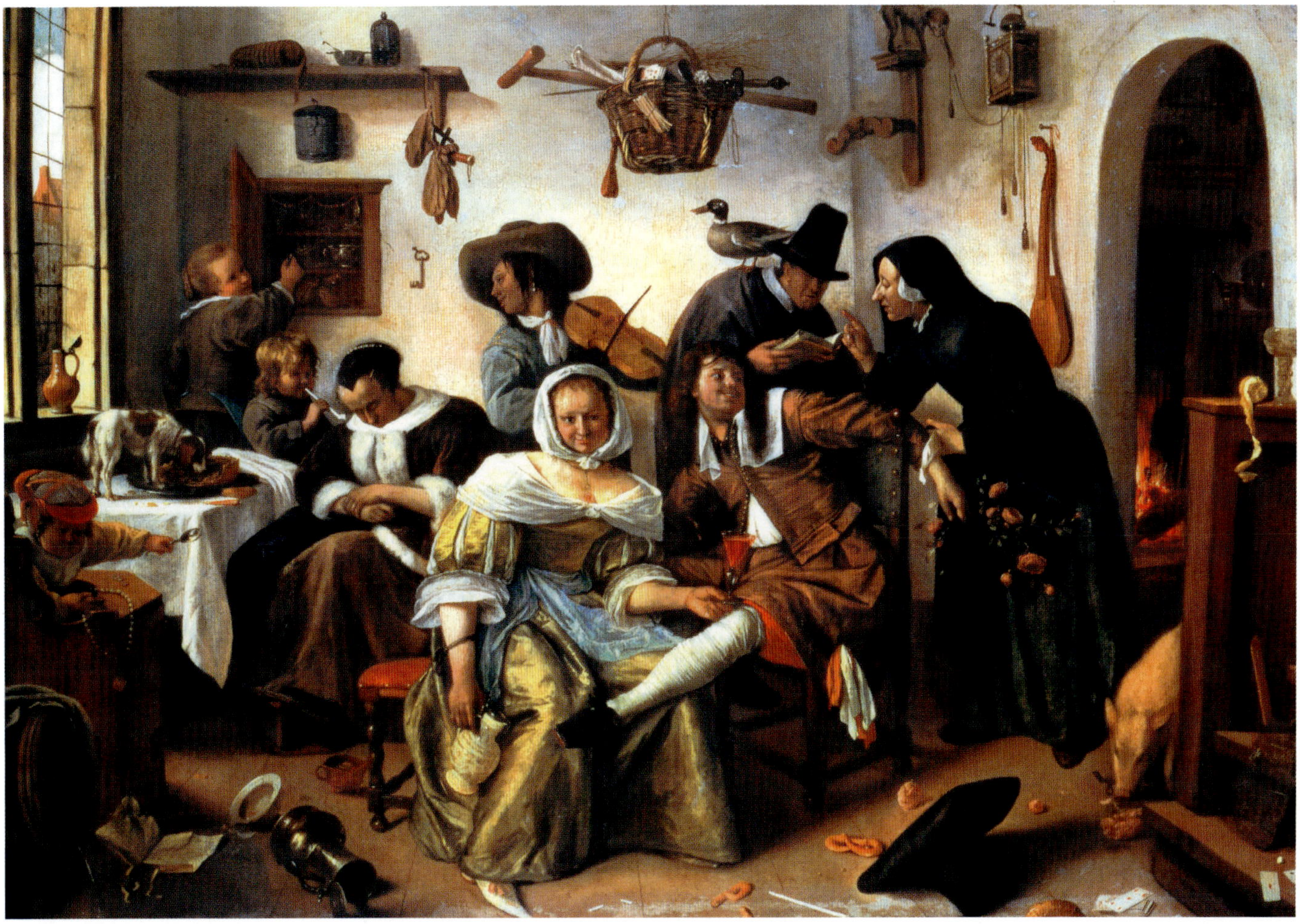

Beware of Luxury, Jan Steen, *c.*1665, oil on canvas, 105 x 145cm (41¼ x 57in), Kunsthistorisches Museum, Vienna, Austria

With a bold look, a young woman compels viewers to look at her. The lady of the house has fallen asleep at the table, leaving the dog to finish a pie. A child steals something from a wall cabinet, and her brother smokes a pipe. The baby plays with a string of pearls, and a man plays a violin, while a Quaker (recognized because of the duck on his shoulder) reads to a nun.

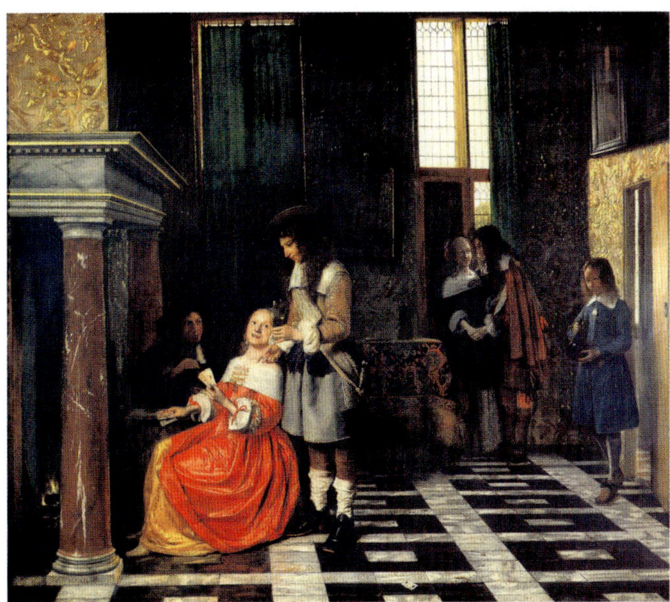

Card Players in an Opulent Interior, Pieter de Hooch, *c.*1663–65, oil on canvas, 67 x 77cm (26⅓ x 30⅓in), Musée du Louvre, Paris, France

In front of a large marble fireplace, a wealthy couple are playing a game of cards. A man is conversing with the woman and a young servant approaches with a carafe to refill his glass. In the background, another couple share an intimate moment. This is no ordinary domestic setting, but a house of pleasure where young men pay for the company of women.

Gamblers Quarrelling, Jan Steen, c.1665, oil on canvas, 70.5 x 88.9cm (27¾ x 35in), Detroit Institute of Art, Michigan, USA

Game-playing for money at an inn has descended into a drunken brawl. Steen draws attention to the ungainliness of the figures as they try to fight with each other. Jugs and hats have been knocked on the floor. In the background, two men pummel each other, elsewhere an amused fiddler plays a lively tune, three men watch, and two maids try to separate two drunks.

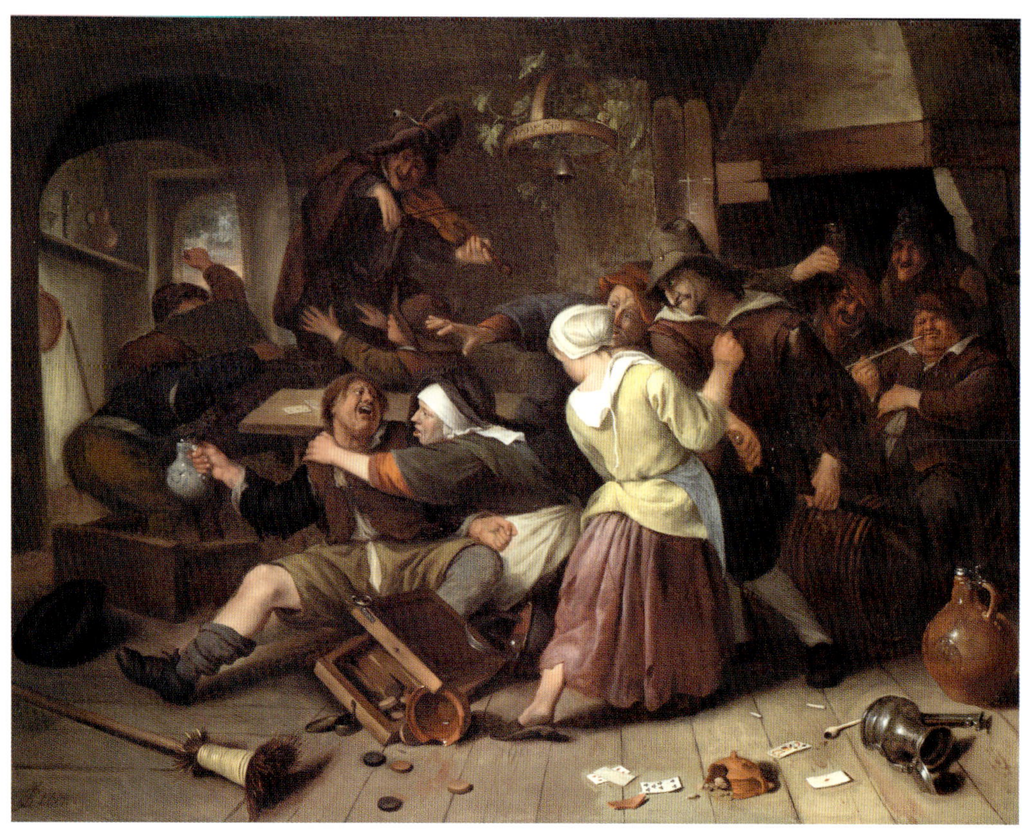

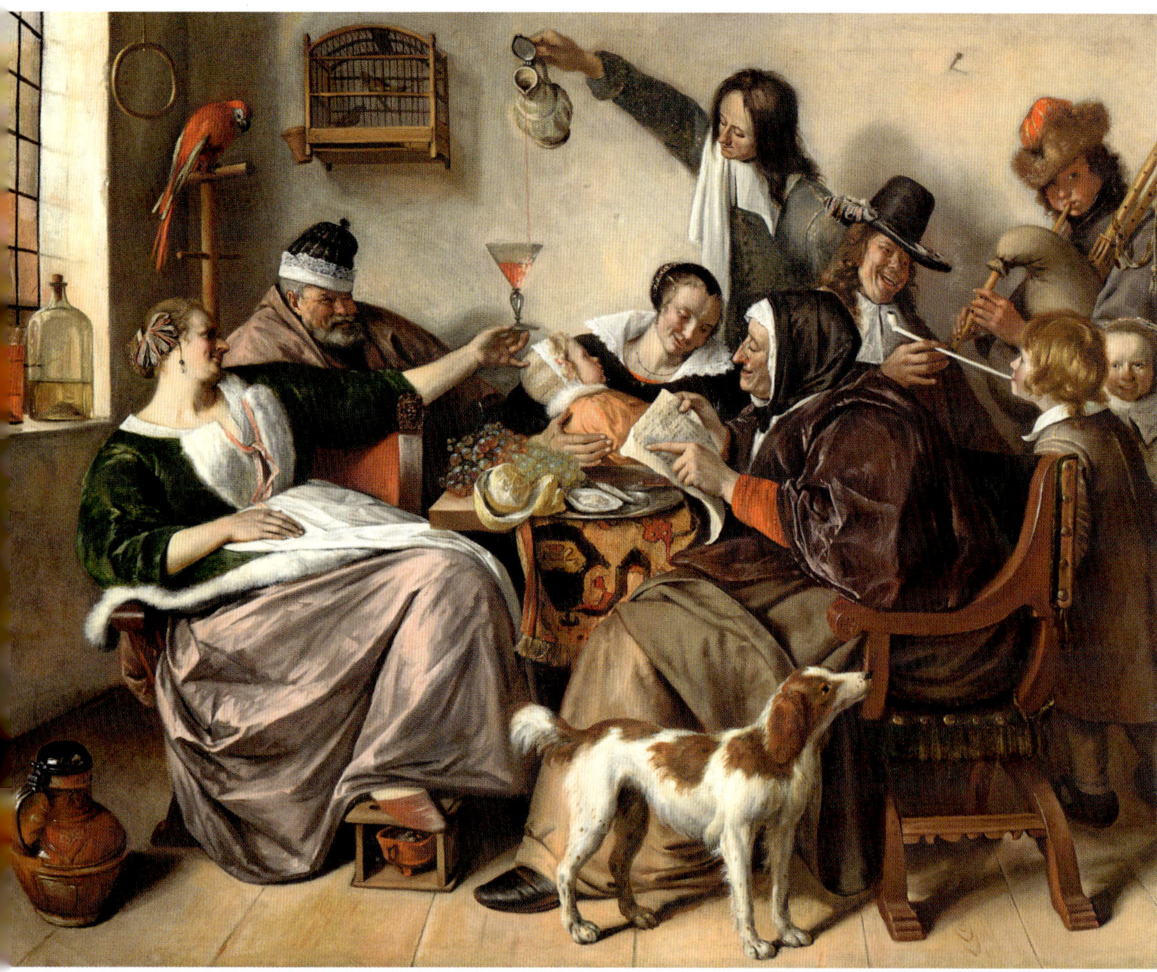

'*The Way you Hear it is the Way you Sing it,*' Jan Steen, c.1665, oil on canvas, 134 x 163cm (52¾ x 64in), Mauritshuis, The Hague, Netherlands

The title refers to a 17th-century Dutch saying, meaning that the young imitate the old. The image shows what a problem this could be if the old do not set a good example. An old woman reads out the saying, while everyone misbehaves. Jan Steen has painted himself in the black hat, passing a pipe to his son Cornelis to smoke, while another of his sons, Thaddeus, plays the bagpipes.

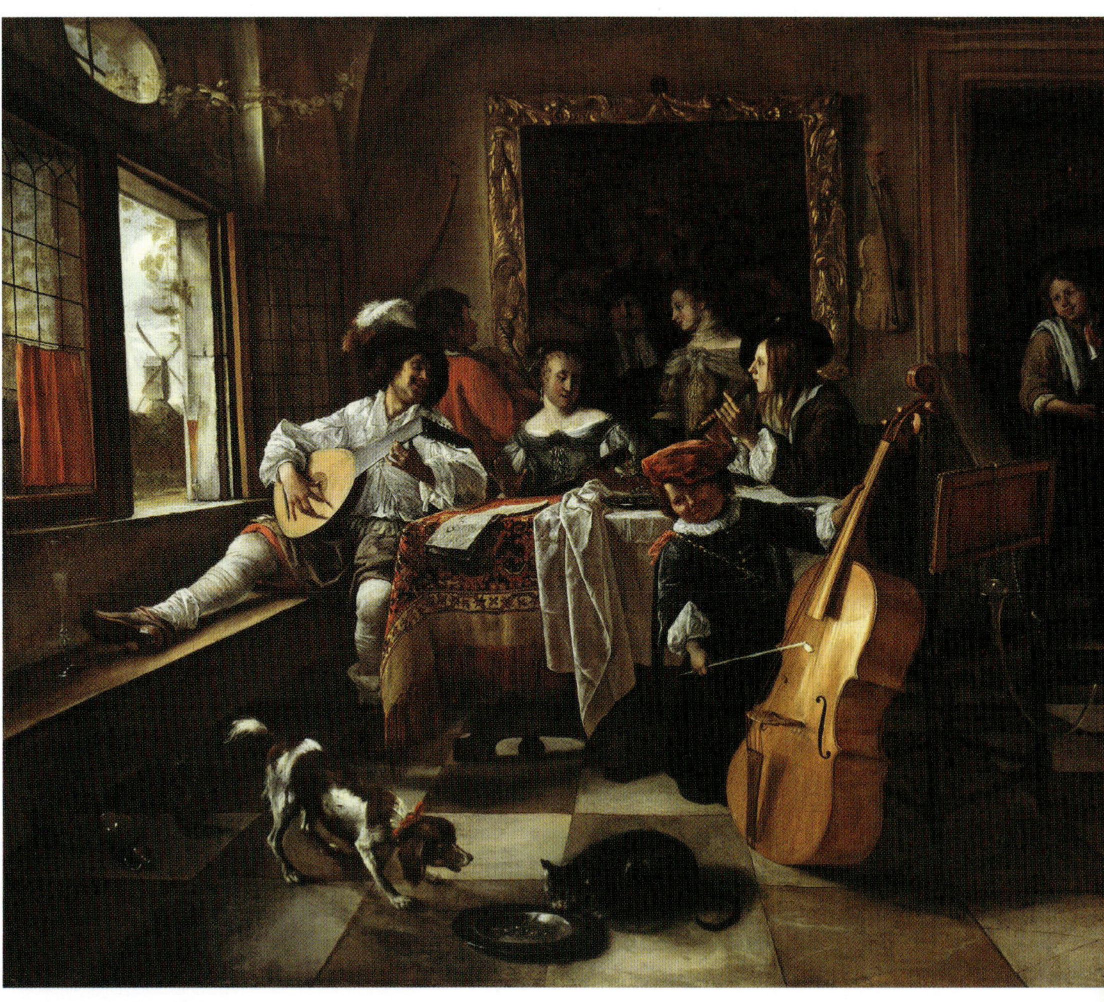

The Family Concert, Jan Steen, 1666, oil on canvas, 86.6 x 101cm (34⅛ x 39¾in), The Art Institute of Chicago, Illinois, USA

Relaxing while making music, this is a family in their well-to-do home. Yet there are some oddities, such as the child playing a cello with a clay pipe. In Dutch painting, clay pipes often symbolized lewd behaviour, while the dog and cat confront each other, suggesting that the family is not as harmonious as it appears. Steen was also criticizing the Dutch fashion for displaying wealth.

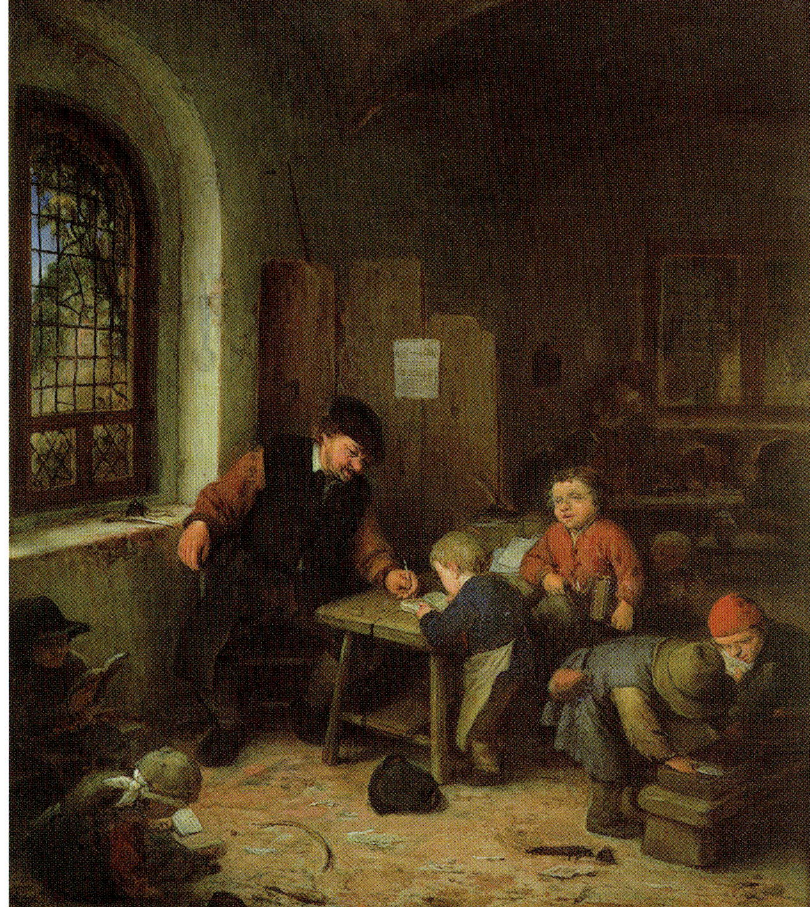

A Schoolroom Interior, Adriaen van Ostade, 1666, oil on oak panel, 22.4 x 18.9cm (8¾ x 7½in), Private Collection

With meticulous brushwork and rich colouring, this small painting conveys the interior of a schoolroom where several boys are working and a teacher helps two of them at his desk. His expression conveys kindness, while behind him light shines through a large window, illuminating the simple, rustic classroom. Happy images of the poor such as this appealed to wealthy buyers.

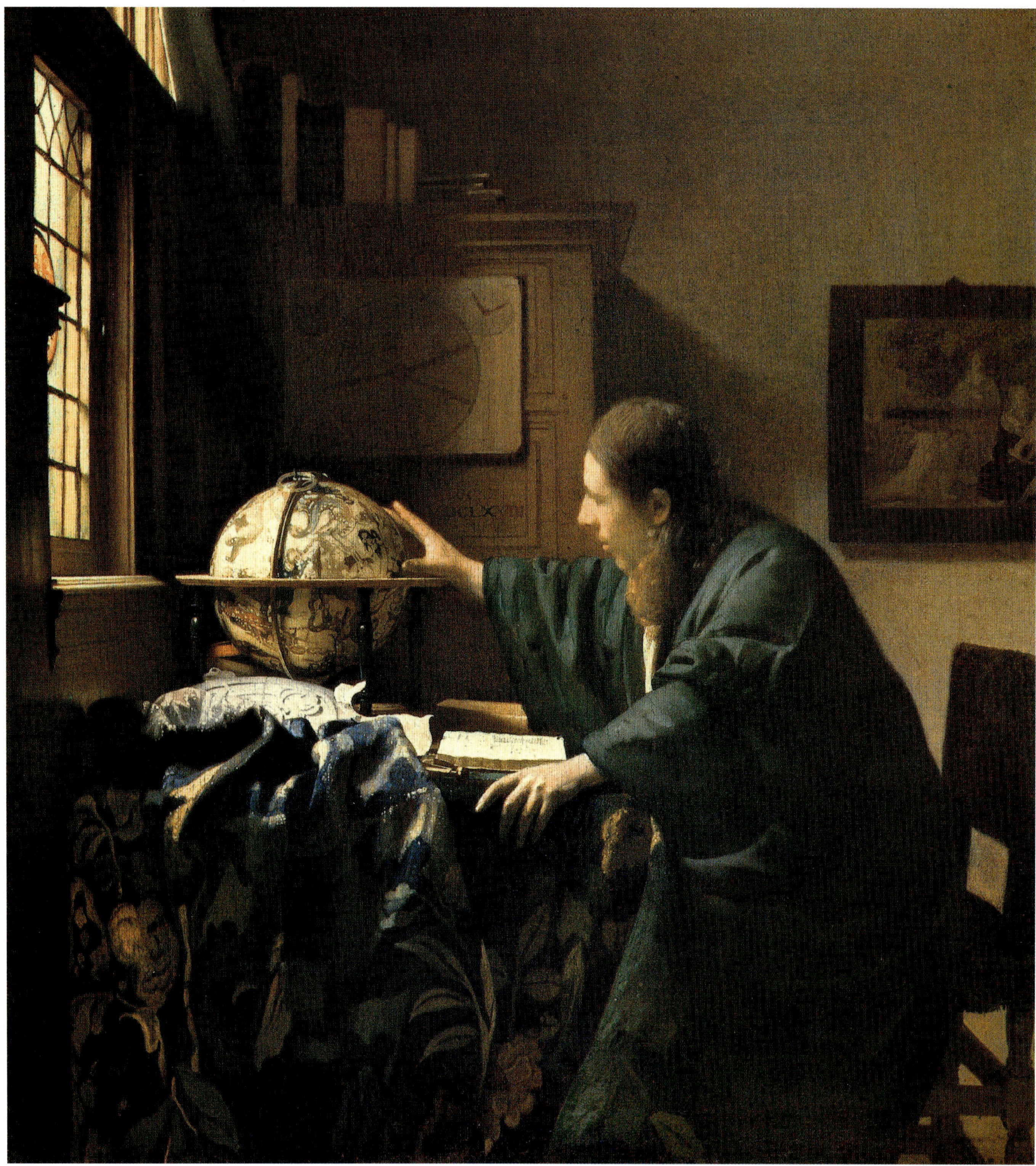

The Astronomer, Johannes Vermeer, 1668, oil on canvas, 50 x 45cm (19½ x 17¾in), Musée du Louvre, Paris, France

In 1667 and 1668, a man in his late 30s posed for Vermeer for at least two paintings and these are now Vermeer's only known paintings that focus on solitary male figures. The paintings are this astronomer with his celestial globe, and *The Geographer* (see page 99). The painting within this painting illustrates the biblical story of the Finding of Moses, perhaps acknowledging the Astronomer's need for divine inspiration.

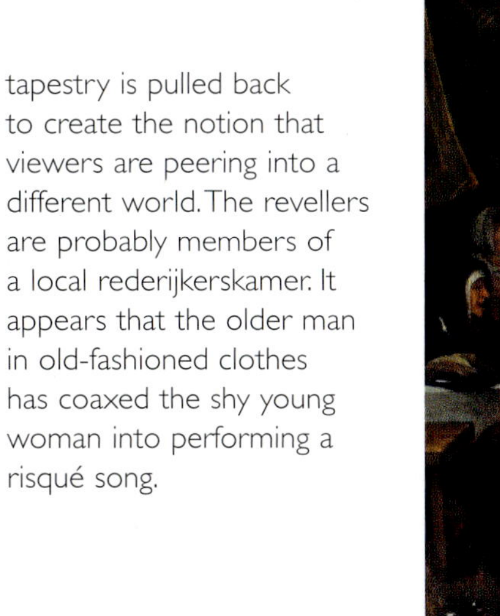

Merry Company, Jan Steen, c.1667–69, oil on oak panel, 44.8 x 37.2cm (17½ x 14½in), Allen Memorial Art Museum, Ohio, USA

People are enjoying themselves in a tavern. The scene is purposefully ambiguous. In a device that Steen often uses, the tapestry is pulled back to create the notion that viewers are peering into a different world. The revellers are probably members of a local rederijkerskamer. It appears that the older man in old-fashioned clothes has coaxed the shy young woman into performing a risqué song.

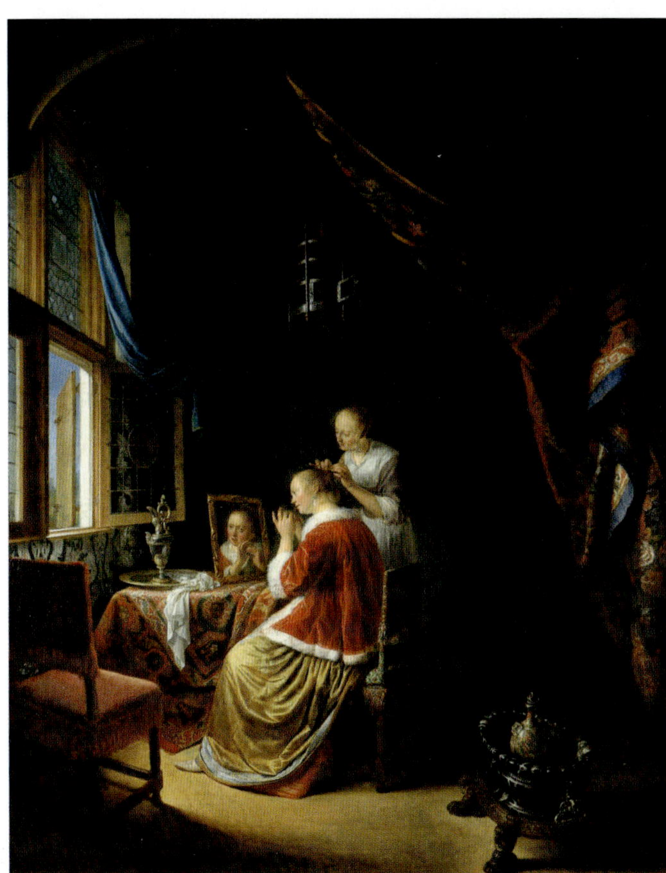

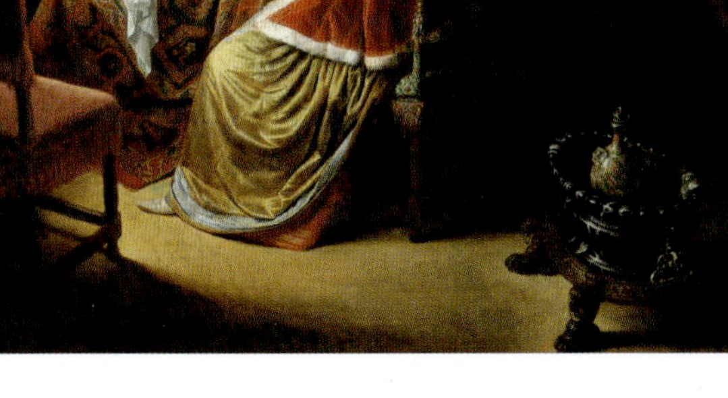

The Fat Kitchen, Jan Steen, c.1660–65, oil on panel, 30.6 x 39.6cm (12 x 15½in), Cheltenham Art Gallery and Museum, Gloucestershire, UK

Steen was the most famous painter of ordinary people and his wealthy patrons enjoyed his hidden moralizing tales. Here the model of the man carving the ham is Steen himself, and the woman in the armchair is his wife Margareta. Copious amounts of meat and cheese hanging from the ceiling, and many pots, dishes and flasks around the room, all suggest that this family is self-indulgent and greedy.

A Young Woman at her Toilet, Gerrit Dou, 1667, oil on panel, 75.5 x 58cm (29¾ x 22¾in), Museum Boijmans van Beuningen, Rotterdam, Netherlands

The young woman's reflection in her mirror can be seen by viewers as she watches her maid pin her hair. A luxurious, heavy curtain has been pulled back so that we can see into the room that is dark apart from the young woman, her dressing table and her maid. A silver ewer and plate are on the table and a wine cooler is in the foreground.

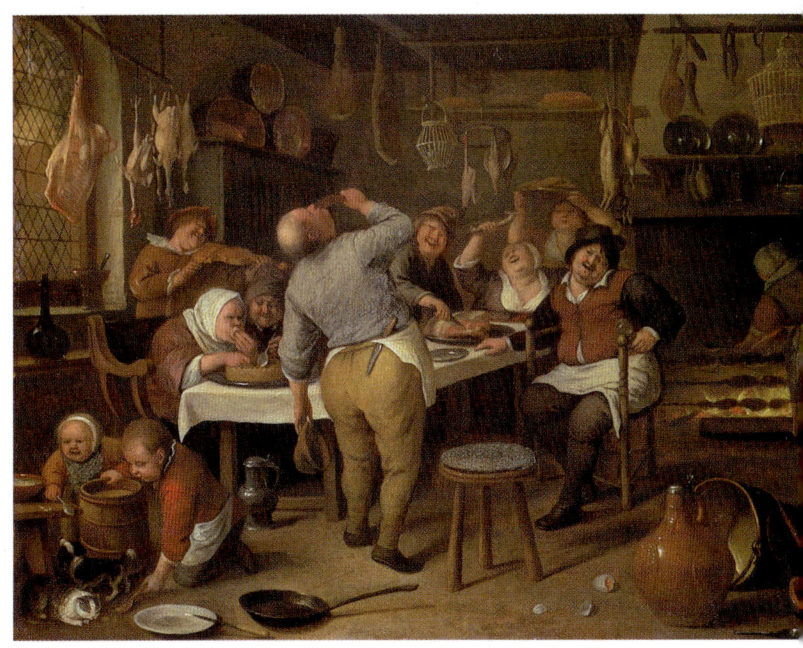

The Music Lesson, Gerard ter Borch, 1665–75, oil on canvas, 63.6 x 50.4cm (25 x 19⅞in), The Art Institute of Chicago, Illinois, USA

After spending time in Madrid, Rome, Münster and possible Brussels, ter Borch moved away from large portraits of notable figures, and he became especially sought after for his later small-scale portraits and genre scenes. Here, a young woman is with a military officer. She sings and plays a double-headed lute, while his position indicates that he might be her music teacher. However, at the time, music-making was a well-known metaphor for love and the ambiguity is intentional; is he looking at the music or at her?

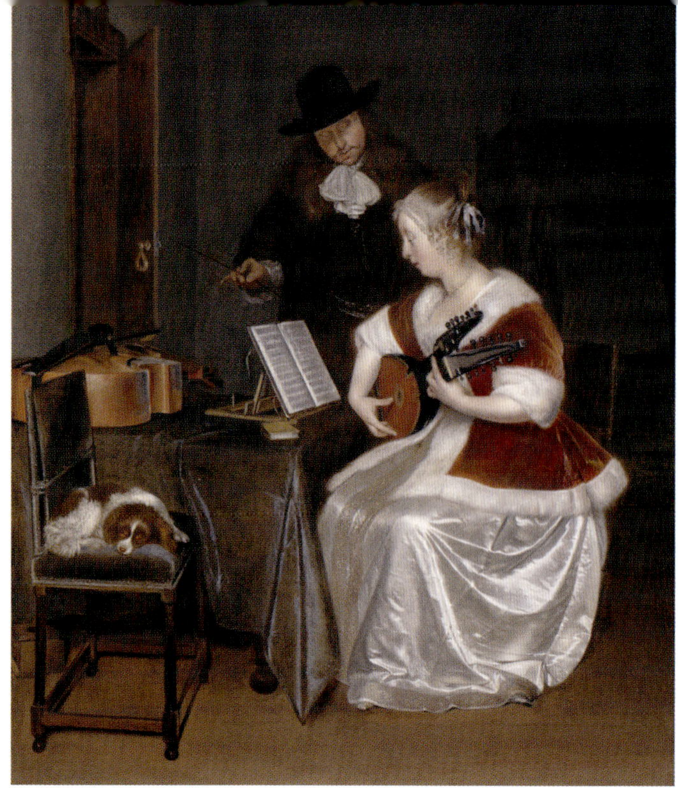

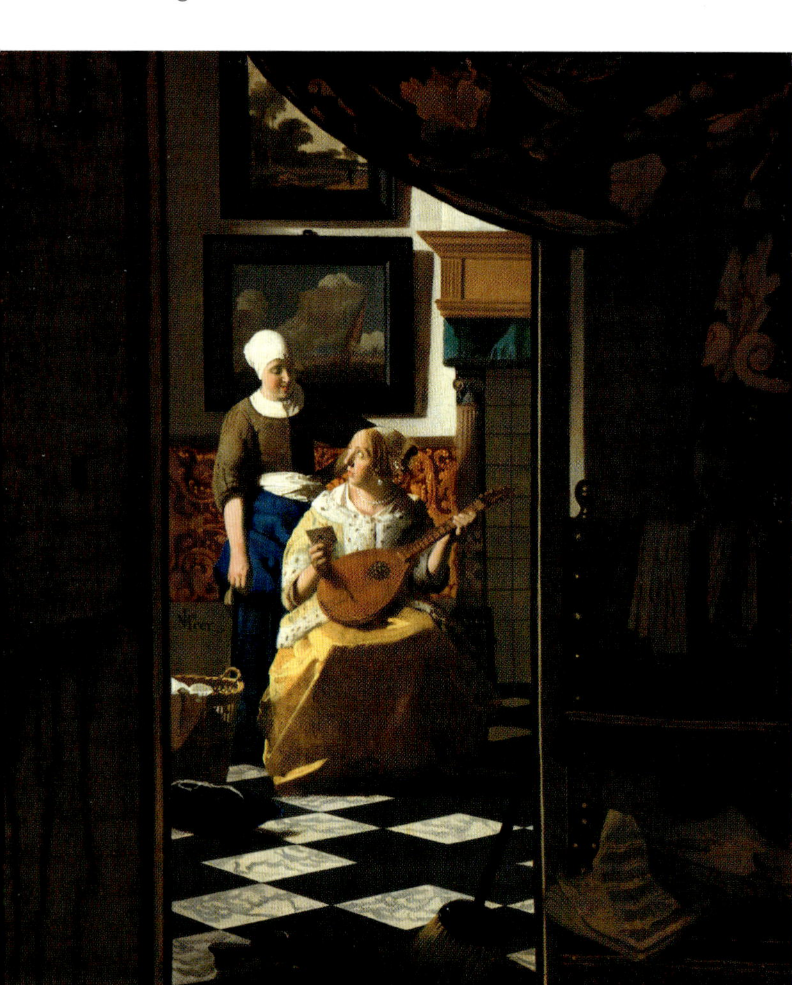

The Love Letter, Johannes Vermeer, *c.*1669, oil on canvas, 38.5 x 44cm (15 x 17¼in), Rijksmuseum, Amsterdam, Netherlands

Beyond a dark space is a brightly-lit room. An expensively dressed woman has paused her music-making to take a letter from her maid. As she turns to look at the maid, her pearl earring catches the light. It seems that the maid is involved in the intrigue between her mistress and the writer of the letter; perhaps he is connected with ships as these are indicated in the painting on the wall.

Messenger of Love, Pieter de Hooch, *c.*1670, oil on canvas, mounted on wood, 57 x 53cm (22½ x 20¾in), Hamburger Kunsthalle, Hamburg, Germany

Also known as *Interior with a Young Woman Receiving a Letter*, this woman greets a man who bears a letter. Characteristic elements of de Hooch's genre works include the clear light and exacting perspective. The view into another room is a doorkijkje. Humanizing elements include the dogs and the painting on the wall. Contemporary viewers would have known that this man was delivering a love letter from his master.

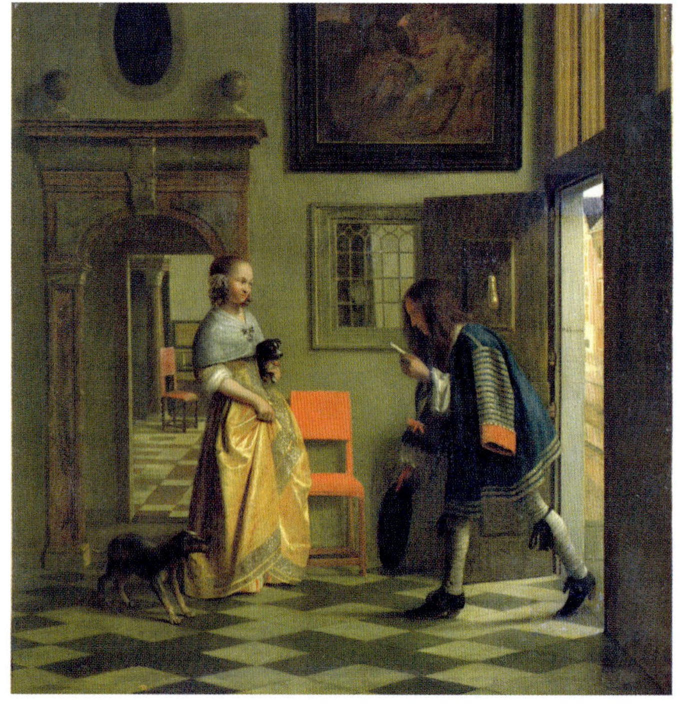

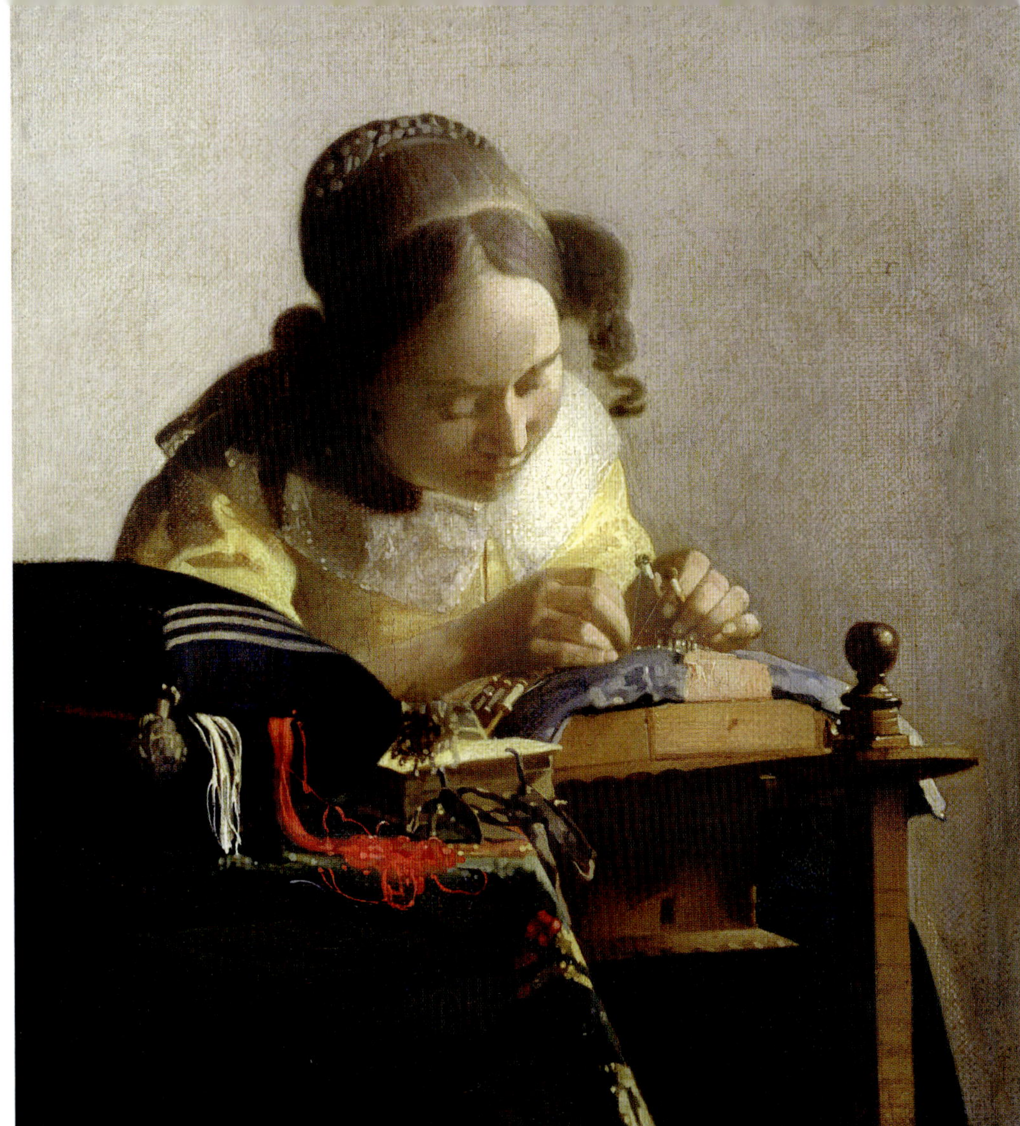

The Lacemaker, Johannes Vermeer, 1669, oil on canvas, 24 x 21cm (9½ x 8¼ in), Musée du Louvre, Paris, France

With her hands on a pale blue lacemaking pillow, this young woman in a yellow and lace dress is making lace. She bends towards her work, concentrating on the task in hand. Both her fashionable hairstyle and clothing show her to be part of Delft's middle class. The book in the foreground is probably the Bible, while the dark blue cushion on the left is used for storing sewing materials.

The Bean Feast, Jan Steen, 1668, oil on canvas, 80 x 105cm (31⅓ x 41¼ in), Gemäldegalerie Alte Meister, Kassel, Germany

On Twelfth Night, or the Feast of the Epiphany, a bean was customarily baked into a cake and whoever found it in their portion was king for the night. Here a cheerful crowd sits around a table, some wearing household utensils on their heads. Wearing the king's crown, a boy drinks a glass of wine, helped by an elderly woman. Steen has included himself and his wife amid the revelry.

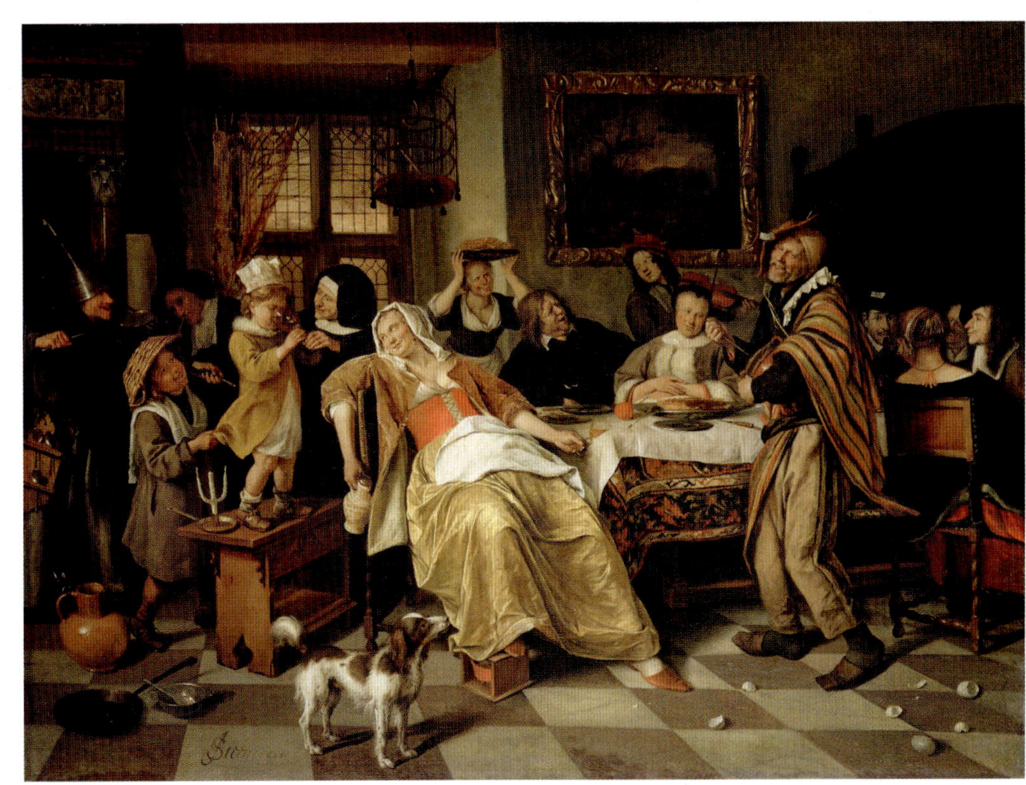

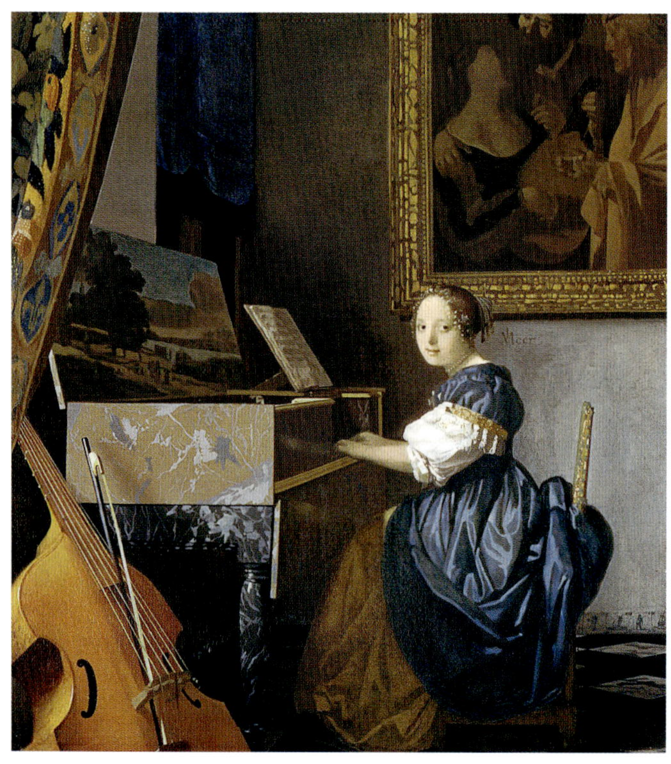

A Young Woman seated at a Virginal, Johannes Vermeer, *c.*1670–72, oil on canvas, 51.5 x 45.5cm (20¼ x 18in), The National Gallery, London, UK

Standing close to the virginal, a well-dressed young woman looks out of the canvas. Propped up in the foreground is a viola da gamba, which suggests that the young woman is expecting someone to join her. On the wall is the painting *The Procuress* by Dirck van Baburen (shown opposite). The purity of this young woman contrasts directly with that promiscuous image.

A School for Boys and Girls, Jan Steen, *c.*1670, oil on canvas, 81.7 x 108.6cm (32¼ x 42¾in), National Gallery of Scotland, Edinburgh, UK

The largest of several schoolroom scenes painted by Steen, this shows chaos in the classroom as the children all misbehave, while the teachers seem oblivious. On a perch is an owl; a traditional symbol of wisdom. A little boy below the owl offers it a pair of spectacles, which refers to the Dutch proverb 'What use are glasses or light if the owl does not want to see?'

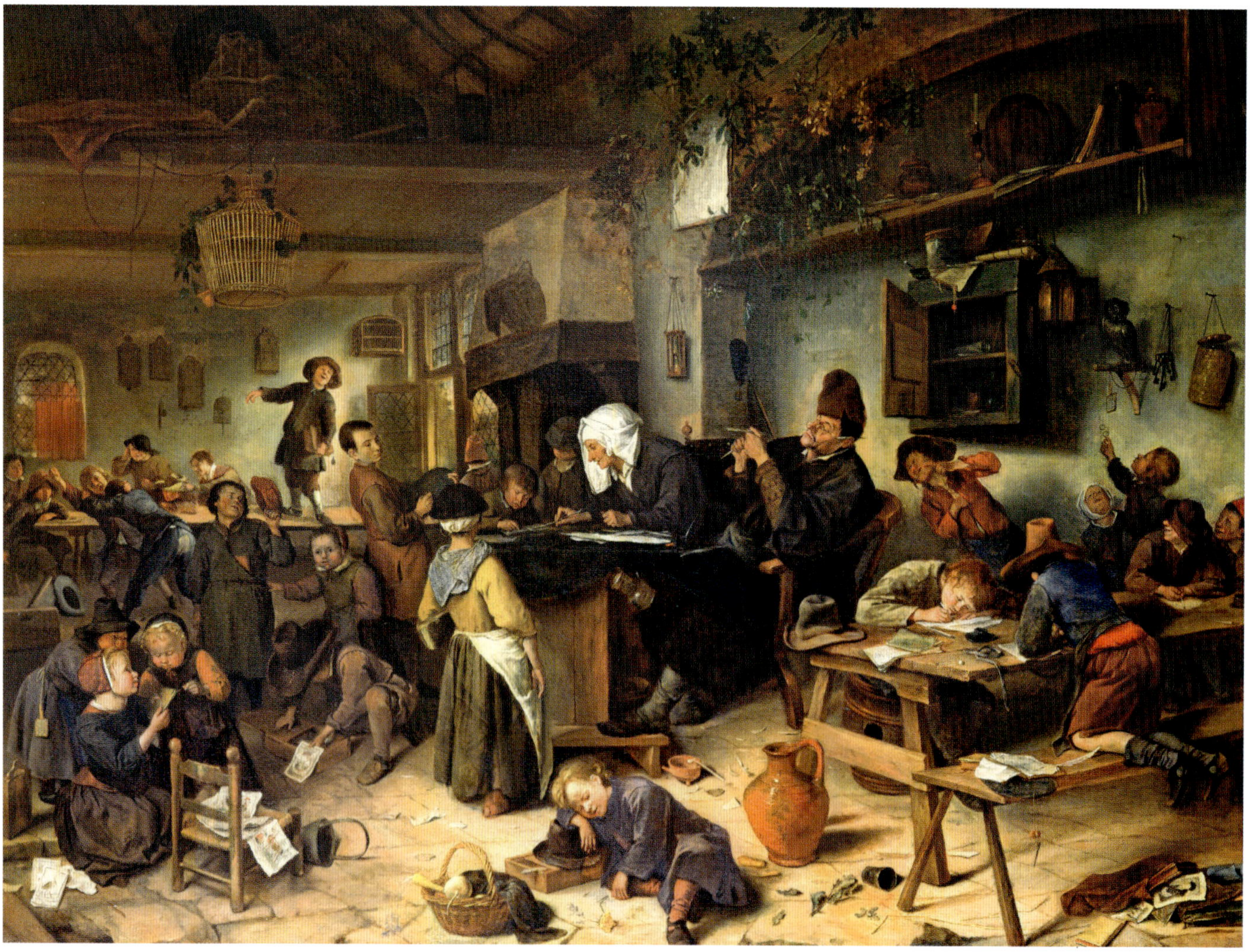

Merry Company on a Terrace, Jan Steen, c.1670, 141 × 131.4cm (55½ × 51¾in), The Metropolitan Museum of Art, New York, USA

A maid looks provocatively at viewers and holds out an empty wine glass. On the far left, slumped in his chair, holding a bottle, flushed with drink and wearing a comical hat, is Steen himself. By his side, with a sausage in his cap, attempting to kiss a serving maid, is 'Hans Worst', a popular figure of comedy from the period.

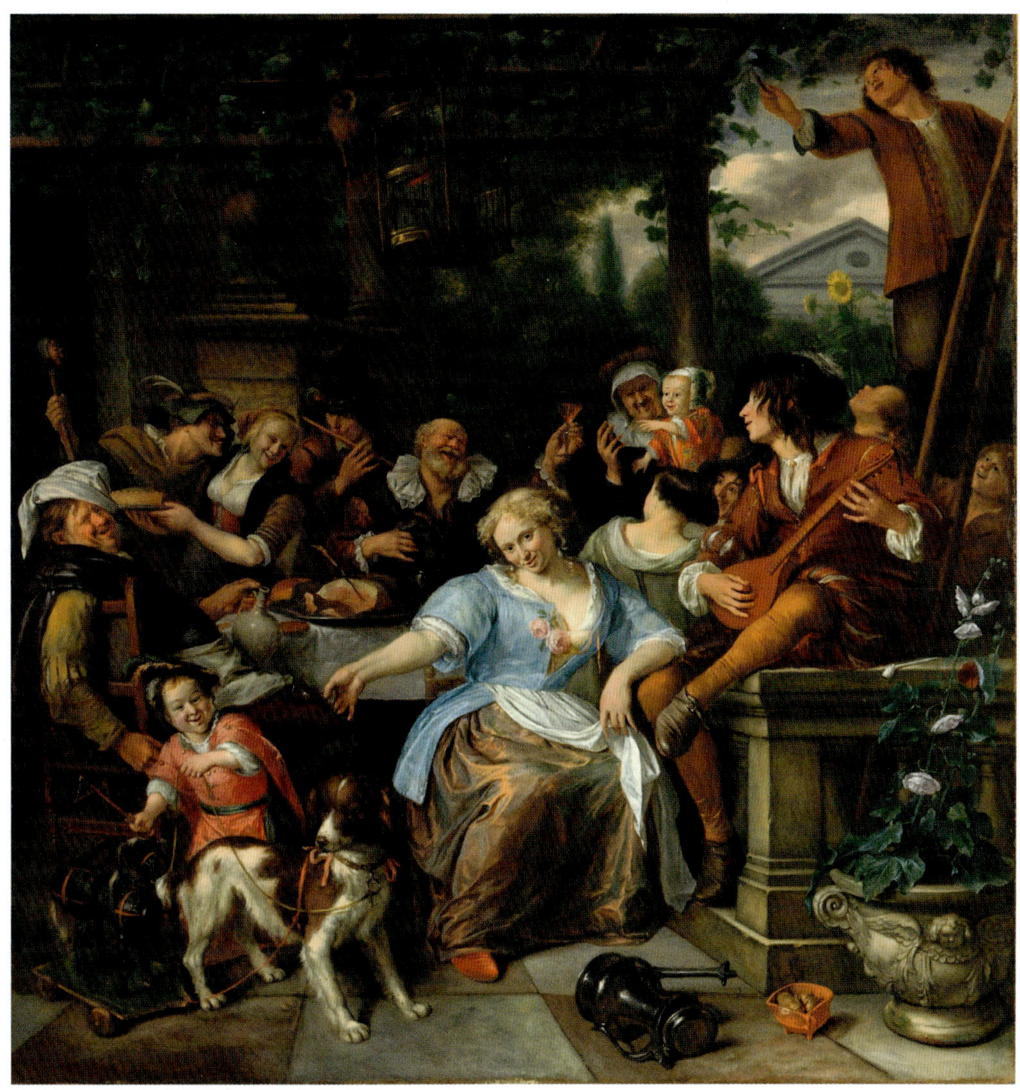

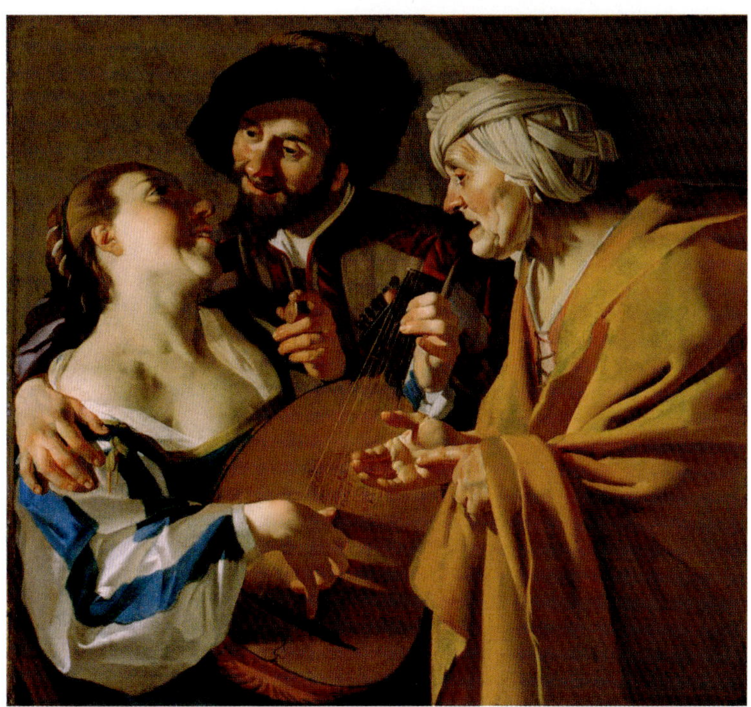

The Procuress, Dirck van Baburen, 1622, oil on canvas, 101.6 × 107.6cm (40 × 42¼in), Museum of Fine Arts, Boston, Massachusetts, USA

One of the Utrecht Caravaggisti, Dirck van Baburen specialized in close-up views of large, half-length figures, solidly modelled with strong contrasts of light and shadow. Here, a prostitute in a low-cut dress is being offered money by a man, while an ageing procuress in a turban barters with him for her services. A symbol of love, a lute, is in the centre of the composition.

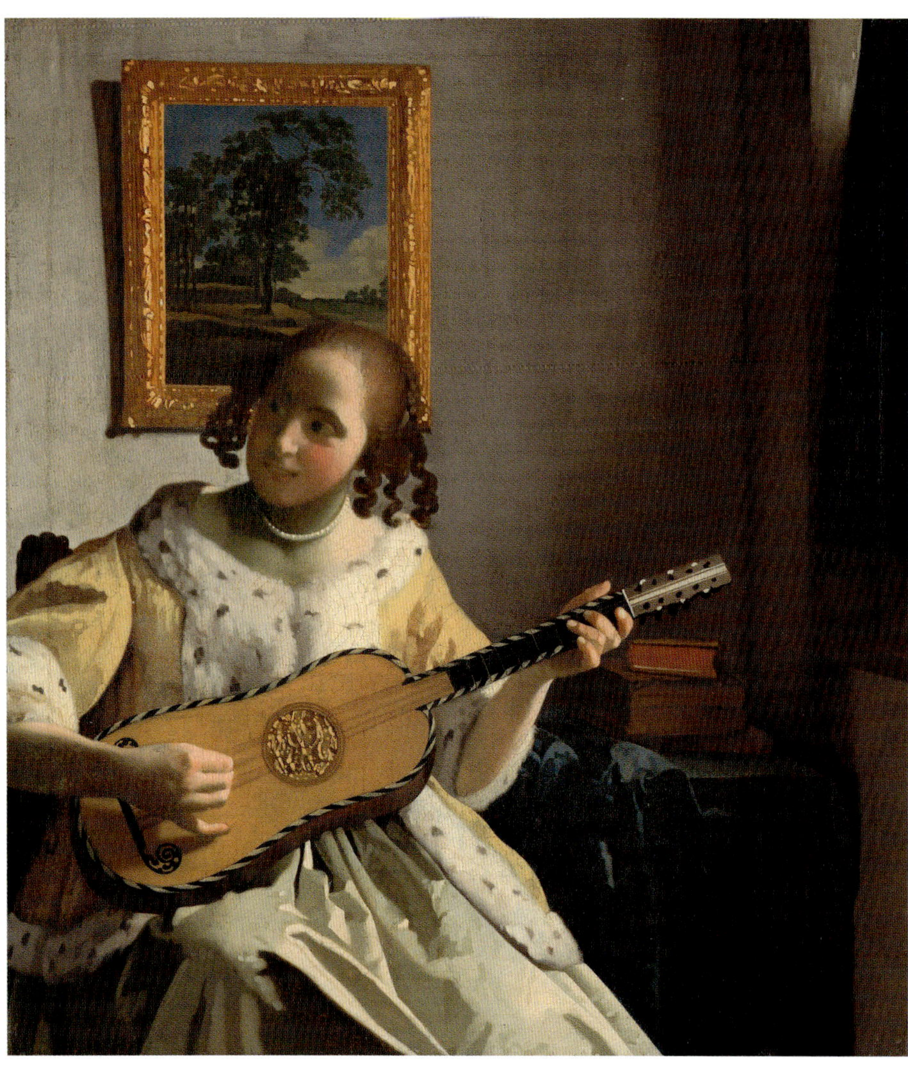

The Guitar Player, Johannes Vermeer, *c.*1670–72, oil on canvas, 53 x 46.3cm (21 x 18¼ in), Kenwood House, London, UK

With its crisp contours and radiant light effects, this is an example of Vermeer's later and most popular style. With freer brushstrokes than in his earlier paintings, he emphasizes patterns of colour over details, subtle modulations of tone over sharp contrasts, and an open expression rather than his earlier, more brooding depictions. Wearing a cream gown and yellow fur-trimmed coat, a girl sits holding a guitar.

The Messenger, Jan Verkolje, 1674, oil on canvas, 59 x 53.5cm (23¼ x 21 in), Mauritshuis, The Hague, Netherlands

A messenger delivers a letter. The woman with her back turned in a satin dress was about to throw a dice. In the background hangs a large shadowed painting of the death of Adonis, but the contents of the letter remain a mystery. Jan Verkolje (1650–93) trained in Amsterdam and was known for his portraits and genre works of elegant couples in interiors. He spent most of his career in Delft working for several powerful patrons.

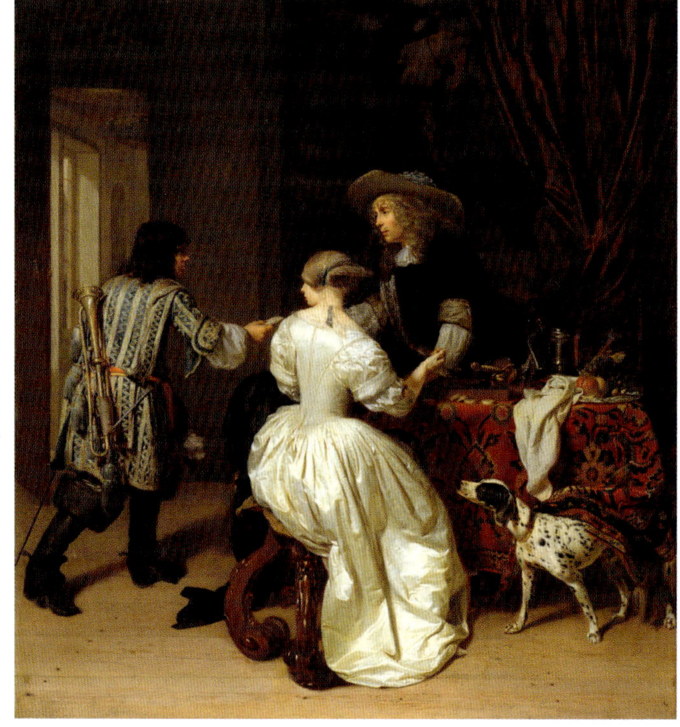

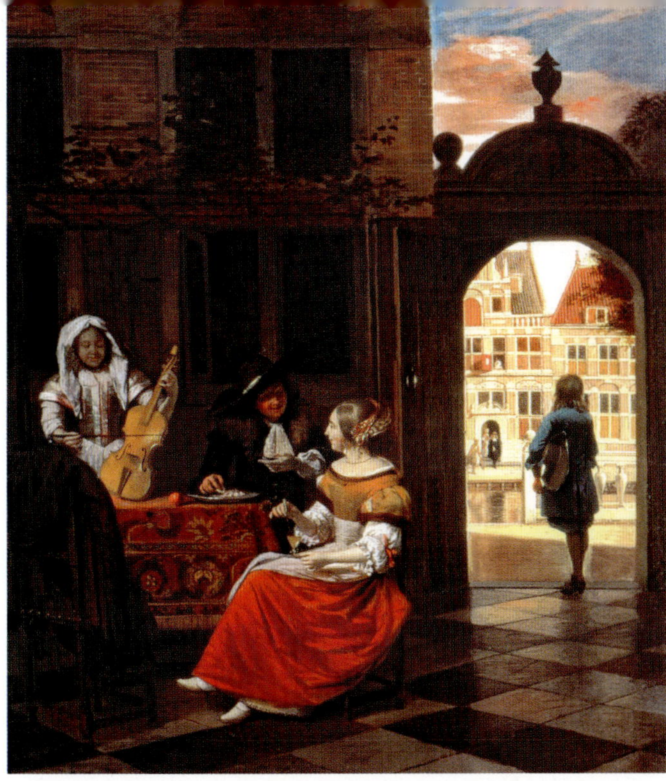

A Musical Party in a Courtyard, Pieter de Hooch, 1677, oil on canvas, 83.5 x 68.5cm (32¾ x 27in), The National Gallery, London, UK

In a shady courtyard, three well-dressed figures sit at a table covered with an expensive carpet. A woman plays a viola da gamba. Almost silhouetted against the light is a man, while beyond him, houses can be seen across a canal. Above the arch, the setting sun streaks the sky with pink and blue. Unlike de Hooch's earlier work, here his figures are elegant and sophisticated.

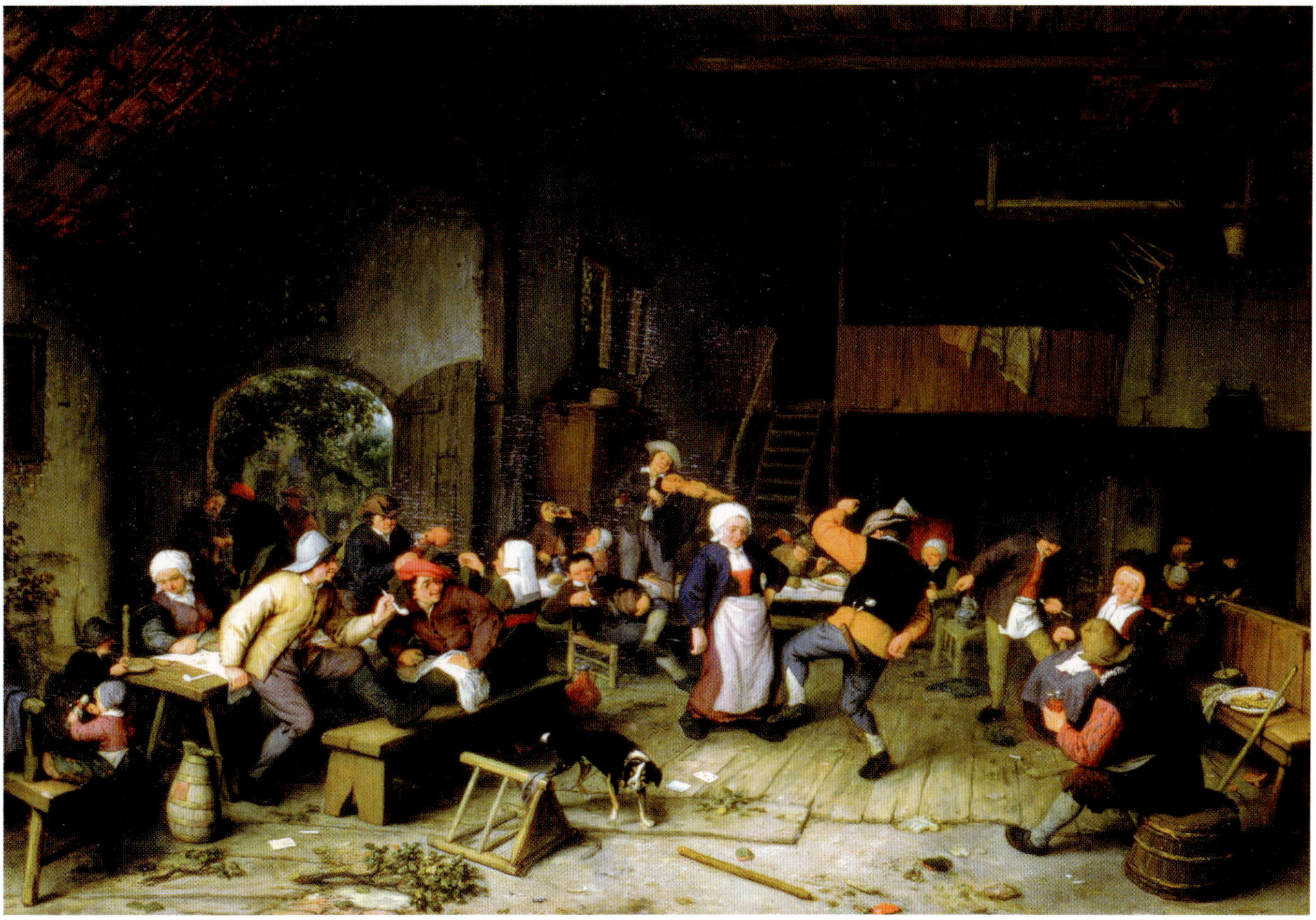

Peasants Dancing in a Tavern, Adriaen van Ostade, 1675, oil on panel, 53.4 x 72.4cm (21 x 28½in), The Harold Samuel Collection, London, UK

In a large room at an inn, a fiddler plays a lively tune. Between the tables, a couple dance a jig, watched by others who are all relaxing and enjoying themselves.

Portrayed from above, van Ostade creates a complex composition with stairs, doorways, a beamed roof and various floorings, all conveying a sense of depth.

In the background at the large door where the moonlight shines through, the landlord gives alms to a beggar.

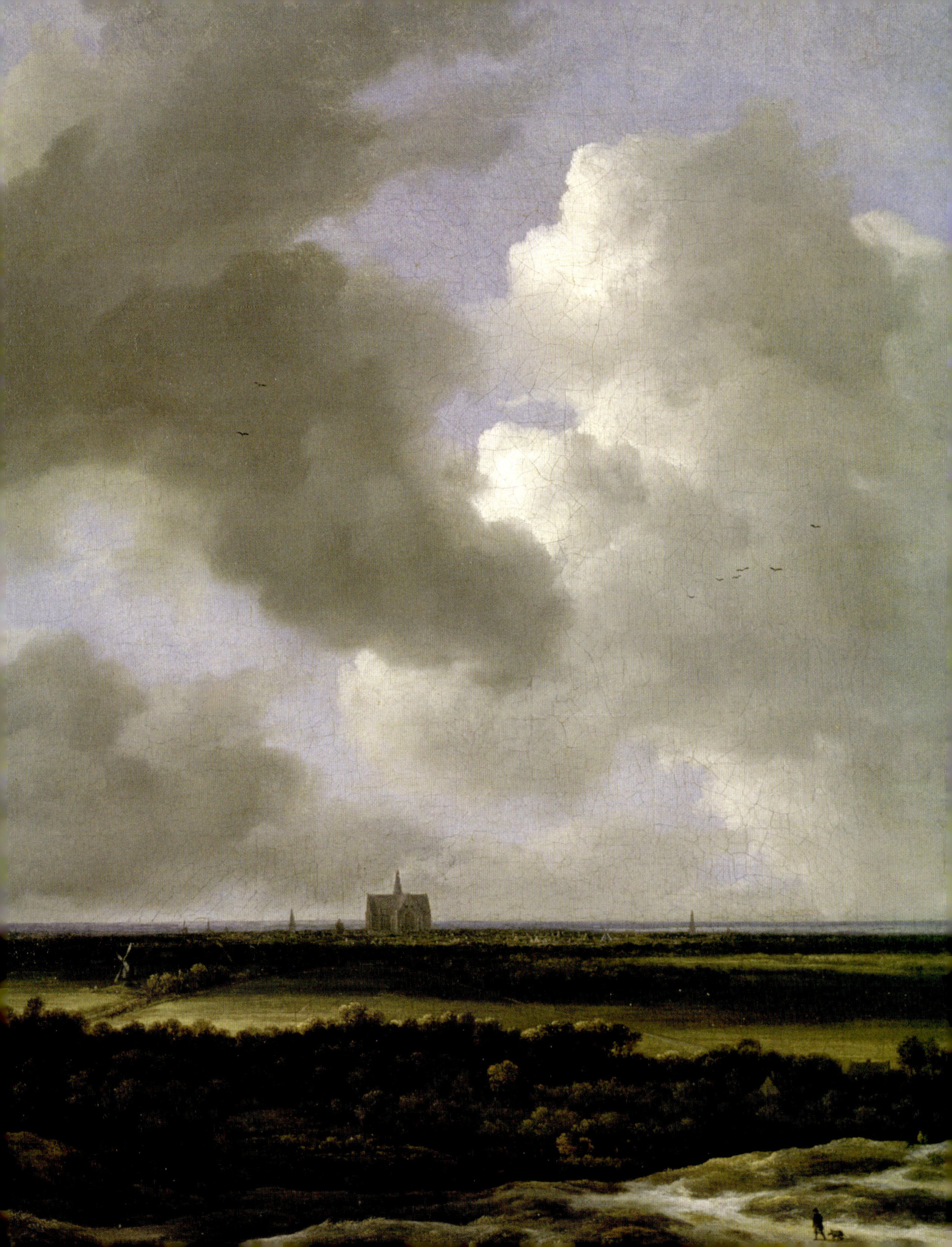

LANDSCAPES

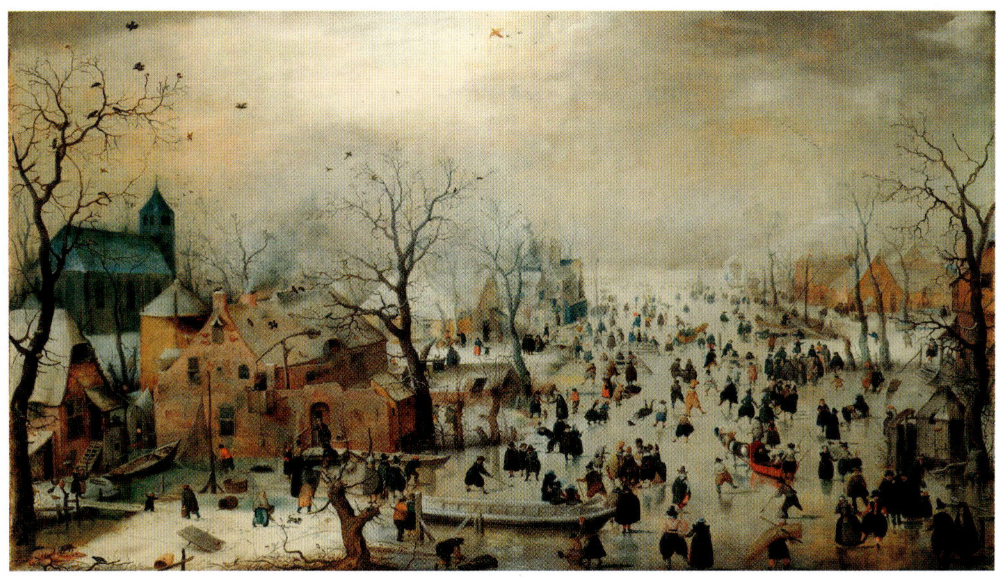

Responding to the unique characteristics of the weather and terrain of the Netherlands, and to a sense of national pride, landscape painting during the Dutch Golden Age became especially respected. As almost 70 percent of the population lived in the towns, views of the country that they rarely saw, of the architecture that they were so proud of, and of the sea, rivers and canals that were so vital to trade, all became fashionable. Country scenes conveyed the imagined bucolic bliss of simple peasant life, while towns and cities represented Dutch pride in their achievements. Several landscape sub-genres developed, including moonlit vistas, panoramas, seascapes and other waters, wintry scenes featuring figures skating, sledging or throwing snowballs, or Italianate views influenced by ancient Rome and Claude Lorrain. Many artists followed Jacob van Ruisdael's atmospheric approach to painting that focused on naturalism and light, but were nonetheless built on scientific observation.

Above: Winter Landscape with Skaters, *c.1608. Hendrick Avercamp was deaf, which adds a further dimension to his view of this frozen canal buzzing with skaters, dancing, playing, gliding and falling over. All life is here: the young, the old, the tragic and the comic, and almost everyone is moving. With no focal point, viewers are compelled to look around the scene, absorbing all the activity. There is no hierarchy between the figures.*

Left: Panoramic View of Haarlem, *c.1670. One of the most significant landscapists of the Golden Age, Jacob van Ruisdael painted several views of Haarlem. The cloudy sky, stretching up from a low horizon, is reflected in the flat countryside in strips of light and shadow.*

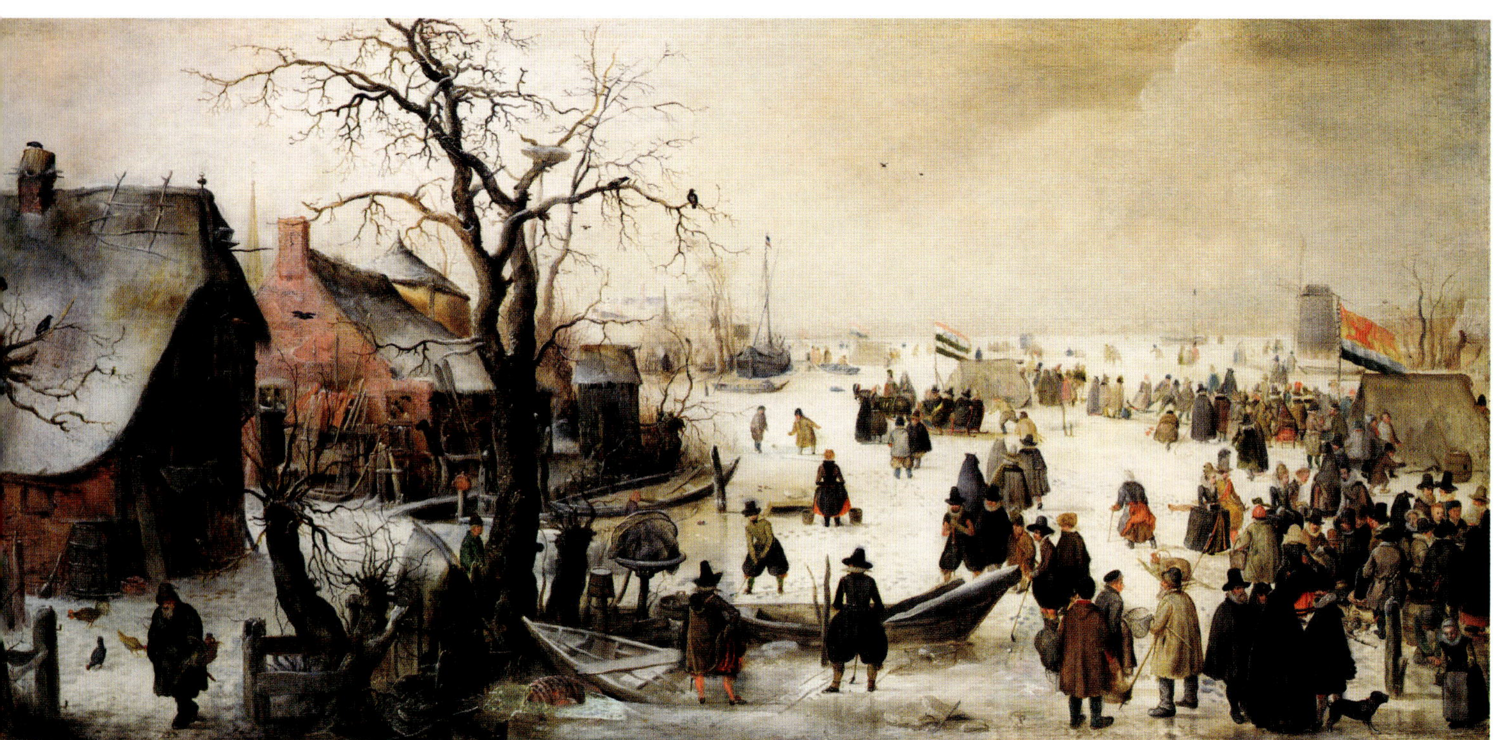

Winter Scene on a Canal, Hendrik Avercamp, 1615, oil on panel, 49.9 x 95.6cm (18¾ x 37½in), Toledo Museum of Art, Ohio, USA

Hendrik Avercamp lived in the small town of Kampen, far from the main towns of the Dutch Republic. This was probably why he painted flat landscapes and winter scenes such as this. Here, people of all ages and backgrounds are skating, sledging and fishing on the frozen canal. As with all his paintings, he uses light colours in the background, brighter in the foreground, and a sense of atmospheric perspective in the distance.

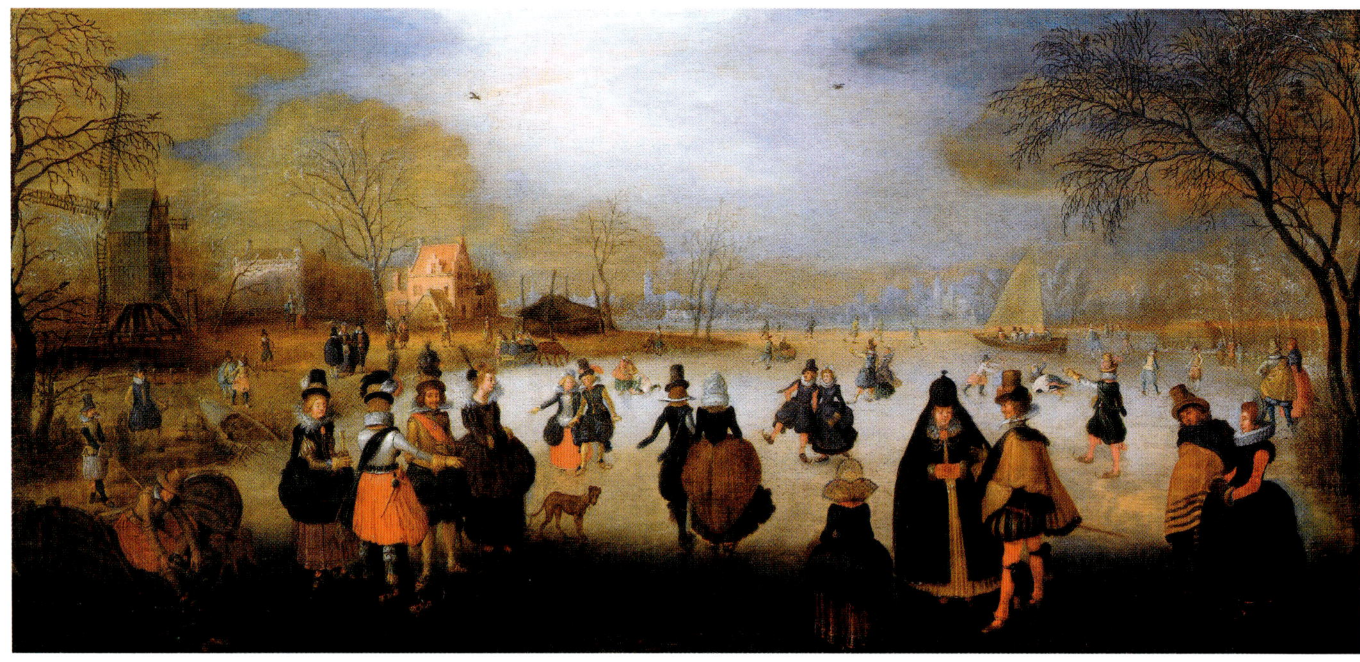

Winter Landscape with Skaters, Adam van Breen, c.1611–15, oil on panel, 47 x 80cm (18½ x 31½in), Private Collection

Little is known about Adam van Breen (1590–1645), but he worked in The Hague between 1611 and 1618 and also spent a great deal of time in Amsterdam and Norway. From 1612–21, he was registered in The Hague's Guild of Saint Luke. His wintry landscapes feature aspects of The Hague and Amsterdam, populated with figures who are often repeated. Van Breen drew inspiration from the Avercamp brothers and David Vinckboons, with whom he possibly trained.

Winter Scene, Hendrick Avercamp, *c.*1605, oil on oak, 29.5 x 46.5cm (11⅔ x 18⅓in), Kunsthistorisches Museum, Vienna, Austria

As well as characterful people having fun (and mishaps) on the ice, Avercamp includes trees with sturdy trunks and delicate bare branches, curving sinuously into the air, creating a foil for the figures and their antics. Here there is no focal point and no hierarchy, deliberately encouraging viewers to consider the entire image, although the large trees and building on the right create a visual anchor.

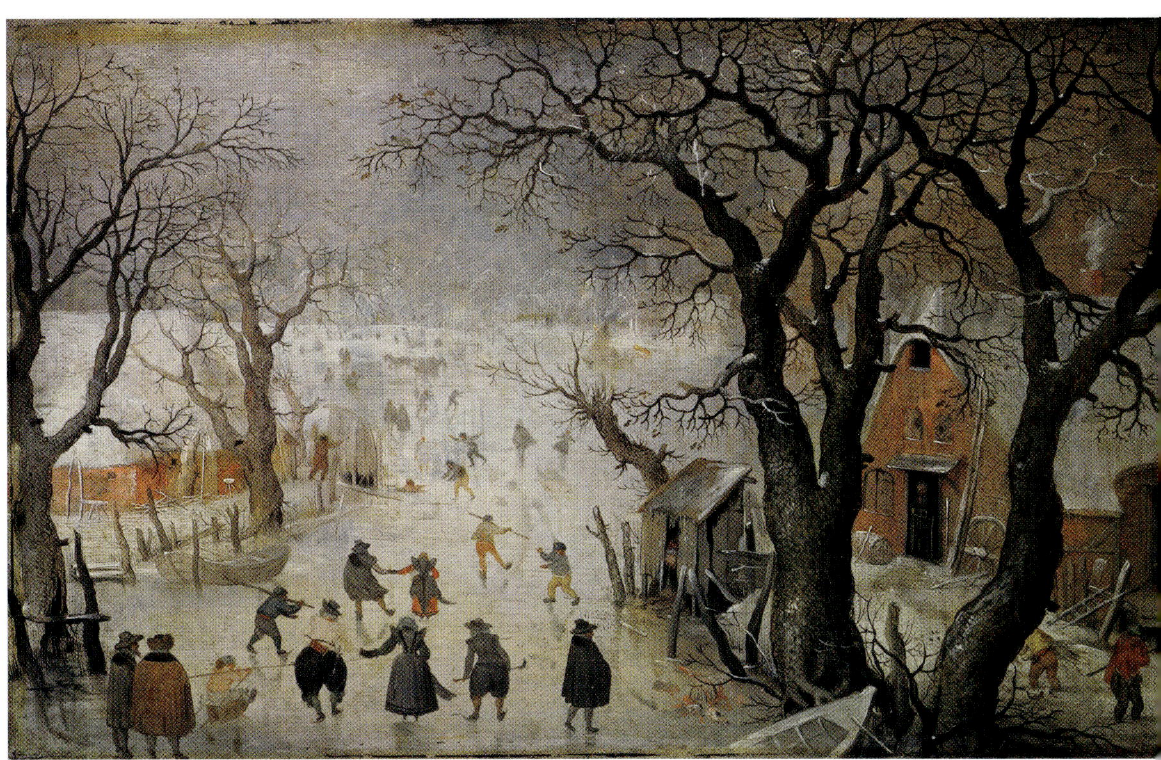

Winter Scene with Skaters near a Castle, Hendrick Avercamp, *c.*1608–09, oil on oak, diameter 40.7cm (16in), The National Gallery, London, UK

Most of Avercamp's paintings are small in scale. This elegant circular image is full of carefully observed details. A spindly, silhouetted winter tree frames the castle in the background, while atmospheric perspective is conveyed through the frosty, misty air. Avercamp imagined this entire scene, but he also includes various carefully observed elements, including smartly dressed figures tentatively skating, children playing excitedly, and a carriage being pulled across the ice.

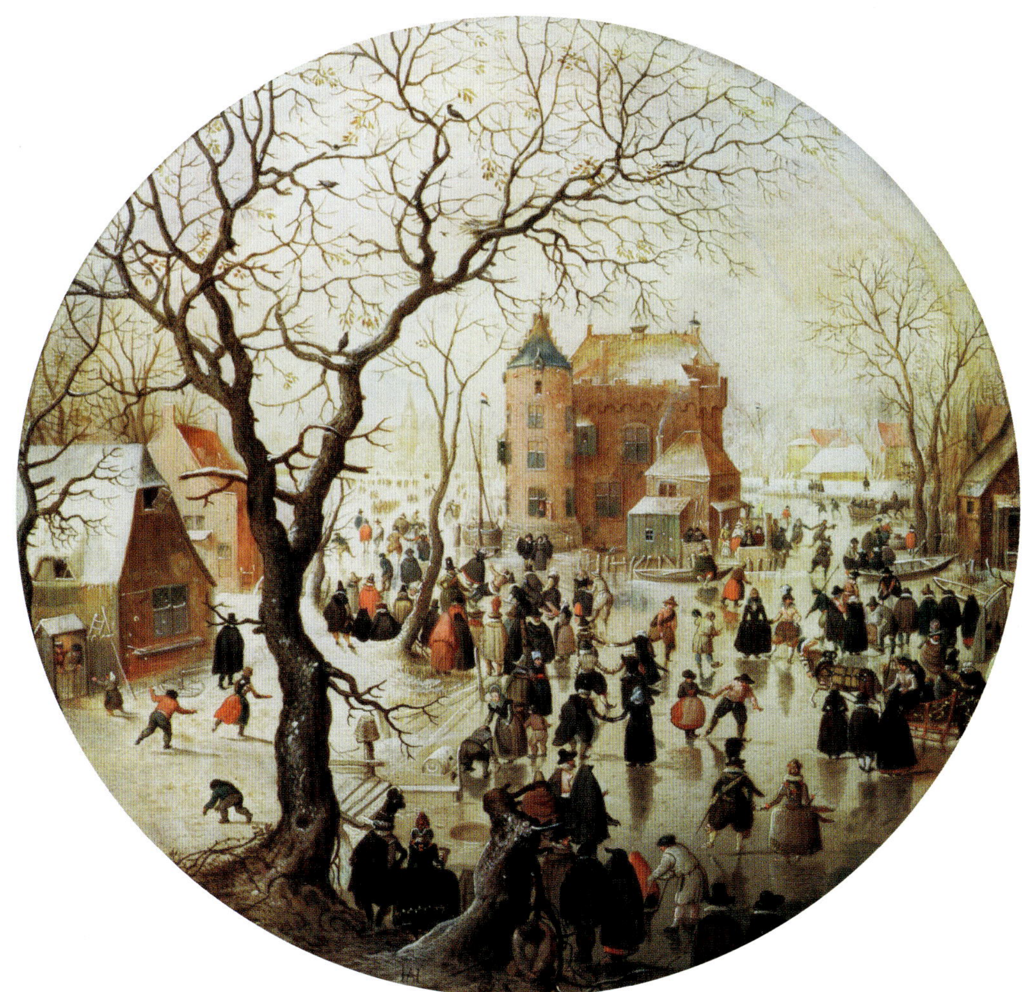

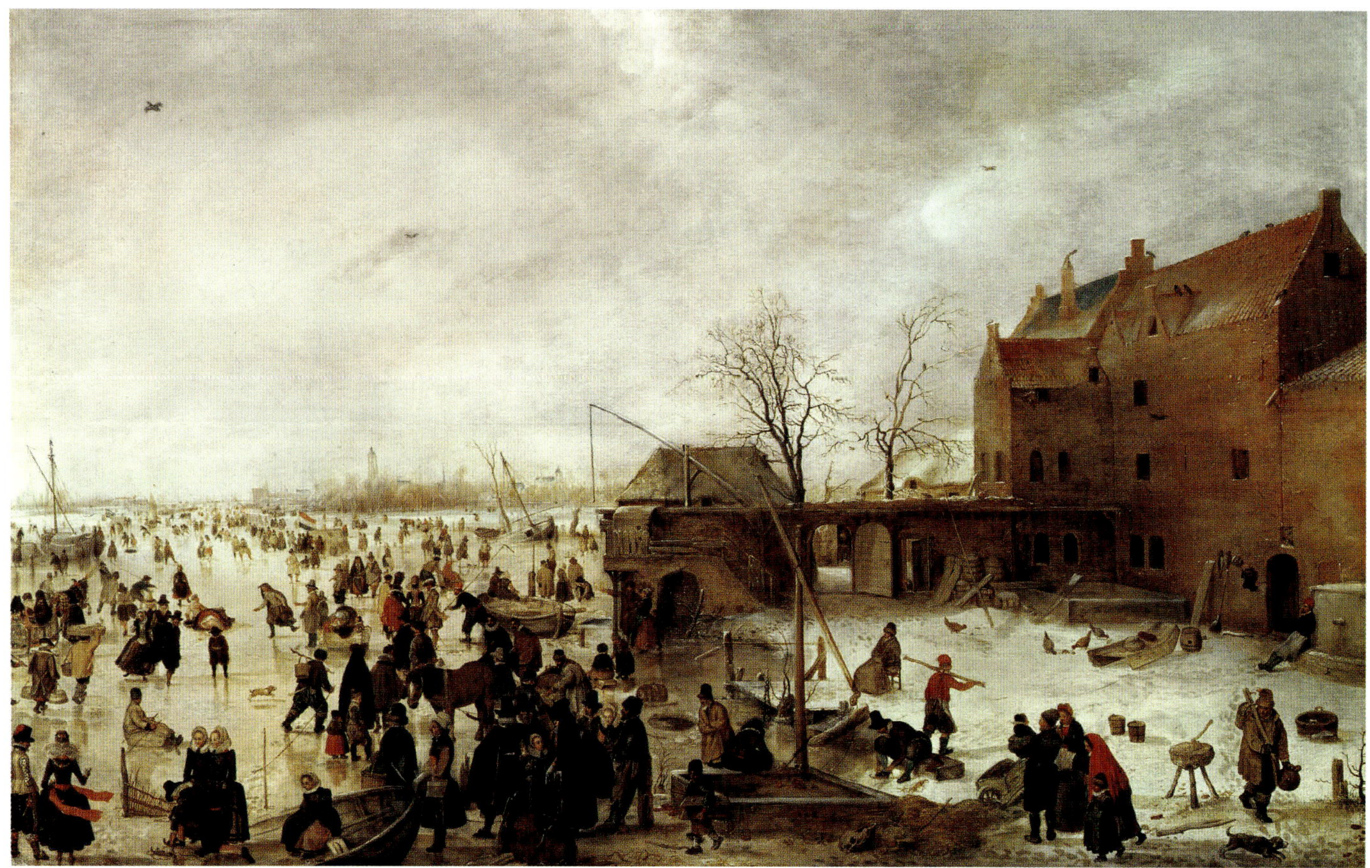

A Scene on the Ice near a Town, Hendrick Avercamp, c.1615, oil on oak, 58 x 89.8cm (22¾ x 35⅓in), The National Gallery, London, UK

As far as the eye can see, figures are entertaining themselves on a frozen river. Wrapped up against the icy cold, some play 'kolf', an early form of golf. Avercamp paints predominantly with muted browns, black and white, judiciously adding touches of red and yellow. As his style changed little over his career, and several paintings such as this are not dated, it is difficult to determine when they were painted.

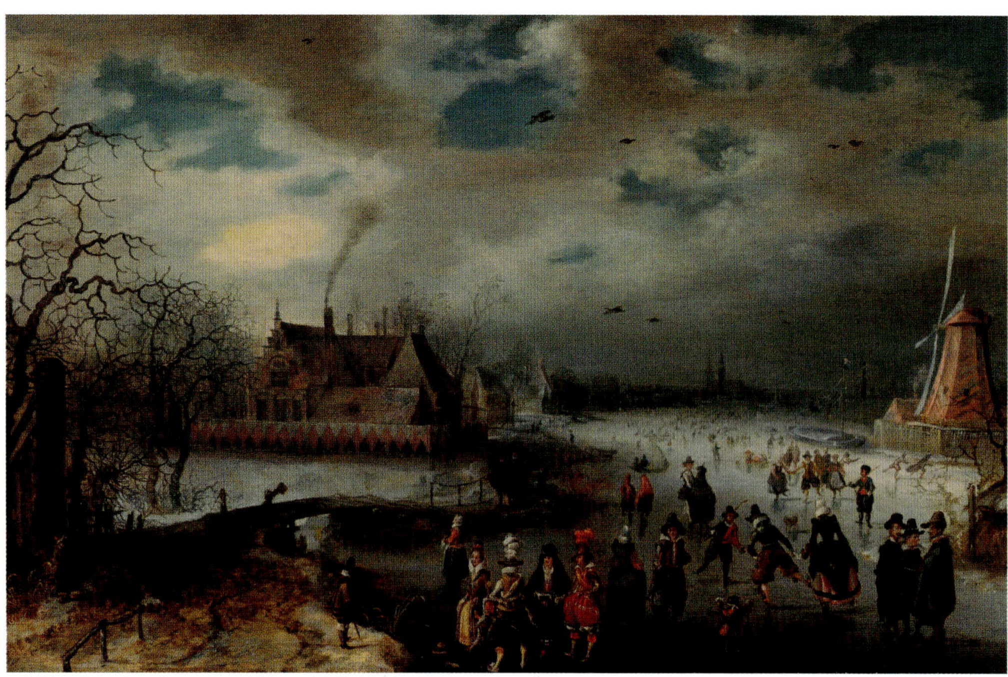

Skating on the Frozen Amstel River, Adam van Breen, 1611, oil on panel, 44.3 x 66.5cm (17½ x 26¼in), National Gallery of Art, Washington DC, USA

Buildings in the middle and far distance help to lead viewers' eyes into and around the frozen river scene. Figures dance, glide, play and chat. Although most of these scenes are imaginary, this depicts an actual location just south of Amsterdam, with its windmill and three churches: the Nieuwe Kerk, the Oude Kerk, and the Zuiderkerk.

A Winter Landscape, Esaias van de Velde, 1623, oil on oak, 25.9 x 30.4cm (10¼ x 12in), The National Gallery, London, UK

Although he grew up in Amsterdam and trained with a landscape artist (van Coninxlo, from Antwerp), from 1610–18 Esaias van de Velde (1587–1630) lived and worked in Haarlem. By the time he painted this, he was living in The Hague. He developed a naturalistic style using broad brushwork and a muted palette. On a cold winter's day, few people are about. A man and a child with a dog walk along the road, while another man carries something on his back and three figures by the cottage play kolf. A church can be seen in the distance.

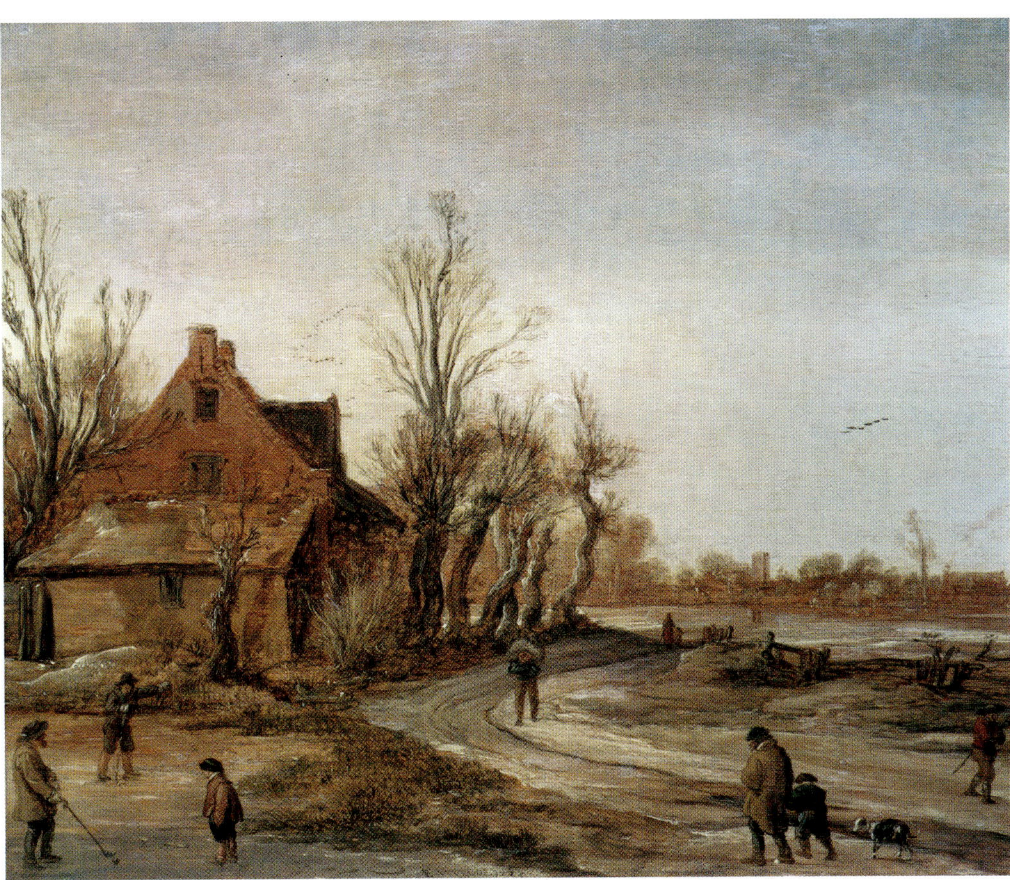

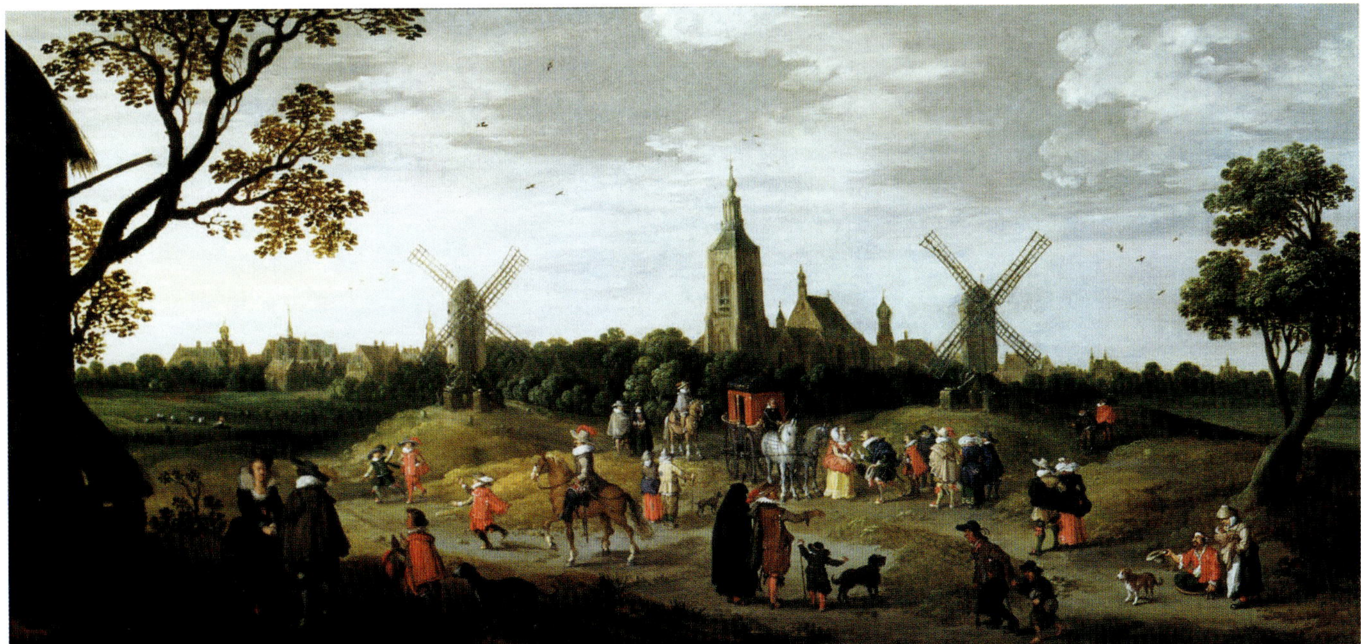

Summer, **Joost Cornelisz Droochsloot**, 1624, oil on oak, 41.3 x 86.5cm (16¼ x 34⅛in), **Private Collection**

One of a pair, this represents summer; its pendant depicts winter. Joost Cornelisz Droochsloot (1586–1666) lived and worked almost his whole life in Utrecht, but this painting seems to have been influenced by artists working elsewhere, such as Esaias van de Velde and Jan van Goyen.

A large part of the painting is sky, with the buildings and trees almost silhouetted against it.

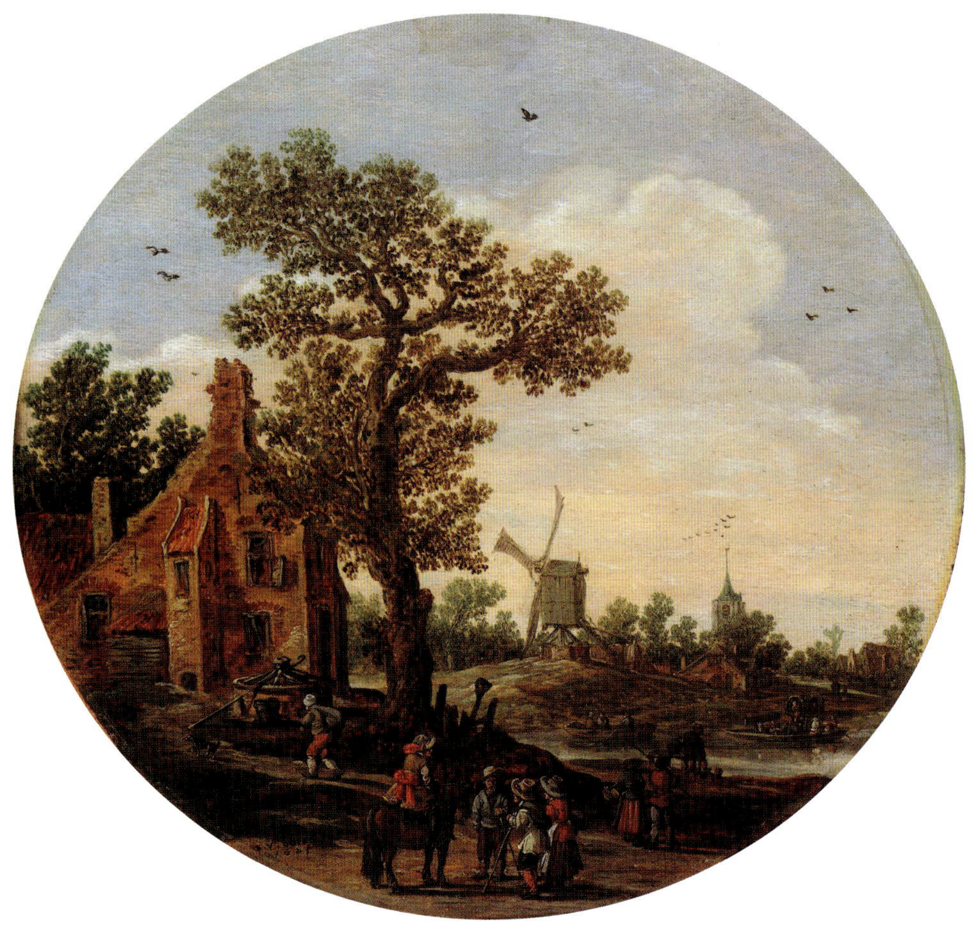

Summer, Jan van Goyen, 1625, oil on panel, diameter 33.5cm (13in), Rijksmuseum, Amsterdam, Netherlands

The idea of depicting different seasons has been popular for centuries. This is one of two paintings by van Goyen representing summer and winter, designed to be pendants to each other. (a pendant is one of two paintings intended as a pair). Such paintings seem to have influenced Droochsloot in his work on the previous page. Here, individual figures undertake typical peaceful occupations of summer, while all is relaxed and calm, the colours are harmonious, and the light is golden.

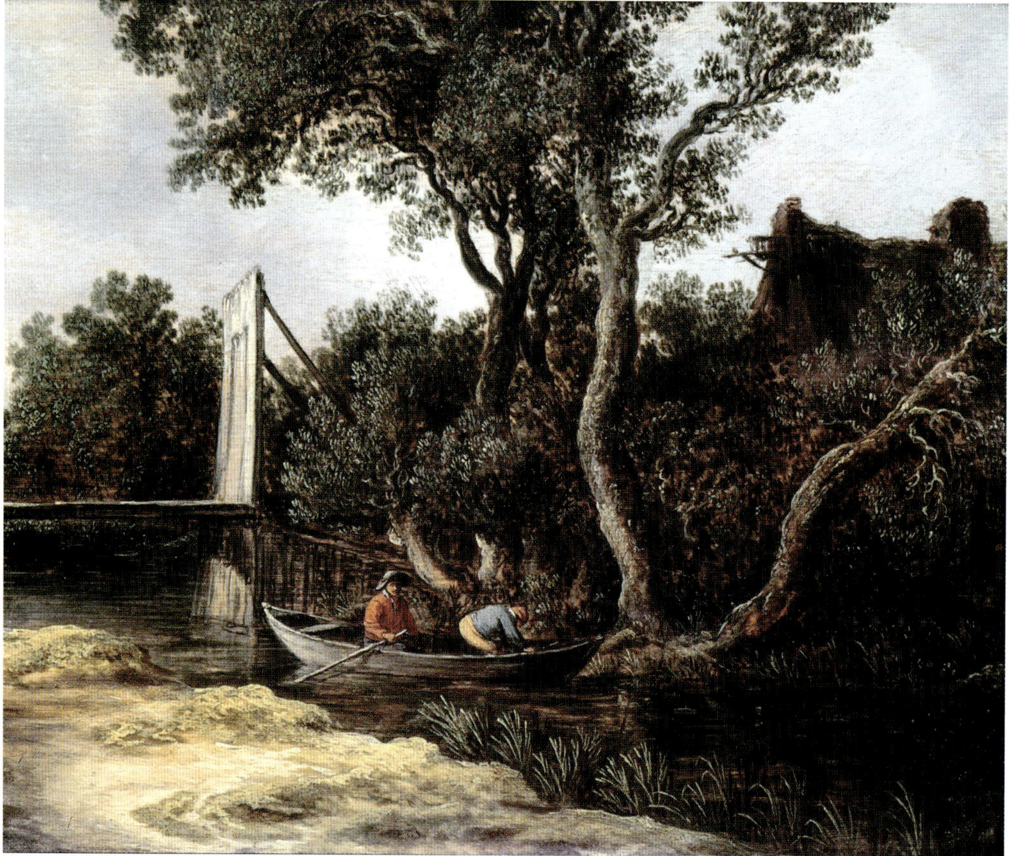

Landscape with Stream, Jan van Goyen, 1628, oil on panel, 25.4 x 30.7cm (10 x 12in), V&A Museum, London, UK

Jan van Goyen has painted this outdoor scene as if it is an interior; a close-up view of a stream, with a wooden bridge in the background and two figures in a small boat. Detailed brushwork builds up the leaves, the flowing water, the foreground path, the wooden boat and the bridge. Although not so apparent here, in many of his works, van Goyen made more use of diagonal lines than most other landscape artists of the period.

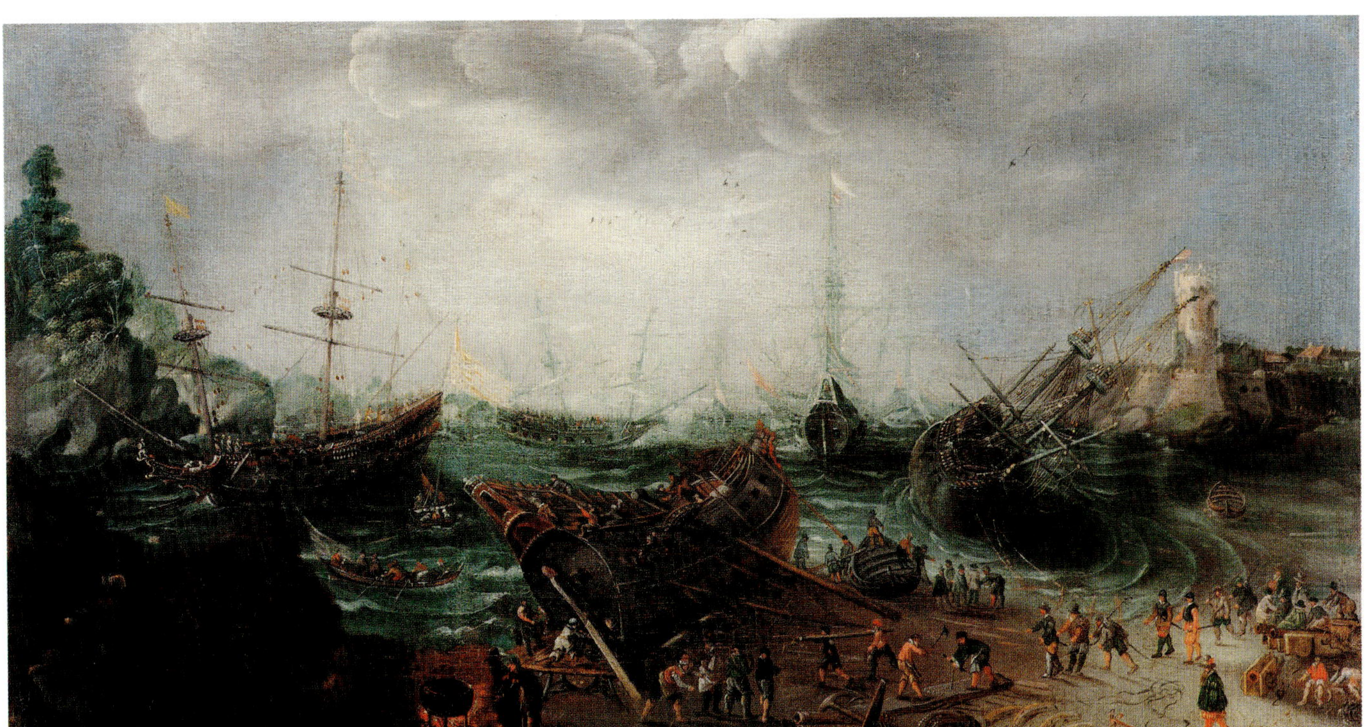

Harbour Scene, Adam Willaerts, *c.*1625, oil on panel, 41 x 72cm (16¾ x 28¼ in), Skokloster Castle, Skokloster, Sweden

Swirling and dynamic, the deep turquoise-green sea undulates around ships clustered around a harbour. Workers are bustling about maintaining and repairing the ships. Adam Willaerts (1577–1664) was born in London to Flemish parents who had fled from Antwerp for religious reasons. By 1585 his family had moved to Leiden. For most of his career, he lived in Utrecht, painting river, sea and canal scenes.

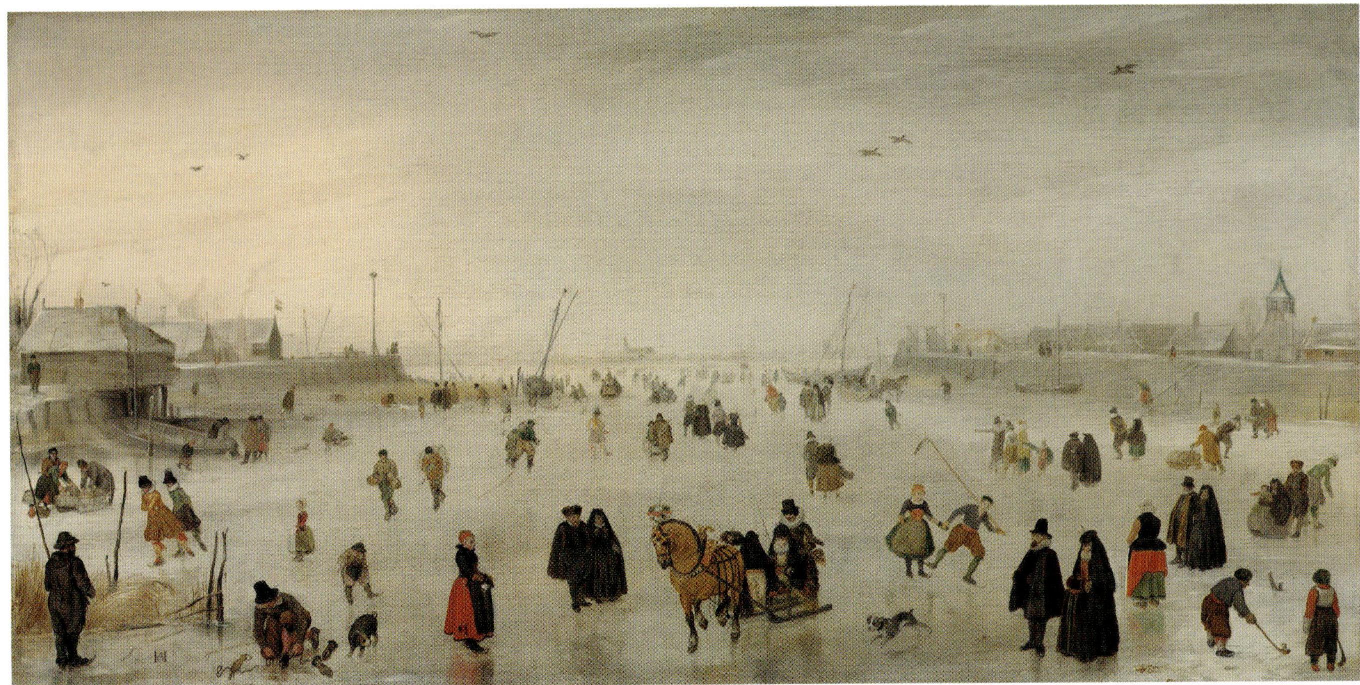

A Scene on the Ice, Hendrick Avercamp, *c.*1625, oil on panel, 39.2 x 77cm (15½ x 30¼ in), National Gallery of Art, Washington DC, USA

In an icy haze, all are out on this frozen river. Most skate, some more elegantly than others. Some are there for recreation while others continue to work. In the lower centre, a groom drives two ladies on a sleigh pulled by a horse, while in the bottom left, two boys play a game of kolf. Avercamp was one of the first European artists to specialize in depictions of winter.

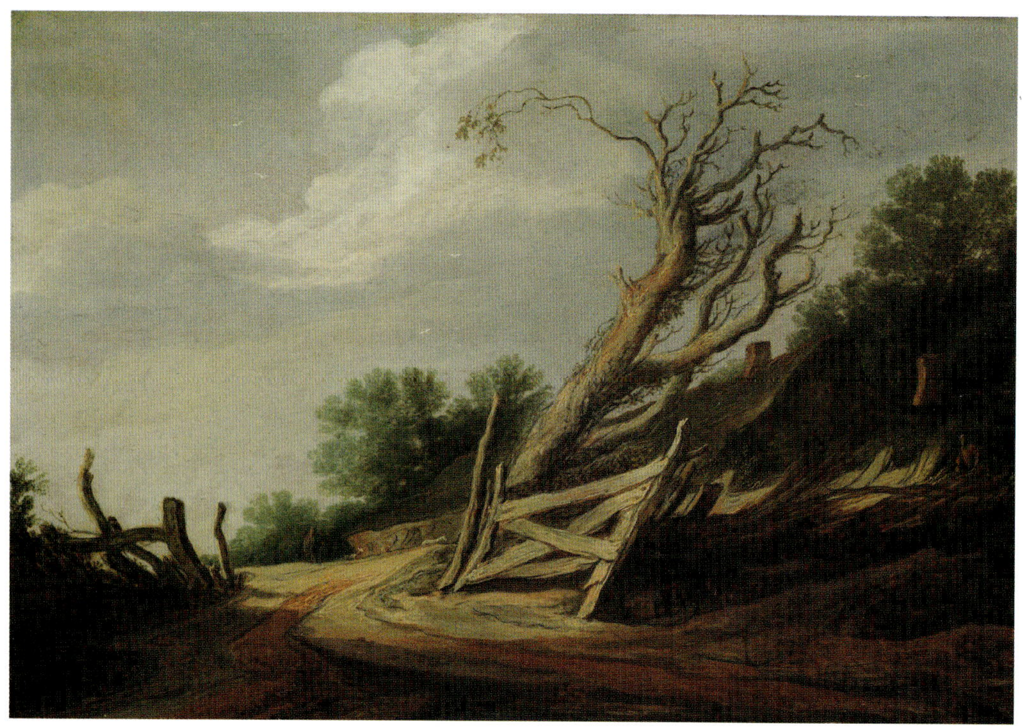

Landscape with an Open Gate, Pieter Molijn, *c.*1630/35, oil on panel, 33.6 x 47.9cm (13¼ x 18¾in), National Gallery of Art, Washington DC, USA

Using diluted paint and fluid brushstrokes, Pieter Molijn, who studied with Gerard ter Borch, captured the sense of the sandy, windswept coast near Haarlem. It is a small work, with a simple but dynamic composition, and it appears to have been painted spontaneously. Viewers are forced to look up and along a lane that meanders off. Molijn's work influenced both Salomon van Ruysdael and Jan van Goyen.

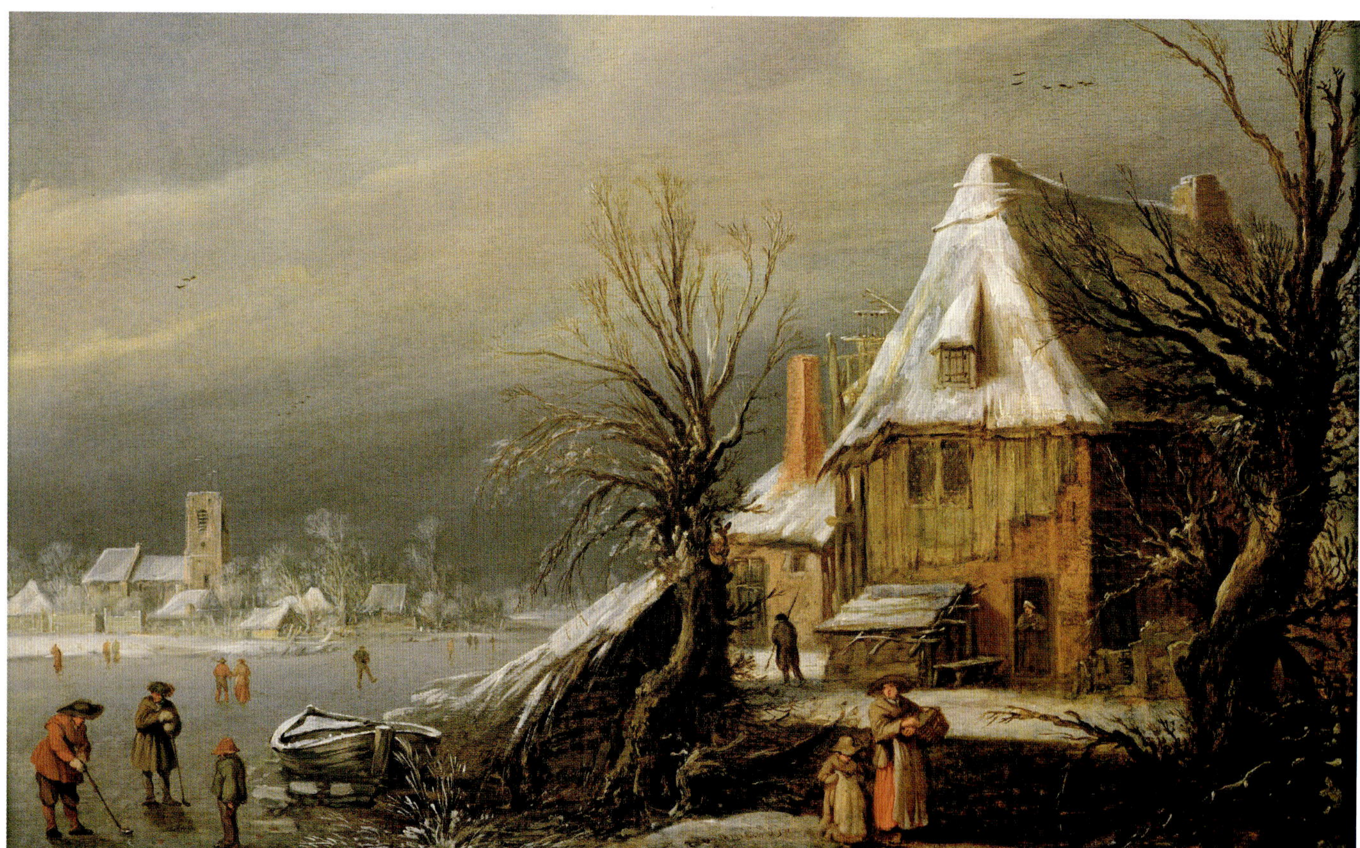

Winter Landscape, **Esaias van de Velde, 1630, oil on panel, 32.8 x 51.3cm (13 x 20in), Private Collection**

By 1630, Esaias van de Velde (no relation to Willem van de Velde) was living in The Hague. As well as painting landscapes there, he was also working as Court Painter to Maurice of Nassau, Prince of Orange and subsequently for Maurice's half-brother, Prince Frederik Hendrik. Most of van de Velde's landscapes are composed with a low viewpoint, with natural-looking figures and trees, and often rural buildings.

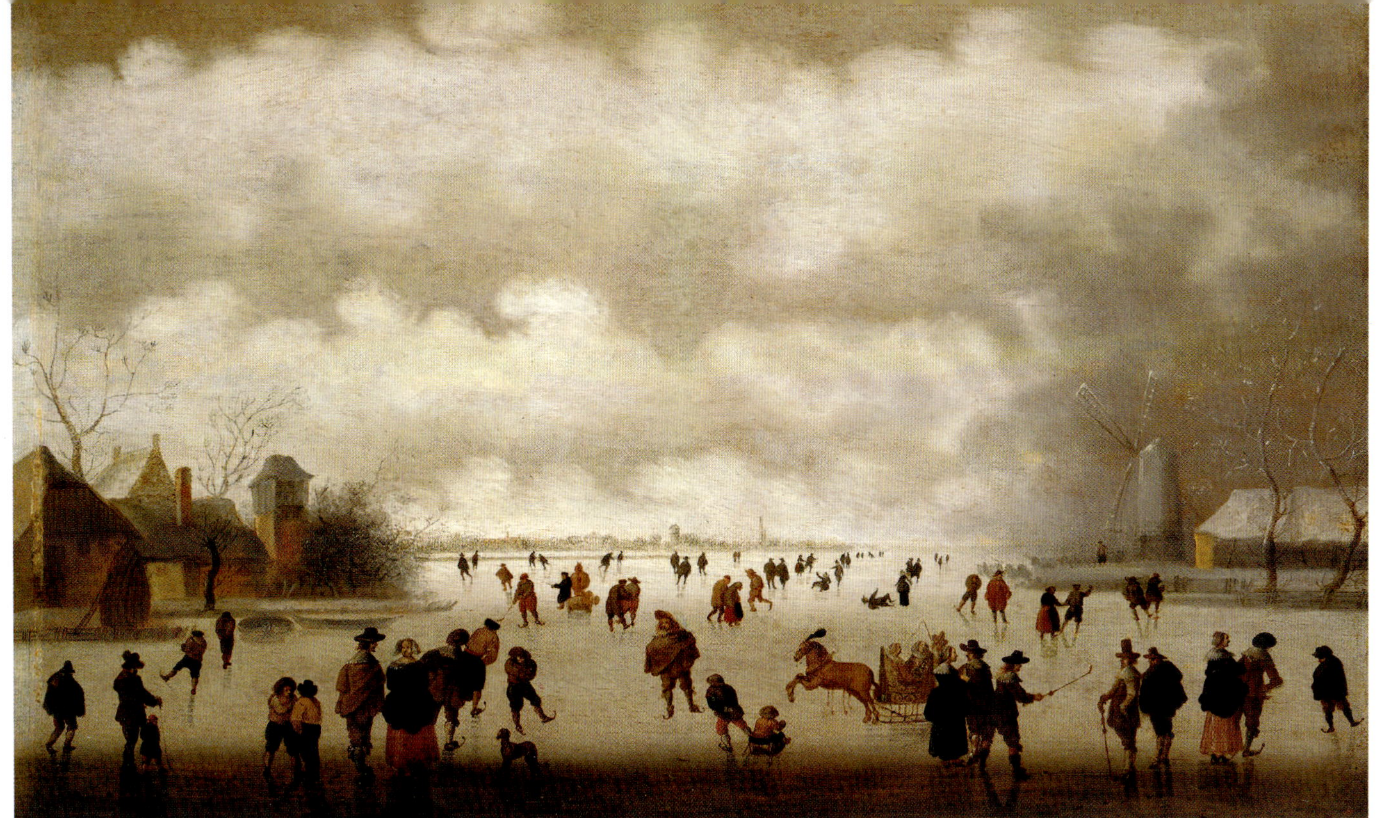

Winter Sport in Holland, Anthonie Verstraelen, *c.*1630–40, oil on panel, 37.5 x 60.3cm (14¾ x 23¾ in), The Heckscher Museum of Art, New York, USA

Although little is known about Anthonie Verstraelen or van Stralen (1593/4–1641), like Hendrick Avercamp, he became best known for his winter landscapes full of busy individual characters. In alignment with many other Dutch landscape painters, his horizon is low. There is no specific focal point as the intention is for viewers to be drawn around the entire composition, to notice each figure in turn.

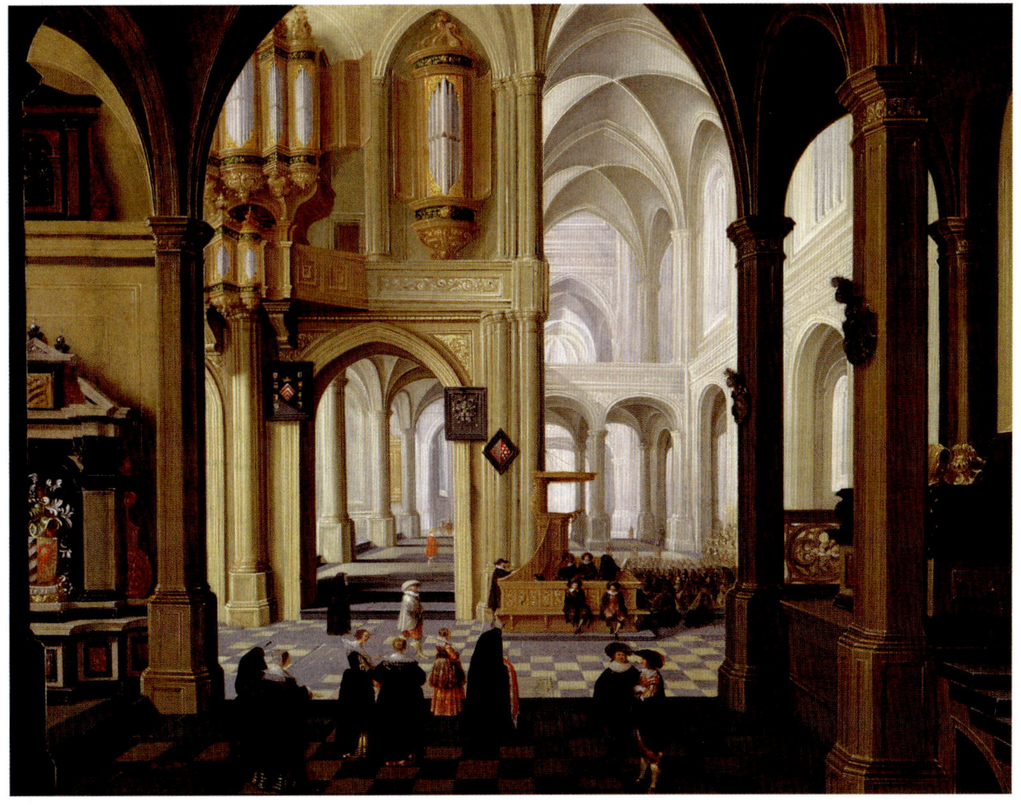

Interior of a Church, with a Sermon and Christening Party in Progress, Dirck van Delen, 1631, oil on panel, 57.1 x 70.2cm (22½ x 27½ in), Private Collection

Little is known about Dirck van Delen's training. His work consists almost entirely of architectural paintings of imaginary palaces and church interiors that show his precise use of perspective and his understanding of light. While most of his church interiors are based on real churches, they are usually amalgamations of architectural details and it is likely that other artists painted his figures.

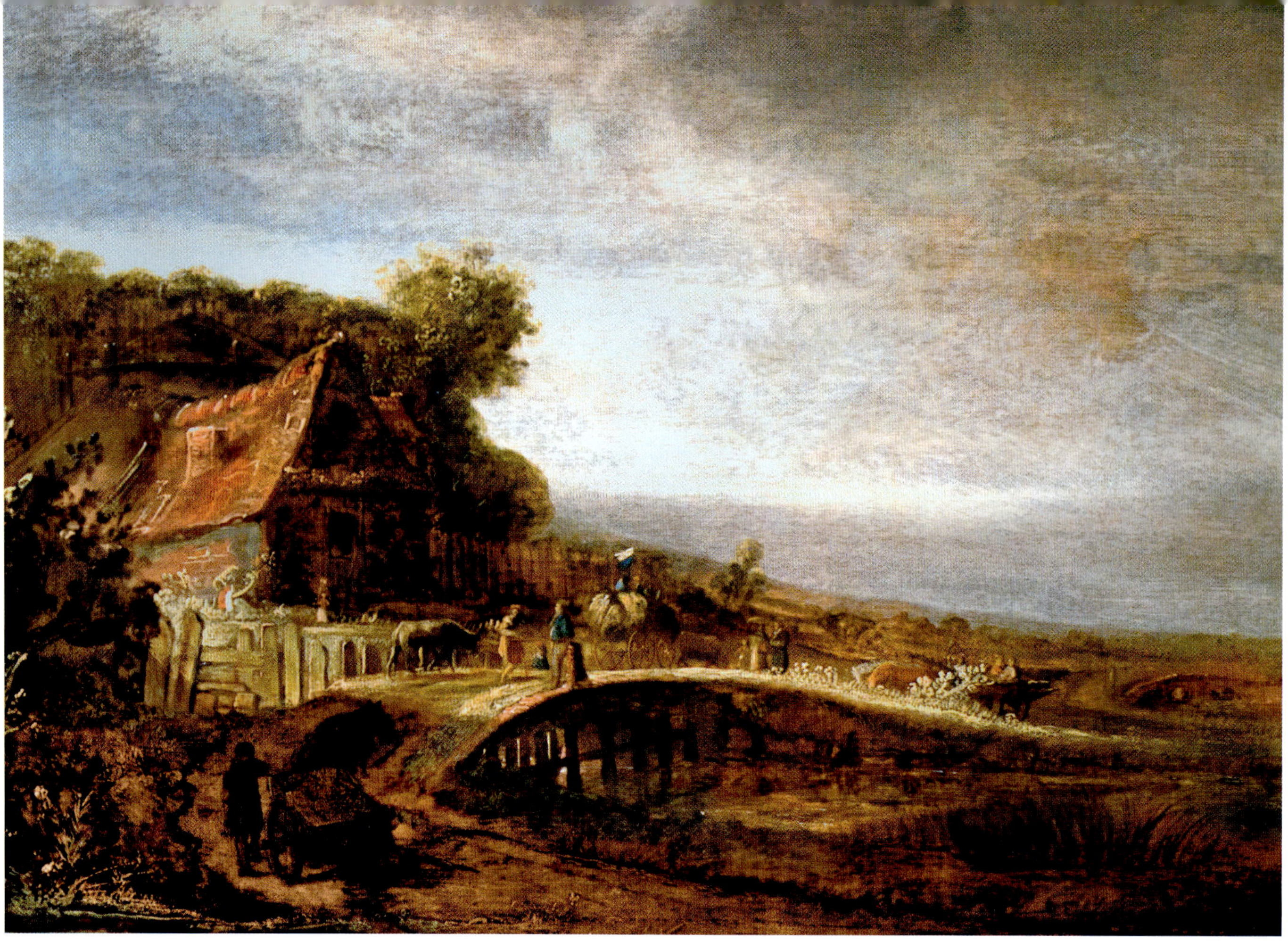

Landscape with a Farm and a Bridge, attributed to Govert Flinck, 1640, oil on panel, 40.7 x 53.5cm (16 x 21in), Museo Nacional Thyssen-Bornemisza, Madrid, Spain

After studying with Rembrandt, Govert Flinck produced history and landscape paintings. The curving bridge draws viewers' eyes into and around the composition while the sunny atmosphere seems to move from Rembrandt's early influence. Only the impasto paint and the palette of colours recall aspects of Rembrandt's approach. As Flinck did not sign this, it is only attributed to him, not verified.

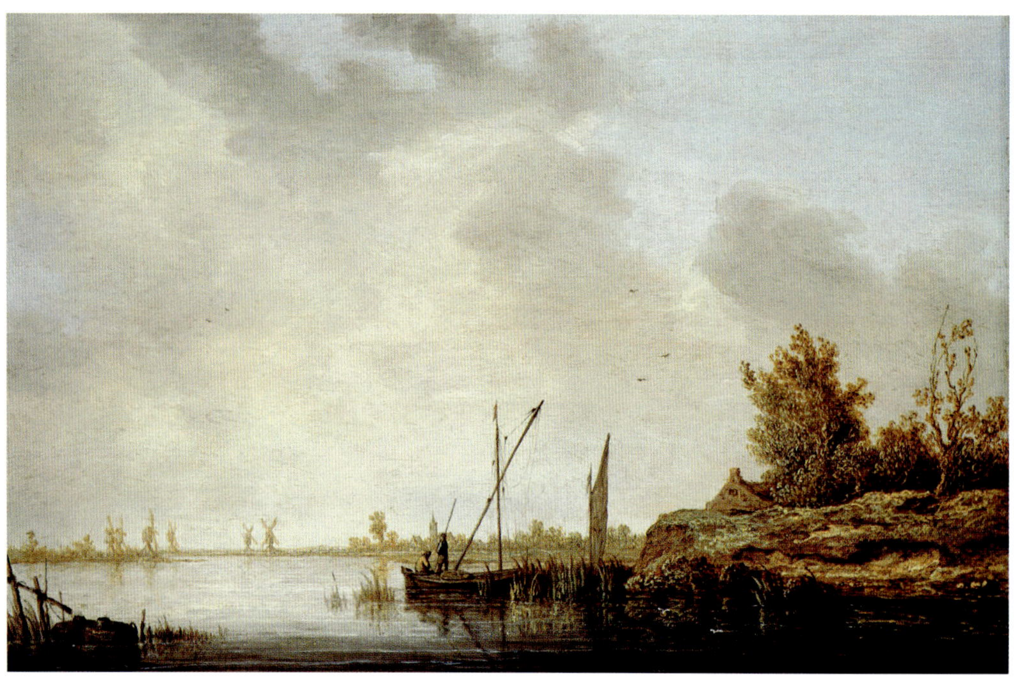

A River Scene with Distant Windmills, Aelbert Cuyp, c.1640, oil on oak, 35.6 x 52.4cm (14 x 20½in), The National Gallery, London, UK

At this point in his career, Aelbert Cuyp was still painting landscapes in a realistic manner, continuing in this way until about 1642, when he visited Utrecht and saw the work of Jan Both who had recently returned from Rome. This work was his own interpretation of a more traditional Dutch style that also builds on ideas of Jan van Goyen.

Peasant Huts with a Well, Jan van Goyen, 1633, oil on panel, 55 x 80cm (21½ x 31½in), Gemäldegalerie Alte Meister, Dresden, Germany

With an elaborate system for drawing up water, this well is being worked by a peasant, while others are getting on with their daily tasks. It was views such as this, showing happy, hard-working peasants in the tranquillity of the countryside that were so admired by the Dutch middle classes. By painting from a direct vantage point, van Goyen made viewers feel part of the idyllic scene.

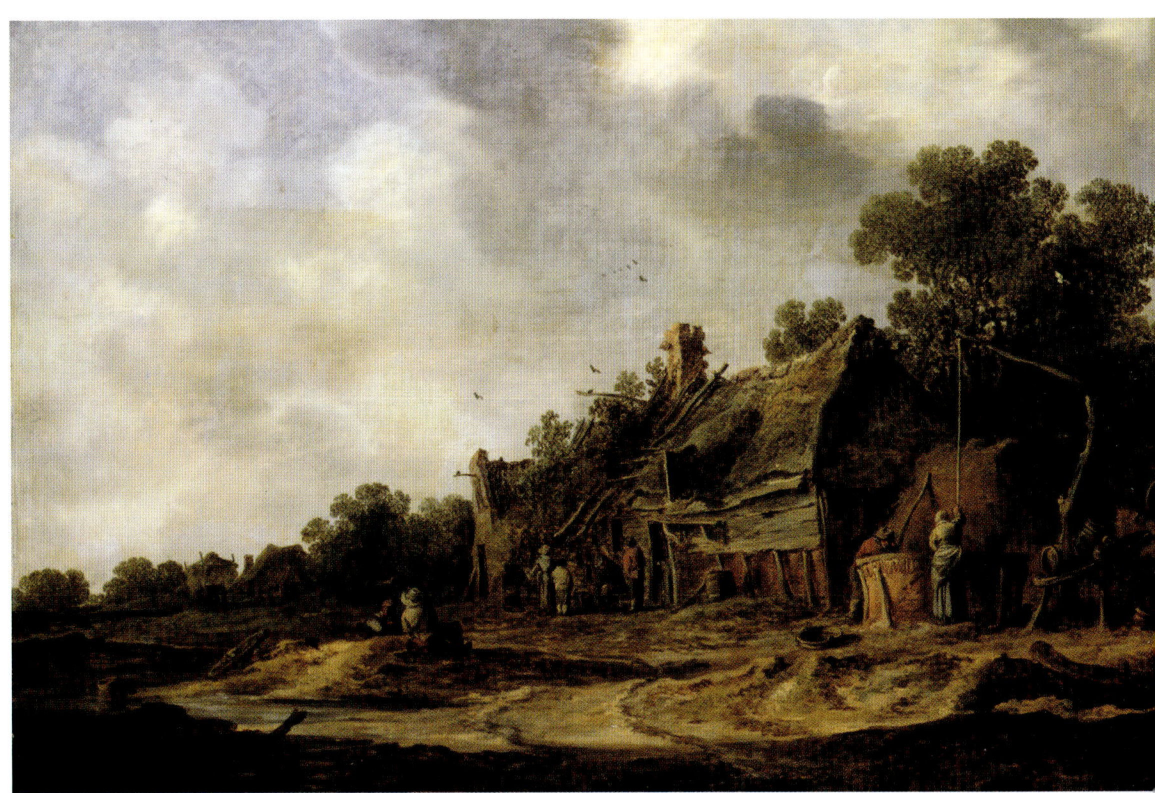

Landscape with an Oak, Jan van Goyen, 1634, oil on canvas, 83 x 105cm (32⅔ x 41⅓in), The State Hermitage Museum, Saint Petersburg, Russia

With dexterous brush-strokes, Jan van Goyen painted prolifically. This is a peasant's cottage that is leaning like the old oak tree next to it, appearing almost a part of nature itself. This is a more painterly style than van Goyen had previously used, and his free use of paint creates a sense of the textures and patterns, such as in the leaves with the variegated greens.

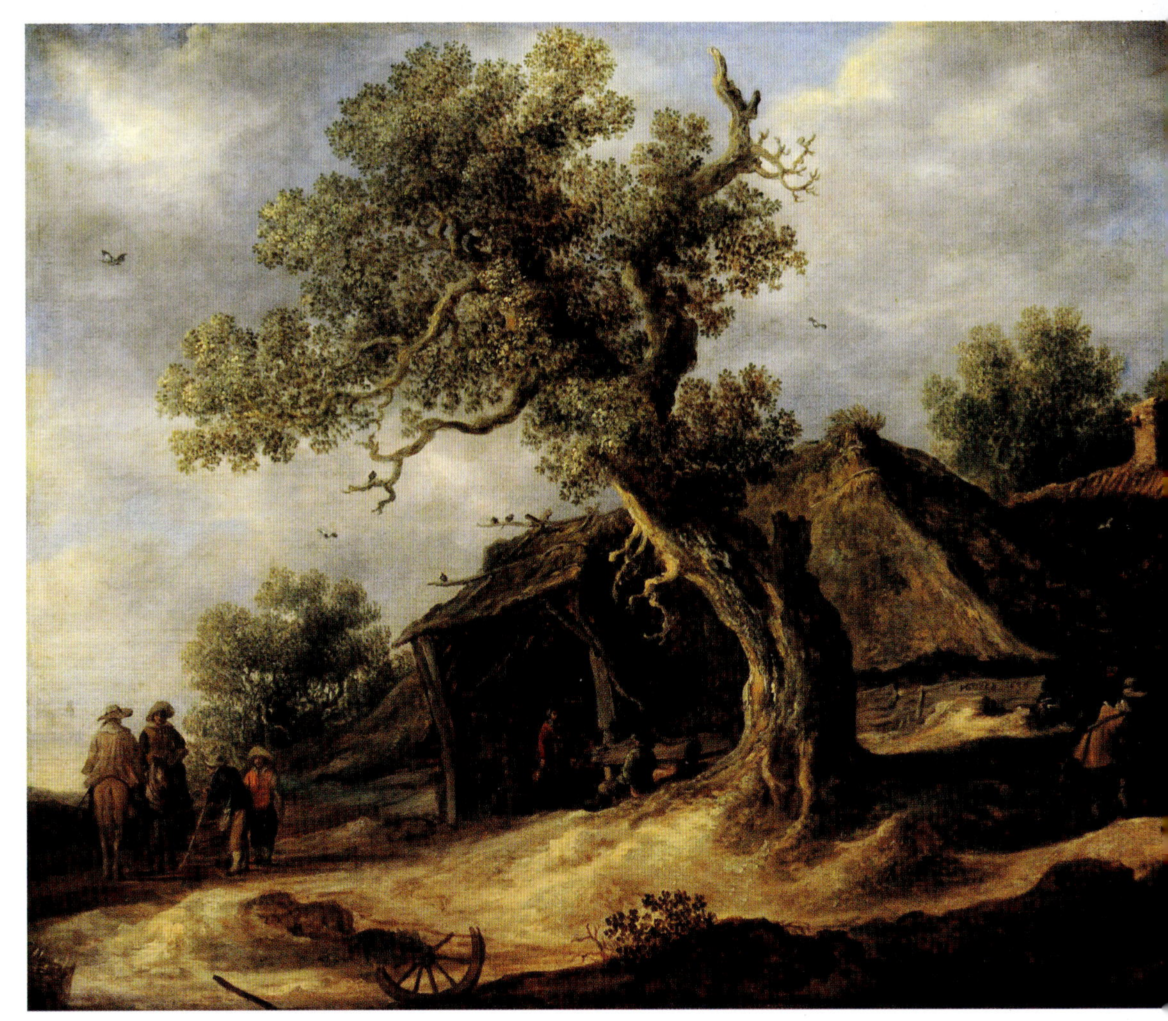

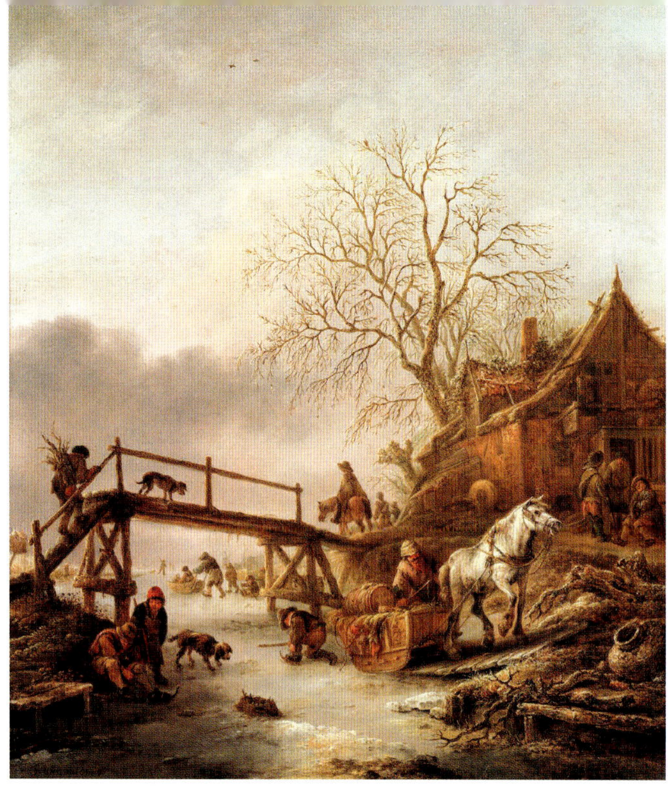

Winter Scene, Isack van Ostade, 1640s, oil on oak, 48.8 x 40cm (19¼ x 15¾in), The National Gallery, London, UK

Although Haarlem-born Isack van Ostade began his studies under his brother Adriaen, he gradually abandoned Adriaen's cottage subjects for landscapes that were more like those of Esaias van de Velde and Salomon van Ruysdael. He began painting landscapes featuring roadside inns, village high streets and travellers, and particularly specialized in winter scenes with frozen canals, horses, figures, hazy or crisp atmospheric effects, and broad tonal contrasts.

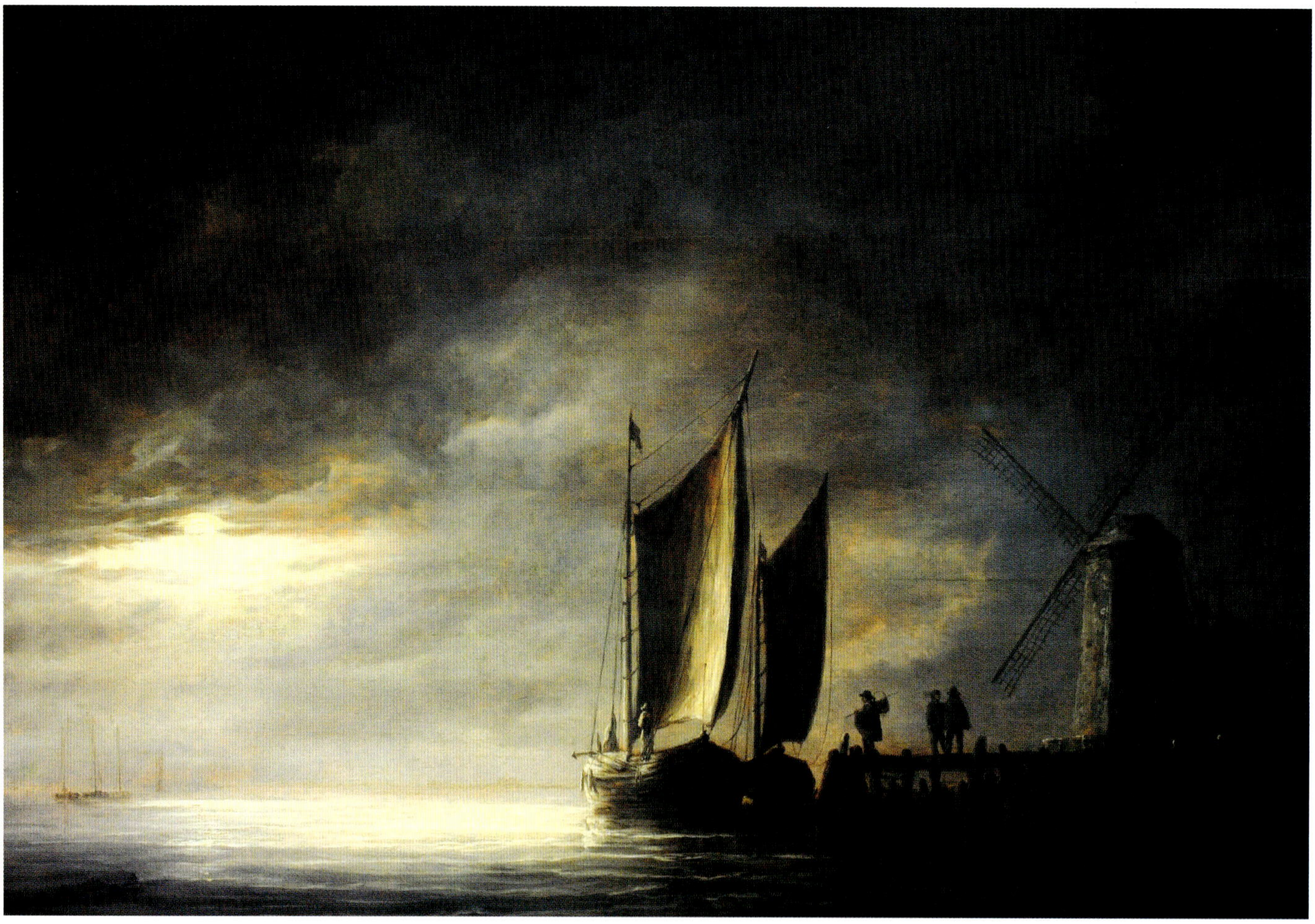

Dordrecht Harbour in Moonlight, Aelbert Cuyp, c.1645–55, oil on panel, 77 x 107cm (30¼ x 42in), Wallraf-Richartz-Museum, Cologne, Germany

Using his new, dramatic backlit style, Aelbert Cuyp painted boats on calm, still water as the moon breaks through the clouds, bathing everything in silvery hues. From the reflective water to the sails and wooden hulls, Cuyp demonstrates his prowess at painting textures. This seemingly simple composition draws the eye directly into the scene with no distractions; no bright or jarring colours, no obvious brushmarks.

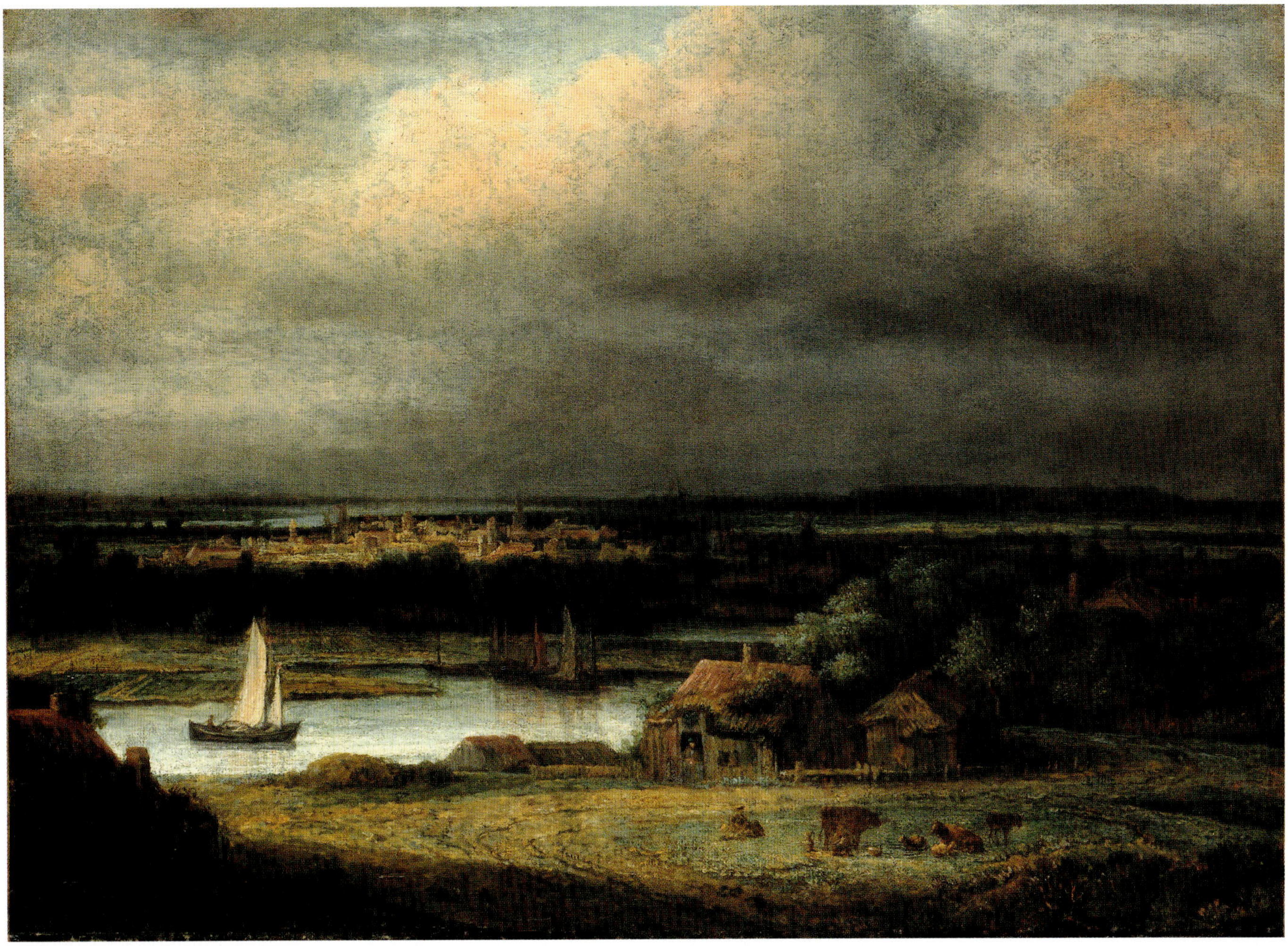

Wide River Landscape, Philips Koninck, 1648–49, oil on canvas, 41.3 x 58.1cm (16¼ x 22¾in), The Metropolitan Museum of Art, New York, USA

Philips Koninck or Philip de Koninck (1619–88) first studied painting in Rotterdam with his landscape artist elder brother Jacob Koninck (c.1615–c.1695), and later possibly trained with Rembrandt in Amsterdam. During the late 1640s, he began painting panoramic landscapes, dividing his canvases approximately in half horizontally, with the sky and land taking up equal space. He painted his scenes from high viewpoints, conveying a sense of space, light and atmosphere.

Interior of the Sint-Odulphuskerk in Assendelft, seen from the Choir facing West, Pieter Saenredam, 1649, oil on panel, 50 x 76cm (19¾ x 30in), Rijksmuseum, Amsterdam, Netherlands

Nine years after first drawing the interior of this church, Pieter Saenredam made a large construction drawing of it, and six years after that, he produced this painting. The perspective is exceptionally accurate and light falls at different angles; its source is on the left. Saenredam includes small figures from his imagination, including a man giving a sermon and a boy reading.

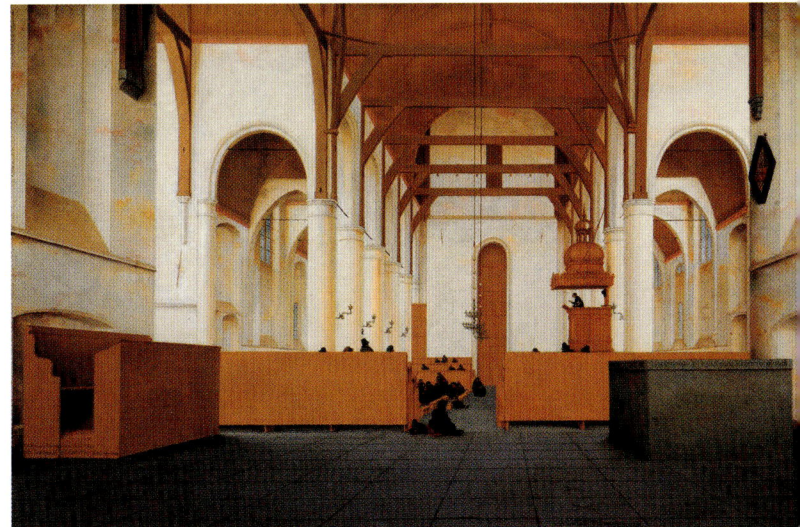

Boatmen Moored on the Shore of an Italian Lake, Adam Pynacker, 1650–70, oil on canvas, 97.5 x 85.5cm (38¾ x 33⅔in), Rijksmuseum, Amsterdam, Netherlands

An artist of the Delft School, Adam Pynacker here creates an Italianate landscape with dark, dramatic tree trunks in the foreground and atmospheric mountains in the background. A golden glow of sunlight bathes the trees, figures and boats. Within the scene are a woman and child and an ox and ass, which suggest that the painting may represent Joseph and Mary's flight to Egypt with the infant Jesus.

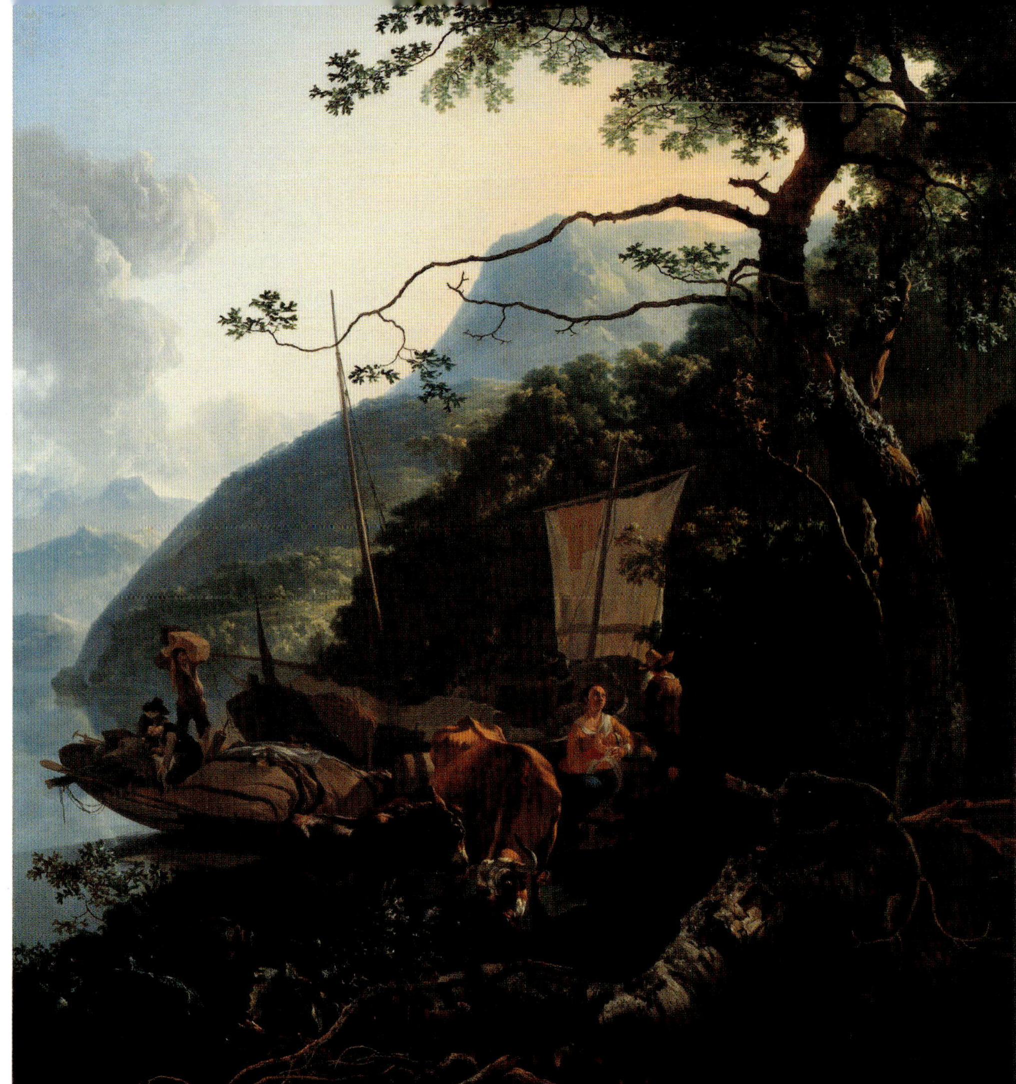

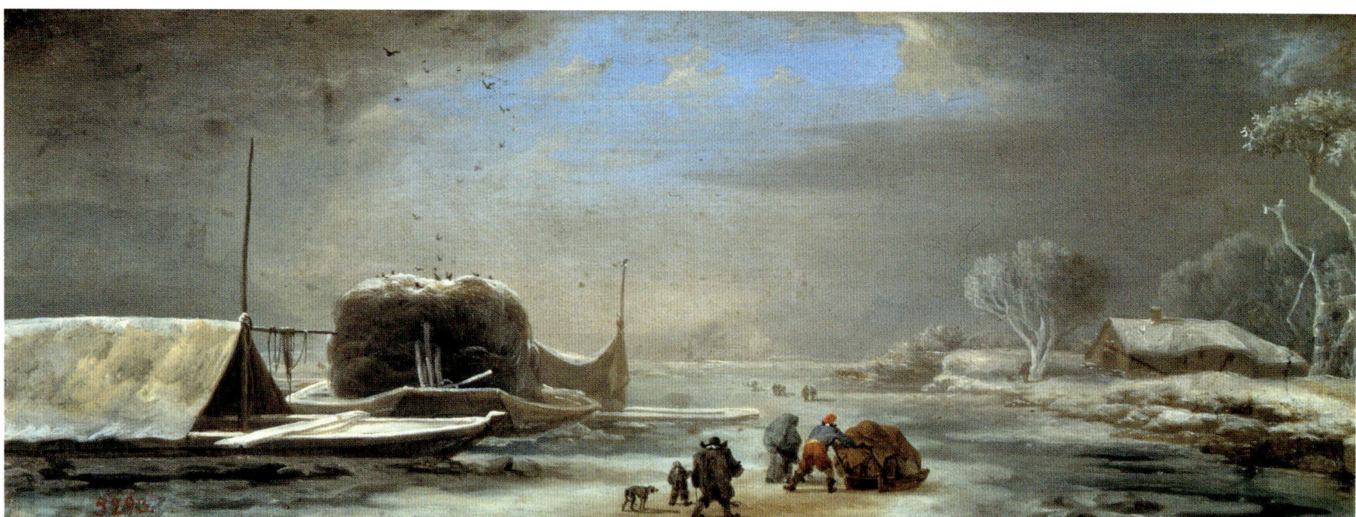

Winter Landscape, Jan Asselijn, 1650, oil on copper, 15 x 38cm (6 x 15in), The State Hermitage Museum, Saint Petersburg, Russia

As a child, Jan Asselijn (c.1610–52) moved with his family to Amsterdam from France. In about 1635, he travelled to Rome, where he became a member of the Bentvueghels (see page 70). His nickname was 'little crab' because he had a deformed left hand. This work also shows an influence of fellow Bentvueghels Pieter van Laer and Jan Both. By the time he painted this, Asselijn was back in Amsterdam.

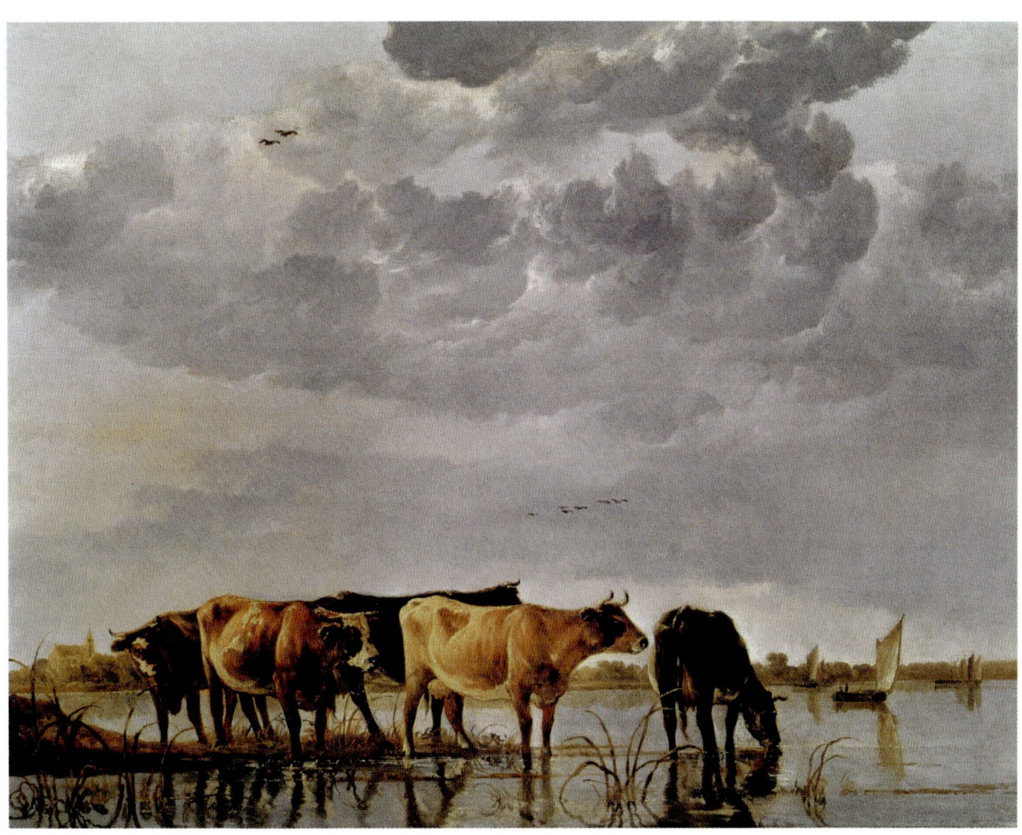

Cows in a River, Aelbert Cuyp, *c.*1650, oil on oak, 59 x 74cm (23¼ x 29in), Museum of Fine Arts, Budapest, Hungary

Portraying the light and atmospheric effects that made him successful, Aelbert Cuyp depicts five cows seeking a drink at the edge of a river. Symbolizing the Earth, fertility and the wealth of the Netherlands, cows often appear in Cuyp's paintings, in fields, along riverbanks or in shallow water. They allowed him to create low horizons and use a palette of predominantly earthy colours with pale blue skies.

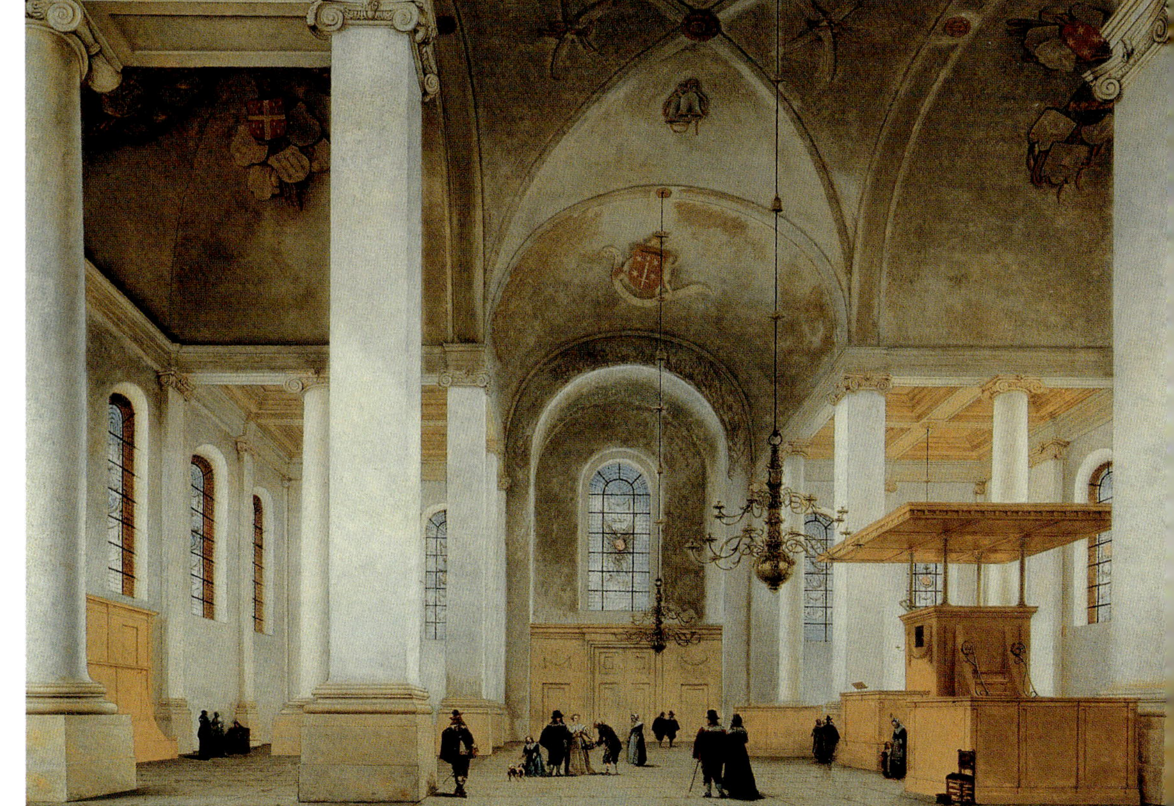

Interior of the Church of Saint Anne in Haarlem, Pieter Saenredam, 1652, oil on panel, 65.5 x 93cm (25¾ x 36½in), Frans Hals Museum, Haarlem, The Netherlands

From 1646–49, the Church of Saint Anne was built in Haarlem, designed by artist and architect Jacob van Campen. His friend Pieter Saenredam painted this interior of it, plus three other paintings and several drawings, although this is not an exact record of its appearance. For instance, although van Campen designed the round columns, they were not all built, and Saenredam has conveyed a larger sense of space.

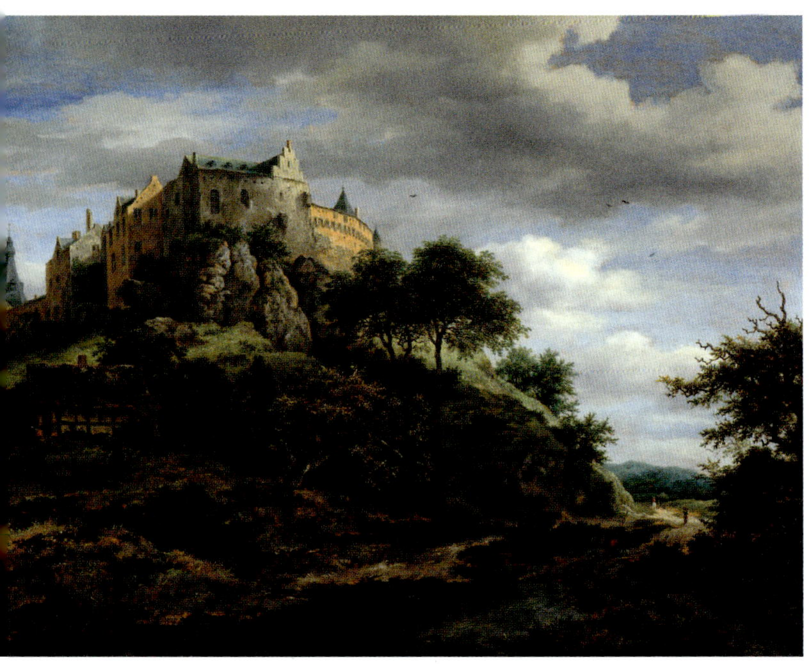

View of Bentheim Castle, Jacob van Ruisdael, *c.*1652–54, oil on canvas, 52 x 67.7cm (20 x 27in), Mauritshuis, The Hague, Netherlands

Jacob van Ruisdael painted several views of Bentheim Castle, showing it as here, high on a rocky hill; depicted higher than it is in reality, the upward view adds to the dramatic effect. Rocky outcrops, trees and a stream fill the foreground, with two tiny figures and a dog by the water, while beyond, a road leads diagonally through the landscape towards mountains in the far distance.

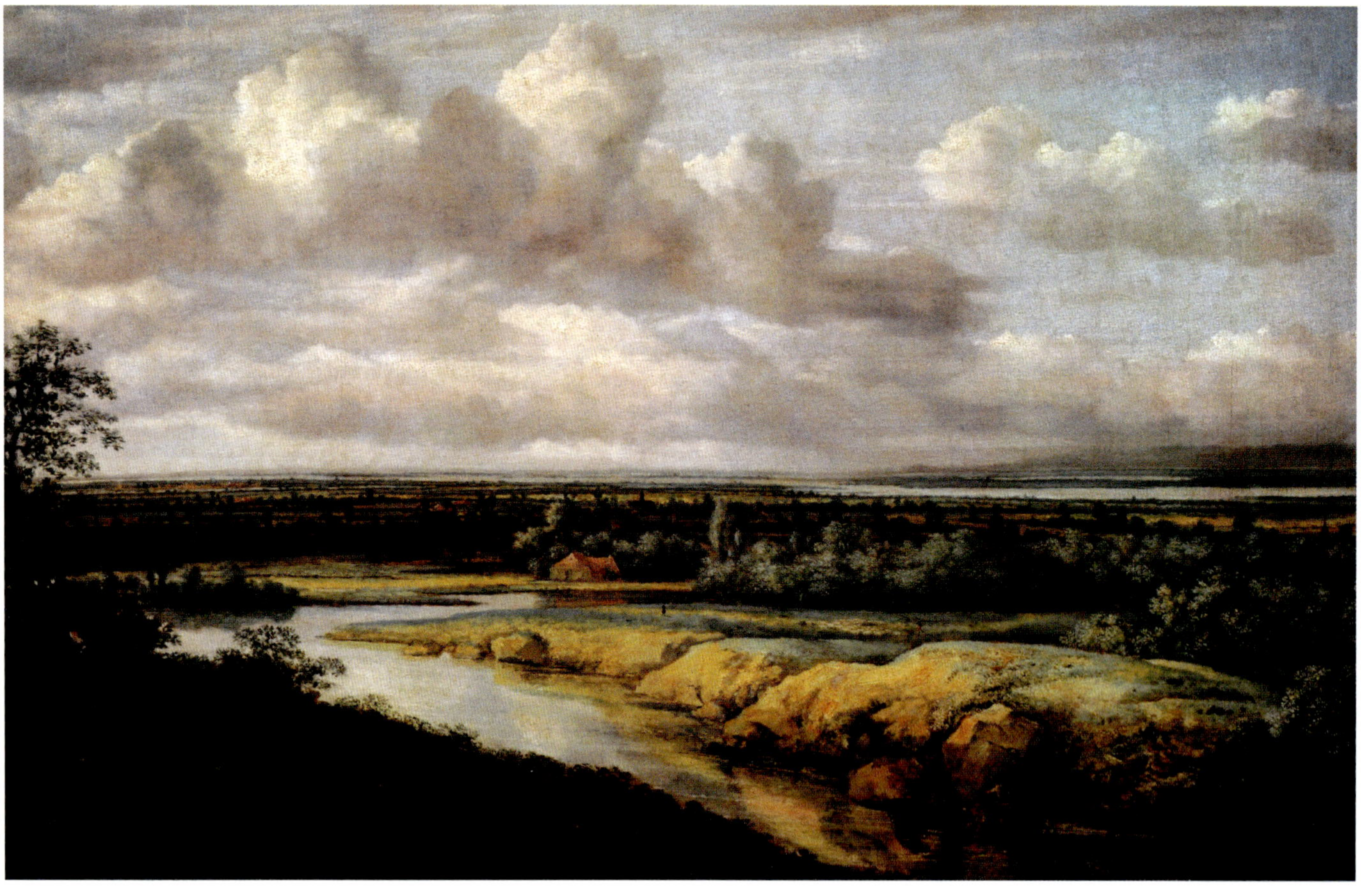

Flat Landscape with Two Anglers, Philips Koninck, 1650–55, oil on canvas, 133.3 x 165.7cm (52½ x 65¼ in), Alte Pinakothek, Munich, Germany

Like many other Dutch Golden Age painters, Philips Koninck supplemented his earnings from paintings with other sources of income. He was also an innkeeper and owned a ferry service that operated between Amsterdam, Leiden and Rotterdam. He mainly painted idealized panoramic views inspired by the countryside around him. Looking down from a high viewpoint, this scene includes lifelike clouds and a distant river.

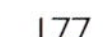

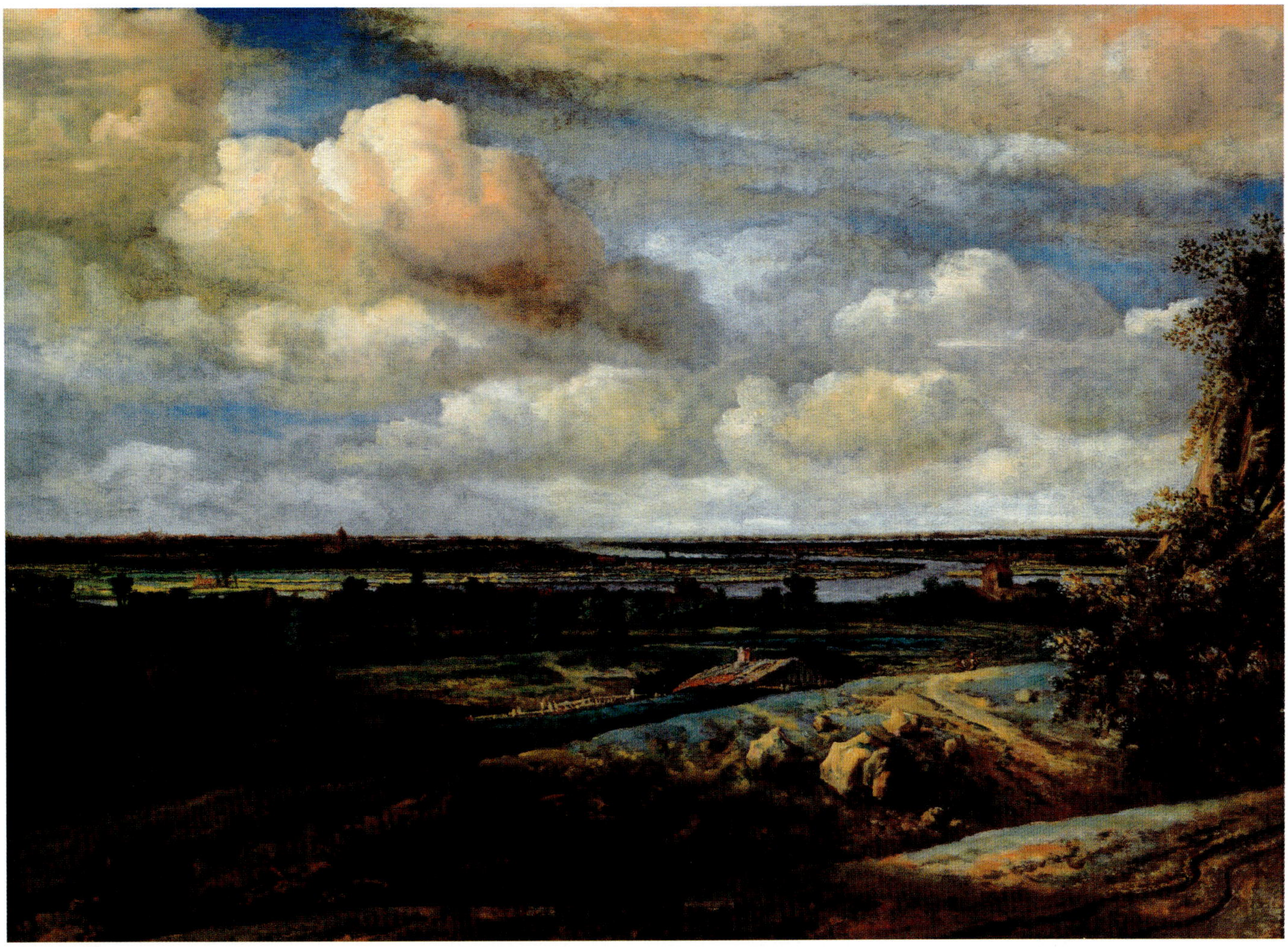

Dutch Panorama Landscape with a Distant View of Haarlem, Philips Koninck, 1655, oil on canvas, 150 x 203cm (59 x 80in), Statens Museum for Kunst, Copenhagen, Denmark

During his lifetime, Koninck was admired for his portraiture and history and genre scenes, but since his death, his landscapes have become more famous. He developed his unique approach of imaginary, idealized panoramic views by about 1650. Here he continues that model, with a high viewpoint, looking down and across the flat landscape. His extremely lifelike clouds are reflecting in the distant water. A particularly large-scale canvas adds to the sense of significance in this majestic scenic painting.

Merry and Rowdy Peasants at an Inn, Philips Wouwerman, 1653, oil on canvas, 69.9 x 111.8 0cm (27½ x 44 0in), Minneapolis Institute of Art, USA

Another landscape combined with a genre painting, this moralizes about the dangers of drinking too much alcohol. While the landscape is painted realistically, the figures are rather comical. Wouwerman painted colourfully-dressed peasants misbehaving in their drunkenness. Some are skinny-dipping, a man is relieving himself on a fence post, another is brandishing a knife while his wife clings to his leg, and others dance, stumble or are helped home.

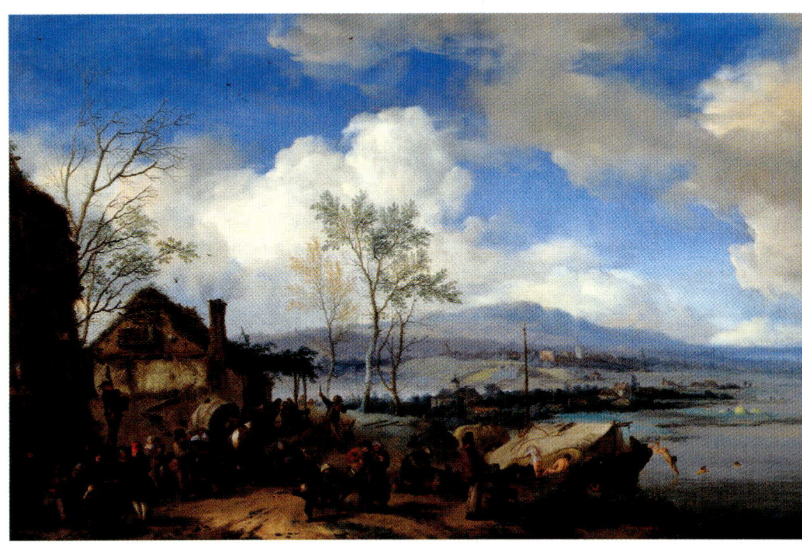

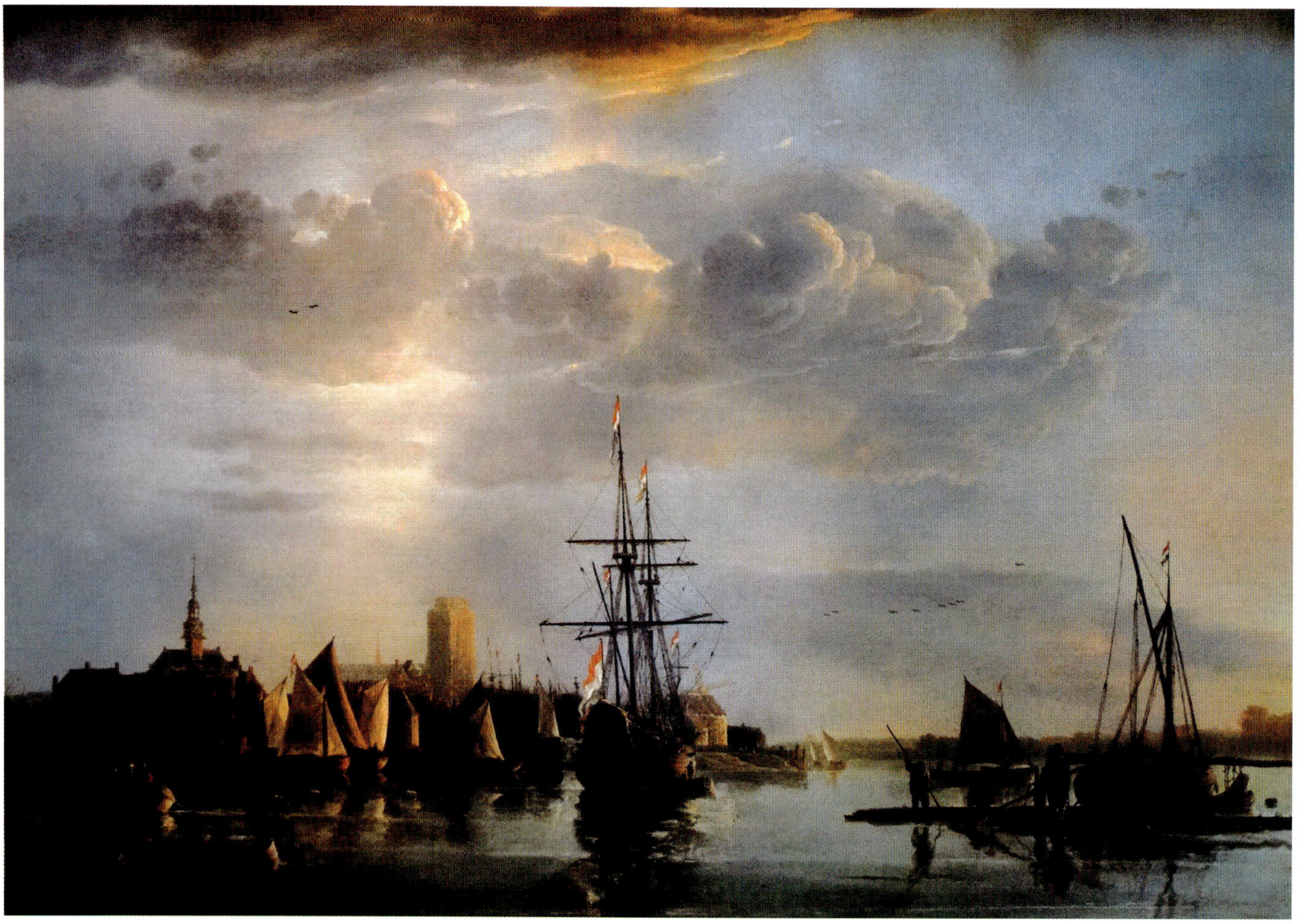

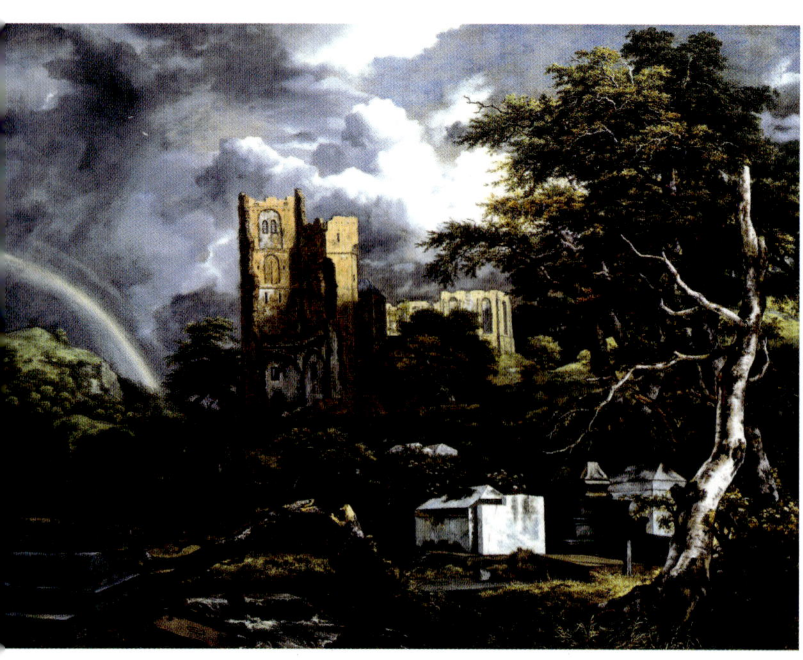

View of Dordrecht, Aelbert Cuyp, *c*.1655, oil on canvas, 97.8 x 137.8cm (38½ x 54¼ in), Kenwood House, London, UK

After abandoning his early grey-green palette, Aelbert Cuyp adopted the style that has become known as 'Italianate.' This work shows that approach; it is a typically Dutch scene, but treated with a golden Italian light. The boats on the River Maas have touches of yellow ochre and white to impart a slightly warmer colour than the usual cool grey-greens, and the sky, though cloudy, has a golden tone.

The Jewish Cemetery, Jacob van Ruisdael, *c*.1654–55, oil on canvas, 142.2 x 189.2cm (56 x 74½ in), Detroit Institute of Arts, Michigan, USA

The ruins of a church and convent can be seen on the hill, while in the middle ground are the marble tombs of the Portuguese Jewish community of Amsterdam. In the foreground is a broken tree, a flowing stream and a tomb of black marble bearing an inscription. The rainbow is an enduring sign from the Bible, which suggests that the picture may imply the promise of the afterlife.

The Castle of Muiden in Winter, Jan Abrahamsz Beerstraten, 1658, oil on canvas, 96.5 x 129.5cm (38 x 51in), The National Gallery, London, UK

Jan Abrahamsz Beerstraaten (1622–66) was a Dutch painter of marine art and landscapes. This is the castle of Muiden, situated about seven miles east of Amsterdam. It probably dates from the 14th century and here, Beerstraaten portrays it from a direct viewpoint, as if he was painting on the spot, capturing the figures out enjoying the icy weather, skating, playing kolf and sliding.

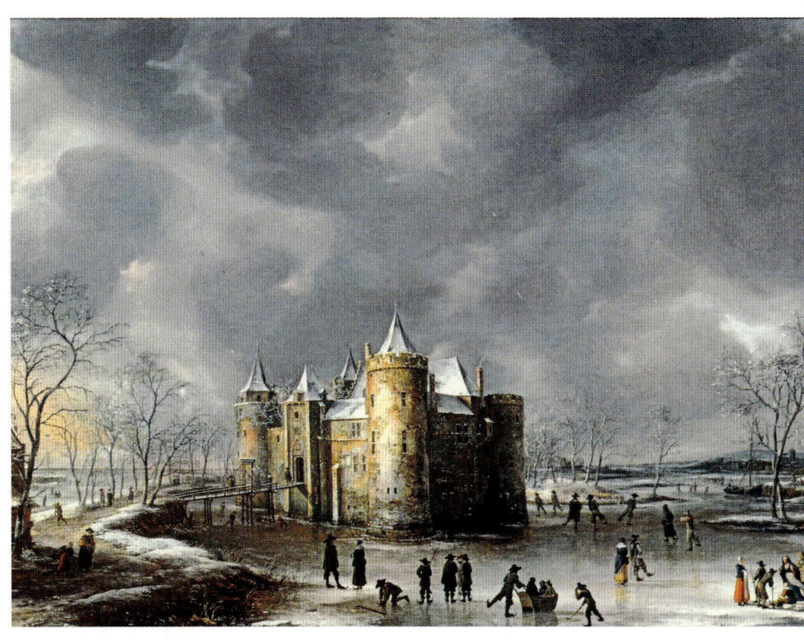

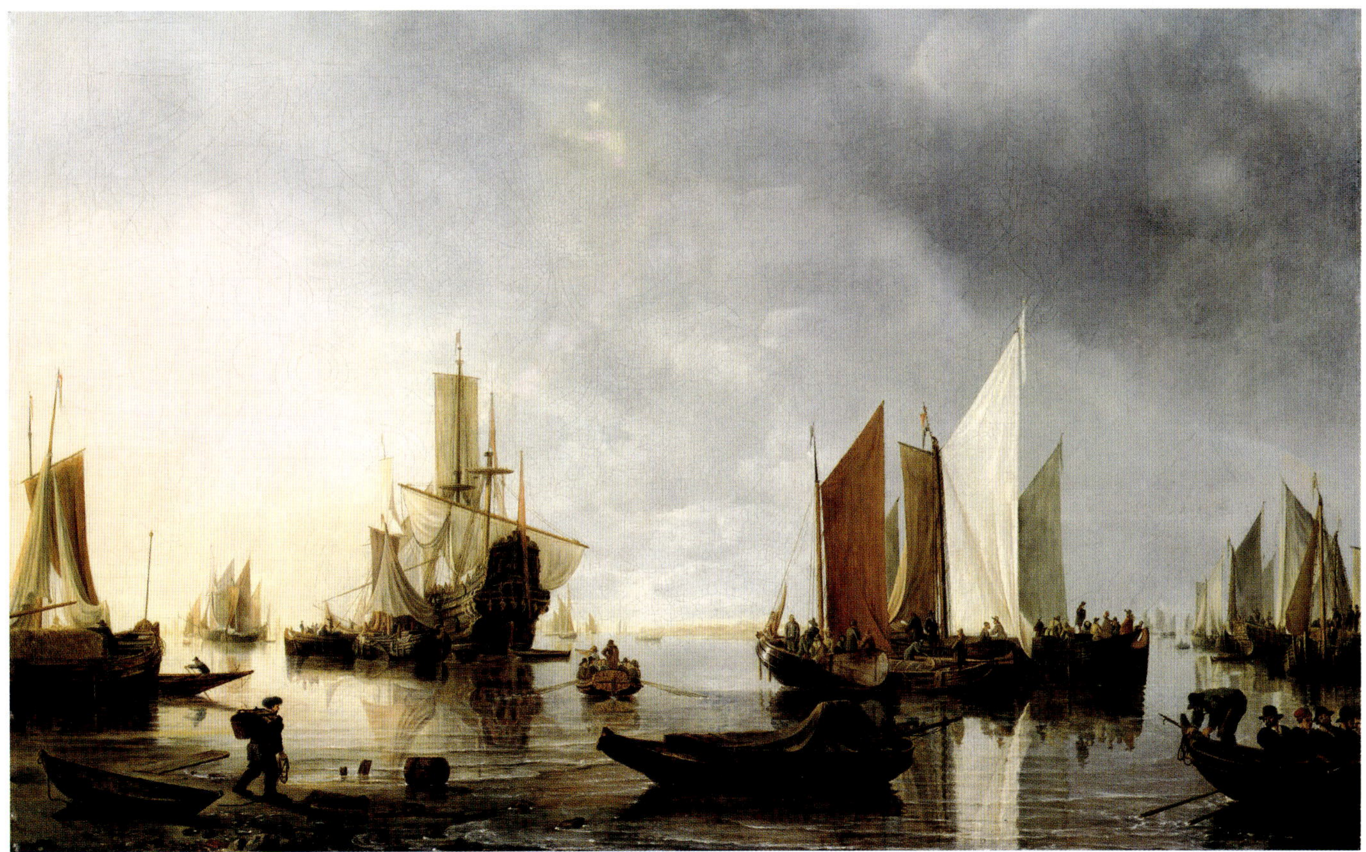

Harbour with Moored Ships, Hendrick Dubbels, 1655–60, oil on canvas, 58 x 90.7cm (22¾ x 35¾in), Gemaeldegalerie Alte Meister, Kassel, Germany

Influenced by Jan van de Cappelle, Hendrick Dubbels (1621–1707) spent his entire career in Amsterdam, painting marine subjects and winter landscapes. During the late 1650s or early 1660s he trained with Ludolf Bakhuizen, who was a leading Dutch marine painter of the time. With its low horizon and atmospheric sky, this tranquil scene depicts a typical Dutch harbour, and conveys Dubbel's prowess in depicting light.

Dunes at Scheveningen, Adriaen van de Velde, c.1659, oil on wood, 24.3 x 32.5cm (9½ x 12¾in), Indianapolis Museum of Art, Indiana, USA

A gentle wind blows the fishing boats to shore at Scheveningen, a town about three miles north of The Hague. Within the scene, meticulously painted figures cast long shadows across the sand. From the 1620s, scenes featuring sand dunes became popular in the Dutch Republic, and here, van de Velde unites the sand and skyline, using pale, harmonious tones and colours.

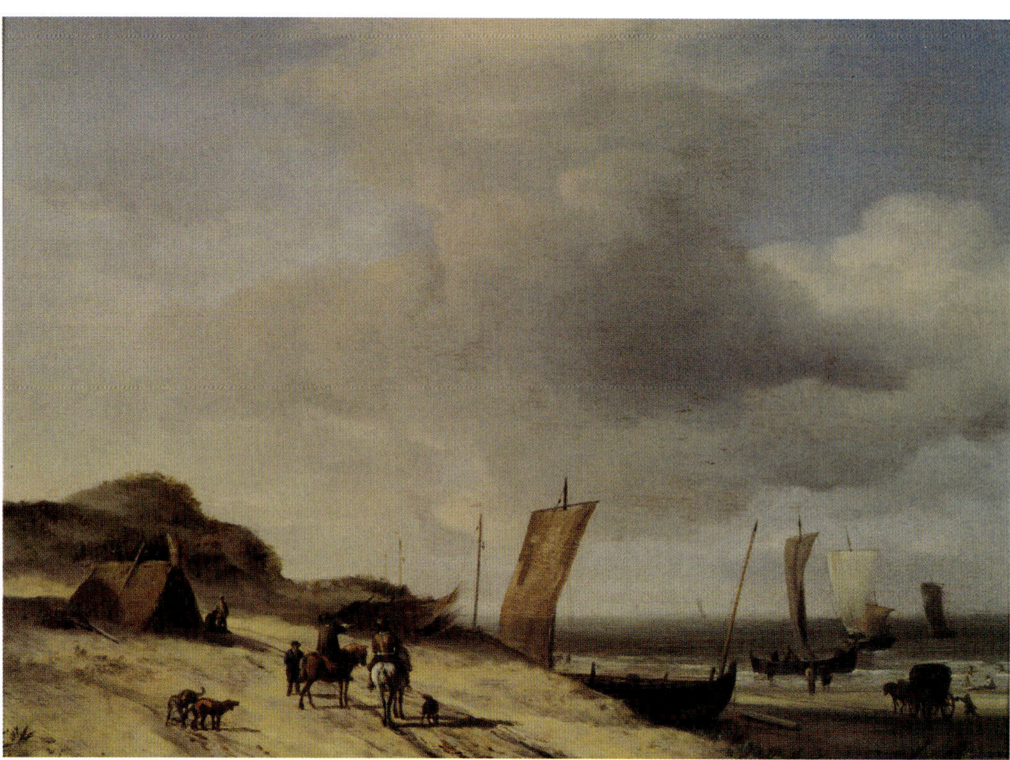

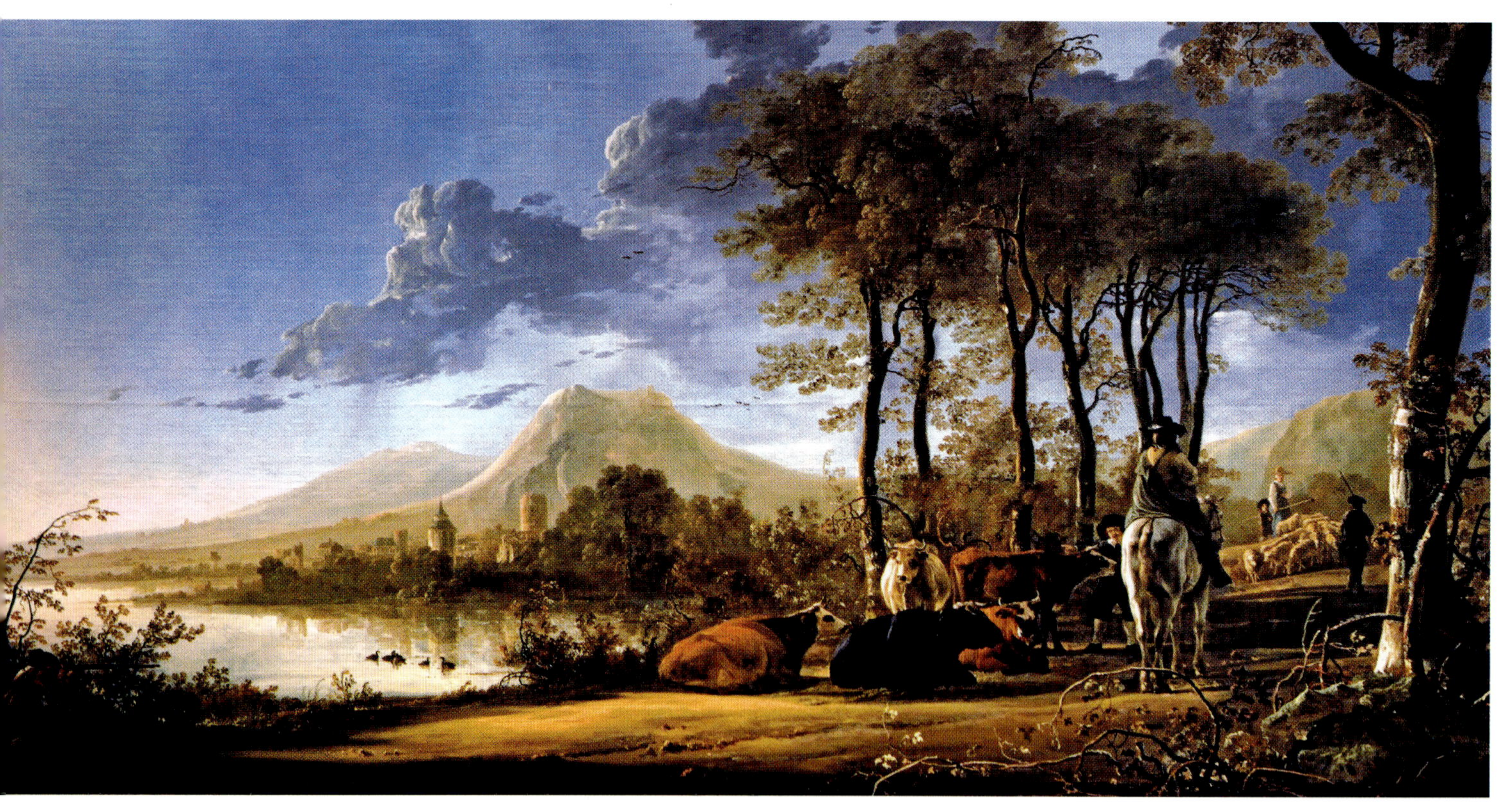

River Landscape with Horseman and Peasants, Aelbert Cuyp, c.1658–60, oil on canvas, 123 x 241cm (48½ x 95in), The National Gallery, London, UK

Bathed in a soft, gentle light, this is the largest known landscape painted by Cuyp. Reflecting the craze for Italian-style scenes at that time, Cuyp depicts hazy, sunlit mountains in the distance that seem to derive from Italy rather than the Netherlands, mainly through his use of a warmer palette. The calm, still water and animals in the foreground or middle ground rather than in the distance were additional features to landscape painting that Cuyp became particularly known for.

A Woodland Landscape,
Jacob van Ruisdael, early
1660s, oil on canvas, 61 x
84.5cm (24 x 33¼ in), The
Barber Institute of Fine Arts,
Birmingham, UK

Within this pastoral scene,
life continues. For instance,
a drover pauses as his
animals cross a river, and
beyond a bridge, sheep
graze in a meadow. Van
Ruisdael's landscapes such
as this presented viewers
with lifelike scenes, but he
idealized them, giving hints
of what might lie beyond
the path and the river but
not revealing anything. The
animals and figures were
probably painted by Adriaen
van de Velde.

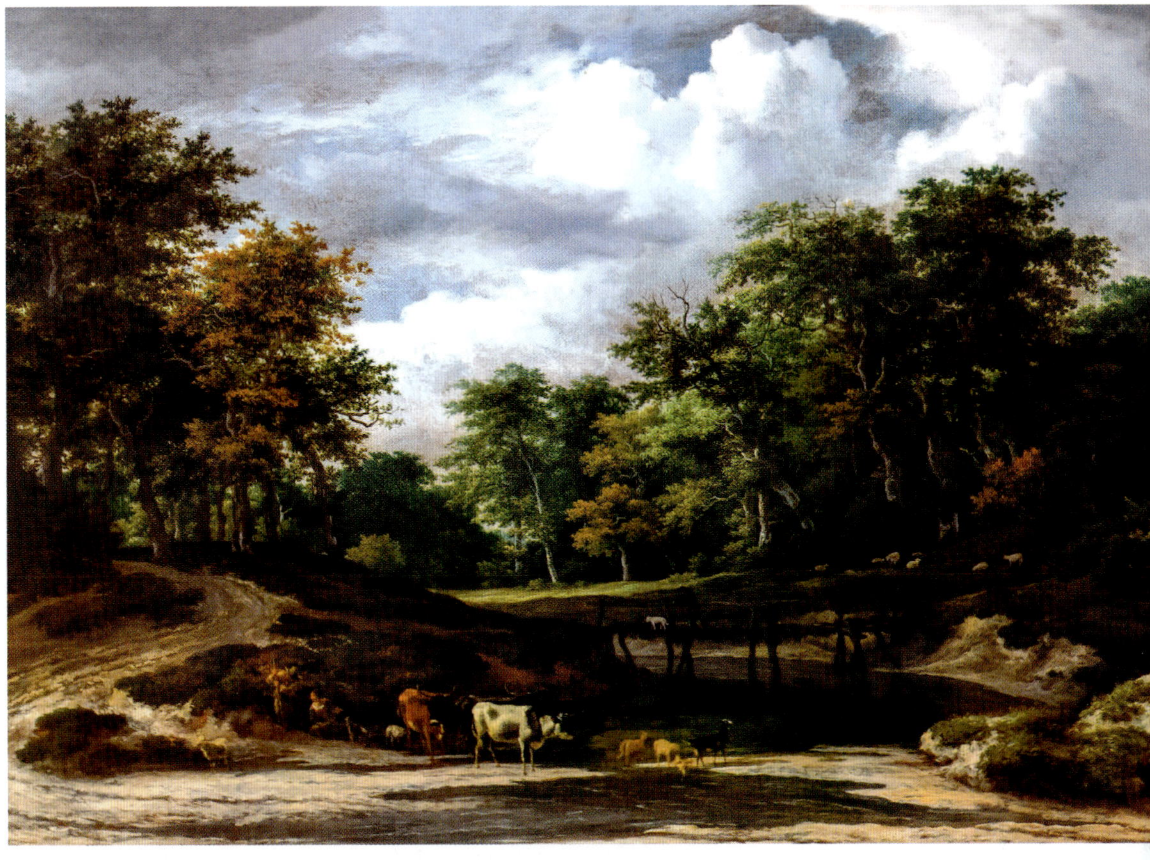

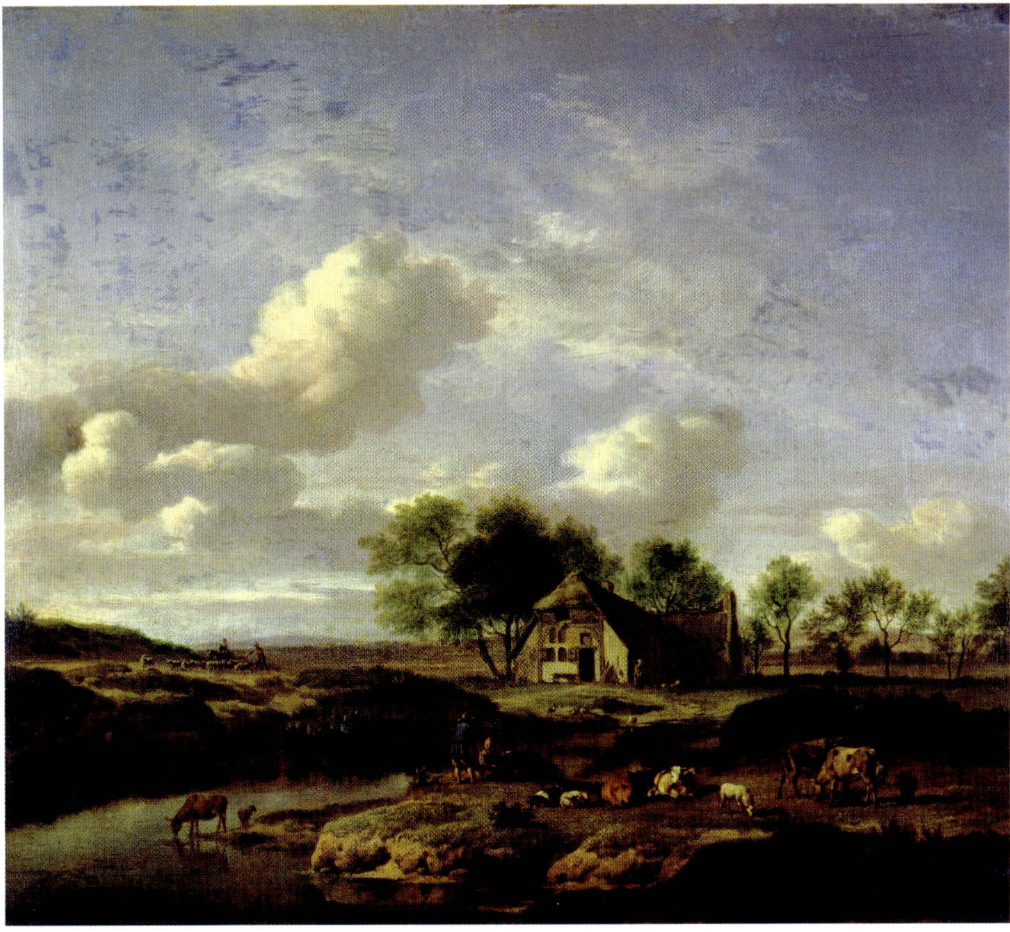

*A Landscape with a Farm by
a Stream,* Adriaen van de
Velde, 1661, oil on canvas,
32.3 x 35.4cm (12¾ x
14in), The National Gallery,
London, UK

With the composition
almost cut in half, this view
stretches over a calm and
peaceful landscape. The eye
is led along the winding river
towards the farmhouse in
the middle distance, while
dramatic cloud formations
create a sense of scale.
The land stretches away,
far beyond the screen of
trees on the right. This is
an imaginary landscape
however, as unlike many of
his contemporaries who
painted views from direct
observation, van de Velde
created his own made-up
scenes.

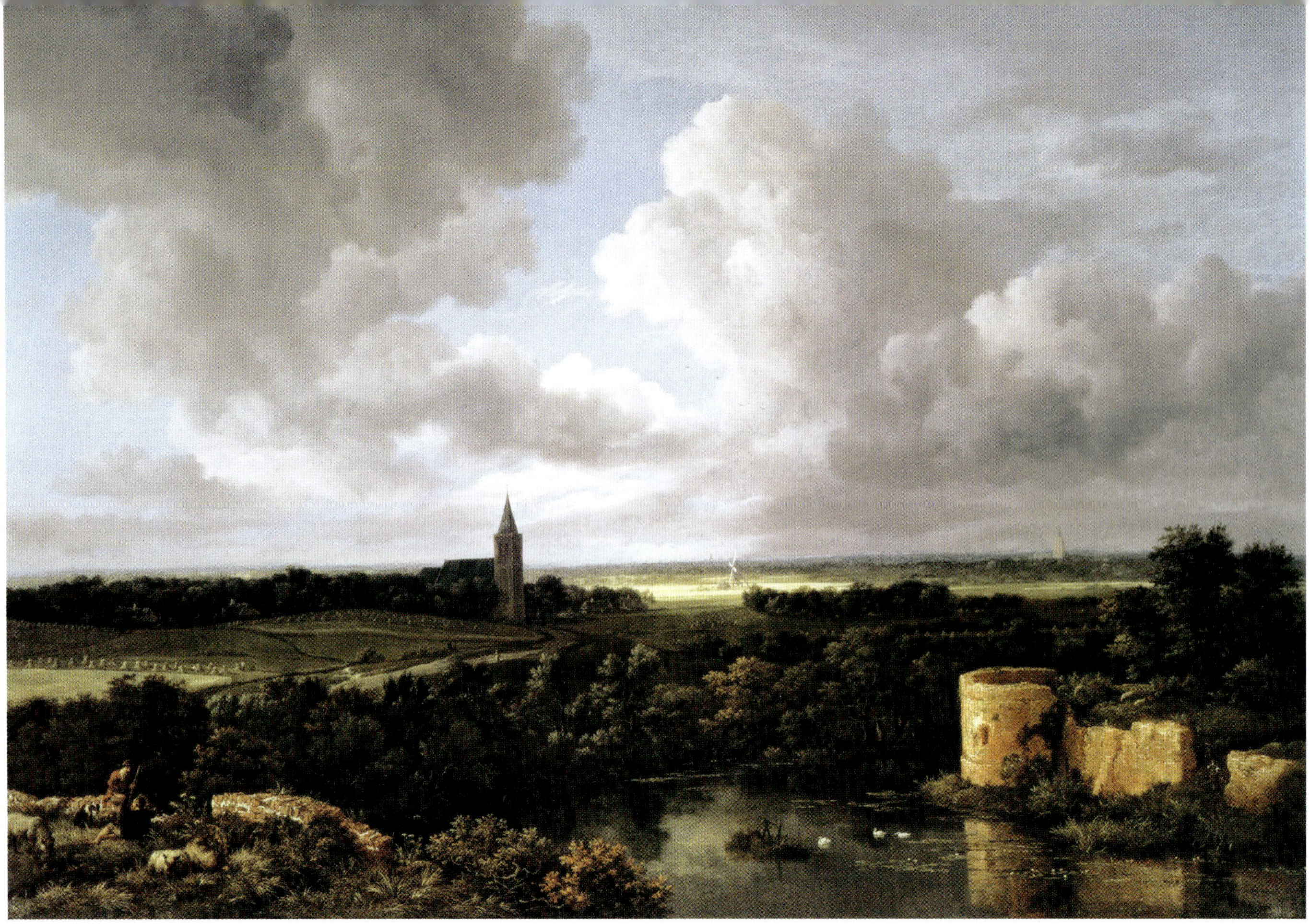

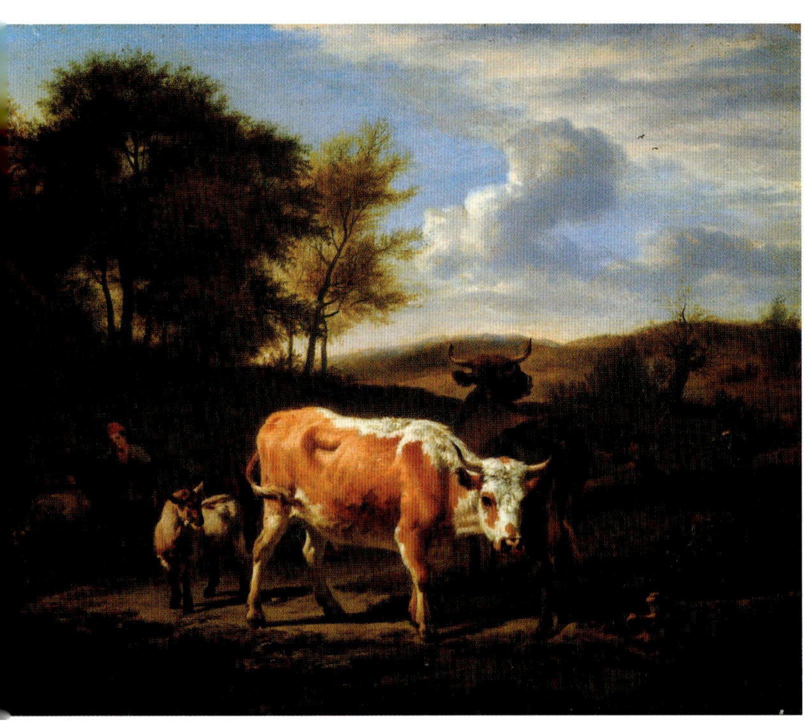

Landscape with a Ruined Castle and a Church, Jacob van Ruisdael, *c.*1665–70, oil on canvas, 109 x 146cm (43 x 57½in), The National Gallery, London, UK

Atmospheric and skilful, this is one of van Ruisdael's most famed landscapes. With a slither of land at the bottom of the composition, the scene is dominated by the heavy clouds with a ray of sunshine filtering through, illuminating fields in the middle distance. While the land is shaped by horizontal lines, the clouds are structured more on diagonals, only interrupted by the vertical lines of the church and ruined castle turret.

Mountainous Landscape with Cows, Adriaen van de Velde, 1663, oil on panel, 30 x 36.5cm (11¾ x 14¼in), Rijksmuseum, Amsterdam, Netherlands

A child prodigy, during his lifetime Adriaen van de Velde was recognized as an outstanding painter of people and animals. He often painted figures in other artists' landscapes and townscapes. His favourite subjects were country scenes, including sheep, cattle and goats, and this landscape with animals shows his attention to detail, his imperceptible brushstrokes, clear understanding of colour, tone and composition, and his skilful draughtsmanship. Van de Velde made meticulous preparatory drawings for landscape paintings such as these.

Despite his success during his lifetime and the massive value placed on his work in the century after he died, van de Velde was plagued with money troubles. His wife ran a linen shop to help make ends meet, but it was not enough. When he died, the sale of all his possessions did not cover the debts.

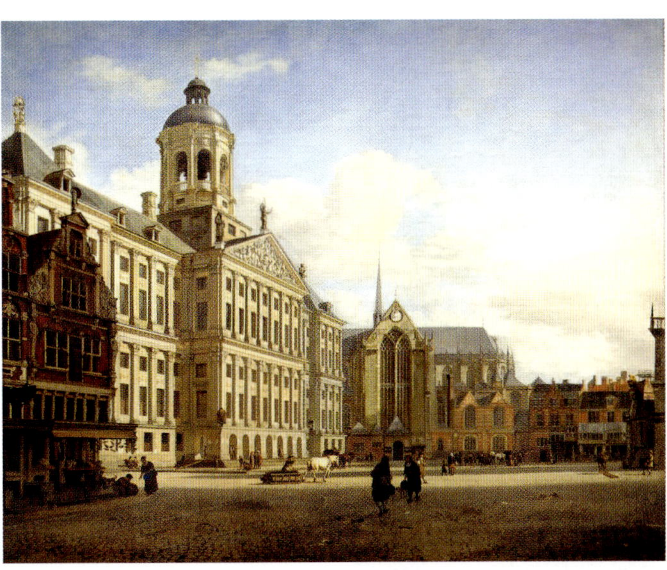

The Dam with the New Town Hall in Amsterdam, Jan van der Heyden, 1668, 73 x 86cm (28¾ x 33¾in), Musée du Louvre, Paris, France

Amsterdam's town hall had started to be built 40 years before Jan van der Heyden painted this view of it standing proudly, set against a soft sky. It later became the Royal Palace. With crisp contours and clear colours, the grandeur of the building is set off in a gentle, golden light. For the people of Amsterdam, the building announced the city's freedom, confidence, individuality and strength.

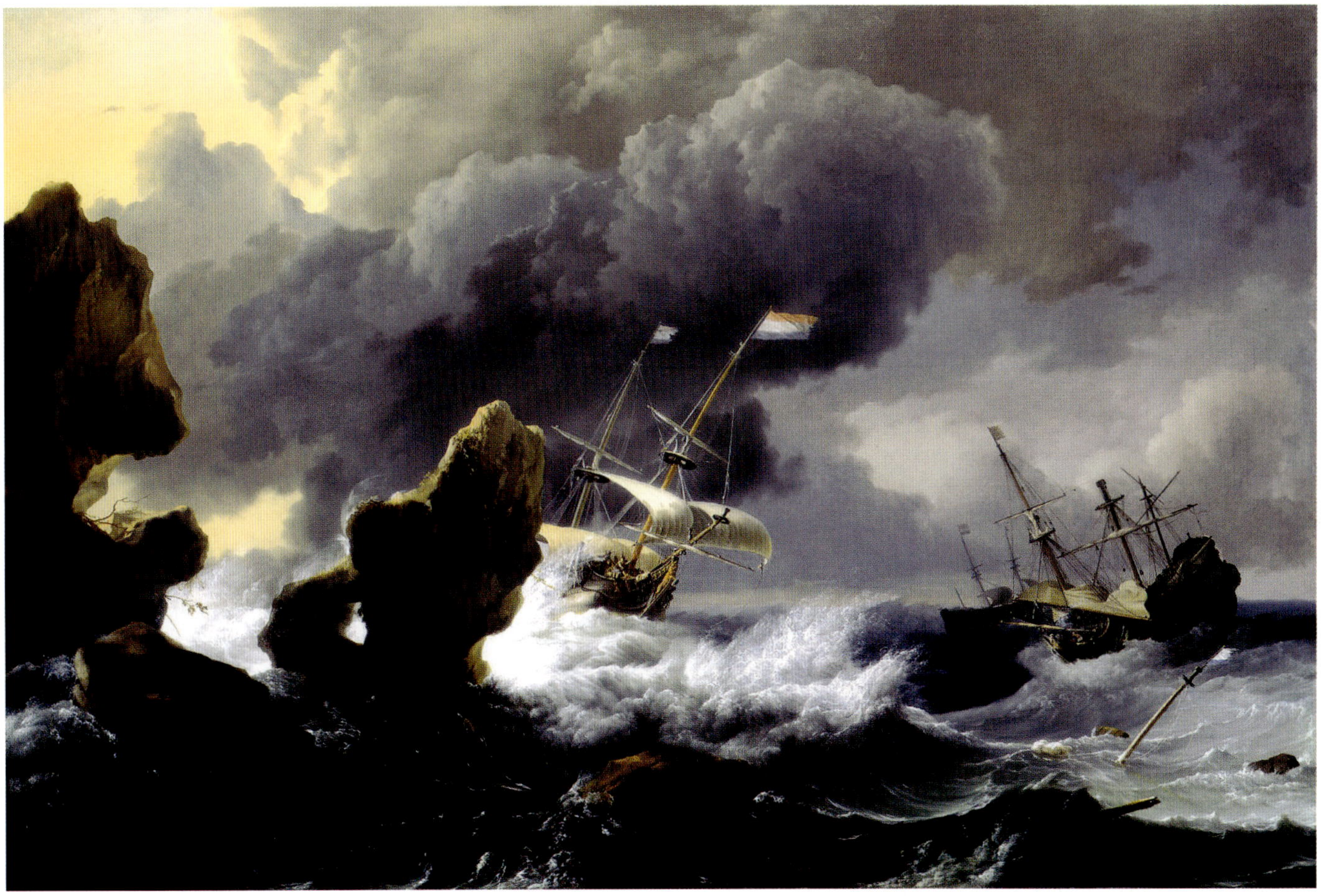

Ships in Distress off a Rocky Coast, Ludolf Bakhuizen, 1667, oil on canvas, 114.3 x 167.3cm (45 x 65¾in), National Gallery of Art, Washington DC, USA

These three cargo ships represent the powerful vessels that helped to generate Dutch wealth in the 17th century. Yet in this violent storm they are in peril, at risk of crashing on to the rocks. In the right foreground, one ship has already been wrecked. Although this painting shows the precariousness of trade by sea travel, it also represents hope as the sun's rays are breaking through the heavy clouds.

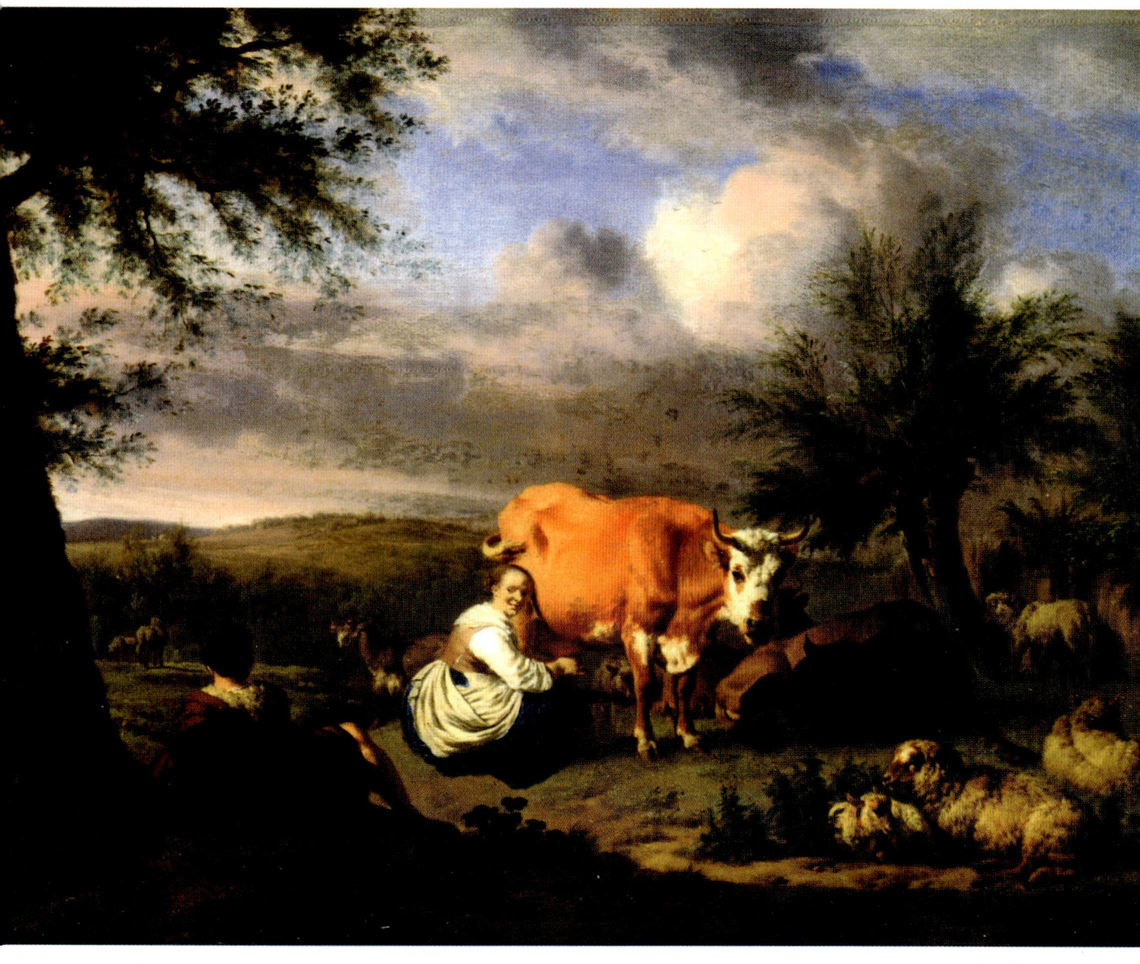

Woman Milking a Cow,
Adriaen van de Velde,
c.1669, oil on canvas, 31.2
x 39.8cm (12¼ x 15⅔in),
Cannon Hall Museum,
Barnsley, UK

Although he painted
Italianate landscapes,
Adriaen van de Velde
never travelled beyond his
native Netherlands. Both
his brother Willem and
their father were marine
painters, but Adriaen chose
to paint landscapes. He
gathered material outdoors
through drawings and
sketches, but unlike most of
his contemporaries, he also
worked from human models
in his studio.

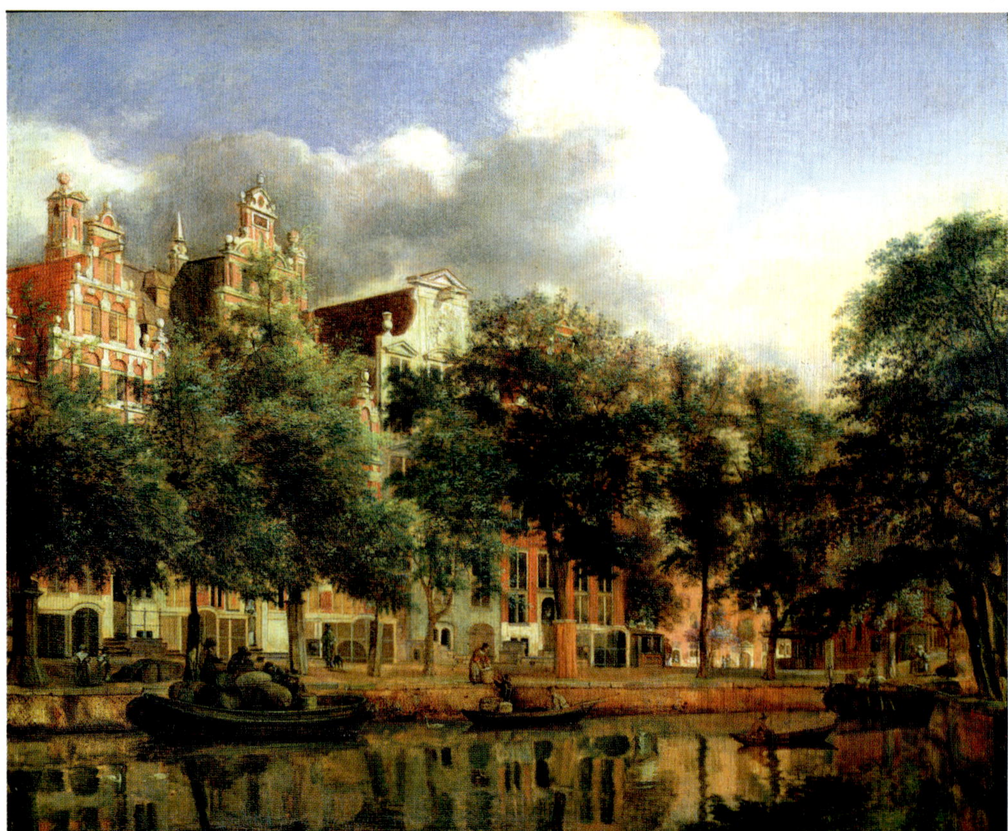

The Herengracht, Amsterdam,
Jan van der Heyden, 1670,
oil on panel, 36.5 x 44cm
(14½ x 17¼ in), Musée du
Louvre, Paris, France

In 1669, the whole of
Amsterdam was illuminated
by Jan van der Heyden's
invention of glass lanterns
and oil lamps. He also
painted views of the city
in natural light like this. His
refined brushwork and
bright colours convey every
detail of the fashionable
Herengracht, a street lined
with huge lime trees that
hide large parts of the
houses flanking the broad
canal.

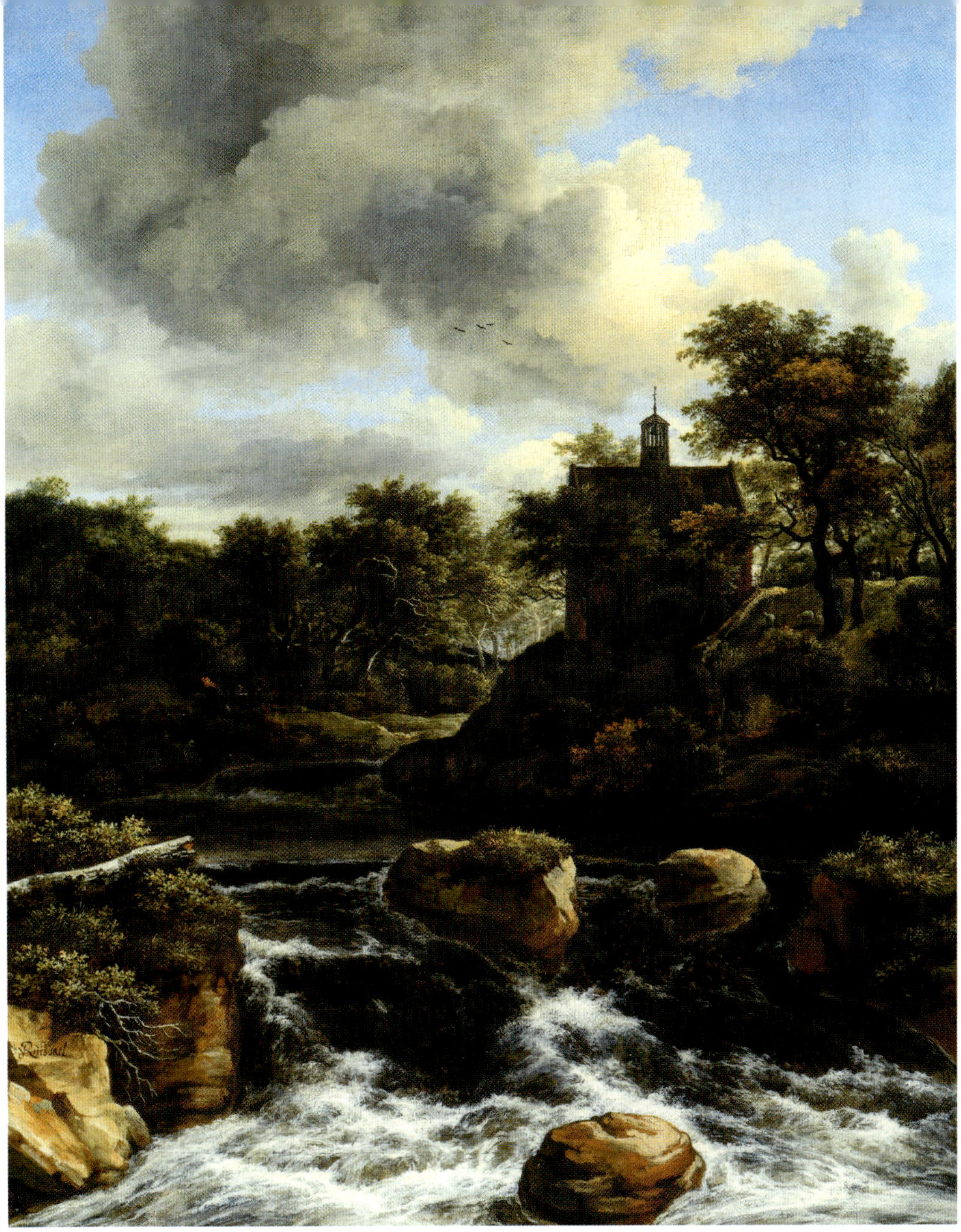

Chapel by a Waterfall, Jacob van Ruisdael, c.1670, oil on canvas, 69 x 53.3cm (27 x 21in), Mauritshuis, The Hague, Netherlands

After being inspired by the work of the Amsterdam artist Allart van Everdingen, who had visited Scandinavia in 1644 and made many drawings of mountainous scenes with waterfalls and torrents, from the late 1650s Jacob van Ruisdael painted many waterfalls. Depicted from a low viewpoint, here a silhouetted church tower rises up in the distance, calm and solid against the wildness of nature.

Landscape with a Shrine, Frederick de Moucheron and Adriaen van de Velde, c.1665–80, oil on canvas, 87.6 x 118.5cm (34½ x 46½in), Cannon Hall Museum, Barnsley, UK

Frederick de Moucheron (1633–86) was born in Emden in Germany. After spending time in France and possibly Italy, he visited Antwerp before settling in Amsterdam. He painted Italianate landscapes, reminiscent of Jan Both and Adam Pynacker, and he became known for his method of painting delicate foliage. This scene with a classical shrine and distant castle are created from aspects of true locations plus de Moucheron's imagination. Adriaen van de Velde frequently painted the figures in his scenes.

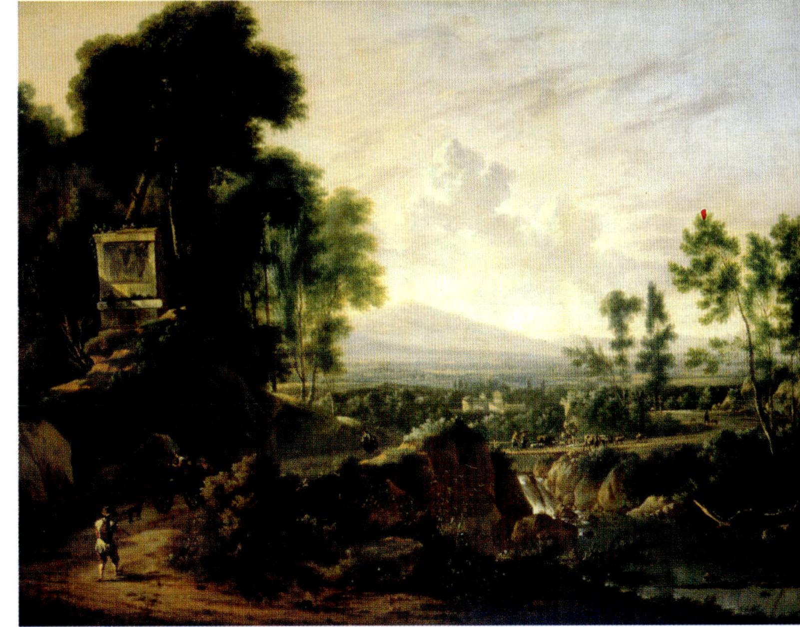

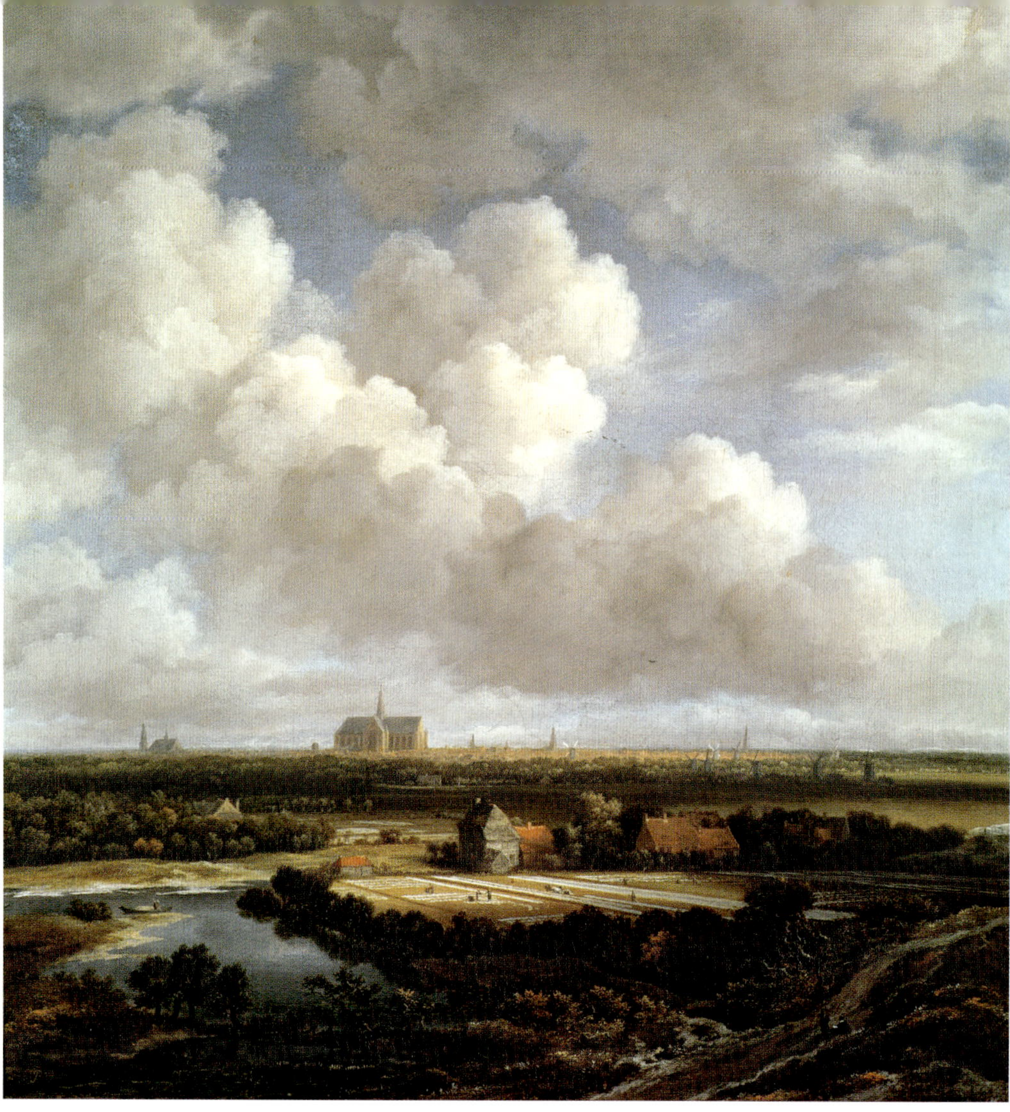

Bleaching Ground in the Countryside, Jacob van Ruisdael, *c.*1670, oil on canvas, 62.2 x 55.2cm (24½ x 21¾in), Kunsthaus Zürich, Zurich, Switzerland

One of van Ruisdael's best-known paintings, this is a pool surrounded with trees and a road leading towards the right. In the middle distance are the bleaching-grounds, which were open areas used for spreading out textiles to be whitened and purified by sunlight. In the painting large pieces of linen can be seen, with figures working. Haarlem is in the distance with the church of Saint Bavo, while above are billowing clouds against a blue sky. Shafts of sunlight illuminate part of the town and the bleaching fields below.

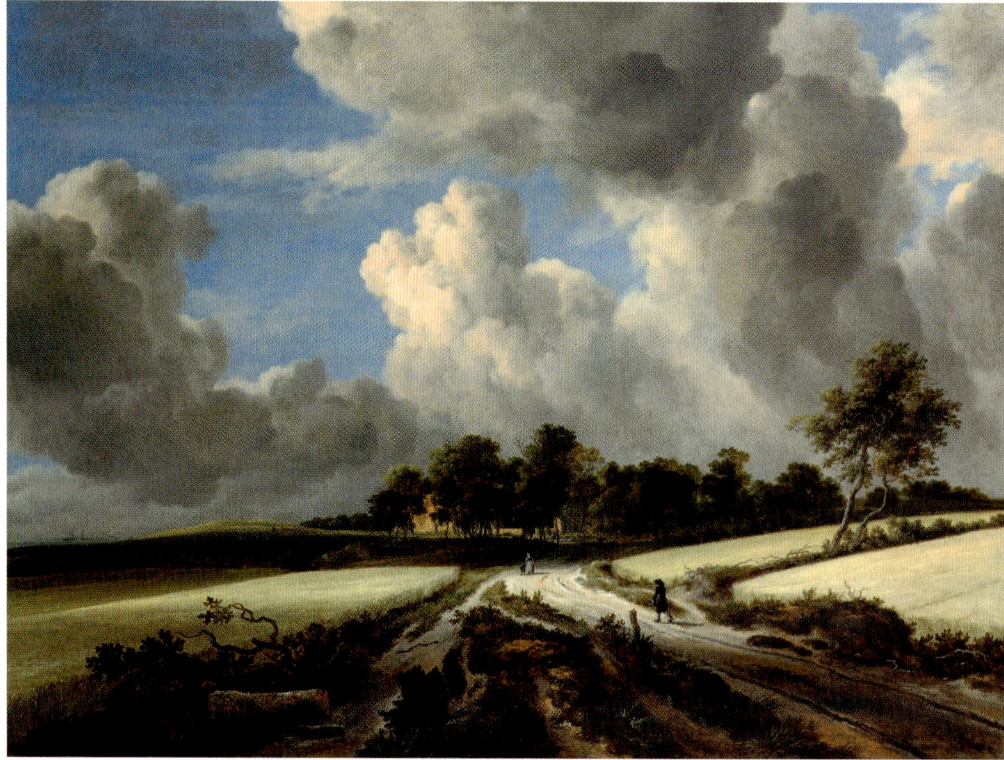

Wheat Fields, Jacob van Ruisdael, *c.*1670, oil on canvas, 100 x 130.2cm (39¼ x 51¼in), The Metropolitan Museum of Art, New York, USA

Leading the eye into this scene is a path overshadowed by clouds. Under the clouds is a man with a traveller's pack, approaching a woman and child. Behind the trees in the distance there are some buildings, but before the travellers reach them, it seems that the rain will start. Even further in the distance, to the left, is an expanse of the sea and boats.

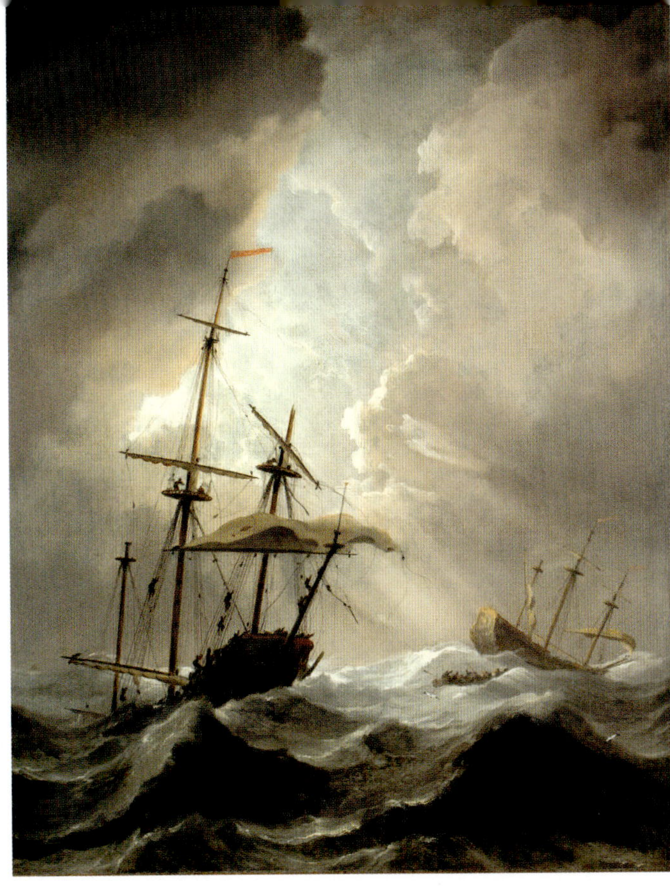

Storm at Sea, Willem van de Velde the Younger, c.1675, oil on panel, 62.5 x 47.3cm (24½ x 18½in), Worcester Art Museum, Massachusetts, USA

The leading Dutch marine painter of the 17th century, Willem van de Velde the Younger moved to England in 1672 and subsequently influenced the development of seascape painting there. This work can be seen to be a forerunner of the work of JMW Turner (1775–1851) although van de Velde's paintings were not usually as emotive as this. In general, they were less dramatic views of ships and events.

Panoramic View of the Amstel, Jacob van Ruisdael, 1675–81, 52.1 x 66.1cm (20½ x 26in), Fitzwilliam Museum, Cambridge, UK

The river fills much of the right-hand side of this painting. Elsewhere is a road with figures, windmills, houses, and a bleaching-ground. The town, with its churches and public buildings, extends in the background. Lilke many of van Ruisdael's landscapes, this painting conveys a harmonious, proud relationship with the land.

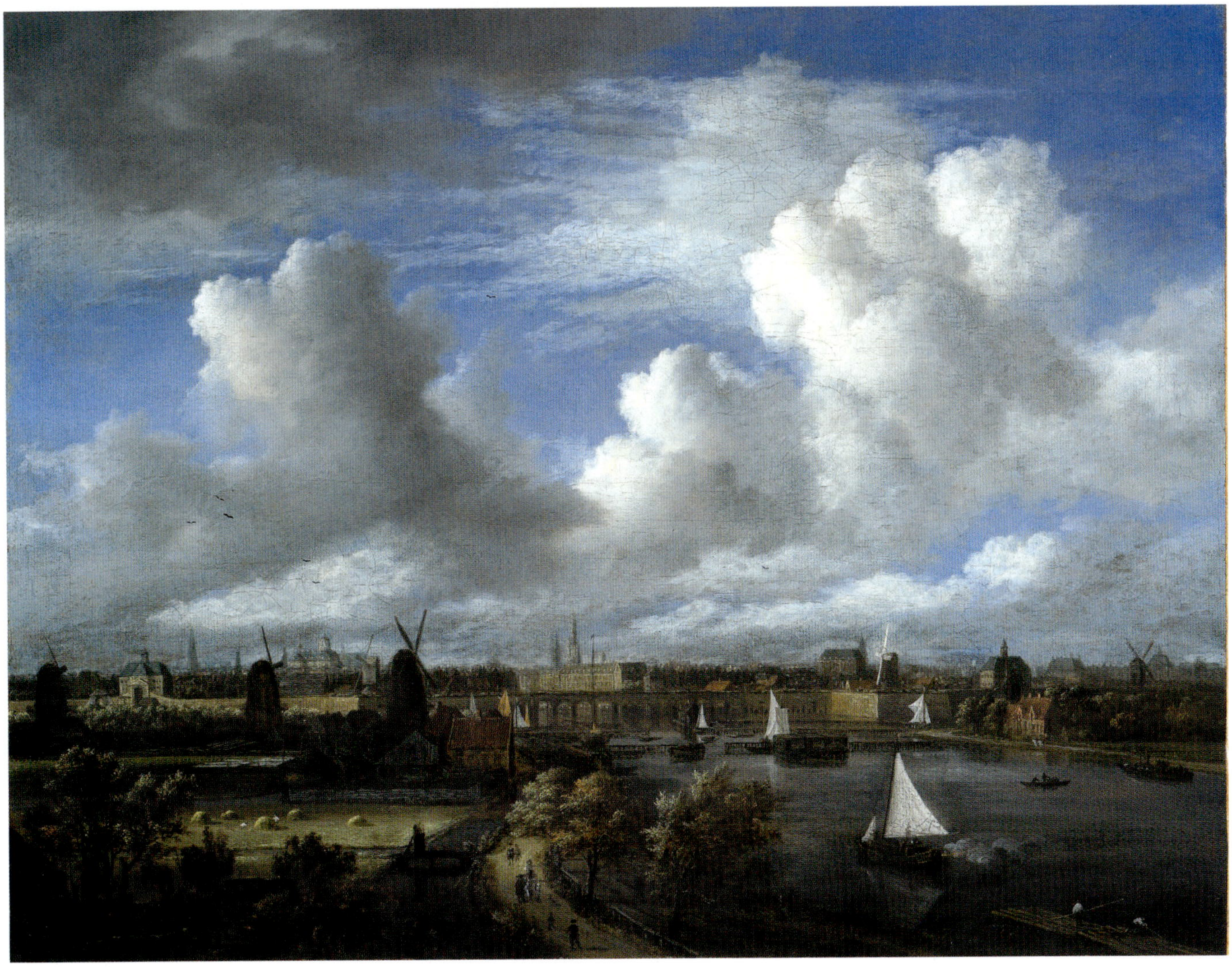

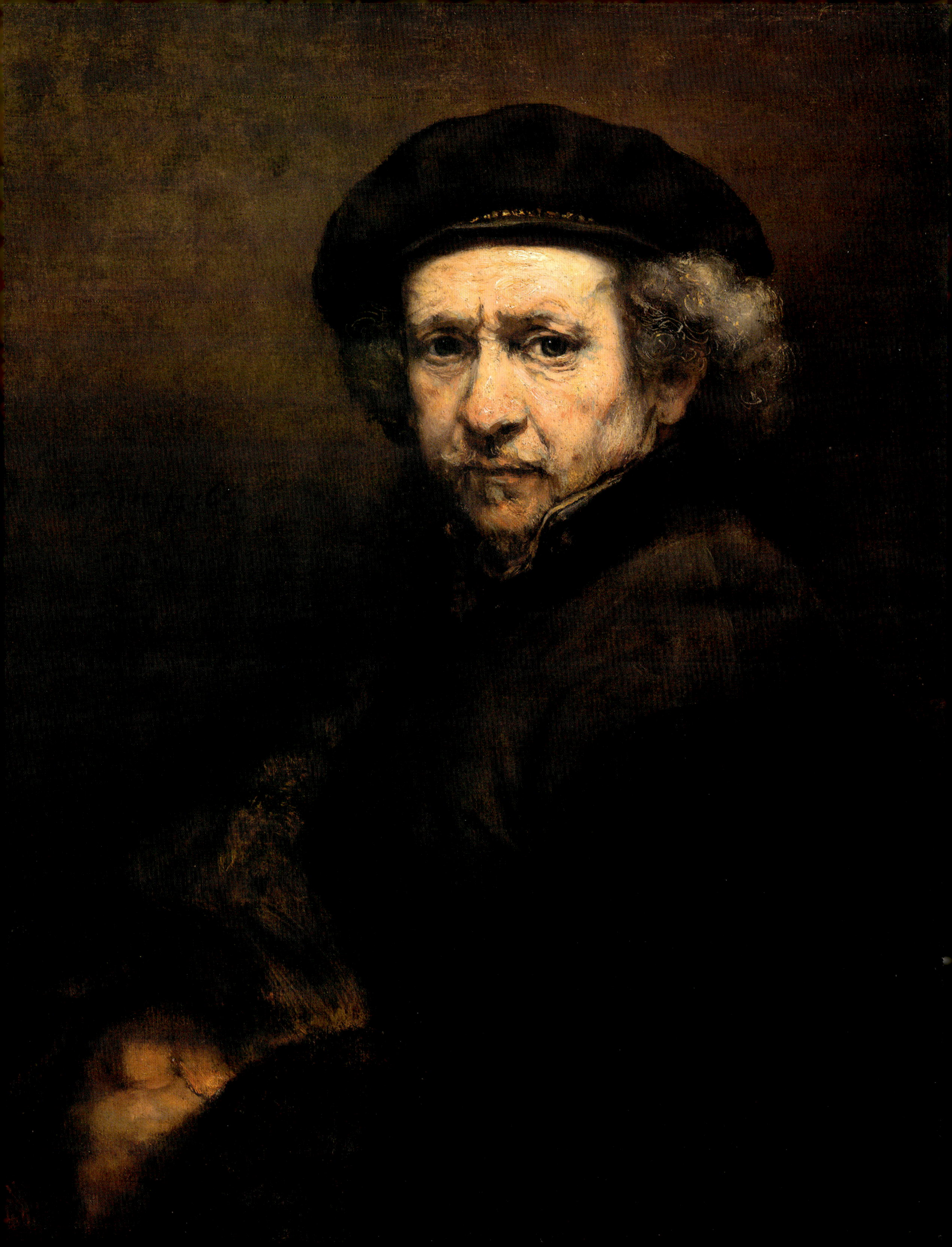

PORTRAITS

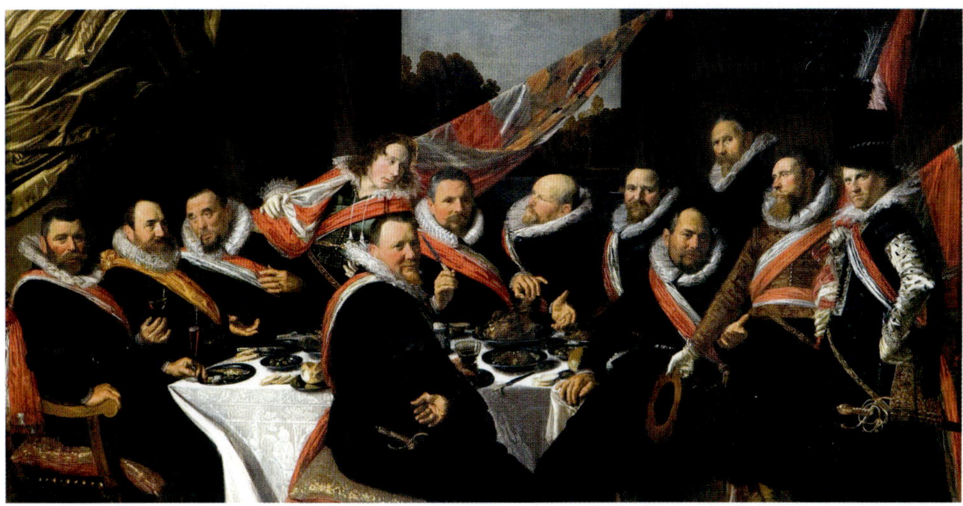

During the Golden Age, merchants and tradesmen with improved financial situations joined the aristocracy and eminent church members in commissioning portraits of themselves, their families, and the guilds to which they belonged. Unlike the more flamboyant Baroque styles fashionable elsewhere in Europe, portraits in the Dutch Republic followed conventions that communicated status, identity and religious attitudes, although there were a number of artists who broke all these rules. Among the greatest portraitists of the period are Rembrandt and Frans Hals, who both abandoned formal restrictions with animated brushwork and relaxed poses. Other successful portraitists include Jan de Bray, Thomas de Keyser, Bartholomeus van der Helst, Ferdinand Bol, Michiel van Mierevelt (1566–1641) and Paulus Moreelse (1571–1638). Self-portraits and tronies continued to be ways in which artists explored their skills. Family and group portraits – largely a Dutch invention – were similarly popular.

Above: Banquet of the Officers of the Saint George Civic Guard Company, *Frans Hals, 1616. Celebrating the vigour and confidence of the new republic, this is the first major group portrait by Hals, depicting the Haarlem civic guard – citizens who undertook military training. After this, many other civic associations commissioned group portraits. Hals, a member of this company, shows great originality by painting each individual vividly.*

Left: Self-Portrait, c.1659. *Three years after he had been forced to declare bankruptcy, after being successful for so long, Rembrandt moved to an artist's quarter in Amsterdam. Here he is 53 years old, and unlike traditional Dutch portraits the painting conveys something of his innermost feelings. It was also inspired by Raphael's portrait of Baldassare Castiglione of c.1514–15, which Rembrandt saw at an auction in Amsterdam in 1639.*

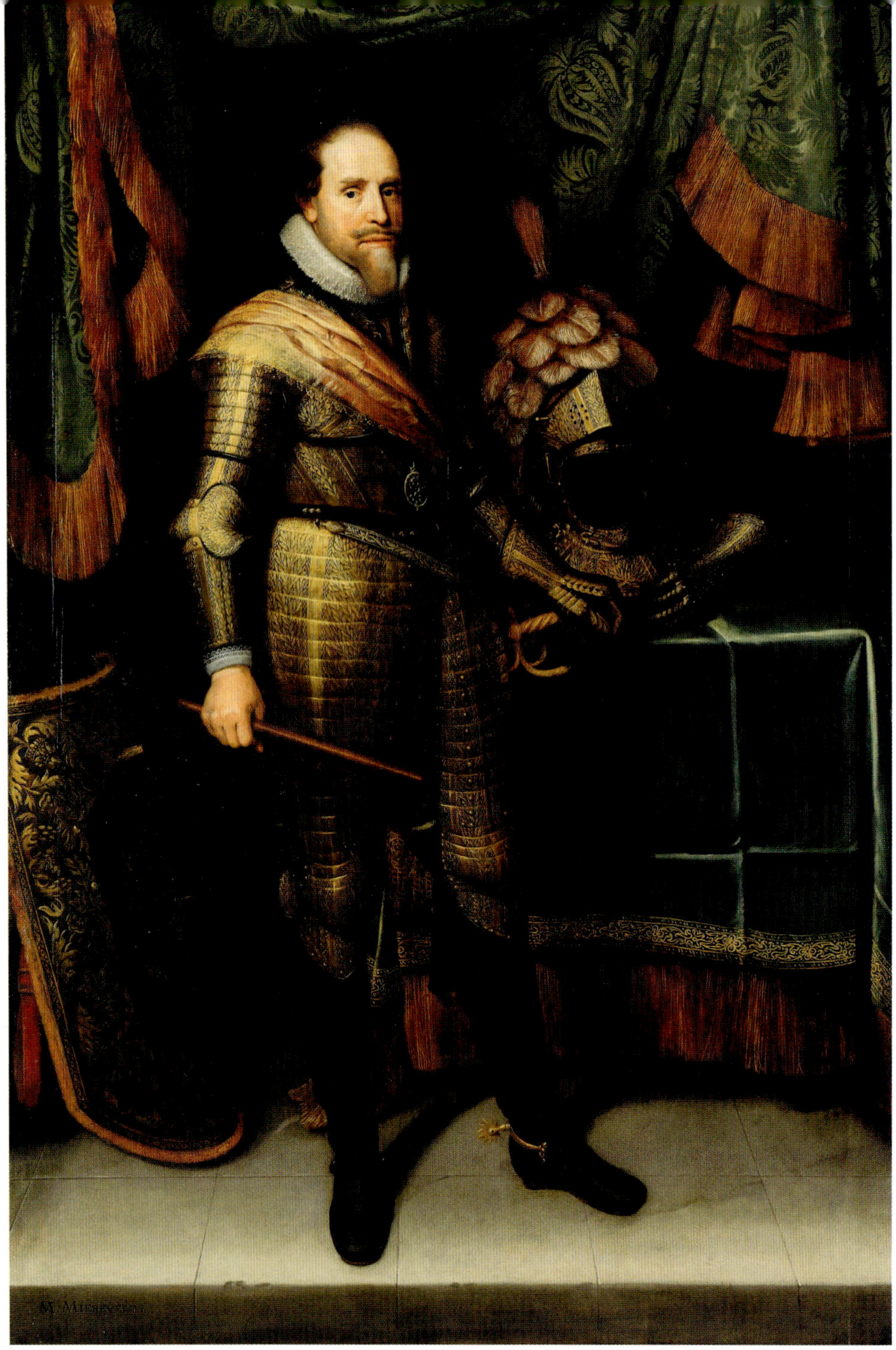

Maurits, Prince of Orange,
Michiel Jansz van Mierevelt,
c.1613–c.1620, oil on panel,
220.3 x 143.5cm (86¾
x 56½in), Rijksmuseum,
Amsterdam, Netherlands

Prince Maurits was
stadtholder of most of the
provinces of the Dutch
Republic. Before he became
Prince of Orange, he was
known as Maurice of Nassau.
Words on the painting state
that he was 40 here, as he
stands in his ceremonial
gilded suit of armour and
orange-plumed helmet with
the staff of office in his right
hand; a sign of his rank as
a general. Van Mierevelt's
detailed portraits made him
one of the most successful
portrait painters of his day
and he employed many
assistants. His use of light and
portrayal of textures were
especially prized.

Hugo Grotius, Jan van
Ravesteyn, 1599, oil on
panel, 31cm (12in) diameter,
Fondation Custodia, Paris,
France

A Catholic and successful
portrait painter at the
court in The Hague, Jan van
Ravesteyn (c.1572–1657)
became one of the founders
of the Confrerie Pictura in
1656; a group of like-minded
painters. Hugo Grotius
(1583–1645), also known
as Huig de Groot or Hugo
de Groot, was a scholar and
prodigy – he was 16 years
old here in this lively three-
quarter profile.

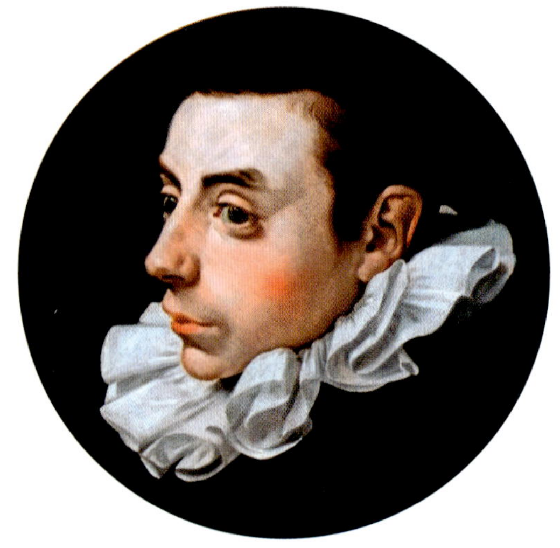

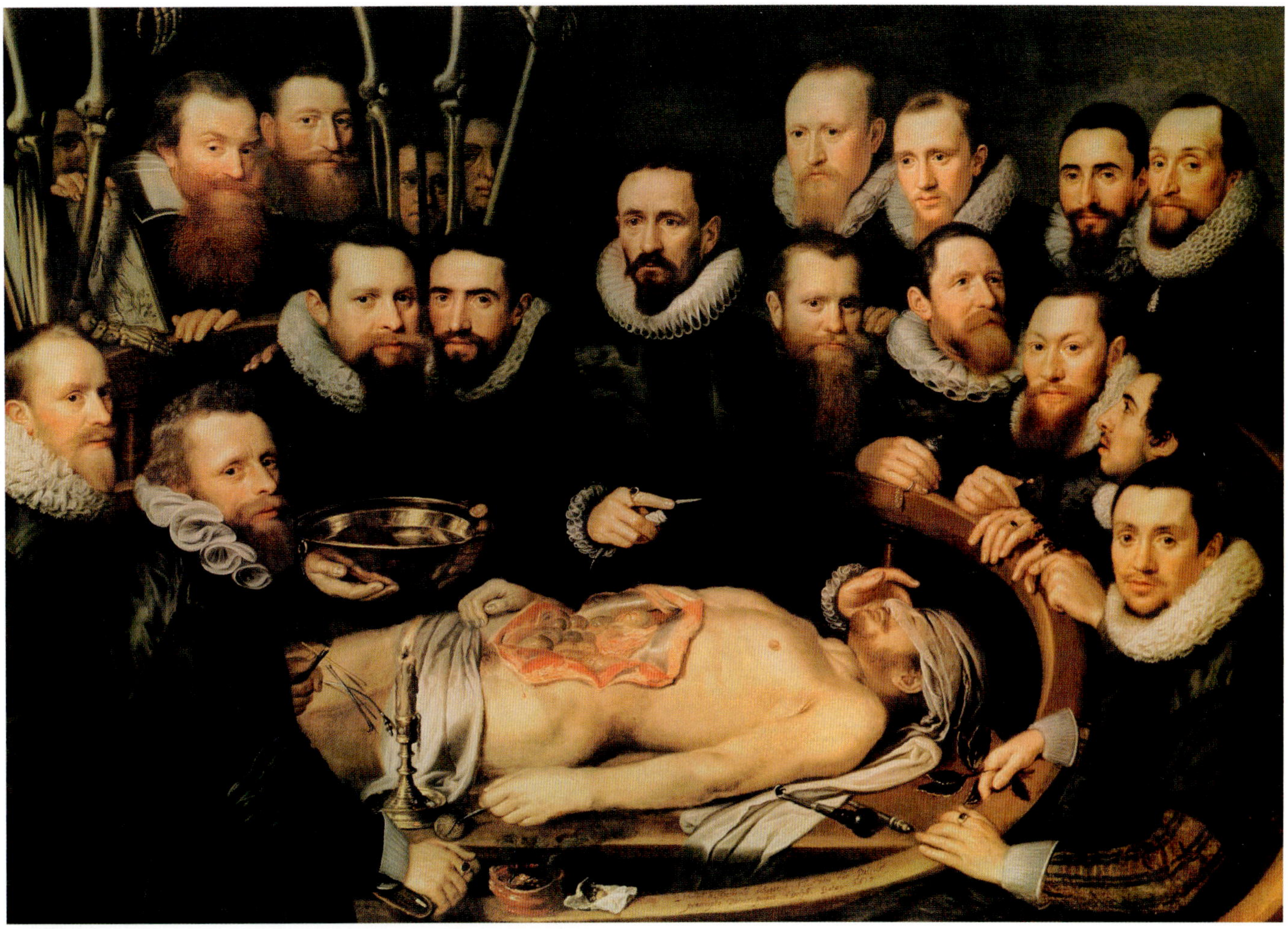

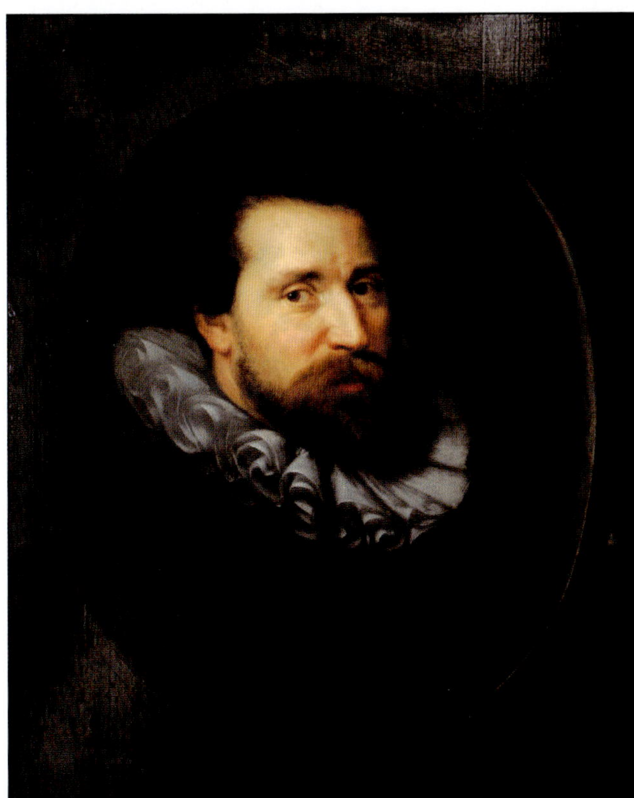

Anatomy Lesson of Dr Willem van der Meer, Michiel Jansz van Mierevelt, 1617, oil on canvas, 144 x 198cm (56⅔ x 78in), Gemeente Musea, Delft, Netherlands

Painted by Michiel Janszoon van Mierevelt (alternatively Miereveld or Miereveldt) (1566–1641) and with the assistance of his eldest son, Pieter Miereveldt (1596–1623), this portrait was commissioned by the surgeon's guild in Delft. It is one of the earliest portraits of this type, showing a doctor giving an anatomy lesson. At that time, van Mierevelt was perceived as the leading painter in Delft.

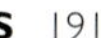

Portrait of Abraham Bloemaert, Paulus Moreelse, 1609, oil on panel, 63.6 x 50.4cm (25 x 21in), Centraal Museum, Utrecht, Netherlands

One of the founders of the Utrecht Guild of Saint Luke, Paulus Moreelse spent time in Italy and on his return became Utrecht's most prominent portraitist. This is his friend and fellow artist Abraham Bloemaert. It is the earliest known portrayal of Bloemaert who was 42 years old at the time. In 1604, Karel van Mander described him as a man of quiet and pleasant character.

Portrait of Laurens Reael, Cornelis van der Voort, *c.*1620, oil on canvas, 223 x 117cm (87 x 46in), Rijksmuseum, Amsterdam, Netherlands

The most important portrait painter in Amsterdam during his career, Cornelis van der Voort (1576–1624) painted Laurens Reael (1583–1637) when the lawyer was in his late 30s. In 1616, Reael had been appointed governor-general of the Dutch East India Company in Asia, and when he returned to the Netherlands, he commissioned van der Voort to paint him full-length; the type of portrait usually only commissioned by royalty or aristocracy.

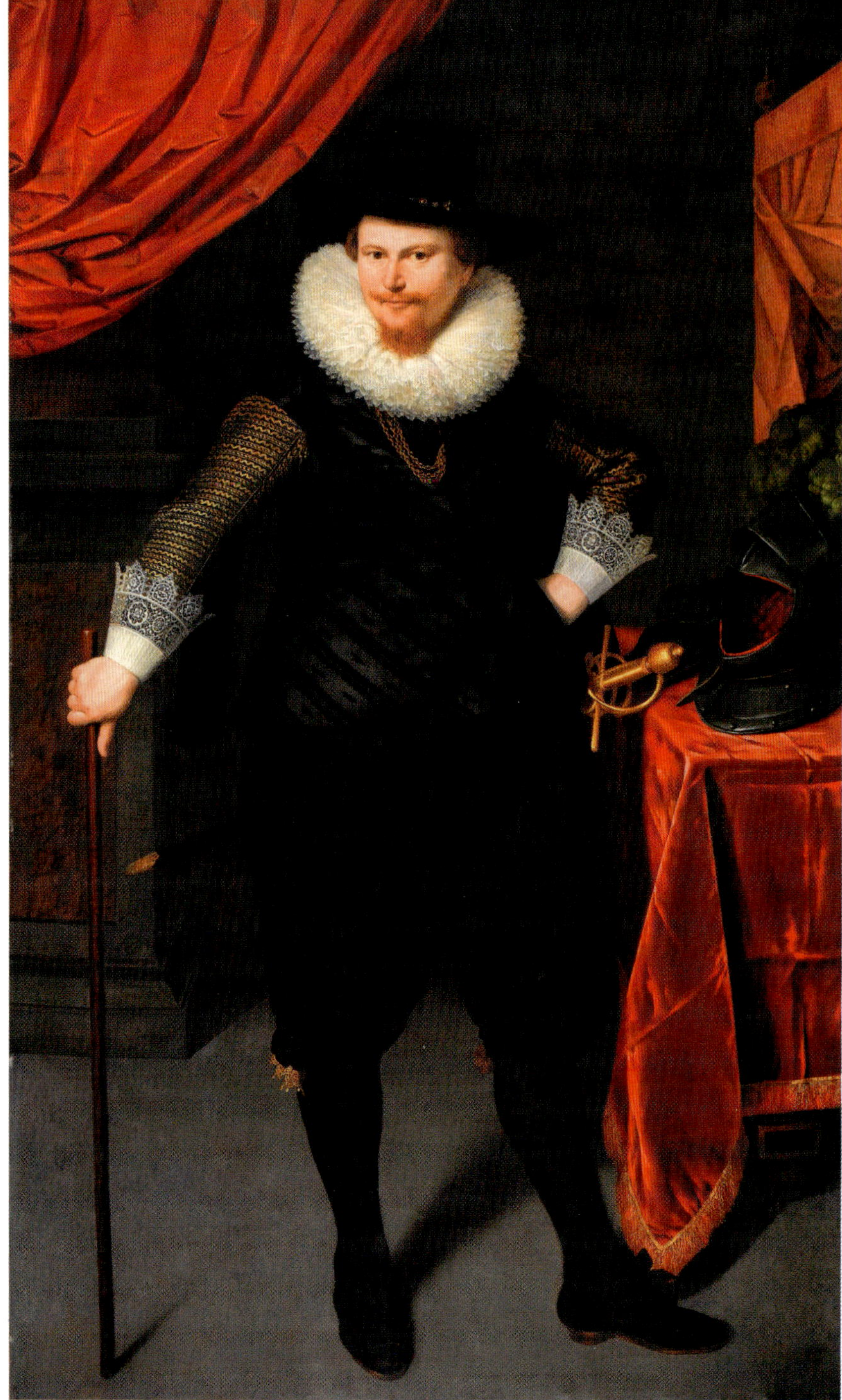

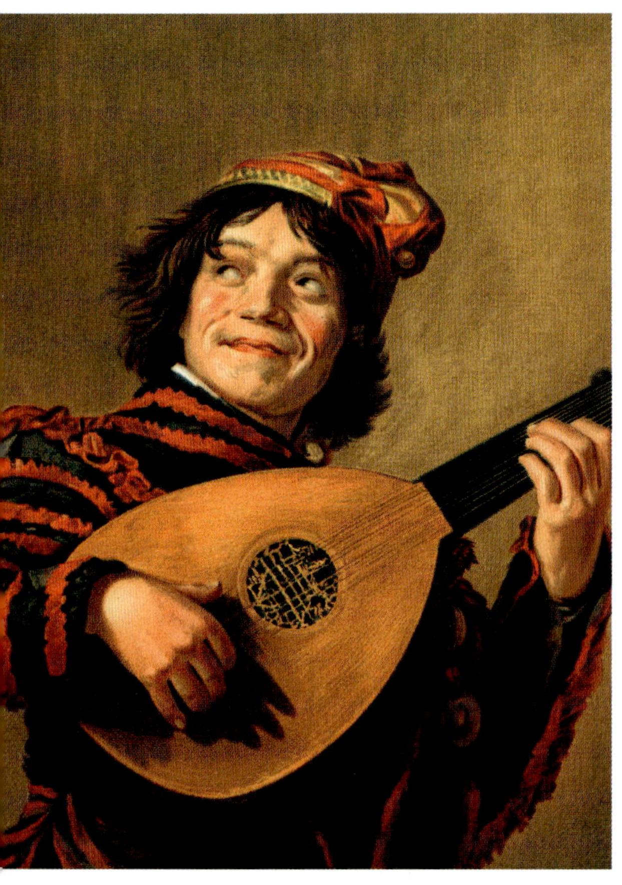

Portrait of a Jester with a Lute, Frans Hals, *c.*1624–26, oil on canvas, 70 x 62cm (28 x 24in), Musée du Louvre, Paris, France

Painted at the start of Frans Hals's 'Caravaggist' period, this man playing the lute appears to project from the canvas. Overall, the sense of dynamism is conveyed as the musician's body and head are twisted in opposite directions and the fingers seem to be plucking the strings. His theatrical 16th-century costume and broad smile create a light-hearted image that exudes a sense of spontaneity.

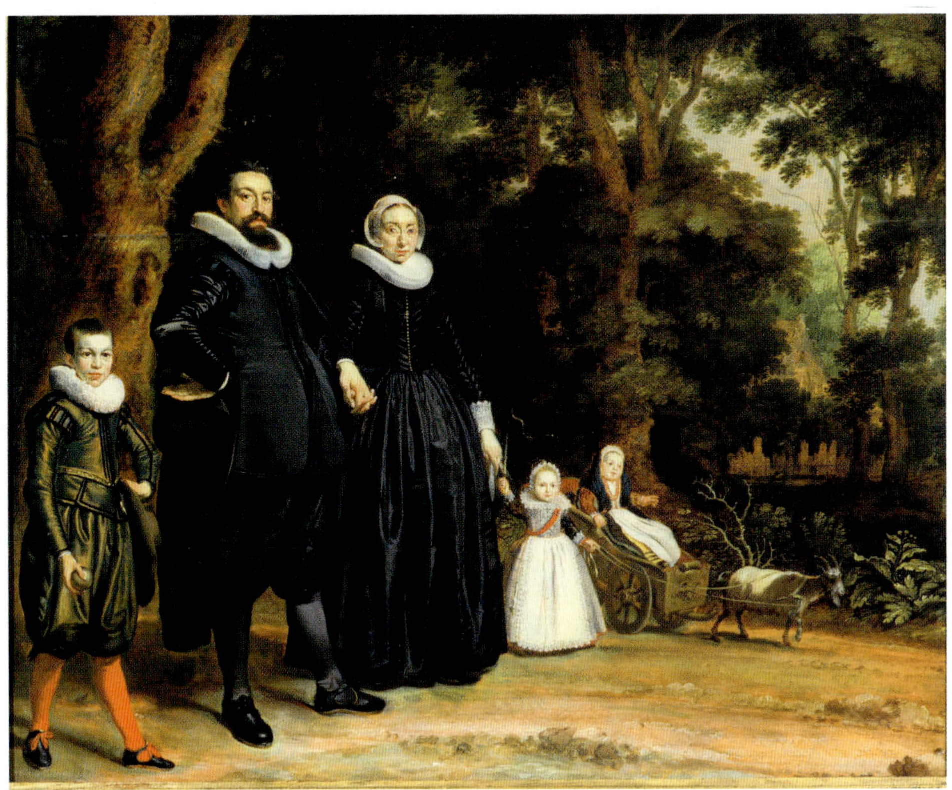

A Dutch Family, Thomas de Keyser, 1624, oil on board, 60.6 x 73.5cm (23¾ x 29in), Schlossmuseum, Schloss Friedenstein, Gotha, Germany

Before Rembrandt's popularity overshadowed Thomas de Keyser (*c.*1596–1667) in the 1630s, he was the most fashionable portrait painter in the Netherlands. He was also an architect, and from 1662 until his death, he oversaw the construction of the new Amsterdam town hall (see page 183). Here, using the traditional composition for such portraits, he has depicted a prosperous Dutch family. Jacob van Ruisdael probably painted the landscape background.

Portrait of a Couple, probably Isaac Abrahamsz Massa and Beatrix van der Laen, Frans Hals, *c.*1622, oil on canvas, 140 x 166.5cm (55 x 65½in), Rijksmuseum, Amsterdam, Netherlands

This couple sit close to each other in a relaxed manner that was highly unusual at the time. In this abandonment of convention, the painting conveys love and probably commemorates the couple's marriage. Both were wealthy and educated; Beatrix was a regent's daughter and Isaac was a merchant and diplomat. Their grinning faces show that through their superior class and wealth, they can make their own rules.

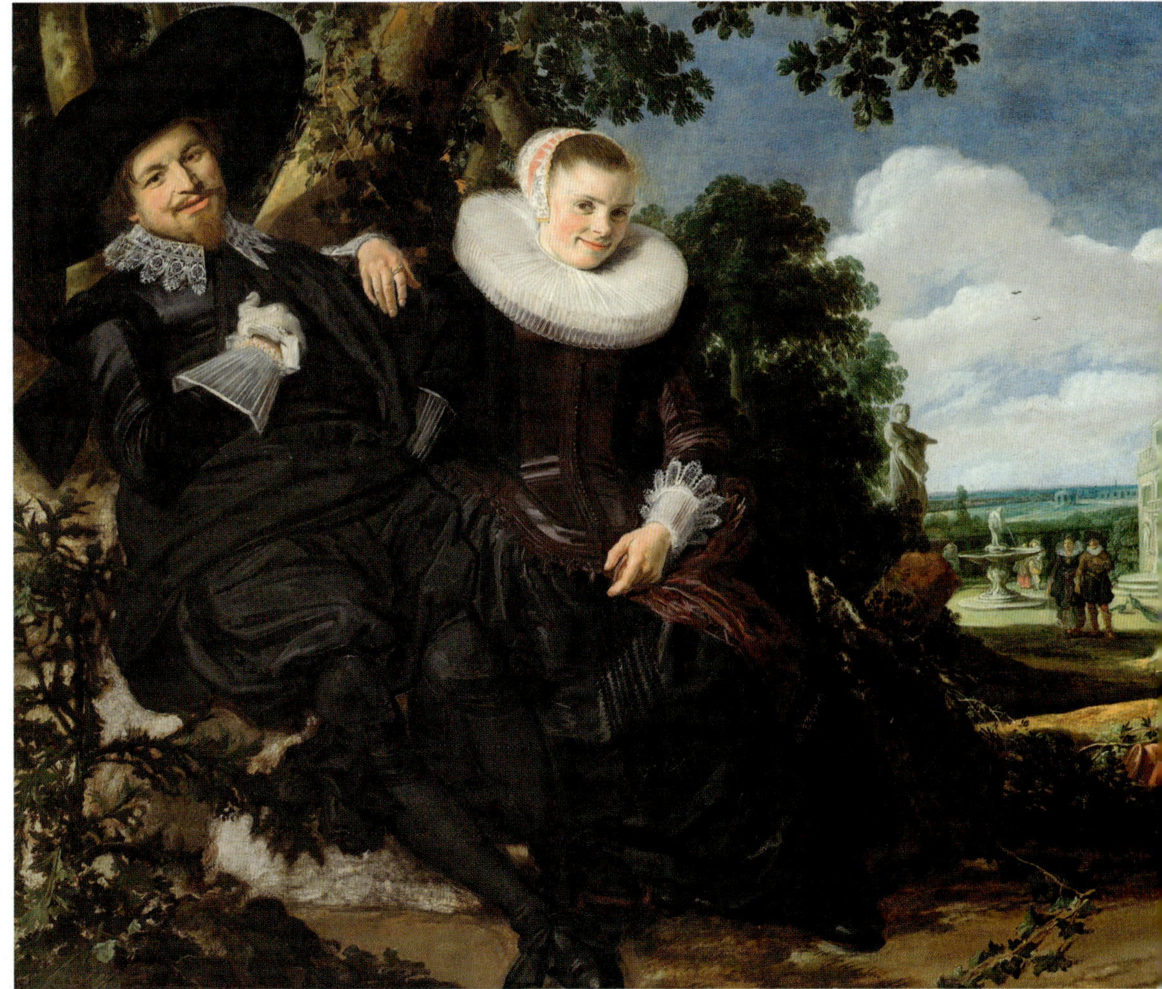

An Old Woman Called the Artist's Mother, Rembrandt, 1617–29, oil on panel, 61.3 x 47.4cm (24 x 19in), Royal Collection Trust, London, UK

Painted towards the end of Rembrandt's time in Leiden just before he moved to Amsterdam, this was a study of old age. The woman's pale, wrinkled skin, narrow lips and large nose are shaded under her purple hood and fur mantle that partially cover a white and yellow embroidered collar. From the start of his career, Rembrandt was fascinated by the ageing process.

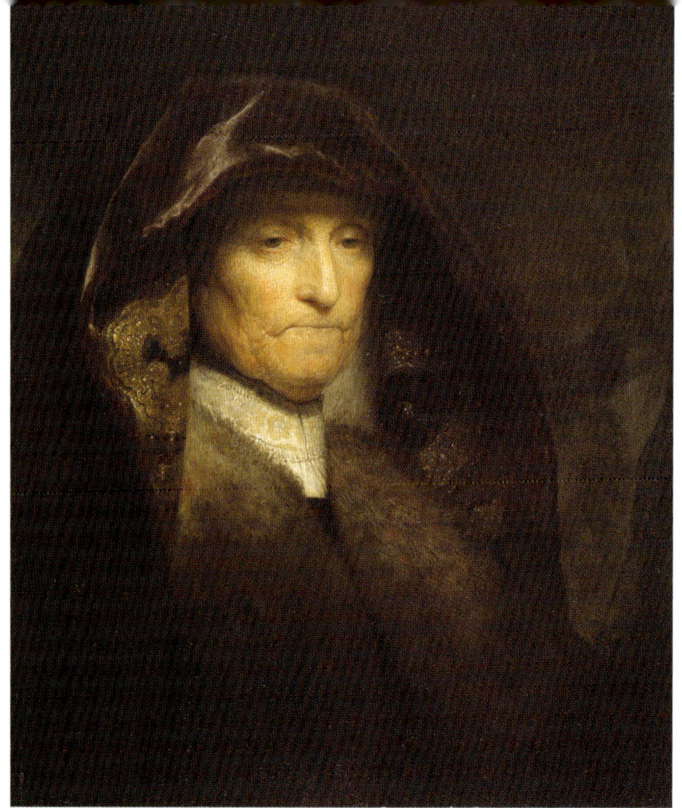

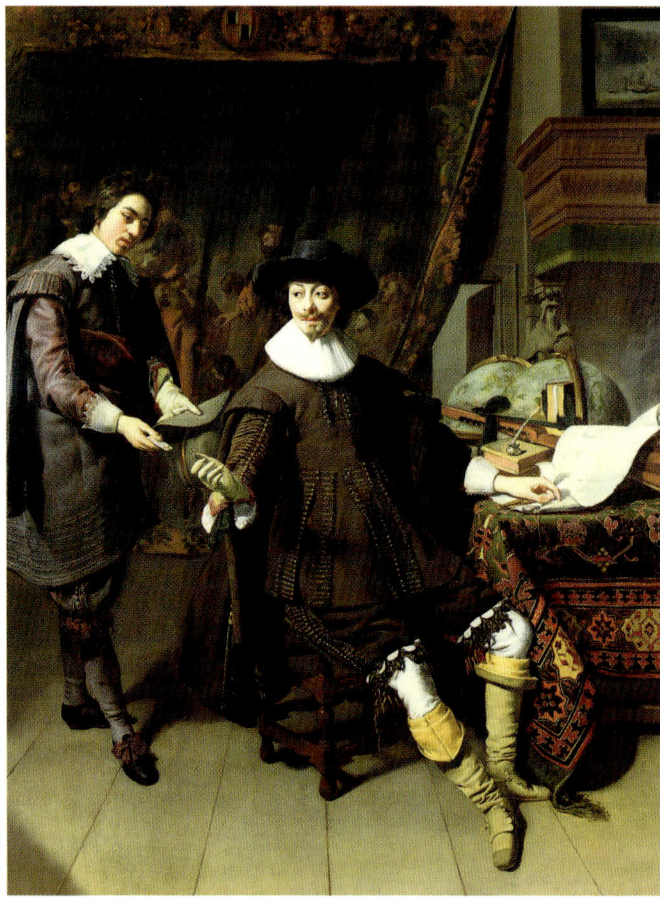

Constantijn Huygens and his Clerk, Thomas de Keyser, 1627, oil on oak, 92.4 x 69.3cm (36¼ x 27¼ in), National Gallery, London, UK

One of the most powerful figures of the period, Constantijn Huygens, Lord of Zuylichem, was secretary to three stadholders, served as ambassador to Venice and England, and was knighted by James I in England in 1622. In this full-length portrait, de Keyser conveys Huygens's importance and worldliness. The tapestry on the back wall features the Huygens coat of arms, while objects surrounding him show his range of interests.

Portrait of a Gentleman, Thomas de Keyser, c.1626, oil on panel, 71.8 x 55.1 cm (28¼ x 21¾ in), North Carolina Museum of Art, Raleigh, USA

Best known for his portraits of important personages in Amsterdam, de Keyser was the son of a distinguished architect and sculptor.

As well as his portraits, de Keyser also produced historical and mythological works, and despite adhering to the somewhat formal expectations of Dutch portraiture, his images are lively and elegant with a golden-based palette and chiaroscuro. Some of his portraits are life-sized, but most are smaller, as here.

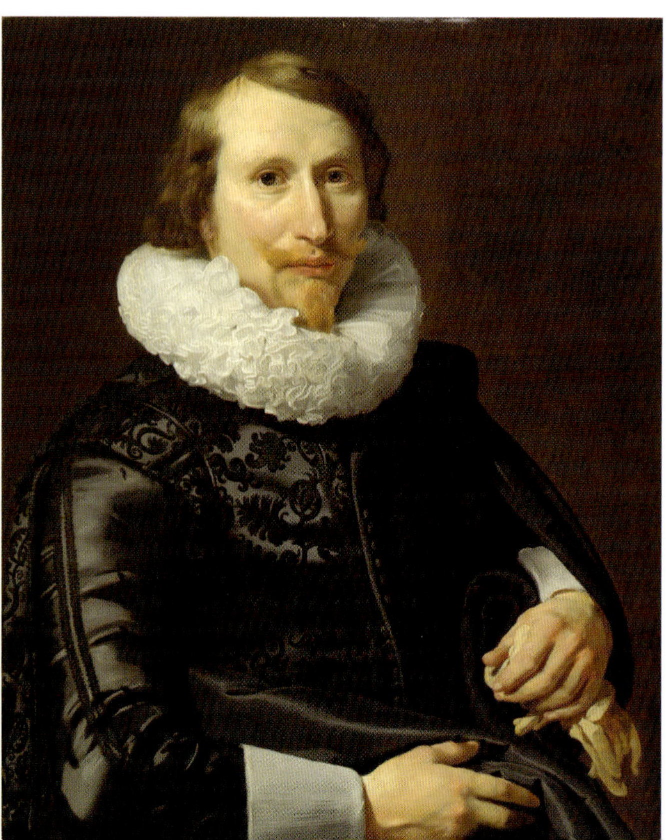

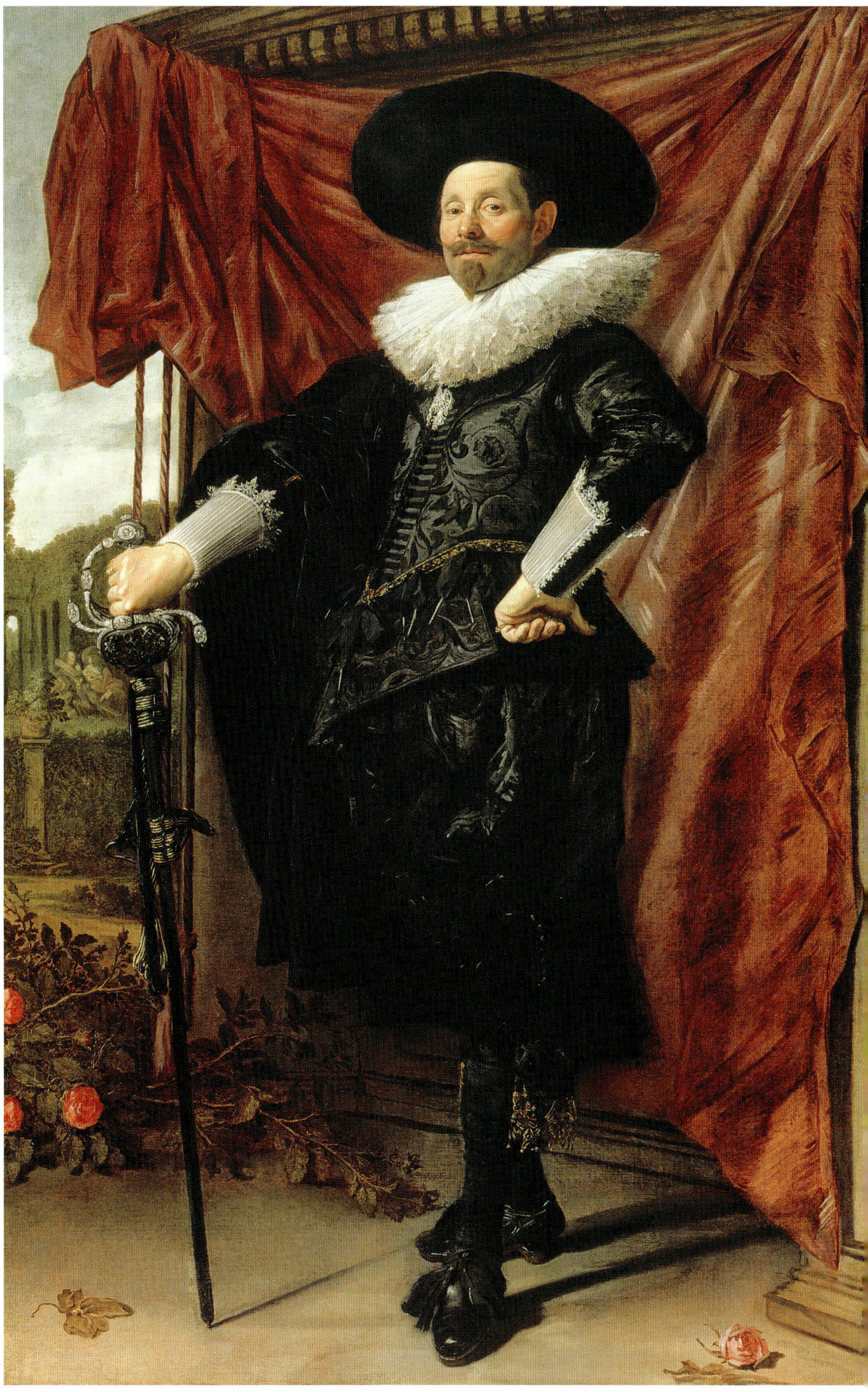

Willem van Heythuysen, Frans Hals, c.1625, oil on canvas, 204.5 x 134.5cm (80½ x 53in), Alte Pinakothek, Munich, Germany

Willem van Heythuysen (1590s–1650), was a Dutch cloth merchant who lived mainly in Haarlem and Weert. He moved to Haarlem as a yarn dealer and became extremely wealthy – and a philanthropist. Among other good works, he founded two poorhouses. Hals painted three portraits of this confident, self-made man. In the foreground of this, he painted wilting roses that symbolize the transience of life.

Self-Portrait, Rembrandt, 1628, oil on panel, 22.5 x 18.6cm (8¾ x 7¼in), Rijksmuseum, Amsterdam, Netherlands

Using his own, softly focused chiaroscuro, Rembrandt painted this self-portrait when he was in his early 20s. Unusually, he painted his face in shadow, covering his eyes and instead illuminating his ear, cheek and neck. To portray his dark, curly hair, he drew curving marks with the end of his brush in the wet paint, creating a unique impression of real texture.

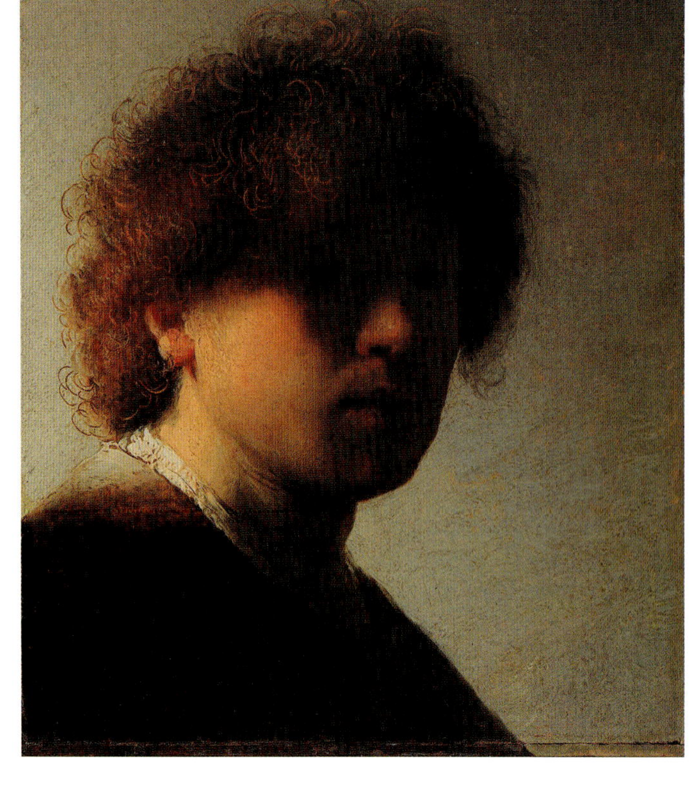

Nicolaes Ruts, Rembrandt, 1631, oil on mahogany panel, 116.8 x 87.3cm (46 x 34¼in), The Frick Collection, New York, USA

Born in Cologne, the merchant Nicolaes Ruts (1573–1638) traded with Russia. Set against a neutral background, draped in a sable-lined gown called a tabbaard and holding a note, he is portrayed with smooth brushmarks, as Rembrandt creates an illusion of various textures and an intense personality.

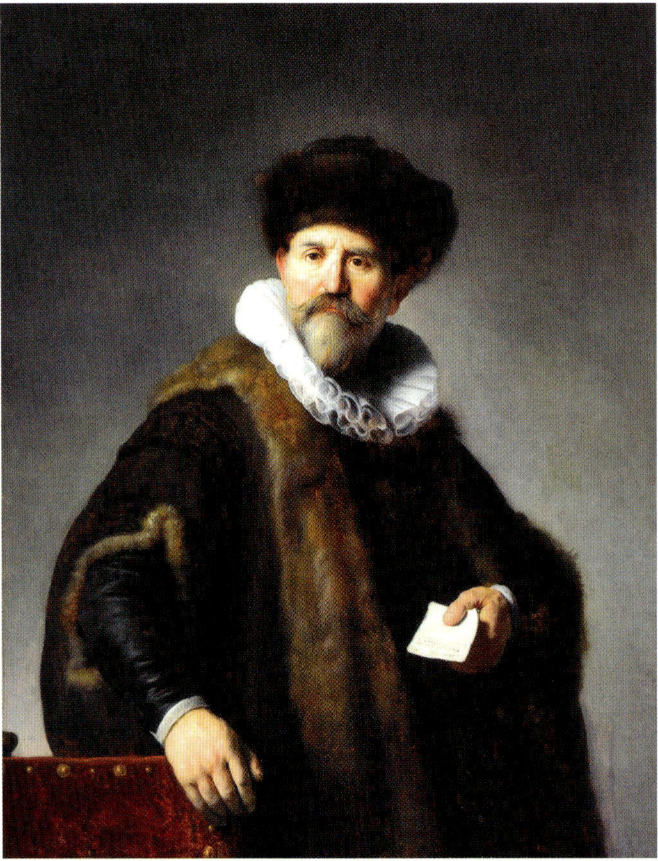

Self-Portrait at the Age of 34, Rembrandt, 1640, oil on canvas, 91 x 75cm (38¾ x 29½in), The National Gallery, London, UK

Influenced by the portraits of Raphael, Titian and Albrecht Dürer, Rembrandt painted himself at the height of his career. Self-assured and wearing an elaborate costume, he seems to be placing himself alongside the tradition of great 'Old Masters' of the past.

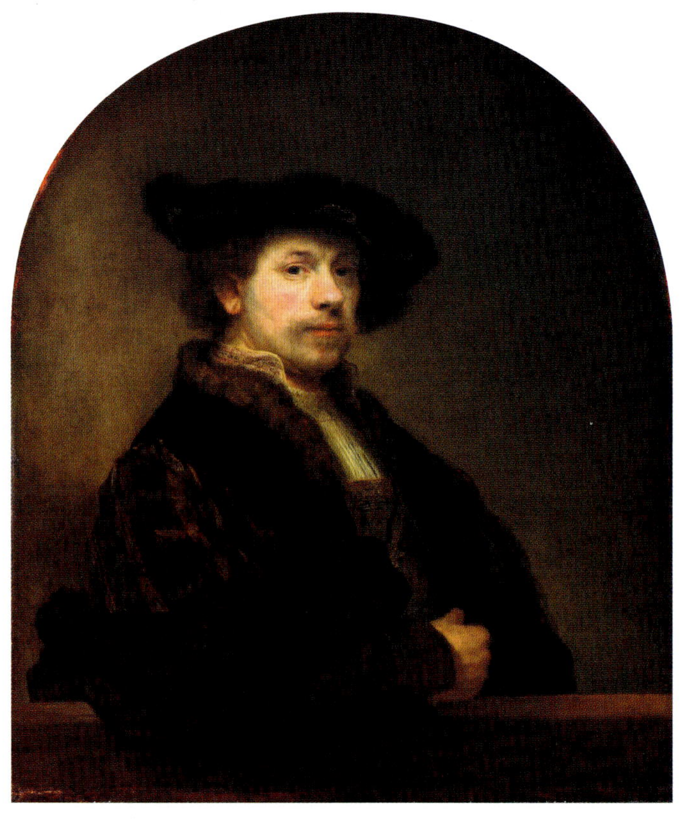

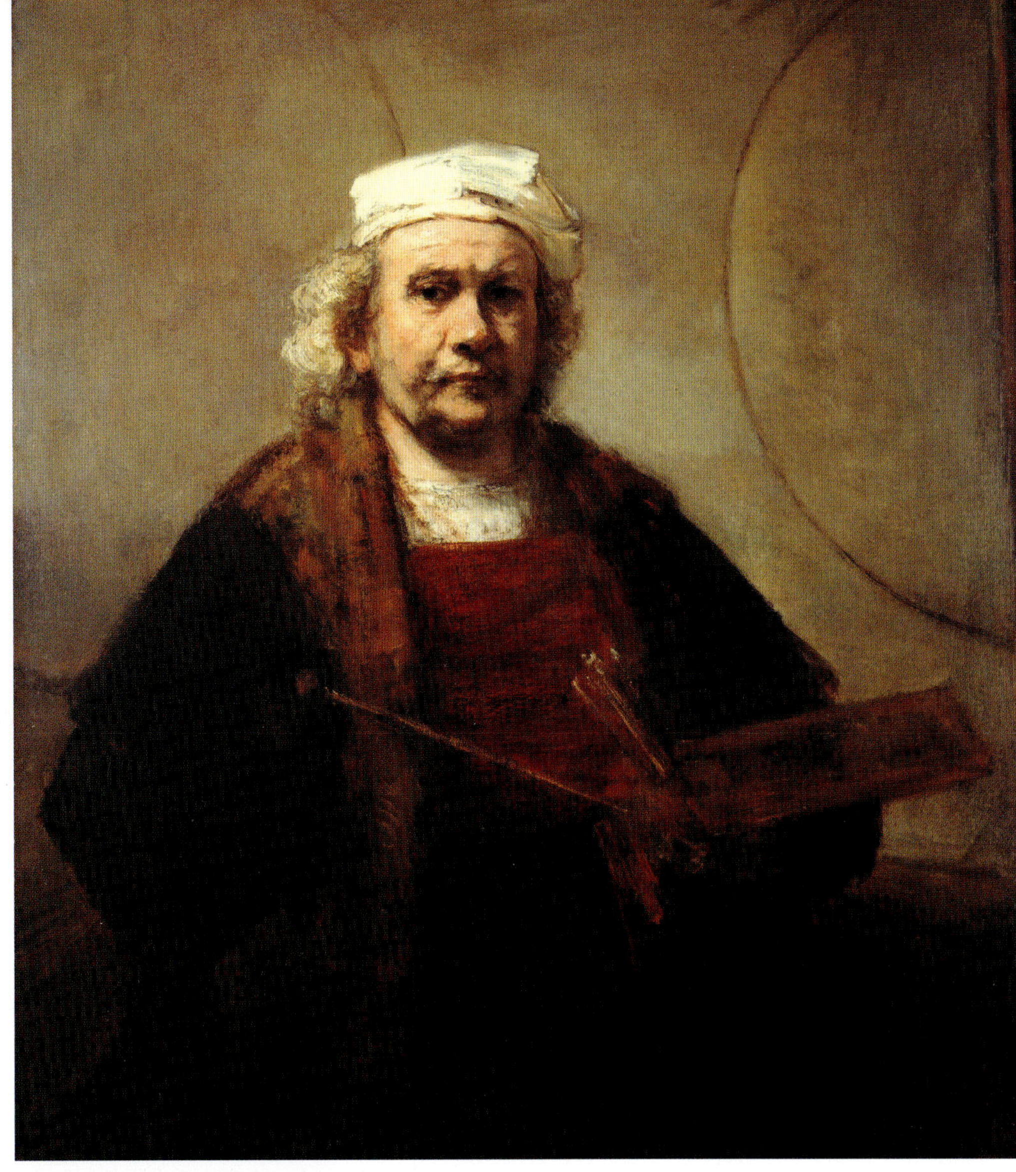

Portrait of the Artist, also known as *Self-Portrait Holding Brushes, Palette and Mahlstick*, Rembrandt, 1659–60, oil on canvas, 114.3 x 94cm (45 x 37in), Kenwood House, London, UK

Although many 'self-portraits' of Rembrandt are now known to have been painted by his pupils, he painted this at the age of about 53. He holds his palette, brushes and mahlstick (a stick with a soft leather top, used by painters to support the hand holding the paintbrush). The two circles in the background remain a mystery. They may allude to circles drawn by Giotto to demonstrate his artistic prowess. As usual, Rembrandt also departs from convention by using the handle of his paintbrush to create a moustache.

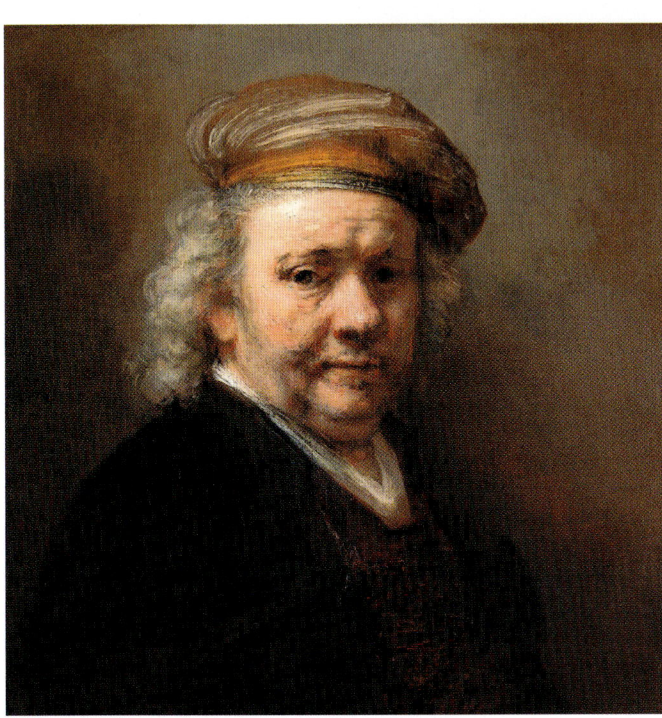

Self-Portrait, Rembrandt, 1669, oil on canvas, 60.2 x 65.4cm (23¾ x 25¾in), Mauritshuis, The Hague, Netherlands

One of Rembrandt's last paintings, here he wears a beret and turning to the right, he looks directly out of the canvas at viewers with a steady gaze. He presents himself in a reflective mood, and uses free, strong brushmarks to apply thick layers of impasto paint, which create a rough surface texture. Chiaroscuro is used masterfully on his face, as even the mottled texture and colours of his skin are apparent. His hair is wispy and grey, his eyes are almost unfathomable, and as usual with Rembrandt's self-portraits, the background is dark, sombre and fairly neutral so that the figure appears to come forward.

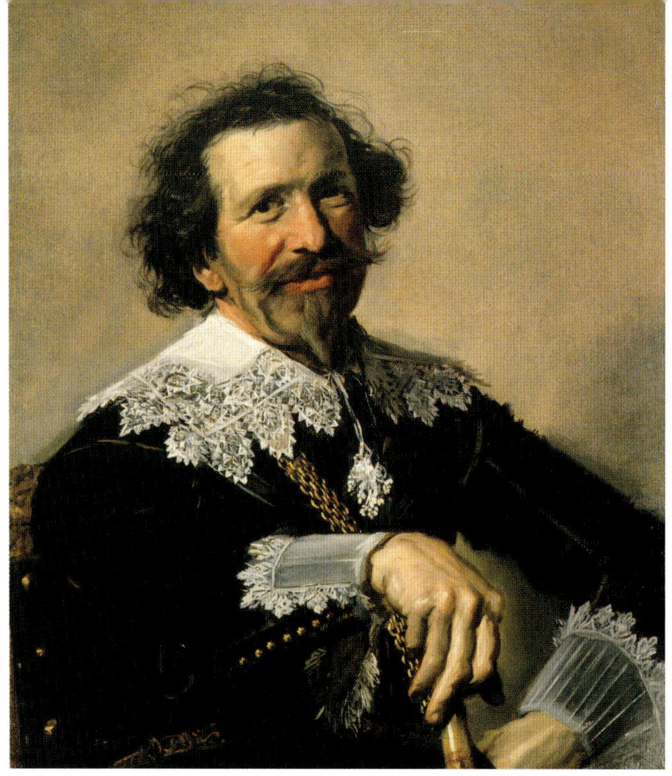

The Merry Lute Player, Frans Hals, *c.*1624–28, oil on canvas, 90.4 x 75 cm (35½ x 29½ in), Guildhall Art Gallery, London, UK

Although this is clearly a portrait of a real person, it is actually a genre painting. The young man appears in several paintings by Hals and here stands in a pose derived from Italian-style paintings, featuring a half-length figure playing music and drinking alcohol. This type of image was inspired by the Dutch Caravaggisti; though Hals did not follow their use of chiaroscuro, he did convey a sense of liveliness and joie de vivre.

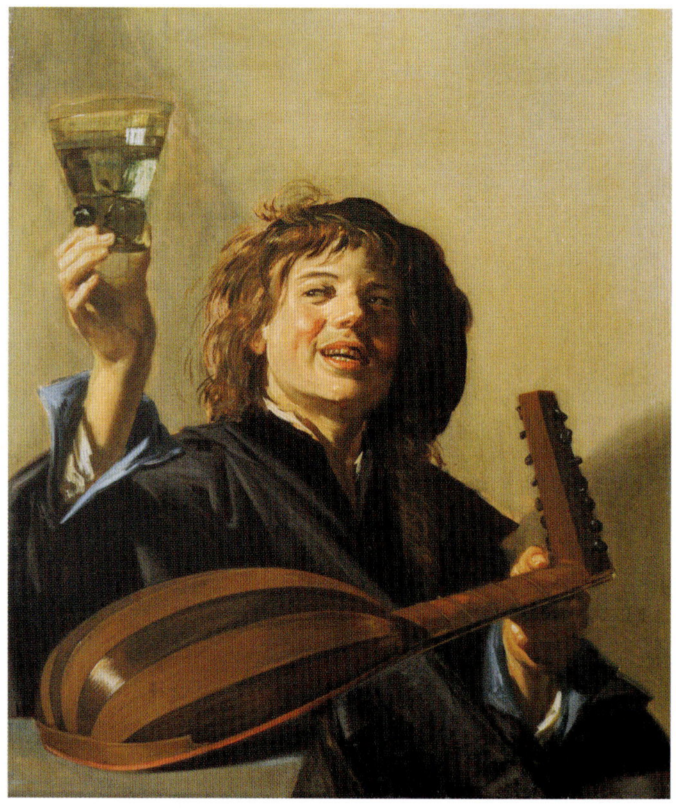

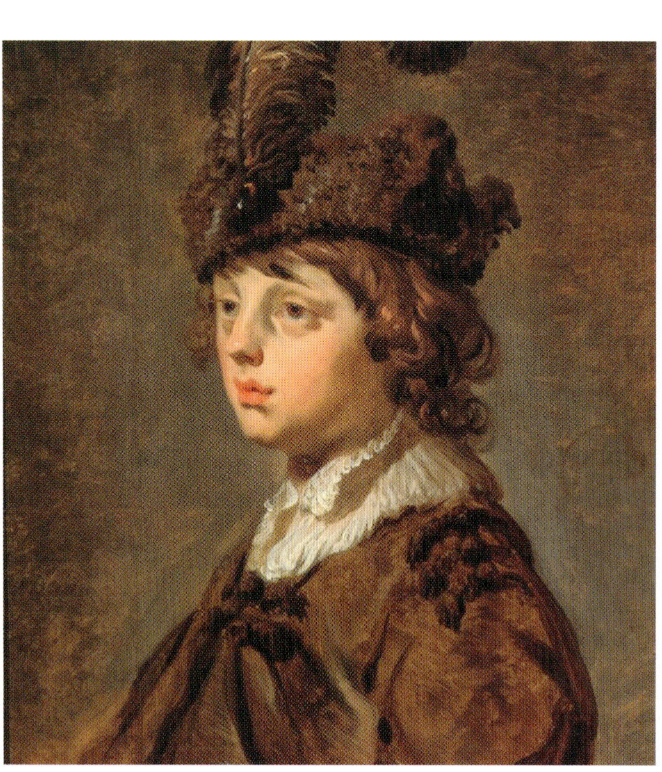

Boy with a Beret, Jacob Backer, *c.*1630/35, oil on panel, 52 x 46cm (20.5 x 18in) Museum Boijmans van Beuningen, Rotterdam, Netherlands

After training in Leeuwarden, Jacob Adriaensz Backer (1608–51) studied with Rembrandt for a while.

He became known as a portraitist although he also painted some mythological and allegorical works. Reminiscent of Rembrandt, broad brushmarks have been used on the feathered fur beret and collar, while the face is painted with smaller marks and more detail. It was probably a tronie.

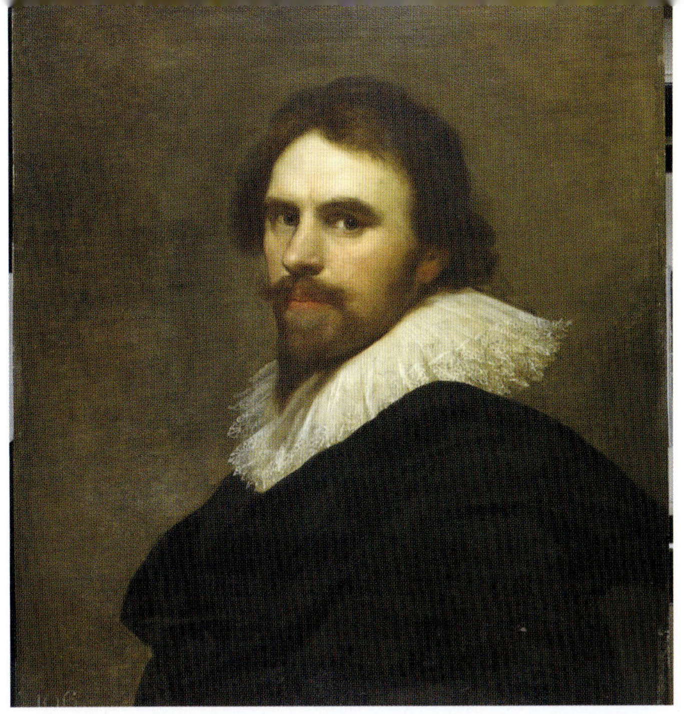

Self-Portrait, Daniel Mytens, 1630, oil on oak, 68.3 x 58.9cm (26¾ x 23¼ in), Royal Collection Trust, London, UK

Daniel Mytens (c.1590–1647) was born in Delft but probably trained in The Hague. By 1618, he was in England, working for James I and then Charles I. However, in 1632 he was displaced by Anthony van Dyck. Eventually he returned to The Hague, where he continued to receive his British royal pension and worked more as an art agent than a painter. In this painting he was still a courtier.

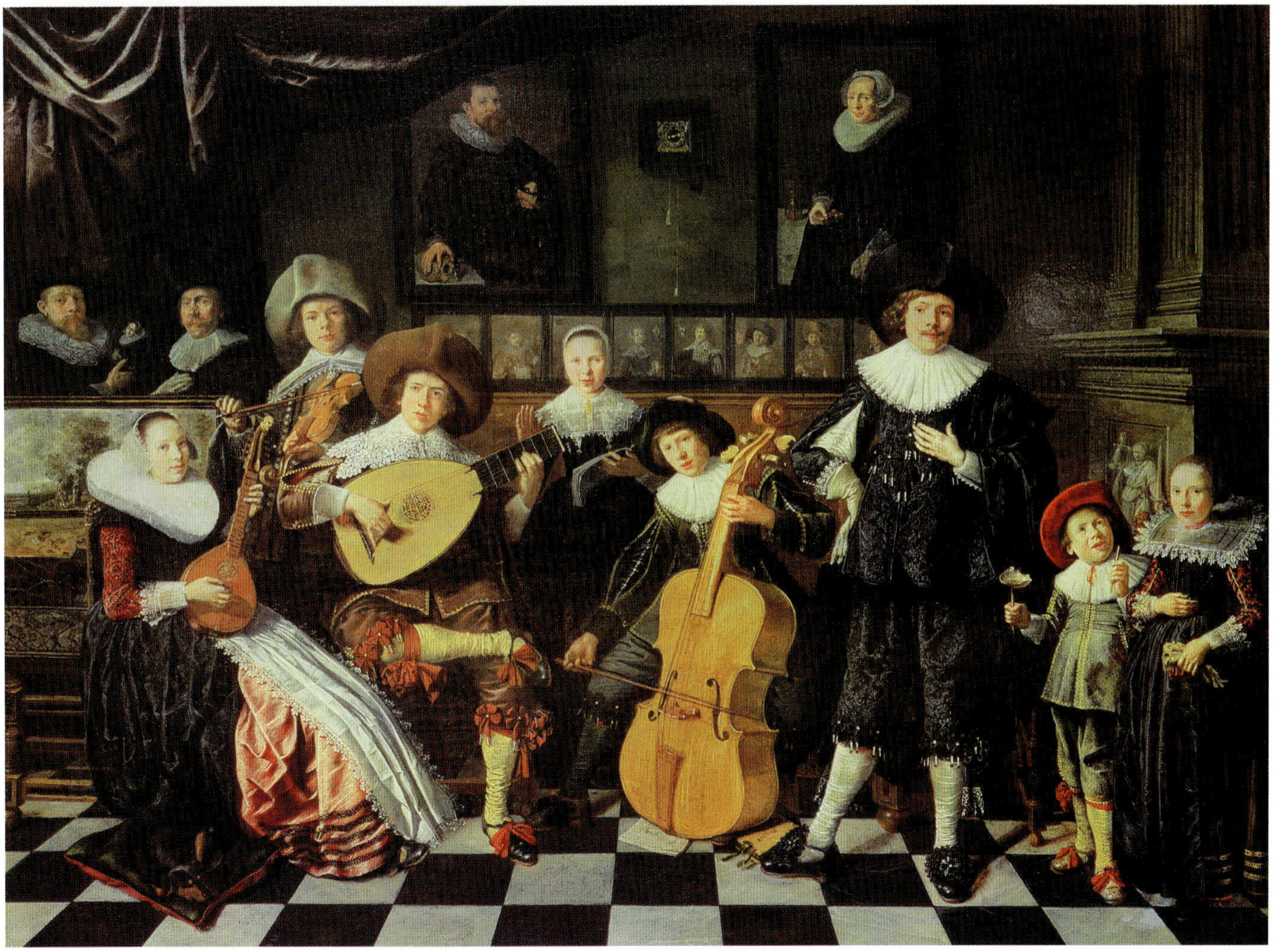

Self-Portrait with Family Members, Jan Miense Molenaer, 1630/40, oil on panel, 62.3 x 81.3cm (24½ x 32in), Frans Hals Museum, Haarlem, Netherlands

Here Jan Miense Molenaer portrays himself with his siblings. A sister Geertruijt plays the zither, Bartholomeus plays the violin, Adriaen the lute, Maria sings and Anthonij plays cello. The youngest children, Nicolaes and Lucia, stand on the right. Nicolaes holds a dish of soapy water and blows bubbles. Behind the harpsichord stand two half-brothers, Meyndert and Cornelis. Music symbolized harmony, bubble-blowing suggested mortality, and the dog represents fidelity.

Self-Portrait Aged 24, Govert Flinck, 1639, oil on oak, 65.8 x 54.4cm (26 x 21½in), The National Gallery, London, UK

As one of Rembrandt's pupils, Govert Flinck was directly influenced by him, as can be seen in this self-portrait, especially in the pose, lighting, paint application and palette used. Along with other artists and educated citizens, Flinck was becoming inspired by new ideas about humanism that were being spread by scholars such as René Descartes (1596–1650) and Baruch Spinoza (1632–77) who lived and worked in the Republic at the time.

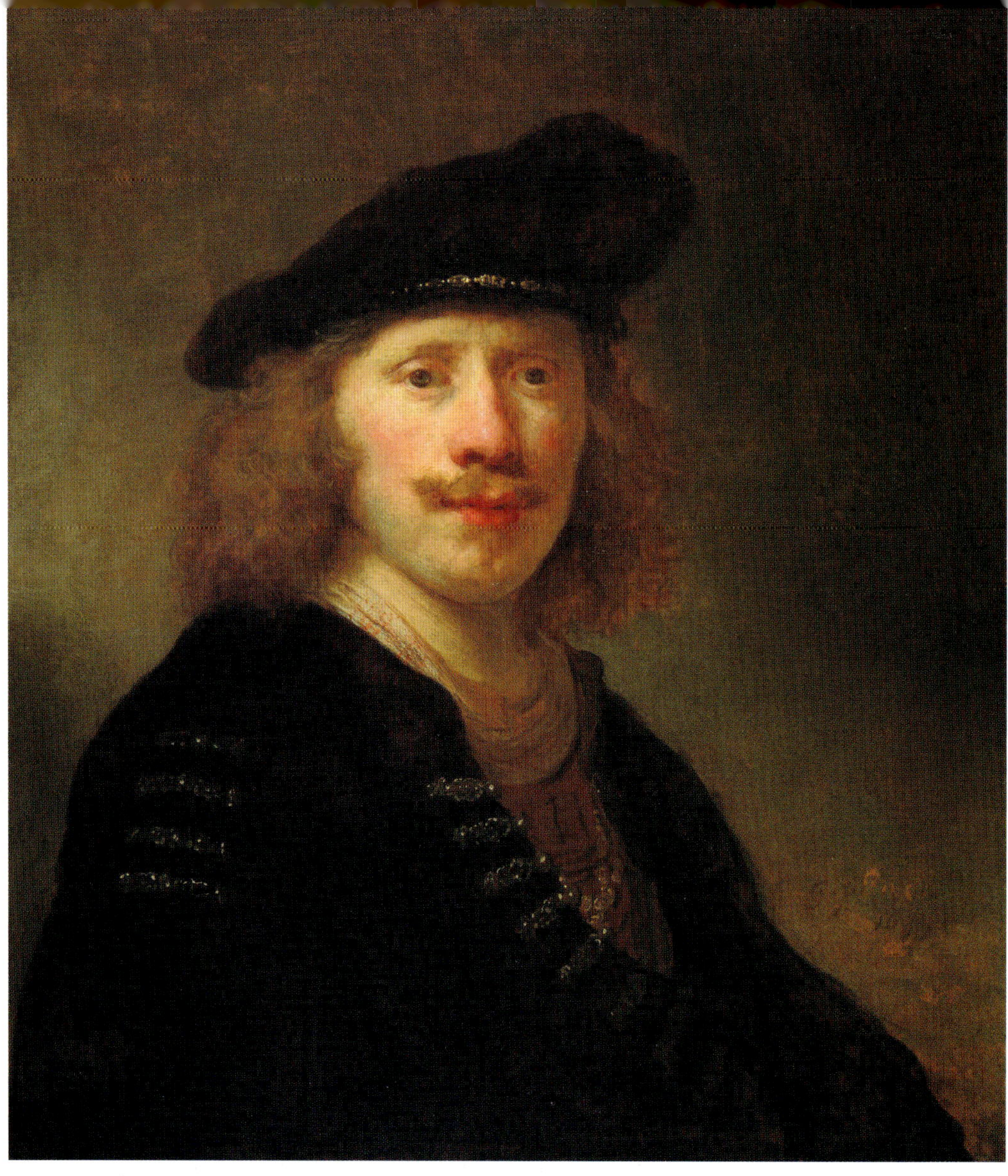

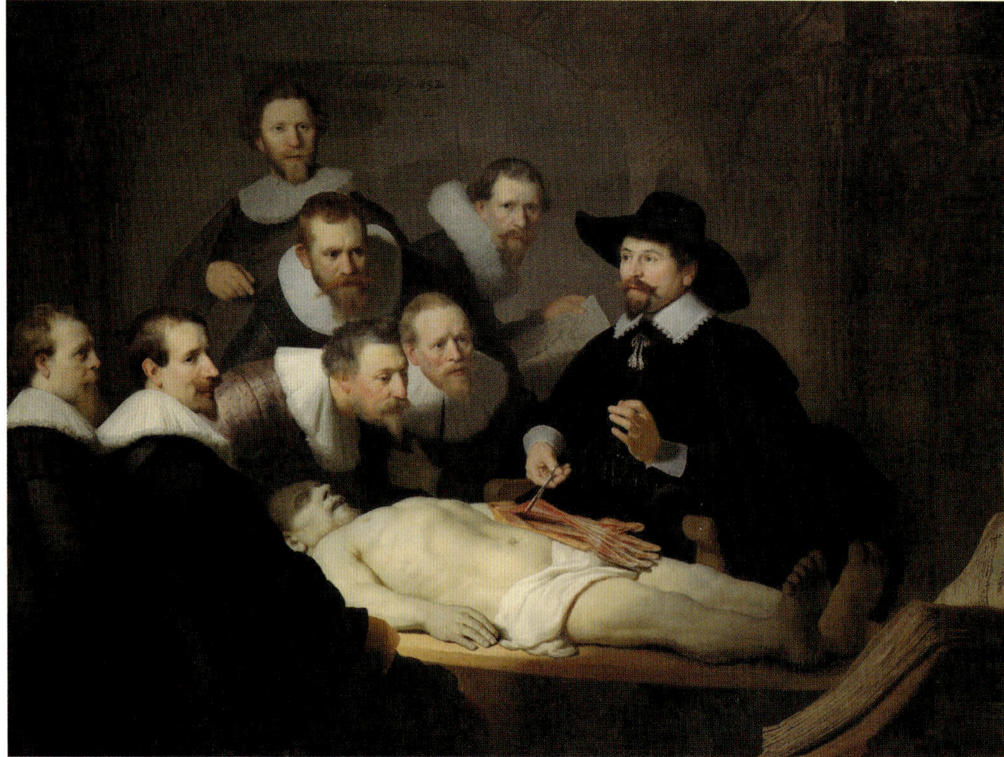

The Anatomy Lesson of Dr Nicolaes Tulp, Rembrandt, 1632, oil on canvas, 169.5 x 216.5cm (85¼ x 66¾in), Mauritshuis, The Hague, Netherlands

It became fashionable for physicians to pose together around a cadaver, suggesting an anatomical lesson. This is the most famous of such portraits. Rembrandt was 25 when he was commissioned to paint these Amsterdam surgeons, showing a lesson given by Dr Nicolaes Tulp in January 1632. He portrays the surgeons each looking at different things. Dynamism is conveyed through the striking contrasts between light and dark.

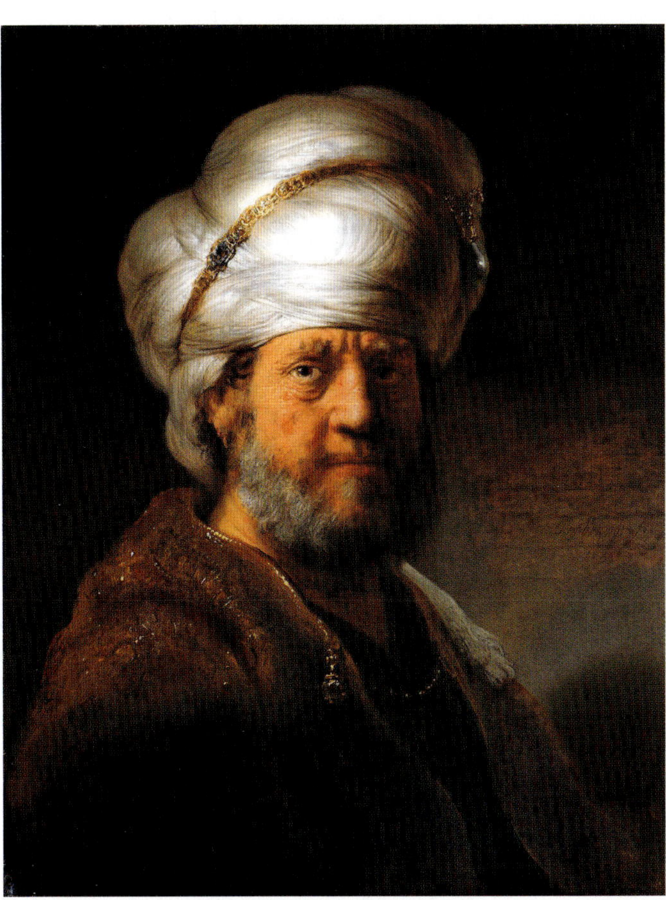

A Man in Oriental Dress, Rembrandt, 1635, oil on panel, 72 x 54.5cm (28¼ x 21½in), Rijksmuseum, Amsterdam, Netherlands

After achieving early success in his career, Rembrandt later experienced personal tragedies and financial adversity. His empathy for depicting the human condition was recognized, and he was later described as 'one of the great prophets of civilization.' Exotic and mysterious images like this were extremely popular in the 17th century, and Rembrandt's were widely copied and imitated, known as 'Turkish tronies'.

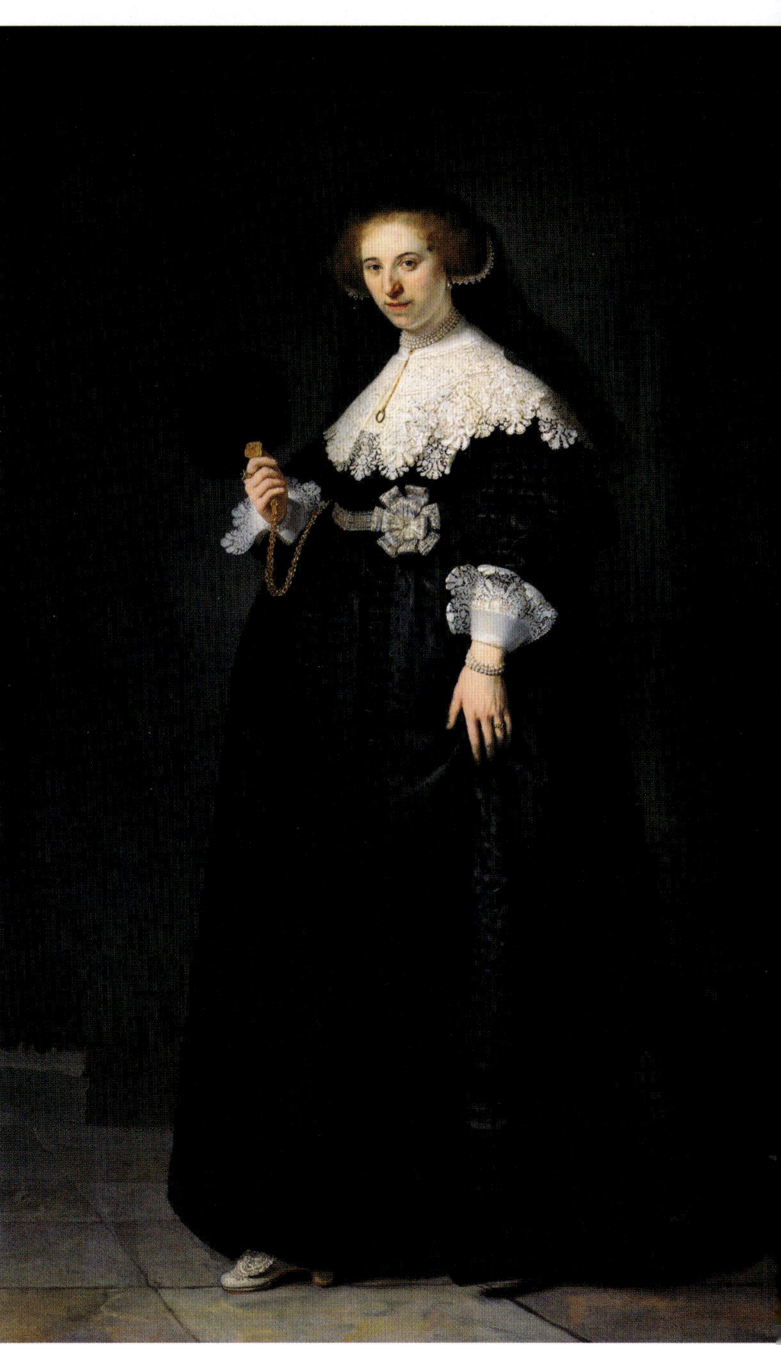

Portrait of Oopjen Coppit, 1634, Rembrandt, oil on canvas, 207.5 x 132cm (81 x 52in), Rijksmuseum, Amsterdam, Netherlands

Rembrandt painted this portrait of Oopjen Coppit (1611–89) when she was about 23 years old and had just married Marten Soolmans. Rembrandt painted the bride and groom as pendant portraits. His meticulous rendering of Oopjen's expensive clothing conveys the pride and affluence of many in the Dutch Republic. Until this time, life-sized, standing portraits were reserved for monarchs and nobles.

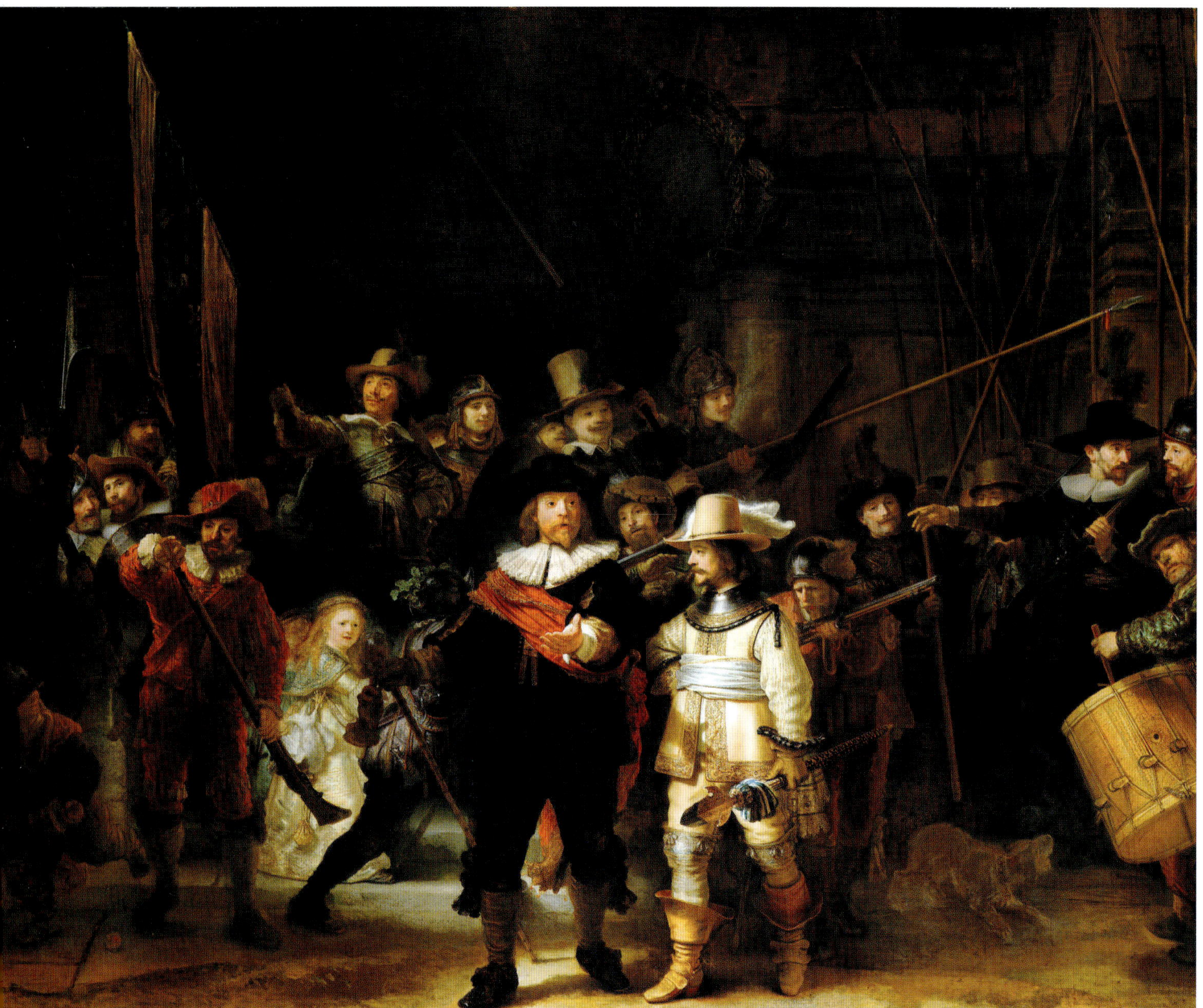

The Night Watch, Rembrandt, 1642, oil on canvas, 363 x 437cm (143 x 172in), Rijksmuseum, Amsterdam, Netherlands

Called *The Night Watch* at the end of the 18th century after it had darkened from layers of dirt and varnish, this group portrait of civic guardsmen should be entitled the *Officers and Men of the Company of Captain Frans Banning Cocq and Lieutenant Wilhelm van Ruytenburgh*. The blonde girl in a gold dress is a mascot, while the burgemeester (mayor) of Amsterdam wears black with a red sash. The composition is powerfully arranged, giving precedence to certain figures and creating a sense of unity. In some areas, Rembrandt has used precise details with small brushmarks and smooth paint, while in others, he applied paint thickly. His creation of tonalities is also extremely accomplished, with certain aspects appearing solid and three-dimensional, such as the captain's hand.

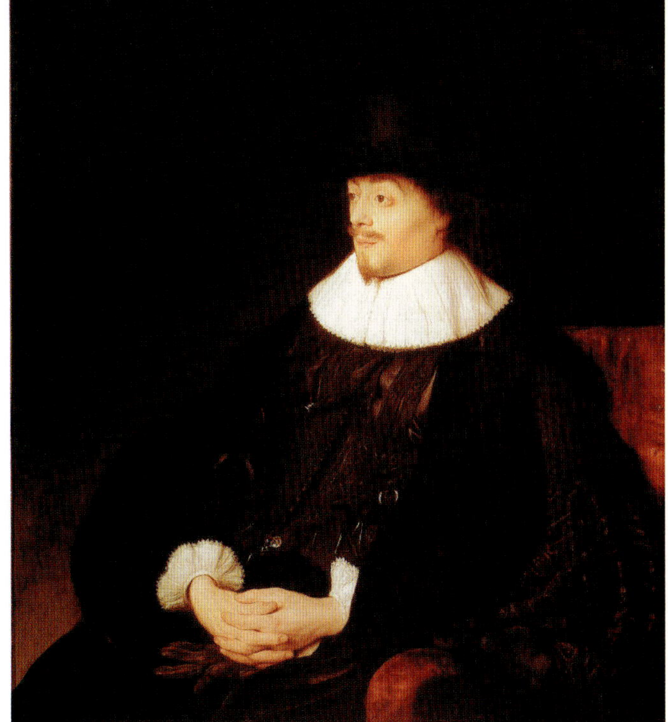

Portrait of Constantijn Huygens, Jan Lievens, c.1628/9, oil on panel, 99 x 84cm (39 x 33in), Rijksmuseum, Amsterdam, Netherlands

When Jan Lievens first met Constantijn Huygens, he asked to paint his portrait (see page 52), and for years after, Huygens supported and promoted Lievens. Here, Lievens has focused on the hands and face, leaving the clothing barely visible against the dark background. As Huygens was so busy, Lievens painted the clothes and hands first, returning later to paint the face.

Portrait of a Woman, possibly Maria Trip, Rembrandt, 1639, oil on panel, 107 x 82cm (42 x 32¼in), Rijksmuseum, Amsterdam, Netherlands

This richly dressed young woman smiles at viewers, displaying her wealth with pride through her adornments, including expensive lace and fine, almost transparent white linen, a rare and valuable folding fan, and pearls around her neck and wrists. It is generally accepted that the sitter is Maria Trip (1619–83), the daughter of a wealthy Amsterdam merchant.

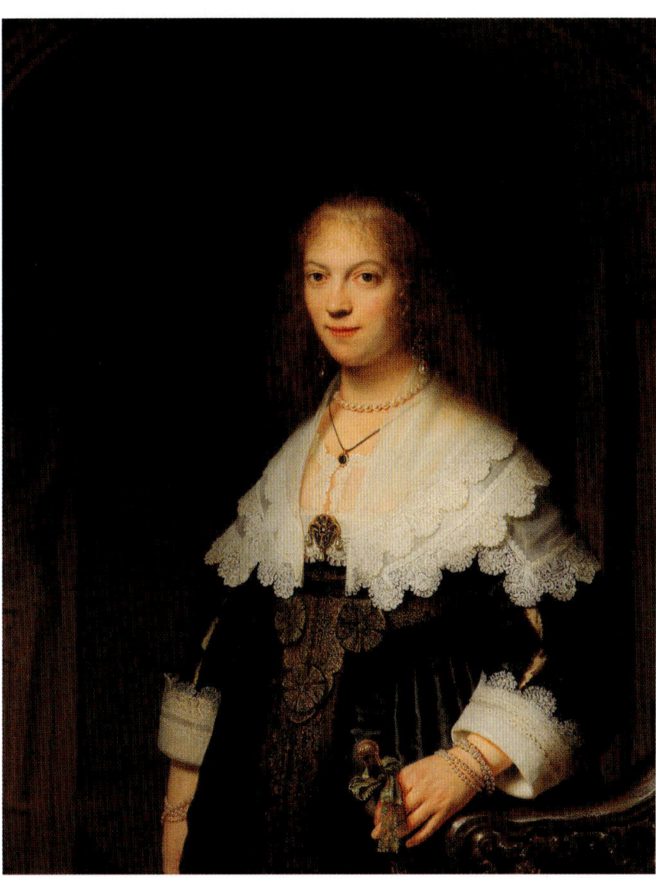

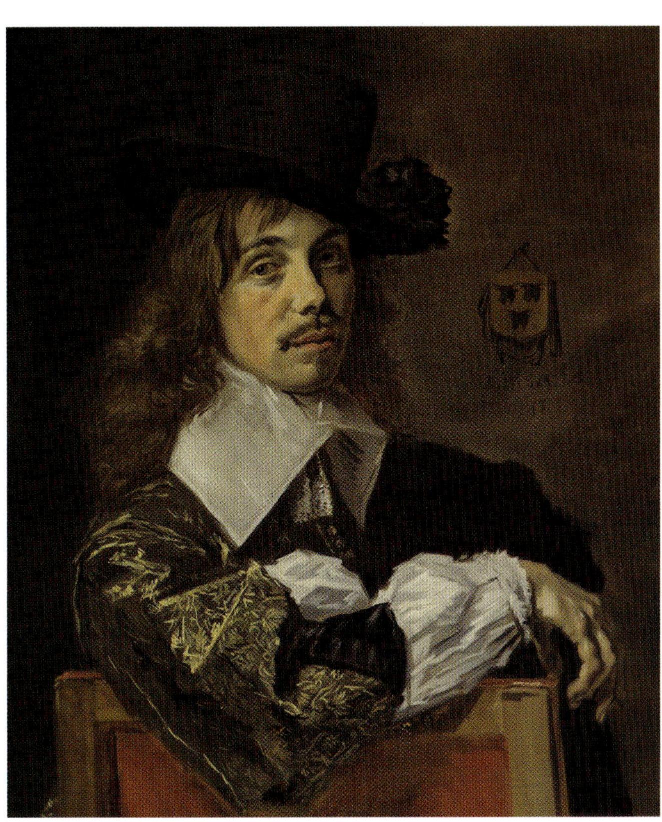

Willem Coymans, Frans Hals, 1645, oil on canvas, 77 x 64cm (30¼ x 25¼in), National Gallery of Art, Washington DC, USA

With his characteristic loose brushwork, Frans Hals has created a portrait of a man who seems to burst out of the canvas. As member of the prosperous Coymans family, Willem could afford to pay the pre-eminent portrait painter in Haarlem to capture his likeness. Hals was famous for his ability to portray his subjects and their clothing using dazzling brushstrokes, and often informal poses.

Bearded Man with a Velvet Cap, Govert Flinck, 1645, oil on wood, 60.3 x 52.4cm (23¾ x 20½in), The Metropolitan Museum of Art, New York, USA

Revealing the influence that Rembrandt had on Flinck, this is a tronie, although unlike his former teacher, this is painted with smooth brushstrokes and thin paint. Originally, the background was painted a deep olive green, but the paint has darkened with age. The man's face seems to emerge from this background; his eyes watch intently, his wispy white beard almost covering his exotic gold medallion.

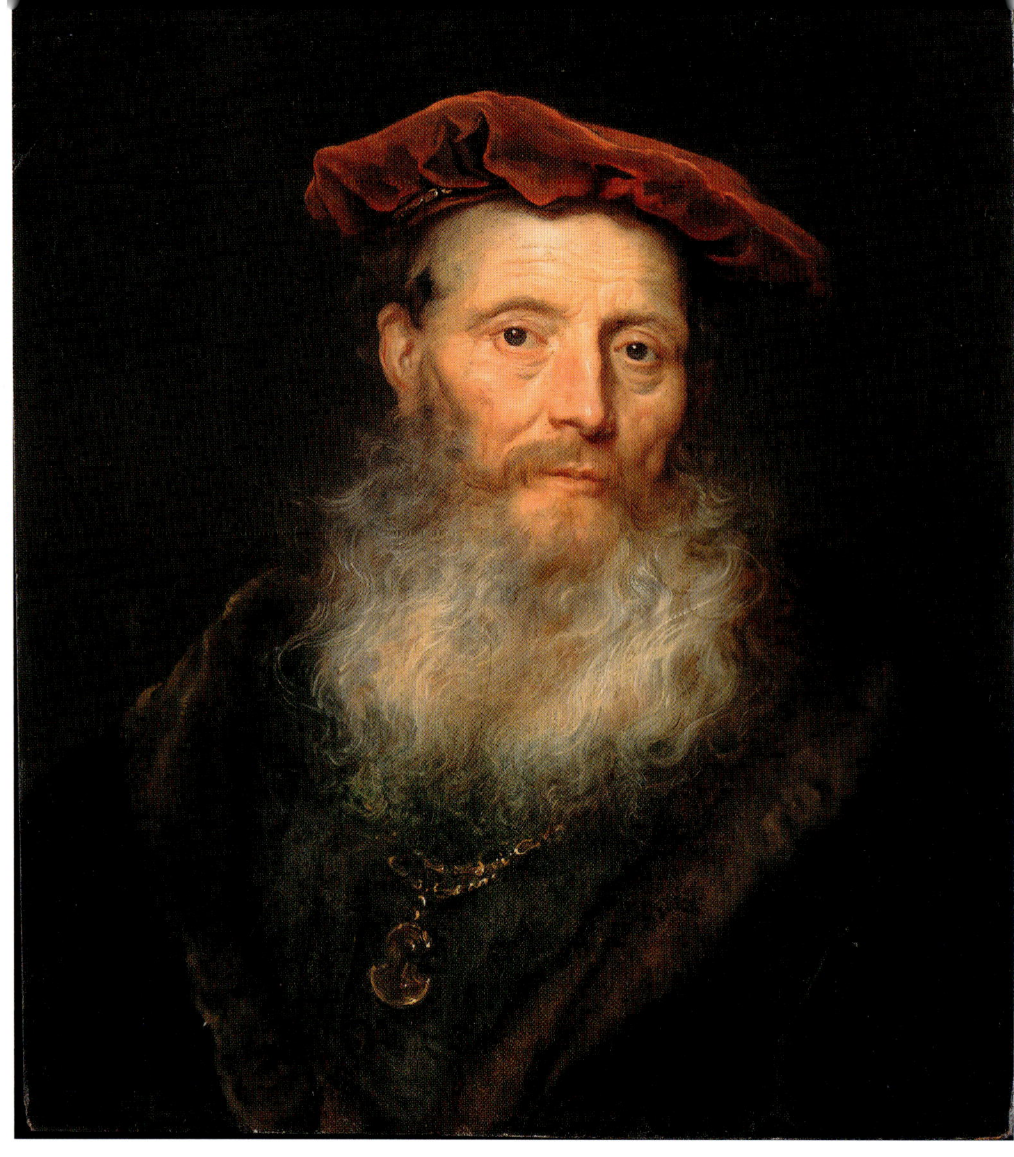

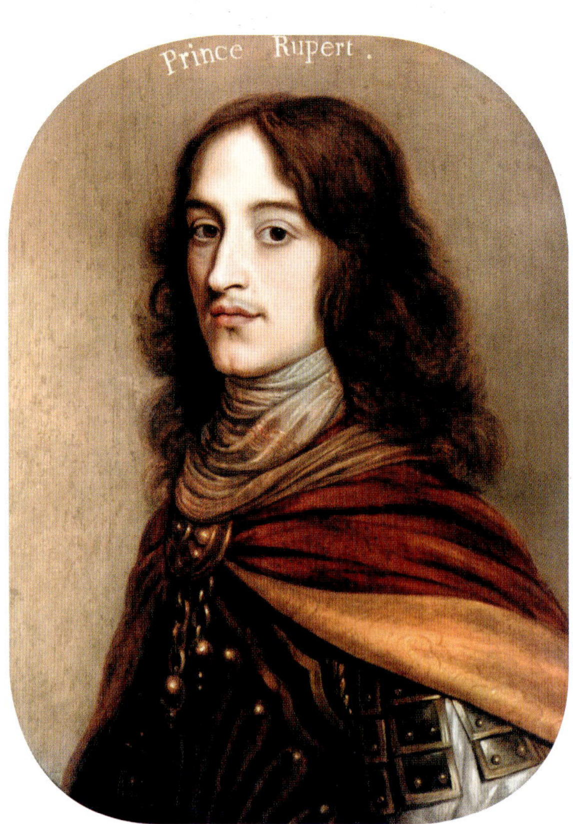

Prince Rupert, Count Palatine, Gerrit van Honthorst, *c.*1641–42, oil on panel, 74.3 x 59.1cm (29¼ x 23¼in), National Portrait Gallery, London, UK

Gerrit van Honthorst is known to have painted over 50 portraits, many of royalty. This is Prince Rupert, Count Palatine (1619–82), Duke of Bavaria, Duke of Cumberland, soldier and patron of science and the son of Frederick V, Elector Palatine and King of Bohemia and Elizabeth of Bohemia. Rather than paint his royal sitter in a restrained pose however, van Honthorst has presented him as rather dashing.

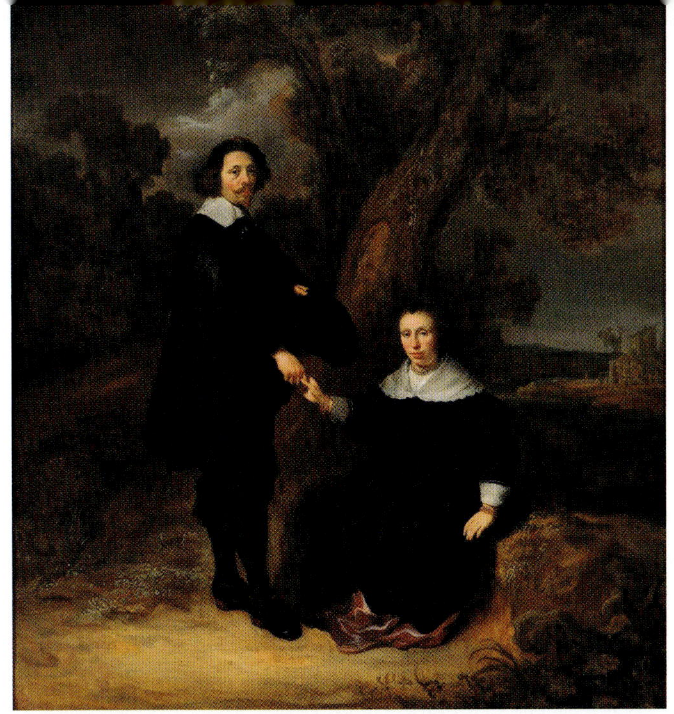

Portrait of Dirck Graswinckel and Geertruyt van Loon, Govert Flinck, 1646, oil on canvas, 107.5 x 91cm (42¼ x 35¾in), Museum Boijmans van Beuningen, Rotterdam, Netherlands

Dirck Graswinckel (1600–66) was a lawyer and author of several books. While his wife Geertruyt van Loon (1600– 75) sits, he stands, holding his wife's hand and looking back at Flinck who was painting the portrait. Despite the formality of Geertruyt's clothing, a pinkish-red underskirt can be seen at the hem of her dress. The chiaroscuro, soft background image and sitters' poses reveal Rembrandt's influence.

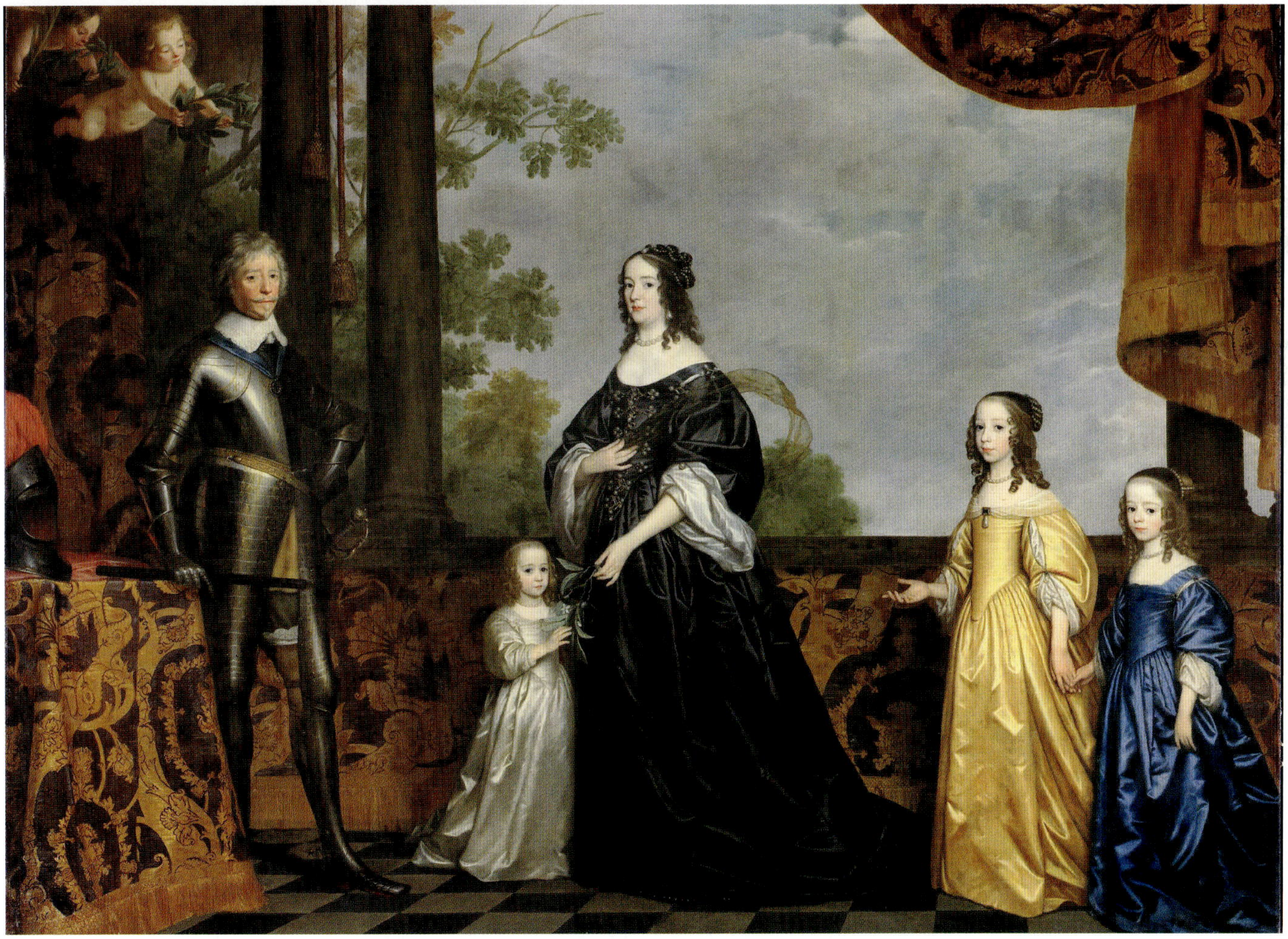

Frederick Hendrik and his wife Amalia van Solms with their Three Youngest Daughters, Gerrit van Honthorst, 1647, oil on canvas, 264 x 348cm (104 x 137in), Rijksmuseum, Amsterdam, Netherlands

Painted in the year of his death, this is Prince Frederick Hendrik (1584–1647) with Princess Amalia van Solms and their three youngest daughters, Maria, Albertine Agnes and Henriette Catharina. At this time, van Honthorst was working as a court painter in The Hague where his polished style was greatly appreciated. The natural background and pulled-back curtain became regular devices in portraits of the monarchy and aristocracy. The painting was commissioned by Amalia for the palace of Huis ten Bosch.

The Kitchen Maid, Rembrandt, 1651, oil on canvas, 78 x 64cm (31 x 25in), Nationalmuseum, Stockholm, Sweden

This is one of a few paintings by Rembrandt with the same title. Using a predominantly warm palette of reds, browns and yellows, the unknown model seems to be projected forward. Rembrandt has conveyed her with his characteristic individuality. She leans her arm on the window-sill, resting her head on her other hand. Her dark hair is held back in a small yellow cap and her neck is adorned with pearls.

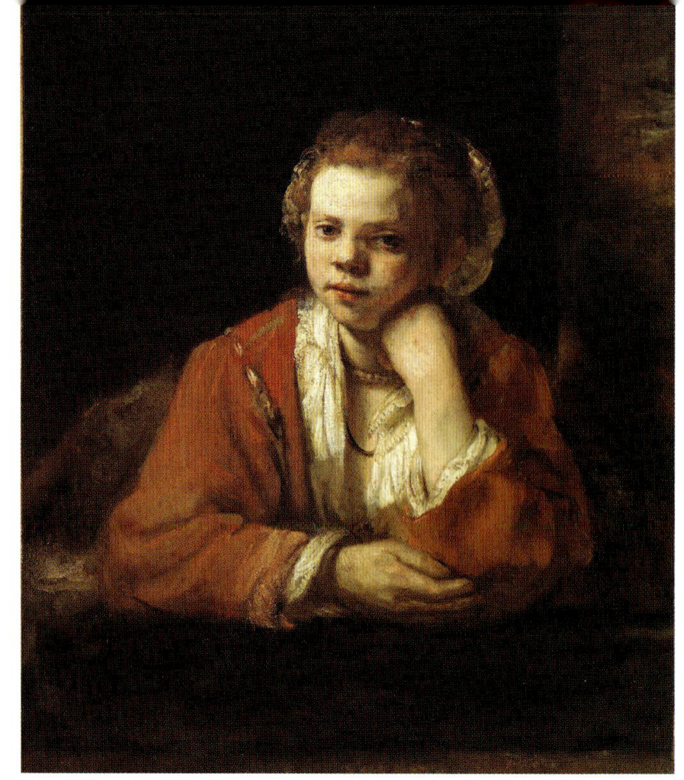

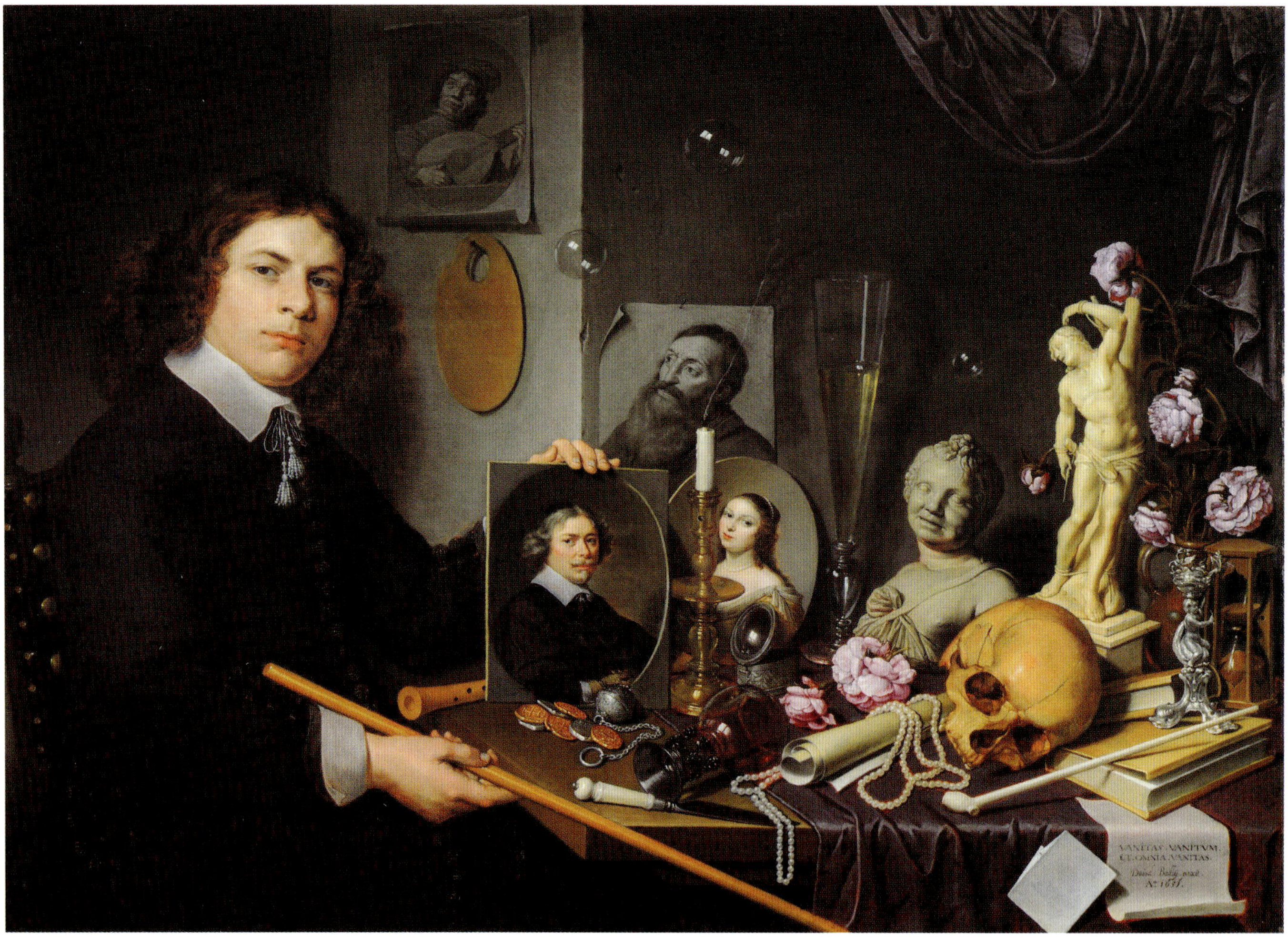

Self-Portrait with Allegorical Still Life, David Bailly, 1651, oil on panel, 89.5 x 122cm (35¼ x 48in), Museum de Lakenhal, Leiden, Netherlands

Standing at a table covered with objects, a young man holds a painting and a mahlstick. Both the young artist and the older man in the portrait are David Bailly (1584–1657). The still life objects surrounding the two ages of self-portrait represent a vanitas, featuring ephemeral items that symbolize the transience of life, a type of painting that Bailly has often been credited with inventing. The oval portrait of the young woman is Bailly's late wife.

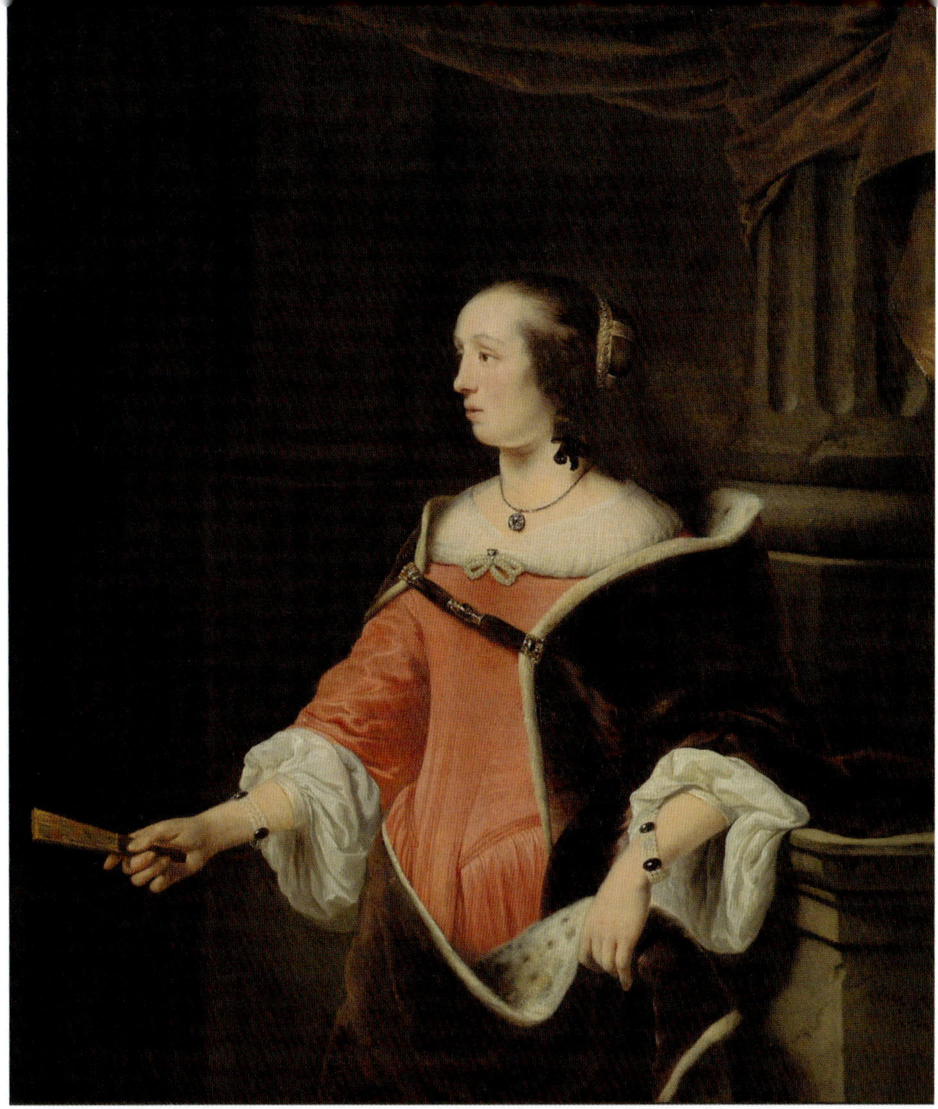

Portrait of a Lady, Ferdinand Bol, 1652, oil on canvas, 108 x 131cm (42½ x 51½in), Museum Boijmans van Beuningen, Rotterdam, Netherlands

This elegant lady's identity is not known. Fur-lined coats were usually only worn by royalty or aristocracy, so she was either extremely rich or posing as such. Along with the mystery of her identity are other issues with this painting. For instance, the fan in her hand replaces an earlier bunch of flowers, but it is not known why such alterations were made.

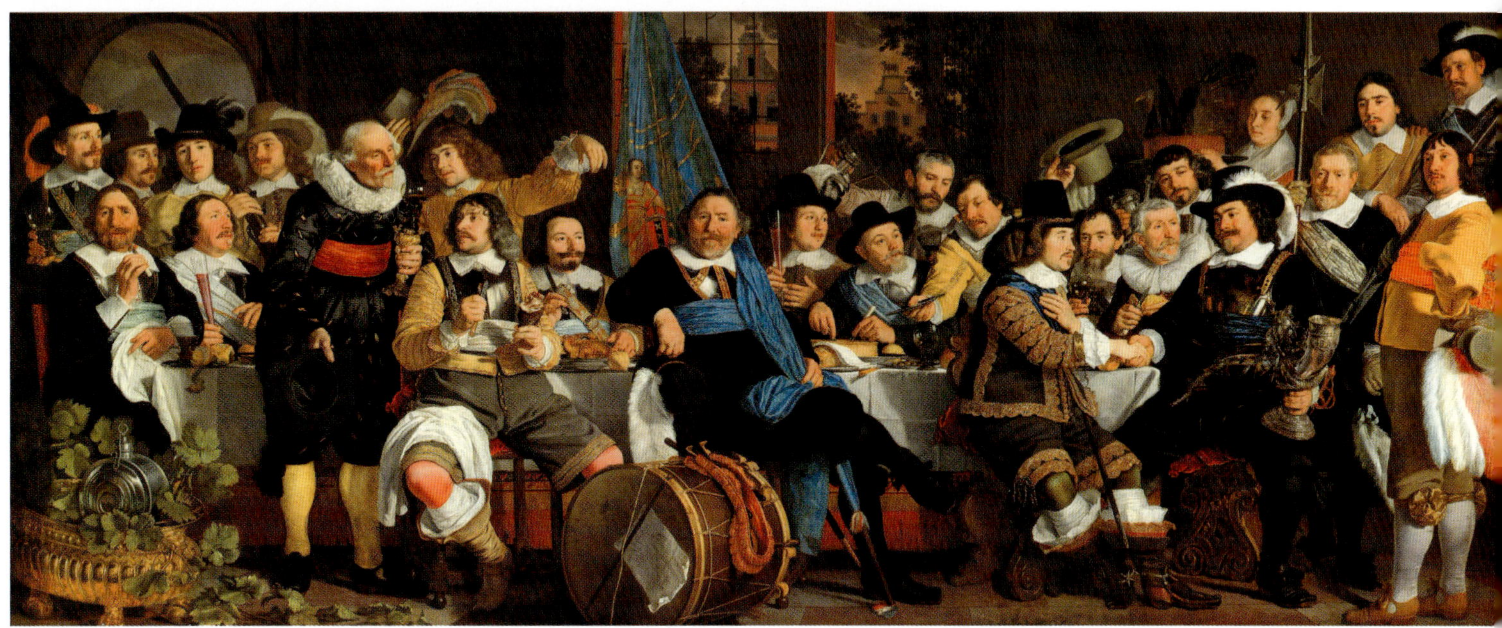

Banquet of the Amsterdam Civic Guard in Celebration of the Peace of Münster, Bartholomeus van der Helst, 1648, oil on canvas, 232 x 547cm (91 x 215in), Rijksmuseum, Amsterdam, Netherlands

One of Rembrandt's greatest rivals, Bartholomeus van der Helst painted this to celebrate the Peace of Münster in June 1648 that marked an end to the war with Spain. The life-sized painting depicts a banquet taking place at the Amsterdam crossbowmen's guild. After years of negotiations the company will retire from active duty. The captains shake hands as a symbol of peace.

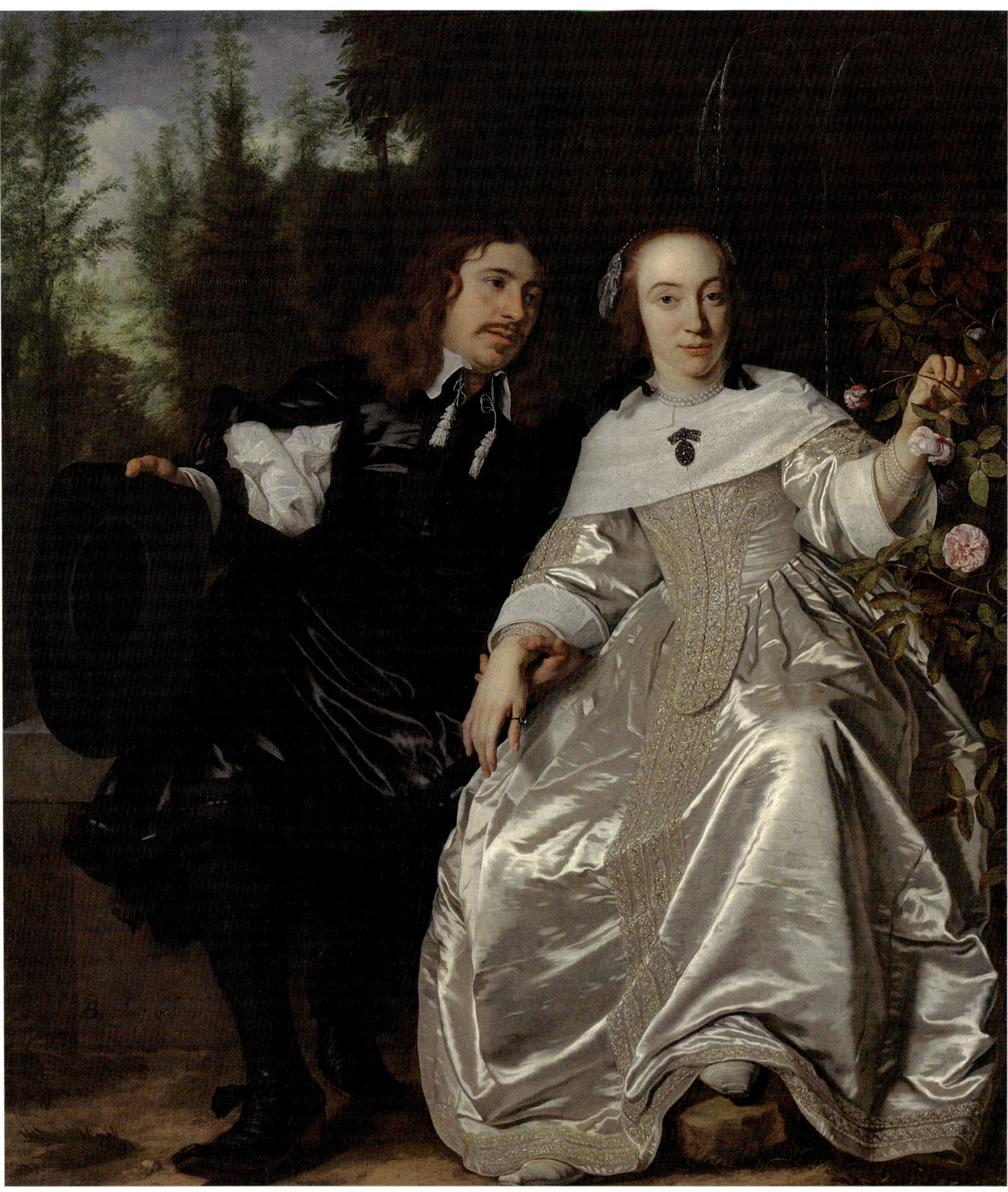

Abraham del Court and his wife Maria de Kaersgieter, Bartholomeus van der Helst, 1654, oil on canvas, 146.5 x 172cm (57¾ x 67¾ in), Museum Boijmans van Beuningen, Rotterdam, Netherlands

Abraham del Court (1623– after 1663) and Maria de Kaersgieter (1631–60) had married four years before Bartholomeus van der Helst painted this portrait of them. Although his style differs from both Rembrandt and Hals, his portraits were just as sought after. His brushmarks are precise and detailed and as he was also a draper, he was particularly interested in depicting the range of fabrics.

Titus at his Desk, Rembrandt, 1655, oil on canvas, 77 x 63cm (30¼ x 24¾in), Boijmans van Beuningen Museum, Rotterdam, Netherlands

Although Rembrandt painted his son Titus van Rijn (1641–68) on many occasions, he always conveyed him with undefined features, making his appearance quite ambiguous. With his long golden curls and big eyes, here he seems an angelic child, only at this time, he was much older than he looks – about 13 or 14 years old. So it seems that his father painted his son from memory of an earlier time.

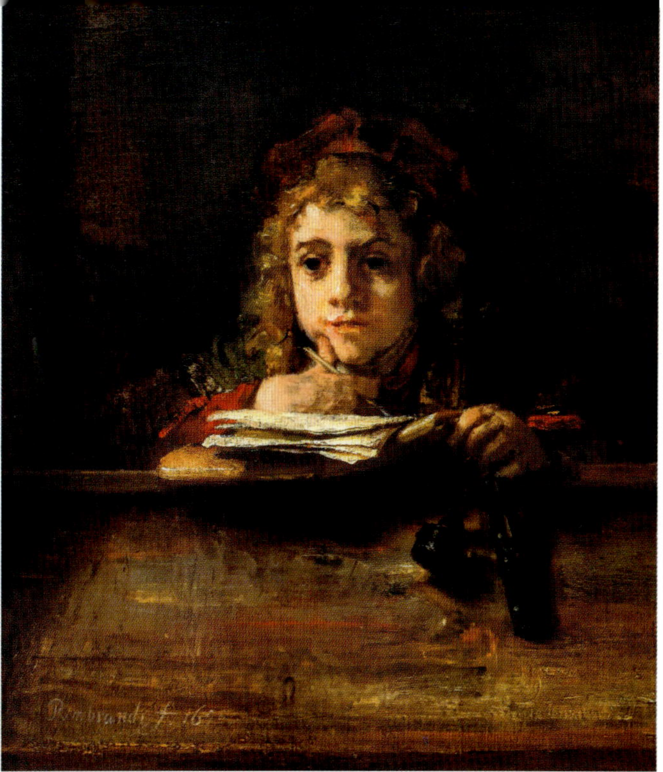

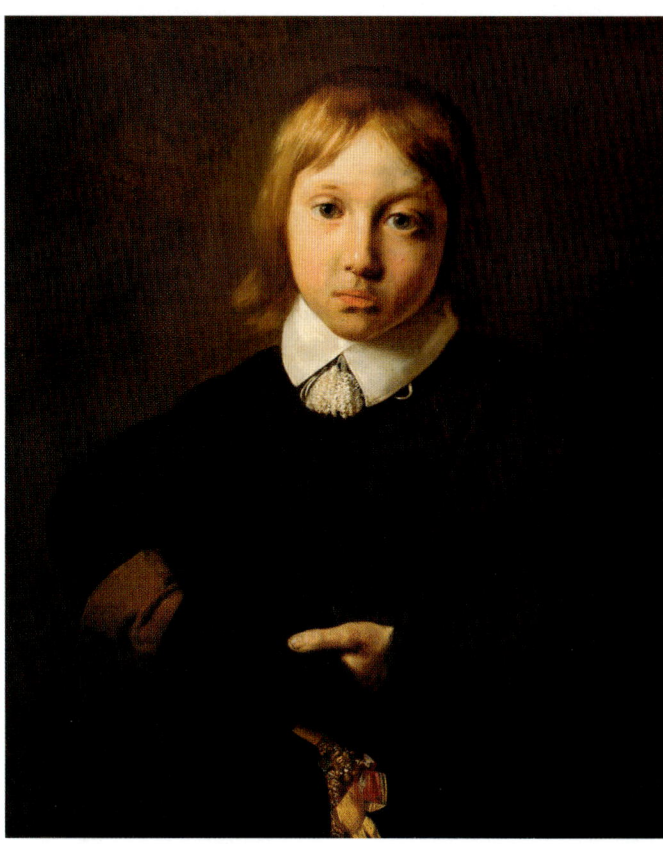

Portrait of a Boy Aged Six, Jan de Bray, 1654, oil on panel, 59.5 x 47cm (23½ x 18½in), Mauritshuis, The Hague, Netherlands

Inclining his head, this little boy who is probably about six to eight years old, looks directly at viewers. One hand is on his hip and the other clutches a ribboned hat. Painted with free yet delicate brushstrokes, the work reveals the artist's mastery in rendering details within a restricted space. Jan de Bray's small brushstrokes build up a smooth image that conveys light coming from the left.

Young Man in a Fur Cap and a Cuirass, Carel Fabritius, 1654, oil on canvas, 70.5 x 61.5cm (27¾ x 24¼in), The National Gallery, London, UK

Wearing a soldier's cuirass and a fur cap, this man stares at viewers. It is generally accepted that this is a self-portrait though it could be of someone else, or a tronie. The three-quarter pose and direct gaze, free paint handling, colours and even the solider's costume with a steel breastplate seem to derive from Rembrandt. This is one of Fabritius's final works. Soon after the painting was completed, Fabritius was killed in the Delft Thunderclap.

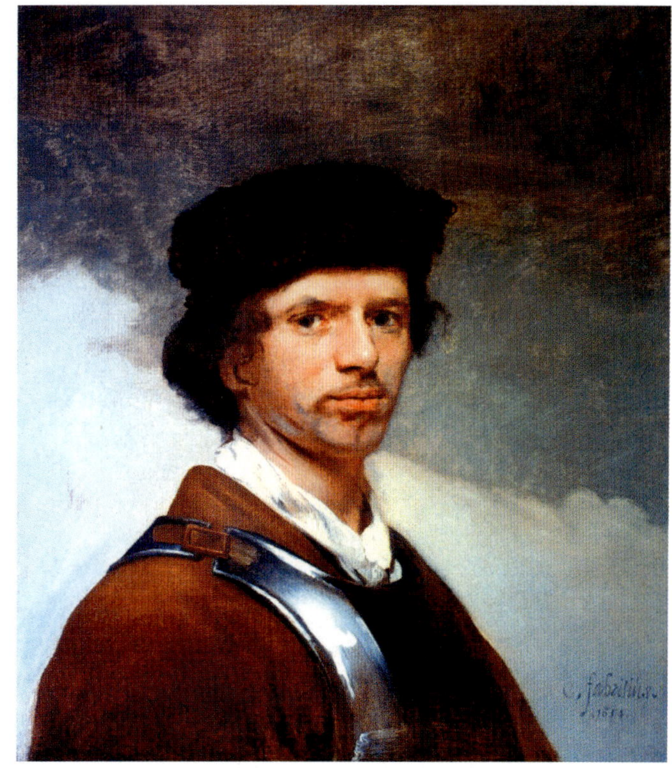

Portrait of Hendrickje Stoffels, Rembrandt, *c.*1656, oil on canvas, 67 × 88.5cm (26¼ × 34¾in), Gemäldegalerie, Staatliche Museen zu Berlin, Germany

A woman is leaning on a half-open door, looking at viewers with her head slightly inclined. She was probably Rembrandt's companion Hendrickje Stoffels, although her relaxed pose and casual clothing follows traditions of images of courtesans. However, the ring on her chain suggests that she was a married woman, and Rembrandt was referring to the disapproval of the Church over her relationship with him.

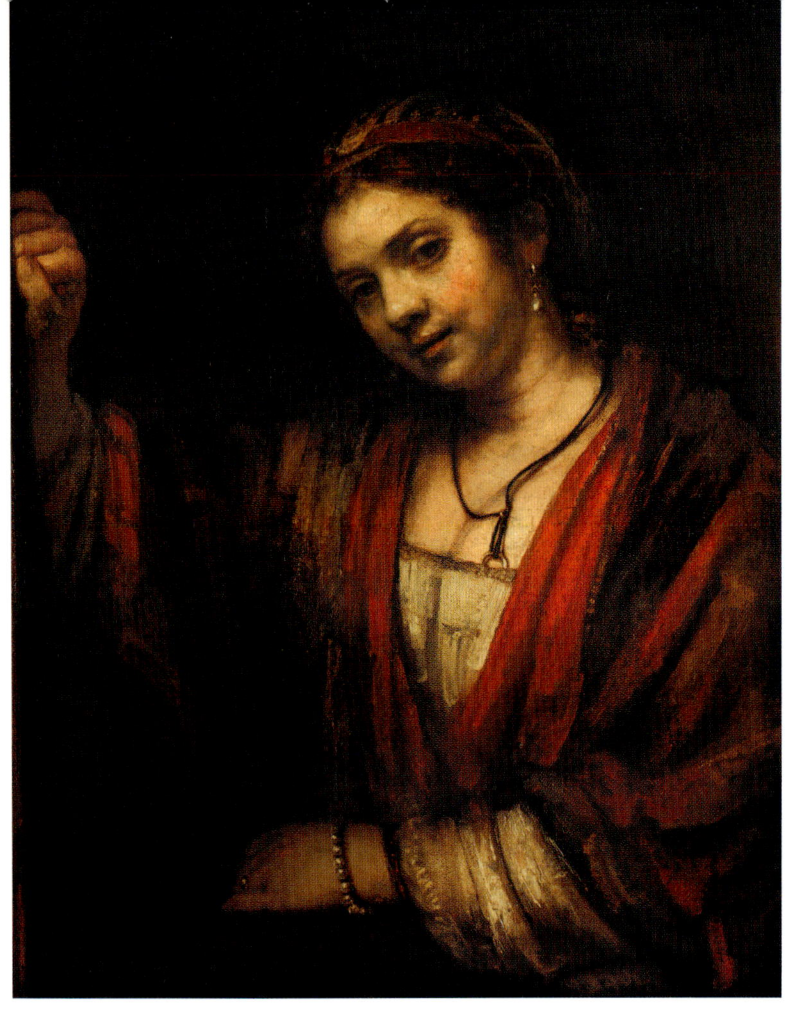

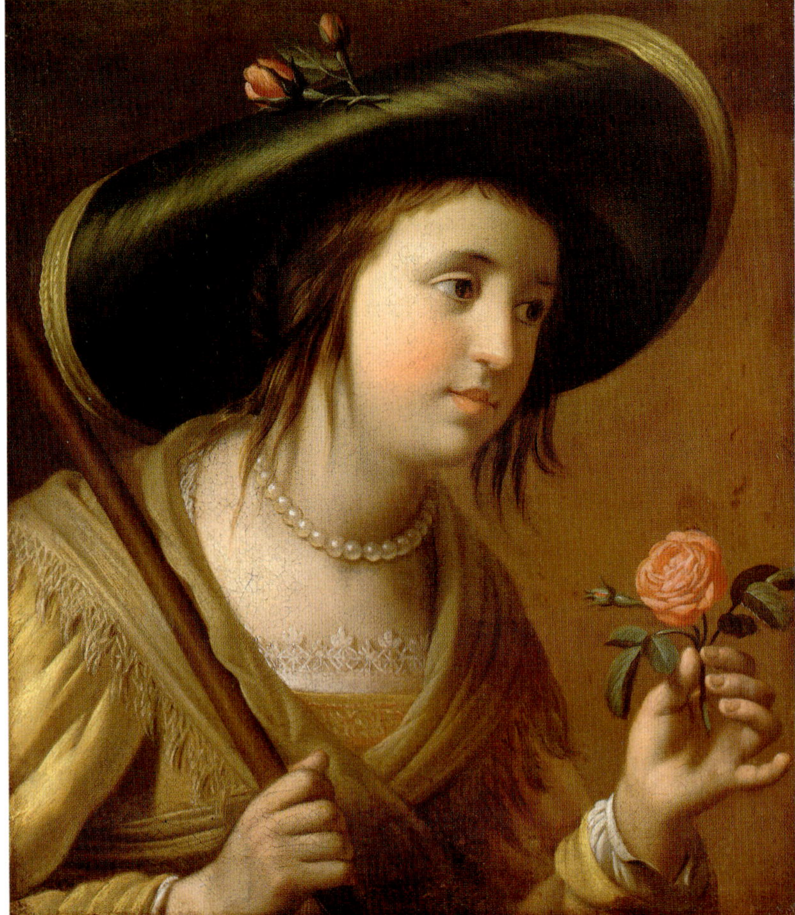

Portrait of Princess Elizabeth II van de Palts as a Shepherdess, Holding a Rose, Gerrit van Honthorst, 1656, oil on canvas, 52 × 44.2cm (20 × 17½in), Private Collection

Princess Elizabeth van de Palts (1618–80) also known as Elisabeth of Bohemia, Princess Elisabeth of the Palatinate, and Princess-Abbess of Herford Abbey, was the eldest daughter of Frederick V and Elizabeth Stuart. Famed for her correspondence with René Descartes, she was known as a philosopher. Van Honthorst's Baroque style particularly appealed to the aristocracy and royalty, and he became especially popular in his portrayal of light. Here he moves away from his usual chiaroscuro by working with a pale, soft palette.

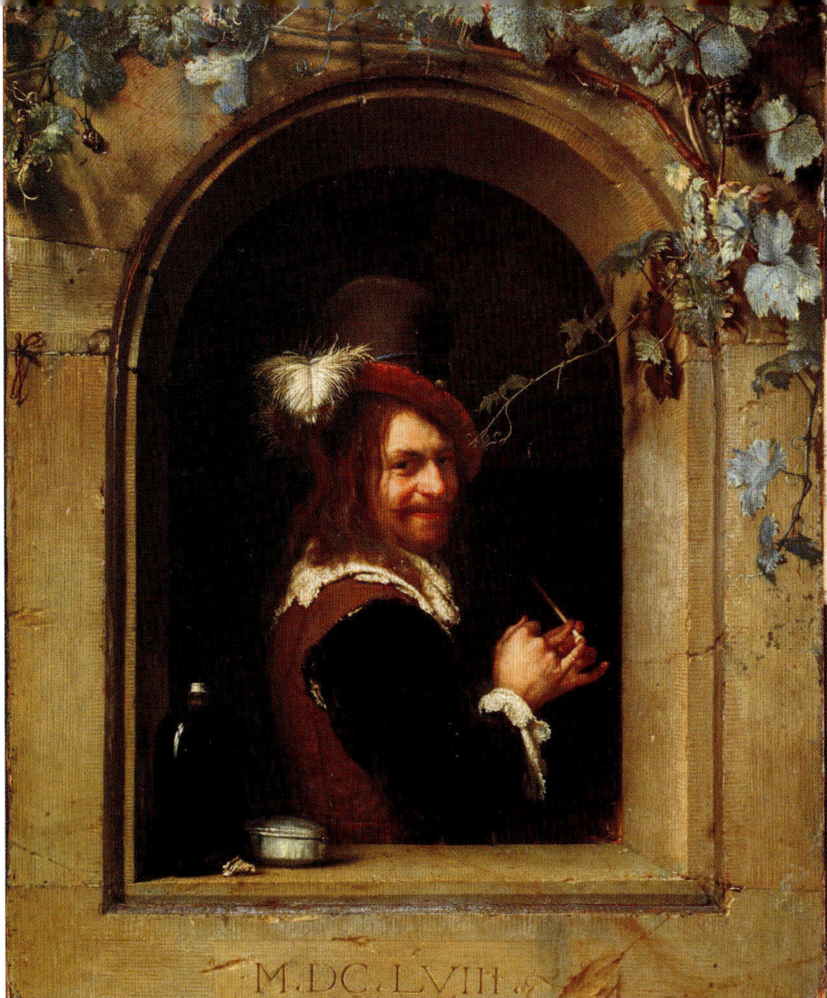

Man with Pipe at the Window,
Frans van Mieris, 1658,
oil on oak, 15.7 x 19.8cm
(6¼ x 7¾in), Brukenthal
National Museum, Sibiu,
Romania

A man tamps his pipe in a
window around which grow
vines, heavy with grapes. On
the window-sill is a bottle
of wine, a silver tobacco
box and a shell. This is one
of a series of portraits by
van Mieris featuring a sitter
at a window. Viewers are
intentionally intrigued, and
objects on the window-sill
seem to link the painting
with the outer world.

*The Baker Arent Oostwaard
and his Wife Catherina
Keizerswaard*, Jan Steen,
1658, 57.8 x 67cm (22¾
x 26¼in), Rijksmuseum,
Amsterdam, Netherlands

In the centre of this
composition, a man with
long hair proudly shows
off his freshly baked
produce. Beside him, his
wife Catharina holds up
a baked item. A little boy
stands nearby. Jan Steen
has incorporated several
genres in one work: a group
portrait, a still life of bread,
and a genre work displaying
a traditional profession and
family business.

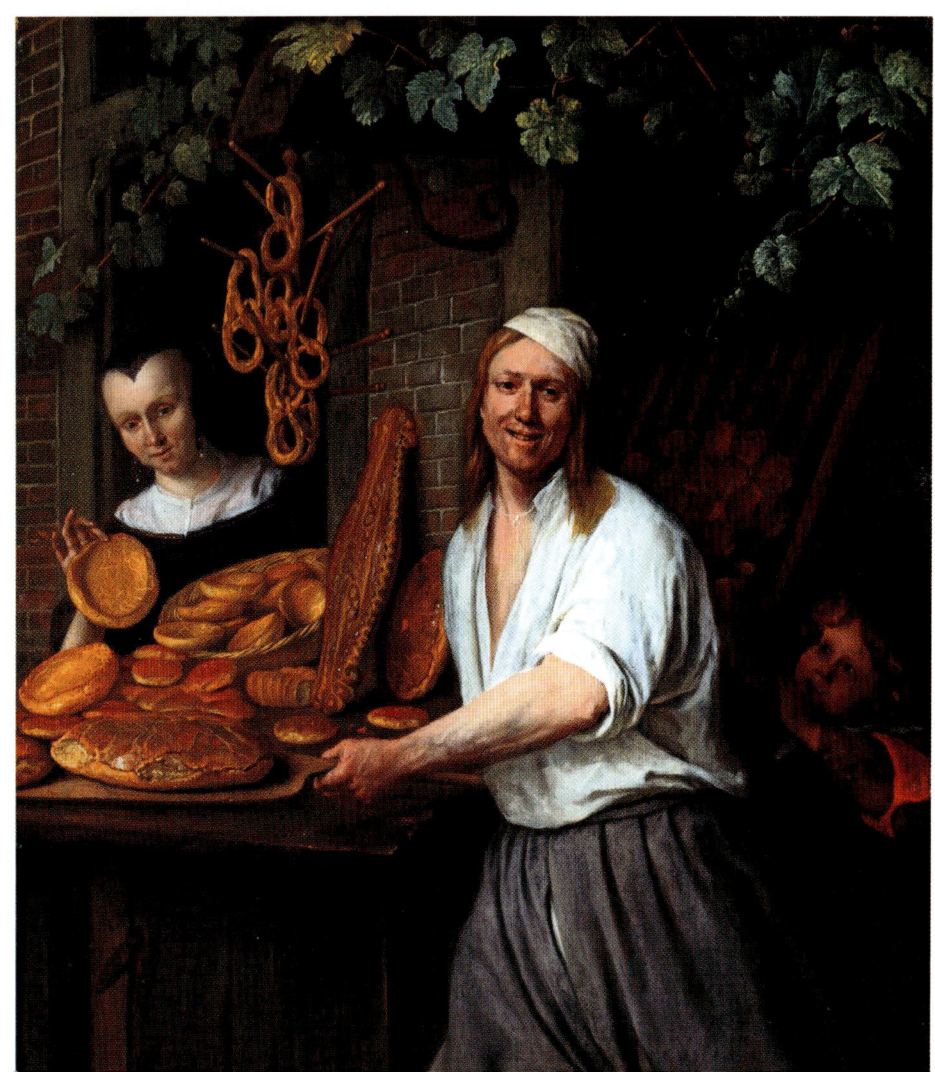

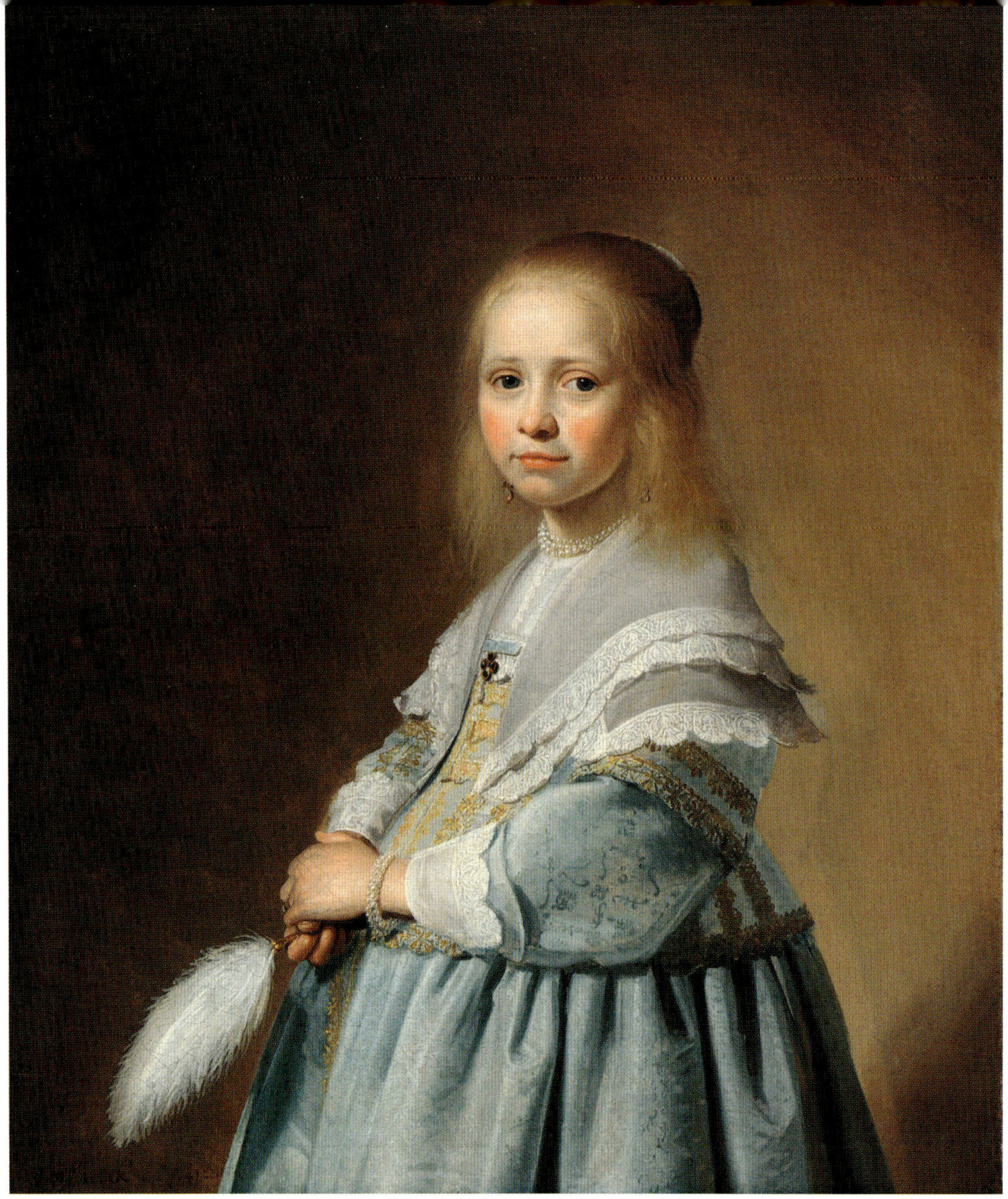

One of the best-known children's portraits from the Dutch Golden Age, this delicate portrait of a child with blonde hair and pink and white skin, dressed in adult finery, including pearls and heavy brocades, was painted in meticulous detail by Johannes Cornelisz Verspronck (1600/03–62) of Haarlem. A contemporary of Frans Hals and possibly his pupil, Verspronck's painting style was quite different. While Hals applied flamboyant, gestural brushmarks, Verspronck worked with a precise, refined style, featuring virtually imperceptible brushstrokes.

This portrait appears quite staid and conventional for the period, with the sitter dressed in black and a somewhat old-fashioned stiff white pleated ruff around his neck. The detailed realism of the sitter however, contrasts with the rather weathered wall behind him. Fabritius was friends with Potter, so perhaps the extremely realistic nail above his signature on this messy-looking wall was a joke between them.

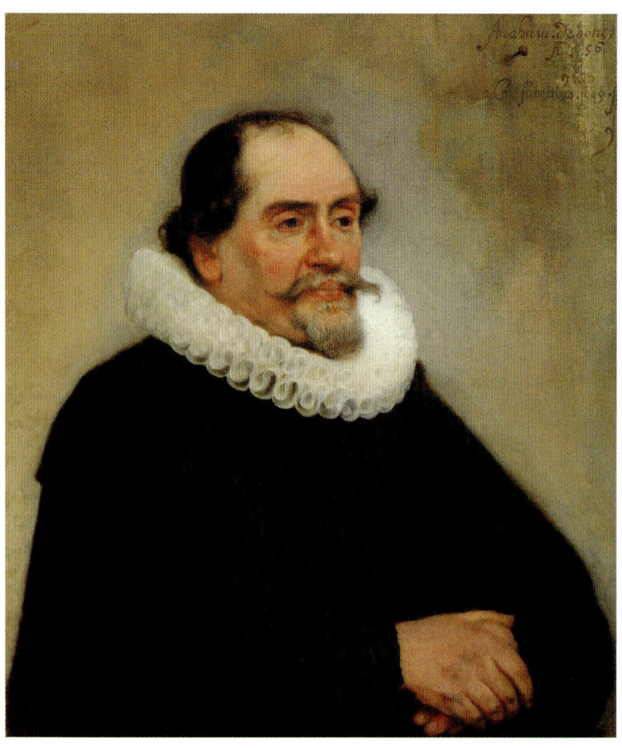

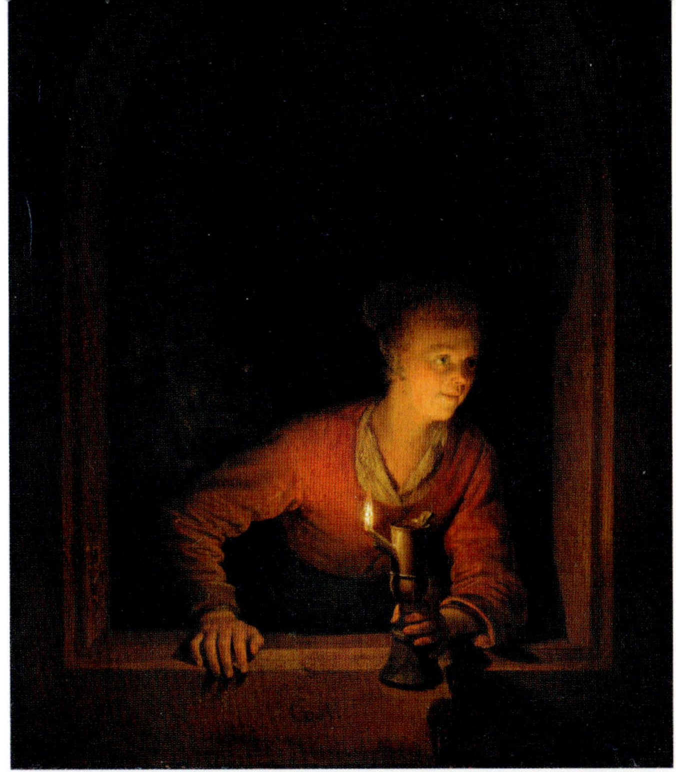

Girl with an Oil Lamp at a Window, Gerrit Dou, c.1645–75, oil on panel, 18.5 x 17.1 cm (7¼ x 6¾ in), Rijksmuseum, Amsterdam, Netherlands

Not strictly a portrait, this is a genre scene, but the tiny painting creates an intimate image of a girl in the darkness, holding an oil lamp and leaning out of a window.

It gave Dou the opportunity to paint with soft, glowing colours and chiaroscuro, using his characteristic brushmarks, and to capture a close likeness of one of his models. Rembrandt's first pupil, Dou became extremely sought after long after his death, but in the late 19th century, he became forgotten for approximately a century, until the 1970s.

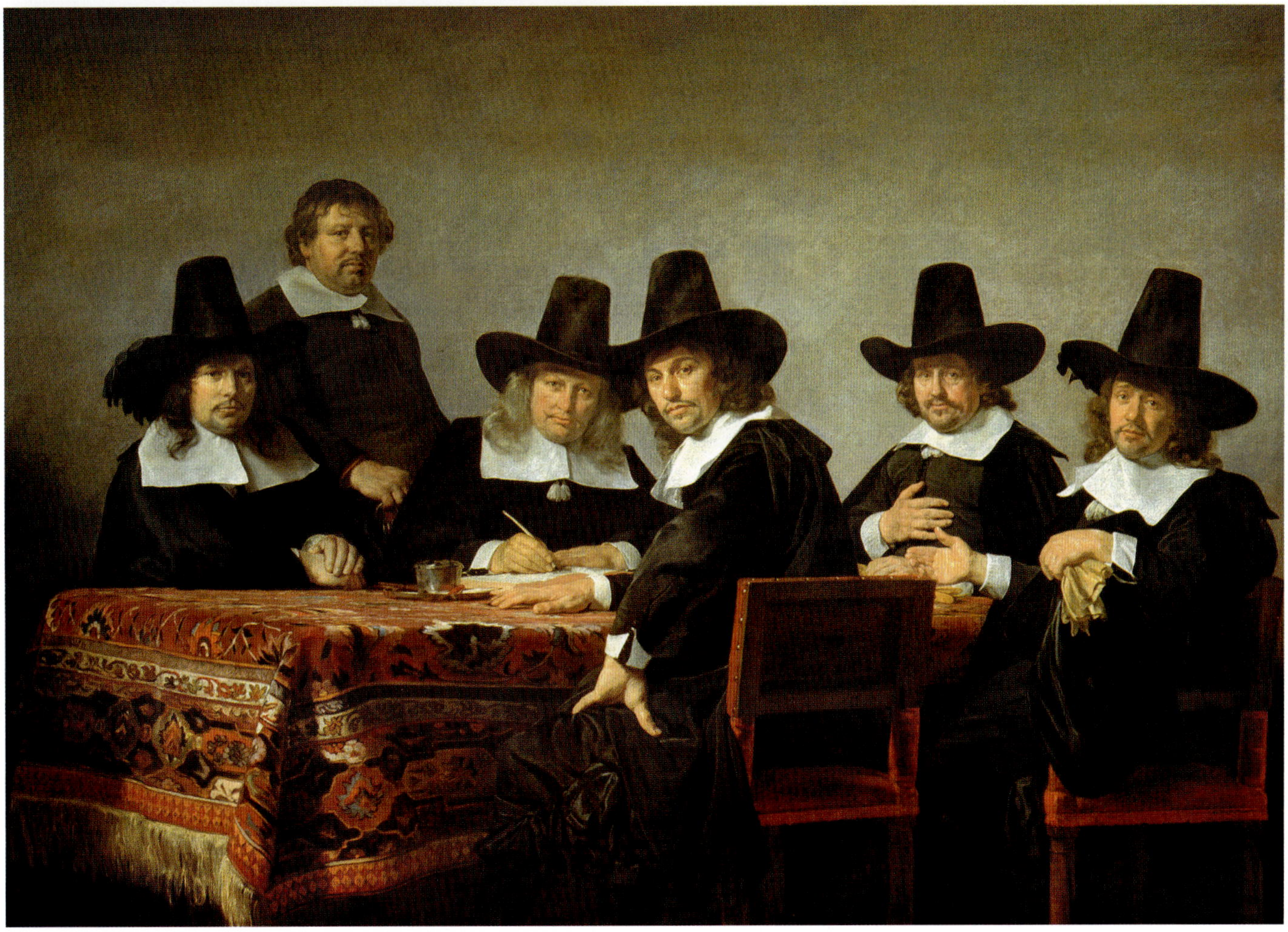

The Regents of the Children's Almshouse in Haarlem, Jan de Bray, 1663. oil on canvas, 187.5 x 249cm (73¾ x 98in), Frans Hals Museum, Haarlem, Netherlands

Jan de Bray painted various group portraits. Also known as *The Regents of the Arme-Kinderhuis in Haarlem*, this lively group picture depicts the male regents of the Children's Almshouse in Haarlem; another painting depicts the female regents. In steep perspective with light falling from the left, the chairman holds his hand on his chest. Although they are formally dressed as usual for the time, each man sits in a different pose and shows his individual personality.

A Girl with a Mirror (Allegory of Profane Love), Paulus Moreelse, 1627, oil on canvas, 106 x 83cm (47¾ x 32½in), Fitzwilliam Museum, Cambridge, UK

One of the important portraitists of the period, Paulus Moreelse was a pupil of another prominent portraitist, Michiel Janszoon van Mierevelt from Delft. Also an architect, Moreelse lived most of his life in Utrecht. While this is an allegory rather than a portrait, the sitter has clearly been painted from life. A voluptuous young woman, she reveals her décolleté to viewers, while on the table are gold jewellery, pearls, rings and a leather case, which reveal her to be a personification of profane love. The painting on the back wall and the text and image in the little book convey ideas about Eros, the ancient Greek god of love.

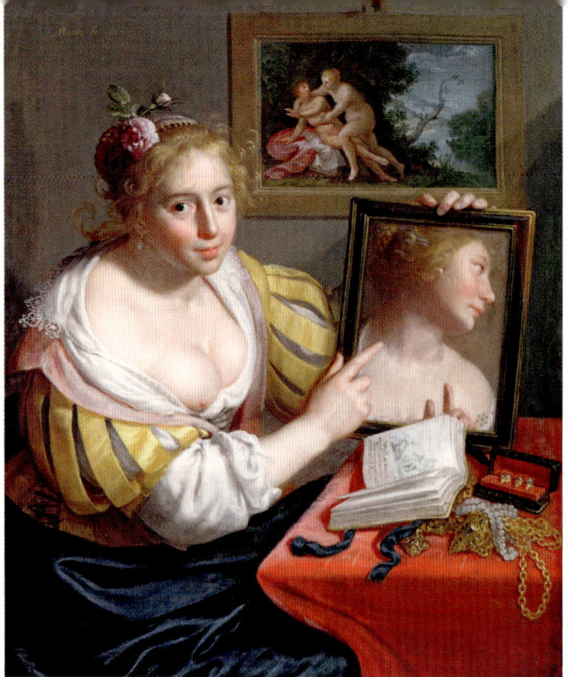

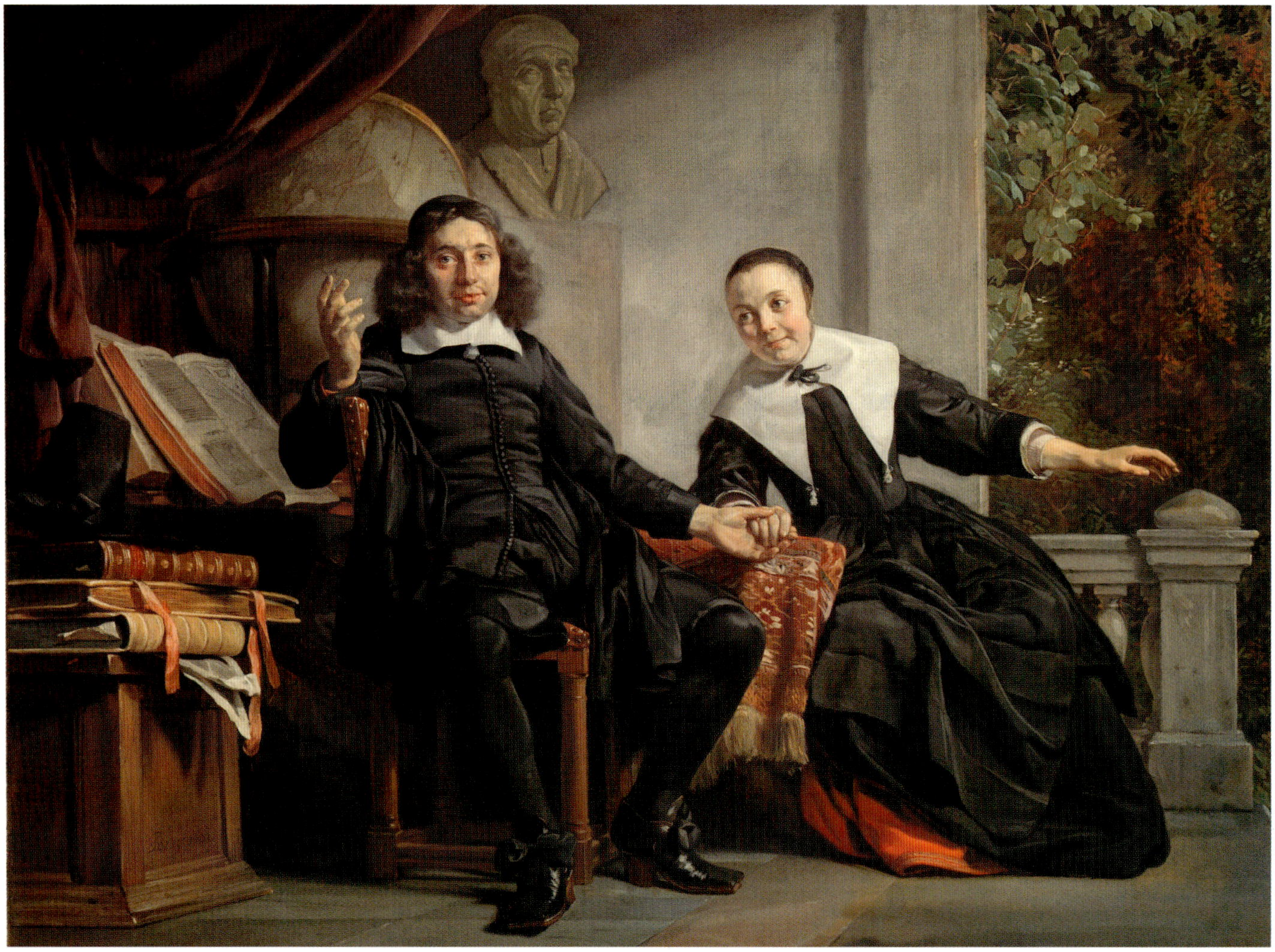

Portrait of Abraham Casteleyn and his Wife, Margaretha van Bancken, Jan de Bray, 1663, oil on canvas, 84 x 108cm (33 x 42½in), Rijksmuseum, Amsterdam, Netherlands

Casteleyn van Brancken was a printer and publisher in Amsterdam. Here he holds the hand of his wife Margaretha to demonstrate his love and fidelity. All around them are references to printing, including a bust of Laurens Jansz Coster (c.1370–1440) who was believed at the time to have invented the printing press, and various books. Indicating van Brancken's use of letters, an A is carved on a pedestal. Despite their restrained clothing, the double portrait is lively and relaxed, with Margaretha leaning across to her husband.

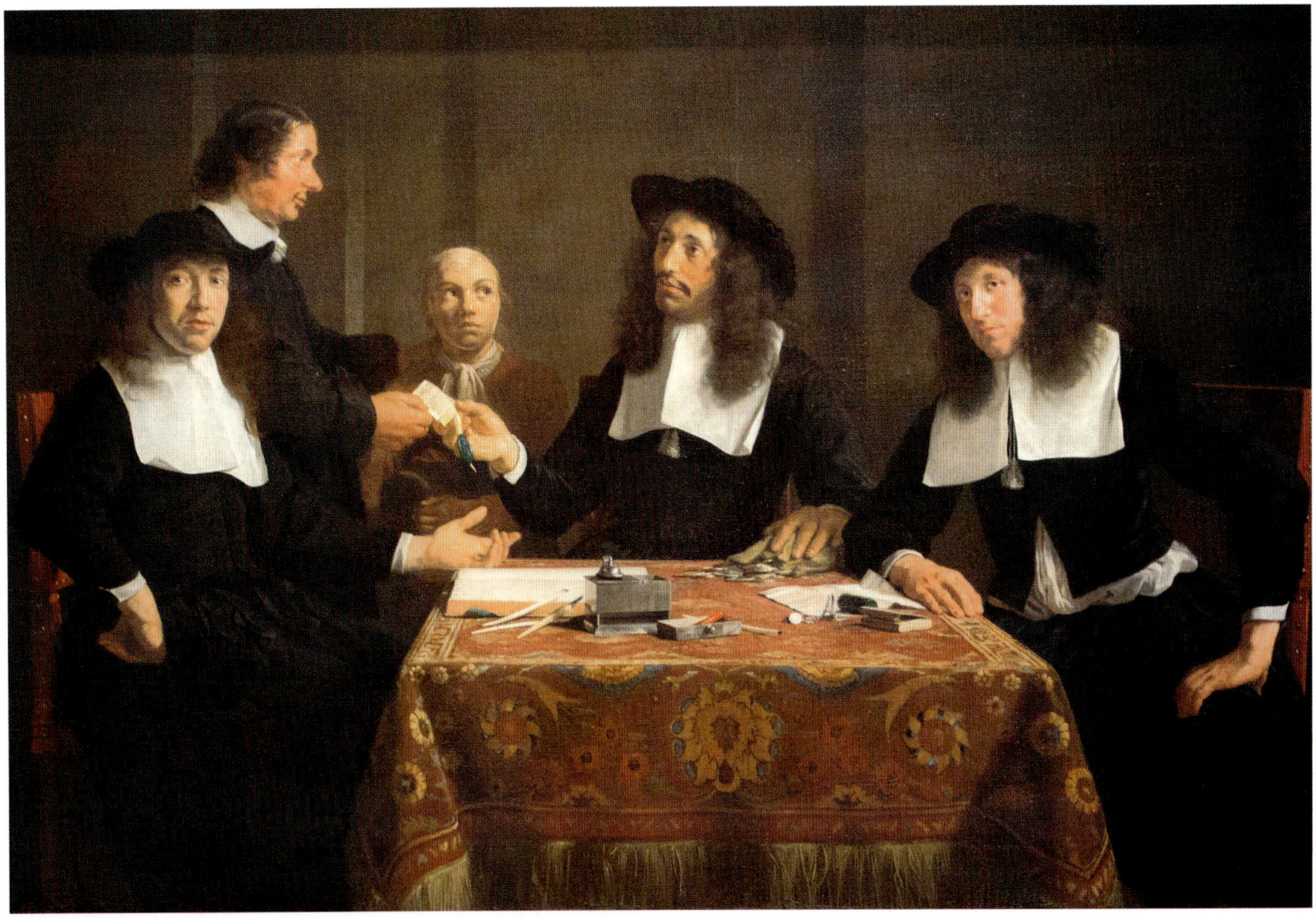

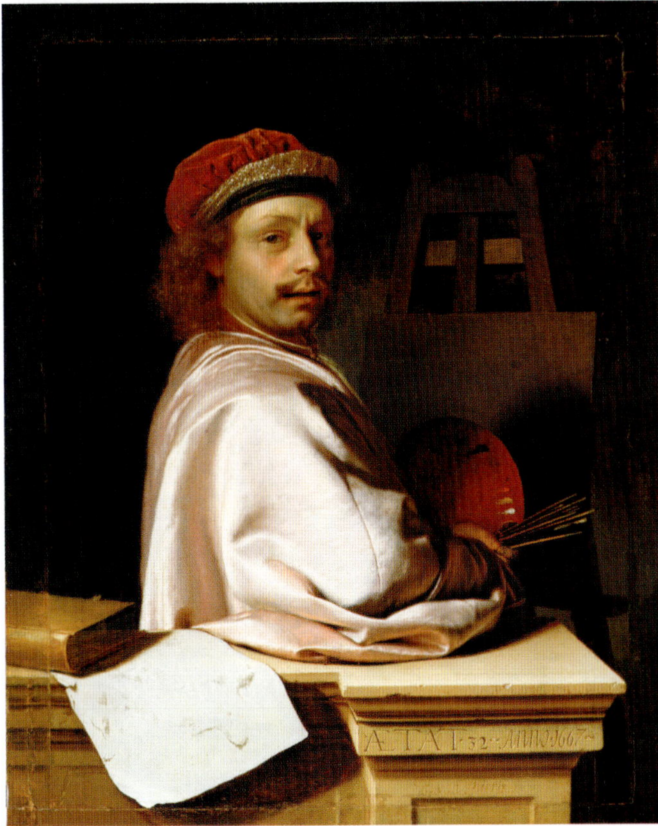

Governors of the Leper Hospital at Haarlem, Jan de Bray, 1667, oil on canvas, 142 x 197.5cm (56 x 77¾in), Frans Hals Museum, Haarlem, Netherlands

From this time, Jan de Bray had become the leading portrait painter in Haarlem and he was commissioned to paint the trustees of the Leper Hospital just outside the town. De Bray's bold composition and animated figures appealed to the trustees, here shown sitting around a table covered by a valuable Indian carpet. Rather than a static portrait, this shows action: a man has brought in a new patient.

The Artist as Virtuoso at his Easel: Self Portrait, Aged 32, Frans van Mieris, 1667, oil on panel, 19 x 15cm (7½ x 6in), Polesden Lacey, Surrey, UK

Demonstrating the importance of the self-portrait as an artist's marketing tool during the 17th century, this painting by fijnschilder Frans van Mieris presents himself as a distinguished gentleman, self-confident and at the height of his fame. He leans on a balustrade, slightly set back from viewers with his materials around him. He holds brushes and a palette and behind him are an easel, a drawing and a book.

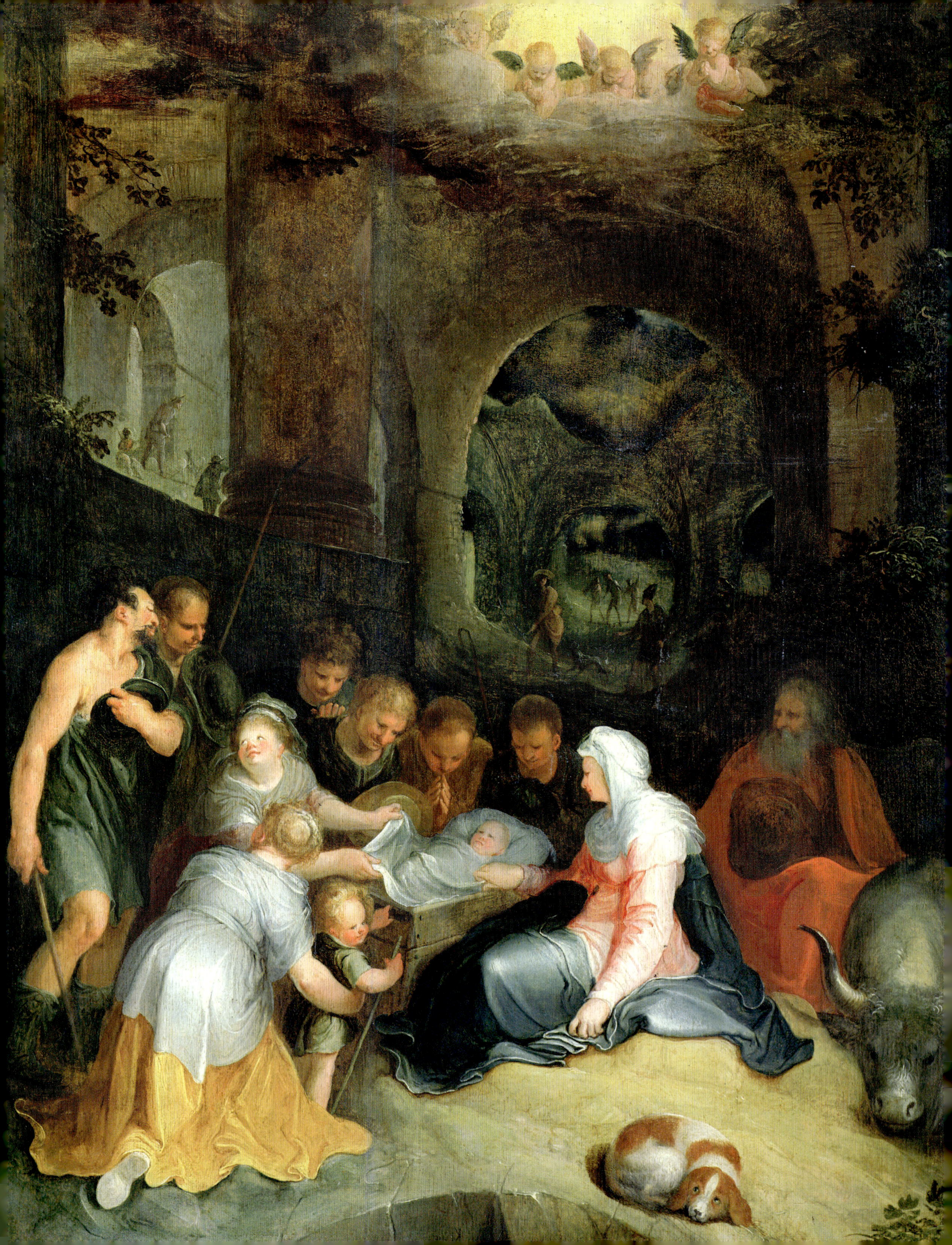

HISTORY AND RELIGION

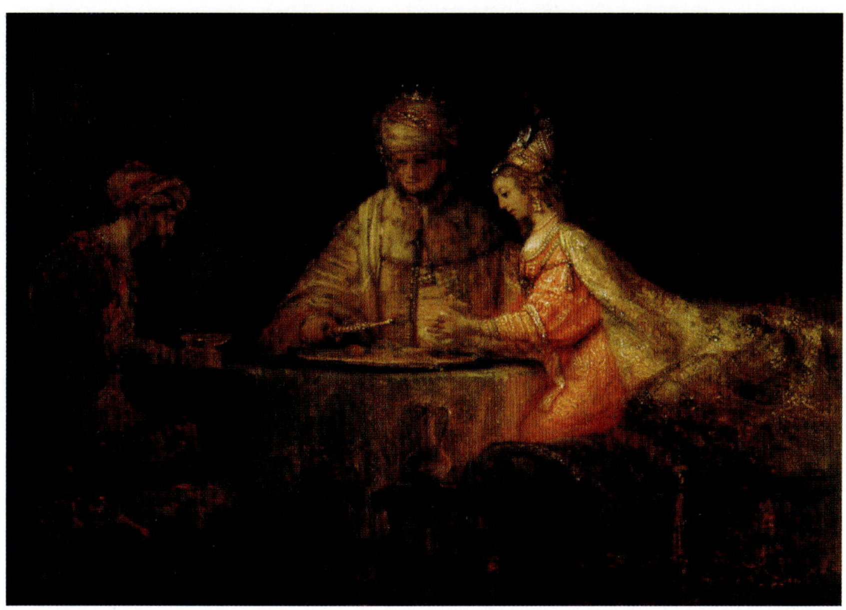

Unlike other European countries where history paintings were of the highest status, in the Dutch Republic, paintings that depicted historical events were not the most popular. Some paintings did portray biblical, mythological, literary and allegorical scenes, but on the whole, as there were few Catholic churches or Baroque mansions to fill, large and dramatic historical or biblical scenes were produced less frequently, and paintings were generally perceived as embellishments for the home. Those history paintings that were created were generally influenced by Italian Baroque painting styles, particularly by Caravaggio, and made heavy use of chiaroscuro. Although religious paintings were rarely commissioned, a fashion did develop for small-scale works featuring Christian messages or moral lessons.

Above: Ahasuerus, Haman and Esther, *1660, Rembrandt. Based on the Old Testament story of Esther, this depicts a banquet held by the Persian King Ahasuerus, whose Jewish wife Esther accuses the king's favourite Haman of plotting to destroy her people. The scene conveys a tense atmosphere.*

Left: The Adoration of the Shepherds, *Karel van Mander, 1598. Van Mander was one of the earliest Dutch Golden Age painters. His book* Het Schilderboeck (The Painter's Book) *in 1604 was the first extensive account of the major Northern European artists, including his views about the theory and practice of painting.*

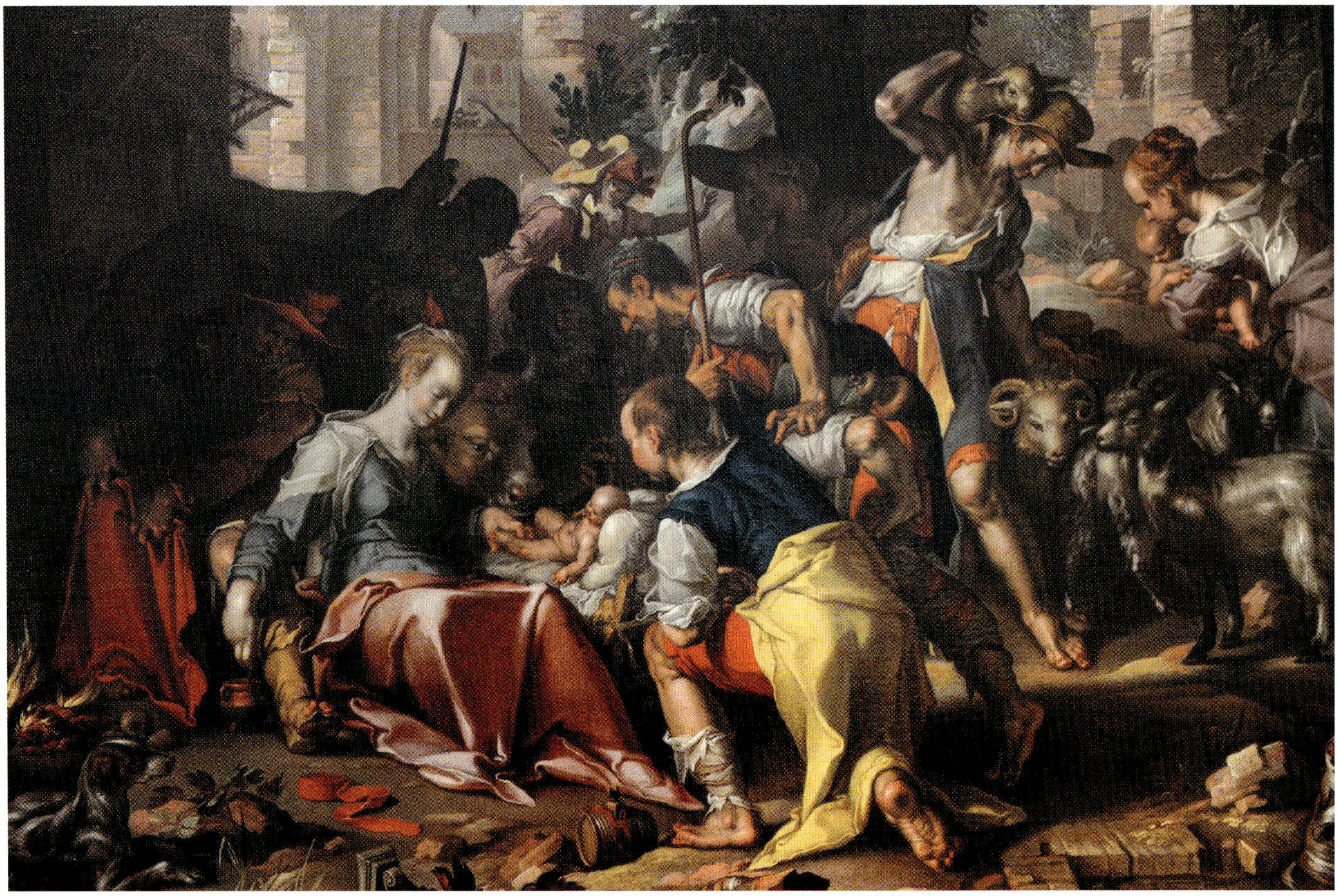

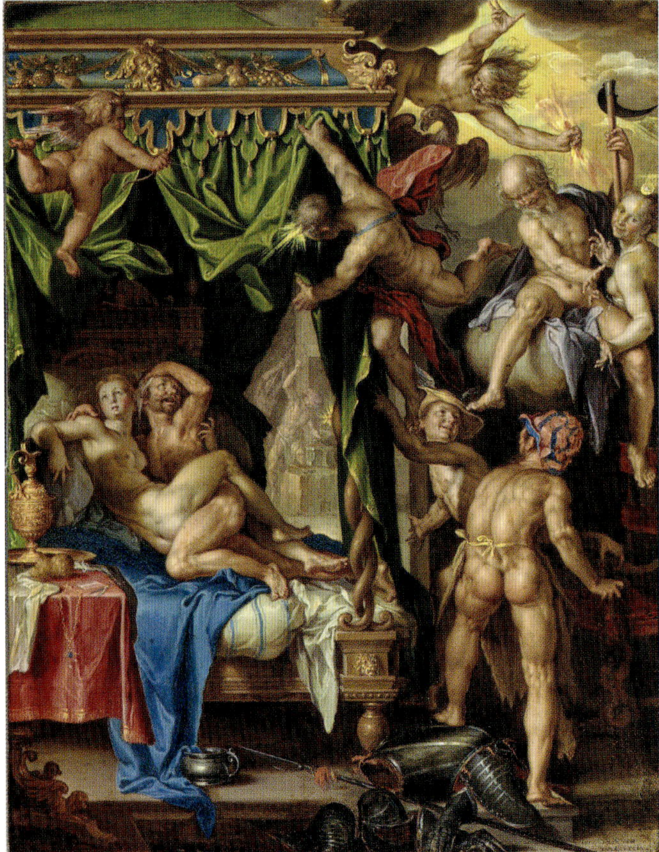

Adoration of the Shepherds, Joachim Wtewael, 1598, 106.9 x 86.7cm (41¾ x 34in), Centraal Museum, Utrecht, Netherlands

Flowing, elegant and flamboyant, this epitomizes Wtewael's Mannerist painting style that continued throughout his career. Utrecht was the main centre of Catholicism in the primarily Protestant country and that was where Wtewael worked. His figures, composition and palette resemble the style of paintings being produced by Flemish artists such as Rubens and reflect the period of four years that he spent studying art in Italy and France.

Mars and Venus Surprised by Vulcan, Joachim Wtewael, *c.*1606–10, oil on copper, 20.3 x 15.5cm (8 x 6in), J. Paul Getty Museum, Los Angeles, USA

One of the leading exponents of Mannerism in the Netherlands, Joachim Wtewael painted with exaggerated, elongated figures in lavish surroundings. Here, the lovers Mars and Venus are in bed when they are surprised by several other gods, including Venus's husband, Vulcan. He stands on Mars's armour, while Cupid and Apollo hover above, holding back the green canopy of the lovers' bed.

The Massacre of the Innocents in Bethlehem, Cornelis van Haarlem, 1591, oil on canvas, 268 x 257cm (105½ x 101in), Rijksmuseum, Amsterdam, Netherlands

In the Bible, King Herod of Judea heard the prophecy of a child born in Bethlehem who would become king of the Jews. To prevent this, he ordered that all baby boys under the age of two must be killed. In this Rubenesque painting, the massacre is taking place.

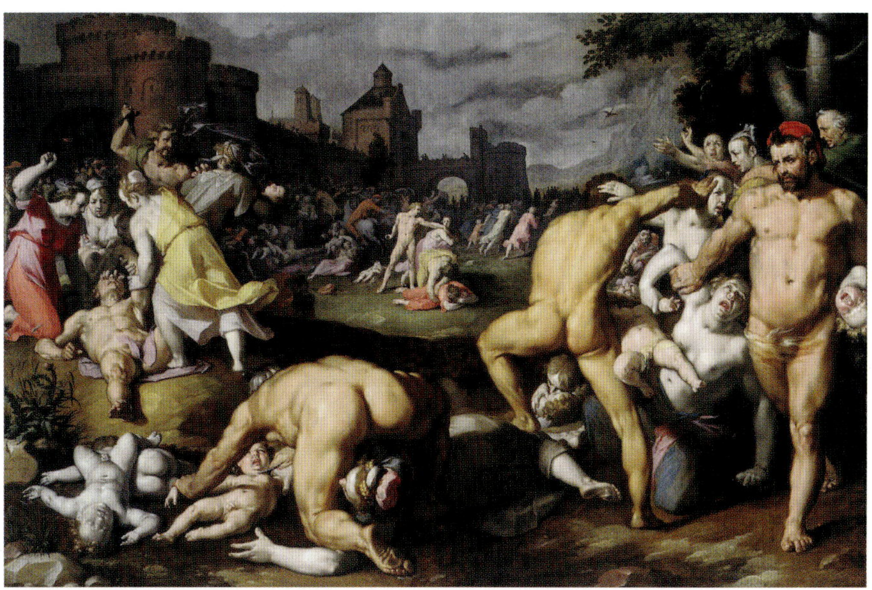

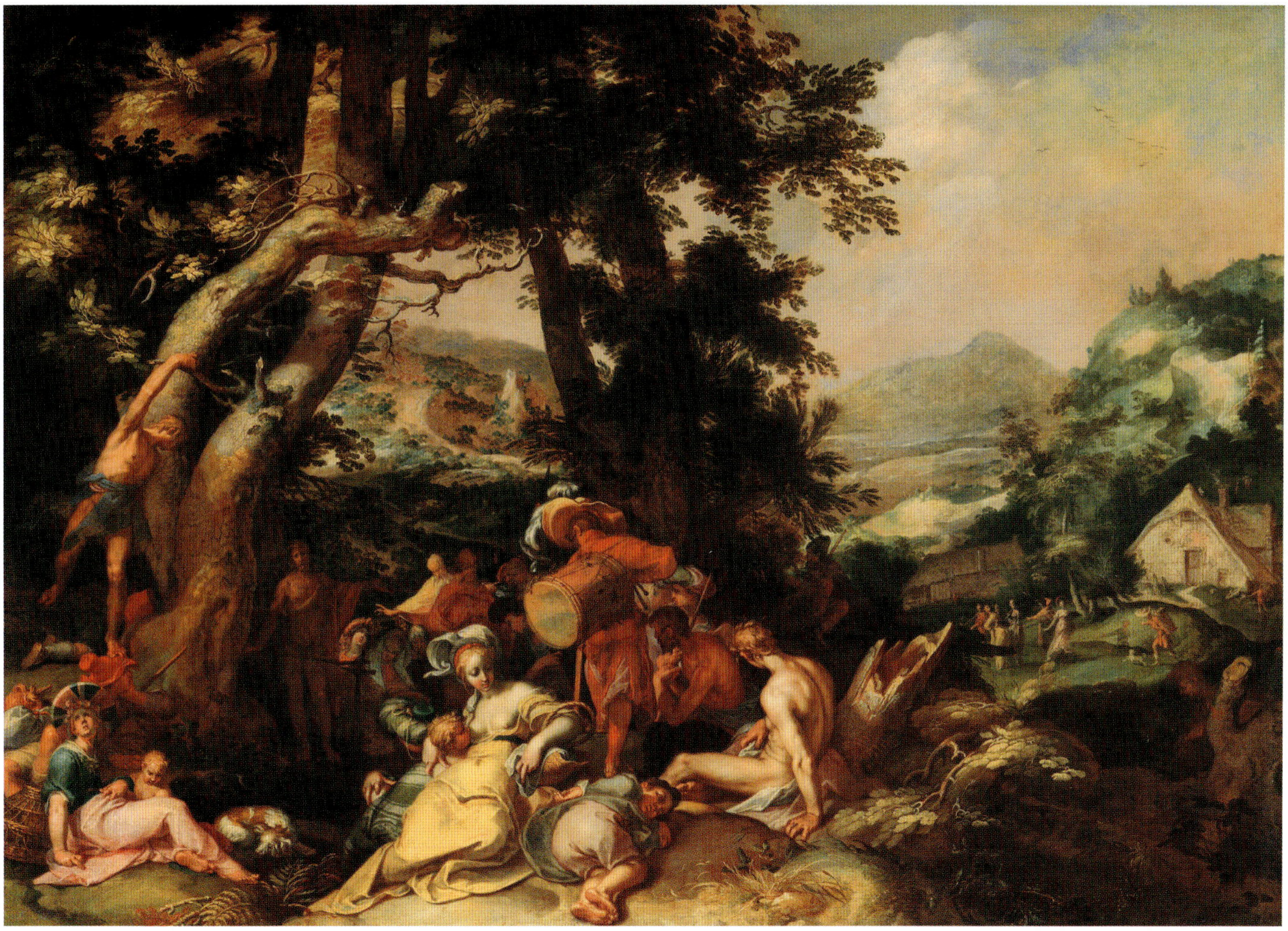

The Preaching of Saint John the Baptist, Abraham Bloemaert, 1590–1610, oil on canvas, 139 x 188cm (54¾ x 74in), Rijksmuseum, Amsterdam, Netherlands

Close to the base of the leaning tree, John the Baptist is preaching in the shadows. Various figures are busy within the scene, several in complicated poses; some are naked and some are dressed in colourful, contemporary fashions, one bangs a drum. Rather than portray a Netherlandish scene, Bloemaert has painted a landscape with mountains in the background, leafy trees and cottages.

Judith with the Head of Holofernes, Gerrit Pietersz Sweelinck, 1605, oil on canvas, 122.5 x 107.5cm (48¼ x 42¼in), Museum Boijmans van Beuningen, Rotterdam, Netherlands

In the Bible, Judith was a Jewish widow of noble rank. After the enemy commander Holofernes attacked her home town, she visited his tent, pretending to want to try to negotiate with him, but after he tried to seduce her, she decapitated him and put his head in a sack held open by a serving woman. Amsterdam-based Gerrit Pietersz Sweelinck (1566–after 1612) was known for his portraits and mythological and religious paintings.

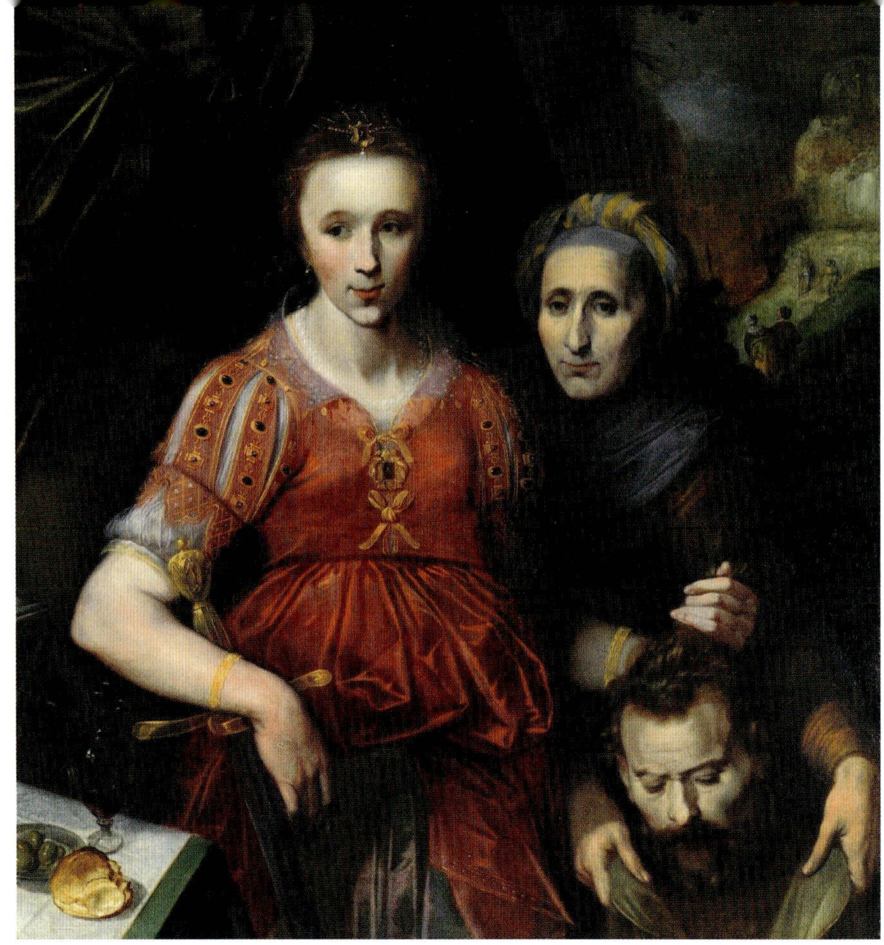

The Martyrdom of Saint Catherine, Hendrick ter Brugghen, c.1618–20, oil on panel, 99.1 x 73.3cm (39 x 28¾in), Chrysler Museum of Art, Virginia, USA

In his usual dramatic style, Hendrick ter Brugghen has illustrated the story of the 4th-century princess, Catherine of Alexandria, who resisted the pagan Roman Emperor Maxentius because of her Christian faith and was sentenced to die. When she survived the tortures of a spiked wheel through God's intervention, Maxentius had her beheaded. Here, with his restrained palette, ter Brugghen includes the broken wheel that is Catherine's saintly attribute.

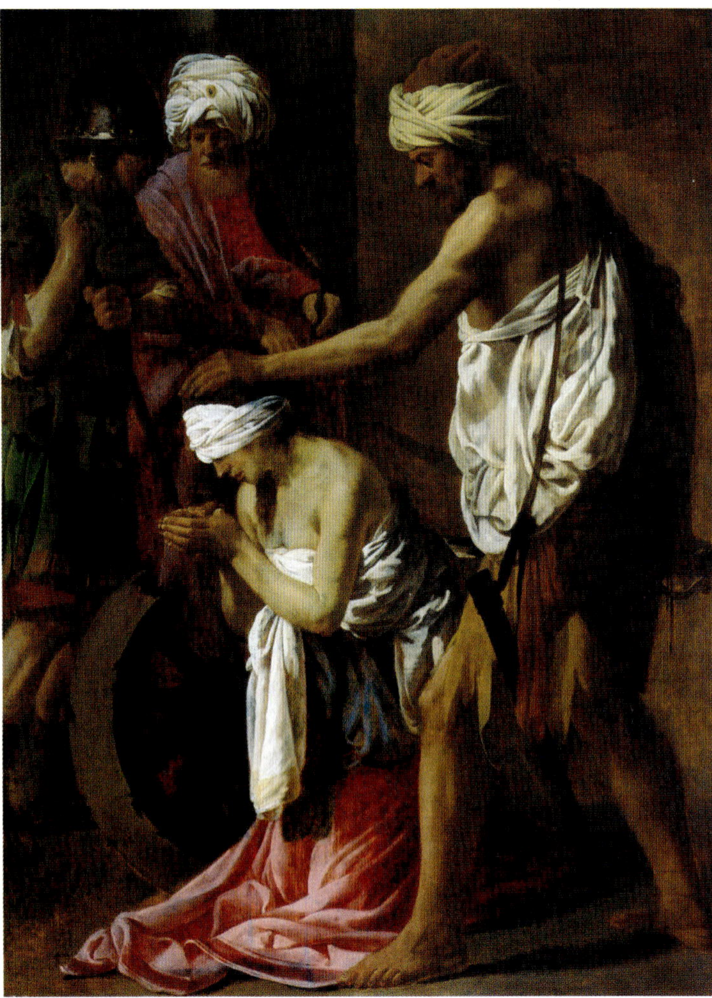

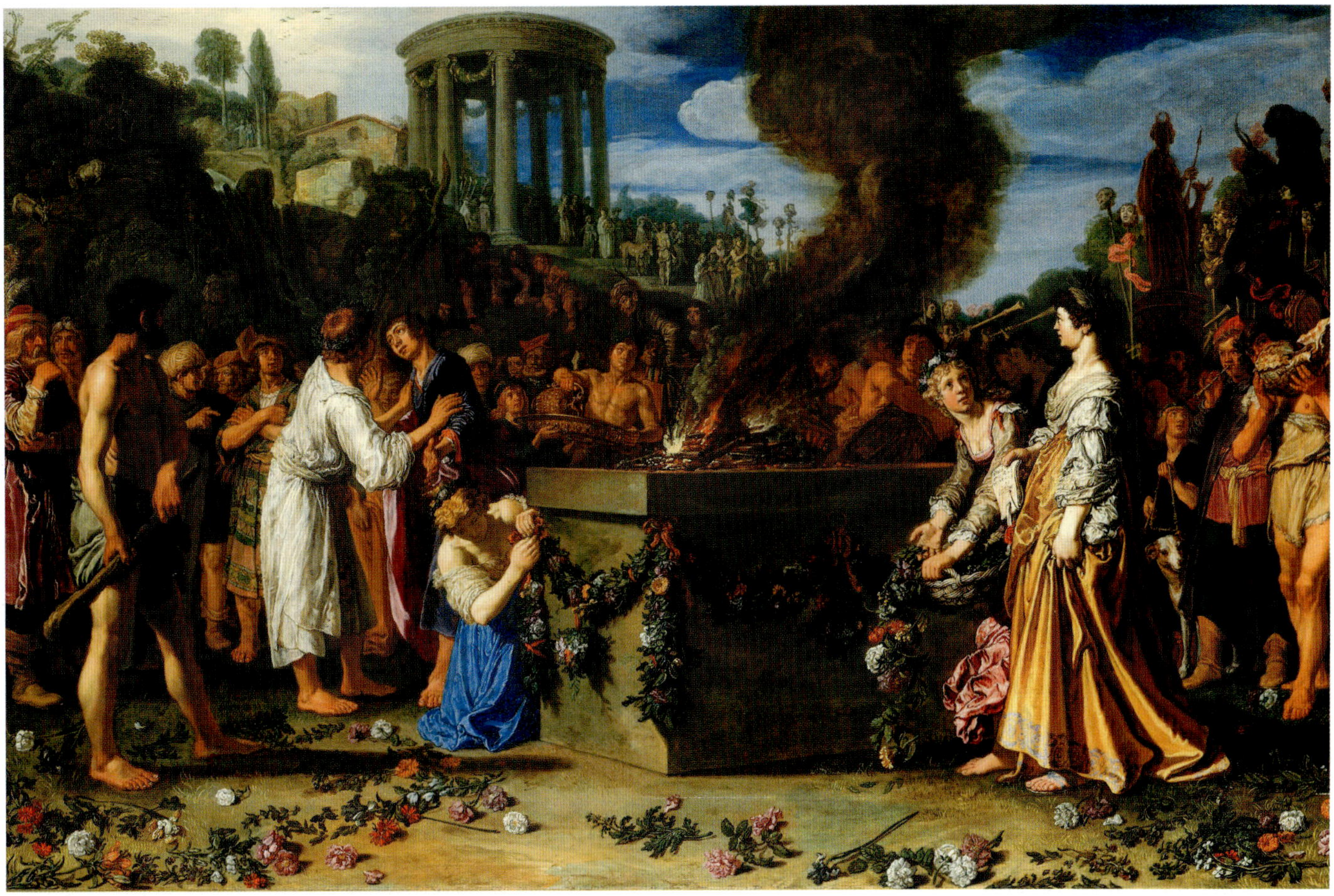

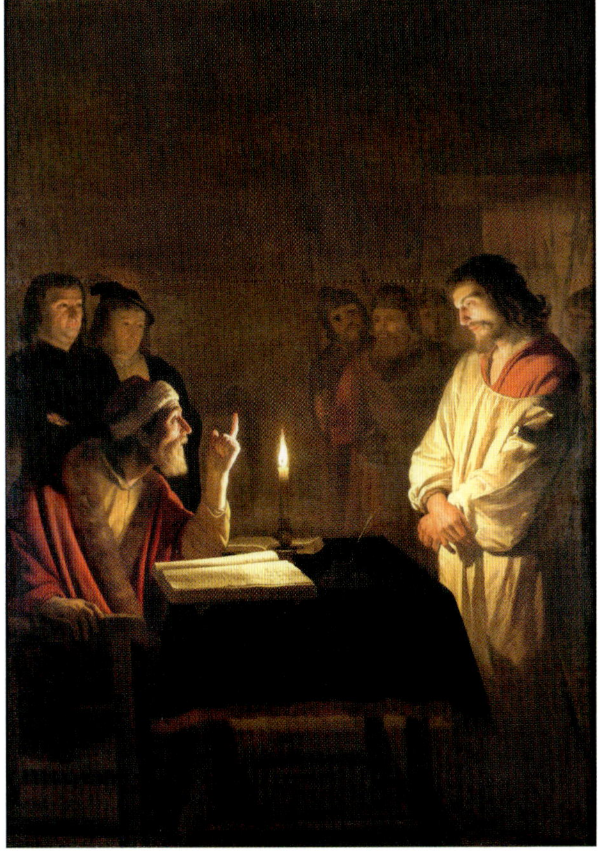

Orestes and Pylades Disputing at the Altar, Pieter Lastman, 1614, oil on panel, 83.2 x 126.1cm (32¾ x 49½in), Rijksmuseum, Amsterdam, Netherlands

Pieter Lastman depicts the ancient Greek myth of the friends Orestes and Pylades, as written by Euripides. The two friends argue about which of them should sacrifice himself, while an executioner stands by with his club, ready to kill one of them. Beside the altar dressed in gold satin is Orestes's sister Iphigenia, who is a priestess of Artemis.

Christ Before the High Priest, Gerrit van Honthorst, c.1617, oil on canvas, 272 x 183cm (107 x 72in), The National Gallery, London, UK

A Catholic in the mainly Protestant Dutch Republic, Gerrit van Honthorst developed his future style while living in Rome. He painted this while he was there and it shows Caravaggio's powerful influence, using subtle contrasts of golden light and deep shadows. In the new Testament, Christ was brought before the High Priest by Roman soldiers, where he was questioned about his teachings and false testimony was called against him.

The Adoration of the Magi,
Hendrick ter Brugghen,
1619, oil on canvas, 133
x 160.5cm (52 x 63 in),
Rijksmuseum, Amsterdam,
Netherlands

On a large canvas, the three
Magi have arrived and are
giving their offerings to the
baby Jesus who is sitting on
his mother's lap. Melchior
is kneeling, with Balthasar
and Caspar standing behind.
Various other figures and
animals are crowded into the
background, each delineated
with careful, detailed, brushmarks, using light and shade
to create solidity and depth.

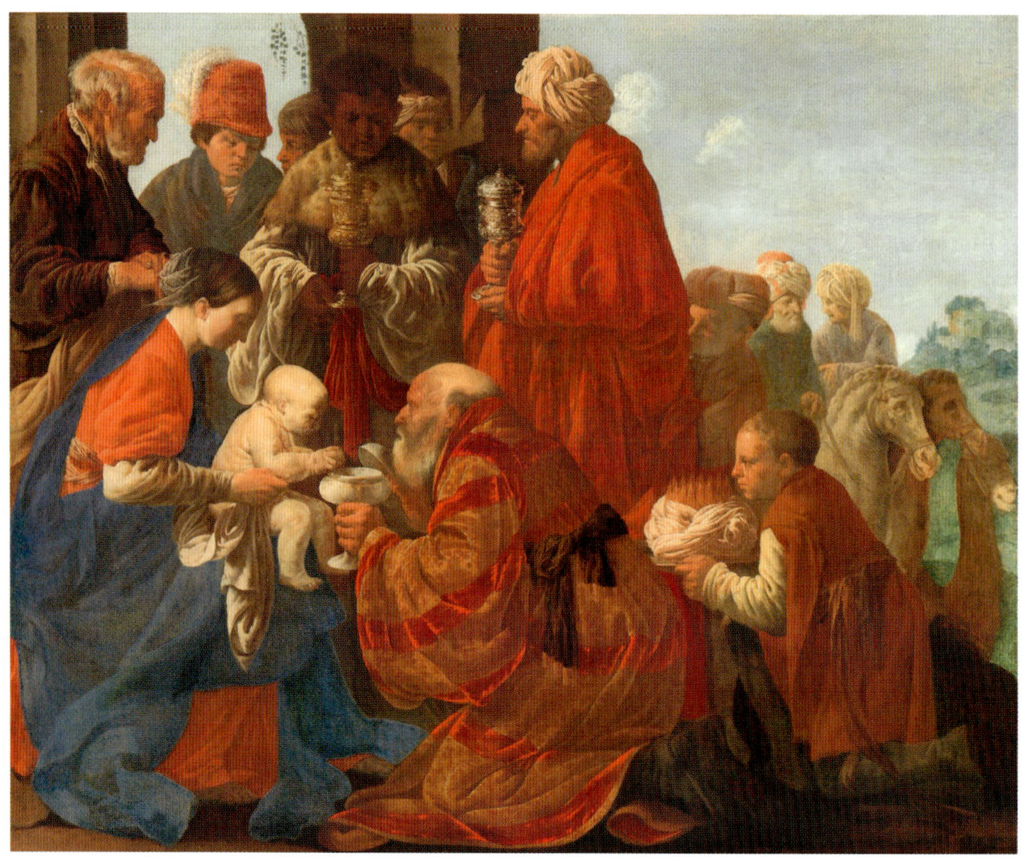

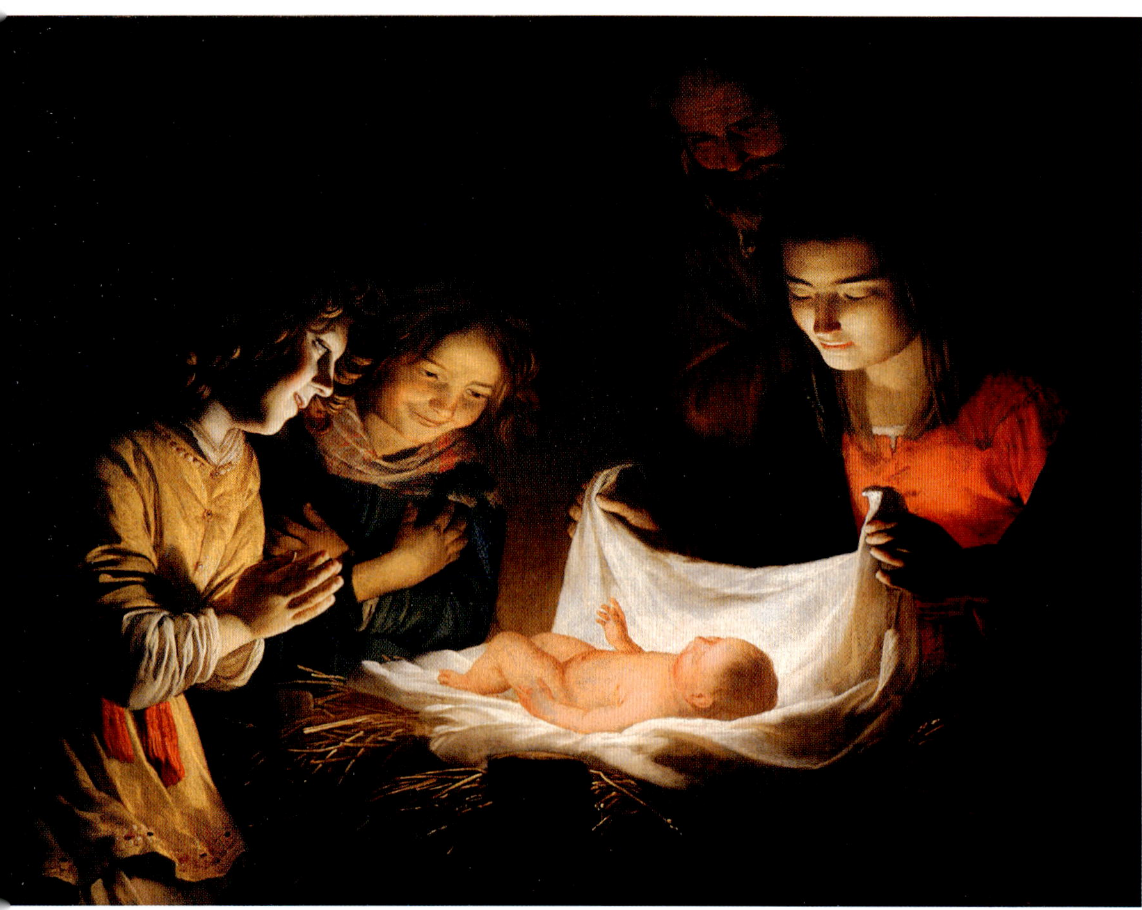

Adoration of the Child, Gerrit
van Honthorst, *c.*1620, oil
on canvas, 131 x 95.5cm
(37½ x 52in), Galleria degli
Uffizi, Florence, Italy

Probably van Honthorst's
most famous work, this
moonlit scene depicts Mary
laying her baby in swaddling
clothes, while Joseph, in
shadow, looks over her, and
two smiling angels lean over
the crib. Light seems to
emanate from the baby and
reflect on the happy, serene
faces gathered around. In
the year this was painted,
van Honthorst returned to
Utrecht from Italy.

Christ Crowned with Thorns, Dirck van Baburen, *c*.1622, oil on canvas, 106 x 136cm (41¾ x 53½in), Museum Catharijneconvent, Utrecht, Netherlands

Great impact is made here through Dirck van Baburen's strong contrasts of light and dark, and the characters he has created through individual facial features and gestures. Despite being just 20 when he painted this, van Baburen has depicted a range of emotions, including the ignorance and belligerence of the executioners and the suffering but acceptance of Christ as the crown of thorns is pressed on to his head.

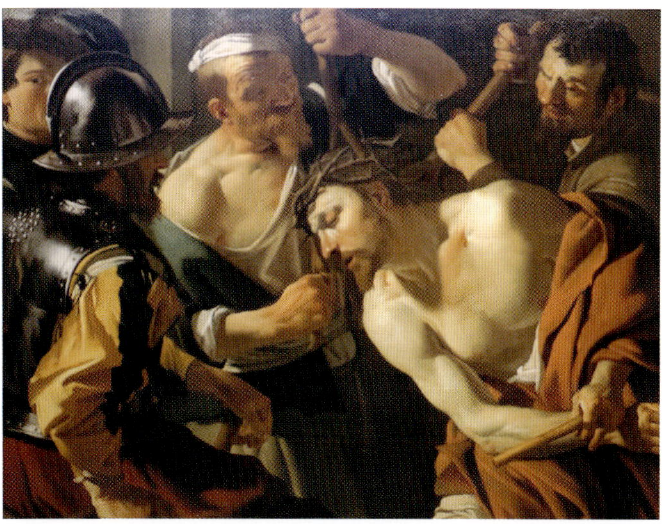

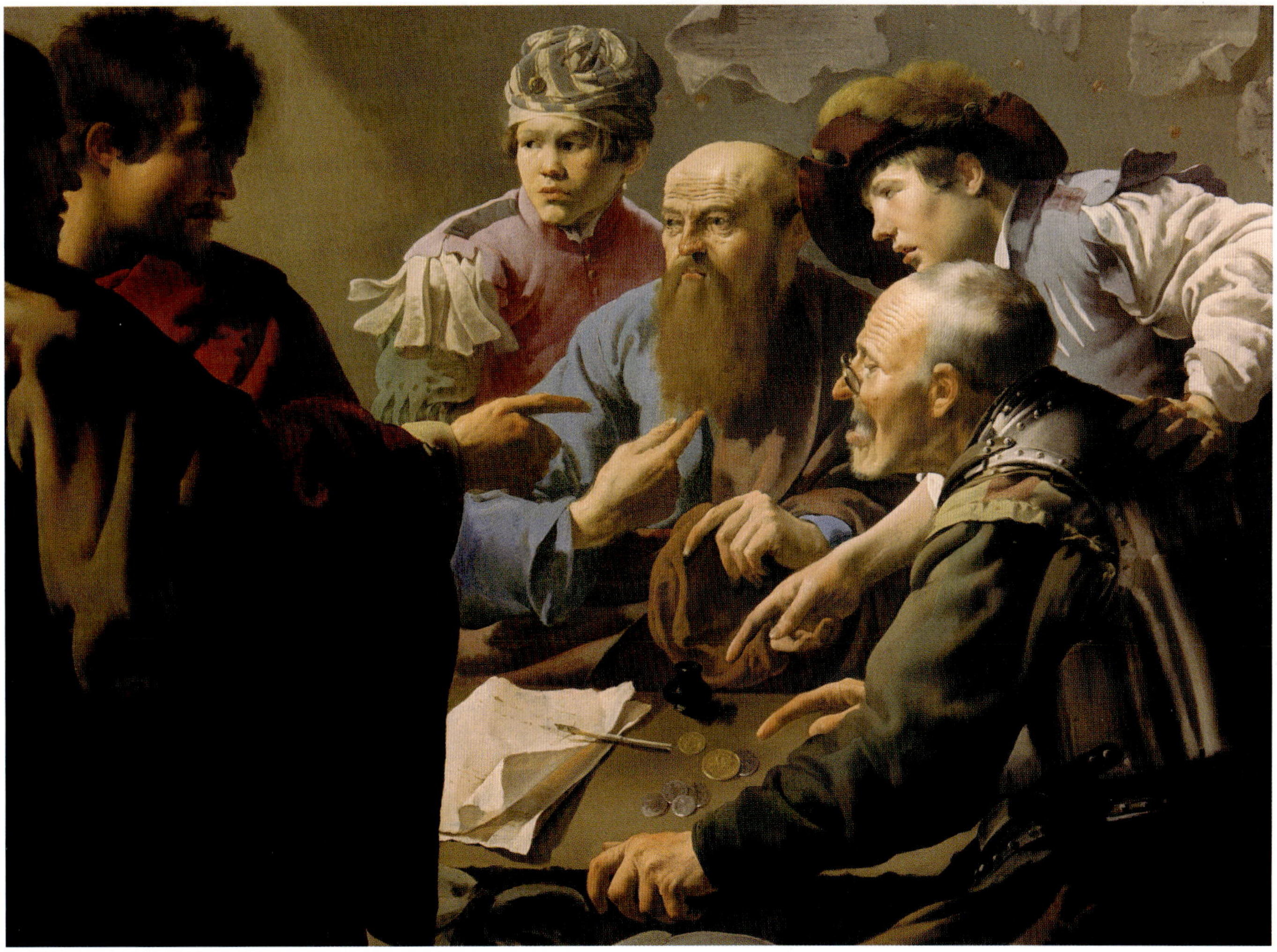

The Calling of Saint Matthew, Hendrick ter Brugghen, 1621, oil on canvas, 162.6 x 129.2cm (64 x 50¾in), Centraal Museum, Utrecht, Netherlands

After returning to Utrecht from Italy in 1614, Hendrick ter Brugghen established his reputation as the most original of the Caravaggisti there. He painted two versions of this subject, following Caravaggio's idea of illustrating the most dramatic moment of the story, as well as his placing of the figures around a table. Yet although this is dramatically lit, it does not adopt Caravaggio's chiaroscuro and the composition is far more compact.

The Triumph of Bacchus, Nicolaes (or Claes) Moeyaert, 1624, 53 × 82.8cm (20¾ × 32½in), Mauritshuis, The Hague, Netherlands

Bacchus, the Roman god of wine, is in a chariot that is being pulled by panthers. Merrily playing music with a reed pipe and a drum, bacchants with goats' feet dance along with the entourage. Some of these followers seem to have drunk too much wine. Nicolaes Moeyaert (c.1592/3–1655) was a Catholic, who probably went to Italy and may have gone into business with Pieter Lastman.

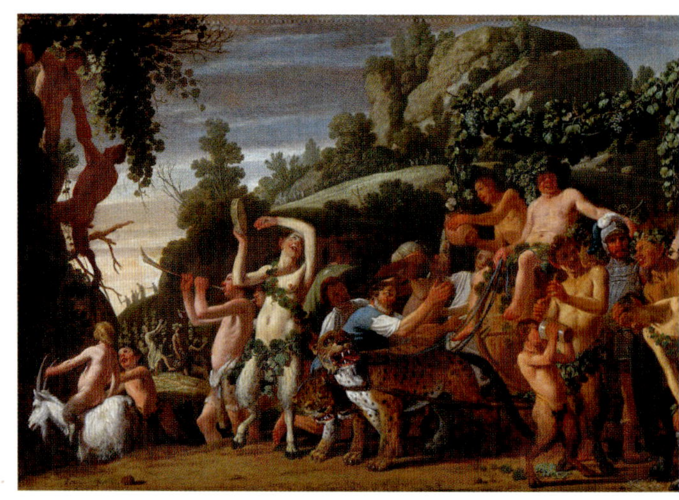

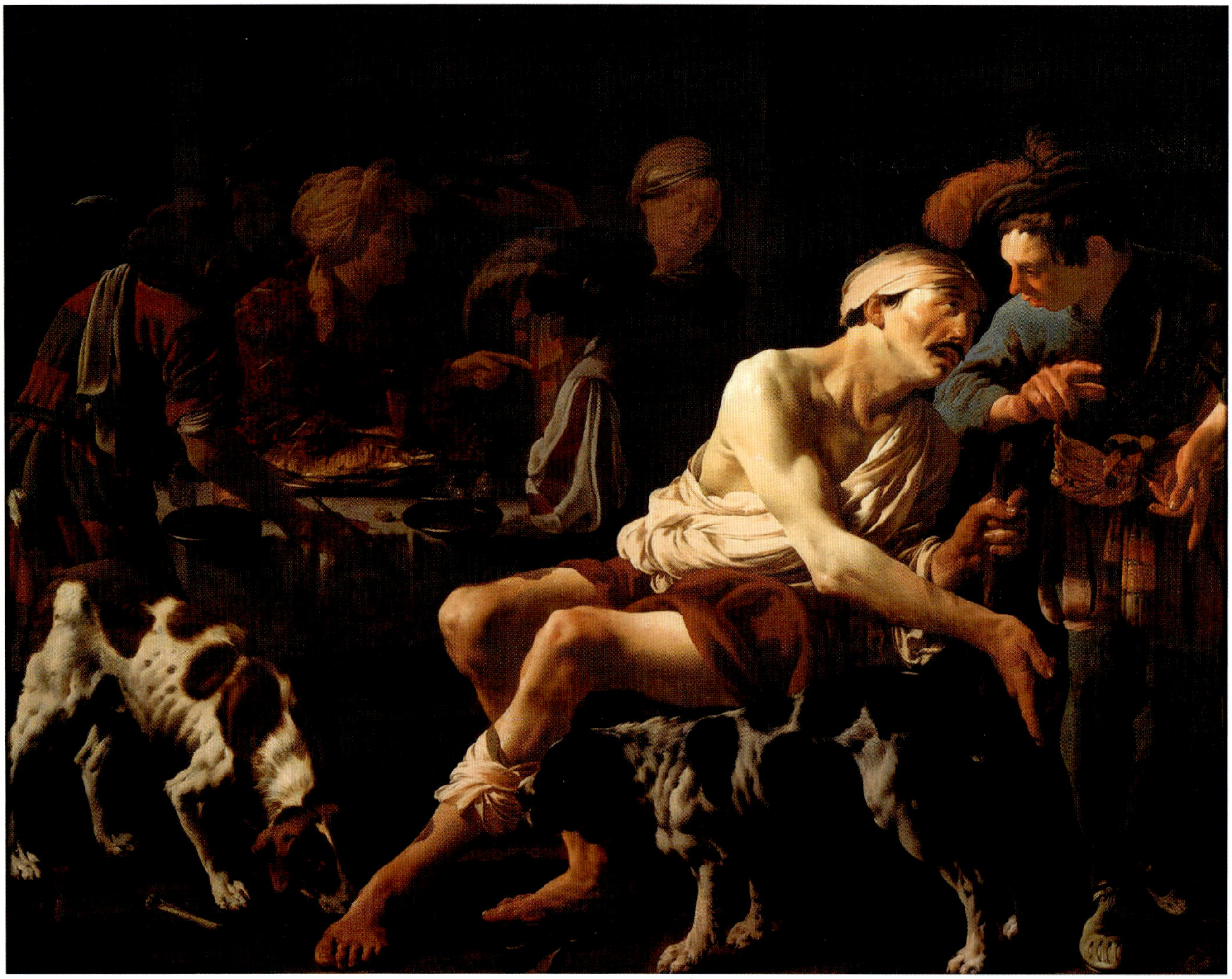

The Rich Man and Poor Lazarus, Hendrick ter Brugghen, 1625, oil on canvas, 167.7 × 207.5cm (66 × 81⅔in), Centraal Museum, Utrecht, Netherlands

As the first important painter to bring the influence of Caravaggio to the Netherlands, Hendrick ter Brugghen used chiaroscuro with outstanding skill, creating the impression of solid three-dimensional forms. Here light shines on the poor starving Lazarus who is begging a servant for some food. Dogs sniff his wounds, but the rich man and his family ignore him, instead continuing to eat at the table.

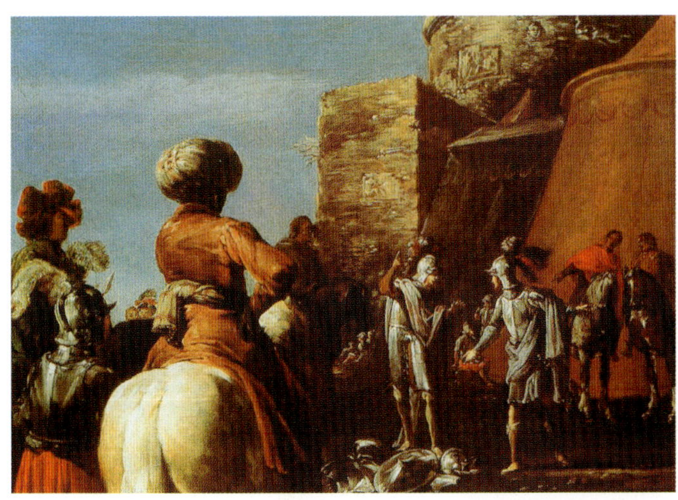

The Quarrel Between Ajax and Odysseus, Leonaert Bramer, c.1623–27, oil on copper, 30 x 40cm (11¾ x 15¾in), Museum Het Prinsenhof, Delft, Netherlands

A few years after this was painted, Leonaert Bramer became classed as one of the artists of the School of Delft, along with the likes of Vermeer, de Hooch and Maes. This painting demonstrates the originality that attracted this acclaim, including the attention-grabbing composition and fluid brushwork. The heroes Ajax and Odysseus are having an argument about who should take the armour that belonged to Achilles before he died.

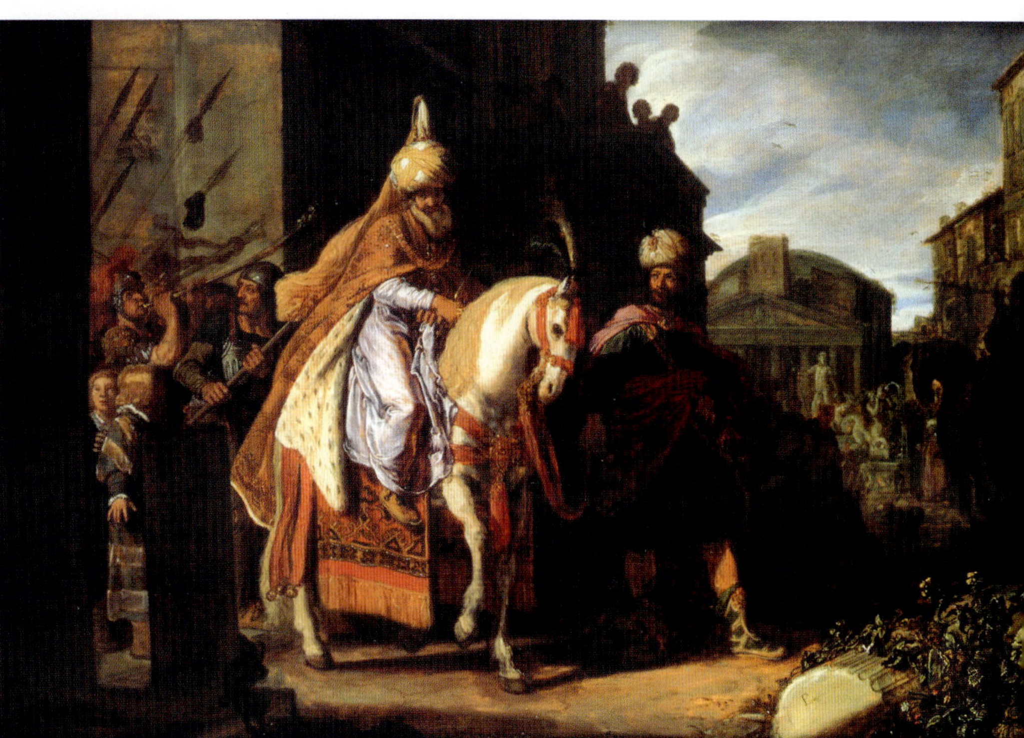

The Triumph of Mordecai, Pieter Lastman, 1624, oil on panel, 52 x 71.5cm (20.5 x 28in), Museum Het Rembrandthuis, Amsterdam, Netherlands

Before his pupils Rembrandt and Lievens began working, Pieter Lastman was considered the most important history painter in Amsterdam and this image demonstrates why he was such an influence on both of those artists. As well as his skill with the brush, he became known for depicting biblical and mythological subjects that were rarely portrayed by Dutch painters. The story of Mordecai is from the Old Testament.

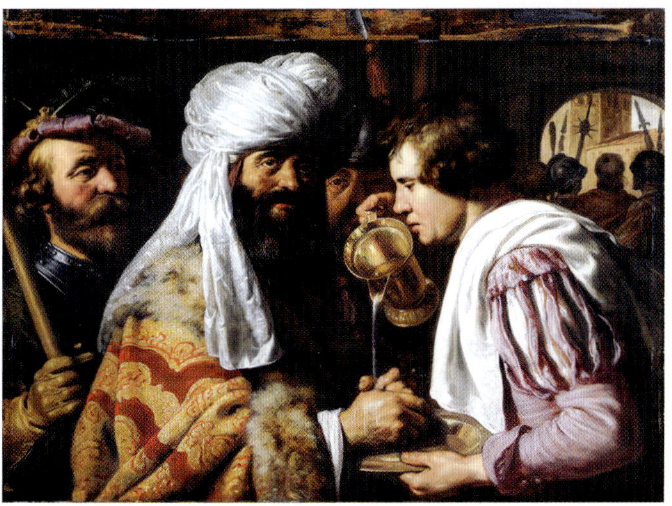

Pilate Washing his Hands, Jan Lievens, c.1626, oil on panel, 83.8 x 106cm (33 x 41¾in), Museum de Lakenhal, Leiden, Netherlands

Standing close to the picture plane in a white turban and fur-trimmed cloak, Pontius Pilate looks out of the image, giving viewers a hard stare as a servant pours water on to his hands. In the background, two soldiers are taking Jesus away through an arch. The strong chiaroscuro that Lievens uses here was probably inspired by the Utrecht Caravaggisti.

The Apostle Paul, Jan Lievens, 1629, oil on canvas, 110.5 x 101.5cm (43½ x 40in), Kunsthalle Bremen, Bremen, Germany

When Jan Lievens painted this, he was sharing a studio in Leiden with Rembrandt and at this time, both Lievens and Rembrandt depicted the Apostle Paul several times. They even sometimes used the same model. This image has been painted with delicate brushwork, smooth paint and a meticulous rendering of tonal contrasts. Paul is writing his Second Epistle to the Thessalonians and has paused for thought.

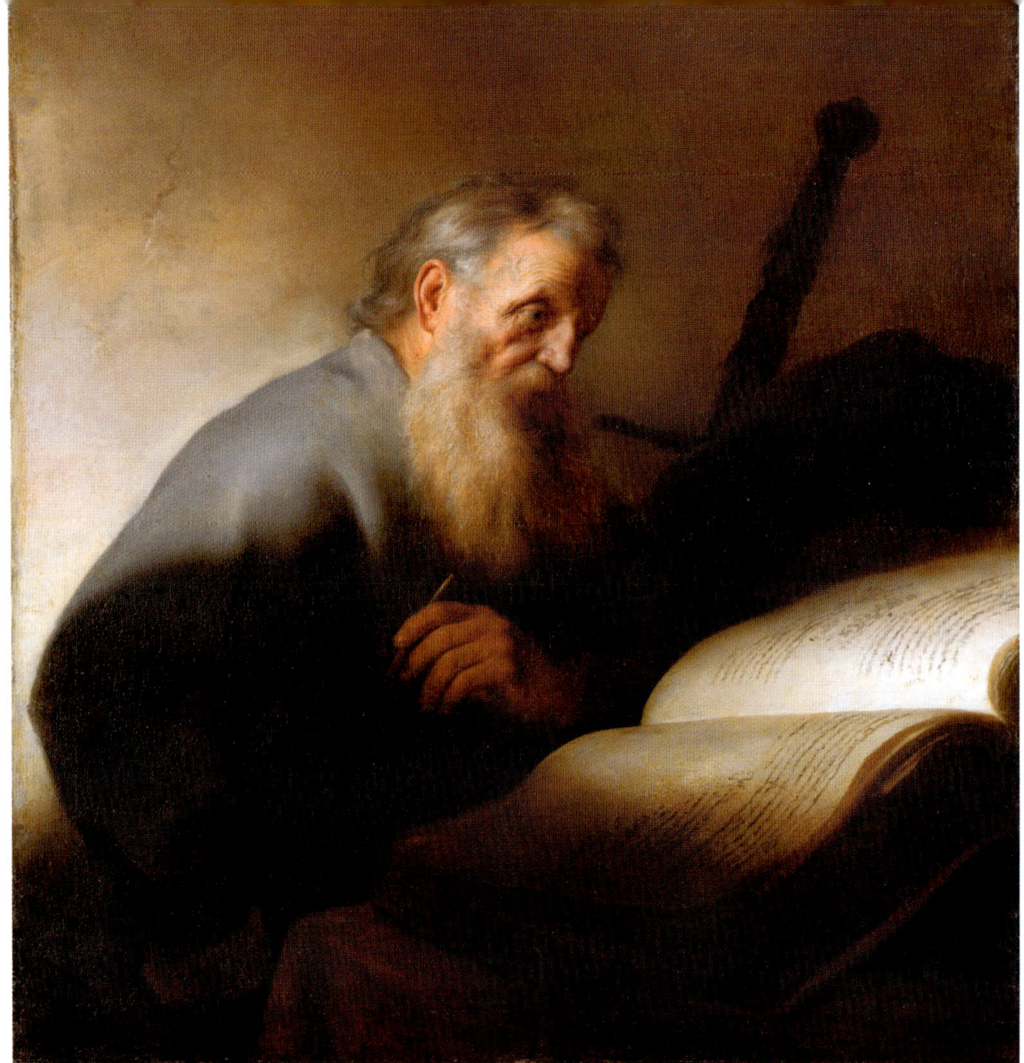

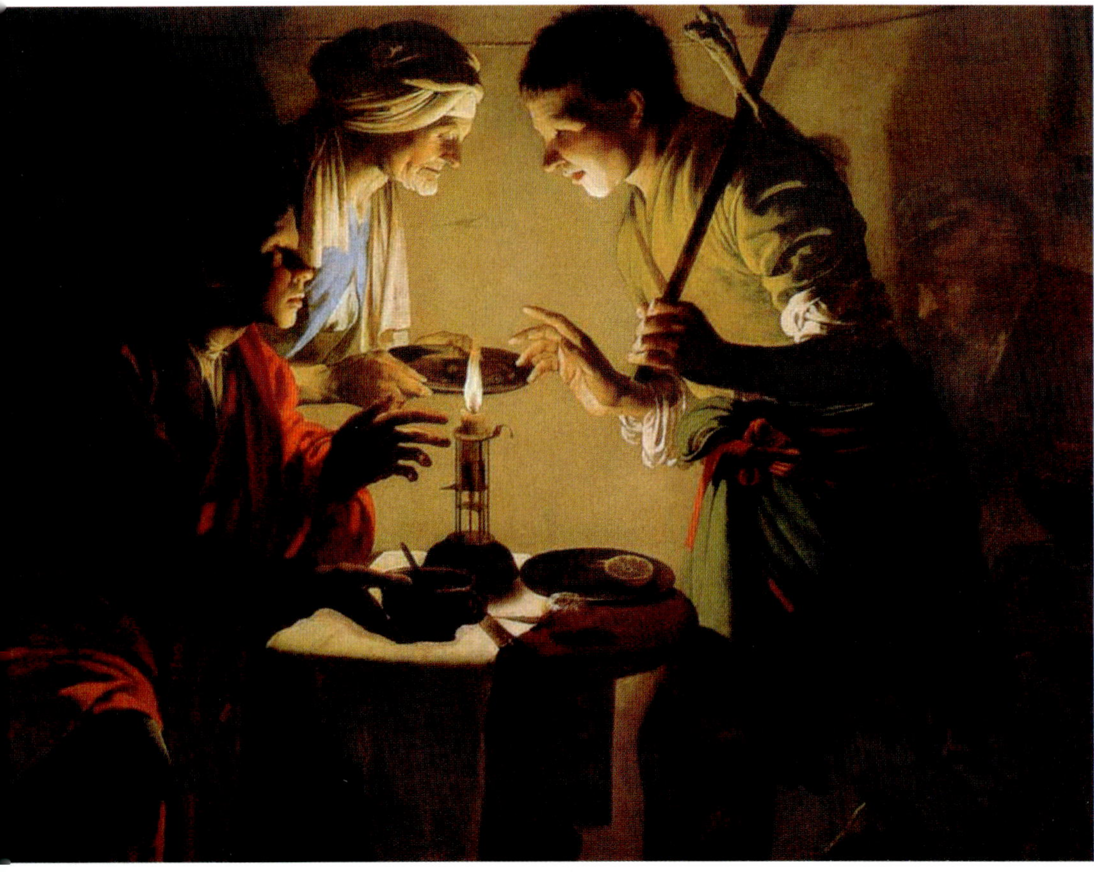

Esau Selling his Birthright, Hendrick ter Brugghen, c.1627, oil on canvas, 106.7 x 138.8cm (42 x 54½in), Museo Nacional Thyssen-Bornemisza, Madrid, Spain

Using a single candle to create dramatic chiaroscuro, Hendrick ter Brugghen depicts a story from the Old Testament. Esau, on the right, has just sold his birthright. On hearing his twin brother do this, Jacob, seated on the left, holds out a bowl containing lentils. Also here is Esau and Jacob's mother Rebecca, holding a plate, and sitting in the shadows in the background, their blind father, Isaac.

Vertumnus and Pomona,
Paulus Moreelse, *c.*1630, oil
on canvas, 130 x 114cm (51
x 44¾in), Museum Boijmans
van Beuningen, Rotterdam,
Netherlands

One of the Metamorphoses
by the Roman poet Ovid,
this is the story of beautiful
Pomona and Vertumnus,
the god of seasons. Here,
Pomona – depicted as
a beautiful 17th-century
Netherlandish girl – has cut
off a bunch of grapes with
a sickle, while Vertumnus
has disguised himself as an
old woman in the hope that
Pomona might pay him some
attention.

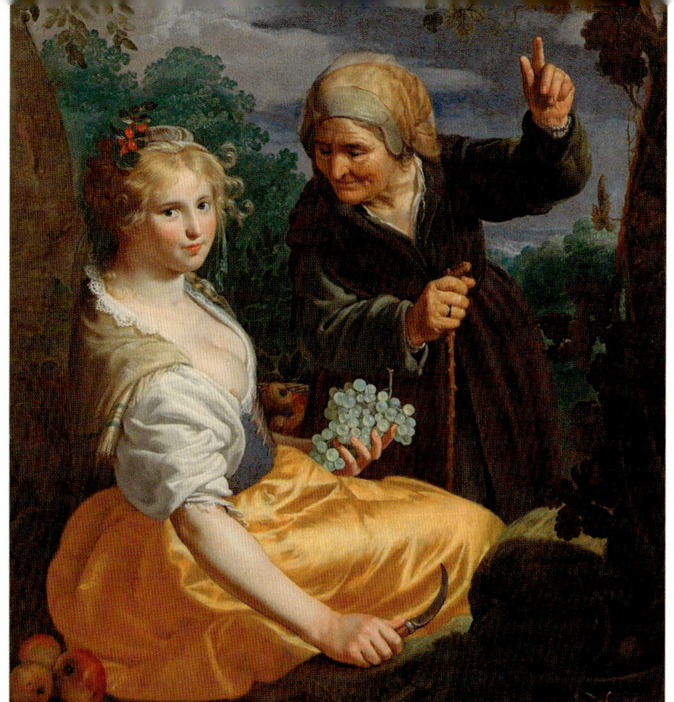

*Jeremiah Lamenting the
Destruction of Jerusalem*,
Rembrandt, 1630, oil on
panel, 58 x 46cm (23
x 18in), Rijksmuseum,
Amsterdam, Netherlands

Lamenting the burning of
Jerusalem that can be seen in
the background, the Prophet
Jeremiah rests his head on
his hand. He had prophesied
about the city's destruction
(Jeremiah, chapters 32, 33).
In the distance, a man holds
his clenched fists to his
eyes; he is the last king of
Judah, Zedekiah, who was
blinded by Nebuchadnezzar.
Jeremiah's pose conveys
his sadness. With powerful
chiaroscuro, Rembrandt
creates a sense of drama.
He used the blunt end of his
brush to scratch in details in
the wet paint.

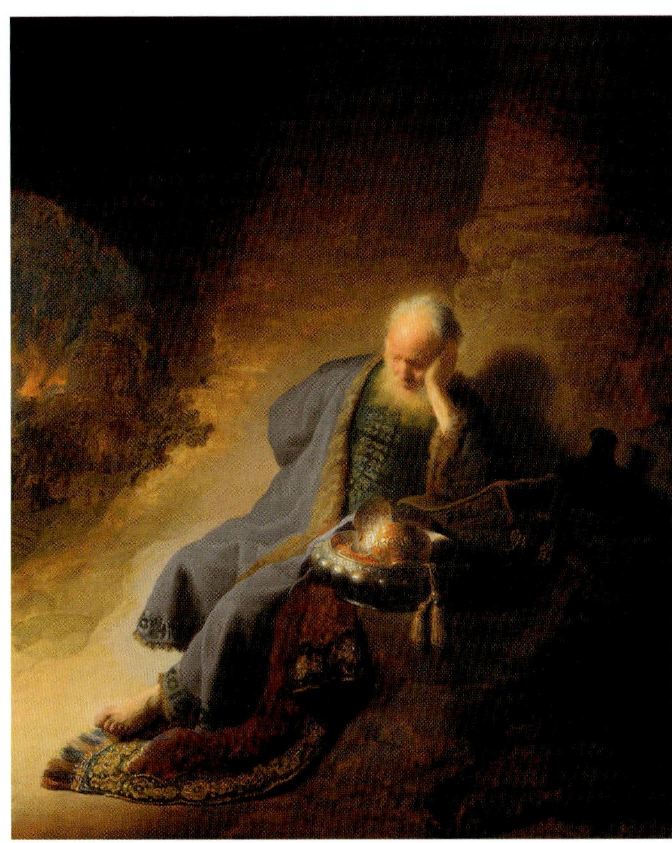

Venus Chastising Cupid, Jan
van Bijlert, 1628, oil on
canvas, 146.1 x 127.6cm
(57½ x 50¼in), Museum of
Fine Arts, Houston, USA

One of the Utrecht
Caravaggisti, Jan van Bijlert
travelled to France and
Rome, but settled back in
Utrecht by 1625. As well
as portraits, he painted
religious, mythological and
genre subjects. In Rome, he
was one of the founders of
the artist group known as
the Bentvueghels. In 1630
he joined the Utrecht Guild
of Saint Luke, and in 1639
he helped form a painter's
school, the 'Schilders-College.'

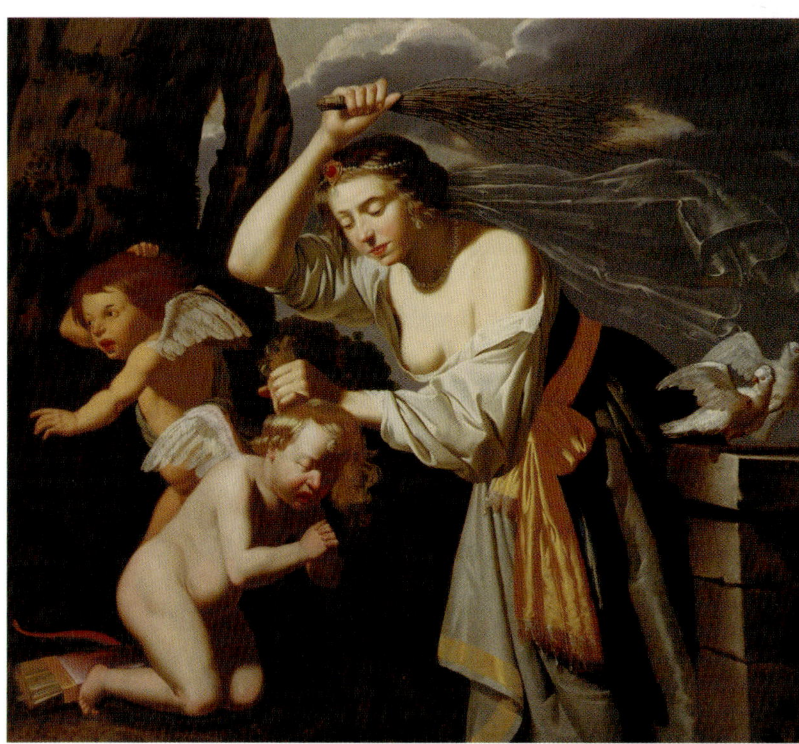

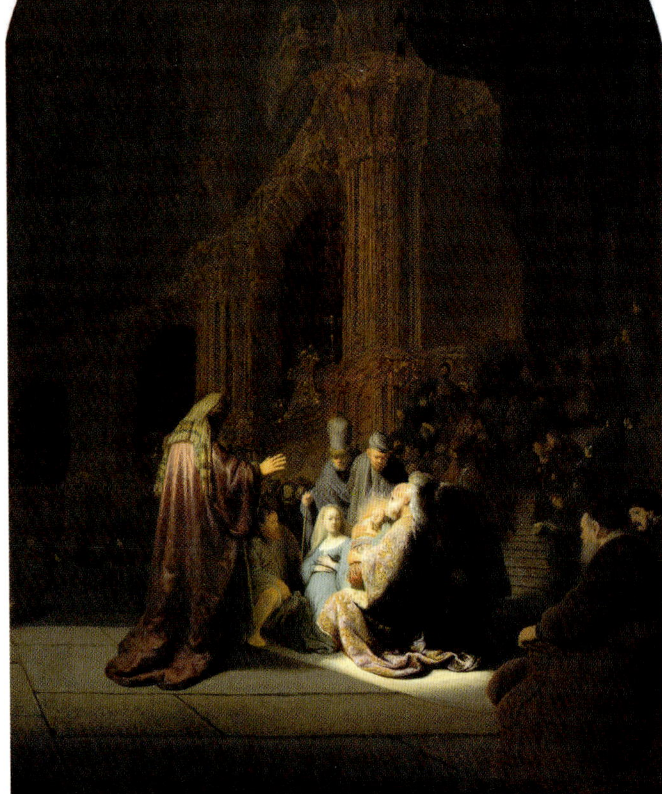

Inside a temple, some figures
are illuminated by a shaft of
divine light. Joseph and Mary
are there to dedicate their
baby to God. Mary sits next
to Simeon who recognizes
Jesus as the Messiah. Anna
stands before them and
they look up to her as she
speaks, although viewers
can only see her long robe
and headdress; her face is
in shadow. Joseph crouches
near her.

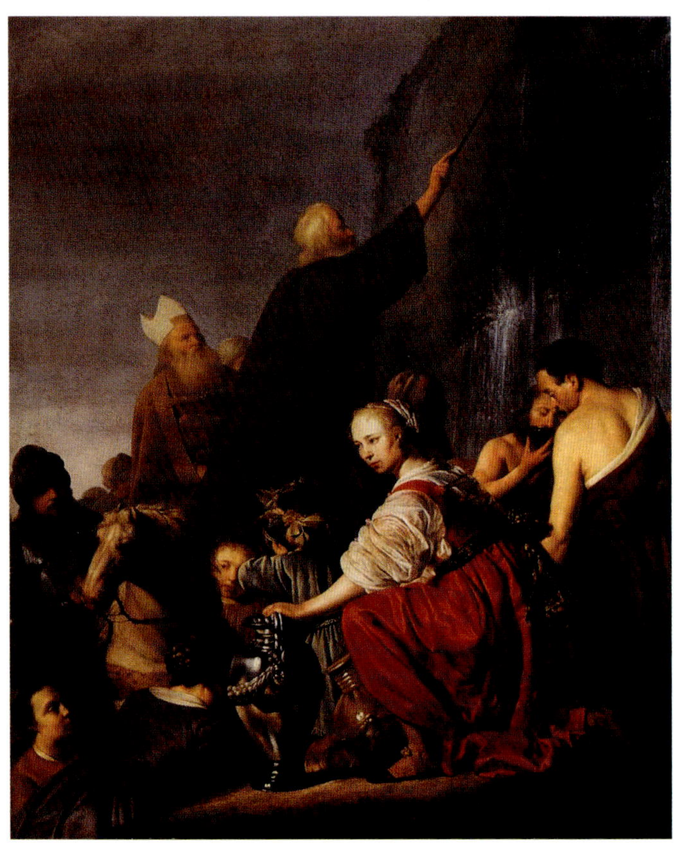

Moses Striking the Rock,
Pieter de Grebber, c.1630,
oil on canvas, 165 x 132cm
(65 x 52in), Musée des
Beaux-Arts, Tourcoing,
France

With a dramatically angled
composition, the eldest
son of Frans Pietersz de
Grebber, Pieter painted this
two years before he became
a member of the Haarlem
Guild of Saint Luke, even
though he had already been
a professional painter for 10
years. This painting shows
the Old Testament story of
Moses striking a rock on
God's instruction and water
pouring forth.

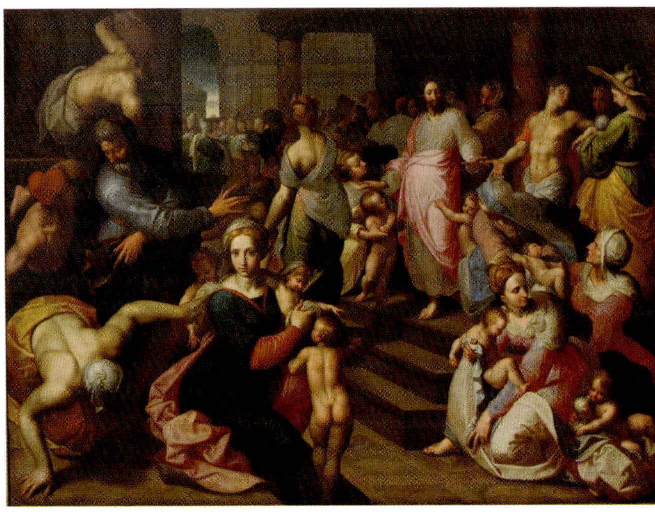

*Let the Children Come to
Me*, Jacob Backer, 1633,
oil on panel, 152 x 180cm
(60 x 70¾in), Maagdenhuis
Museum, Antwerp, Belgium

Jacob Backer (1608–51)
was especially influenced
by Rubens and Abraham
Bloemaert. He spent most
of his life in Amsterdam and
was a friend of Govert Flinck.
He became an important
portrait painter, recognized
in particular for his speed
in completing his paintings.
He was also known for his
religious and mythological
paintings as here in this
depiction of Christ's words:
'Let the little children come
to me.'

Samson and Delilah, Jan Lievens, 1630–35, oil on canvas, 131 x 111cm (51½ x 43¾in), Rijksmuseum, Amsterdam, Netherlands

Painted while Lievens was working in Leiden with Rembrandt, this depiction of the Old Testament story of Samson and Delilah (Judges 16:19) shows the moment when Samson is asleep in the lap of his beloved Delilah. Unaware that anything is amiss, he sleeps contentedly as Delilah hands a pair of scissors to a Philistine – one of Samson's enemies. Samson had just told Delilah that his uncut hair was the secret of his great strength. Rembrandt's influence can be seen in the painting's chiaroscuro and in the expressiveness of the faces. He was also influenced here by Gerrit van Honthorst.

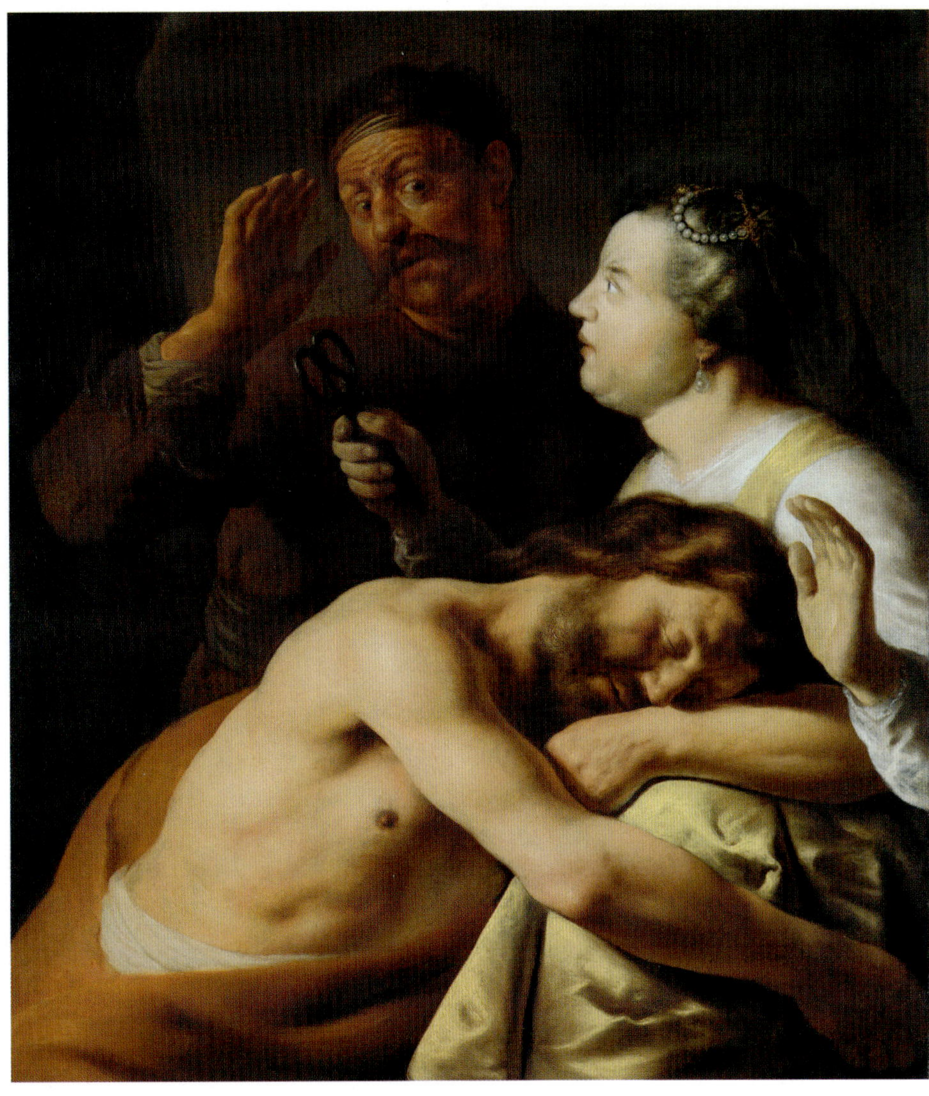

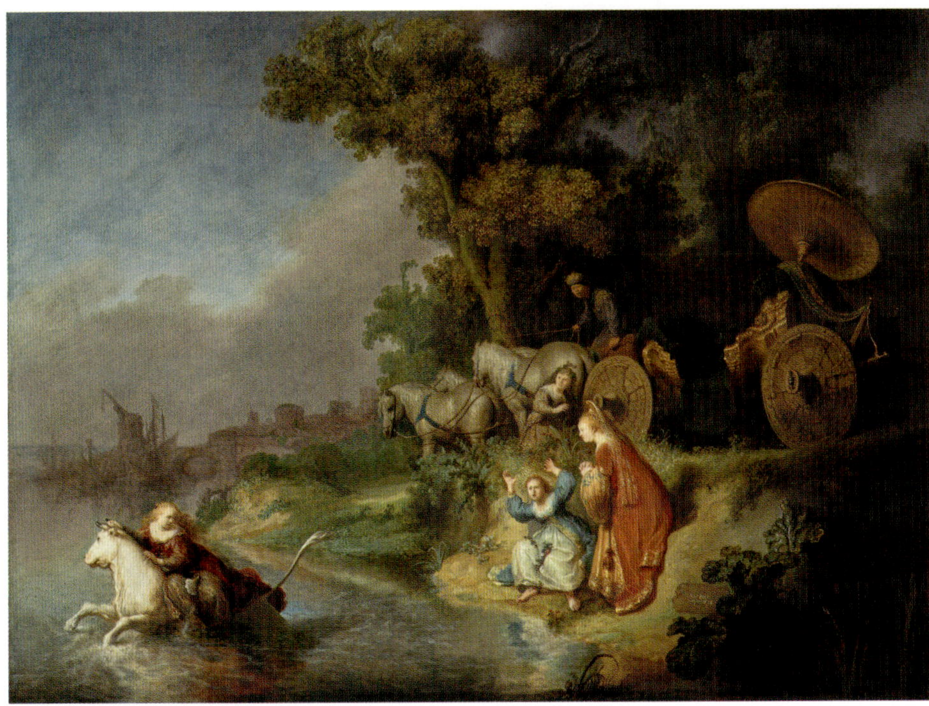

The Abduction of Europa, Rembrandt, 1632, oil on oak, 78.7 x 64.6cm (31 x 25½in), J. Paul Getty Museum, Los Angeles, USA

In Ovid's *Metamorphoses,* the god Jupiter disguised himself as a white bull to seduce the princess Europa and carry her across the sea to a distant land that would bear her name. Rembrandt rarely painted mythological subjects, but using dramatic gesture and visual effects, he conveys the story in a unique way as the bull escapes with Europa and her friends are helpless at the water's edge.

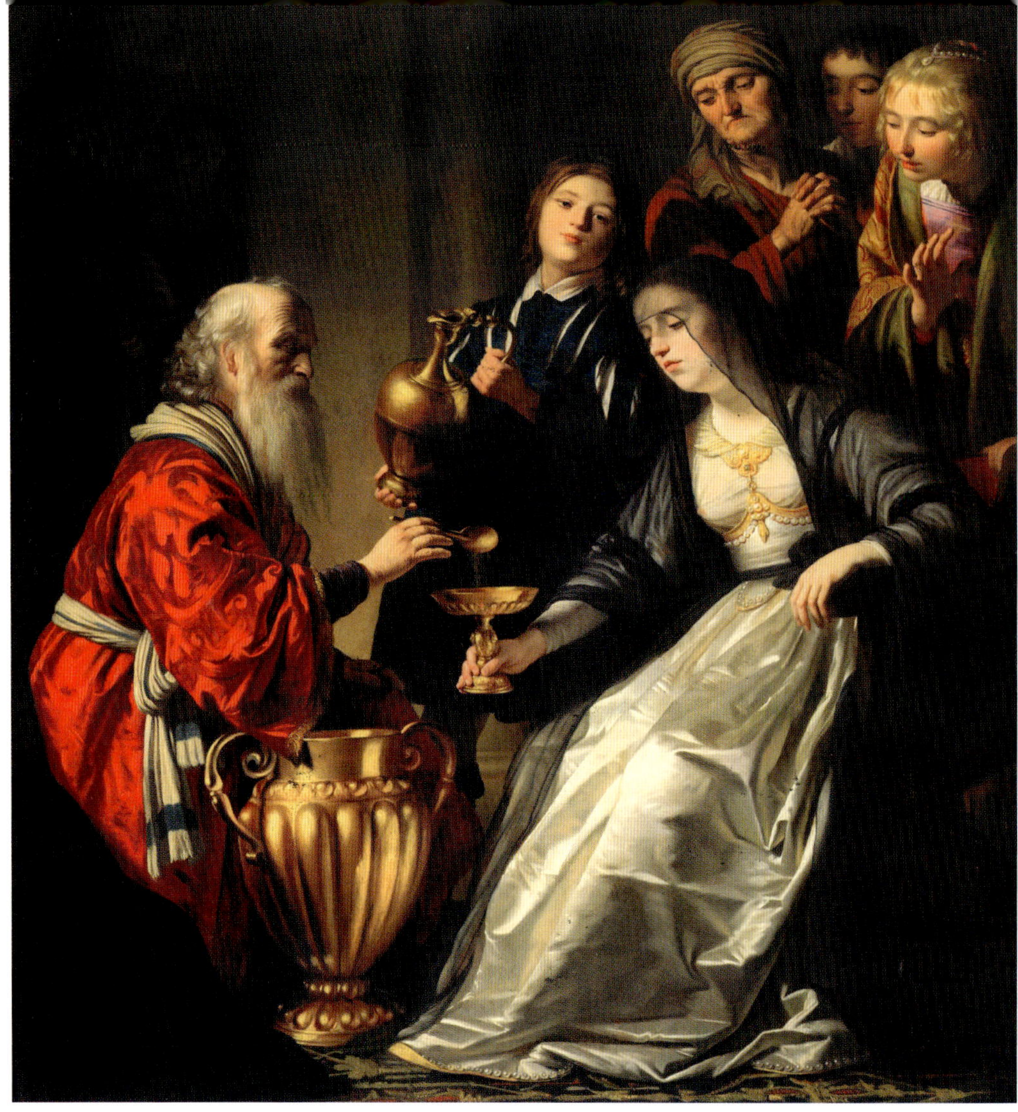

Artemisia, Gerrit van Honthorst, *c.*1635, oil on canvas, 170 x 147.5cm (67 x 58in), Princeton University, New Jersey, USA

Queen Artemisa of Halicarnassus in Asia Minor was said by ancient authors to have mourned her husband, Mausolus, by building a mausoleum for him, which became one of the Seven Wonders of the World. She then drank his ashes mixed with wine in order to become his living tomb and it is this act that van Honthorst illustrates here. By this time, he was back in Utrecht, and building a highly respected reputation.

Jael, Deborah and Barak, Salomon de Bray, 1635, oil on panel, 86.5 x 71.5cm (34 x 28in), Museum Catharijneconvent, Utrecht, Netherlands

With her breasts almost completely exposed, Jael scowls. She holds a hammer and a tent peg covered in blood. She has used the tent peg to murder Sisera, the leader of the Canaanites, by nailing a peg into his head while he was asleep in her tent. The prophet Deborah stands next to Jael and next to her is the commander Barak, who defeated Sisera's troops. An architect as well as painter, Salomon de Bray painted in a fairly old-fashioned style for the time, using smooth paint and often half-length figures as here. His technique was skilful and accomplished, but unfortunately for him, it had become rather old-fashioned in comparison to a freer approach used by several younger artists. By the time he painted this, his work was showing more of an influence of Rembrandt.

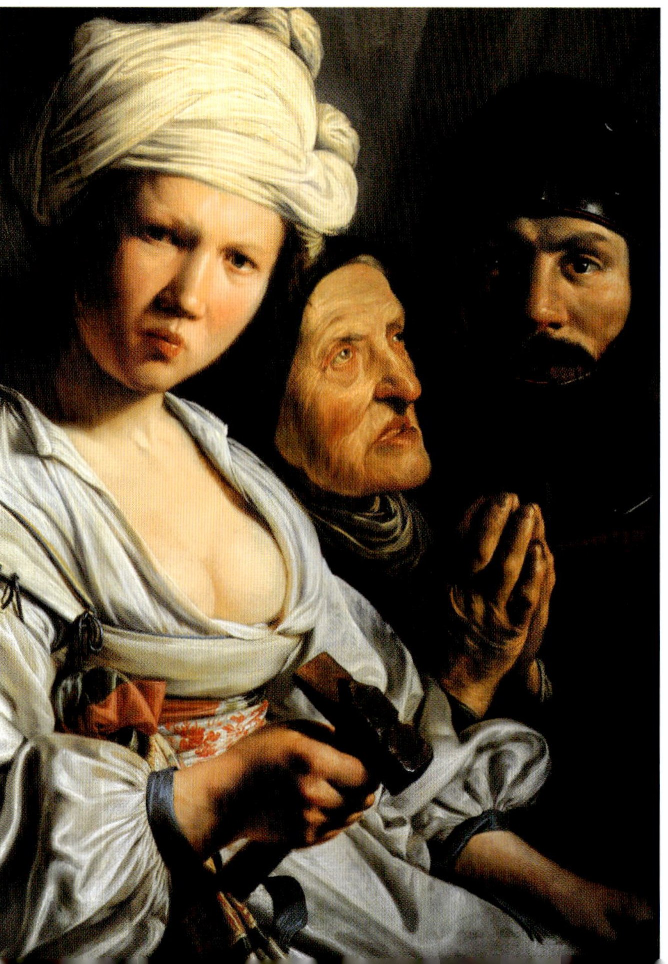

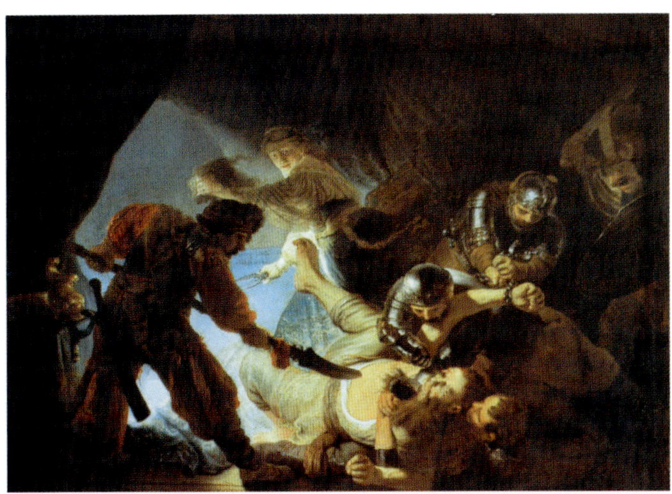

The Blinding of Samson, Rembrandt, 1636, oil on canvas, 236 x 302cm (93 x 119in), Städelsches Kunstinstitut, Frankfurt, Germany

One of Rembrandt's most powerful biblical scenes, this conveys Samson's agony as he is tied up and blinded by enemy soldiers. The figures are life-sized and the gruesome deed is depicted with directness, using a dramatic composition. Rembrandt has used chiaroscuro to theatrical effect, with the figures around Samson emerging from the darkness, and a harsh beam of light streaming on to him as he suffers.

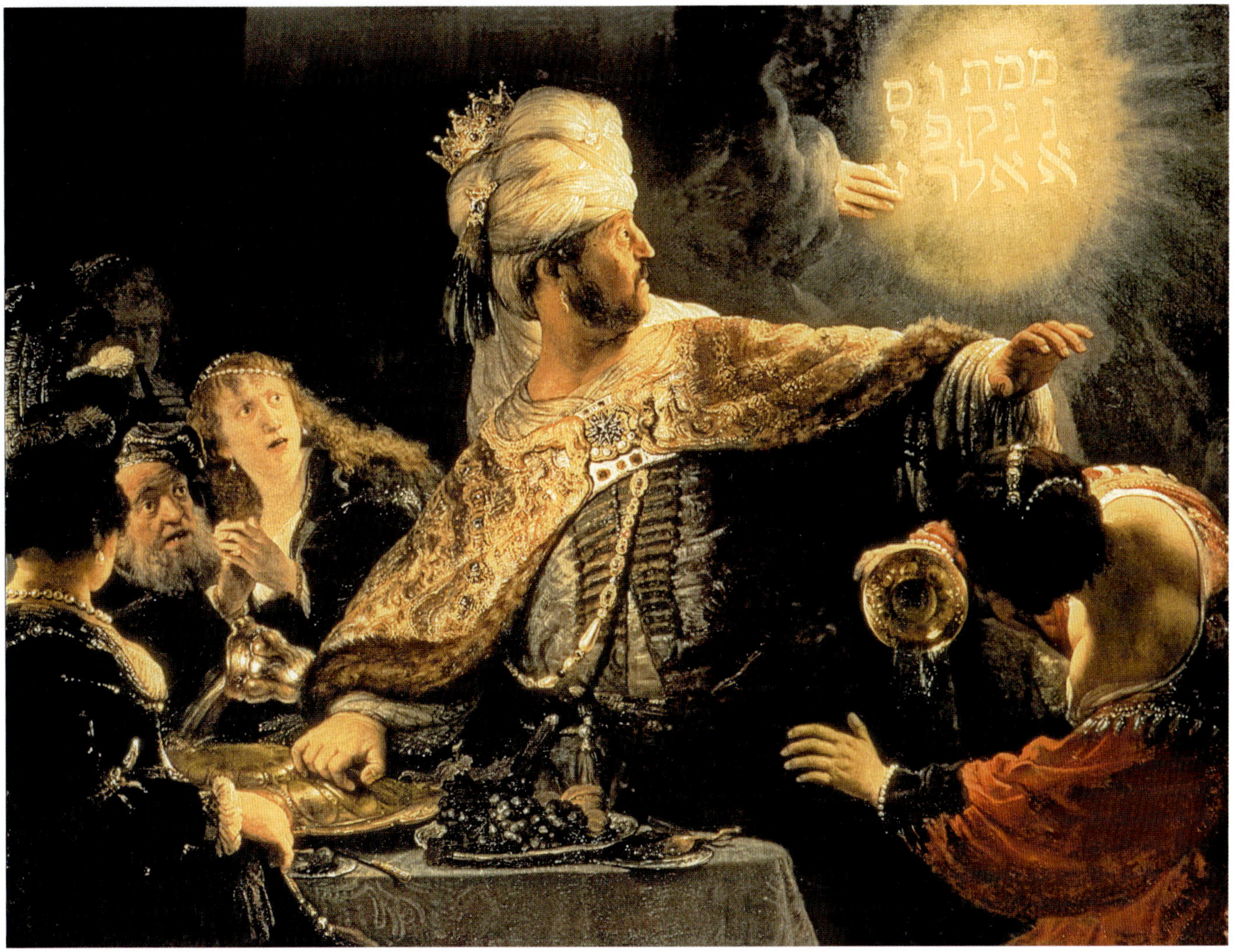

Belshazzar's Feast, Rembrandt, 1636–38, oil on canvas, 167.6 x 209.2cm (66 x 82¼ in), The National Gallery, London, UK

From the Old Testament Book of Daniel, this painting depicts the story of the Babylonian King Belshazzar, who had been feasting with friends using sacred vessels that had been stolen by his father Nebuchadnezzar from the Temple of Jerusalem. In terror, Belshazzar watches as a disembodied hand writes on the wall in Hebrew, that his kingdom is about to end. As usual, Rembrandt conveys expression, dynamism and drama.

The Infancy of Zeus, Nicolaes Berchem, 1648, oil on canvas, 202 x 262cm (79½ x 103in), Mauritshuis, The Hague, Netherlands

When Zeus, the ruler of the gods was a baby, his father threatened to eat him. So his mother sent him away to be brought up by a princess. In this large-scale work, Berchem depicts the princess sitting in the open air, with the baby Zeus sleeping peacefully in her lap. A faun is carrying a heavy barrel filled with milk and healthy-looking animals surround them.

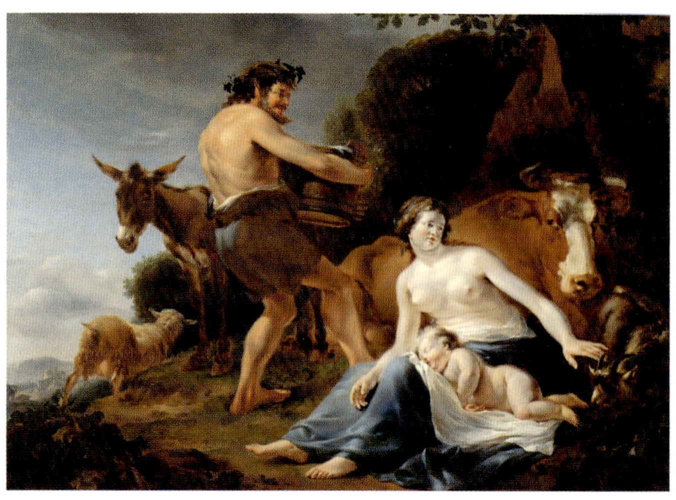

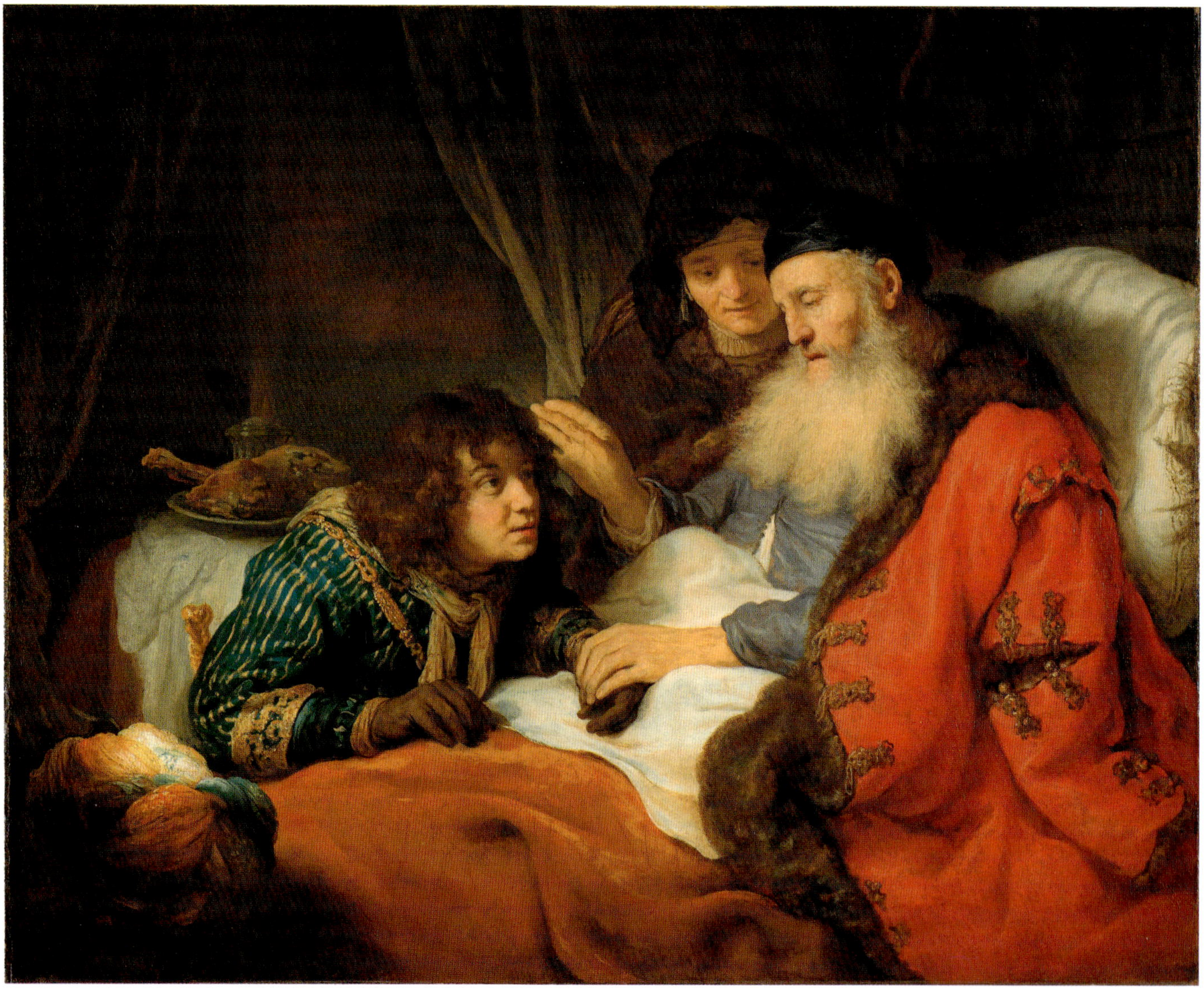

Isaac Blessing Jacob, Govert Flinck, 1638, oil on canvas, 117 x 141cm (46 x 55in), Rijksmuseum, Amsterdam, Netherlands

In the Bible story, Isaac, who is blind, wants to bless his son Esau, but Isaac's wife Rebecca tells her son Jacob to take Esau's place. To trick Isaac, she tells Jacob to cover his smooth hand with the skin of a goat so that his father will think it is Esau's hairy hand. Here, Isaac blesses Jacob while Rebecca watches, smiling as her trick has worked.

The Sacrifice of Abraham, Jan Lievens, 1638–40, oil on canvas, 180.8 x 136.9cm (73 x 54in), Herzog Anton Ulrich Museum, Lower Saxony, Germany

A relieved father and son hug each other. This is an episode from the Old Testament. Moments before, Abraham had been following God's command and was about to to sacrifice his son Isaac, but just in time, an Angel intervened and instructed Abraham to kill a ram instead as a sacrifice as God was merely testing Abraham's faithfulness. Lievens was living in Antwerp when he painted this, and had been influenced by Anthony van Dyck.

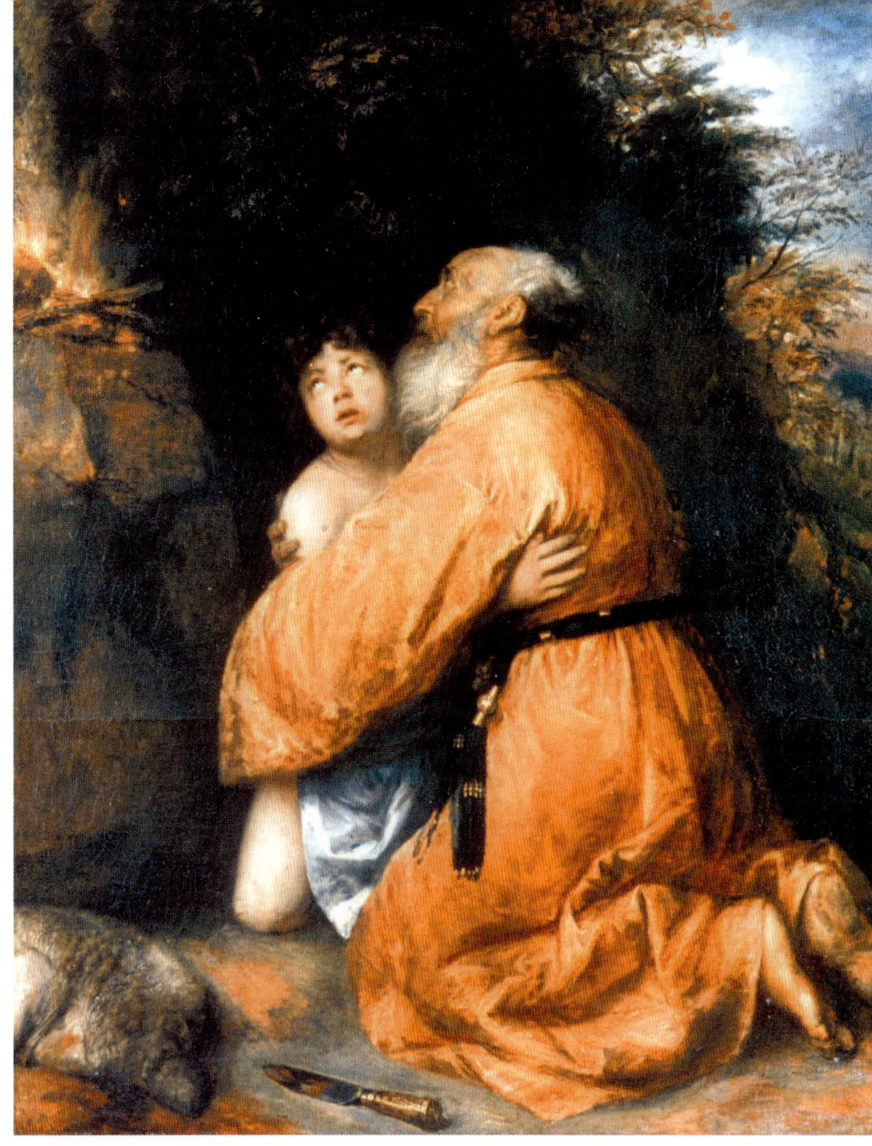

Christ and Mary Magdalene at the Tomb, Rembrandt, 1638, oil on panel, 61 x 49.4cm (24 x 19½in), Royal Collection Trust, London, UK

Showing his incredible imagination, Rembrandt depicts Mary Magdalene at Christ's tomb on the morning after his Crucifixion. The massive stone at the tomb's entrance has been moved and two angels guard it. A gardener approaches and this is the moment that Mary Magdalene turns round to appeals to him for information, when he calls her by her name and she suddenly recognizes him as Christ.

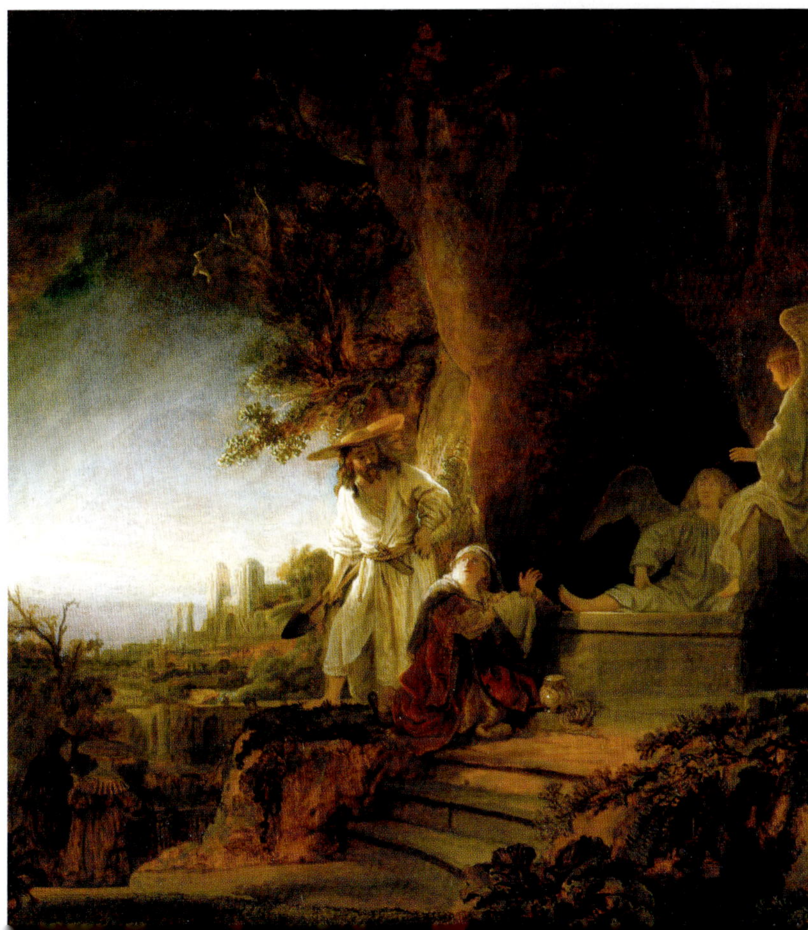

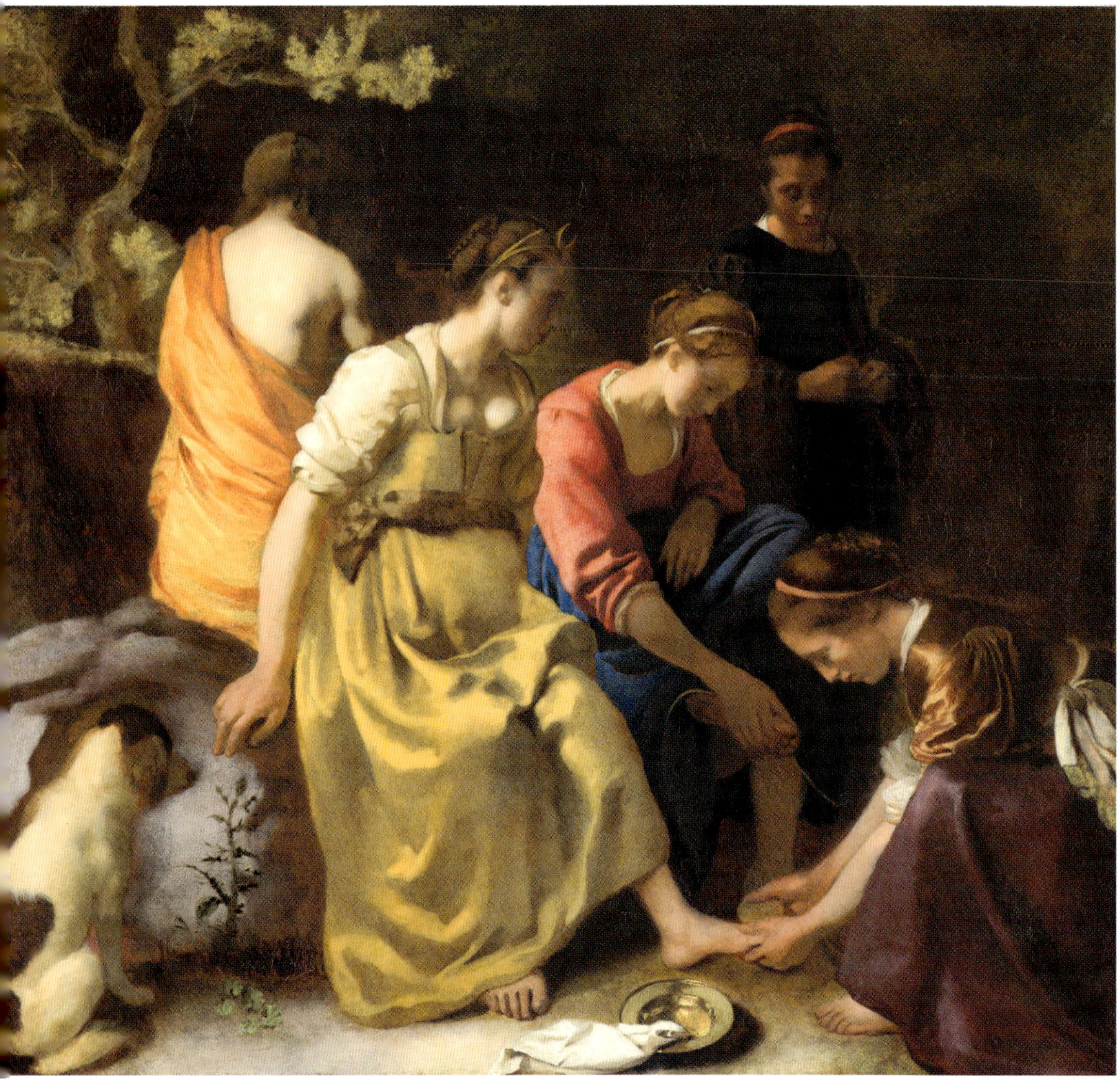

Diana and her Nymphs, Johannes Vermeer, c.1653–54, oil on canvas, 97.8 x 104.6cm (38½ x 41in), Mauritshuis, The Hague, Netherlands

Although best known for his small paintings of softly illuminated interiors with few figures, Vermeer actually painted some larger biblical and mythological works early in his career, including this depiction of Diana, the goddess of hunting and of the night resting with her nymphs. The dog at her feet convey her links with hunting and the moon on her forehead suggests her connection with the night.

Bathsheba with King David's Letter, or *Bathsheba at her Bath*, Rembrandt, 1654, oil on canvas, 142 x 142cm (56 x 56in), Musée du Louvre, Paris, France

Bathsheba is at her bath, considering King David's letter summoning her to his palace, even though she was married to one of his generals. Rembrandt was rare in his painting of the nude during the Dutch Golden Age. The painting conveys intimacy and thoughtfulness; Bathsheba is visibly disturbed by the royal message. Rembrandt painted her from life and used rich colours and chiaroscuro to emphasize the soft flesh, drapery and jewellery.

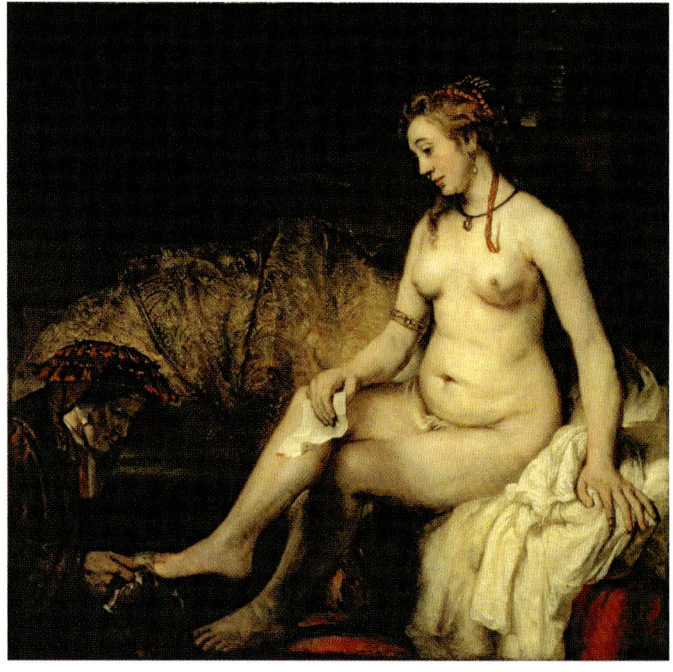

Boaz and Ruth, Gerbrand van den Eeckhout, 1655, oil on canvas, 75 x 82cm (29½ x 32¼ in), Museum Boijmans van Beuningen, Rotterdam, Netherlands

Illustrating a passage from the biblical story of Ruth, Gerbrand van den Eeckhout has painted Ruth talking to Boaz. She has been gleaning in his field and he tells her she can also drink water from his pitchers if she wishes, because she deserves a reward for the care she takes of her family. Here, in her skirt, she is holding the wheat she has gleaned.

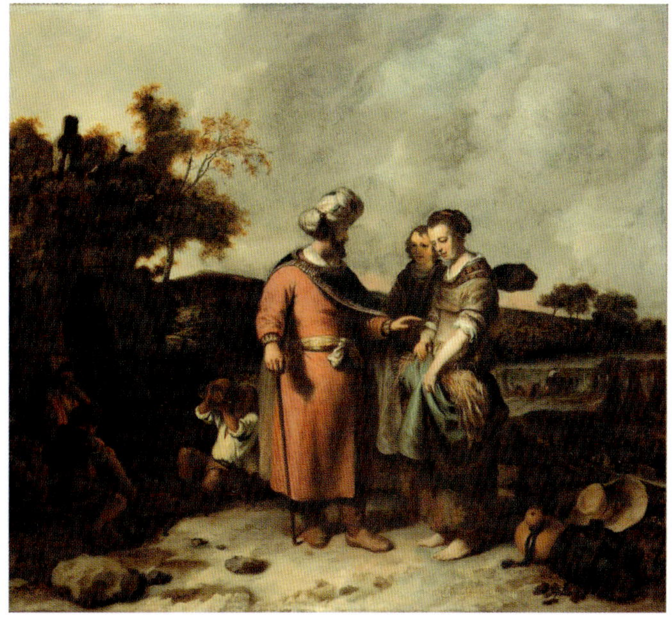

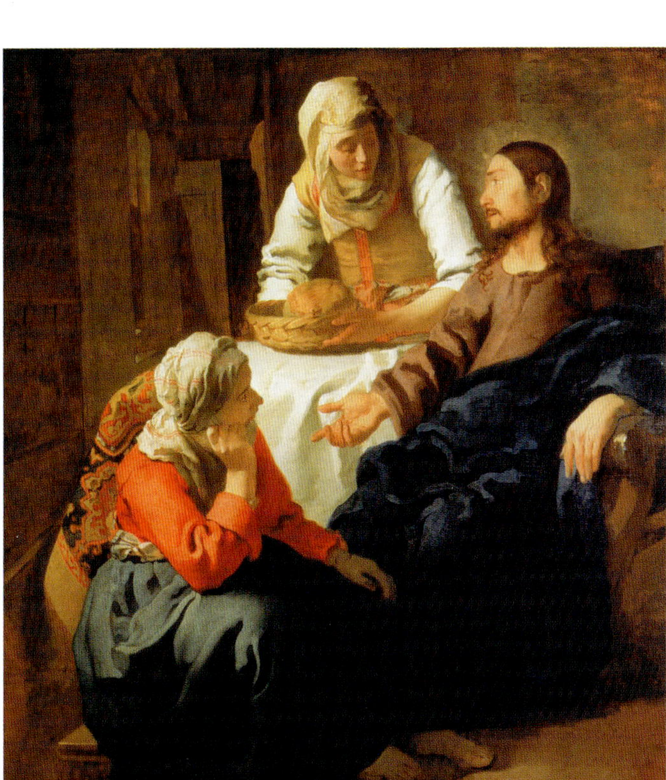

Christ in the House of Martha and Mary, Johannes Vermeer, c.1654–56, oil on canvas, 158.5 x 141.5cm (62½ x 55½ in), Scottish National Gallery, Edinburgh, UK

Vermeer's only known painting of a biblical subject, this illustrates a scene from the Gospel of Saint Luke when Christ visits the sisters Martha and Mary. In their house, he praises Mary for sitting and listening to his teachings, while Martha remains preoccupied with housekeeping. The brilliant light and shadow that Vermeer conveys seem to derive from the example of artists from Utrecht, who in turn were influenced by Caravaggio's art.

Pharaoh's Daughter and her Handmaids with Moses in the Reed Basket, Jan de Bray, 1661, oil on canvas, 121 x 164cm (47⅔ x 64½ in), Museum Boijmans van Beuningen, Rotterdam, Netherlands

After the Pharaoh gave the order that all baby Hebrew boys were to be murdered, one mother put her baby into a basket and placed it in the rushes of the River Nile. When the Pharaoh's daughter discovered the basket, she kept the baby, hiring his real mother as a wet nurse. This depicts the finding of the baby, with his real mother looking on hopefully.

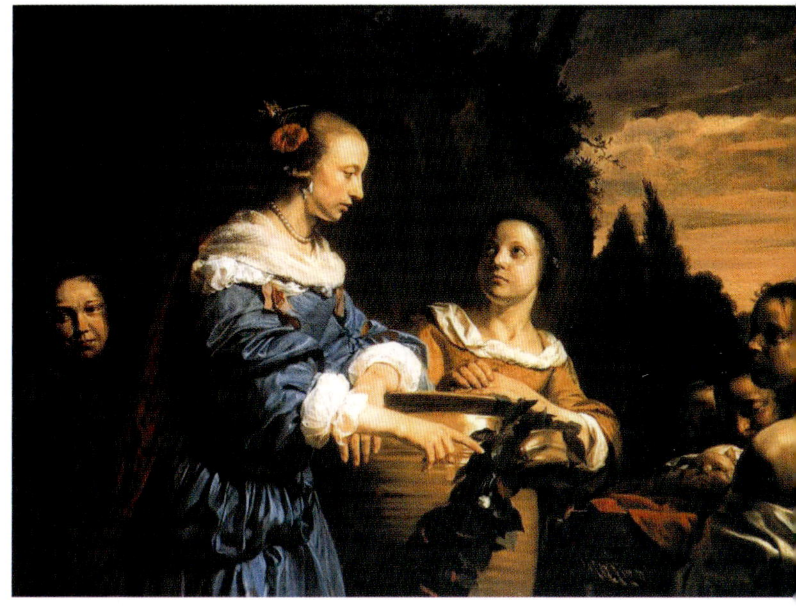

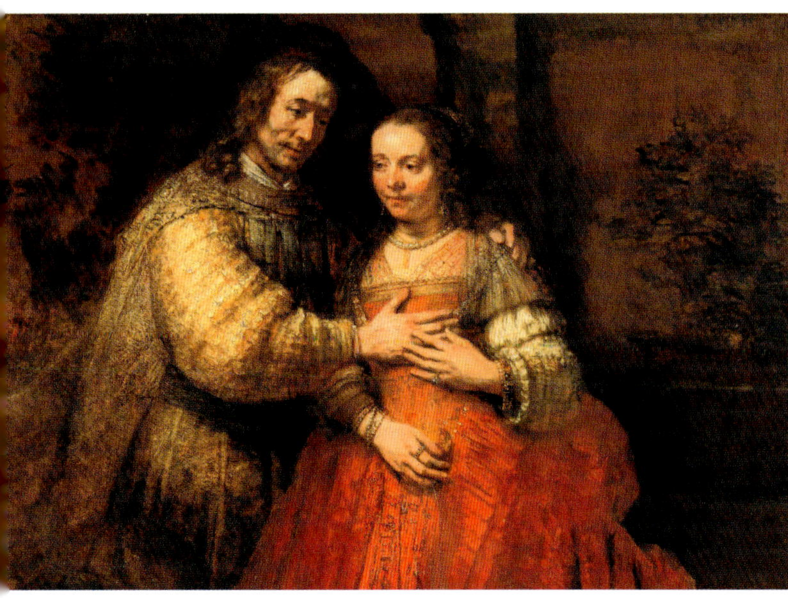

Isaac and Rebecca, known as 'The Jewish Bride', Rembrandt, *c.*1665–69, oil on canvas, 166.5 x 121.5cm (65½ x 47¾in), Rijksmuseum, Amsterdam, Netherlands

Depicting a married couple who pose as the biblical figures Isaac and Rebecca, Rembrandt uses paint that is so thick in places, such as on Isaac's sleeve, that it conveys the texture almost in three-dimensions. As well as the setting, pose and style of painting, the exotic clothing was also derived from Rembrandt's imagination. The sitters probably asked him to portray them as the biblical couple.

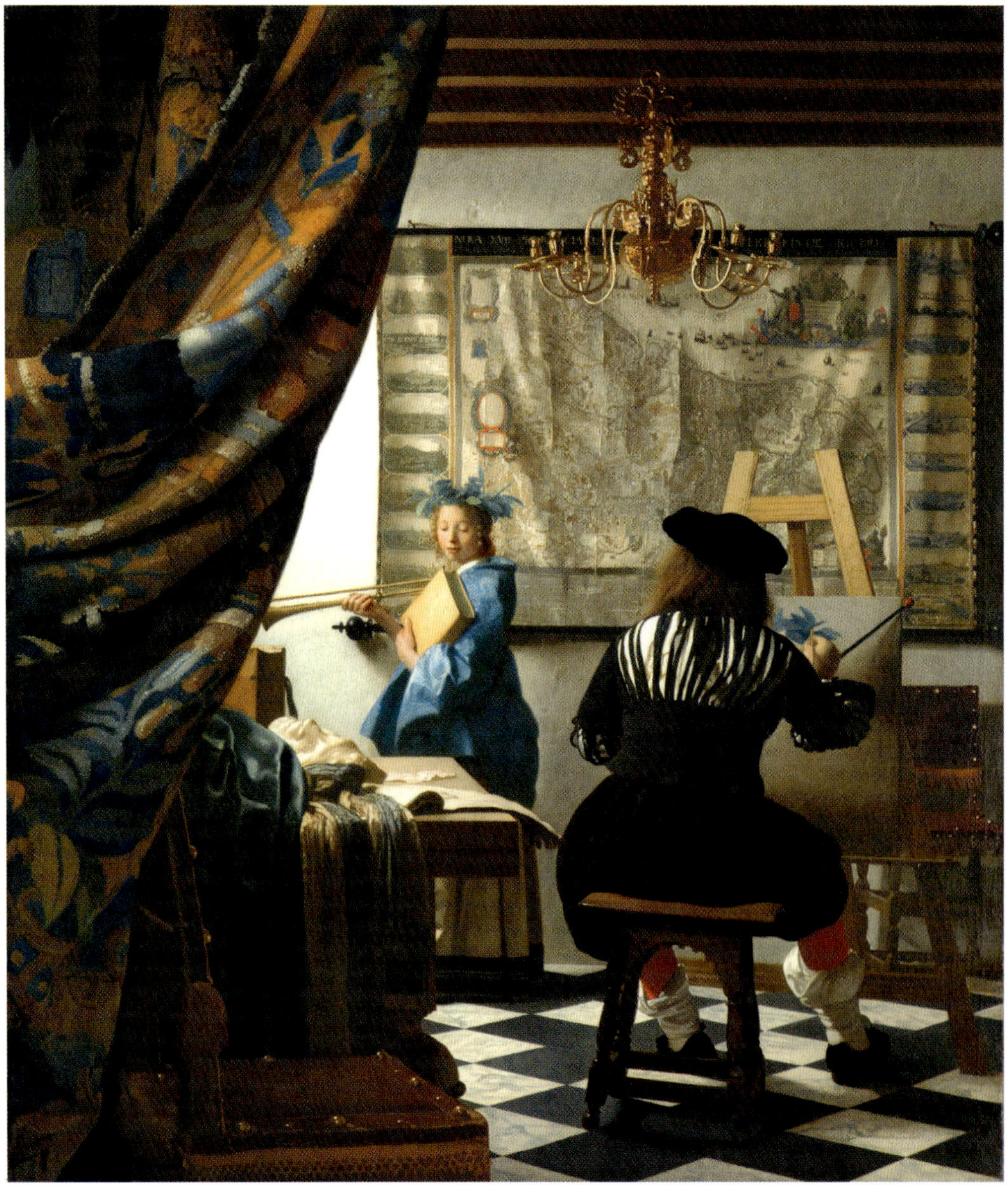

Allegory of Painting, Johannes Vermeer, *c.*1665–67, oil on canvas, 120 x 100cm (47¼ x 39¼in), Kunsthistorisches Museum, Vienna, Austria

While this looks like an artist's studio, the artist is dressed formally, and the image represents an allegory of the art of painting. For example, the model is dressed as Clio, the goddess of creative innovation, while her trumpet is a symbol of fame. The pulled-back curtain reveals a room bathed in light from an unseen window and on the back wall is a map of the Netherlands.

The Annunciation, Adriaen van de Velde, 1667, oil on canvas, 128 x 176cm (50¼ x 69¼ in), Rijksmuseum, Amsterdam, Netherlands

The New Testament relates the story of the angel who comes down from the heaven to tell Mary that she will give birth to the son of God even though she is a virgin. Here, van de Velde depicts the moment when Mary is both surprised and shocked at the angel's arrival and news. He probably painted the work for a secret Catholic church in Amsterdam.

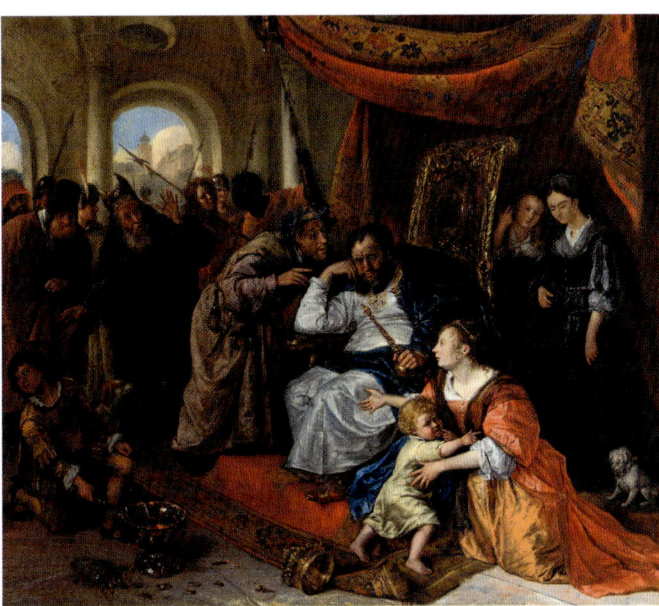

Moses and the Pharaoh's Crown, Jan Steen, c.1670, oil on canvas, 78 x 79cm (30.7 x 31.2in), Mauritshuis, The Hague, Netherlands

This is one of few religious scenes painted by Steen. He portrays the story of Moses who, as a child, was regarded by the Pharaoh's counsellors as a threat to Egypt. To test him, the Pharaoh and his men make him choose between gold and a dish of glowing coals. In innocence, he picks up a coal and burns himself — and runs crying to his foster mother.

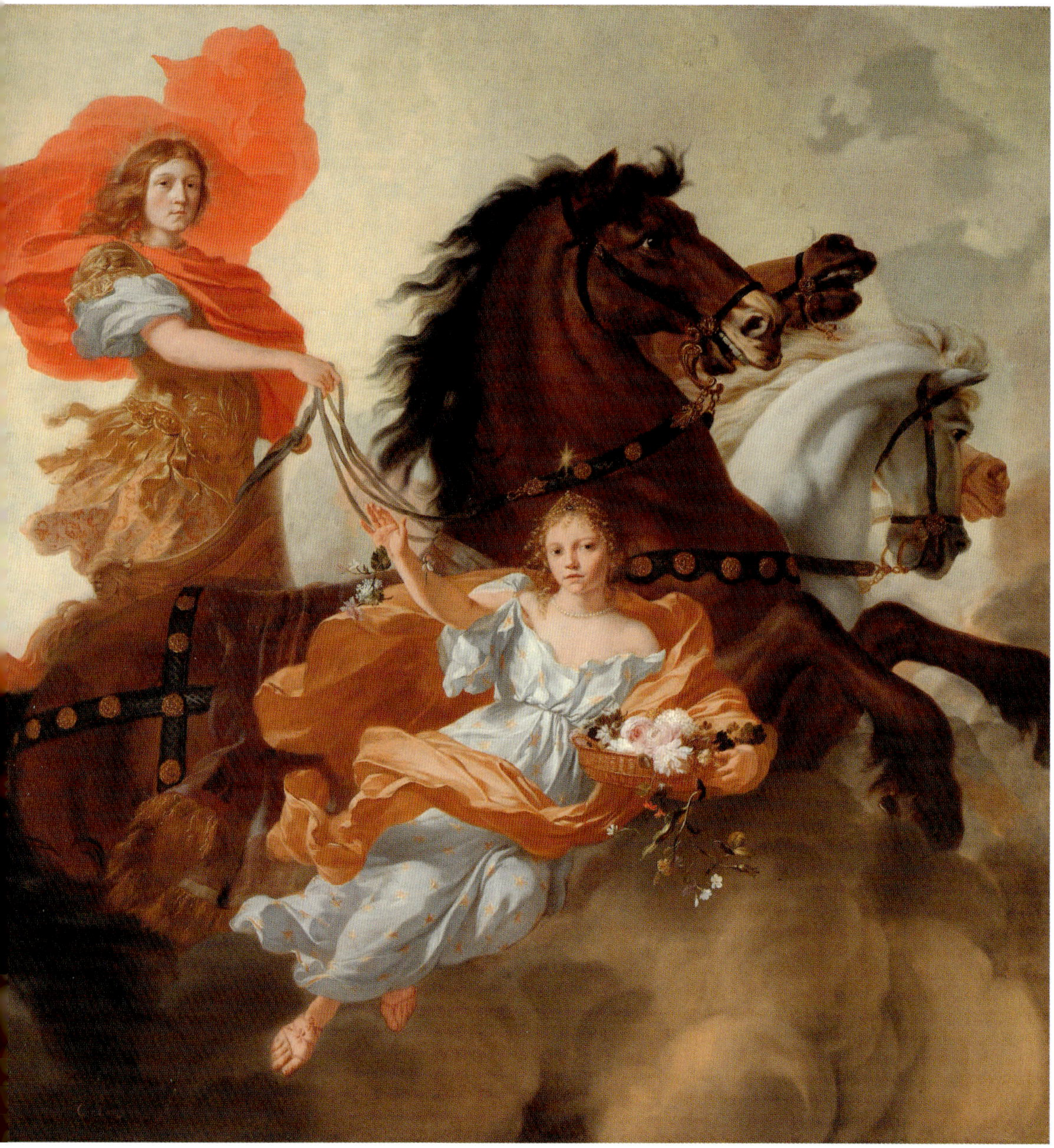

Apollo and Aurora, Gerard de Lairesse, 1671, oil on canvas, 204.5 x 193.4cm (80½ x 76in), The Metropolitan Museum of Art, New York, USA

French-born Gerard de Lairesse (1641–1711) was a painter and art theorist who settled in the Netherlands. During his lifetime, he was was celebrated as a painter. This painting portrays the sun god Apollo with Aurora, the goddess of the dawn. The subject was popular at the time and it has been speculated that this may be the portrait of a newly married couple.

The Banquet of Ahasuerus, Arent de Gelder, 1680s, oil on canvas, 111.8 x 139.7 cm (44 x 56 in), J. Paul Getty Museum, Los Angeles, USA

Drunken King Ahasuerus leans on the table, spilling wine on to his lap from a goblet. This scene is from the biblical Book of Esther.

After seven days of feasting and drinking, King Ahasuerus summons the beautiful Queen Vashti, but when she refuses to appear, Ahasuerus is livid and chooses Esther as his wife instead. Dordrecht-born Arent de Gelder (1645–1727) was one of Rembrandt's last pupils in Amsterdam.

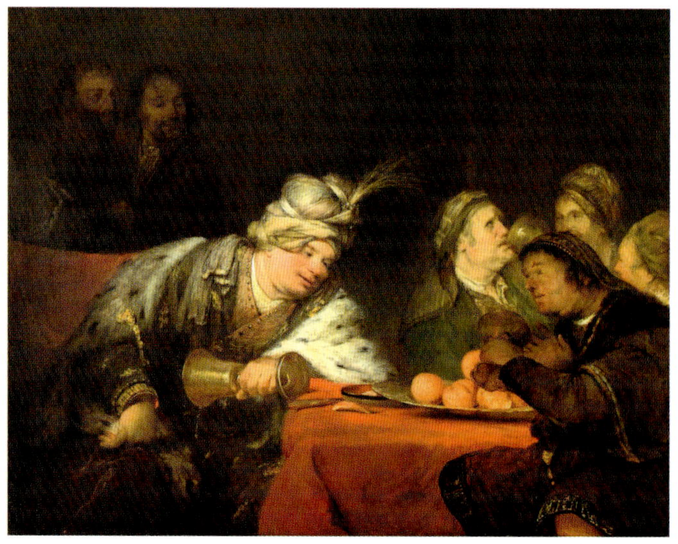

The Expulsion of Heliodorus from the Temple, Gerard de Lairesse, 1674, oil on canvas, 89 x 77cm (35 x 30¼in), Private Collection

Admired for his idealization that was based on his study of classical antiquity, Gerard de Lairesse has here painted Heliodorus being expelled from the Temple in Jerusalem, caught by a horseman and angels. Heliodorus had been sent by the king of Syria to sneak in and evaluate the wealth of the temple in Jerusalem. Here his terror is evident, as Lairesse proves his adroitness at portraying emotion and textural details.

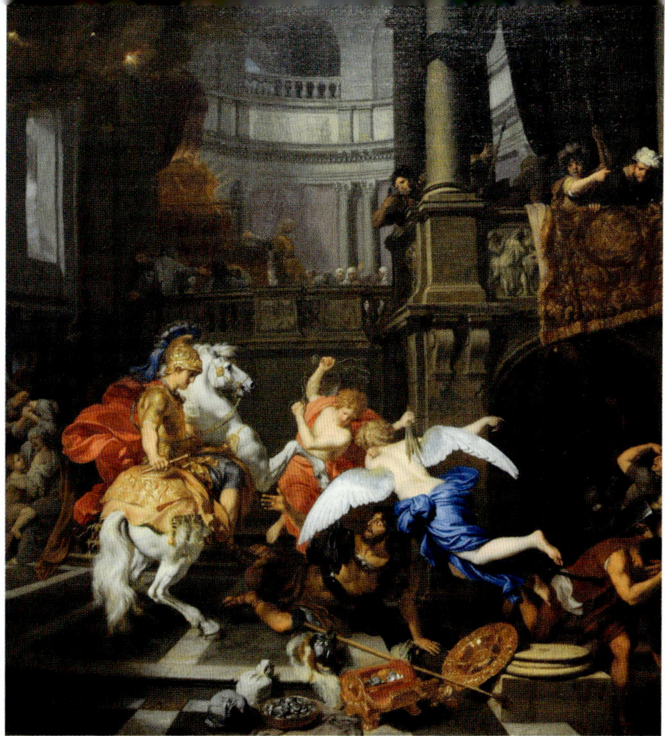

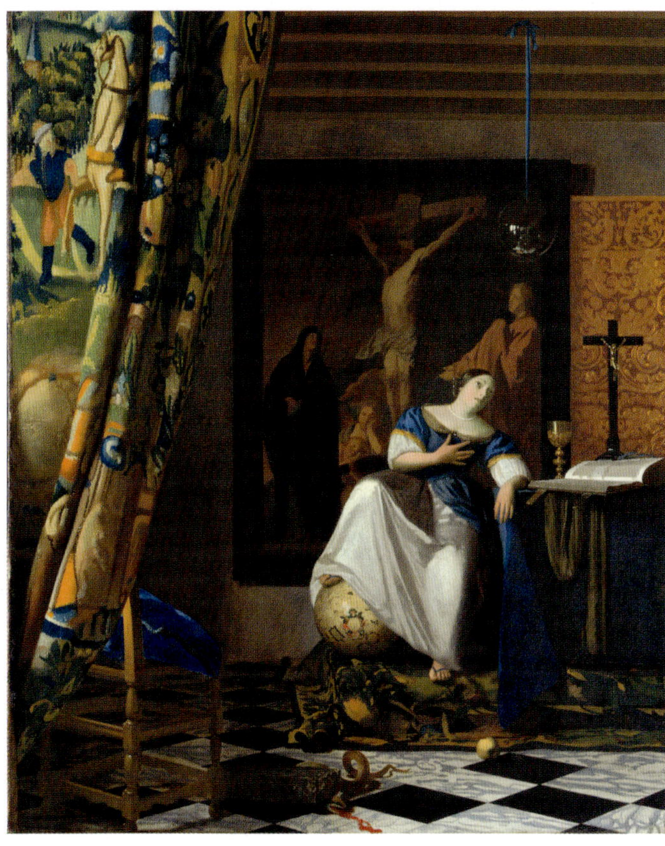

Allegory of the Catholic Faith, Johannes Vermeer, 1670s, oil on canvas, 114.3 x 88.9cm (45 x 35in), The Metropolitan Museum of Art, New York, USA

When Vermeer painted this, public celebrations of the Mass were forbidden in the Dutch Republic, yet a patron commissioned it. A woman, symbolizing the Church, has one foot on a globe. In the foreground, the cornerstone of the church crushes the serpent of evil. On a table are a chalice, missal and crucifix, probably referring to the celebration of the Mass in private homes.

Allegory of Frederik Hendrik as the Bringer of Peace, Jan de Bray, 1681, oil on canvas, 217 x 218cm (85½ x 85¾in), Frans Hals Museum, Haarlem, Netherlands

Here, the personification of Virtue crowns Frederik with a laurel wreath, while Bravery holds a shield. As Prince Frederik Hendrik had been so helpful in the Dutch fight against the Spanish, 34 years later, Jan de Bray was commissioned to depict him as a peacemaker. De Bray painted it to hang above a fireplace in the Princenhof, where the ruling Orange family stayed when they were in Haarlem.

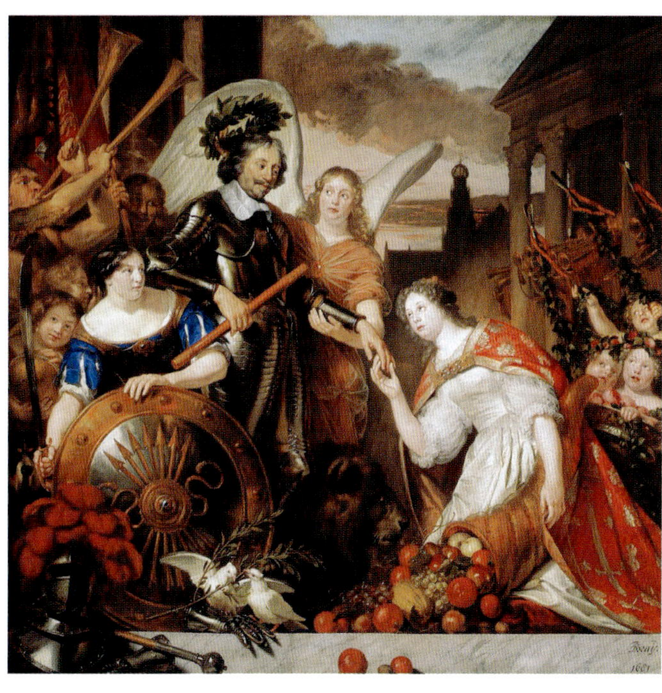

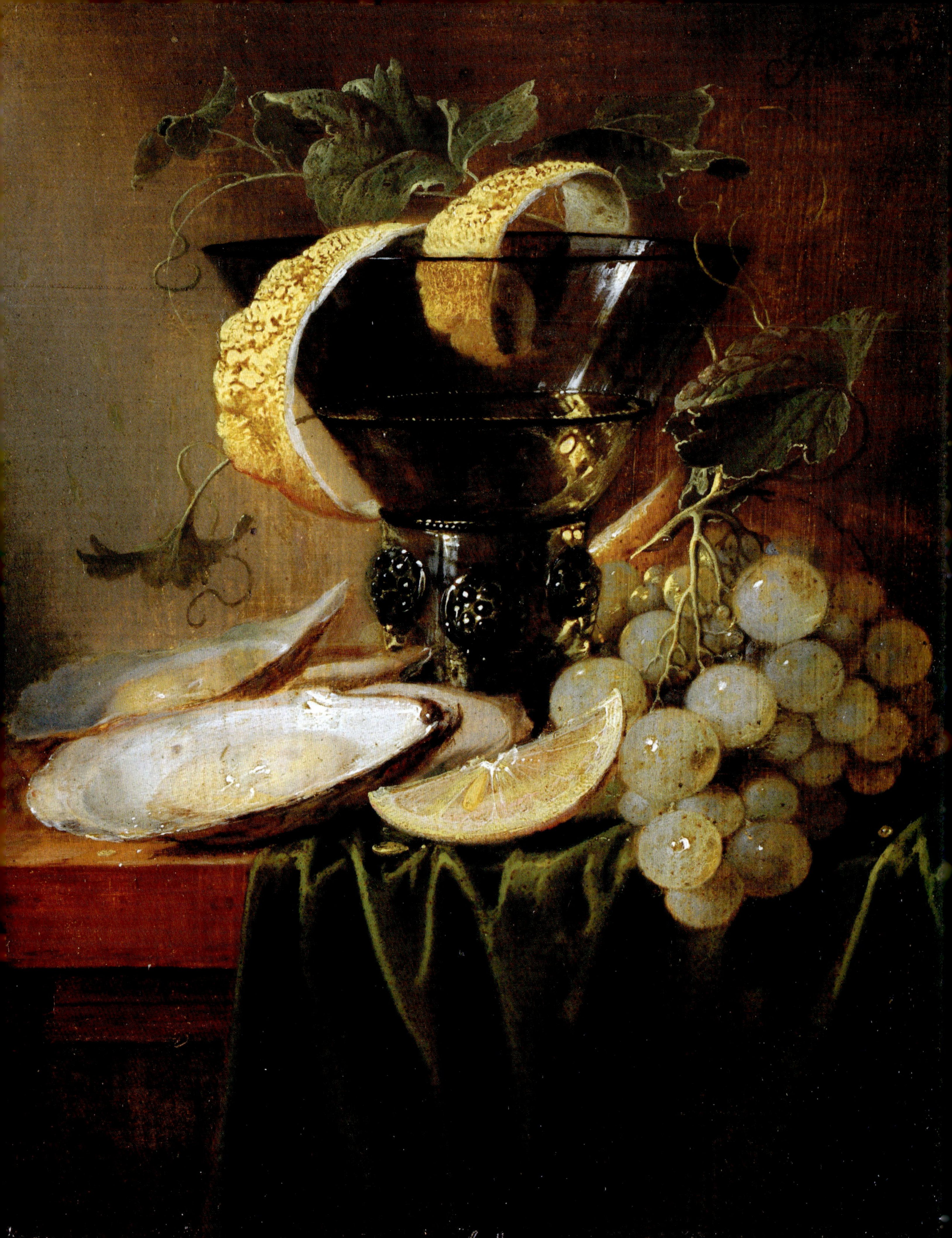

STILL LIFE

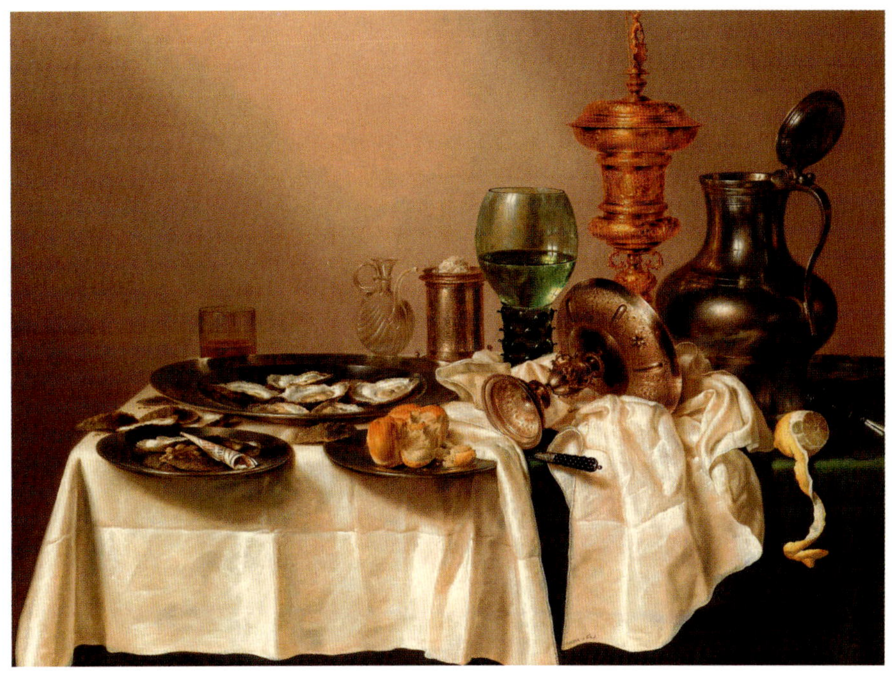

Like genre and landscape, still life painting was pioneered in Haarlem and Amsterdam during the 16th century and spread throughout the Republic. The Dutch became one of the first consumer societies, with new wealth being spent on valuable goods and expensive foodstuffs, and with artists conveying these in realistic-looking paintings. Still life specialisms included flowers or banquet (banketje) and breakfast (ontbijtje) pieces, pronkstillevens and vanitas. Invented in the Dutch Republic, the term vanitas comes from the Old Testament book: 'Vanitas vanitatum... et omnia vanitas' or 'Vanity of vanities, all is vanity'. Although Samuel van Hoogstraten called still life painters 'foot soldiers in the army of art,' meaning that still life was the lowest of the genres, these paintings were hugely popular, attracting some of the finest artists and commanding high prices.

Above: Still life with Gilt Cup, Willem Claesz Heda, 1635. *Throughout his career, Heda painted still lifes using a cool, harmonious palette. Here, he demonstrates his skill in rendering textures and light reflections, especially on materials such as pewter, silver, damask, glass and mother-of-pearl. A lemon complements the monochrome.*

Left: Still Life with Glass and Oysters, Jan de Heem, c.1640. *Featuring a mix of some of the most familiar objects used in Dutch Golden Age still life, including lemon peel, a roemer (or rummer) glass and oysters, this small painting is precisely painted and lifelike. Oysters, grapes and lemons were high-status delicacies.*

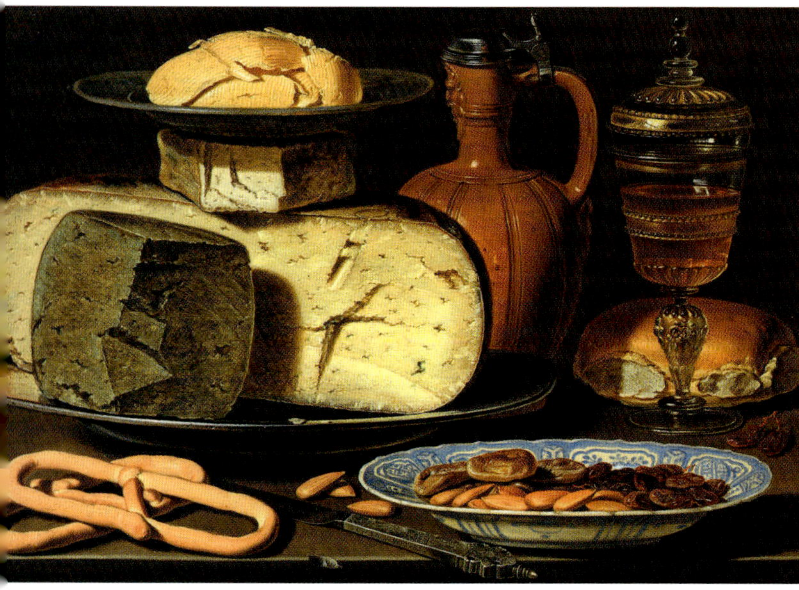

Still Life with Cheeses, Almonds and Pretzels, Clara Peeters, c.1615, oil on panel, 34.5 x 49.5cm (13½ x 19½in), Mauritshuis, The Hague, Netherlands

Arranged on a table are a delicate Venetian wine glass, a Chinese Wan-Li porcelain dish, several cheeses, pretzels, nuts and figs. Clara Peeters has also included a tiny reflected self-portrait on the pewter lid of the earthenware jug, and added her signature on the silver knife. For most of her career, Peeters painted opulent or costly objects in banketje still lifes as here.

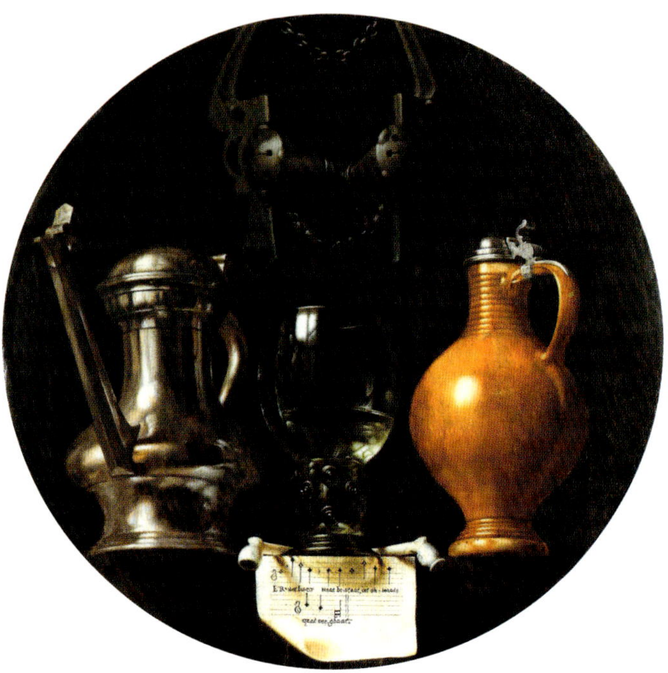

Emblematic Still Life with Flagon, Glass, Jug and Bridle, Johannes van der Beeck, 1614, oil on panel, 52 x 50.5cm (20½ x 20in), Rijksmuseum, Amsterdam, Netherlands

Johannes (Jan) Symonsz van der Beeck (1589–1644) was also known as Johannes Torrentius (Torrentius is a Latin equivalent of the surname van der Beeck, meaning 'of the brook' or 'of the river'). He was born and worked in Amsterdam but few of his paintings survive as most were burned after he was accused of being a Rosicrucian with atheistic and Satanic beliefs and imprisoned for two years.

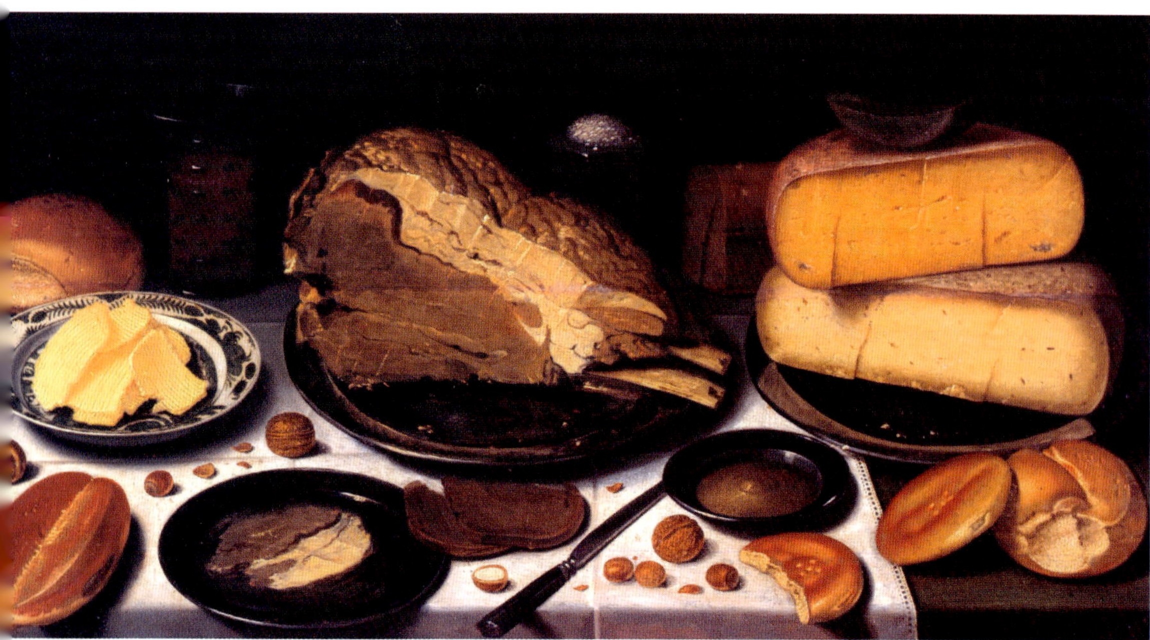

Breakfast, Floris van Schooten, 1615–20, oil on panel, 84 x 47cm (33 x 18½in), Kröller-Müller Museum, Otterlo, Netherlands

Van Schooten (1585/8–1656) painted many breakfast pieces, market and kitchen scenes. As a young man, he and his Catholic family moved from Amsterdam to Haarlem, where Catholicism was more accepted. He served as the dean of the Haarlem Guild of Saint Luke. This meticulous painting is an ontbijt.

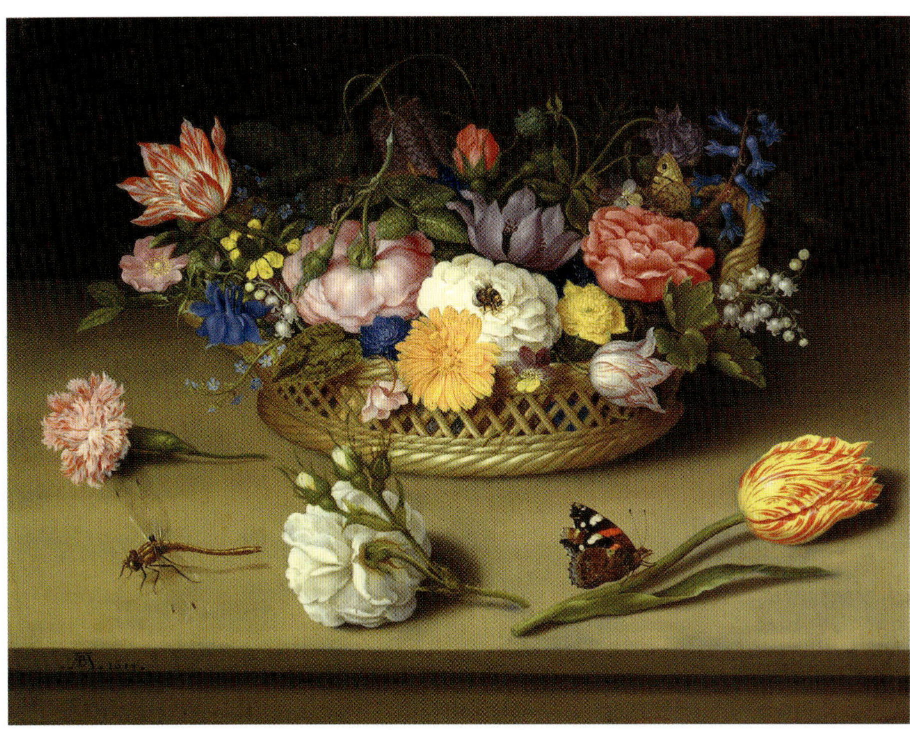

Still Life of Flowers, Ambrosius Bosschaert the Elder, 1614, oil on copper, 30.5 x 38.9cm (12 x15¼in), J. Paul Getty Museum, Los Angeles, USA

A pink carnation, white rose and a yellow tulip with red stripes are scattered in front of a basket of brightly coloured flowers that would usually bloom at different times. In painstaking detail, Ambrosius Bosschaert the Elder applied delicate brushmarks to capture the flowers and insects to convey the brevity of life. Bosschaert was the first great Dutch specialist of fruit and flower paintings.

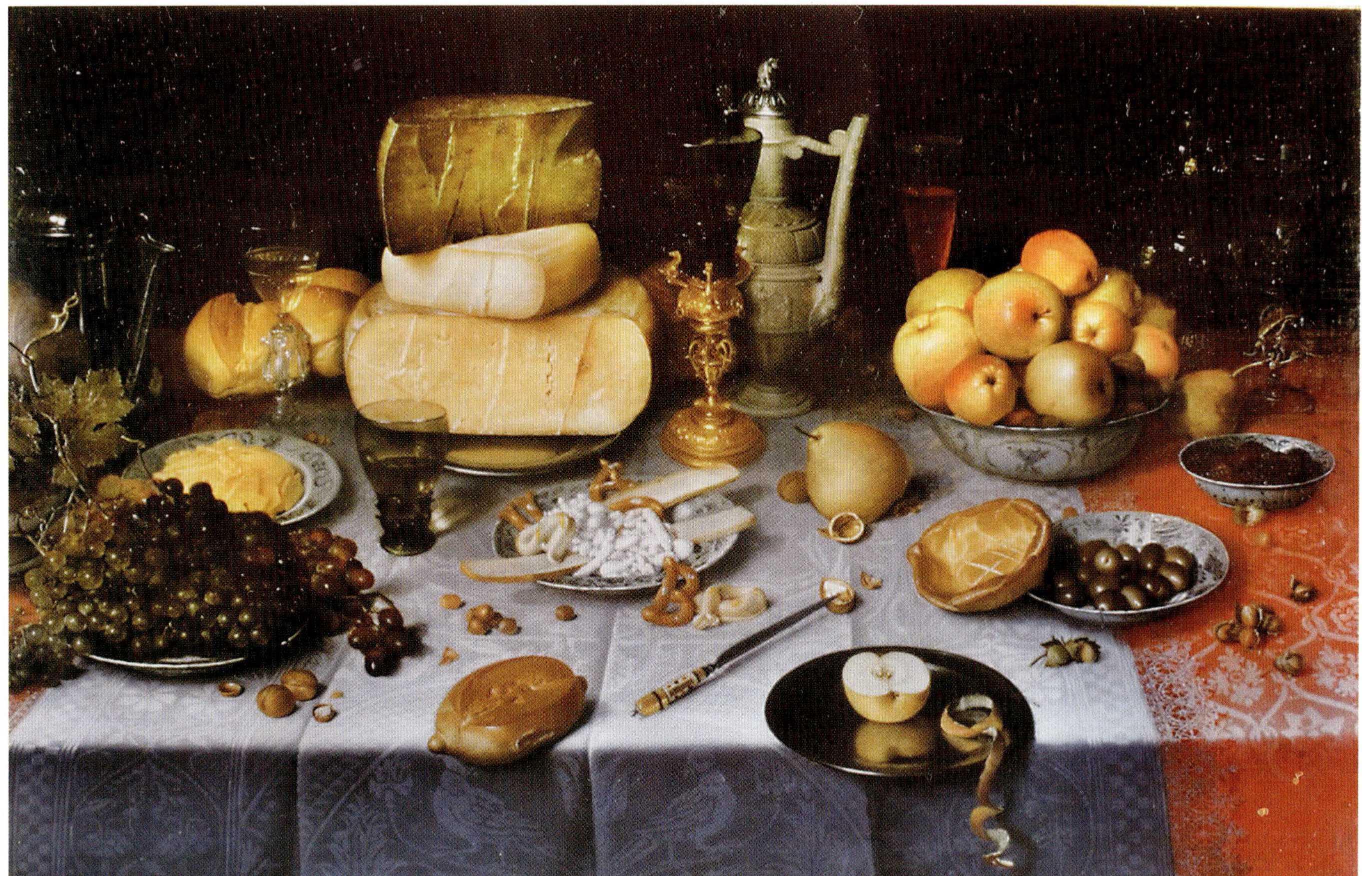

Laid Table with Cheese and Fruit, Floris van Dyck, 1610, oil on oak panel, 73.7 x 113cm (29 x 44½in), **Private Collection**

Depicting the objects from a high viewpoint, symmetrically arranged platters of fruit, cheese, nuts, sweets, glasses, jugs and knives are displayed on a table. Floris van Dyck renders every texture as faithfully as possible, and 17th-century viewers were amazed and delighted with such realism in paint. Many of these items, including the fruit, Chinese Wan-Li porcelain, damask tablecloth, silver plate and glasses were status symbols.

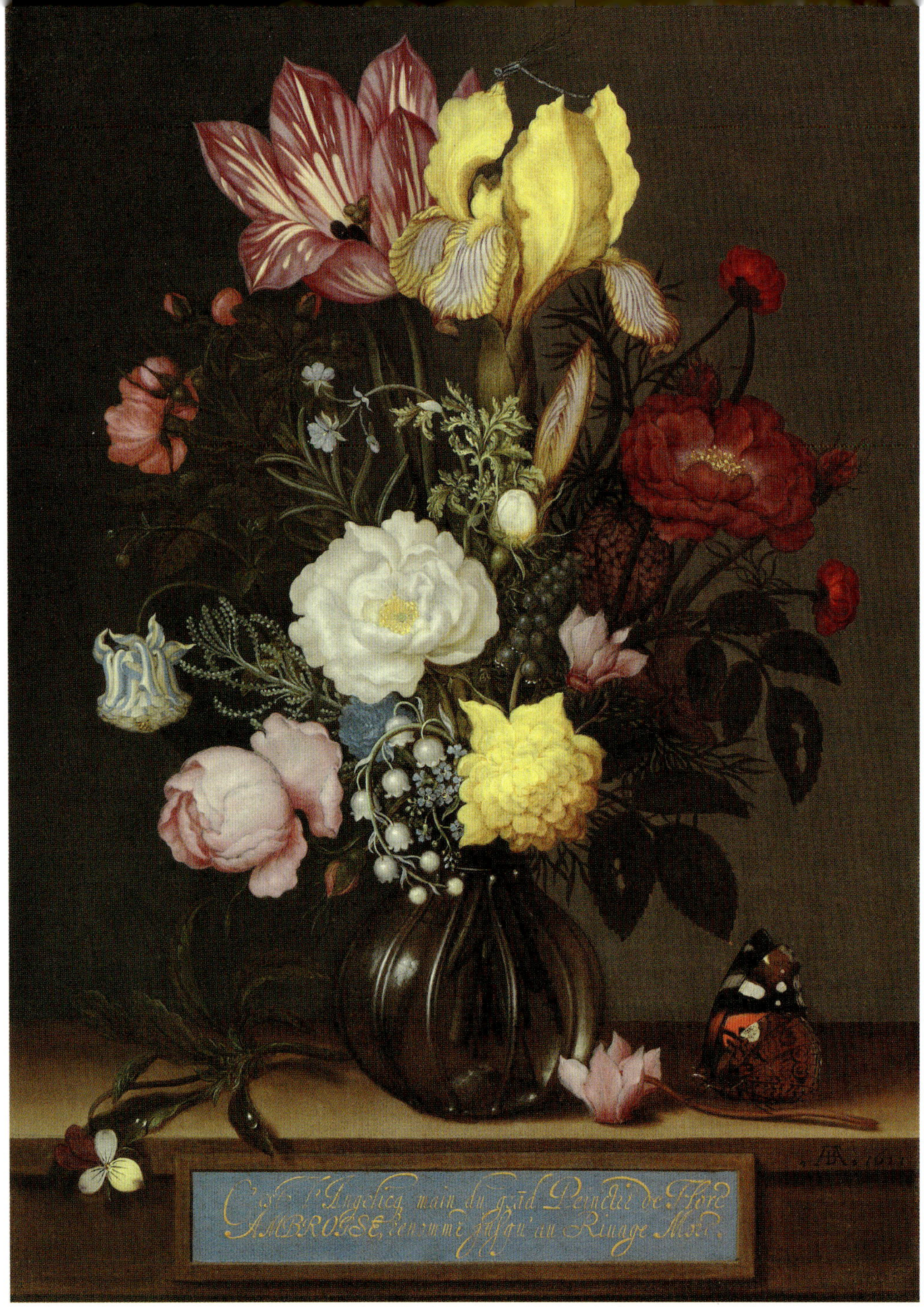

Bouquet of Flowers,
Ambrosius Bosschaert the
Elder, 1621, oil on copper,
216 x 316cm (85 x 124¼in),
National Gallery of Art,
Washington DC, USA

Ambrosius Bosschaert
created numerous paintings
of flowers of different
colours and shapes that
in nature would never
blossom at the same time.
Always set against a dark
background, among other
flowers here are a yellow iris,
a highly desirable red-and-
white striped tulip, roses, a
columbine, a hyacinth and
lily of the valley. A dragonfly
has landed on the iris and
a butterfly rests on the
cyclamen.

Basket of Flowers, Balthasar
van Ast, c.1622, oil on panel,
18.4 x 24.4cm (7¼ x 9½in),
National Gallery of Art,
Washington DC, USA

This was probably produced
for Princess Amalia van
Solms. With its wicker basket
overflowing with flowers, and
surrounded by plump, ripe
fruit and shells, the image
conveys the abundance
and beauty of nature.
Trained by his brother-in-law
Ambrosius Bosschaert, van
der Ast made many detailed
preparatory studies from
life, from which he produced
further paintings without
needing the actual objects in
front of him.

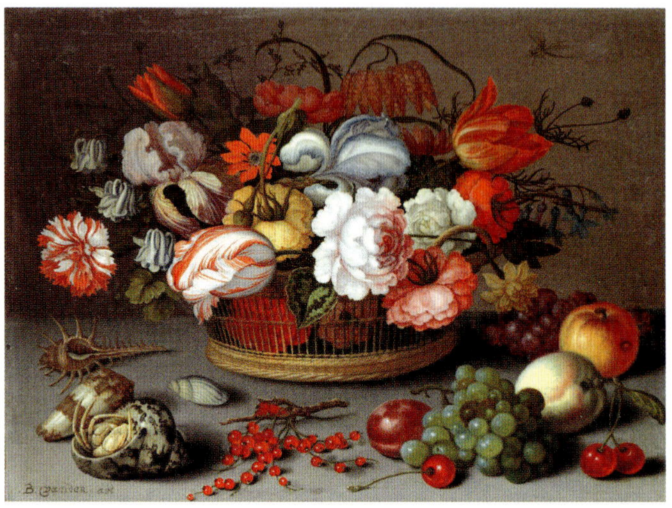

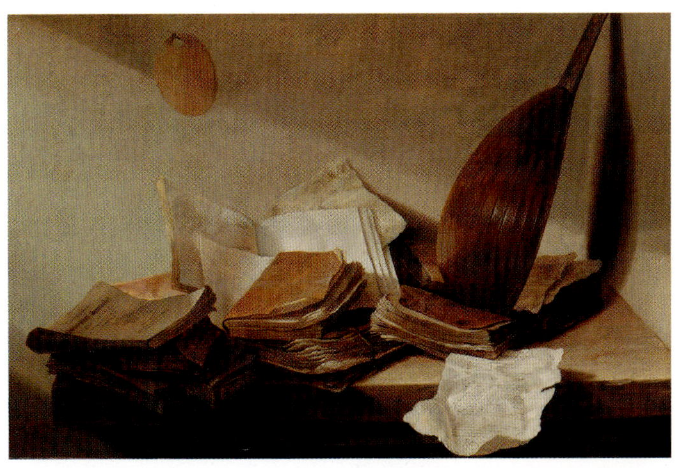

Still Life with Books, Jan Davidsz de Heem, 1625–30, oil on panel, 26.5 x 41.5cm (10½ x 16⅓in), Rijksmuseum, Amsterdam, Netherlands

This monochrome still life of books, each with curling pages, and a lute leaning against the wall, alludes to the ephemerality of life. Worn and well-read books are similar to the notion of producing music; both reading and listening to music are momentary pleasures and this is a reminder that death comes to us all. The word: 'finis' on the paper at the edge of the table is a literal reference to the end of life.

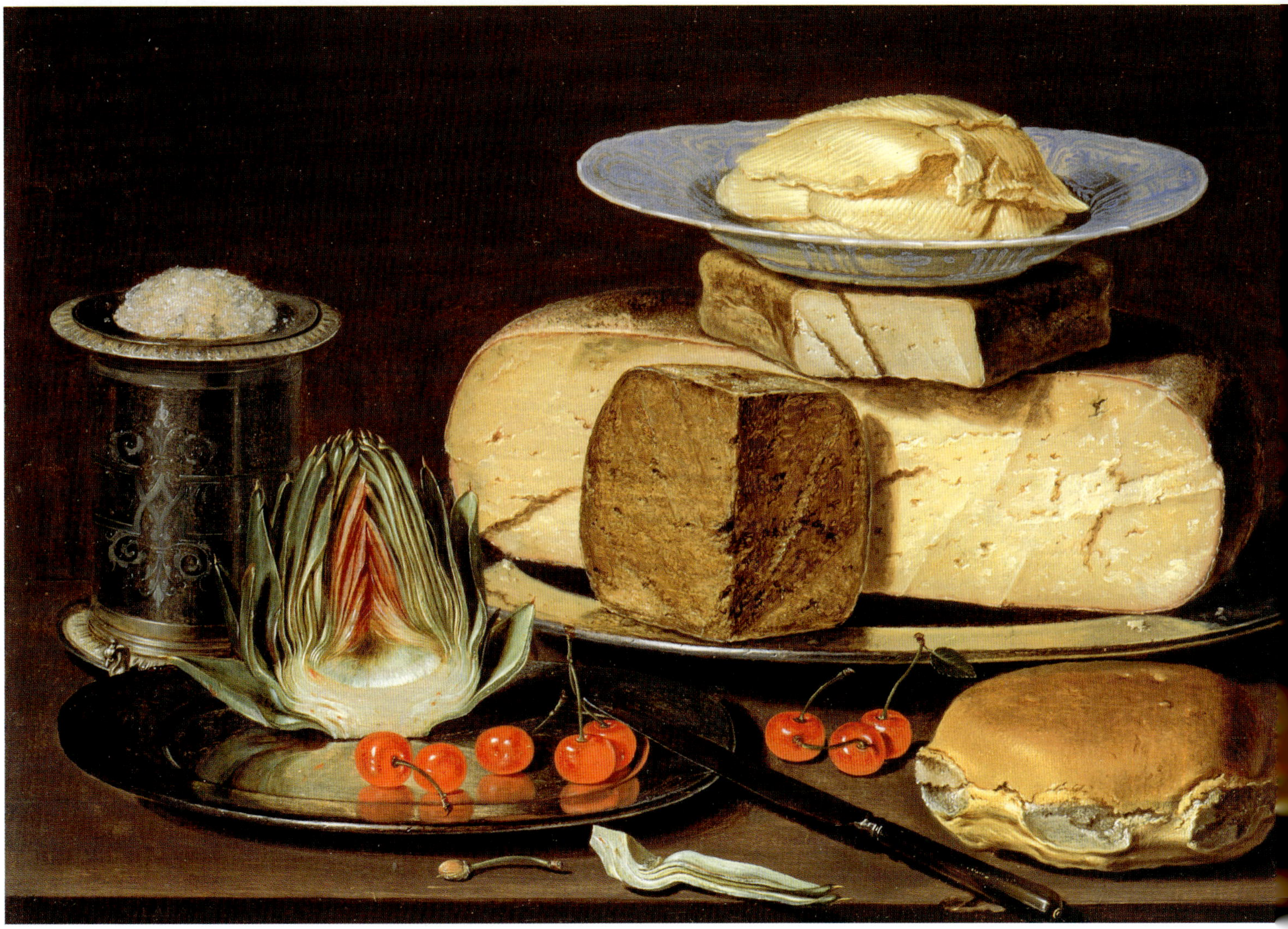

Still Life with Cheeses, Artichoke and Cherries, Clara Peeters, 1625, oil on wood, 46.7 x 33.3cm (18¼ x 13in), Los Angeles Museum of Art, California, USA

As an early Dutch Golden Age still life painter, Clara Peeters was prominent in the development of ontbijtjes. With props of unadulterated food and plain but valuable vessels, here, she painstakingly depicts the textures and colours of the shiny silver plates and cutlery, salt, butter, chunks of cheeses on top of each other, small, glossy red cherries, a bread roll and a delicate globe artichoke cut in half.

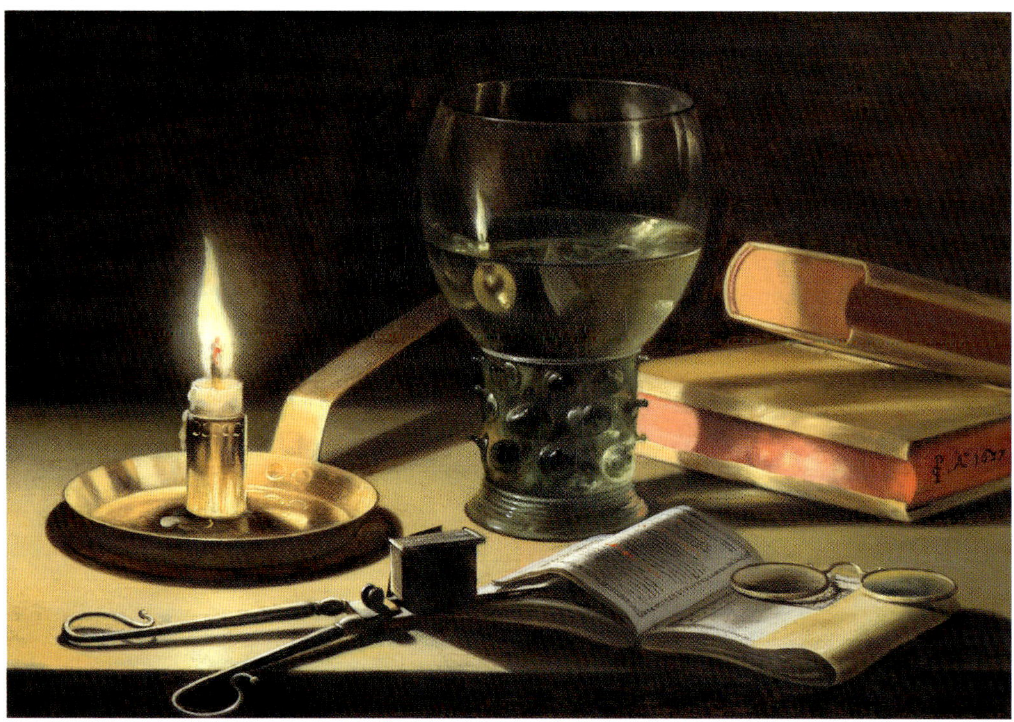

Still Life with Lighted Candle, Pieter Claesz, 1627, oil on panel, 26.1 x 37.3cm (10¼ x 14⅔in), Mauritshuis, The Hague, Netherlands

Using a restrained palette, Pieter Claesz conveyed convincing depictions of various materials, such as the glass containing wine, brass candlestick, pewter candle snuffer and books. Powerfully painted highlights, shine, reflections and shadows using fine brushwork and smooth paint create a sense of solidity and realism, while the dark background, table edge and dramatic play of light are all characteristic of his style.

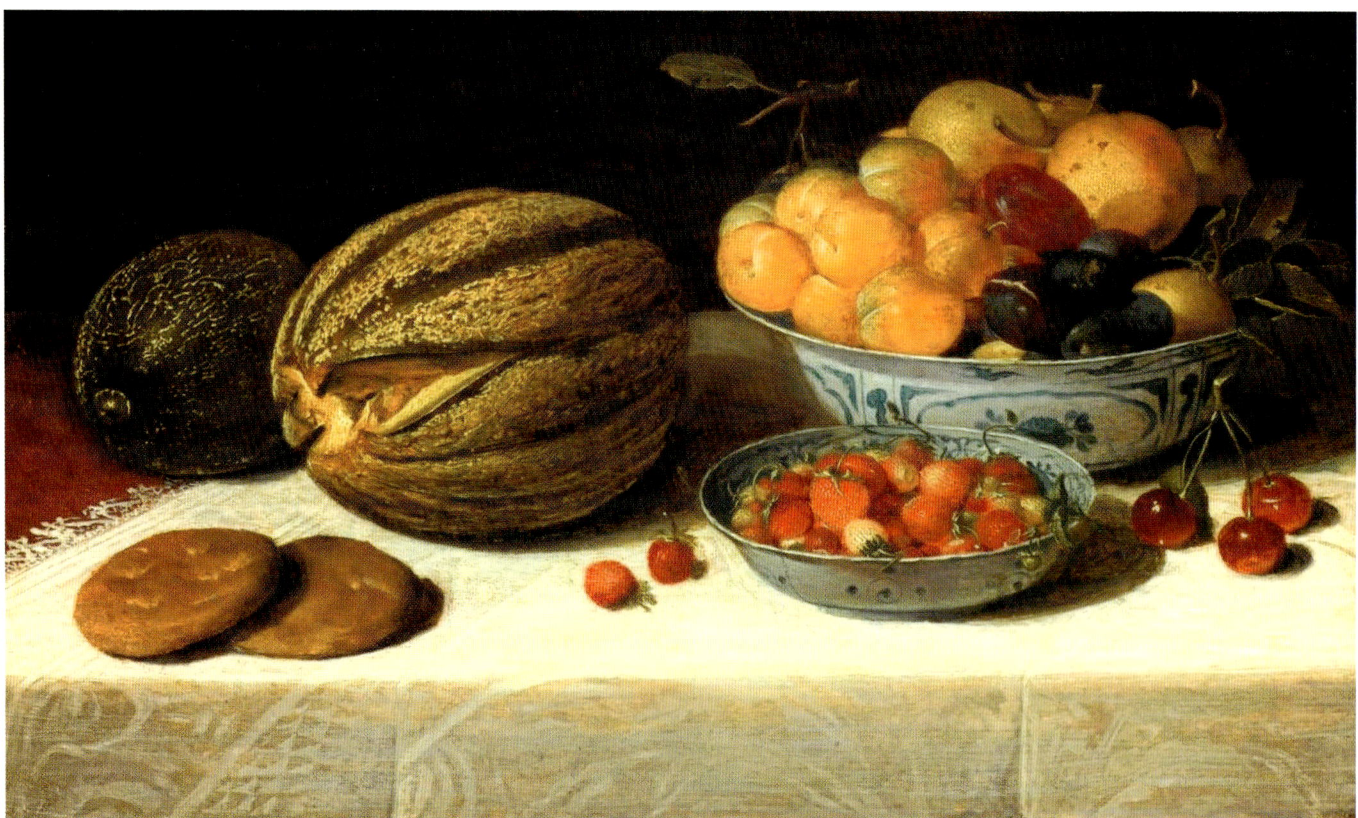

Still life with Melons, Plums, Cherries, Floris van Dyck, 1628, oil on oak panel, 28 x 45.5cm (11 x 18in), Private Collection

One of only seven dated works by Floris van Dyck, this small painting combines several of his favourite objects, including fruit, bread and a white tablecloth. Unlike van Dyck's earlier paintings, this table contains expensive but fewer items than usual. Each object is larger than in many of his works and closer to the picture plane.

Vanitas Still Life, Pieter Claesz, 1630, oil on panel, 39.5 x 56cm (15½ x 22in), Mauritshuis, The Hague, Netherlands

An extinguished candle stub, an empty glass, a quill, a watch and a skull. Each of these objects communicated clearly to original viewers that this alludes to the fact that we will all die, so our lives should be spent morally and honestly. Unlike many other Dutch still lifes that contain allusions to the fragility and brevity of life, the symbolism here is blatant.

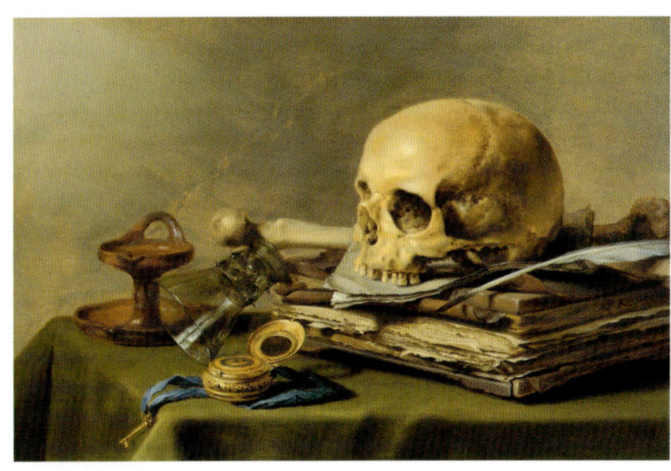

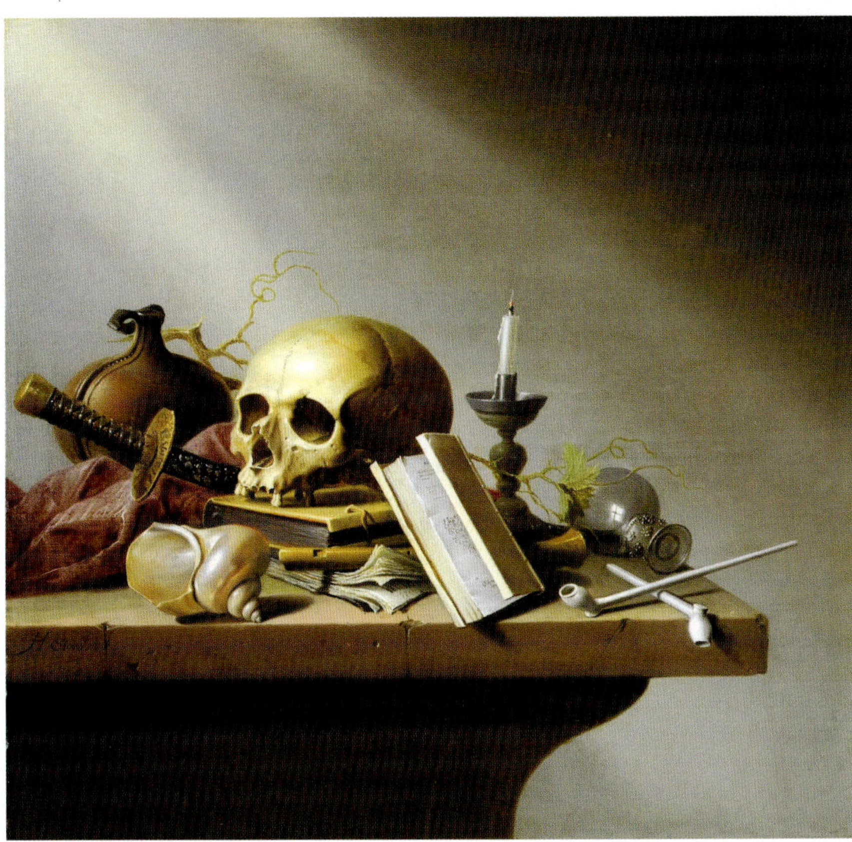

Vanitas, Harmen Steenwyck, c.1650, oil on panel, 37.7 x 38.2cm (14¾ x 15in), Museum de Lakenhal, Leiden, Netherlands

Born in Delft, Harmen Steenwyck and his brother Pieter were taught by their uncle David Bailly in Leiden. Bailly is often credited with the invention of the vanitas, for which Steenwyck became its leading exponent. In this smoothly painted vanitas, books represent knowledge, musical instruments and clay pipes convey worldly pleasures, while the Japanese sword, rare shell and expensive Venetian glass all symbolize earthly wealth.

Vanitas Still Life, Pieter Claesz, 1625, oil on canvas, 29.5 x 34.4cm (11½ x 13½in), Frans Hals Museum, Haarlem, Netherlands

A candlestick with a candle that is almost burned down, a pocket watch, a letter, a quill and a pot of ink, a flower, a skull and a walnut are arranged on a table. Together, they comprise a vanitas, or an allusion to the passing of time and the brevity of life. At the edge of the table is an anemone. Although this beautiful flower is brightly coloured now, it will soon wilt and die.

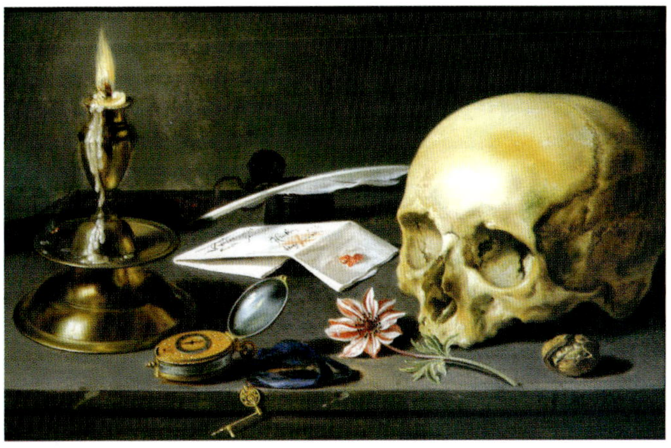

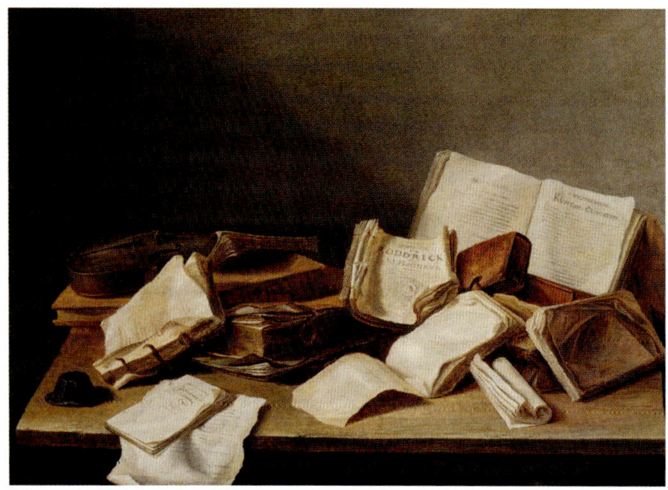

Still Life with a Basket of Fruit, Judith Leyster, 1635–40, oil on canvas, 62.5 x 68cm (24½ x 26¾in), The Kremer Collection, Amsterdam, Netherlands

Judith Leyster painted this at around the time she married Jan Miense Molenaer (1636). The painting features a tilted wicker basket full of apples and grapes. In front of the basket are two more apples and a bunch of grapes hanging over the edge of the table. The pewter wine jug, the half-filled roemer and the dark shadow serve to anchor the objects in the composition.

Still Life with Books and a Violin, Jan Davidsz de Heem, 1628, oil on panel, 36.1 x 48.5cm (14¼ x 19in), Mauritshuis, The Hague, Netherlands

De Heem is known mainly for the colourful flower still lifes he painted from 1650, but as here, previously he painted simple still lifes in virtually monochromatic colours. Well-educated viewers would have recognized the titles of the books and understood that the image focuses on the concept of fate, which alludes to the notion of mortality.

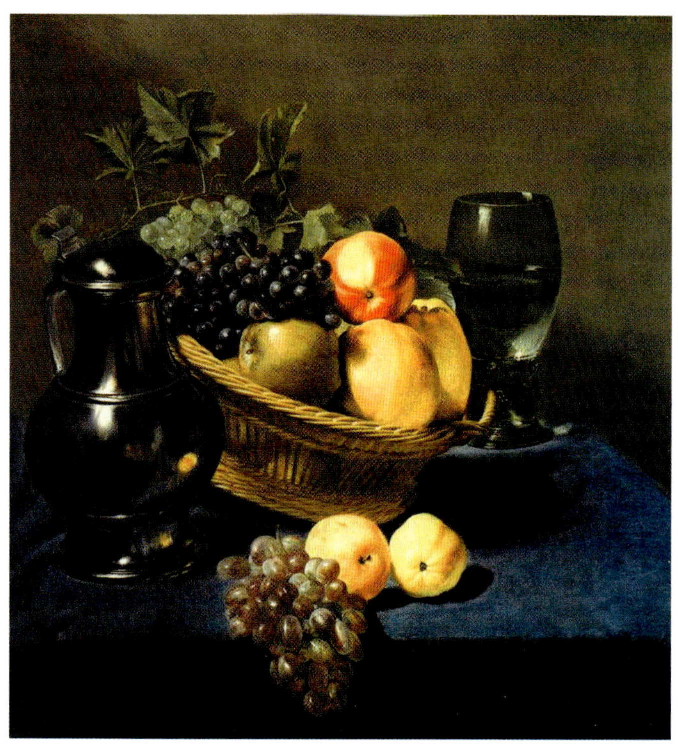

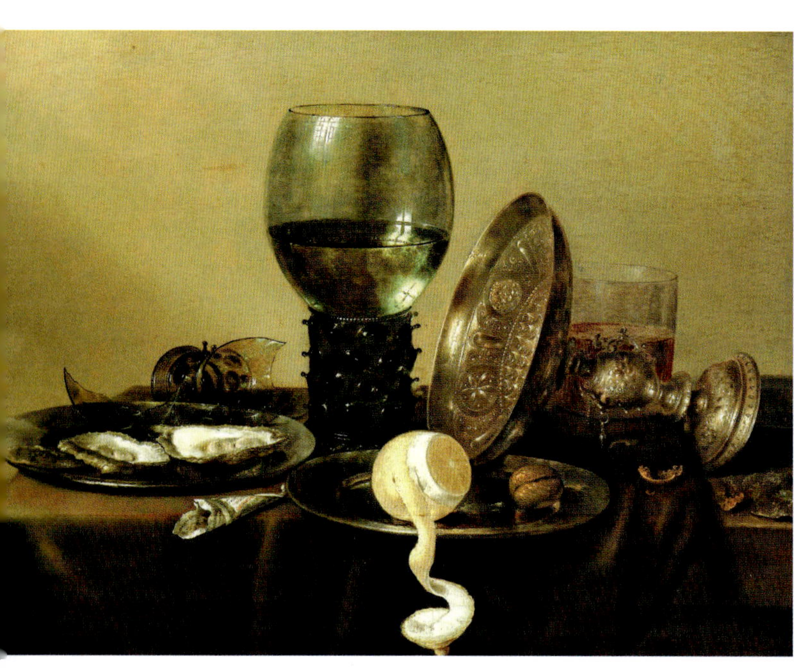

Still Life with Oysters, a Rummer, a Lemon and a Silver Bowl, Willem Claesz Heda, 1634, oil on panel, 43 x 57cm (17 x 22½in), Museum Boijmans van Beuningen, Rotterdam, Netherlands

Willem Heda frequently painted the same still life objects and here his glassware, silver bowl and pewter plate with opened oysters are familiar. Another common element is the lemon, an exotic and expensive fruit in the 17th-century Netherlands. It adds an accent to the predominantly monochrome image that as usual has an underlying message; the half-filled glass suggests moderation in all things.

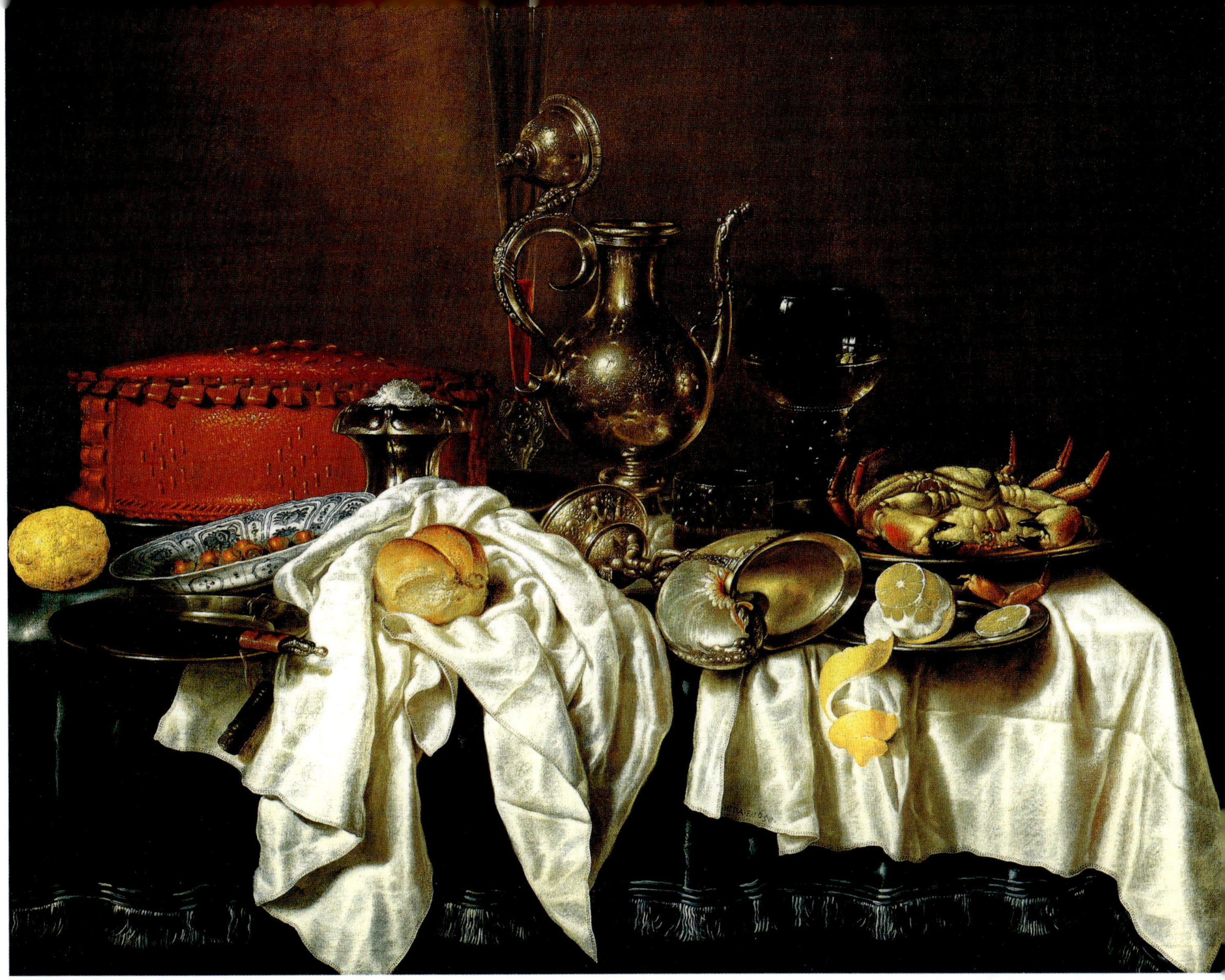

Still Life with Pie and Silver Ewer, Willem Claesz Heda, 1658, oil on canvas, 103 x 123cm (40½ x 48½in), Frans Hals Museum, Haarlem, Netherlands

From 1640, Willem Heda painted still lifes that became increasingly busy, filled with a great variety of objects. His meticulous painting style was greatly admired for its realism and harmony. Compared with Heda's later compositions, this is quite simple, and particularly focuses on the reflective qualities of shiny materials. In the silver jug, for instance, are reflections of a window, the nautilus shell cup and the crab.

Still Life with Crab, Shrimps and Lobster, Clara Peeters, c.1635–40, oil on wood, 70.8 x 108.9cm (27¾ x 42¾in), The Museum of Fine Arts Houston, Texas, USA

Although information about Clara Peeters is scant, in six of her known paintings she includes the same ornate knife inscribed with her name and a silver mark from Antwerp. At that time knives were given as wedding gifts and also taken to others' houses when invited to dine. Nearly all of Peeters's paintings are still lifes using a fairly limited palette and close cropping, as here.

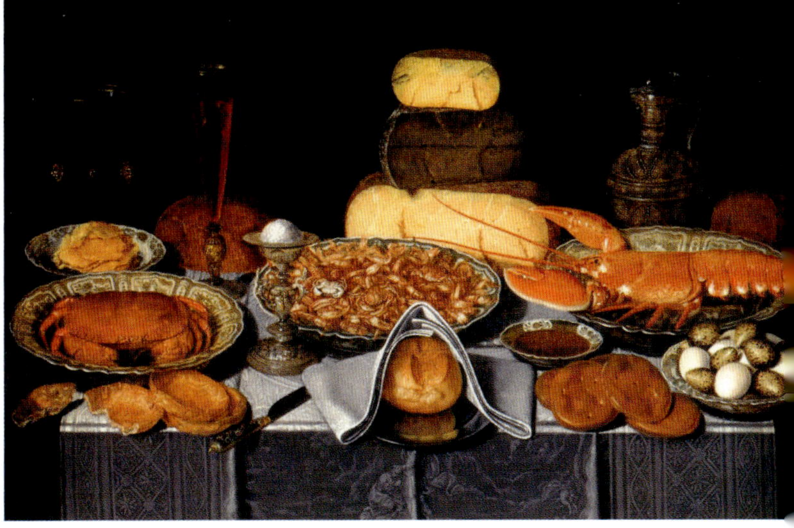

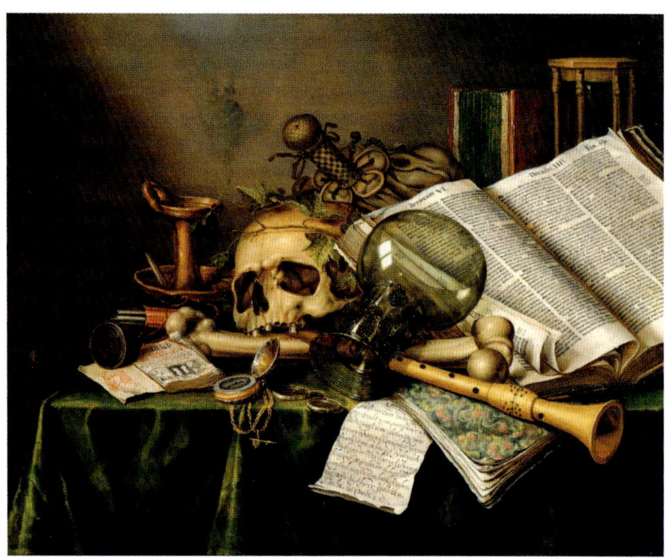

Still Life with Books and Manuscripts and a Skull, Evert Collier, 1663, oil on panel, 70 x 56.5cm (27½ x 22¼ in), The National Museum of Western Art, Tokyo, Japan

Evert Collier trained in Haarlem and specialized in vanitas and trompe l'oeil still lifes, depicting such things as books, glasses, globes and musical instruments, warning about vanity, greed, the impermanence of life and the pointlessness of pleasure. Many of his works include documents containing texts, often in English as he lived in London for a while, although he was also successful in Leiden, Haarlem and Amsterdam.

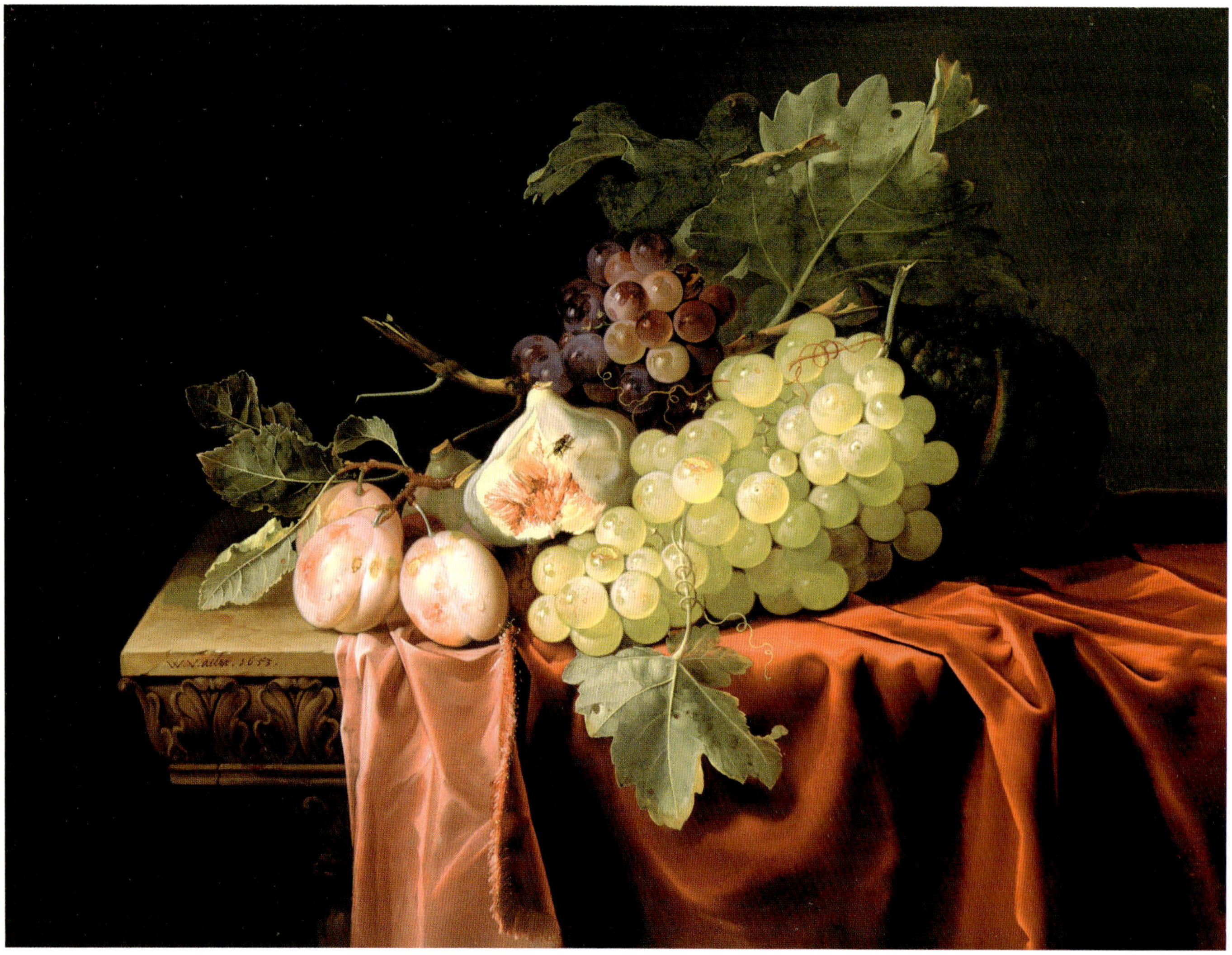

Still Life, Willem van Aelst, 1653, oil on canvas, 41.2 x 53cm (16¼ x 20¾ in), Private Collection

Between 1645/6 and 1651, Willem van Aelst lived in France, then in Italy until 1656. While he was in Italy, he worked for various wealthy patrons including the Medici family, and on his return to the Netherlands, after a brief stay in Delft, he eventually settled in Amsterdam. The realism of these grapes, plums, figs and melon resting on a velvet cloth and stone ledge reveal his outstanding skills.

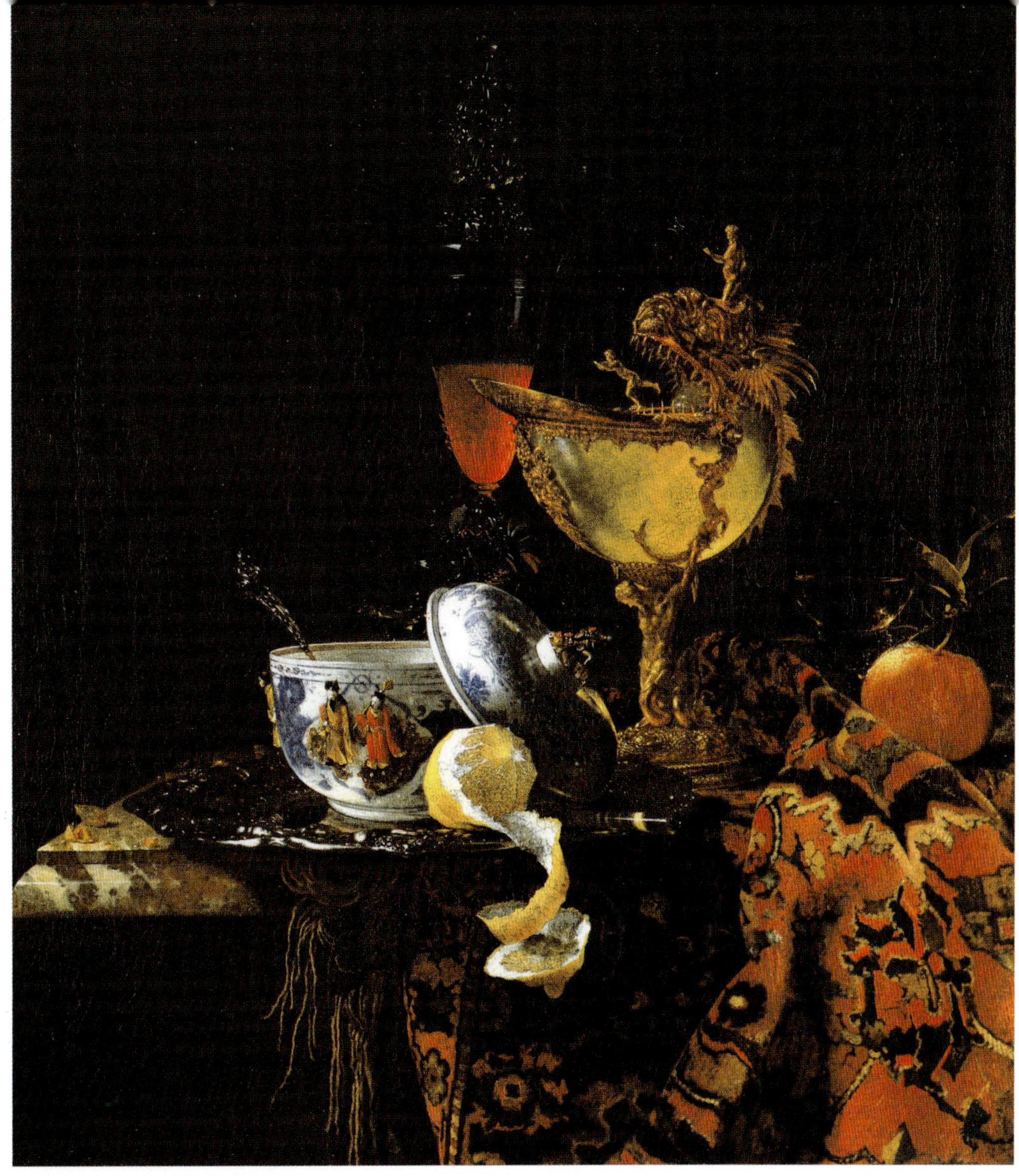

Still Life with a Chinese Bowl, Willem Kalf, 1662, oil on canvas, 79 x 67cm (31 x 26¼ in), Museo Thyssen-Bornemisza, Madrid, Spain

Willem Kalf was especially recognized for his pronkstillevens that portrayed rare, costly or ornate objects. Here he depicts some of the luxury goods that were being imported to the Netherlands, including an expensive Chinese Ming porcelain bowl, a nautilus cup and a Persian carpet. He used meticulous marks to create bright highlights and to convey shining reflections and a range of different textures.

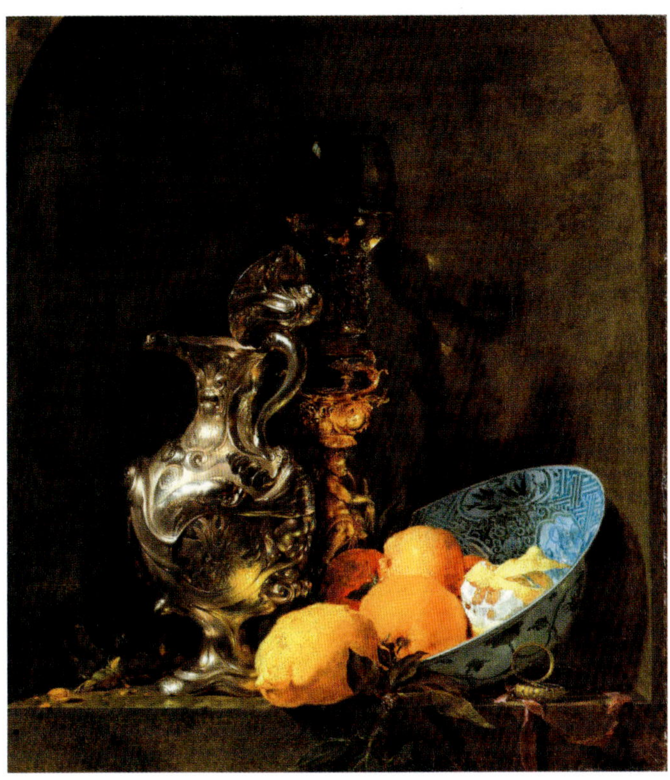

Still Life with Silver Jug, Willem Kalf, 1655–60, oil on canvas, 73.8 x 65.2cm (29 x 25½in), Rijksmuseum, Amsterdam, Netherlands

Against the traditional dark background of Dutch still lifes, costly objects are arranged, including an ornate silver jug, silver glass holder and a Wan-li porcelain bowl. Kalf selected objects especially in order to explore their reflective qualities and contrasts of texture. As with many pronkstillevens, most of the painting is fairly monochromatic, having the effect of thrusting the lemons and blue bowl into sharp focus.

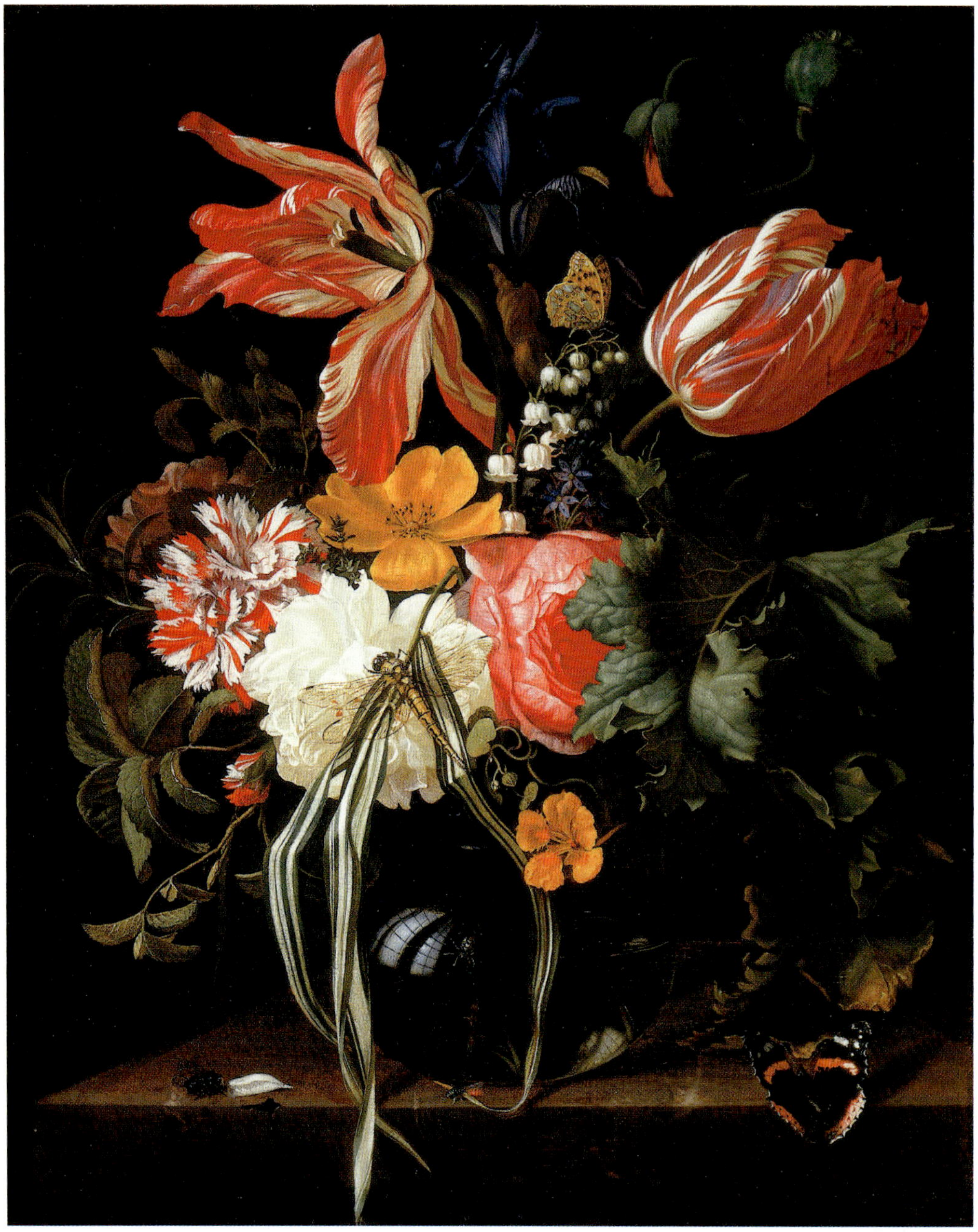

Still Life of Flowers, Maria van Oosterwijck, 1669, oil on canvas, 46 x 37.1cm (18 x 14½in), Cincinnati, Ohio, USA

Bright flowers that bloom at different times, this luscious bouquet is not just comprised of flowers: within the image are a dragonfly, a spider, butterflies and flies. The windows of van Oosterwijck's studio are reflected in the glass vase. Since Tulpenwindhandel (see page 37), the tulip had become a symbol of Dutch national pride. The elegance and luminosity of her depictions of flowers made van Oosterwijk an extremely sought-after artist.

Letter Rack, Evert Collier, c.1698, oil on canvas, 61.5 x 48.5cm (24¼ x 19in), Art Gallery of South Australia

Evert Collier signed himself 'Edwaert Colyer' in his Dutch works but was known as Edward Collier in the 1690s when he moved to London and painted letter racks with trompe l'oeil effects, featuring newspapers, pamphlets and brochures. Although he returned to the Netherlands occasionally, he achieved his greatest success in England. Here, every item, including musical instruments and scores, newspapers and a quill are included to remind viewers of life's impermanence.

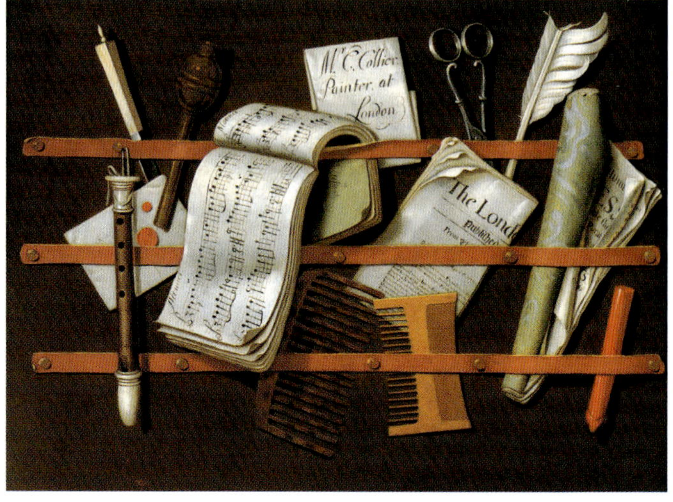

Trompe l'Oeil, Samuel van Hoogstraten, 1664, oil on 46 x 58cm (18 x 22¾in), Dordrechts Museum, Dordrecht, Netherlands

Paintings that deceive the eye – trompe l'oeil – became extremely popular during the Dutch Golden Age and Samuel van Hoogstraten, the son of a goldsmith, engraver and painter, and who studied under Rembrandt, was a pioneer in the field. This type of still life reached unprecedented levels of expertise during the period, as seen here with these illusionistic effects, that sought such realism that the painting 'fooled the eye.'

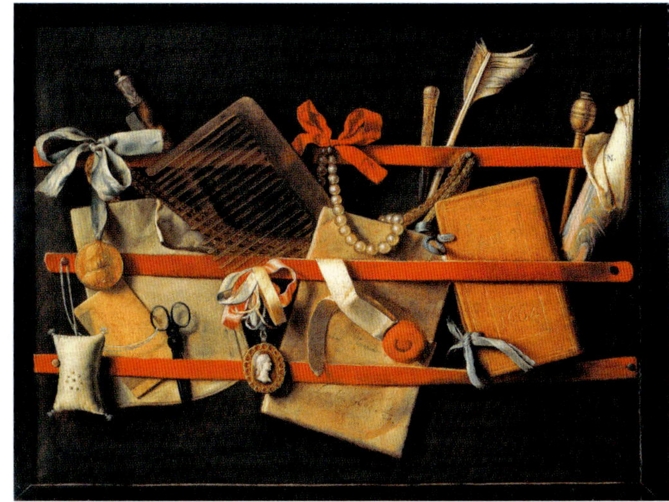

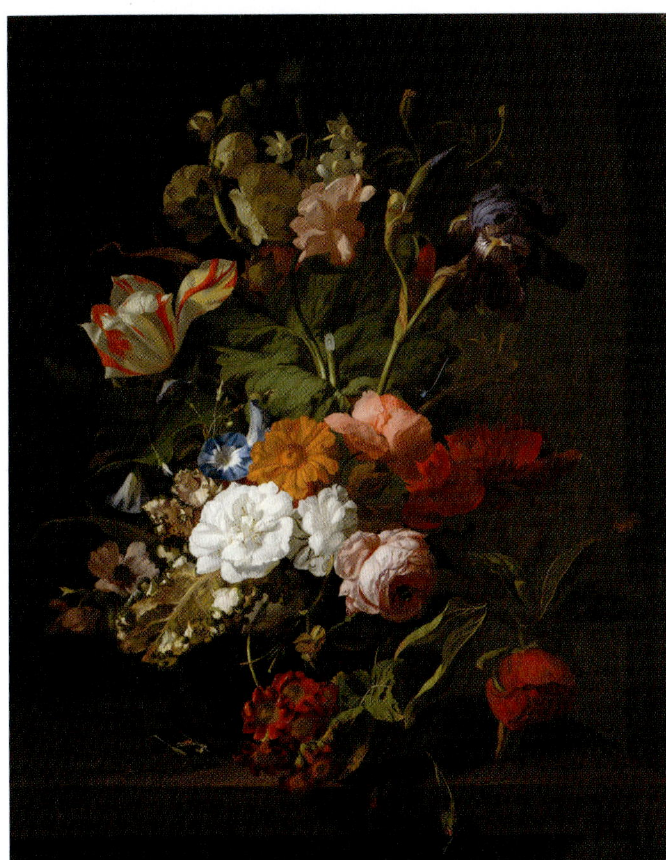

Vase with Flowers, Rachel Ruysch, 1700, oil on canvas, 79.5 x 60.2cm (31¼ x 23¾in), Mauritshuis, The Hague, Netherlands

Hugely successful, Rachel Ruysch's paintings often sold for more during her lifetime than Rembrandt's sold in his. As the daughter of the head of Amsterdam's botanical gardens, she used knowledge learned from her father to paint precise images of plants and insects. Here she uses her characteristic dramatic lighting to convey flowers with astonishing realism. Several are beginning to wilt, conveying the brevity of earthly life – and perhaps also the waning of the Dutch Golden Age.

Still Life with a Bouquet in the Making, Dirck de Bray, 1674, oil on panel, 40.5 x 35.7cm (16 x 14in), Mauritshuis, The Hague, Netherlands

Unlike many Dutch flower still lifes that were generally lavishly arranged and featured flowers that bloom in different seasons, this bouquet is still being arranged and the flowers, that include anemones, tulips, narcissi and columbines, all blossom together in the spring. As well as painting flowers, Dirck de Bray was also a skilled printmaker in etching and woodcut, but in the late 1670s he entered the Gaesdonck monastery in Brabant.

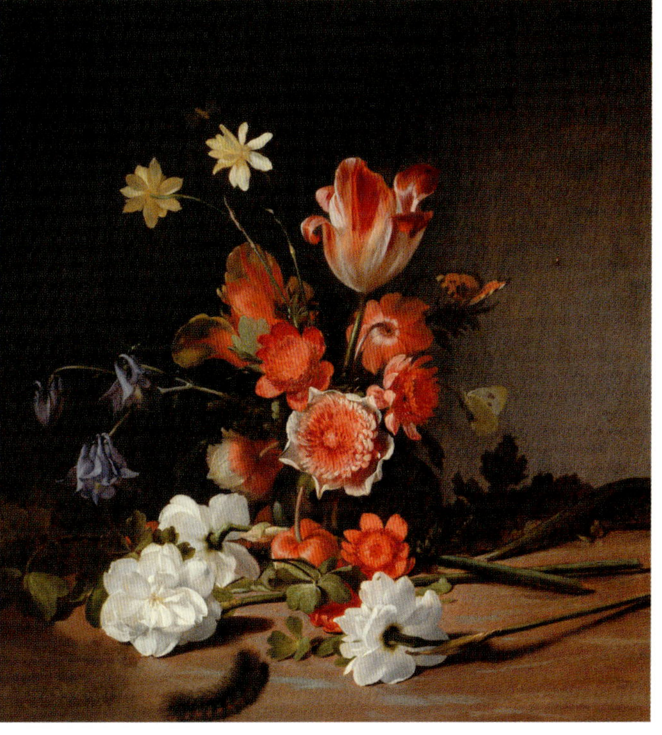

INDEX

Page numbers in *italic* refer to illustrations

Aelst, Willem van 95, 110
  Still Life 250
'alla prima' method 26–7
Amberger, Christoph, *Charles V, Holy Roman Emperor 7*
Ampzing, Samuel 34, 35, 42, 54
animals in paintings 70, 71, 76–7
architectural painting 40–1, 66–7, 107
Asselijn, Jan, *Winter Landscape 174*
Ast, Balthasar van der 24–5
  Basket of Flowers 244
  Still Life of Flowers, Fruit, Shells and Insects 25
Avercamp, Hendrick 28–9, 44, 83
  Figures Skating in a Dutch Landscape 29
  Fishermen at Moonlight 28
  River Landscape in Winter with Skaters 29
  A Scene on the Ice 167
  A Scene on the Ice near a Town 164
  Winter Landscape on the River Ijsel near Kampen 28
  Winter Landscape with Skaters 161
  Winter Scene 163
  Winter Scene on a Canal 162
  Winter Scene with Skaters near a Castle 163

Baburen, Dirck van 31, 32
  Christ Crowned with Thorns 223
  The Procuress 156, 157
Backer, Jacob
  Boy with a Beret 198
  Let the Children Come to Me 228
Backhuysen, Ludolf, *The Dutch Fleet of the Dutch East India Company 18*
Bailly, David, *Self-Portrait with Allegorical Still Life 206*
Bakhuizen, Ludolf 61, 179
  Ships in Distress off a Rocky Coast 183
Bamboccianti 70, 77
Barbari, Jacopo de 75
Bassen, Bartholomeus van 35, 40
  Interior View of a Church 41
Beeck, Johannes van der, *Emblematic Still Life 242*
Beerstraten, Jan Abrahamsz, *The Castle of Muiden in Winter 179*
Beert, Osias 24, 25, 39
Bellevois, Jacob Adraensz, *A Dutch Merchantman with a Wijdschip 18*
Bentvueghels 70, 227
Berchem, Nicolaes Pieterszoon 38, 39, 86, 90
  The Infancy of Zeus 232
  Landscape with a Hunting Party 39
  On the Ice Near a Town 39
Bijlert, Jan van 32, 67
  Venus Chastising Cupid 227
Bloemaert, Abraham 30, 32, 65, 98, 191, 228
  The Adoration of the Magi 20
  The Preaching of Saint John the Baptist 219
Bol, Ferdinand 51, 64, 65, 189
  Governors of the Wine Merchant's Guild 19

Moses and Jethro 65
Portrait of a Lady 207
Six Regents and the Beadle of the Nieuw Zijds Institute 65
Borch, Gerard ter 68–9, 105
  Curiosity 68
  The Glass of Lemonade 69
  The Letter 69
  The Parental Admonition 132
  The Ratification of the Treaty of Münster 11, 69
  A Woman Playing the Theorbo-Lute and a Cavalier 135
  Woman Writing a Letter 68
Borch, Gesina ter 68
Borch, Moses ter 68
Bosschaert the Elder, Ambrosius 24
  Bouquet of Flowers 244
  Still Life of Flowers 243
Both, Jan 70, 72, 73, 170, 185
Bramer, Leonaert 92, 98
  The Quarrel Between Ajax and Odysseus 225
Bray, Dirck de 84, 85
  Flowers in a Glass Vase 5, 85
  Still Life with a Bouquet in the Making 253
Bray, Jan de 84, 85, 189
  The Adoration of the Shepherds 84
  Allegory of Frederik Hendrik as the Bringer of Peace 239
  The Banquet of Cleopatra 84, 85
  Governors of the Leper Hospital at Haarlem 215
  Pharaoh's Daughter and her Handmaids with Moses in the Reed Basket 235
  Portrait of Abraham Casteleyn and his Wife 214
  Portrait of a Boy Aged Six 209
  The Regents of the Children's Almshouse in Haarlem 213
Bray, Joseph de 84, 85
  Still Life in Praise of the Pickled Herring 85
Bray, Salomon de 34, 84–5
  Jael, Deborah and Barak 230
  Young Woman Combing her Hair 84
Breen, Adam van
  Skating on the Frozen Amstel River 164
  Winter Landscape with Skaters 162
Brouwer, Adriaen 27, 46–7, 53, 56
  Drunken Peasants at an Inn 124
  Innkeeper Singing 129
  Interior with Smokers 47
  Peasants 46
  Peasants Brawling at Cards 127
  Playing Cards 46
  The Smokers (1635–38) 47
  The Smokers (c.1636) 129
Bruegel the Elder, Pieter 15, 21, 29
Brugghen, Hendrick ter 30–1, 32
  The Adoration of the Magi 222
  The Calling of Saint Matthew 223
  Christ Crowned with Thorns 31
  Esau Selling his Birthright 226
  A Lute Player Carousing with a Young Woman 118
  The Martyrdom of Saint Catherine 220
  Melancholia 31
  The Rich Man and Poor Lazarus 224

The Concert 31
A Violin Player with a Glass of Wine 30
Burgh, Hendrick van der 15, 90, 91

camera obscura 101
Campen, Jacob van 64, 65, 175
Camphuysen, Jochem Govertsz 44
Camphuysen, Rafaël 44
Cappelle, Jan van de 82–3, 179
  Seascape with Ships 83
  A Shipping Scene with a Dutch Yacht Firing a Salute 83
  A Small Dutch Vessel Before a Light Breeze 82
  A Small Vessel in Light Airs 82
Caravaggio 15, 30, 32, 48–9, 50, 67, 75, 100, 119, 217, 221, 223
chiaroscuro 30
Claesz, Pieter 38–9, 94
  Still Life 21
  Still Life of a Banquet 38
  Still Life with Lighted Candle 246
  Still Life with Musical Instruments 38
  Vanitas Still Life (1625) 247
  Vanitas Still Life (1630) 247
Claude Lorrain 72
Collier, Evert 75
  Letter Rack 252
  Still Life with Books and Manuscripts and a Skull 250
Coninxloo, Gillis van 44
Cuyp, Aelbert 72–3, 76
  Child Playing Golf 20
  Cows in a River 175
  Dordrecht Harbour in Moonlight 172
  Flora 73
  A Herdsman with Five Cows 73
  The Maas at Dordrecht 72
  River Landscape with Horseman and Peasants 180
  A River Scene with Distant Windmills 170
  Sunset over the River 72
  View of Dordrecht 178
Cuyp, Jacob Gerritsz 65, 72
  Abel Janszoon Tasman and Family 19

Delen, Dirck van 35
  Iconoclasm in a Church 11
  Interior of a Church 169
Delft School 15, 91, 174
Delft Thunderclap 74, 78, 98
Delft tiles 14
Diest, Jeronymus van, *View of the Merwede off Dordrecht 21*
doorkijkje (see-through door) device 91, 142, 154
Dou, Gerrit 16, 48, 51, 62–3, 88, 89, 104, 105
  Anne and Tobias, or Reading the Bible 63
  Astronomer by Candlelight 62
  The Doctor 130
  An Evening School 133
  Girl with an Oil Lamp at a Window 213
  A Girl Chopping Onions 14
  Maid at the Window 134
  Old Woman with Candle 143
  Old Woman Reading 126

Self-Portrait 63
A Sleeping Dog with a Terracotta Pot 130
Trumpet Player in Front of a Banquet 62
The Urine Doctor 144
A Woman Playing a Clavichord 148
A Young Woman at her Toilet 153
Droochsloot, Joost Cornelisz 166
  Summer 165
Dubbels, Hendrick 82
  Harbour with Moored Ships 179
Dujardin, Karel 70, 77
Dutch Classical architecture 64
Dutch Golden Age art 14–15
  apprenticeships 21
  dealers 19
  decline of 111
  genres 20–1
  guilds 16–17
  influences on 15, 21
  market for 12–13, 14, 18–19, 60
  pricing 19
Dutch Republic, history of 6–13
Dyck, Anthony van 53, 61, 103, 199, 233
Dyck, Floris van 24
  Laid Table with Cheese and Fruit 243
  Still Life with Cheese 24
  Still Life with Fruit, Nuts and Cheese 24
  Still Life with Melons, Plums, Cherries 246

Eeckhout, Gerbrand van den 82
  Boaz and Ruth 235
Everdingen, Allaert van 86, 185

Fabritius, Barent 74
  Young Painter in his Studio 17
Fabritius, Carel 15, 41, 51, 66, 74–5, 90, 92, 98, 100
  The Beheading of John the Baptist 75
  The Goldfinch 74
  Portrait of Abraham de Potter 212
  The Sentry 74
  Young Man in a Fur Cap and a Cuirass 209
fijnschilders 15, 19, 62, 79, 89, 100, 105, 215
Flinck, Govert 51, 64–5, 228
  Bearded Man with a Velvet Cap 204
  Calvary, or Golgotha 64
  First Councillor and Director-General of the Dutch East India Company 65
  Isaac Blessing Jacob 232
  Landscape with a Farm and a Bridge 170
  Portrait of Dirck Graswinckel and Geertruyt van Loon 205
  Self-Portrait Aged 24 200
floral paintings 21, 95, 110–11, 243, 244, 252, 253
'frame within a frame' pictures 63
Frankenthal School 44

Gelder, Arent de, *The Banquet of Ahasuerus 238*
genre painting 15, 21, 27, 35, 46–7, 55, 56–7, 62–3, 67, 68–9, 78–81, 88–93, 98–105, 114–59

Gogh, Vincent van 27, 51
Goyen, Jan van 19, 36–7, 39, 42, 72, 76, 78, 83, 84, 168, 170
   Castle by a River 36
   Landscape with an Oak 171
   Landscape with Stream 166
   Landscape with Two Oaks 36
   Peasant Huts with a Well 171
   River Scene with a Fortified Shore 37
   Summer 166
   A View of Leiden 37
   Winter Landscape with Skaters 37
Grebber, Frans Pietersz de 40, 54, 88
Grebber, Pieter de 39
   Moses Striking the Rock 228

Haarlem, Cornelis van 84
   The Massacre of the Innocents 219
Hals, Dirck 27, 34, 35, 55
   An Elegant Party Making Music 34
Hals, Frans 26–7, 31, 35, 54, 55, 56, 70, 82, 83, 85, 189
   Banquet of the Officers of the Saint George Civic Guard Company 189
   Daniel van Aken Playing the Violin 27
   The Gypsy Girl 126
   The Laughing Cavalier 1, 26
   Malle Babbe, the Witch of Haarlem 128
   The Merry Lute Player 198
   A Militiaman Holding a Berkemeyer or *The Merry Drinker 125*
   Peeckelhaering 128
   Pieter van den Broecke 198
   Pieter Verdonck as Samson 27
   Portrait of a Couple 193
   Portrait of a Jester with a Lute 192
   Portrait of a Woman 27
   The Rommel Pot Player 117
   Willem Caymans 203
   Willem van Heythuysen 195
   Young Man and Woman in an Inn 121
Heda, Willem Claeszoon 34–5, 39, 84, 94
   Breakfast Still Life 34, 35
   Still Life with Gilt Beer Cup 35
   Still Life with Gilt Cup 241
   Still Life with Oysters, a Rummer, a Lemon and a Silver Bowl 248
   Still Life with Pie and Silver Ewer 249
Heem, Jan Davidsz de 25, 53, 94, 95, 111
   Still Life with Books 245
   Still Life with Books and a Violin 248
   Still Life with Glass and Oysters 240
Helst, Bartholomeus van der 27, 60–1, 85, 189
   Abraham del Court and his Wife Maria de Kaersgieter 208
   Banquet of the Amsterdam Civic Guard 60, 207
   Militia Company of District VIII 60, 60, 61
   Portrait of Jacobus Trip 61
   Portrait of a Lady in Black Satin 60
   A Young Woman Celebrating Wine 61
Heyden, Jan van der 106–7
   A Capriccio of a Town Square 3, 107
   Cityscape with a Church and a Square 107
   The Dam with the New Town Hall in Amsterdam 183
   A Fortified Moat or Canal 106

The Herengracht 184
View of the Boterbrug with the Tower of the Stadhuis, Delft 106
history painting 20, 50, 61, 65, 85, 216–39
Hobbema, Meindert 59, 86, 108–9
   The Avenue at Middelharnis 109
   The Watermill 108
   Wooded Landscape with Merrymakers in a Cart 109
   Wooded Landscape with Water Mill 108
Honthorst, Gerrit van 31, 32–3, 126, 229
   Adoration of the Child 222
   Adoration of the Shepherds 33
   Artemisia 230
   Christ Before the High Priest 221
   The Concert (1623) 121
   The Concert (1626–30) 125
   The Concert Group 122
   The Debauched Student 123
   The Dentist 119
   Dinner with a Lute Player 117
   The Duet 120
   Feast Scene with a Young Married Couple or *The Wedding Supper 116*
   Frederick Hendrik and his wife Amalia van Solms 205
   The Laughing Violinist 123
   Merry Company 33
   The Merry Fiddler 120
   Merry Group Behind a Balustrade 32
   Musical Group on a Balcony 118
   Musical Group by Candlelight 119
   Portrait of Princess Elizabeth II van de Palts 210
   Prince Rupert, Count Palatine 204
   The Procuress 122
   Saint Peter Released from Prison 15
   Singing Cornett Player 32
   The Violin Player 124
Hooch, Pieter de 15, 69, 90–3, 100, 101, 102
   The Bedroom 92, 93
   A Boy Bringing Bread 92, 92
   Card Players in an Opulent Interior 149
   Card Players in a Sunlit Room 139
   The Courtyard of a House in Delft 139
   A Dutch Courtyard 23, 140
   The Gold Weigher 114
   Interior with a Woman Knitting 92, 93
   Interior with Women Beside a Linen Cupboard 144
   Man Reading a Letter to a Woman 92, 92
   Messenger of Love 154
   Mother Lacing her Bodice Beside a Cradle 140
   A Musical Party in a Courtyard 159
   Two Soldiers and a Serving Woman with a Trumpeter 90
   The Visit 138
   Woman and Child in a Courtyard 91
   Woman with a Child in a Pantry 91
   A Woman Delousing her Child's Hair or *A Mother's Duty 5*
   Woman and Maid in a Courtyard 90
   A Woman Peeling Apples 147
   Young Woman Drinking 138
Hoogstraten, Samuel van 74, 75, 101, 241

Perspective View with a Woman Reading a Letter 75
Trompe l'Oeil 253
A Trompe l'Oeil of Objects 13
Houckgeest, Gerard 15, 40, 41, 66
   Interior of the Oude Kerk Delft 40
   The New Church in Delft with the Tomb of William the Silent 40
   The Tomb of William the Silent in the Nieuwe Kerk in Delft 41
houding 108

Iconoclastic Fury 9, 10

Jongh, Ludolf Leendertsz de 66, 67, 90, 94, 96
   Paying the Hostess 67

Kalf, Willem 19, 94–5
   Still Life with a Chinese Bowl (1662) 251
   Still Life with a Chinese Bowl (1669) 94
   Still Life with a Pilgrim Flask 94
   Still Life with Silver Jug 251
Keyser, Thomas de 189
   Constantin Huygens and his Clerk 194
   A Dutch Family 193
   Portrait of a Gentleman 194
Knupfer, Nicolaus 78, 89
Koninck, Philips
   Dutch Panorama Landscape with a Distant View of Haarlem 177
   Flat Landscape with Two Anglers 176
   Wide River Landscape 173

Laer, Pieter Bodding van 70, 130
Lairesse, Gerard de
   Apollo and Aurora 238
   The Expulsion of Heliodorus from the Temple 239
landscape painting 20, 21, 28–9, 36–7, 39, 42–5, 59, 72–3, 86–7, 96–7, 106, 108–9, 160–87
Lastman, Pieter 48, 49, 52, 84, 224
   Orestes and Pylades Disputing at the Altar 221
   The Triumph of Mordecai 225
Leonardo da Vinci 50
Leyster, Judith 27, 54–5, 84
   Man Offering Money to a Young Woman 127
   Self-portrait 55
   Serenade 55
   Still Life with a Basket of Fruit 248
Lievens, Jan 48, 52–3, 83, 89
   The Apostle Paul 226
   Bearded Man with a Beret 53
   Christ at the Column 52
   Fire and Childhood 52
   Pilate Washing His Hands 225
   Portrait of Constantijn Huygens 203
   The Sacrifice of Abraham 233
   Samson and Delilah 229
   Still Life with Books 53
   The Young Artist or *The Little Draughtsman 53*
Lingelbach, Johannes 70, 97, 106
Little Ice Age 28–9, 45

Maes, Nicolaes 51, 92, 102–3
   The Account Keeper 135
   Eavesdropper with a Scolding Woman 132
   The Idle Servant 102
   The Lacemaker 103
   The Listening Housewife 137

Lovers with a Woman Listening 102
Old Woman Saying Grace 137
The Spinner 136
Vegetable Market 136
Young Woman Peeling Apples 133
A Young Woman Sewing 103
Mander, Karel van 17, 20, 24, 26, 191
   The Adoration of the Shepherds 216
marine painting 42, 58–9, 82–3, 179, 183, 187
'Master of the Small Landscapes' 15
Metsu, Gabriel 63, 69, 78, 88–9, 101
   A Man and Woman Seated by a Virginal 88
   Man Writing a Letter 89
   The Vegetable Market 88
   Woman Reading a Letter 89
Mierevelt, Michiel Jansz van 189, 214
   Anatomy Lesson of Dr Willem van der Meer 191
   Maurits, Prince of Orange 190
Mieris, Frans van 63, 80, 89, 104–5
   The Artist as Virtuoso at His Easel: Self Portrait, Aged 32 215
   The Doctor's Visit 104
   The Dutch Charlatan 105
   Lady at her Toilet 105
   Man with Pipe at the Window 211
   An Old Alchemist and his Assistant 16
   The Painter's Studio 104
   Woman at a Harpsichord 104
Moeyaert, Claes (Nicolaes) Cornelisz 39, 76, 84
   The Triumph of Bacchus 224
Molenaer, Jan 27, 54, 55
   Self-Portrait with Family Members 199
   Twelfth Night 55
   Young Man Playing a Theorbo and Young Woman Playing a Cittern 54
Molijn, Pieter 42, 69
   Landscape with an Open Gate 168
Mor, Anthonis, *William I the Silent 10*
Moreelse, Paulus 189
   A Girl with a Mirror 214
   Portrait of Abraham Bloemaert 191
   Vertumnus and Pomona 227
Moucheron, Frederick de, *Landscape with a Shrine 185*
Mytens, Daniel, *Self-Portrait 199*
mythological painting see history painting

Neer, Aert van der 44–5
   Landscape at Sunset 45
   Moonlit Landscape with Bridge 44
   Sports on a Frozen River 45
   Winter Scene with Figures Skating 44
nocturnes 44

Oosterwijck, Maria van 94, 95
   Bouquet of Flowers in a Vase 95
   A Floral Still Life with Yellow and White Lilies 95
   Still Life of Flowers 252
'Oriental' portrait genre 52, 201
Ostade, Adriaen van 27, 47, 55, 56–7, 78, 84, 90, 105
   An Alchemist 57
   A Peasant Family at Home 57
   Peasants Dancing in a Tavern 159
   The Schoolmaster 56
   A Schoolroom Interior 151
   The Painter in his Workshop 17
   Village Inn with Backgammon and Card Players 57

Ostade, Isack van 57
   Winter Scene 172

peasant painting 56, 57, 124, 127,
   129, 130, 159, 171, 177
peep boxes 75
Peeters, Clara 24, 25, 39, 94
   Still Life with Cheeses, Almonds and
     Pretzels 242
   Still Life with Cheeses, Artichoke and
     Cherries 245
   Still Life with Crab, Shrimps and
     Lobster 249
   Still Life with Fish and Cat 25
Pickenoy, Nicolaes Eliasz 60
portrait painting 20–1, 26–7, 48–9,
   52–3, 60–1, 65, 69, 85, 103,
   188–215
Post, Pieter 64, 110
Potter, Paulus 60, 76–7, 92
   Cattle in a Field 76
   The Farmyard 76
   The Piebald Horse 77, 77
   Punishment of a Hunter 77
   A Spaniel 77
pronkstillevens 94, 95, 251
Pynacker, Adam 15, 91, 96, 185
   Boatmen Moored on the Shore of
     an Italian Lake 174

Rampjaar (Year of Disaster) 19, 80,
   101, 103, 111
Ravesteyn, Jan van, *Hugo Grotius 190*
Rederijkerskamers 79, 153
religious paintings 15, 217
   see also history painting
Rembrandt van Rijn 14, 16, 19, 31,
   33, 47, 48–51, 52, 53, 57, 61,
   63, 64, 65, 74, 75, 82, 83, 85,
   102, 170, 189, 198, 204, 205,
   226, 238
   The Abduction of Europa 229
   Ahasuerus, Haman and Esther 217
   The Anatomy Lesson of Dr Nicolaes
     Tulp 50, 200
   Artist in his Studio 51
   Bathsheba with King David's Letter
     or Bathsheba at her Bath 234
   Belshazzar's Feast 50, 231
   The Blinding of Samson 231
   Christ and Mary Magdalene at the
     Tomb 233
   Danaë 50
   Daniel and Cyrus Before the Idol
     Bel 50
   The Deposition 51
   Isaac and Rebecca ('The Jewish
     Bride') 50, 236
   Jeremiah Lamenting the Destruction
     of Jerusalem 227
   The Kitchen Maid 206
   A Man in Oriental Dress 201
   The Mill (engraving) 49
   Nicolaes Ruts 196
   The Night Watch 50, 60, 202
   An Old Woman Called the Artist's
     Mother 194
   Portrait of Hendrickje Stoffels 210
   Portrait of the Mennonite Preacher
     Cornelius Claesz Anslo and his
     Wife 13
   Portrait of Oopjen Coppit 201
   Portrait of a Woman 203
   Self-Portrait (1628) 196
   Self-Portrait (c.1659) 188
   Self-Portrait (1669) 197
   Self-Portrait at the Age of 34 196
   Self-portrait with Hat and Two
     Chains 48

Self-portrait Holding Brushes, Palette
   and Mahlstick 50, 197
Simeon's Song of Praise 228
The Storm on the Sea of Galilee 49
Titus at his Desk 209
A Young Scholar and his Tutor 48
Reynolds, Sir Joshua 61
Rhetoric Rooms 47
Rombouts, Gillis
   The Announcement of the Peace
     Treaty of Münster 12
   The Workshop of a Weaver 17
Rubens, Peter Paul 31, 32–3, 47, 53,
   64–5, 83, 103, 228
Ruisdael, Isaak van 42, 86
Ruisdael, Jacob van 39, 43, 59, 86–7,
   96, 108, 109, 193
   Bleaching Ground in the Countryside
     186
   Chapel by a Waterfall 185
   An Extensive Landscape in Summer
     112–13
   The Jewish Cemetery 178
   Landscape with a Ruined Castle
     and a Church 182
   Landscape with a Stream 87
   Panoramic View of the Amstel 187
   Panoramic View of Haarlem 160
   View of Bentheim Castle 176
   View of the Hekelveld, Amsterdam,
     in Winter 87
   A Watermill 87
   Wheat Fields 186
   Windmill on the Banks of a River
     86
   A Woodland Landscape 181
Ruysch, Rachel 110–11
   Flowers and Insects 111
   A Still Life of Flowers in a Vase on a
     Ledge 110
   A Still Life on a Marble Ledge 110
   Still Life of a Tulip, a Melon and
     Flowers on a Ledge 111
   Vase with Flowers 253
Ruysdael, Jacob Salomonsz van 43,
   86
Ruysdael, Salomon van 42–3, 56, 84,
   86, 108, 168, 172
   A Battle Scene 43
   A Country Road 43
   Fishing Boats on a River 42
   Marine 42
   River Landscape with Fishermen at
     Work 43

Saenredam, Pieter Jansz 40–1, 66, 92
   Interior of the Church of Saint Anne
     in Haarlem 175
   Interior of the Sint-Odulphuskerk in
     Assendelft 173
   St Katherine's Church, Utrecht 40
Schooten, Floris van, *Breakfast 242*
Schrieck, Otto Marseus van 110
schutterij 85
Sorgh, Hendrink, *View of the Great*
   Market in Rotterdam 131
Steen, Jan 15, 36, 55, 57, 76, 78–81,
   89, 92, 105
   'As the Old Sing, So Pipe the Young'
     154
   The Bad Company 79
   The Baker Arent Oostwaard and
     his Wife Catherina Keizerswaard
     211
   The Bean Feast 155
   Beware of Luxury 149
   Celebration of the Birth 148
   The Dissolute Household 146
   The Doctor's Visit 80

Easy Come, Easy Go 142
The Effects of Intemperance 21
The Family Concert 151
The Fat Kitchen 153
Gamblers Quarrelling 150
Girl Eating Oysters 140
Grace Before Meat 78
Merry Company 153
Merry Company on a Terrace 157
The Merry Family 81
Moses and the Pharaoh's Crown 237
Peasant Family at Meal Time 78
Revelry (Merrymaking) 79
A School for Boys and Girls 156
Skittle Players Outside an Inn 81
The Sleeping Couple 134
The Tavern Garden 146
Twelfth Night Feast 81
The Village Fiddler 80
'The Way You Hear it is the Way You
   Sing it' 150
Steenwyck, Harmen
   An Allegory of the Vanities of
     Human Life 15
   Vanitas 247
still life painting 21, 24–5, 34–5, 38–9,
   94–5, 240–53
Sweelinck, Gerrit Pietersz, *Judith with*
   the Head of Holofernes 220

tenebrism 30
through-the-keyhole genre 102
Titian 50, 196
   Philip II of Spain 7
town- and cityscapes 106–7
trompe l'oeil 75, 252–3
tronies 46, 51, 189, 201, 204
Truth Presenting a Mirror to the
   Vanities of the World (anon) 13
Tulip Mania 36, 37, 78, 95, 252

Utrecht Caravaggisti 15, 31, 32, 49,
   52, 54, 67, 100, 118, 126, 225,
   235

vanitas paintings 21, 24, 34, 94, 206,
   241, 247, 250
Velázquez, Diego 69
Velde, Adriaen van de 58, 59, 77,
   97, 107
   The Annunciation 237
   Dunes at Scheveningen 180
   Haymakers Resting in a Field 59
   A Landscape with a Farm by a
     Stream 181
   Landscape with a Shrine 185
   Mountainous Landscape with Cows
     182
   Portrait of a Couple with Two
     Children and a Nurse in a
     Landscape 59
   Woman Milking a Cow 184
Velde the Elder, Willem van de 58, 82
   A Hoeker Alongside a Kaag at
     Anchor 58
Velde the Younger, Willem van de
   58–9, 82
   The Battle of Texel 58
   The Hampton Court 59
   Storm at Sea 187
Velde, Esaias van de 36, 42, 44, 172
   A Winter Landscape (1623) 165
   Winter Landscape (1630) 168
Verkolje, Jan, *The Messenger 158*
Vermeer, Johannes 14, 15, 19, 31, 57,
   69, 90, 91, 93, 98–101, 102
   Allegory of the Catholic Faith 239
   The Allegory of Faith 98
   Allegory of Painting 236

The Astronomer 152
Christ in the House of Martha and
   Mary 235
Diana and her Nymphs 234
The Geographer 99, 152
Girl Interrupted in her Music 141
Girl with a Pearl Earring 98
Girl with a Red Hat 101
Girl with a Wine Glass 2
The Glass of Wine 100
The Guitar Player 5, 158
The Lacemaker 155
Lady Writing a Letter with her Maid
   98
The Love Letter 154
The Milkmaid 142
Mistress and Maid 100
The Music Lesson 143
View of Delft 8–9
View of the Houses in Delft, or The
   Little Street 101
Woman Holding a Balance 147
Woman with a Lute 99
Woman Reading a Letter 144
Young Woman with a Pearl
   Necklace 145
A Young Woman Seated at a Virginal
   156
Young Woman with a Water Pitcher
   6
verre eglomisé 106
Verspronck, Johannes Cornelisz 27
   Portrait of a Girl Dressed in Blue
     212
Verstraelen, Anthonie, *Winter Sport in*
   Holland 169
Vlieger, Simon de 58, 82, 83
Vliet, Hendrick Cornelisz van 41, 66
Voort, Cornelis van der, *Portrait of*
   Laurens Reael 192

Weenix, Jan Baptist 39, 89
Wieringen, Cornelis Claesz van,
   Battle of Gibraltar 10
Willaerts, Adam, *Harbour Scene 167*
Witte, Emanuel de 15, 41, 66–7, 91
   Interior of a Church 66
   Interior of the Portuguese Synagogue
     in Amsterdam 66
   Interior with Woman Playing on a
     Virginal 115
   Portrait of a Family in an Interior 67
women artists 25, 54–5, 95, 110–11
Wouwerman, Jan 70
Wouwerman, Philips 59, 70–1, 76,
   96, 97
   Cavalry Battle in Front of a Burning
     Mill 71
   The Grey Horse 70
   Landscape with a Large Number of
     Peasants Merrymaking 130
   Merry and Rowdy Peasants at an
     Inn 177
   Riders Watering their Horses 71
   Travellers with Pack Horses and
     Wagons 70, 71
Wouwerman, Pieter 70
Wtewael, Joachim Anthonisz 31
   Adoration of the Shepherds 218
   Mars and Venus Surprised by Vulcan
     218
Wynants, Jan 96–7
   A Dune Landscape with Figures 96
   A Hunting Party in a Classical
     Landscape 97
   Landscape with Figures 97
   Wooded River Landscape with
     Peasants on a Path 96
Wyntrack, Dirck 96

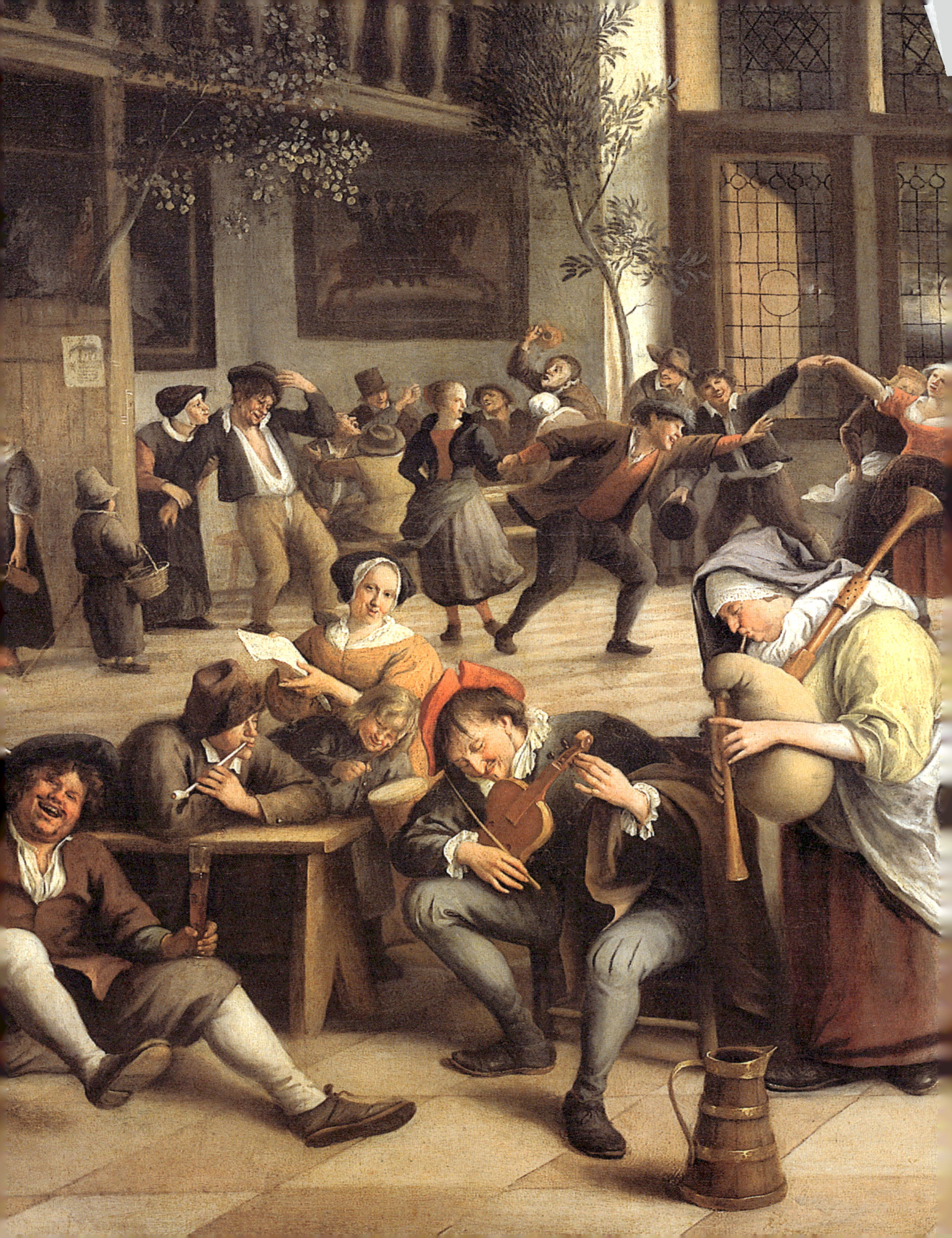